SO YOU LIKE THE NAME BRIANNA?

Although the other baby-name books might mention that *Brianna* is an Irish na... that means "strong" and "vi... only *What's In A Na...*

Its root name is *Bria...* Celtic name, *Bran,* ... tations include "vi... "eloquent," but the... personalities who ca...

There are many f... liest for which there is a record seems to be *Briana,* a name found in the second book of Edmund Spenser's *Faerie Queene* (1596).

◉ Number

Eight. It's not wise to cross people of this number. When it comes to a battle of wills, an eight usually wins.

☾ Astrological sign

Gemini. Gemini is a "voice" sign, and a large number of entertainers are born under this zodiac sign.

✳ Color

Black. *Dhu* means "black" in Celtic and represents Bran, ancient god of the underworld.

◆ Stone

Schorl. This gem is a black tourmaline with opaque prismlike crystals. Today, it is thought to attract love and money.

♆ Element

Quicksilver represents Gemini's ruling planet of Mercury.

⚘ Herb

Bryony *(Bryonia alba).* Bryony is a cultivated climbing plant, but it also grows wild in moist soil and vineyards in Europe.

WHAT'S IN A NAME?

WHAT'S IN A NAME?

Susan Osborn

Produced by The Philip Lief Group, Inc.

POCKET BOOKS

New York   London   Toronto   Sydney   Singapore

An *Original* Publication of POCKET BOOKS

POCKET BOOKS, a division of Simon and Schuster Inc.
1230 Avenue of the Americas, New York, NY 10020

Contributors:
   Hilary Mac Austin
   Marilyn Brooks
   Elizabeth McGinley Soltan
   Marylou Webster Ambrose
   Catherine Peck
   Diane Rhodes

ISBN: 0-671-02555-4

First Pocket Books trade paperback printing November 1999

10   9   8   7   6   5   4   3   2   1

Book design by Nancy Singer Olaguera
Cover design by Jeanne M. Lee; front cover photo credits: © Bill Losh 1995/FPG
International; © Myrleen Ferguson Cate/Photo Network/PNI; © Ken Sherman/
Bruce Coleman/PNI; © Fotopic/Stock South/PNI

Printed in the U.S.A.

RRDH/✠

Introduction

Naming your baby is one of the most emotionally satisfying decisions you will ever make. If you are like most parents, you will consider a potential name from several angles. How does it sound when you say it aloud? How does it fit into your family's genealogy? What historical significance does it carry? Most baby-naming books offer a line or two explaining what names "mean." But where do you go if you want the whole story? *What's in a Name?* presents the most detailed history available for the most popular and prevalent names in use today.

Included in this volume are fascinating facts not only about the origin and meaning of each name but also about the reasons it survived over the course of generations and how it evolved as it traveled around the globe. *What's in a Name?* is the only book to offer, in addition, a contemporary analysis of the numerological significance of each root name, its astrological association, and its relationship with particular herbs, colors, metals, and stones. Thanks to *What's in a Name?*, you *can* know the whole story behind your baby's name, a story that's woven with many interconnected threads.

For their first thread, names draw on key qualities suggested by their histories. The name *Judith,* for example, clearly inspires the image of strength from biblical history, just as the name *Abraham* suggests leadership. Qualities of a famous person who held the name may have been considered as well. Such qualities are then balanced with the numerology for the root name.

The numbers were assigned using the Pythagorean system of numerology, in which each letter of the name is worth a particular number (1 through 9, corresponding with certain personality descriptions or traits).

1	2	3	4	5	6	7	8	9
A	B	C	D	E	F	G	H	I
J	K	L	M	N	O	P	Q	R
S	T	U	V	W	X	Y	Z	

The sum of all the numbers must be less than 10. For example, the name *Allison* is 1+3+3+9+1+6+5 = 28. Keep adding the single digits until you get to a number under 10. So, *Allison*'s 2+8 = 10, which in turn is 1+0 = 1. Note that variations in spelling may change the number for a name. To be completely accurate, a person's full name (first, middle, and last name) should be calculated.

Obviously the astrological signs may not correspond exactly with a person's actual date of birth. Nevertheless, the name itself has some metaphysical affinity or connection with this sign. For example, a name's meaning often corresponds with a basic astrological element—earth, air, fire, or water—or other characteristics of an astrological sign, including color, stone, herb, or metal. Cancer, Pisces, or Scorpio, for instance, could be linked to a name with water in its meaning.

There are other natural connections as well. The supergemstones, with their own incredible histories, attach well to very strong names. Herbs may be compatible because of their own essential purpose or appearance, some connection with their Latin name, and so on. In all, the metaphysical entries flesh out the real personality or "soul" of each name.

The majority of parents choose names from among variations on a few hundred traditional root names. With that fact in mind, this book has included all the most popular contemporary variants along with references to their deep historical roots. For example, the name *Wendy* has only relatively recently been used as an independent name for girls, and it stands very nicely on its own. But readers wishing to learn more about *Wendy* are referred to the intriguing history of the name *Jennifer*. What's the connection? Would you have guessed it is in the ancient name *Guinevere*? Making the link between the venerable origins of names and their modern significance is what *What's in a Name?* is all about.

So before you make the all-important decision on your baby's name, curl up and enjoy learning what really is in that name.

A word of caution about the herbs listed in the book: The uses of herbs described here are from traditional sources, from various cultures both past and present. The descriptions are for historical interest only. The use of herbs for medicinal purposes should be practiced only under the guidance of a licensed health practitioner. *Never* use them without proper supervision or instruction on their preparation and usage. Some are highly poisonous in their raw state, but benign when cooked. Some people can have severe, and even life-threatening allergies to various plants, while others may not be affected at all.

Names for Boys

-A-
Aaron
Aatami
Abarran
Abe
Abie
Abraham
Abrahamo
Abrahan
Abram
Abrami
Abramo
Abramovitch
Abrams
Abramson
Abran
Ad
Adam
Adamo
Adams
Adan
Adao
Addie
Addis
Addison
Ade

Adhamh
Adiran
Adnet
Adrian
Adriano
Adrik
Adryan
Aharon
Aidan
Aindrea
Al
Alair
Alaire
Alan
Aland
Alanson
Alasdair
Alastair
Alec
Alejandro
Alek
Alessandre
Alex
Alexander
Alexei
Alexio

Alexis
Allen
Alley
Aloysius
Ambert
Ambre
Ambrogio
Ambrose
Ambrosine
Ambrosio
Amby
Anders
André
Andrea
Andreena
Andrei
Andres
Andrew
Andrezj
Andy
Ange
Angel
Angelo
Angy
Anno
Anntoin

Anthony
Antin
Antoine
Anton
Antonello
Antonio
Arel
Ari
Arik
Arin
Arke
Arlo
Arnie
Aron
Arram
Arrigo
Art
Artair
Arthur
Artie
Artis
Artur
Arturo
Artus
Arye
Ash

Ashlan
Ashleigh
Ashley
Ashlinn
Augie
August
Augustin
Augustine
Augustino
Augustus
Austin
Austyn
Avram

-B-
Band
Bari
Barnard
Barney
Barnhard
Barrie
Barris
Barry
Bastian
Bear
Beatham
Ben
Benek
Beniamino
Benjamin
Benjamon
Benji
Bennie
Benson
Bern
Bernard
Bernardo
Bernarr
Bernie
Berry
Bev
Beverleigh

Beverly
Beyren
Bill
Billy
Binyamin
Biron
Blair
Blaire
Blake
Blakelee
Blakeleigh
Blakeley
Blayr
Bo
Bob
Bobby
Brad
Bradlea
Bradleigh
Bradley
Bradney
Braham
Bram
Branden
Brendan
Brendon
Brennan
Brent
Brentan
Brentyn
Bret
Brett
Brette
Bretton
Brian
Briano
Briant
Britt
Brock
Brockley
Brook
Brooke

Brookes
Brookie
Brooks
Brose
Bruce
Brucie
Bryan
Bryant
Brynn
Buiron
Burnard
Byran
Byrom
Byron

-C-
Caelan
Cal
Cale
Caleb
Cam
Cameron
Camron
Carl
Carlos
Carmen
Carmine
Carolus
Carroll
Cary
Cecil
Cecilius
Celio
Chad
Charles
Charlie
Charlton
Charmaine
Chas
Che
Chick
Chico

Chip
Chris
Christian
Christoffer
Christoforo
Christophe
Christopher
Christophoros
Christos
Christy
Chuck
Claas
Clarence
Clark
Clarke
Claude
Claudius
Claudy
Clerc
Clerk
Cliff
Clifford
Clive
Clovis
Clyfford
Cob
Coby
Colas
Cole
Coleman
Colin
Con
Connie
Connor
Conor
Conrad
Conrade
Conrado
Constant
Constantine
Corey
Cort

Costa
Courtenay
Courtney
Craig
Curcio
Curry
Curt
Curtis

-D-
Daemon
Dafydd
Dai
Dale
Dalen
Daley
Dallan
Damian
Damiano
Damien
Damion
Damon
Damyon
Dan
Dana
Danal
Dandie
Dane
Danie
Daniel
Danit
Dannon
Danny
Danyal
Daran
Daren
Dario
Daron
Darrel
Darren
Darrick
Darrin

Darrion
Darrol
Darron
Darryl
Daryn
Dave
Davey
David
Davide
Davidson
Davies
Davin
Davis
Davon
Davy
Dayle
Dean
Deen
Demenico
Demingo
Den
Dennet
Dennis
Dennison
Denny
Deon
Derek
Deric
Derk
Derrick
Derril
Derron
Deryke
Deryll
Dewitt
Deyn
Dick
Diego
Dino
Dion
Dionysius
Diot

Dirk
Dolph
Dom
Domenico
Domingo
Dominic
Don
Donald
Donall
Donalt
Donaugh
Donnell
Donny
Doug
Douglas
Doyle
Drew
Drud
Drugi
Dugaid
Duncan
Dunn
Dwight
Dylan

-E-
Eamon
Ean
Eberman
Ed
Edan
Eddie
Eden
Edik
Edmonde
Edmund
Edmundo
Edouard
Eduardo
Edvard
Edward
Egor

Eli
Elias
Elie
Elihu
Elijah
Elliot
Ellis
Eloi
Eloy
Ely
Emil
Emilij
Emilio
Emmet
Emmott
Enrico
Enrique
Enzio
Eric
Erich
Erico
Erik
Erin
Eryk
Esteban
Estevan
Etan
Ethan
Etienne
Eugene
Eugenio
Eugenius
Evan
Evgeny
Ewart

-F-
Federico
Fedor
Felipe
Felippo
Ferenc

Feri
Filip
Fran
Francesco
Franchot
Francis
Francisco
Franco
François
Franio
Frank
Frankie
Frants
Franz
Frasco
Frascuelo
Fred
Freddie
Frederick
Frederico
Fridrick
Friedel
Friedrich
Fritz
Fritzchen
Fritzi

-G-
Gabby
Gabe
Gabriel
Gabriello
Gaby
Gareth
Garrett
Garrin
Gary
Gaultier
Gauthier
Gavriel

Gavrilo
Gayle
Gene
Geoff
Geoffrey
Geordie
Georg
George
Georges
Georgie
Gerald
Geraldo
Gerard
Gerhard
Gerome
Geronimo
Gerrick
Gerry
Giacomo
Gian
Giordano
Giorgio
Giovanni
Giulio
Giuseppe
Giustino
Glen
Glendon
Glenn
Glennie
Glin
Glynis
Godfrey
Goran
Gorden
Gordie
Gordon
Gordy
Gorgeina
Graig

Greer
Greg
Gregoire
Gregorio
Gregory
Gregos
Grigor
Grigorio
Grzegorz
Gualterio
Guglielmo
Guillaume
Guillermo
Gus
Gyuri

-H-
Hadrian
Hagan
Hal
Haleigh
Haley
Hallie
Hamish
Hank
Hannes
Hans
Hanschen
Hansel
Haroun
Harry
Hayleigh
Hayley
Heath
Heathcliff
Heindrick
Heinrich
Heinz
Henerik
Henning

Henri
Henry
Hew
Hierome
Hilaire
Hilario
Hilarius
Hilary
Hollis
Howard
Howie
Huey
Hugh
Hughes
Hugo
Hunter

-I-
Iacopo
Iago
Iakob
Ian
Ibrahim
Igor
Ike
Ilario
Ioannis
Iosep
Isaak
Isacco
Iskander
Issaac
Itzak
Ivan
Izak

-J-
Jace
Jack
Jackie

Jacko
Jackson
Jaco
Jacob
Jacques
Jago
Jaime
Jaisen
Jake
James
Jameson
Jamie
Jan
Janek
Janos
Jarad
Jared
Jarell
Jarrod
Jase
Jason
Jay
Jayson
Jeff
Jefferies
Jeffers
Jeffrey
Jem
Jemmy
Jeoffroi
Jerald
Jeramie
Jere
Jeremiah
Jeremy
Jeroen
Jerome
Jerrid
Jerrold
Jerry

Jerzy
Jess
Jesse
Jessie
Jesus
Jim
Jimmy
Jiri
Jock
Jody
Joe
Joel
Joey
Johann
John
Johnny
Jolyon
Jon
Jonah
Jonas
Jonathan
Jordan
Jorgan
Jorge
Jory
Jose
Joseph
Josetto
Josh
Joshua
Josip
Josy
Jourdan
Jovan
Joyce
Jozef
Jozua
Juan
Jules
Julian

Julien
Julio
Jurek
Jurgen
Justin
Justinian
Justino
Justinus
Justo
Justus

-K-
Kaleb
Karel
Karl
Karmen
Karoly
Keith
Kelly
Kelsey
Ken
Kennet
Kenneth
Kenny
Kent
Kenton
Kenyon
Kenzie
Keon
Kevin
Kevon
Kevyn
Kilen
Kiley
Kim
Kimball
Kimberleigh
Kimberly
Kit
Klarance

Klaudio
Klaus
Konrad
Konstantin
Konstanz
Kourtney
Kris
Kristo
Kristofer
Kristos
Kristy
Kurt
Kurtis
Kyle
Kym

-L-
Lalo
Laren
Larrance
Larry
Lars
Laurel
Laurence
Laurus
Lawrence
Lee
Leigh
Len
Lenci
Lennard
Lenny
Leo
Leon
Leonard
Leonardo
Leroy
Les
Leslea
Lesley

Leslie	**-M-**	Maximilian	Nelson
Lew	Mac	Maxwell	Nichol
Lewis	Mack	Mazo	Nicholas
Lex	Mackenzie	Mckenzie	Nick
Lezley	Madison	Meredith	Nicky
Liam	Maks	Meredyth	Nicolo
Lieb	Malcolm	Micah	Nigel
Lind	Malcolum	Michael	Nikita
Lindsay	Malkolm	Michel	Nikki
Lindsey	Marc	Mick	Nikolai
Lodovico	Marcel	Micky	Nikos
Lon	Marco	Miguel	Niles
Lonny	Marcos	Mihail	Nilos
Lorenzo	Marcus	Mikayla	Nils
Loritz	Marinos	Mike	Noach
Lorne	Mario	Mikey	Noah
Lory	Marion	Mikhail	Noak
Lothair	Marius	Mikhos	Noé
Lothar	Mark	Mikkel	Noll
Lothario	Mart	Miles	Nyle
Lou	Martell	Milo	
Louie	Martijn	Mincho	**-O-**
Louis	Martin	Misha	Oliver
Loukas	Martino	Mitch	Oliverio
Luc	Marty	Mitchell	Olivier
Luca	Massimo	Morgan	Ollie
Lucas	Mat	Morgen	Osip
Lucho	Mateo	Mykell	Ostynn
Lucien	Mathias	Myles	Owen
Lucio	Mats		
Lucius	Matt	**-N-**	**-P-**
Lucky	Matthaus	Naldo	Paavo
Ludovic	Matthew	Nat	Pablo
Ludwig	Matthias	Nate	Pacho
Luigi	Mattie	Nathan	Paco
Luis	Matvey	Nathaniel	Paddie
Luke	Matz	Neale	Padhraig
Luken	Max	Ned	Pancho
Lutero	Maxie	Neil	Paolo
Luther	Maxim	Nels	Paquito

Pat	Randy	Rogelio	Scot
Patricio	Ray	Roger	Scott
Patrick	Rayment	Rogers	Scottie
Patrik	Raymond	Rogiero	Scotto
Patrizius	Raymonde	Roi	Seamus
Patton	Raymundo	Ron	Sean
Paul	Reg	Ronald	Seb
Paulus	Reggie	Ronny	Sebastian
Pauly	Reginald	Rory	Sebastiano
Pavel	Reginalt	Ross	Sebo
Peadar	Reinhold	Rosse	Sepp
Pedro	Reinwald	Rossell	Seth
Pepe	Renault	Rousell	Shamus
Perrin	René	Roy	Shanan
Perry	Rex	Ruggiero	Shane
Pete	Rey	Rupert	Shannen
Peter	Reynaldo	Rush	Shannon
Phil	Reynolds	Russ	Shawn
Philip	Ricardo	Russel	Shem
Philly	Ricciardetto	Russell	Shimon
Pierce	Rich	Rusty	Si
Pierre	Richard	Rutger	Sid
Piers	Rick	Ruy	Siddie
Pietro	Ricky	Ryan	Sidney
Pino	Rico	Ryon	Sidon
Pippo	Riik	Ryszard	Sidonio
Pol	Rikkert	Ryun	Sikander
Poul	Rinaldo		Sim
Pyotr	Riobard	-S-	Simeon
	Rip	Sacha	Simmons
-R-	Ritchie	Sam	Simmy
Rab	Ritshard	Sammy	Simon
Raemond	Rob	Samuel	Simpson
Raimondo	Robby	Samuello	Sinclair
Raimund	Robert	Sanders	Spence
Rainault	Robin	Sandor	Spencer
Ramon	Robinson	Sandy	Spenser
Randall	Rodge	Sascha	Staffan
Randolf	Rodger	Sashi	Stefan
Randolph	Rog	Saunder	Stefano

Steffel
Stephan
Stephanos
Stephanus
Stephen
Steve
Steven
Stevenson
Stevie
Steward
Stewart
Stu
Stuart
Syd
Sydney
Symms
Symon
Szymon

-T-
Tailer
Tailor
Tamek
Tamsin
Tandie
Tarrance
Tayler
Taylor
Teador
Ted
Teddie
Teemofe
Tennyson
Tenton
Teodoor
Teren
Terence
Terencio
Terry
Thaniel
Theo

Theodor
Theodore
Theodorus
Theodosios
Thom
Thomas
Thompson
Thumas
Tiennot
Tilar
Tim
Timmie
Timo
Timofei
Timoscha
Timoteo
Timothee
Timotheo
Timotheus
Timothy
Timoty
Tino
Tobe
Tobiah
Tobias
Tobin
Tobit
Toby
Tod
Todd
Tom
Tomaso
Tomasz
Tome
Tomek
Tomlin
Tommie
Tonetto
Tonio
Tony
Traver

Travers
Travis
Travys
Trefor
Trevar
Trevor
Tris
Tristam
Tristan
Tristram
Troi
Troy
Troye
Trystan
Tudor
Ty
Tylar
Tyler
Tymon
Tymoteusz

-U-
Ugo

-V-
Val
Valerian
Valerio
Valery
Valther
Vanek
Vanko
Vic
Vicente
Vicenzio
Vickie
Victor
Victorien
Vidor
Viktor
Vilhelm

Vin
Vince
Vincent
Vincents
Vincenzio
Vincien
Vinny
Vinzenz
Vittore
Vittorio
Vittorios

-W-
Wain
Walder
Wally
Walt
Walter
Walther
Ward
Ware
Waring
Warren
Warriner
Wat
Watkins
Wayn
Wayne
Wes
Wesley
Westleigh
Westley
Wilek
Wiley
Wilhelm
Wilhelmus
Wilkes
Wilkie
Wilkinson
Will
Willem

William
Williamson
Wills
Willson
Willy
Wilmar
Wilmot
Wilson
Wim
Winston
Winton
Wintsen
Witt

Wynston
Wynstonn

-X-
Xan
Xander
Ximenes

-Y-
Yakov
Yanni
Ygor
Yitzhak

Yochanan
Yosef
Yuri
Yurik
Yusuf
Yuszel

-Z-
Zacaria
Zaccheus
Zach
Zachaios
Zachariah

Zacharias
Zachary
Zack
Zak
Zan
Zander
Zane
Zaz
Zekariah
Zeke
Zindel

Names for Girls

-A-
Abagael
Abagil
Abaigeal
Abame
Abarrane
Abbe
Abbie
Abbye
Abbygail
Abigail
Abra
Abrahana
Ada
Adama
Adamina
Adamine
Adan
Adana
Addie
Adelice
Adrea
Adria
Adrian
Adriana
Adrie

Adrienah
Adrienne
Aidan
Aiden
Aila
Aileen
Aimee
Aindrea
Airika
Ala
Alaina
Alana
Alandra
Alani
Alanis
Alasdair
Alastair
Alastrina
Alecia
Aleethia
Alejandra
Alekia
Aleni
Alessandra
Alex
Alexa

Alexandra
Alexandria
Alexia
Alexis
Aleyna
Aliana
Alice
Alikah
Alina
Alisha
Alison
Alissa
Allaire
Allena
Allis
Ally
Allyson
Aloysia
Alysa
Alyssa
Amada
Amalie
Amalina
Amanda
Amandi
Amandine

Amara
Amaris
Amata
Amber
Amberetta
Amberly
Ambra
Ambrosia
Amelia
Ammy
Amy
Andra
Andreas
Andrei
Andrel
Andresa
Andrette
Andrewena
Andriána
Andy
Anechka
Anela
Ange
Angel
Angela
Angelica

Angelina
Angeline
Angelique
Angiola
Angy
Anika
Anita
Ann
Anna
Annabel
Annale
Anne
Annelise
Annette
Anngel
Annie
Annis
Annisa
Annjela
Annora
Antoinette
Antonia
Anya
Aoiffe
Aretha
Ariana
Arie
Ariel
Ariela
Ariellah
Ariellel
Arina
Arnina
Arona
Artheia
Arthuretta
Arthurine
Artice
Artina
Artlette
Ashla

Ashlan
Ashleigh
Ashley
Augusta
Augustina
Austina

-B-
Babe
Babette
Babs
Baibin
Bairbre
Barb
Barbara
Barbary
Barbette
Barbie
Barbro
Bari
Barrie
Barry
Basha
Basia
Bauby
Bebe
Becca
Becky
Becs
Belinda
Belle
Bennie
Berbera
Berna
Bernadene
Bernadette
Bernadine
Bernette
Bernie
Bernita
Berry

Berta
Bertie
Bess
Beth
Bethanne
Bethannie
Bethany
Betsy
Bette
Bettina
Bettine
Betty
Bev
Beverly
Bevlyn
Bevvy
Bibi
Billy
Blair
Blaire
Blake
Blakelee
Blakenee
Bo
Bobbie
Bobette
Bobinette
Bon
Bonne
Bonnebell
Bonni
Bonnie
Borbala
Brad
Bradlea
Bradleigh
Bradley
Brana
Breanna
Bree
Bren

Brenda
Brenna
Brenndah
Brett
Brette
Bria
Brianna
Brianne
Bridget
Brina
Briny
Britney
Britt
Britta
Brittany
Brook
Brooke
Brookes
Brookie
Brooks
Brucie
Brucina
Brucine
Brynne
Buffy
Bunnie

-C-
Cait
Caitlin
Cam
Cameron
Camron
Caraleen
Caren
Carey
Cari
Carla
Carlene
Carlie
Carlin

Carlotta

Carly

Carma

Carmelia

Carmelita

Carmella

Carmen

Carmencita

Carmina

Carmine

Carmita

Carmyna

Carol

Caroline

Carolynn

Carrie

Casandera

Cass

Cassandra

Cassandry

Cassie

Cat

Catalina

Catherine

Cathleen

Cathy

Caty

Cece

Cecely

Cecil

Cecile

Cecilia

Cecily

Cele

Celene

Celia

Celie

Celine

Celyna

Cesya

Charin

Charlayne

Charlene

Charlie

Charlotta

Charlotte

Charmaine

Chellie

Chelsea

Chelsey

Cheri

Cheryl

Chessie

Chiara

Chris

Chrissa

Chrissy

Christa

Christal

Christan

Christiana

Christie

Christina

Christine

Christy

Chrystel

Cilla

Cinda

Cindy

Cinny

Cintia

Cissie

Clair

Clara

Clarabel

Clare

Clarice

Clarissa

Clarisse

Claudetta

Claudette

Claudia

Claudine

Claudy

Colette

Colleen

Collie

Colline

Con

Connie

Constance

Constancia

Constanta

Constanz

Constanza

Corey

Corri

Cortnee

Cory

Cosette

Courtenay

Courtland

Courtnee

Courtney

Cristal

Crysta

Crystal

Cybele

Cybil

Cyn

Cynda

Cynthia

-D-

Daile

Daisee

Daisy

Dalanna

Dale

Dallana

Damia

Damienne

Damya

Dana

Danay

Dane

Daneal

Danella

Danet

Danetta

Danette

Dani

Danica

Danice

Danielle

Danika

Danill

Danise

Danita

Danitza

Danna

Danne

Danny

Dannyce

Danya

Darel

Darryl

Darrylene

Darylin

Dasha

Dasie

Davina

Davita

Davrat

Dayann

Dayle

Dayna

Deanna

Deanne

Deb

Debbie

Debera

Debora

Deborah

Debra	Donna	Ekaterina	Etty
Dede	Donnell	Elaine	Eugenia
Deena	Donnelle	Elan	Eva
Den	Donni	Elana	Eve
Denise	Doortje	Eleanor	Evelina
Denny	Dora	Elena	Evelyn
Denys	Dorat	Elisa	Evennia
Deva	Doretta	Elise	Evetta
Devora	Dori	Elissa	Evie
Devorit	Dorika	Eliza	Evika
Di	Dorinda	Elizabeth	Evita
Diahanne	Dorlissa	Ella	Evonne
Diana	Doro	Ellen	Evvy
Diandra	Dorota	Ellie	Eyrica
Diane	Dorothea	Ellma	
Dinny	Dorothy	Ellspet	-F-
Dionysia	Dorrit	Eloise	Fannie
Dita	Dory	Elsa	Farica
Divina	Dosha	Elsie	Fedora
Dobra	Dot	Elspeth	Felipa
Dodie	Dotty	Em	Fifi
Dodo	Dreena	Emalee	Fran
Dolly	Drew	Emelda	Frances
Domenica	Dvora	Emelina	Francesca
Domina	Dvoshke	Emeline	Francetta
Dominca	Dyanne	Emilia	Francine
Dominga	Dylana	Emilija	Frank
Domini	Dylane	Emily	Frankie
Dominique		Emma	Franny
Dominizia	-E-	Emmalyn	Fred
Domitia	Eba	Emmy	Freda
Dona	Edma	Emyln	Fredalena
Donalda	Edmée	Engracia	Freddie
Donaldina	Edmonda	Enrichetta	Frederica
Donaleen	Edmunda	Erica	Fredrika
Donella	Edwarda	Erika	Frieda
Donelle	Edwardine	Erin	
Donette	Eileen	Erina	-G-
Donia	Eire	Erynn	Gabby
Donica	Eirene	Etana	Gabriella
Donita	Eiryn	Etta	Gabrielle

Gaby
Gail
Gaila
Galina
Gavra
Gavrielle
Gayel
Gayle
Geena
Geenia
Gelya
Gemma
Gena
Gene
Genevieve
Genna
Gennie
Gennifer
Georgeann
Georgeina
Georgette
Georgia
Georgie
Geralda
Geraldine
Gerianne
Gerri
Gianna
Gina
Ginelle
Ginerva
Ginetta
Ginger
Ginia
Ginny
Giorgia
Giuditta
Giulia
Giuseppina
Giustina
Glen

Glenda
Gleneen
Glenn
Glenna
Glennie
Grace
Gracia
Gracie
Gratia
Gratiana
Grazia
Grazielle
Graziosa
Grazyna
Greer
Gregoria
Greta
Gretchen
Guglielma
Guillelmina
Guinevere
Gus
Gusta
Gwen
Gwendolyn

-H-
Hadria
Hadrienne
Hailea
Haleigh
Halina
Halle
Hallie
Hanna
Hannah
Hannelore
Hattie
Hayleigh
Hayley
Heather

Hedy
Heida
Heidi
Helen
Helena
Helène
Hellenor
Helma
Helmina
Helminette
Heloise
Hendrika
Henie
Henka
Henrietta
Henrika
Hilaria
Hilary
Hilliary
Hollie
Hollis
Holly
Honor
Huette
Hughina

-I-
Ileana
Ilene
Ilona
Ilse
Ilysee
Ilyssa
Ina
Ira
Iranda
Irene
Iriana
Irina
Isabelle
Iva

-J-
Jackette
Jackie
Jacqueline
Jacquenetta
Jacqui
Jamie
Jan
Jana
Jane
Janet
Janette
Jania
Janice
Janine
Janis
Janna
Jaquith
Jardena
Jasia
Jayne
Jean
Jeanie
Jeannette
Jeannine
Jeena
Jelena
Jelika
Jemma
Jen
Jenella
Jenelle
Jeni
Jenna
Jennie
Jennifer
Jennora
Jenny
Jeraldeen
Jeralee
Jere

Jeremia	Joycelyn	Kelcey	Kourtney
Jeri	Joyous	Kellee	Kris
Jerrie	Juanita	Kellina	Krista
Jerry	Judite	Kelly	Kristen
Jess	Judith	Kelsa	Kristle
Jessa	Judy	Kelseigh	Kristy
Jessalin	Julia	Kelsey	Krystal
Jesse	Juliana	Kelsie	Krystle
Jessica	Julie	Kena	Kyle
Jessie	Juliette	Kendra	Kym
Jinia	Justina	Kenia	Kynthia
Jinna	Justine	Kenna	
Jinnie	Justy	Kennice	-L-
Jo	Jutta	Kenza	Ladonna
Joan		Kenzie	Lana
Joanna	-K-	Kevina	Lara
Joanne	Kaatje	Kevyn	Larin
Jody	Kaitlin	Kikelia	Larissa
Joela	Kara	Kilan	Laura
Joelin	Karen	Kiley	Laureen
Joelle	Kari	Kim	Lauren
Joely	Karina	Kimba	Laurette
Joelynn	Karmen	Kimberleigh	Laurie
Joey	Karmina	Kimberly	Lea
Joice	Karoline	Kimberlyn	Leah
Jolette	Kassandra	Kimette	Leanne
Joline	Kata	Kimiko	Leanora
Jonelle	Kate	Kimmie	Lee
Joni	Katharyn	Kirsten	Leena
Jordan	Katherine	Kirsty	Leese
Jordana	Kathleen	Kit	Leia
Jorgina	Kathy	Kitty	Leigh
Jorie	Katie	Klaire	Lena
Josepha	Katinka	Klaretta	Lenda
Josephine	Katja	Klaryce	Leneen
Josetta	Katrina	Kolleen	Lenette
Josy	Kay	Konstance	Lenia
Jourdan	Kayla	Konstantija	Lenna
Jowella	Kaylee	Konstantina	Lennette
Joy	Kealy	Korry	Lenore
Joyce	Keely	Kosta	Leona

Leonarda	Lori	Mala	Marlo
Leonie	Lorin	Malena	Marquita
Leonora	Lorna	Malgorzata	Marsha
Les	Lory	Mallie	Mart
Leslea	Louisa	Mamie	Marta
Lesley	Louise	Manda	Martella
Leslie	Lu	Mandi	Martha
Lexie	Ludovica	Manon	Marthe
Lezley	Ludwiga	Mara	Marthena
Lib	Luisa	Marabelle	Marti
Libby	Luka	Marcene	Martina
Licha	Lulu	Marcia	Marty
Lidija	Lydia	Marcille	Mary
Lin	Lydie	Marcy	Marylin
Lina	Lyndel	Maren	Mattea
Lind	Lynelle	Maretta	Matthaus
Linda	Lynette	Marga	Matthea
Lindsay	Lynn	Margaret	Mattia
Lindsey	Lynne	Marge	Mattie
Lindy	Lyssa	Margery	Maude
Lindzy		Margit	Maura
Linell	**-M-**	Margo	Maureen
Linzy	Mackenzie	Margot	Maxanne
Lioa	Mada	Marguerita	Maxie
Lisa	Maddie	Marguerite	Maxine
Lisbette	Madel	Maria	May
Lise	Madeleine	Mariah	Mckenzie
Lisette	Madelena	Marian	Meg
Lissa	Madge	Marianne	Megan
Lissandre	Madlen	Marie	Meggie
Lita	Madonna	Mariel	Meghan
Liv	Maegan	Mariet	Meghanne
Livvie	Mag	Marilyn	Mel
Liz	Magdalena	Marina	Melania
Liza	Maggie	Marion	Melanie
Lois	Maida	Marissa	Melantha
Lola	Maighdlin	Marjorie	Melinda
Lolita	Maighread	Marla	Melisenda
Lora	Maira	Marleih	Melissa
Loreen	Maire	Marlene	Melita
Loretta	Maisie	Marlina	Mella

Mellicent	Morgance	Nonie	Perrine
Melly	Morganne	Nonnie	Pet
Melonie	Morgen	Nora	Peterina
Melosa	Muriel	Norah	Petra
Meredith	Myles	Noreen	Petronella
Merridie	Myra	Norina	Petronija
Merry			Petrova
Mia	-N-	-O-	Philippa
Michaela	Nan	Ohndrea	Phillippine
Micheline	Nancy	Olive	Philly
Michelle	Nanette	Olivette	Pierette
Micky	Nani	Olivia	Piero
Miguela	Nanon	Olivine	Pietra
Mika	Naoma	Ollie	Pippa
Mikayla	Naomi	Olva	Polly
Mikhayla	Nat	Orina	
Mikko	Nata		-R-
Mila	Natalia	-P-	Rachel
Milena	Natalie	Pam	Rachelle
Miles	Nataline	Pamela	Rae
Milica	Natasha	Pamelina	Raisa
Milka	Nathalie	Pamilla	Ramona
Millie	Nathania	Pammie	Rana
Mimi	Natividad	Paola	Randi
Min	Nattie	Pat	Raquel
Mina	Navitt	Patrice	Rashelle
Minnie	Neda	Patricia	Rasia
Mira	Nelda	Patricka	Rayna
Miranda	Nell	Patsy	Reba
Miriam	Nellie	Pattie	Rebbie
Misha	Nessa	Paula	Rebecca
Missy	Nessie	Paule	Rebekah
Mitzi	Netta	Paulette	Reenie
Moira	Nettie	Paulin	Regina
Molly	Nicole	Pauline	Rena
Mona	Nicolette	Pauly	Renata
Monica	Nikki	Pavia	Rene
Monique	Nikolia	Pavla	Renie
Morgan	Nina	Peg	Rennie
Morgana	Nomi	Peggy	Reyna

Rheba
Rhoda
Rica
Ricarda
Richelle
Richia
Rickie
Rina
Rita
Riva
Rivi
Robby
Roberta
Robertene
Robin
Rochelle
Roline
Romonde
Ron
Ronica
Ronnie
Rory
Rosa
Rosalind
Rosalinda
Rosalyn
Rose
Roseann
Roselind
Roseline
Rosella
Rosemarie
Rosemary
Rosetta
Rosie
Rosita
Roslyn
Rosslyn
Roze
Rozele

Rozsi
Ruperta

-S-
Sabilla
Sacilia
Sadie
Saffi
Sal
Saleena
Sally
Sam
Samantha
Sammie
Samuela
Sandera
Sandra
Sandy
Sara
Sarah
Sarena
Sari
Sarine
Sarita
Sasa
Saundra
Sebastiana
Sebastiane
Seelie
Sefa
Seila
Selene
Selia
Selina
Selinda
Semanntha
Sena
Shana
Shane
Shani

Shanna
Shannen
Shannon
Shara
Sharel
Shari
Sharia
Sharla
Sharleen
Sharmain
Sharolyn
Sharon
Sharona
Sharonda
Shawna
Shayla
Sheela
Sheena
Sheila
Sheilagh
Shelly
Sheri
Sheron
Sherry
Sheryl
Shoshana
Sib
Sibbie
Sibella
Sibyl
Sid
Sidney
Sile
Simantha
Simona
Simone
Simonetta
Sindy
Sinead
Sioux

Sissela
Sissy
Sofie
Sohndra
Sondra
Sonia
Sonja
Sonnie
Sonya
Soosanna
Sophia
Sophie
Sorcha
Stefa
Steffi
Stephana
Stephanie
Stephine
Stevana
Stevie
Stina
Sue
Suki
Susan
Susanetta
Susannagh
Susannah
Suschen
Susette
Susie
Suzanne
Suzette
Suzy
Sybille
Sydel
Sydelle
Sydney
Sydnie
Symantha
Symone

Synda
Synthia

-T-
Tailor
Tammie
Tara
Tarah
Taresa
Tarra
Taryn
Tasha
Tayler
Taylor
Tea
Teddie
Tedra
Teena
Tera
Terena
Teresa
Teresita
Terezinha
Teri
Terry
Teryna
Tess
Tessa
Thea
Theodora
Theodosia
Theophanie
Theresa
Thèrése
Theresina
Theresita
Thoma
Thomasina
Thomazine
Tibbie
Tiffany
Tiffenie

Tiffie
Tiffney
Timmie
Timothea
Tina
Tine
Tiny
Tobe
Toby
Toinette
Toma
Tommie
Toni
Tonia
Tonye
Tova
Tracy
Tresha
Tressa
Tressie
Tricia
Trina
Trinette
Trisha

-V-
Val
Valaria
Vale
Valeria
Valerie
Valery
Vallie
Valorie
Valry
Van
Vanessa
Vanetta
Vanija
Vanna
Vanya
Varina

Varvara
Veera
Velma
Venetta
Vera
Verlee
Verlye
Verohnicca
Veronica
Veronice
Veronika
Veronike
Veronique
Vic
Vicenta
Vicentia
Vicentine
Vickie
Victoria
Victorina
Victorine
Viktorija
Vilma
Vincentine
Virge
Virgie
Virginia
Virginie
Vittoria
Vonnie

-W-
Wendy
Willa
Willabella
Willamina
Wilma
Wilmette
Wilna
Winifred
Wylma

-X-
Xan
Xandra

-Y-
Yarina
Yekaterin
Yelena
Yetta
Yettie
Ylisabette
Yosepha
Ysabel
Yudi
Yulia
Yvonne

-Z-
Zahra
Zan
Zandra
Zanna
Zara
Zarita
Zita
Zoe
Zoelie
Zoeline
Zoelle
Zoey
Zofi
Zofia
Zondra
Zoya
Zsa Zsa
Zsofe
Zsofia
Zusa
Zuza

WHAT'S IN A NAME?

♥ ♂ **AARON**   Aharon Ari, Arin, Arnie, Arnina, Aron, Arona, Haroun, Ron, Ronny: The biblical Aaron, the first High Priest of the Israelites, was ultimately renowned as a great peacemaker. But he is best known for helping his younger brother Moses and his sister Miriam liberate the children of Israel from slavery in Egypt. When the brothers appeared before the pharaoh to demand freedom, Aaron acted as Moses' spokesman, since Moses was a stutterer. Aaron demonstrated the power of the Hebrew God by throwing his staff down onto the floor in front of the pharaoh, where God miraculously transformed it into a snake. Another miracle associated with Aaron's staff occurred when God commanded it to burst into bloom, thus creating the flower that became known as the goldenrod.

There is some dispute as to whether the name *Aaron* comes from the Egyptian word *haron*, meaning "high mountain" or "mountain of strength," or from the Hebrew word *aharon*. *Aharon* means "light" or "bright" and is also related to words that mean "to sing" and "to enlighten"—a fitting choice for this high priest who taught his people, lit the menorah in the desert sanctuary, and sang holy songs.

The Arab version of the name is *Haroun*. Haroun-al-Raschid (Aaron the Just), was a powerful ruler in eighth-century Persia. Also known as the Caliph of Baghdad, Haroun is the hero of *The Arabian Nights*.

Early in the Middle Ages, Jewish parents chose biblical names for their children, but the practice didn't become popular among Christians until the sixteenth century, when Protestants shunned names that did not have religious associations. By that time, *Aaron* was a revered name because of Saint Aaron, who was martyred under the Roman emperor Diocletian.

During the seventeenth century in the American South, the wives and daughters of plantation owners were given the duty of renaming slaves when they refused to reveal their African names. More often than not, the women chose biblical names. *Aaron* was especially popular, which is ironic in light of the original Aaron's role in helping to lead his people out of bondage. Perhaps because of this association with liberation, the name enjoyed a revival among African Americans beginning around 1915.

By the late 1800s, *Aaron* had spread across Europe, North America, and Australia and was among the top 100 names worldwide. Jewish immigrants to North America and Australia breathed new life into the name by using it as a surname. It was a Jewish tradition to take as a surname the appellation of a priest or king, and add *bar, off, vitch,* or *kin*—all of which mean *son of*—to the end of it. *Bar Aron* (son of Aaron) became *Baron. Aranoff, Aronovitch, Arkin,* and *Aaronson* all thrived as last names among immigrants, and they are still prevalent among Jewish Americans and in Israel. A Yiddish nickname for *Aaron* was *Haare* or *Hurre,* and many with that nickname adopted *Hirsh* or *Harris* as a surname in the New World.

Aaron is widely used among the Amish, and in the general population it remains a popular first name among Jews and non-Jews alike. In Hawaii, *Aaron* is known as *A'alona.* It is still among the top 40 most-used male names in the United States.

⊚ Number

Four. Above all, fours are dependable. Many are born leaders, with a natural proclivity for making their way to the top in their chosen field.

☾ Astrological sign

Aries. Ruled by the planet Mars and charged by its element of fire, Aries people are dynamic and courageous, and they exude self-confidence.

☀ Color

Brownish red. Brown is a color of security and promotes a feeling of ease. The combination of brown and red helps to allay fear and stress, acting as a stabilizer against anxiety.

◆ Stone

Jet. Since Roman times, jet has been used by travelers as a safety charm for hazardous journeys. It was also burned as incense. It was believed that a jet necklace united the body and soul and that once one wore it, one should never part with a jet stone.

🌿 Element

Gold. Gold enhances and is an excellent complement to the powers of jet.

⚘ Herb

Goldenrod *(Solidago virgaurea).* The flowering tops and leaves of the goldenrod plant, brewed as a tea by herbalists, are used for kidney problems and whooping cough.

♂ AATAMI: From the root name *Adam*.

♀ ABAGAEL: From the root name *Abigail*.

♀ ABAGIL: From the root name *Abigail*.

♀ ABAIGEAL: From the root name *Abigail*.

♀ ABAME: From the root name *Abraham*.

♂ ABARRAN: From the root name *Abraham*.

♀ ABARRANE: From the root name *Abraham*.

♀ ABBE: From the root name *Abigail*.

♀ ABBIE: From the root name *Abigail*.

♀ ABBY: From the root name *Abigail*.

♀ ABBYE: From the root name *Abigail*.

♀ ABBYGAIL: From the root name *Abigail*.

♂ ABE: From the root name *Abraham*.

♂ ABIE: From the root name *Abraham*.

♥ ♀ **ABIGAIL   Abagael, Abagil, Abaigeal, Abbe, Abbie, Abby, Abbye, Abbygail, Gail, Gaila, Gayel, Gayle:** Taken from the Hebrew *Avigayil,* a contraction of *avi* (father, or source) and *gil* (joyous stirrings or joyous happenings), *Abigail* literally means "the source of joy." In the Old Testament accounts, Samuel referred to Abigail, the wife of King David, as a woman of common sense and efficient action.

The name gained popularity among non-Jews during the sixteenth century, when it began to appear in English birth registers alongside many other biblical names. One hundred years later, though, Abigail fell from favor in England. The Puritans may have been most responsible for the drop in popularity. As a group, they frowned on *Abigail,* possibly because of the biblical Abigail's scandalous behavior in marrying King David immediately after her first husband's death. Also in England, a series of popular playwrights used Abigail for the characters of servants. Consequently, *abigail* became a slang term for a maid.

Rarely did *Abigail* appear in early colonial birth records, but the appellation did become common after 1675 in non-Puritan communities. Although chosen regularly throughout the eighteenth century, *Abigail* suffered the same fate as all biblical names in the early part of the nineteenth century. Then in the mid-1800s, a hugely popular Abigail surfaced as a spirited innkeeper in Charles Dickens's *Our Mutual Friend,* and, perhaps owing to Dickens's fame, the name took off once again.

In the United States, *Abigail* began a rapid rise in popularity during the 1970s, and its current revival places it among the top 50 U.S. girls' names. Girls named *Abigail* are frequently called by the diminutive *Abbie,* sometimes spelled *Abby. Abbie* is sometimes used as an independent name.

Gail (with variants of *Gayle and Gaila*) started as a pet name for *Abigail,* but is now considered to be a given name in its own right. *Gail* reached its height of popularity in the United States in the 1940s, and continued to be used regularly until the late 1970s.

☉ Number

Five. People of this number have an abundance of energy and are happiest when in the company of others. Spirituality is a large part of their lives. Fives can be restless, and they experience intense moodiness.

☾ Astrological sign

Aquarius. One of the noblest traits of Aquarians is their humanitarianism. But Aquarius is an air sign, and its natives approach interpersonal relationships with free spirits. They fare best when they are independent of restrictions in life or love.

✹ Color

Sky blue. This color is associated with peace and promotes imagination. It also placates a troubled mind.

◆ Stone

Sodalite. Sodalite has been discovered in ancient tombs and was once mistaken for turquoise because of its similarity in color. Egyptian priests used sodalite to dispel guilt and fear and to strengthen the power of mind over body.

♔ Element

Calcite. Calcite is usually found in sodalite, appearing as white veins or patches throughout the blue stone, making sodalite resemble clouds and sky.

♔ Herb

Lady's Mantle *(Alchemilla vulgaris)*. This plant is found in eastern North America, Greenland and northern Asia. The stems can be bluish green with small green flowers. Herbalists brew lady's mantle into a tonic to increase appetite and soothe stomach ailments. Early dentists found it useful to stop bleeding after pulling teeth.

♀ ABRA: From the root name *Abraham*.

♥ ♂ **ABRAHAM** **Abame, Abarran, Abarrane, Abe, Abie, Abra, Abrahamo, Abrahan, Abrahana, Abram, Abrami, Abramo, Abramovitch, Abrams, Abramson, Abran, Arram, Avram, Braham, Bram, Eberman, Ibrahim:** The biblical Abraham was originally called Abram, or Av-ram, meaning "exalted father." *Abraham* is a Hebrew name, but *Av-ram* most likely is not. Many linguists believe it derives from the ancient language spoken in Mesopotamia, where Abraham was born. In any case, when God appointed Av-ram patriarch of the Israelites, God changed the name to *Abraham,* meaning "father of multitudes."

Although Abraham was himself much revered, there were no rabbis in the Talmud who took his name, perhaps out of respect, and Abraham seems to have been neglected for several centuries. When the name appears next in a historical context, it is among the Christians, not the Jews. The appellation appeared twice in the land of the patriarch's birth. In the fourth century, a Mesopotamian hermit, Saint Abraham, was added to the Coptic and Eastern Orthodox calendars, and another Abraham was martyred. One hundred years later, yet another pair of Mesopotamian Abrahams were made saints. Before his death, one of these two saints made his way to France and, it is believed, introduced the name to that country.

The biblical Abraham is the patriarch of the Muslim faith as well as of the Jewish and Christian faiths. During the rise of Islam, after the sixth century A.D., *Ibrahim* became one of the most widely used names for boys among Arab Muslims, and it has never gone out of favor. With a growing population of Arab Americans, *Ibrahim* is becoming a commonly heard name in the United States.

Abraham finally came into common use among Jews—in England—during the twelfth century. British Christians didn't choose *Abraham* until after the Reformation in the sixteenth century when it gained popularity throughout the British Isles. By 1644, *Abraham* had traveled to the Netherlands, where it was shortened to *Abram, Bram,* and *Abra,* the latter being the feminine form.

Abraham came to the New World with the Pilgrims in the seventeenth century, but it fell out of favor for the next two hundred years. By the mid-nineteenth century, it was considered to be old-fashioned, though after the Civil War the shorter *Abram* caught on, most likely as a "modernized" tribute to President Lincoln.

Surnames have arisen from *Abraham* and are found worldwide as *Abrams, Abramson, Abramovitch, Braham,* and *Eberman.*

Number

Eight. Eights often have deep natures and great strength of character. Although sometimes set in their ways, they believe that nothing is impossible and are willing to work hard to make things happen.

Astrological sign

Capricorn. Capricorn is an earth sign, which means that it is concerned with the body and the physical world. Capricorns are ruled by the planet Saturn and the number eight. They are possessed of great courage and fortitude.

Color

Nile green. This shade of green represents metaphysical balance. Dark green is a color of Capricorn.

Stone

Andradite garnet. This rare type of bright green garnet is highly valued for its unusual color.

Element

Titanium. Andradite garnets contain titanium, the strongest metal on earth.

🦎 Herb

Sage *(Salvia officinalis)*. Dried sage has been used since ancient times as a brewed tea to relieve symptoms of tuberculosis and other respiratory illnesses. The tea is still quite popular in the Middle East and other regions. The native peoples of North America burn bundles of sage to cleanse the air both physically and spiritually.

♂ ABRAHAMO: From the root name *Abraham*.

♂ ABRAHAN: From the root name *Abraham*.

♀ ABRAHANA: From the root name *Abraham*.

♂ ABRAM: From the root name *Abraham*.

♂ ABRAMI: From the root name *Abraham*.

♂ ABRAMO: From the root name *Abraham*.

♂ ABRAMOVITCH: From the root name *Abraham*.

♂ ABRAMS: From the root name *Abraham*.

♂ ABRAMSON: From the root name *Abraham*.

♂ ABRAN: From the root name *Abraham*.

♂ AD: From the root name *Adam*.

♀ ADA: From the root name *Adam*.

♥ ♂ **ADAM** **Aatami, Ad, Ada, Adama, Adamina, Adamine, Adamo, Adams, Adan, Adana, Adao, Addie, Addis, Addison, Ade, Adhamh, Adnet, Mina:** Although *Adam* is associated with the Judeo-Christian myth of the first man, our modern use of the name may very well derive from *Adam*'s resemblance to the pagan Celtic name *Aedh*, or "fire."

In the Old Testament, *Adam* comes from *adamah*, a

Hebrew word meaning "red." Scholars believe the word *red* referred to clay or to red-colored earth—specifically, the red earth from which the first man was created. It may also allude to ruddy skin (thus was the biblical Esau surnamed Edom, or "ruddy"). Yet another interpretation links it to the word that means "likeness." In the book of Genesis, *adamah* signifies all of humankind.

Although one of the oldest proper names with Hebrew roots, *Adam* was not commonly used in Jewish communities (although *Eve* was). Its popularity as a Christian child's name began in England, Ireland, and Scotland during the late Middle Ages, thanks to the ninth abbot of Iona; Adamnan, or Adam the Little. Adamnan was a local man who bore the Celtic name of *Aedh*. When he was christened, his pagan name was forsworn in favor of *Adam*, which sounded similar. Adam the Little was instrumental in creating Adamnan's Law, which served to protect women, children, and the clergy during warfare.

After his death, the much-loved Adamnan was canonized, and different versions of his name appeared throughout the British Isles. Common variants included *Awnan*, *Ennan*, and *Onan*. Evidence of Adam's popularity can be seen in the number of surnames that were coined from it in the period following Adamnan's death, among them *Adams, Addison, Atkins,* and *MacAdam*. *Adam* caught on particularly well in Scotland. In the nineteenth century it evolved into a popular girls' name, as many baby girls were baptized *Adamina*. *Adam* became *Adamo* in Italy and *Adan* in Spain. It also traveled to Scandinavia, where it took root as *Aatami*.

In America, the Puritans shunned the name because of its association with the doctrine of Original Sin. So ingrained was this doctrine that it appeared as the first entry in the *New England Primer,* the basic textbook for all Puritan children from 1737 on:

In Adam's fall
We sinned all

Adam came into vogue in the United States and Great Britain in the 1960s. A 1976 London survey revealed that *Adam* was among the top 10 names chosen by women connoting sex appeal and manliness. In the United States, *Adam* now ranks among the top 50 boys' names.

✹ Number

Five. People of this number can be idealistic and impulsive. They seem to have no middle ground, and although they usually have a positive outlook on life, if they tend toward the negative, they will be strongly so. Above all, they possess enormous curiosity and get along with everyone, particularly other fives.

☽ Astrological sign

Taurus. The sign of the bull works well for Adam because its element is earth and because it is associated with the physical body. Taureans are best known for their practical, down-to-earth natures. They are warm and loving but can turn bullish when crossed.

✳ Color

Red. Civilizations of the past associated this color with birth and death. It is still considered a sacred color in many cultures.

◆ Stone

Chrysoprase. Chrysoprase is a rare chalcedony, or variety of quartz agate. Chrysoprase contains patterns of organic matter that enhance its elemental energy properties. It was highly prized by the Greeks and Romans for its beauty and translucent apple green color.

♛ Element

Nickel. The presence of the mineral nickel gives chrysoprase its brilliant hue.

🐉 Herb

Wild jalap *(Ipomoea pandurata)*. This herb is commonly called man-in-the-earth, or manroot. It is a native North American plant with tuberous roots and reddish purple trailing stems. Traditionally, balms made from the root were used to treat a variety of skin ailments.

♀   ADAMA: From the root name *Adam*.

♀   ADAMINA: From the root name *Adam*.

♀   ADAMINE: From the root name *Adam*.

♂   ADAMO: From the root name *Adam*.

♂   ADAMS: From the root name *Adam*.

♀♂ ADAN: From the root names *Adam* and *Aidan*.

♀   ADANA: From the root name *Adam*.

♂   ADAO: From the root name *Adam*.

♀ ♂ ADDIE: From the root name *Adam*.

♂   ADDIS: From the root name *Adam*.

♂   ADDISON: From the root name *Adam*.

♂   ADE: From the root names *Adam* and *Adrian*.

♀   ADELAIDE: From the root name *Alice*.

♀   ADELICE: From the root name *Alice*.

♂   ADHAMH: From the root name *Adam*.

♂   ADIRAN: From the root name *Adrian*.

♂   ADNET: From the root name *Adam*.

♀   ADREA: From the root name *Adrian*.

♀   ADRIA: From the root name *Adrian*.

♥ ♀♂ **ADRIAN**   Ade, Adiran, Adrea, Adria, Adriana, Adriano, Adrie, Adrien, Adrienah, Adrienne, Adrik, Adryan, Hadria, Hadrian, Hadrienne: *Adrian* is a Latin name, indicating someone who hailed from the region of Italy's Adriatic Sea. The root *adria* means "black."

One of history's most prominent bearers of the name was the Roman Emperor Publius Aelius Hadrianus. He reigned from A.D. 117 to 138 and built the famed Hadrian's Wall across northern England. The wall was a celebrated feat of engineering for its time.

There were several Saint Adrians, but the most influential was a member of the Roman army who converted to Christianity after witnessing the intense conviction of the early martyrs. He was eventually martyred himself. His bones were taken to Constantinople, then moved to Rome, and finally housed in several abbeys throughout Flanders (modern-day Belgium and parts of France and Holland). Because of the supposed miracles associated with these relics, his name became common in that region as *Arje, Janus, Arrian,* and *Arne.* The French developed a fondness for *Adrien* and added the feminine form *Adrienne.*

Another important Saint Adrian was born in Africa. In the eighth century, he became the first Abbot of Saint Augustine's in Canterbury. This Adrian was a learned scholar, and under his directorship Saint Augustine's became renowned for academic excellence.

Although *Adrian* does not appear often in early English history, the name surfaces with more frequency after the Norman Conquest in 1066. It was given a boost in the twelfth century when Nicholas Breakespear, the only English pope, took it as a papal name, becoming Adrian IV. However, *Adrian* has always been rare in birth records until its inexplicable resurgence—both in its masculine and feminine forms—in Great Britain and Australia in the 1950s.

The name remained popular throughout England, Wales, and Australia through 1975, when it began to disappear. Although *Adrian* has seen revival in some European countries, the feminine form *Adriana* is used more often in the United States. It has ranked among the top 100 girls' names. Another feminine form of the name, *Adria,* is more rare.

Number

Two. Numerologists and astrologers link the number two to the moon. Twos are usually gentle people. They are sentimental, make friends easily, and they form lifelong commitments to those they love.

☾ Astrological sign

Cancer. Cancers tend to be tender-hearted and romantic. Cancer is a water sign, which means that those born under this sign are in touch with the mysterious side of life.

✳ Color

Azure. This shade of blue lightens the heart and lifts the soul.

◆ Stone

Black coral. Ancients believed that wearing coral protected sea travelers and repelled shark attacks. Coral was also reputed to protect children. Black coral is rare, found only off the coasts of the West Indies and Australia.

♔ Element

Silver. Mystics consider silver to be a protective metal that enhances the already formidable power of black coral.

🌿 Herb

Seaweed *(Laminaria spp.)*. This plant, also called kelp or sea vegetable, grows in ocean "forests" throughout the world. It is favored by many Eastern cultures as a dietary staple. Seaweed is high in calcium and iron. It has been suggested that seaweed can protect against the absorption of harmful metals by the bones.

♀   ADRIANA: From the root name *Adrian*.

♂   ADRIANO: From the root name *Adrian*.

♀   ADRIE: From the root name *Adrian*.

♂   ADRIEN: From the root name *Adrian*.

♀   ADRIENAH: From the root name *Adrian*.

♀   ADRIENNE: From the root name *Adrian*.

♂   ADRIK: From the root name *Adrian*.

♂   ADRYAN: From the root name *Adrian*.

♂   AGOSTIN: From the root name *Austin*.

♂   AHARON: From the root name *Aaron*.

♥ ♀♂ **AIDAN**   **Adan, Aiden, Edan, Eden:** *Aidan* comes from a diminutive of the ancient Celtic name *Aodh,* meaning "fire." It is related to the Greek *aitho,* which is the source of our word *heat.*

There are a number of Welsh myths, which may be based on Druidic myths, that recount the exploits of the sun god Hu Gadran. Tales of Hu Gadran also mention someone called Aedh Mawr. Because *aedh* is "fire," experts believe that this may have been another name for the solar deity.

Various forms of *Aedh* were so prevalent in Wales, Scotland, and Ireland that 200 young men bearing some variant of the name were recorded as having been killed in

15

the early medieval Battle of Maghrath. Eventually several surnames evolved as boys were given the second name of *MacAedh* (son of Aedh), which became also *Magee, Mackey,* and *MacHugh*. In sixth century Scotland, *Edan,* or *Aidan,* was a ruler who is said to have given his name to the capital city, Edinburgh (although some linguists dispute this).

The seventh-century Saint Aidan was an Irish monk who founded the famous church on the isle of Lindisfarne off the coast of England. He had been called to convert the pagans of northern England after previous missionaries had failed, claiming the Anglo-Saxons were so barbaric as to be unteachable. Aidan's gentle ways and compassionate behavior soon brought multitudes to the church.

Thereafter, *Aidan* became less common, though it was briefly revived during a nineteenth-century British religious movement within the Church of England. Beginning with the turn of the twentieth century, *Aidan* has been growing steadily in popularity in Ireland and elsewhere. Although the old Irish *Eithne* for a girl is now obsolete, *Aidan* is still found as a girl's name in modern Wales. *Aidan* reached a peak in the 1960s and declined again in the 1970s. With the current interest in Irish names, though, it is enjoying a revival today both in the United States and Great Britain.

◉ Number

Two. This number is most often associated with the natural world. Two represents opposites, such as male and female or night and day. People of this number are imaginative and prone to restlessness.

☽ Astrological sign

Aries. The sign of the ram is ruled by the planet Mars and by the element of fire. Aries people are assertive, outspoken, and passionate about everything they do.

Color

Burnt orange. This fiery shade, the color of sunrise and sunset, helps to focus meditative energy.

 ## Stone

Red spinel. Spinel, a member of the crystal family, was once believed to boost physical strength during times of exhaustion. Although this gem comes in a variety of colors, red spinel is valued for its resemblance to rubies.

 ## Element

Iron. The distinctive hue of the red spinel comes from its high iron content. In mythology, iron represented the god Mars.

Herb

Pilewort *(Erechtites hieracifolia)*. Commonly called fireweed, this plant is found in fields and burned-over wastelands. A tonic of the crushed plant was once used to reduce fever.

♀   AIDEN: From the root name *Aidan.*

♀   AILA: From the root name *Helen.*

♀   AILEEN: From the root name *Helen.*

♀   AIMEE: From the root name *Amanda.*

♀♂ AINDREA: From the root name *Andrew.*

♀   AIRIKA: From the root name *Eric.*

♂   AL: From the root names *Alan/Allen* and *Alexander.*

♀   ALA: From the root name *Alice.*

♀   ALAINA: From the root name *Alan/Allen.*

♂   ALAIR: From the root name *Alan/Allen.*

♂   ALAIRE: From the root name *Hilary.*

♥ ♂ **ALAN/ALLEN**   Al, Alaina, Alair, Alana, Alaine,
Alaina, Aland, Alandra, Alani, Alanis, Aianna, Alanson,
Aleyna, Allan, Allena, Allene, Alley, Alleyene, Lana, Lena:
Alan means "cheerful" in its English form; its Celtic form,
Allen, means "harmony." The Latin *Aelianus* translates to
"sun-bright," and *Alun* is Gaelic for "fair and beautiful."

In tracing *Alan* back through Welsh genealogies, we find
that it first may have appeared as Alwn Aulerv, brother of
Bran the Blessed. According to Welsh and Druidic myths,
Bran, accompanied by Alwn, obtained a magic bowl in
Ireland that cured mortal wounds and raised the dead. The
bowl was counted as one of the 13 wonders of the British
Isles.

Alan also has musical connections, for an *Alawn,* meaning "light," was one of the great bards of ancient Britain.
Although there was no real historical connection, the Welsh
linked *Alawn* to the ancient Greek poet Olen, lauded as the
first to write hymns in hexameter and whose name actually
means "flute player." Further lyrical association comes from
the Robin Hood legend of Alan-a-dale, a famous bard noted
for his agility and cleverness. This Alan may well have contributed to the name's popularity in the Middle Ages.

The spelling *Alan* seems to have come to England in the
twelfth century with the count of Brittany, Alan Fergeant.
The count, a friend of William the Conqueror's, lent an aura
of nobility to the name, and thereafter many highborn sons
were christened *Alan.* Several barons bore the name, and so,
owing to intermarriage, the name made its way into
Scotland and then throughout Europe. It was one of the
most common names of seventeenth-century England.

Although the spelling of the name varied, it was mainly
seen as *Allen* or *Alan* in England and Scotland. In Wales,
Alun was used, most likely due to the prominence of the
Alun River, after which a large region was also named.
However, the French preferred *Alain* and the Germans

altered it to *Alane*. Several feminine derivatives arose, including *Alaine, Allene, Alanna, Alana,* and *Alleyene*. However, *Alana* can also be traced to Hawaiian roots meaning "light and buoyant," and to Hebrew roots meaning "the little tree." In the United States *Lana* and *Lena* both became somewhat common as names unto themselves in the 1930s, but they quickly fell out of favor.

Alan's popularity continued to ebb and flow throughout Europe and the world, peaking in the 1950s in North America, perhaps owing to the growth of the movie industry and the celebrity of Alan Ladd, who made many movies throughout the 1940s and 1950s. Although *Alan*'s usage declined after the 1950s, it never entirely faded and is once again returning to favor.

Number

One. This number represents highly creative people. Ones are focused and imaginative. They usually have piercing or otherwise unusual eyes.

Astrological sign

Sagittarius. Sagittarians are usually enthusiastic and cheerful. Although they can be overly assertive and downright rowdy, they are never malicious. They are interested in religion and spirituality.

Color

Bronze. A combination of yellow and brown, bronze is a color of warmth. It is associated with communication in the form of voice projection, such as singing or broadcasting.

Stone

Falcon's-eye. Falcon's-eye is a stone from the chrysoberyl family and is classified as an "animal-eye stone." The falcon's-eye is considered one of the "strongest" eye stones and has long been thought to aid in self-control.

⚜ Element

Tin. Tin is one of the metals connected with Sagittarius. It is used to coat alloys such as bronze.

⚜ Herb

Linden *(Tilia europaea)*. Found in the forests of Europe, the yellow-brown flowers and bark of this tree have been used to treat coughs and laryngitis.

♀ ALANA: From the root name *Alan/Allen*.

♂ ALAND: From the root name *Alan/Allen*.

♀ ALANDRA: From the root name *Alexander*.

♀ ALANI: From the root name *Alan/Allen*.

♀ ALANIS: From the root name *Alan/Allen*.

♂ ALANSON: From the root name *Alan/Allen*.

♀♂ ALASDAIR: From the root name *Alexander*.

♀♂ ALASTAIR: From the root name *Alexander*.

♀ ALASTRINA: From the root name *Alexander*.

♂ ALEC: From the root name *Alexander*.

♀ ALECIA: From the root name *Alice*.

♀ ALEETHIA: From the root name *Alice*.

♀ ALEJANDRA: From the root name *Alexander*.

♂ ALEJANDRO: From the root name *Alexander*.

♂ ALEK: From the root name *Alexander*.

♀ ALEKIA: From the root name *Alexander*.

♀ ALENI: From the root name *Alice*.

♀   ALESIA: From the root name *Alice*.

♀   ALESSANDRA: From the root name *Alexander*.

♂   ALESSANDRE: From the root name *Alexander*.

♀♂ ALEX: From the root name *Alexander*.

♀   ALEXA: From the root name *Alexander*.

♥ ♂ **ALEXANDER** **Al, Alandra, Alasdair, Alastair, Alaster, Alastrina, Alec, Alejandra, Alejandro, Alek, Alekia, Alesche, Alessandra, Alessandre, Alesandro, Alex, Alexa, Alexandr, Alexandra, Alexandre, Alexandria, Alexe, Alexandrina, Alexandrine, Alexei, Alexia, Alexio, Alexis, Ally, Cesya, Iskander, Lex, Lexie, Lissandre, Sacha, Sanders, Sandor, Sandra, Sandro, Sandy, Sascha, Sashi, Saunders, Saundra, Sikandra, Sondra, Xan, Xander, Xandra, Zan, Zander, Zandra, Zindel, Zondra:** *Alexander* originated from the Greek *alexios* (defender) and *ander* (man). Paris, the son of Priam, king of Troy, earned the title "defender of man" when he helped protect the local shepherds from raiders.

Alexander later became a family name among Macedonian kings and gained universal prominence when Alexander the Great, king of Macedonia (356-323 B.C.) expanded his empire and influence throughout the known world. During that period the name became so popular that even Maccabean Jews used it, spreading it throughout Judea. In the postclassical period New Testament figures and many Christian saints were named Alexander. An early convert to Christianity bore the name (a son of the apostle Simon) and carried the cross for Jesus on the road to Calvary.

Pope Alexander I headed the Catholic Church in the second century until he was martyred. Eight more popes have taken *Alexander* as a name since. In the fifth century a young Roman noble named Allexius took monastic vows to avoid a forced marriage. After 17 years in seclusion, he returned home disguised as a pilgrim and spent another 17 years begging scraps from his father's kitchen. He endured abuse by the servants until his dying moments when he made himself known to his family. He was canonized Saint Alessio, and his feast day, July 17, is still observed in Greece and in Rome.

Alexander took hold in Scotland during the thirteenth century when three kings reigned in succession from 1214 to 1285. In the Highlands, the name changed to *Alaster* and eventually evolved into the surname MacAlister. In the American South, the name contracted to *Alick* and *Saunders* (*Sander*), and was eventually used in surnames such as *Saunderson, Sanders,* and *Sanderson.* These forms of *Alexander* traveled to all English-speaking countries.

Other variations evolved as *Alexander* traveled the world. Germans favored *Alexandr* or *Alexio,* and the French favored *Alexandre* or *Alexe.* Italians shortened *Alessandro* to *Sandro* and Spaniards took *Alejandro.* Russians preferred *Alexei* and *Alescha. Alexis* became popular for Englishmen and -women, but *Alexander* remains the form of choice in the United States. It was consistently in the top 40 throughout the early 1990s.

Feminine versions are well established: *Alexia* in Germany and *Alexandrine* in France. *Alexandra, Alexandrina* and *Alexa* are found in English-speaking areas as well as in Russia. It is said that the mother of the fourteenth-century Saint Thomas of Canterbury was named *Alisaundre. Alexandrina* and *Alexandra* were popularized in England when Queen Victoria's son Edward VII (1841-1910) married Princess Alexandra of Denmark. The feminine diminutive, *Sandra,* is popular worldwide, but it has been most prevalent in the United States, especially during the 1940s, the 1960s, and the 1970s. Currently, *Alexandra* is among the top 50 girls' names, along with *Alexandrina* and *Alexis.*

Unusual pet names include *Xander* (or *Zander*) for men

and *Xan* (or *Zan*) for men and women. Sascha is a nickname for Russian men named *Alexander*. Common nicknames in the United States include *Alex, Alec,* and *Al.* Such celebrities as Alec Baldwin keep these names fresh and popular. *Alex* and *Alec* have both ranked in the top 100 United States boys' names in recent years.

Number

Eight. These people have the ability to drive themselves and others. They are excellent organizers. Eights are born leaders and like to conquer what seems impossible. Sometimes eights can be relentless risk-takers.

Astrological sign

Capricorn. Capricorn is an earth sign and is ruled by the number eight. Capricorns often achieve their goals through relentless persistence.

Color

Cyprus brown. This earth tone is associated with stability. It calms the emotions, promoting inner serenity.

Stone

Alexandrite. Alexandrite is a rare and valuable gem with the unusual ability to change color. In daylight it can appear blue-green, but incandescent light alters it to golden or reddish brown. Alexandrite is said to draw luck and love to those who wear it.

Element

Beryllium. Beryllium is a corrosion-resistant metallic element used in alloys because of its stability.

🌿 **Herb**

Plantain *(Plantago lanceolata)*. This herb is also called sheep's herb. Farmers plant it for their flocks to graze on, but it also grows wild from seaside meadows to mountaintops. It has tiny white flowers with brown sepals. Practitioners of traditional Chinese medicine use plantain to treat lung problems, especially asthma and bronchitis. Crushed fresh leaves can be applied to wounds and insect bites to stop bleeding and encourage healing.

♀   ALEXANDRA: From the root name *Alexander.*

♀   ALEXANDRIA: From the root name *Alexander.*

♂   ALEXEI: From the root name *Alexander.*

♀   ALEXIA: From the root name *Alexander.*

♂   ALEXIO: From the root name *Alexander.*

♀♂   ALEXIS: From the root name *Alexander.*

♀   ALEYNA: From the root name *Alan/Allen.*

♀   ALIANA: From the root name *Helen.*

💙 ♀ **ALICE** **Adelaide, Adelice, Ala, Alecia, Alesia, Aleethia, Aleni, Alicia, Alikah, Alisha, Alison, Allis, Allison, Ally, Allyson, Elissa, Ella, Elsa, Ilysee, Leese, Licha:** *Alice* is no stranger to royalty. The name means "of noble kind." It derived from the Old German name *Adelaide* (which also turned into *Adeline,* which in turn became *Adele*). In Old German, *athal* is "noble" and *haidu* is "sort" or "kind." But *haidu* also sounds like the Old German word for "cheer," and thus many name experts translate *Alice* as "of noble cheer." In Norman French, *Adelaide* became *Adelais,* then *Aaliz,* and finally *Aliz.* By the twelfth century, the name was being spelled *Alesia* and *Alicia* and was very popular in both England and France.

Alice was exceptionally common throughout the Middle Ages, but it fell into decline during the Reformation and by American Colonial times had nearly disappeared. By then, it had become associated with an old-fashioned, rural lifestyle. However, *Alice* saw a revival in the nineteenth century with the surge of interest in the romances of the Middle Ages. With the publication of Lewis Carroll's *Alice's Adventures in Wonderland* (1865) and *Through the Looking Glass* (1871), the popularity of *Alice* soared in English-speaking countries. By the turn of the twentieth century, *Alice* was second only to *Mary*, and it remained so in the United States through the 1930s and 1940s. By the mid-1950s, however, Alice all but vanished as a given name.

Some say that *Alison* is a French derivative of *Alice*—first used during the Middle Ages—that just happened to have caught on particularly well in Scotland. Other experts believe the popular Scottish *Alison* originated as a feminine version of *Louis* (famous warrior) and that the name evolved from *Aloys* to *Heloise* to *Alison*.

Whatever its origin, *Alison* traveled to France in the thirteenth century where it retained its stature as an independent name. In England, Geoffrey Chaucer, author of the enormously popular *Canterbury Tales,* brought recognition to the name in 1386, and it remained popular through the seventeenth century. *Alison* eventually appeared in northern England as *Alieen*.

Spellings appeared as *Allyson* or *Alisone,* and the creative combination of *Alice* and *Anne* yielded *Alisanne* and *Alysanne. Alison* became a name of social status in England when *Alice*'s popularity fell after 1925. *Alison* skyrocketed to the United States and even had enough fuel to explode in Australia as a wildly popular name. It's still a favored name in both places. *Ally* is another derivative that's been gathering favor (especially among television fans of the show *Ally McBeal*).

It seems logical to link *Alice* with *Alyssa* or *Alissa*. But *Alyssa*'s history is firmly connected to Greece, and it is considered an independent name of different roots.

 Number

Three. Threes are ambitious, and many are found in positions of authority. They are exceptionally trustworthy and possess a keen sense of justice.

 Astrological sign

Leo. This sign symbolizes nobility. Leo's planetary ruler is the sun, and its element is fire. Leos are known for their fiery enthusiasm, and like their lion totem, Leos are proud. Leos should guard against arrogance.

 Color

Tawny gold. This shade of yellow promotes self-confidence and psychic awareness. Gold is considered a protective color on the metaphysical plane, and various shades of it were worn during ancient rites to enhance mystical visualization.

 Stone

Ruby. Rubies rank among the top-valued gemstones. They are a variety of corundum, one of the hardest stones known. With the overmining of rubies, there is no longer an abundance of this gem, which increases its value even more. Historically, the ruby has been honored as the queen of gems, and it symbolizes the sun.

 Element

Platinum. Platinum, long linked with nobility, is the perfect setting to complement the ruby.

🦎 Herb

Lemon verbena *(Aloysia triphylla)*. Another name for this herb is queen-of-the-meadow. It grows as a large shrub or small tree, and has a strong lemon scent. Herbalists brew the dried leaves into tea, which they use as a sedative. The dried leaves are also used for long-lasting sachets and potpourris.

♀ ALIKAH: From the root name *Alice.*

♀ ALINA: From the root name *Helen.*

♀ ALISHA: From the root name *Alice.*

♀ ALICIA: From the root name *Alice.*

♀ ALISON: From the root name *Alice.*

♀ ALISSA: From the root name *Alyssa.*

♀ ALLAIRE: From the root name *Hilary.*

♂ ALLAN: From the root name *Alan/Allen.*

♀ ALLENA: From the root name *Alan/Allen.*

♂ ALLEY: From the root name *Alan/Allen.*

♀ ALLIS: From the root name *Alice.*

♀ ALLISON: From the root name *Alice.*

♀ ALLY: From the root names *Alexander* and *Alice.*

♀ ALLYSON: From the root name *Alice.*

♀ ALOYSIA: From the root name *Louis.*

♂ ALOYSIUS: From the root name *Louis.*

♀ ALYSA: From the root name *Alyssa.*

♀ **ALYSSA** **Alissa, Alysa, Ilyssa, Lissa, Lyssa:** *Alyssa* derives, quite simply, from the alyssum, a delicate flower with small greenish white, purple, or yellow blossoms and a sweet fragrance. The name may also be related to another plant—the alusson, whose name means "sane," so called because the plant is thought to cure rabies.

Some researchers link *Alyssa* to *Elissa* or *Lissa*. However, *Elissa* is more commonly associated with *Elizabeth*, the given name of Greek mythology's Queen Elissa Dido of Carthage. Also from Greek mythology, *Lissa*, a short form of *Melissa*, comes from the story of Melitus ("honey-sweet"), the priestess-nymph who taught humankind about the tricks of using honey.

As a point of interest, although flower names seem to have originated with the Greeks, many Anglo-Saxon names also came from plants or animals, and these were especially popular among the Scottish. Flower names were virtually unknown among the ancient Romans but surfaced in Europe in the late nineteenth century. The trend toward naming girls after flowers became extremely fashionable by the turn of the twentieth century. Names such as *Hazel, Violet, Ivy, Daisy,* and *Rosemary* cropped up throughout Europe and North America. Unusual names bloomed as well, such as *Cherry, Daffodil, Fern, Laurel,* and *Iris.*

Although the popularity of flower names saw a rapid demise in the early twentieth century, they experienced revival in the 1970s. *Alyssa* is among the top 25 most popular names. Two other flower and plant names that have regained popularity in recent years include Holly (from the Old English, meaning "to prick") and *Jasmine. Jasmine* is from the Persian word *yasemin,* and it is now one of the top 100 girls' names.

Number

Five. People of this number usually make friends easily but can be mercurial in disposition and somewhat high-strung. They crave excitement and tend to be open-minded freethinkers.

 Astrological sign

Gemini. This sign of the zodiac is ruled by the number five and by the element of air, which represents the mind and sanity. Typical Geminis are quick-witted and resourceful and love to talk.

Color

Citron yellow. *Alyssa*'s color is pale yellow, matching her floral namesake. Yellow is long believed to stimulate the intellect and enhance conversation.

Stone

Lace agate. Agates represent reliability. A lace agate in a yellow shade aids attitude and mental strength. Some believe lace agates ease depression by supporting the mind and increasing energy flow. Agates were used as healing amulets by the ancient Greeks, Egyptians, and Babylonians.

Element

Silver. Silver complements lace agates by acting as a metallic stabilizer for the gem's power. Mercury, also called quicksilver, is Gemini's ruling planet.

Herb

Lemon balm *(Melissa officinalis).* This herb has yellow splotched leaves and tiny fragrant flowers. Related to the mint family, its crushed leaves can be used in a poultice to soothe insect bites and skin injuries. Brewed as tea, it is purported to strengthen the brain and aid against cold and flu. According to an old Arab legend, lemon balm makes the heart merry.

♀   AMADA: From the root name *Amanda*.

♀   AMALIE: From the root name *Emily*.

♀   AMALINA: From the root name *Emily*.

♥ ♀ **AMANDA Aimee, Amada, Amadeus, Amandi, Amandine, Amaris, Amata, Ammy, Amy, Mabel, Manda, Mandi, Mandie, Miranda:** *Amanda* is a name linked to love. It began as a Latin word whose root, *amo*, means "to be loved." It made its way, virtually unchanged, into European languages as *Amanda* ("fit to be loved").

Gaelic Christians liked to name their children with derivatives of *Amanda*, and unusual forms were created such as *Amabilis* ("lovable"). *Amabilis* traveled to France as *Aimable*.

A Norman heiress of Gloucester was named Amabel, and this form gained favor among Old English families. Later it was shortened to *Mabel*, and another variation came from the Earl of Leicester when he named his daughter Amicia.

Just as feminine versions arose from male names, so did masculine forms derive from *Amanda*. One in particular, *Amadeus* ("loving God") belonged to famed Austrian composer Wolfgang Amadeus Mozart (1756–1791). Among other popular forms were *Amator* ("a lover"), *Amatus* and *Amata* ("loved"), and simply *Amand*. Sir Amadas was listed as one of King Arthur's Knights of the Round Table.

Amandus ("about to be loved") was borne by various saints from the fourth through seventh centuries. In the informal calendar of name or feast days that was created to commemorate various saints, the days for Amandus and Amatus are August 20 and February 6, respectively.

Amanda's popularity increased in the seventeenth century, possibly thanks to its use in many plays and books, including Daniel Defoe's 1724 romance *Roxana*. It has not gone completely out of fashion since. By 1975, *Amanda* ranked at the top of naming lists in England and Australia. *Amanda*'s popularity came more slowly to the United States, but during the 1980s and 1990s, it was a top name of choice, and it remains strong today.

Although *Amy* is chosen as a girl's name independently of Amanda, it was probably adapted from the French diminutive for *Amanda, Aimee*. The diminutive skyrocketed to popularity in the United States during the nineteenth century and is still a favored girl's name. *Amy*, like *Amanda*, appears frequently in literature. Characters such as Amy Dorrit in Charles Dickens's *Little Dorrit* and the little sister, Amy, from Louisa May Alcott's *Little Women*, brought popularity to the name.

Another variant of *Amanda* is *Miranda*, which comes from the Latin *mirandus* ("admirable") or *mirari* ("to wonder at, admire"). Some say that Shakespeare invented the name specifically for his heroine in *The Tempest*.

Pet names for *Amanda* include *Ammy, Manda,* and *Mandi*. Another literary connection is found with *Mandie*, a character in a popular children's series of middle-grade adventures set in the early 1900s.

Number

Seven. This number is usually associated with independence and with people who love to travel. Sevens are dreamers and seekers of truth.

Astrological sign

Cancer. This sign is ruled by the moon. Its element is water, which represents the soul. Cancers are sensitive to the feelings of those around them but are sometimes overly sensitive when criticized by others.

Color

Primrose pink. Pink has long been connected to love, and it promotes peace and joy.

 ## Stone

Watermelon tourmaline. Tourmalines are of the silicate family. Their name comes from the ancient Singhalese word *turmali* (mixed-color gemstone). The watermelon variety has an interior of red or pink surrounded by green. Medieval lore labeled this tourmaline as a balancer of male and female energies, and many used it to attract love.

 ## Element

Silver, the metal most often associated with the moon.

Herb

Lovage *(Levisticum officinale)*. Also called sea parsley, lovage is a wild herb found in Europe and Asia Minor. Ancients brewed its roots to aid various digestive troubles, as well as to treat rheumatism and fever. Skin problems were sometimes treated by soaking in a bath of lovage water. The plant has a pungent, aromatic scent.

♀   AMANDI: From the root name *Amanda*.

♀   AMANDINE: From the root name *Amanda*.

♀   AMARA: From the root name *Mary*.

♀   AMARIS: From the root name *Amanda*.

♀   AMATA: From the root name *Amanda*.

♀ **AMBER** Amberetta, Amberly, Ambert, Ambra, Ambre, Ambrogio, Ambrose, Ambrosia, Ambrosine, Ambrosio, Amby, Brose, Emrys: Though the name *Amber* did not come into use until the nineteenth century, the history of its namesake gemstone and of its antecedent names adds luster to its current popularity.

Amber is the fossilized resin of extinct conifer trees and was highly valued in ancient times. Artisans used it for decoration and carvings, but more important, early doctors prescribed ground amber powder and water as an aid for various stomach ills. Mixed with honey or oils, it was used as a salve to heal wounds. Worn as a gem, it supposedly protected against illness. It also was thought of as an elixir to heal everything except broken hearts!

Ancient Greeks called it *elektor,* which means "sun's glare." They considered it to be solid sunlight because it was warm to the touch. Another Greek link to *amber* came from *ambrose,* meaning "divine and immortal" or "pertaining to the immortals," with *ambrosia* being the name of a legendary life-giving elixir.

A point of interest: In the early 1700s, King Frederick I of Prussia became so enamored of the gemstone that he built a room using 100,000 pieces of amber, including rare shades of blue and green. Courtesans said they felt like they were inside a jewel when the sun shone through the windows. During World War II, the room was dismantled, and at the end of the war the cartons containing the pieces could not be found. Their whereabouts remains unknown.

Before the name *Amber* gained popularity in the nineteenth century, the masculine name *Ambrose* and its feminine form *Ambrosia* (now infrequently chosen) were prominent. *Ambrose* traveled west from Greece and became well known in the person of the bishop of Milan (A.D. 374). Saint

Ambrose, as he was better known, was one of the four great Latin doctors of the church. By the mid-fifteenth century, *Ambrose* was used regularly, and it experienced a rise in popularity in the 1600s.

The feminine form, *Ambrosia*, was made popular through the sister of Sir Philip Sidney in the sixteenth century. She was named after her uncle, Ambrose, Earl of Danwick. In Wales, *Ambrose* changed to *Emrys*, and the French altered it to *Ambre* and *Ambrosine*. Other variations occurred with *Amberetta* and *Ambert*, from the German meaning "bright and shiny."

Amber rose to prominence thanks to a popular nineteenth-century naming tradition using gemstones and minerals as names. Other popular gem names of the time included *Jewel, Amethyst, Jade, Diamond,* and *Ruby. Amber*'s popularity in the twentieth century seems inexorably tied to Kathleen Winsor's widely read 1944 novel *Forever Amber,* which is considered the prototype for the modern romance. The name enjoyed another boost when the book was made into a movie in 1947.

Although it faded somewhat in the 1970s, *Amber* revived and became a stylish girl's name from 1980 through the mid-1990s. It ranks among the top 40 girls' names.

Number

Three. Numerologically, this number describes people who are in touch with their environment. Threes have nurturing qualities—anything organic, be it plants, animals, or people, fares well under their care.

Astrological sign

Capricorn. In ancient legends, Capricornus was nurse to the young sun god, one of the oldest gods in history. Ruled by the planet Saturn, Capricorn's element is earth, which is a fitting association for *Amber.*

Color

Red-orange. The two components of this color are symbolic of the sun's glow. The combination of the two hues projects warmth and positive energy and, in some cultures, signifies divinity.

 ## Stone

Amber. Amber is an organic gemstone that has been revered by ancient cultures dating back to the beginning of recorded history. Its color usually ranges from yellow-brown to cherry-orange, depending on where it is found. In many Eastern civilizations, burnt amber was used for its disinfectant abilities, and midwives sterilized birthing areas with it.

 ## Element

Uranium. This silvery-white metallic element, used in research and as nuclear fuel, has powerful radioactive energy—using it is akin to harnessing a piece of the sun.

Herb

Everlasting *(Gnaphalium polycephalum)*. This plant, also called life everlasting, is a fragrant annual found in dry fields and pine woods along the Atlantic coast and as far west as Texas. Traditional lore suggests the plant be brewed into a tea and used for lung problems.

♀ AMBERETTA: From the root name *Amber*.

♀ AMBERLY: From the root name *Amber*.

♂ AMBERT: From the root name *Amber*.

♀ AMBRA: From the root name *Amber*.

♂ AMBRE: From the root name *Amber*.

♂ AMBROGIO: From the root name *Amber*.

♂ AMBROSE: From the root name *Amber*.

♀ AMBROSIA: From the root name *Amber*.

♂ AMBROSINE: From the root name *Amber*.

♂ AMBROSIO: From the root name *Amber*.

♂ AMBY: From the root name *Amber*.

♀ AMELIA: From the root name *Emily*.

♀ AMMY: From the root name *Amanda*.

♀ AMY: From the root name *Amanda*.

♂ ANDERS: From the root name *Andrew*.

♀ ANDRA: From the root name *Andrew*.

♂ ANDRÉ: From the root name *Andrew*.

♀ ANDRÉE: From the root name *Andrew*.

♂ ANDREA: From the root name *Andrew*.

♀ ANDREANA: From the root name *Andrew*.

♀ ANDREAS: From the root name *Andrew*.

♀ ANDREENA: From the root name *Andrew*.

♂ ANDREI: From the root name *Andrew*.

♀ ANDREL: From the root name *Andrew*.

♂ ANDRES: From the root name *Andrew*.

♀ ANDRESA: From the root name *Andrew*.

♀ ANDRETTE: *From the root name* Andrew.

♀ ANDREWINA: From the root name *Andrew*.

♥ ♂ **ANDREW** Aindrea, Anders, Andra, André, **Andrea, Andreas, Andreena, Andrei, Andrel, Andres, Andresa, Andrette, Andrewina, Andrezj, Andriana, Andy, Dandie, Deena, Drew, Drud, Drugi, Ohndrea, Rena, Tandie:** *Andrew* is a Greek name derived from *andros,* meaning "a man" or "strong" (manly). The name's first notable association is with Andreas the Galilean fisherman, known as Andrew, the first disciple of Jesus and brother of Simon Peter, also a disciple. Andrew was martyred at Patras in Achaea; from there, some of his relics eventually journeyed to Scotland, where Saint Andrew's Metropolitan See was established in the fourth century.

One of the relics, Saint Andrew's cross, became the symbol on the Scottish national emblem, making Saint Andrew a patron saint and later "Knightly Champion of Scotland." Other relics went to Constantinople, and after the fall of that city, they were spread throughout Europe. Philip the Good of Burgundy obtained several relics and made Saint Andrew the patron of the Order of the Golden Fleece. The travels of a saint's relics or bones almost always sparked the spread of the saint's name.

Saint Andrew's widespread popularity during the Middle Ages is illustrated by the 637 churches dedicated to him in England alone. Because of the devotion of his followers, many subsequent religious figures took the name. Owing to the number of saints with Andrew's name, there are several days honoring him: February 4, March 19, May 13 and 21, July 4, October 20, and November 10 and 30.

Andrew was a cherished name in sixteenth-century England and traveled easily across the sea to the Colonies. It took root in new soil and has never gone out of favor. *Andrew* reached a peak in popularity during the 1950s, faded in the 1960s, then rose again during the 1970s and 1980s. It shows up consistently among the top 10 boys' names today. The variation *André* is popular among African American families. *Andrew* also remains one of the top names in Great Britain, Scotland, and Australia and is common as the surname *Anderson* (son of Andrew).

The English feminine derivative *Andrea* grew popular in the United States during the 1980s and remains a popular girl's name. The French prefer *Andrée*, whereas *Andreana* is found in Italy. Unusual forms sometimes appear, such as *Andreena, Andrewina,* and *Andrette.* Independent feminine versions are scarce but have surfaced as *Dreena* or *Rena,* and *Drew* and *Andy* are used as a diminutive with both males and females.

Pet names once included *Dandie* and *Tandie* in Scotland, but were changed to *Andy* in English. Today, *Andy* is so often used that it's almost become an independent form itself.

⊚ Number

Two. Twos are sensitive and have strong instincts. If they follow their intuition, they will most likely keep themselves out of trouble. Some are passive, preferring to let others take the lead.

☾ Astrological sign

Pisces. Pisces—the Fishes—is an appropriate sign for Andrew, since one of the name's most notable carriers was a fisherman. Pisces's element is water, and those under this sign are ruled by the planets of Jupiter and Neptune.

✳ Color

Penncross green. When seen in someone's personal aura, green indicates peacefulness. On the physical plane, green represents lushness and new growth. Penncross grass is found on many golf courses. (The game of golf originated in Scotland, and today, its rules are established by the Royal and Ancient Golf Club at Saint Andrews in Scotland.)

◆ Stone

Amazonite. Also called Amazon stone, amazonite is a blue-green form of feldspar. Legends refer to it as the "hope stone"—it was worn to inspire faith and hope and to boost physical endurance under stress.

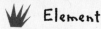 Element
Lead. The amazonite's striking color is due to its lead content.

☙ Herb
Myrrh *(Commiphora myrrha).* The clear, fragrant resin of the myrrh tree has been used since ancient times as incense in religious ceremonies. According to the Old Testament, Moses was instructed by God to use myrrh in holy oil to anoint priests. Myrrh was also believed to have been a gift from one of the wise men to the infant Jesus. Medicinally, myrrh powder was applied as a disinfectant for wounds.

♀ ANDREWENA: From the root name *Andrew.*

♂ ANDREZJ: From the root name *Andrew.*

♀ ANDRIANA: From the root name *Andrew.*

♀♂ ANDY: From the root name *Andrew.*

♀ ANECHKA: From the root name *Anna.*

♀ ANELA: From the root name *Angela.*

♀♂ ANGE: From the root name *Angela.*

♀♂ ANGEL: From the root name *Angela.*

♥ ♀ **ANGELA Anela, Ange, Angel, Angelica, Angelina, Angeline, Angelique, Angelita, Angelo, Angelyne, Angie, Angiola, Angy, Anngel, Annjela, Gelya:** When the name *Angela* is spoken, angels take notice! It originates from *angelos,* a Greek term meaning "spiritual messengers." Some say the name actually comes from Hebrew, where the last of the

Old Testament prophets, Malachi, was considered "the angel or messenger of God."

The Greek version seems to have first become a matter of record in the Byzantine Empire, where it was used to describe one Konstantinos Angelos, a man whose physical beauty captured the heart of Princess Theodora Komnena. She took him for her consort around the year 1100.

Around 1200, the nuns of the Order of Our Lady of Carmel claimed a Saint Angelo as their saint, and his name took root in Italy. Variations arose with *Agnolo, Annillo,* and *Angiola* for boys and *Angelica* for girls. Saint Angela Merici founded the Order of Saint Ursula of teaching nuns in Italy and France in 1535. In addition, there were three revered Italian saints named *Angelina.*

Angel, used mostly as a man's name in England, became popular with Angel Clare, the male protagonist in Thomas Hardy's novel *Tess of the D'Urbervilles* (1891). It fell out of fashion as a boy's name in the United States in the early 1900s but slowly increased in popularity for girls, particularly among African American families in the 1950s. It has always been a favored name for boys among Latinos in the Americas, and with the growing Latino population in the United States, *Angel* is becoming prevalent. In fact, it is among the most popular boys' names in the United States.

Although most European countries used feminine forms of *Angela, Angelina,* and *Angelica,* the French preferred *Angeline* or *Angelique.* Unusual versions found in Germany are *Angelita, Angelyn,* and *Angelika. Angela* is a favored name in Australia as well.

Angela rose to the top 50 girls' names in the United States by 1975 and is still among the top 100 names. *Angelica* has also found great favor with many American families today. *Angie* seems to be the only pet name associated with *Angela.*

☽ Number

Four. Honesty and dependability are always connected with this number. Fours are often attracted to social issues and are not impressed by material wealth.

☾ Astrological Sign

Gemini, a sign symbolized by twins. Geminis have the ability to see both sides of a situation. They are usually quick-witted and resourceful. Gemini's element is air, which represents the mind. Another Gemini trait is a love of conversation—a perfect sign for the name of a heavenly messenger.

✺ Color

Alabaster white. In many metaphysical beliefs, white is the color of receptiveness. Since white is actually a combination of all colors, many believe it attracts luck because it carries the power of all the colors of the spectrum.

◆ Stone

Citrine. Stones of the quartz family are best known as conductors of energy. Citrine, a form of quartz, is thought to empower communication.

♛ Element

Brass, which enhances the intuition-boosting properties of quartz.

♘ Herb

Angelica (*Angelica archangelica*). An herb from the parsley family, angelica is found in Europe and Asia. The plant has greenish white flowers and exudes a honeylike scent. When the bubonic plague hit Europe, legend tells of an angel that appeared to a monk in his dreams and revealed that angelica would cure the disease.

♀ ANGELICA: From the root name *Angela*.

♀ ANGELINA: From the root name *Angela*.

♀ ANGELINE: From the root name *Angela*.

♀ ANGELIQUE: From the root name *Angela*.

♀ ANGELITA: From the root name *Angela*.

♂ ANGELO: From the root name *Angela*.

♀ ANGELYN: From the root name *Angela*.

♀ ANGIOLA: From the root name *Angela*.

♀♂ ANGY: From the root name *Angela*.

♀ ANIKA: From the root name *Anna*.

♀ ANITA: From the root name *Anna*.

♀ ANN: From the root name *Anna*.

♥ ♀ ANNA   Anica, Anice, Anechka, Anika, Anita, Ann,
**Anna, Annabel, Annale, Anne, Annelise, Annette, Annie,
Annis, Annissa, Annora, Anya, Hanna, Hannah, Hannelore,
Nan, Nancy, Nanette, Nani, Nanon, Nettie, Nina, Nonie:**
Anna is from the Hebrew *hanah,* which means "grace(ful),"
"favor," or "mercy." The name was first known as *Hannah,*
mother of the ancient prophet Shmueil (Samuel); the Bible
tells of her blessing when God rewarded her faithful devotion with a pregnancy after years of barrenness.

Hannah came into use with the Phoenicians (present-day
Lebanon and Syria) and may have traveled to Greece among
traders. Somewhere along the way, it was translated to
Anna. In Greek mythology, Anna was the sister of Dido and
Pygmalion of Carthage. She is sometimes referred to as Anna
Perenna, who was worshiped as the nymph of the River
Numicius.

In a classical interpretation, Ovid, in the *Fasti,* wrote that
Anna is the name of the moon because "by its months it fills

up the year."Another Roman, Macrobius, said in his work *Saturnalia* that Anna's festival on March 15 (the Ides of March) celebrates the return of spring, tying the name with the cyclic year (*annus*).

The Gospels refer to the Blessed Virgin's mother Anna, making Saint Anna a favorite with the Byzantines. In 550, Emperor Justinian built a church in honor of Saint Anna, and by 710, her relics were enshrined there.

As *Anna*'s popularity spread, variants surfaced according to the dictates of various world cultures: *Annot* in Scotland, *Anglarawd* in Wales, *Annette* in France, and *Anita* in Spain. Pet derivatives were made with endings of *-ice* and *-issa,* as in *Anice* and *Annissa.*

Around 1584, a fashion arose among European Catholics of combining the names of the Blessed Virgin and her mother. *Anne Marie, Marianne,* and *Mariana* were among the ingenious combinations that gave us new names. Other derivatives using *Anna* or *Anne* in combination with other names include *Joann, Joanne,* or *Joanna; Julianne* or *Juliana;* and *Annabel, Annabella,* and *Annalie. Anne,* like *Marie,* was also sometimes added to men's names in France, as seen with Lord Anne Hamilton (1709-1748), named after his godmother, Queen Anne. *Ann,* or *Anne,* remains the most widely used middle name in the English language, perhaps for its compatibility with every given name imaginable.

Anna was immensely popular in the 1600s after the Restoration in England. The name flourished in the United States around the same time when it crossed the Atlantic with English settlers. Many variants of *Anna* or *Anne* became popular independent names among English-speaking peoples, including *Nancy, Annie, Anita,* and *Annette. Nanette* and *Nanon* grew independently in France. Italians created *Annica. Annika* rose in Denmark, and *Annali* came from Switzerland. *Nina* and *Annora* are also found abroad, but not much in the United States.

Anna was the second most popular girl's name in the United States in the late 1800s, seeing regular use in England along with *Annie, Annale* and *Hannah*. Even today, *Anna* is a top name in both countries, but *Hannah* has surpassed *Anna,* now placing among the top 10 U.S. girls' names.

◉ Number
Two. This number includes people who have a gentle nature. They are most often patient. Some have an uncanny sense of direction and are extremely perceptive.

☾ Astrological sign
Virgo. The constellation Virgo symbolizes Mother Earth, the goddess of fertility. Virgos are usually faithful and modest but sometimes try to live by impossible standards.

❋ Color
Annatto. This color is a shade of pink that symbolizes devotion.

◆ Stone
Pink Sapphire. According to folklore, sapphires are considered to be gems of destiny, especially in connection with the bestowal of divine favors on those who own them. Although most sapphires are blue, the pink sapphire is prized for its rarity. Pink sapphires are thought to protect from illness when worn against the skin.

♛ Element
Electrum. An alloy of gold and silver—and sometimes platinum, electrum was used centuries ago by ancient magicians. Ancient Egyptian rulers used electrum cups to test for poisons. Naturally occurring electrum is rare.

🌿 Herb

Rue *(Ruta graveolens)*. The common name for this aromatic plant is herb-of-grace. In European folk medicine, rue was used to relieve colic, improve failing appetites, and aid in digestion. Later uses included treatment of gout, rheumatic pains and nervous heart problems.

♀ ANNABEL: From the root name *Anna*.

♀ ANNALE: From the root name *Anna*.

♀ ANNE: From the root name *Anna*.

♀ ANNELISE: From the root name *Anna*.

♀ ANNETTE: From the root name *Anna*.

♀ ANNGEL: From the root name *Angela*.

♀ ANNIE: From the root name *Anna*.

♀ ANNIS: From the root name *Anna*.

♀ ANNISA: From the root name *Anna*.

♀ ANNJELA: From the root name *Angela*.

♂ ANNO: From the root name *John*.

♀ ANNORA: From the root name *Anna*.

♂ ANNTOIN: From the root name *Anthony*.

♂ ANTEK: From the root name *Anthony*.

♥ ♂ **ANTHONY Anntoin, Antin, Antoine, Antoinette, Anton, Antonello, Antonia, Antonio, Antwan, Antwon, Netta, Nettie, Tasha, Tenton, Toinette, Tonetto, Toni, Tonia, Tonio, Tony, Tonye:** The historical journey of *Anthony* spans nearly two millennia. Traced from Latin roots, *Anthony* means "inestimable" or "priceless." As with many Latin names, it is not easy to pinpoint origins, but

Antonius seems to have risen from *Antius,* a son of Hercules. The name became infamous thanks to two men who made their marks on history: Marcus Antonius (Mark Antony), avenger of Caesar and lover of Cleopatra (around 41 B.C.), and Marcus Aurelius Antoninus, Roman philosopher and emperor (A.D. 88–217).

Among early Christians, Antonius, the legendary hermit of the fourth century, was an ascetic, a lifestyle that later became the basis for the monastic system. Saint Antony the Great, as he came to be known, was of Egyptian birth, and his conflicts with Satan brought him admiration in Eastern churches. During the Crusades, he gained many followers who brought his story and his name to the West. The temptation of Saint Antony was a favorite subject in medieval art

Because Saint Antony was regarded as a patron of swineherds, the term *Saint Antony* or *Tantony* was given to a litter's runt in an attempt to ensure its survival. A skin disease that became an epidemic around the year 1089 was named Saint Antony's Fire because many claimed miraculous healing after praying to him for a cure. Somewhere in its travels, *Antony* was altered to *Anthony.* This small change seems to be tied to the Dutch, who added the silent *h.* However, the British avoid the *th* sound, regarding it as a mispronunciation similar to the one produced by adding a *k* sound to *knife* or a *b* sound to *doubt.*

Antony remained a popular name in England throughout the late 1800s, and it traveled as a favorite to the New World with the Pilgrims.

Once a frequently given slave name, *Anthony* has been handed down through generations of African American families. Modern versions such as *Antwaine, Antwan,* and *Antwon* gained immense popularity by the 1990s.

Ethnic variations are found with *Tonio* and *Tonetto* in Italy, *Antoine* in France, and *Tenton* in Germany. *Anton* is preferred in Russia and *Antek* and *Antos* are used in Poland. *Tony* remains a universal nickname.

As with most classic male names, feminine forms have arisen. *Antonica* and *Antoinette* are well known in Europe. In Greek, *Antonia* means "flower," "flourishing," or "beautiful" and seems to be the most widely used female variation. Literary associations are made with British novelist Lady Antonia Fraser and with Willa Cather's novel *My Antonia*. *Anthony* is also prevalent as a surname.

 ## Number

Seven. Some numerologists regard seven as the number of military prowess, whereas others connect seven to spirituality. All agree that sevens show remarkable resilience and a fierce will, whether as military or spiritual warriors. Sevens have the ability to rise above life's obstacles through intellect and intuition.

 ## Astrological Sign

Leo. Ruled by the sun and the element of fire, Leos live up to their leonine image. Most project regal auras and have fiery spirits.

 ## Color

Burgundy. Throughout the ages, shades of red have been associated with both vitality and nobility. Modern connotations include aggressive energy and fervor.

 ## Stone

Pyrope. Pyrope, also called garnet, is a blood-red stone that was used in healing rites to help patients regain vigor. Many ancients believed pyropes would drive off demons and banish nightmares.

 ## Element

Antimony. Small pieces of this white metal were worn into battle for protection. Antimony was also used to repel evil.

♔ Herb

Feverweed *(Gerardia pedicularia)*. As its name implies, feverweed has been used to combat high fevers as far back as the Middle Ages. Tonics were also created from this herb to be used as a sedative.

♂ ANTIN: From the root name *Anthony*.

♂ ANTOINE: From the root name *Anthony*.

♀ ANTOINETTE: From the root name *Anthony*.

♂ ANTON: From the root name *Anthony*.

♂ ANTONELLO: From the root name *Anthony*.

♀ ANTONIA: From the root name *Anthony*.

♂ ANTONIO: From the root name *Anthony*.

♂ ANTWON: From the root name *Anthony*.

♀ ANYA: From the root name *Anna*.

♂ AGOSTINO: From the root name *Austin*.

♀ AOIFFE: From the root name *Eve*.

♂ AREL: From the root name *Ariel*.

♀ ARETHA: From the root name *Arthur*.

♂ ARI: From the root names *Aaron* and *Ariel*.

♀ ARIANA: From the root name *Ariel*.

♀ ARIE: From the root name *Ariel*.

♥ ♀ **ARIEL** **Arel, Ari, Ariana, Arie, Ariela, Arieli, Ariellah, Arielle, Arik, Arke, Arye, Lieb:** Although *Ariel* appears to have links to mythology, the name has strong connections to the word *ari,* which means "lion of God" in Hebrew. Some say this leonine connection is the true basis for the name. In fact, a passage from the book of Ezra in the Torah and the Bible describes Ariel (called "God as a lion") as a commander summoned to lead a mission to Jerusalem (whose symbol is a lion). Also, *aryeih* is Hebrew for "lion of strength and fearlessness."

Ariel is a water-spirit in the demonology of the Cabala (mystical teachings of rabbinical origins). Ariel is also known as an elemental entity of air in various medieval fables. The name's airy qualities were immortalized by William Shakespeare in *The Tempest*, in which the breezy servant of Prospero is named Ariel and portrayed as an airy spirit. Shakespeare can be thanked for the propagation of many names. After new plays appeared in England, certain names from the plays would obviously catch the public's fancy and begin to appear on birth records.

During the eighteenth century, the name gained new fame in England as the sylph named Ariel in Alexander Pope's enormously popular poem *Rape of the Lock*.

Probably because of its biblical origins, *Ariel* has historically had a masculine connotation. It is a familiar man's name in Israel, often shortened to *Ari*. Different versions are found there as well with *Arel, Arye,* and *Arieli*. From these names, surnames were formed such as *Ari, Arik,* and *Arke* and even *Lieb,* which is "lion" in Yiddish.

Although traditionally bearers of the name have been men, modern U.S. culture associates the terms *airy* or *breezy* with femininity. For this reason perhaps, Ariel never became a popular boy's name in the United States. However, *Ariel* found great favor among Amish women living in the northeastern United States. Many take the name and spell it *Arie*. Other feminine variations have appeared, such as *Ariellah* and *Arielle*. The female version of choice seems to be *Ariana,* which is, in fact, among the top 100 girls' names.

Ariel has become increasingly popular as a girl's name in recent years among Jews and non-Jews alike. With this relatively recent gender-usage change for *Ariel,* women have adapted the original Hebrew translation as "lioness of God" or "God as a lioness."

🌀 Number

Nine. In numerology, nine is associated with righteousness. People of this number are thought to be strong-willed and inclined to fight for their beliefs. However, nines are more likely than other numbers to act in haste.

🌙 Astrological sign

Libra. In history and myth, this autumn sign is depicted by the balanced scales of justice. Libra's element is air, which relates to the mind. *Ariel* brings a balance of spirit and strength to any Libran so named.

☀ Color

Reddish blue. The colors red and blue stimulate spiritual reflection, and when combined, they enhance the balance of energies between heart and mind.

◆ Stone

Mexican lace agate. Agates were used in amulets dating back to the time of the ancient Greeks. Lace agates have a circular pattern like ripples in a pond. Although lace agates come in many shades, the Mexican variety has a deep reddish hue and is believed to boost emotional strength and energy.

🌿 Element

Copper. Copper complements agate and is the metal related to Libra's ruling planet, Venus.

🦎 Herb

Lion's foot *(Prenanthes alba).* This herb has a smooth, purple-tinged stem that contains a milky juice. Ancient herbalists believed that drinking this juice would protect against wounds from poisonous snakes. They also made a poultice from its pulverized leaves to treat insect bites and nonpoisonous snakebites.

♀ ARIELA: From the root name *Ariel*.

♂ ARIELI: From the root name *Ariel*.

♀ ARIELLAH: From the root name *Ariel*.

♀ ARIELLE: From the root name *Ariel*.

♂ ARIK: From the root name *Ariel*.

♂ ARIN: From the root name *Aaron*.

♀ ARINA: From the root name *Irene*.

♂ ARKE: From the root name *Ariel*.

♂ ARLO: From the root name *Charles*.

♂ ARNIE: From the root name *Aaron*.

♀ ARNINA: From the root name *Aaron*.

♂ ARON: From the root name *Aaron*.

♀ ARONA: From the root name *Aaron*.

♂ ARRAM: From the root name *Abraham*.

♂ ARRIGO: From the root name *Henry*.

♂ ART: From the root name *Arthur*.

♂ ARTAIR: From the root name *Arthur*.

♀ ARTHEIA: From the root name *Arthur*.

♥ ♂ **ARTHUR** **Aretha, Art, Artair, Artheia, Arthuretta, Arthurina, Arthurine, Artice, Artie, Artina, Artis, Artlette, Artur, Arturo, Artus:** *Arthur* may have come from the Celtic *artos* ("bear") or from an ancient Briton word *arcturus* ("the bear's tail"). In Welsh, *arth* is "bear" and *ur* is "man," meaning *Arthur* translates to "bear-man" or "heroic man of strength." The pronunciation of the last letter of *ard* in the Celtic tongue sounds like *th,* not *d,* and the word *ard* means "high" or "noble." Among the Celts, then, *Arthur* means "high courage" or "chief."

The rise of *Arthur* is linked to a fifth- or sixth-century British king. However, King Arthur's popularity seems more than a little ironic because ancient Welsh bards and poets created much of their lore around a man who supposedly subjugated their people under English rule. Even so, no Celtic name is as renowned as is that of the leader of the Knights of the Round Table.

Although legends abound, virtually no historical facts exist about King Arthur. It is known that a son (Arthur or Arthwys) was born to Uther Pendragon in Cornwall, England. This Arthur took the throne after the death of Pendragon and reigned for 40 years, apparently dying during a treacherous coup instigated by a disgruntled nephew.

In legend, of course, Arthur was conceived through magic and hidden until his father's death. His claim to the throne was validated by his pulling the sword Excalibur from a stone. With his famous band of knights, he took vows of Christianity and went on a quest for the elusive Holy Grail. During this undertaking, he suffered betrayal by his wife, Queen Guinevere, and his knight Lancelot. His death came from a mortal wound in a battle with his ill-begotten son Mordred (some legends call Mordred a nephew of Arthur). But before his demise, Arthur threw Excalibur into a river as a signal to the fairies, who came and bore him away to a hidden isle to die.

Arturius was the name of an Irish prince killed in 596, and in Irish legends, Art Oenfer ("Art the Lonely"), son of Conn Cetchathach ("Conn of the Hundred Battles") overcomes trials and dangers to win his bride, Delbchaem. The name *Art MacCormac* appears in another legend while *Art* and *Arth* pop up in Irish Highland pedigrees.

Arthur, Duke of Brittany, was the nephew of King John, and Arthur Tudor was the heir of Henry VII. A Welsh Arthur appeared in Scotland in the thirteenth century; the name was carried by marriage to the English Hamiltons.

Arthur gained popular favor through Mallory's prose in the fifteenth century and Alfred Lord Tennyson's *Idylls of the King* in the nineteenth. Popularity in the nineteenth century is also tied to Arthur Wellesley, Duke of Wellington, who was the victor over Napoleon at Waterloo. Wellington had several godsons named after him, including the Duke of Connaught, son of Queen Victoria.

Throughout *Arthur*'s travels, variations arose, such as *Arthgallo* and *Artegal*. In Italy, the name became *Arturo;* the French took on *Artus*. *Arthmael* was used in Ireland with other early Irish forms, such as *Azer* and *Azor(ius)*, found around 1086. *Acur* is traced back to the early 1200s.

Female forms were rare but included *Arthurine, Arthurina, Artina, Artlette,* and *Artheia*. *Artis* and *Artice* traveled to the United States and became popular with African American families in the 1970s, along with *Arthetta* and *Artra*. The name *Aretha* may be a variant of these forms.

From the 1870s into the 1930s, *Arthur* found great favor in the United States and even more so in England and Wales. By 1950, it had fallen in popularity but was still common. However, it all but disappeared within the next generation (25 years). Although it is a name of history and legend, it appears infrequently today.

Nicknames for *Arthur* include *Art* and *Artie*.

⌾ Number

Five. Often considered to be perfect companions, fives like to surround themselves with friends. However, they treasure freedom and don't like restrictions. Many fives have a religious bent and engage in idealistic pursuits.

☾ Astrological sign

Aries. Aries people are highly motivated and like to be in charge. However, they are advised to be cautious lest the single-minded pursuit of a goal make them ruthless.

✺ Color

Red and white. These colors represent power with a capital P. Red symbolizes the essence of vitality and the life force of blood; white contains the combined energy of the entire spectrum. According to legend, King Arthur's banner bore a red pendragon on a white background.

◆ Stone

Fire opal. According to stone lore, the fire opal ensures for its wearer personal happiness. Although most opals are milky white, the fire opal ranges in color from orange to scarlet and is iridescent in bright light. No other stone on earth resembles it.

♨ Element

Iron. Metaphysically speaking, iron is connected to the planet Mars. The Romans drove iron nails into the walls of their homes to keep the occupants healthy, especially during the plague.

❧ Herb

Bearberry (*Arctostaphylos uva-ursi*). A small evergreen shrub found in Europe and the northern United States, the bearberry has white blossoms and bright red or pink berries. Herbalists use a brew of the leaves to relieve kidney stones and bronchitis.

♀   ARTHURETTA: From the root name *Arthur*.

♀   ARTHURINA: From the root name *Arthur*.

♀   ARTHURINE: From the root name *Arthur*.

♀   ARTICE: From the root name *Arthur*.

♂   ARTIE: From the root name *Arthur*.

♀   ARTINA: From the root name *Arthur*.

♀♂ ARTIS: From the root name *Arthur*.

♀   ARTLETTE: From the root name *Arthur*.

♂   ARTUR: From the root name *Arthur*.

♂   ARTURO: From the root name *Arthur*.

♂   ARTUS: From the root name *Arthur*.

♂   ARYE: From the root name *Ariel*.

♂   ASH: From the root name *Ashley*.

♀   ASHLA: From the root name *Ashley*.

♀♂ ASHLAN: From the root name *Ashley*.

♀♂ ASHLEA: From the root name *Ashley*.

♀♂ ASHLEIGH: From the root name *Ashley*.

♥ ♀♂ **ASHLEY Ash, Ashla, Ashlan, Ashlea, Ashleigh, Ashlinn, Ashlynn:** *Ashley* originates from the Old English *ash* ("wood") and *lea* or *ley* ("glade/clearing") so the entire name translates as "from the ash tree meadow."

Ashley was a renowned surname in England from as early as the thirteenth century. A man of note who bore it was a wealthy landowner named Robert de Ashley. A record of a marriage license for Richard Reeve and Anne Ashley in 1617 was traced back to de Ashley's roots. Surnames such as *Ashman* from the Anglo-Saxon word *aescmann* ("shipman") are linked to an early English work-related naming pattern of taking one's occupation for a surname. *Aescmann* identified someone as a sailor, ship-builder, or seagoing trader.

Ashton, from *ash* ("tree") and *tun* ("enclosure or settlement") was also a common English surname and found as a local place name from numerous areas in Great Britain. There are Ashley Parishes in Canterbury, Gloucester, Bristol, Winchester, and Oxford, and at least 15 counties of the name scattered throughout England.

The giving of surnames as Christian names was somewhat popular for several centuries and was mainly a practice found among families with titles and land. This type of naming pattern became more prevalent in the nineteenth century, mostly through marriage. Brides from powerful families would christen a first child with their maiden name to symbolize the joining of two dynasties, bringing harmony to avoid feuds or increase wealth. In the case of *Ashley,* its rise to prominence as a given name most likely came from admiration for Anthony Ashley Cooper, the seventh Earl of Shaftesbury (1801–1885) and creator of the Ten Hours Bill. This humanitarian legislation made it illegal for children to work more than 10 hours a day in factories and workhouses.

Ashley's use as a Christian name for men grew in the late 1800s, becoming popular first in England and later in Australia. It didn't find much favor in the United States until the publication of Margaret Mitchell's *Gone with the Wind* (1936), with its famous protagonist, Ashley Wilkes. The name's use flourished after the blockbuster movie, starring Vivien Leigh and Clark Gable, hit the silver screen.

Today, *Ashley* is rarely used as a boy's name, but it is one of the most popular transferred surnames in use as a girl's name in the United States. It has been one of the top 10 names throughout the 1990s.

Spelling variations have arisen with its current female popularity, including *Ashleigh* and *Ashlea* or a combination of *Ashley* and *Lynn,* which became *Ashlynn.*

◎ Number

Seven. Sevens are hailed as people of intellect whose hunger for knowledge leads them to seek information through travel and books.

☾ Astrological sign

Taurus. Many Taureans are considered to be the "salt of the earth" by those who know them well. Strong in heart and mind, people of this sign are determined in their pursuits, whether it be in business or love.

☀ Color

Forest green. This color of the deep woods fosters tranquillity and joy. It can cool the blistering heat of anger.

◆ Stone

Dioptase. Dioptase is a vivid green with a hint of blue. It is crystalline in nature and translucent. Many collectors honor it for its color and rarity.

♕ Element

Copper. When dioptase is set in copper, its beauty and energy are enhanced, encouraging a sense of well-being and peace for those who wear it.

⚜ Herb

Bird's tongue *(Fraxinus excelsior)*. Commonly called European ash, this deciduous tree grows throughout the British Isles and often reaches heights of 130 feet. Preparations of the grayish green bark have healing attributes and were used by traditional herbalists as a substitute for quinine in treating fever.

♀ ASHLINN: From the root name *Ashley*.

♀ ASHLYNN: From the root name *Ashley*.

♂ AUGIE: From the root name *Austin*.

♂ AUGUST: From the root name *Austin*.

♀ AUGUSTA: From the root name *Austin*.

♂ AUGUSTIN: From the root name *Austin*.

♀ AUGUSTINA: From the root name *Austin*.

♂ AUGUSTINE: From the root name *Austin*.

♂ AUGUSTINO: From the root name *Austin*.

♂ AUGUSTUS: From the root name *Austin*.

♥ ♂ **AUSTIN** **Augie, Agostin, Agostino, August, Augusta, Augustin, Augustina, Augustine, Augustino, Augustus, Austina, Austine, Austyn, Gus, Gusta, Ostynn, Tina:** *Austin* has imperial origins, as illustrated by its Latin root meaning "venerable" or "consecrated." The modern *Austin* derives from a slow melding of *Augustinus* and *Augustine/August*. Some believe *Austin* is also related to *avigur* or *augur* ("chatter of birds"), which is synonymous with clairvoyance and precognition. In the Teutonic language, *aege* means "awe."

As *Augustine*, the name came to denote royalty. *Augustus* was given to the second Caesar by the Roman Senate. In that context, the name's meaning was altered to mean "revered."

After the reign of the Roman emperor Diocletian (A.D. 245-313), *Augustus* became a venerable title for men, and a royal woman was referred to as "the Augusta." The Welsh used a form of *Augustus* (*Awst*), but the name did not appear with any frequency until the middle of the sixteenth century after a German princess named her son August (of

Anhalt Plotzgau) and another August (of Wolfenbüttel) named his daughter Anne Augusta.

The route from *Augustus* to *Austin* seems to have many twists and turns. International variations included *Augustino* in Spain, *Augustin* in France and Germany, *Agostino* in Italy, and *Agostin* in Poland.

August traveled to England with the Hanoverians, where it became *Augustin*. Spelling changes over the centuries altered it to *Austin*. This name found honor in association with the famous order of the Austin Friars, who took their name from Saint Augustine, first Archbishop of Canterbury (A.D. 597). From there it became one of the top Christian names in the Middle Ages.

Austin lost much of its appeal as an English given name after the Restoration, but related surnames arose in the forms of *Austen, Astin,* and *Ostin*. British novelist Jane Austen (1775-1817) and American patriot Stephen F. Austin (1793-1836), for whom Texans named their state capital, bore the name with distinction on different continents.

When *Austin* appeared in the United States it became fashionable with African American families in the 1950s. It faded for a generation or so, then surfaced to become one of the top 10 names in recent years.

Although *Austin* remains more common among boys, it is gaining favor as a girl's name and is becoming one of the gender-mixing traditionals like *Kelsey, Lindsay, Jordan,* and *Elliot*. The female variation *Austine* rarely makes an appearance.

🌀 Number

Three. This is a number long associated with ambition and inspiration. Threes have a sharp awareness of environmental problems and the need for ecological preservation.

☾ Astrological sign

Leo. Referred to as the sign of royalty, Leos are ruled by the sun and fueled by its element of fire. They are born leaders.

☀ Color

Roman ocher. Formed from the union of red and yellow, this orange hue is often associated with motivation and organization.

◆ Stone

Yellow diamond. The rare yellow diamond, known as the king of gems, was worn by aristocratic families to ward off the plague in medieval times. Diamonds are stones of high energy and are prized for their prismatic fire.

♛ Element

Gold. In the metaphysical realm, gold is believed to be the best metal to enhance the power of a diamond.

♋ Herb

Imperial masterwort (*Imperatoria ostruthium*). Once used for a variety of ailments, from digestive problems to rheumatism, masterwort was also recommended by ancient healers for bronchitis and fever.

♀   AUSTINA: From the root name *Austin.*

♀   AUSTINE: From the root name *Austin.*

♂   AUSTYN: From the root name *Austin.*

♂   AVRAM: From the root name *Abraham.*

B

♀ BABE: From the root name *Barbara*.

♀ BABETTE: From the root names *Barbara* and *Elizabeth*.

♀ BABS: From the root name *Barbara*.

♀ BAIBIN: From the root name *Barbara*.

♀ BAIRBRE: From the root name *Barbara*.

♀ BARB: From the root name *Barbara*.

♥ ♀ BARBARA Babe, Babette, Babs, Baibin, Bairbre, Barb, Barbe, Barbary, Barbette, Barbie, Barbara, Barbro, Basha, Basia, Bauby, Bebe, Berbera, Bibi, Bobbie, Borbala, Varvara, Varinka: *Barbara*'s history is a saintly one despite its barbarous roots. The Greek word *barbar* means "stranger," and the term was used by Greeks to describe anyone who couldn't speak their language. In Latin, *barbarus* translates loosely as "wild cruelty," "rude ignorance," or "ill-gotten splendor." Thus, the modern word *barbarian* (*barbaric*) describes uncivilized people or behavior.

Barbara, one of the four virgin saints exalted in the Roman Catholic Church, was a maiden whose story became legend through her (barbaric) demise. She was believed to be a maiden from Heliopolis. Her Christian devotion was tested when she insisted that her bath chamber be built with three windows to honor the Holy Trinity.

This request infuriated Barbara's father and he beheaded her. Immediately after this brutal deed (so it's said) he was immediately smitten by a bolt of lightning. From this story, Barbara emerges as a symbol of artistic devotion, consecrating architecture and art for religious expression. Consequently, Saint Barbara became the patroness of architects and engineers as well as protectress from thunder and lightning (artillery). Her name was invoked to bring protection against storms and before going into battle.

Among the less reverent, she may be considered the patron saint of bathrooms, as is apparent today aboard French ships, where the term *la sainte Barbe* is still used for powder rooms.

Barbara spread mainly through the daughters of artisans and soldiers. It was fairly common from the late twelfth century onward. It traveled to Scotland where it became *Babie,* and when it reached France it became *Barbe* and *Babette.* In Russia, it is *Varvara* and *Varinka.* The English, Italians, Germans, and Danes kept the original saintly form, but its use faded during the Reformation when Puritans rejected Catholic rites and saints. Although *Barbara*'s popularity as a given name faded, *Barbara* turned up in surname form as *Barbot, Barberry, Barbata,* and *Babbs.*

Through the 1950s, it was one the top five girls' names in the United States and found great favor among African American and Jewish families. It also flourished in Canada, Great Britain, and Australia.

Although spelling variations are rare, a contracted form is used by entertainer and film director Barbra Streisand. *Barbara* is popularly used in conjunction with other names, yielding the once-common *Barbara Ann* and *Barbara Ellen.* The American South still uses this type of blending for many names; *Bobbie,* a nickname for *Barbara,* was a favorite producing popular derivatives like *Bobbie Sue, Bobbie Jo,* and *Bobbie Jean.*

By 1960, *Barbara* was considered a dated name in the United States, but remained among the top 50 girls' names into the 1970s. Although pet names for *Barbara* are few—*Babs* and *Barb* are diminutives—*Barbie* is very common as a nickname.

 Number:

Seven. This number is linked to artists and craftspeople. Ancient folk beliefs also link seven to healing and spirituality.

 Astrological sign:

Pisces. This sign's element is water, which represents the soul. One of Pisces's ruling planets is Neptune, which is also tied to the number seven. The name *Barbara* works well for a Pisces, as people born under this sign are creative and compassionate.

 Color:

Deep sea green and red. Green is a healing color, and when linked with red, represents religion and magic.

 Stone:

Bloodstone. Bloodstone, a member of the jasper family, is a dark green opaque rock with blood red or deep orange spots. According to a medieval legend, the stone was formed when droplets of Christ's blood hit the ground and turned to stone. Bloodstone was believed to have exceptional wound-healing powers.

 Element:

Iron, a metal of force. The term *iron will* describes a person's power of conviction or strength of character.

🌿 **Herb**

Barberry *(Berberis vulgaris).* A bushy shrub found throughout Europe, its leaves resemble three-forked spines. When ripe, the berries resemble scarlet teardrops. The root bark and berries were used by ancient healers to relieve liver ailments and to soothe throat irritations.

♀   BARBARY: From the root name *Barbara.*

♀   BARBETTE: From the root name *Barbara.*

♀   BARBIE: From the root name *Barbara.*

♀   BARBRA: From the root name *Barbara.*

♀   BARBRO: From the root name *Barbara.*

♀♂ BARI: From the root name *Barry.*

♂   BARNARD: From the root name *Bernard.*

♂   BARNEY: From the root name *Bernard.*

♂   BARNHARD: From the root name *Bernard.*

♀♂ BARRIE: From the root name *Barry.*

♂   BARRIS From the root name *Barry.*

❤   ♀♂ **BARRY** **Bari, Barrie, Barris:** There is some dispute as to the origin of the name *Barry,* though all agree that it originally came from a Celtic language. Most believe that it is a derivation of the word *bearach* or *bearrach,* meaning "spear" or "javelin." Names historian Charlotte Yonge writes that the name means "looking straight at the mark." There is another theory, though, that *Barry* is an Anglicization of the Irish name *Barra—barr* in Ancient Erse is "head." A third possibility (though not as commonly held) is that the name is from the Welsh and means "son of Harry," as in *Ap-Harry* or *Ab-Harry.*

Barry was originally a place name in both Scotland and Wales. It then was adopted as a last name. In the nineteenth century it came into use more frequently as a first name, and the rise of its popularity can be connected with both the popular poet and songwriter Barry Cornwall (1787–1874), whose original name was Bryan Waller Procter, and a novel, *The Luck of Barry Lyndon* (1844), by William Thackeray.

The turn of the century provided two well-known Barrys who helped keep the name in the public mind: Irish actor Barry Fitzgerald (1888–1961), whose original name was William Shields, and American actor Barry Sullivan (1912–1994), whose original name was Patrick Barry, were both wildly popular. Sir James Barrie (1860–1937), who wrote *Peter Pan,* may have inspired parents to use that spelling for their children's first name. Though *Barry* remained popular through World War II, the use of the name has dropped off dramatically since midcentury in the United States.

Number

One. Sometimes physical attributes are assigned to numbers, and a one's dominant feature is the eyes. Ones are often drawn to creative endeavors.

Astrological sign

Sagittarius. According to myth, Sagittarius was a centaur who raised Jason, Achilles, and Aeneas. He loved freedom and taught respect for nature.

Color

Magenta, a shade of reddish purple that stimulates the psychic third eye and boosts physical strength.

Stone

Bull's-eye quartz. Eye stones are part of the star chrysoberyl family and carry a rich history of mystic lore. Ancient superstitions included beliefs that people owning or wearing such a gem could see another's private thoughts or could even see behind closed doors. Bull's-eye quartz is mahogany in color with stripes of fibrous-looking minerals and is found mainly in South Africa. It resembles an iris and pupil when cut and polished.

Element

Tin. Tin is the metal tied to Jupiter, ruling planet of Sagittarius, and was believed to have powers that aided seers in predicting the future.

 Herb

Spearmint *(Mentha spicata).* Found in wet or moist soils and warmer climates, spearmint grows about two feet high and has pale purple flowers. The herb has been used for digestive ills, including heartburn and nausea. Some healers combined spearmint and horehound to help reduce fever, especially for children.

♀ BASHA: From the root name *Barbara*.

♀ BASIA: From the root name *Barbara*.

♂ BASTIAN: From the root name *Sebastian*.

♀ BAUBY: From the root name *Barbara*.

♂ BEAR: From the root name *Bernard*.

♂ BEATHAM: From the root name *Benjamin*.

♀ BEBE: From the root name *Barbara*.

♀ BECCA: From the root name *Rebecca*.

♀ BECKY: From the root name *Rebecca*.

♀ BECS: From the root name *Rebecca*.

♀ BELINDA: From the root name *Linda*.

♀ BELLE: From the root name *Linda*.

♂ BEN: From the root name *Benjamin*.

♂ BENEK: From the root name *Benjamin*.

♂ BENIAMINO: From the root name *Benjamin*.

♥ ♂ **BENJAMIN**   **Beatham, Ben, Benek, Beniamino, Benjamon, Benji, Bennie, Benny, Benson, Binyamin, Mincho:** *Benjamin* is an ancient Hebrew name that has several possible origins. The most accepted is taken from the biblical Benjamin who was Jacob's twelfth son and a patriarch of one of the 12 tribes of Israel. The story of Benjamin's name begins with his mother, Rachel. As she lay dying after giving birth to her youngest son, she named him Ben-Oni, which means "son of sorrow." Jacob is said to have later changed the boy's name to Benjamin, which means "son of my right hand." This has led some scholars to suggest that the name first meant "son of the south," for if you face the rising sun, your right hand is toward the south, and Benjamin was patriarch of a southern tribe. Still other scholars take this even further and believe that *Benjamin* was possibly a more generic term for the southern tribe and that the patriarch was given the name because he represented that tribe.

Regardless of what origins the scholars ascribe to the name, the interpretation of the name is connected to the person known as Benjamin. With passing generations, the name took on many associations in honor of the patriarch, including "strong," "fortunate" and "a gift from God." It is surprising that with such an interesting and powerful background, *Benjamin* did not achieve immediate popularity.

Even among Jews, the name was not common until the twelfth century, when the adventurer Benjamin of Tudela became famous.

Most historians believe that the name came into use among Christians in the late sixteenth century when Protestants, particularly Puritans, cast aside saints' names and returned with great zeal to biblical names. Charles Waring Endell Bardsley, in his book *Curiosities of Puritan Nomenclature* (1880), notes that the Puritans, fond as they were of the name *Benjamin,* were even fonder—by a ratio of six to one—of *Benoni.* In the mid-seventeenth century, a man named John Cromwell split the difference by naming his son Ben-oni-jamin.

Benjamin traveled quite successfully with the Puritans to the American colonies. Benjamin Franklin (1706–1790), inventor and founding father of the United States, certainly helped maintain the popularity of the name. The name of Benjamin Banneker (1731–1806), an architect and inventor who created the first wholly American-made clock and took over from Pierre L'Enfant in surveying and designing Washington, D.C., attested to the early use among free African Americans of the name *Benjamin.*

Use of the name did not decline until the middle to late nineteenth century, when Jewish immigration to America increased. By the early twentieth century, *Benjamin* had come to be considered "traditionally Jewish," and its use declined among white Christians. In the 1960s, however, the name began a powerful revival. Some historians have noted that the baby boomers who embraced the counterculture of the 1960s and 1970s revived the use of Old Testament names in general. Since the 1960s, *Benjamin* has never really lost ground among boys' names in the United States, and it's continually popularized by the likes of such well-known figures as screen star Ben Affleck.

Common variations for *Benjamin* include *Binyamin* (Yiddish), *Beniamino* (Italian), *Benek* (Polish), *Beatham*

(Scottish), and *Benja* and *Mincho* (Spanish). Among the most popular diminutives and nicknames are *Ben, Bennie, Benny* and *Benjie*.

 ## Number

Five. Numerologists connect the number five to the planet Mercury. While many fives are multi-talented, they can become depressed if they find themselves in the wrong profession.

 ## Astrological sign

Gemini. Being ruled by Mercury and the number five helps make Geminis adaptable and resourceful. Even when the chips are down, they will find a way to come out on top.

 ## Color

Vermeil bronze. This gilded yellow hue cheers all who look on it, lifting even the heaviest cloud of sorrow.

 ## Stone

Quartz crystal. Highly regarded for centuries for its amazing ability to elevate physical and psychic energies, quartz crystals are also beautiful. Simply rubbing this gem stimulates the electrons, producing rainbow flashes within. The ancients claimed that the sun and a universe of light lived within the stone. Today, quartz crystals are used in lenses, lamps, and precision instruments such as clocks and watches.

 ## Element

Electrum, a mixture of metals. Ancient magicians used an electrum of gold, silver, and platinum to draw on the supreme elemental power represented by these precious metals.

🌿 Herb

Bennet *(Geum urbanum)*. This plant prefers the shade and grows around hedges and fences and in forests. Its rootstock and the flowering herb have medicinal uses, including as an excellent gargle for gum and breath cleansing. It also promotes appetite. The star-shaped flowers are bright yellow.

♂ BENJAMON: From the root name *Benjamin*.

♂ BENJI: From the root name *Benjamin*.

♀♂ BENNIE: From the root name *Benjamin*.

♂ BENNY: From the root name *Benjamin*.

♂ BENSON: From the root name *Benjamin*.

♀ BERBERA: From the root name *Barbara*.

♂ BERN: From the root name *Bernard*.

♀ BERNA: From the root name *Bernard*.

♀ BERNADENE: From the root name *Bernard*.

♀ BERNADETTE: From the root name *Bernard*.

♀ BERNADINE: From the root name *Bernard*.

♥ ♂ **BERNARD** **Barnard, Barney, Barnhard, Bear, Bern, Berna, Bernadene, Bernadette, Bernadine, Bernardo, Bernarr, Bernette, Bernie, Bernita, Berry, Burnard:** It is generally thought that the name *Bernard* comes from the Teutonic Frank tribes and was originally *Biornhard* or *Berinhard,* which means literally "bear" and "stern" (or "bold" or "brave"). This is taken to mean "having the resolution of a bear." The name appears in Old English as *Beornheard.* The French variation *Bernard* came to the British Isles after the Norman Conquest in 1066. The English then developed their own variation of the French name: *Barnard*. In Ireland, *Bernard* was sometimes used as the Anglicized form of the Erse name *Brian* or *Bryan*.

The earliest famous *Bernard* didn't appear until the eleventh century, and he is still undoubtedly the most famous person to have borne the name. Saint Bernard of Menthon was the monk who founded the famous alpine shelters for travelers, many of whom were on pilgrimages to Rome. Two alpine passes were named for him, as was the bearlike breed of dogs.

Despite the current fame of the Saint Bernard of Menthon, in medieval Europe the name became truly famous because of a twelfth-century figure, Saint Bernard of Clairvaux. A Cistercian monk, this second Saint Bernard was the main organizer of the second Crusade. As an advisor to no fewer than five popes, he also helped define Roman Catholicism during a particularly fractious period.

After being extremely common in England during the Middle Ages, *Bernard* lost its shine after the Reformation—when the names of most nonbiblical saints fell out of fashion—and the name did not travel well to the American colonies. In both the United States and Great Britain, Bernard did not truly revive until the nineteenth century. Its return to popularity may be linked with the French feminine variation of the name, *Bernadette*.

Marie-Bernard Soubirous (1844–1879), a young girl who saw a vision of the Virgin Mary at Lourdes in France, was called Bernadette. Her story became instantly famous, and she soon had namesakes all over the world, including in the United States and England. (Canonized in 1933, Saint Bernadette was made even more famous by the film *The Song of Bernadette,* released in 1943.) Beyond Saint Bernadette, the influence of Irish and Italian immigration to the United States during the middle and late nineteenth century must also be taken into account when examining the possible reasons for *Bernard*'s revival here. It was still among the top 50 boys' names in the United States in 1925, but soon thereafter, its popularity began to decline. Today, it is somewhat rare.

 ## Number
Eight. Eights usually have deep convictions and follow their chosen paths with zeal and courage.

 ## Astrological sign
Scorpio. Piety and resolution are traits common in people of this sign.

 ## Color
Bordeaux brown. Any shade of brown promotes a feeling of emotional safety. It's also one of the colors of the famous Saint Bernard dog breed.

 ## Stone
Brown jasper. Jasper is an opaque gemstone with the hardness of an agate. The histories of these two gems have mingled throughout the centuries and can be traced back to past civilizations. In the biblical book Revelation, a description of God recounts an "appearance like a jasper stone." Brown jasper is considered a stone of security and one that induces both physical and mental stability.

 ## Element
Silver, which acts as a metaphysical stabilizer when coupled with certain gemstones. Additionally, it is considered to promote self-improvement.

♨ Herb

Bear's garlic *(Allium ursinum).* The entire plant has medicinal use. Bear's garlic is found in large patches, mainly in moist wooded or shady areas. It has an onionlike root and grows to a height of about 16 inches. It is noticeable for its rather pungent scent. Herbal lore suggests this plant works to reduce blood pressure and acts to combat hardening of the arteries.

♂   BERNARDO: From the root name *Bernard.*

♂   BERNARR: From the root name *Bernard.*

♀   BERNETTE: From the root name *Bernard.*

♀♂ BERNIE: From the root name *Bernard.*

♀   BERNITA: From the root name *Bernard.*

♀   BERRY: From the root name *Bernard.*

♀   BERTA: From the root name *Robert.*

♀   BERTIE: From the root name *Robert.*

♀   BESS: From the root name *Elizabeth.*

♀   BETH: From the root names *Bethany* and *Elizabeth.*

♀   BETHANNE: From the root name *Bethany.*

♀   BETHANNIE: From the root name *Bethany.*

♥ ♀ **BETHANY** Beth, Bethanne, Bethannie: *Bethany*'s origins are complex. Some say it came from *beath,* which in the Celtic language means "life." The Swiss translation of the same word is "God's oath." However, stronger ties are found in its link to *bethia,* which means "house" in Hebrew and Aramaic.

There are references to *Betha,* an old English hereditary name and to the Latin *Bega* (*Begga*), a saint also called

Hayne who lived around A.D. 620, Although Begga (Hayne) was of Irish birth, she went with Celtic missionaries to northern England, where Saint Aidan consecrated her at Whitby as the first nun in Northumbria.

In Hebrew, *bayit* ("beth") is also the second letter of the alphabet. Its symbol is shaped like a house. Semitic translations can be hard to pinpoint, though. In Hebrew, *beth te' ena* or *beth te' enimf* is thought to mean "house of figs." However, in Aramaic, the root *ena* means "poverty," so the meaning changes to "house of poverty."

Although the exact origins may never be clarified, a pharaoh and his wife, Mered, named their daughter Bethia, which is said to have been taken from the Hebrew *bith-yah* meaning "daughter (worshiper) of Jehovah."

Many biblical references link the name to such places as Bethel on the Jordan River, where Jacob dreamed of the ladder reaching to heaven and made a vow to go to his father's house in peace. Bethesda—from the Hebrew meaning "house of mercy," was also a sacred pool in Jerusalem said to have healing powers. Bethlehem, of course, is traditionally held to be the birthplace of Jesus. And the town of Bethany itself, lying just southeast of Jerusalem below the Mount of Olives, is where Jesus is said to have spent a great deal of time with his friends Mary and Martha. Bethany is also traditionally held to be the site of the tomb of their brother Lazarus.

Perhaps because of all these biblical connections, *Bethany* became a name favored by Roman Catholics. During Puritan times (1600s–1700s), the name appeared often in Christian England, which seems odd, since the Puritans avoided the names, saints, and religious ideals of the Catholics. But one might imagine that the beauty of the name and its link to the life of Christ kept *Bethany* from disappearing from the Protestant records the way many Catholic and Hebrew names did at the time.

In America, *Bethany* became somewhat visible in the 1950s, but its use was short-lived, and the name faded by the 1970s. Today its popularity has revived, as often happens for many names, and it is again among the most popular names for girls. The practice of combining two names may have also contributed to its recent favor, as in the blending of *Beth* and *Ann* to form *Bethannie, Bethann(e),* and *Bethania.*

⊚ Number
Three. Threes find inspiration in everyday life and may pursue artistic careers. They have a deep sense of responsibility and thrive in an environment of harmony.

☾ Astrological sign
Pisces. Pisces is a water sign, which means its natives are comfortable in the realm of the soul. They are compassionate and empathetic. Pisces is ruled by the planet Jupiter and the number three.

☀ Color
Lilac. Ancient Europeans associated the number three with the color lilac. Metaphysically, lilac is linked to heightened intuition.

◆ Stone
Lepidolite. Folk legends call this brilliant, lilac-colored mineral "the stone of peace" or "the stone of reconciliation" for its purported ability to neutralize anger. In lore, lepidolite is tied to Jupiter and Neptune.

♆ Element
Lithium. Lepidolite is a mica stone rich in lithium.

Herb

Betony *(Stachys officinalis).* The flowering herb of this plant was used by healers of the past for heartburn and varicose veins. Betony juice was also used to treat cuts, sores, and mild sprains.

♀ BETSY: From the root name *Elizabeth*.

♀ BETTE: From the root name *Elizabeth*.

♀ BETTINA: From the root name *Elizabeth*.

♀ BETTINE: From the root name *Elizabeth*.

♀ BETTY: From the root name *Elizabeth*.

♀♂ BEV: From the root name *Beverly*.

♂ BEVERLEIGH: From the root name *Beverly*.

♀♂ **BEVERLY**   Bev, Beverleigh, Bevlyn, Bevvy, Buffy, Verlee, Verlye: *Beverly* comes from two sources: first from a place name in England and later from the transference of a surname into a given name. In English-speaking countries, many surnames are converted, a trend that grew throughout the eighteenth and nineteenth centuries. *Beverly* has been used for both boys and girls in Europe, and the male variation is usually spelled *Beverley*.

Its origins in Britain come from a place in Humberside, named in Old English for *beofor* ("beaver") and *leac* ("stream"). *Beverley* is the original spelling, but when it sailed across the ocean to the United States, *Beverly* apparently lost its third *e* overboard.

Another translation may have come from the Old English *belvoir* ("beautiful prospect") with *ley* ("place or field"). Some believe the name came from *beverlac* ("lake of beavers") from the beavers that thrived in the Hull River.

In the United States, the name was actually first used as

the name of a place, which eventually gave rise to its popularity as a first name almost exclusively for girls. The spelling (without the third *e*) is apparently found only in the United States; *Beverley* seems to be the spelling of choice in most other English-language nations.

At the turn of the twentieth century, when President Taft was in office (1909–1913), the name was constantly in the press because he visited and spent his vacations at a place called Beverly Farms, a practice that seems to have catapulted *Beverly* into being a name with high-class associations.

Beverly received another boost early in the twentieth century when the wealthy and glamorous movers and shakers of the film industry set up shop in Beverly Hills, California. By 1925, *Beverly* had become one of the top 50 American female names. It remained in the spotlight of popular names for the next 25 years.

The name spread from the United States throughout the world and was especially popular in Canada, Great Britain, Australia, and New Zealand. Although still associated with an aura of luxury, the name has faded in the United States and is not represented in the most popular names of the 1990s.

The spelling of *Beverlee* was sometimes used; the only pet name associated with *Beverly* (male or female) is *Bev*.

 ## Number

Three. Modern numerologists associate this number with people who appreciate nature. Threes are particularly sensitive to any turmoil in the environment around them. The number three is also connected to inspiration and inner balance.

Astrological sign

Scorpio. This sign is ruled by Pluto. Its element is water. Scorpios are unusually persistent when pursuing their desires in love or business. They can be temperamental and aggressive, but above all, they are passionate in love.

Color

Crimson. This sunset hue is linked to desire and personal power.

 Stone

Red jasper. Native Americans of the Southwest used jasper in rain-making ceremonies, calling it "the rain bringer." Some Eastern cultures believed that jasper warded off drought and guarded against sight defects. European lore held that red jasper could send negativity back to its source.

 Element

Plutonium. This silvery element has immense natural powers.

Herb

Watercress *(Nasturtium officinale)*. This plant is native to Europe but was brought to North America with the colonists. It thrives in clear, cold streams. Traditionally, the roots and young shoots are used to treat lung ailments and digestive distress. It has a high vitamin C content and is rich in iron and iodine.

♀ BEVLYN: From the root name *Beverly*.

♀ BEVVY: From the root name *Beverly*.

♂ BEYREN: From the root name *Byron*.

♀ BIBI: From the root name *Barbara*.

♂ BILL: From the root name *William*.

♀♂ BILLY: From the root name *William*.

♂ BINYAMIN: From the root name *Benjamin*.

♀ BIRGITTA: From the root name *Brittany*.

♂ BIRON: From the root name *Byron*.

♀♂ **BLAIR** **Blaire, Blayr:** Blair was originally probably a Scottish place name. It is certainly Celtic in origin and is most often said to mean "a level piece of ground" or "a plain." In Scotland, where the name seems to have first appeared, tribal clans selected plains or open fields for their battle sites and the word *blair* came to signify battle. As with many place names, *Blair* first came into use as a surname, then as a first name. Several names historians describe *Blair*'s transition from place name to first name quite lyrically when they state that, as a given name, *Blair* means "child of the fields."

When used as a first name, *Blair* has historically been masculine. It is so rare that most names historians make no mention of it in their dictionaries of given names, even those published as recently as 1979.

Blair began being used as a feminine name during the 1980s, especially in the United States. The feminine *Blair* has only very recently transformed into the alternate spelling, *Blaire*. Why, how, or exactly when the *e* began to be added to the name is a mystery. It probably can be traced to a long-standing tradition of differentiating between the masculine and feminine variations of names.

Number

Six. People of this number are magnetic. Always determined to carry out their plans, they are sometimes obstinate. More than any other number, sixes thrive when surrounded by adoration.

Astrological sign

Taurus. With six as the ruling number of Taurus, *Blair* fits well with this sign. Taurus's element of earth represents the body, and people who are practical in nature. Taureans can be stubborn.

Color

Meadow brook green. This earthy color promotes peace and tranquillity, which is most helpful in calming an enraged bullheaded Taurean.

 Stone

Green anglesite, a fragile crystalline stone that is usually nearly colorless. It is found in Wales and the Leadhills district of Scotland. The content of lead sulfate adds a pale greenish hue to this sparkling gem. It is valued by collectors and is often faceted in a fancy cut to increase its worth.

Element

Copper, which is associated with the planet Venus, Taurus's ruling planet.

Herb

Eyebright *(Euphrasia officinalis).* This small, downy herb is common in meadows and pastures throughout the world. Some herbalists believe a distilled solution of this plant makes an excellent eyewash, and they use it to treat eyestrain and other eye ailments. When brewed as a tea, it helps alleviate symptoms of hay fever and colds.

♀♂ BLAIRE: From the root name *Blair.*

♥ ♀♂ **BLAKE**   Blakelee, Blakeleigh, Blakeley, Blakenee: *Blake* comes from the transference of a surname to a given name of distinction, a trend that has grown popular in the last two centuries. Previously, the use of transferred surnames was chiefly found among "landed" families. The practice became more prevalent in the nineteenth century, and in most instances the names were given because of a relationship between families, usually through marriage. Brides from rich and powerful families would christen their first children with their maiden names, symbolizing the union of the two names and bringing harmony between families.

Although traditionally used for men, *Blake* is also beginning to appear as a first name for girls, following a recent trend of androgynizing monikers formerly reserved for men, as with *Morgan, Kelsey, Austin,* and *Elliot.*

Originating in England, *Blake* seems to have two etymologies, one being the Old English *blaec* (black) and the Old English form *blac* (pale, or white). However, in Anglo-Saxon it means "to bleach or whiten" and is linked to an early English work-related naming pattern of taking one's occupation for a name. In this case, someone named Blake would be one who bleached cloth or linens for a living.

Some believe *Blake* is a "corruption" of the British *Ap-Lake* with *Ap* meaning "from" or "son" and *Lake* meaning the body of water—therefore, the son of Lake. According to this version, the family name went to Ireland with the warrior Strongbow, where it changed to *Blake*. Ap-Lake was also one of the knights of King Arthur's Round Table.

Blake recently placed in the top 100 popular names for boys, and its popularity among both boys and girls continues to rise.

 ## Number

Four. Fours often appear to view issues from the opposite perspective of those around them. Although this may make them seem quarrelsome, it is their innate sense of honesty that compels them to question everything.

☾ Astrological sign

Pisces. Pisces is a water sign, which means that Pisceans understand the language of the soul. They tend to be indecisive, but that is only because they can sympathize with all sides of an issue.

❋ Color

Slate. The mixing of black and white yields a striking slate gray. The combination of two such powerful colors enhances self-control and clear inner vision.

◆ Stone

Onyx. In ancient ceremonial magic, amulets of onyx were used to protect against hexes and curses. This black stone is from the chalcedony family and is often banded with streaks of white.

♣ Element

Silver, which encourages strong positive emotion.

♫ Herb

Dyer's Broom *(Genista tinctoria)*. The flowering twigs of this plant were once used to stimulate the central nervous system and to help raise the blood pressure. It grows in meadows and pastures worldwide.

♀♂   BLAKELEE: From the root name *Blake*.

♂   BLAKELEIGH: From the root name *Blake*.

♂   BLAKELEY: From the root name *Blake*.

♀   BLAKENEE: From the root name *Blake*.

♂   BLAYR: From the root name *Blair*.

♀♂ BO: From the root name *Robert*.

♂ BOB: From the root name *Robert*.

♀ BOBBIE: From the root name *Barbara*.

♂ BOBBY: From the root name *Robert*.

♀ BOBETTE: From the root name *Robert*.

♀ BOBINETTE: From the root name *Robert*.

♀ BON: From the root name *Bonnie*.

♀ BONNE: From the root name *Bonnie*.

♀ BONNEBELL: From the root name *Bonnie*.

♀ BONNI: From the root name *Bonnie*.

♥ ♀ **BONNIE**   **Bon, Bonne, Bonnebell, Bonni, Bunnie:**
The name *Bonnie* comes from a Latin root. It traveled by
way of France through the word *bonne,* meaning "good,"
and—most probably after the Norman Conquest—landed in
Scotland, where it developed as a slang term meaning "pretty," "healthy," "good," or "charming." The name *Bonita*,
which is Spanish for "good," developed independently of the
Scottish *Bonnie*. Today, *Bonnie* is used both as an independent name and as a diminutive of *Bonita*.

Most names historians report that the term *bonnie* didn't
become the name *Bonnie* until the early twentieth century. It
is possible, however, that the transformation began even earlier. The song "My Bonnie Lies Over the Ocean" became a
hit in the 1880s and certainly must have helped influence the
term's transformation into a given name. An early twentieth-
century reference to the name is a character in the novel
Over Bemerton's (1908) by Edward Verrall Lucas. The first
important historical figure with the name was Bonnie Parker
(1910–1934), the famed bank robber—the Bonnie of the
duo Bonnie and Clyde.

Though all these earlier Bonnies helped make the use of the name more widespread, Margaret Mitchell deserves the credit for being the name's biggest influence. In her classic novel *Gone With the Wind* (1936), Mitchell gave Rhett Butler and Scarlett O'Hara's daughter the nickname Bonnie. She was born Eugenie Victoria, but Rhett coined the nickname when he commented that his daughter's eyes were "as blue as the bonnie blue flag." It is surprising, therefore, that notwithstanding the name's popular history and the fact that it seems to be such a "typical" girl's name, Bonnie has never broken into the top 50 girls' names in the United States. Its use has declined in the past few decades with the trend toward names with more historical depth.

 ## Number

Five. Although fives often make excellent companions and have many friends, tying a five down is like trying to control the ocean tides.

 ## Astrological sign

Pisces. A Piscean is at home around water, whether in it or on it.

 ## Color

Oceanic blue, which shows depth of spirit in a person's aura and represents serenity.

 ## Stone

Abalone. No two abalone shells are alike. Found in many shapes, sizes, and a rainbow of colors, they are used for buttons, jewelry, and other decorative ornaments. The iridescent abalone, also called paua, is one of the most beautiful. Shell items unearthed in ancient South American Indian archaeological sites show that many tribes used shells for trade and considered them symbols of wealth. Abalone necklaces or bracelets were highly valued.

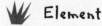 Element

Silver, a precious metal associated with the moon. It adds strength and beauty to abalone.

🌿 Herb

Bluebonnet *(Centaurea cyanus)*. Native to the Mediterranean region but cultivated anywhere, bluebonnet has several uses. Its large blue flowers are attractive to bees and have medicinal value. The dried flowers were usually mixed with other herbs and brewed in teas to settle upset stomachs. Sometimes the flowers were used in eyedrops and soothing compresses for tired eyes. According to Greek lore, the genus name *Centaurea* was given to the plant because it healed a wounded centaur. *Cyanus* means blue.

♀ BORBALA: From the root name *Barbara*.

♀♂ BRAD: From the root name *Bradley*.

♀♂ BRADLEA: From the root name *Bradley*.

♀♂ BRADLEIGH: From the root name *Bradley*.

♥ ♀♂ **BRADLEY** **Brad, Bradlea, Bradleigh, Bradney:** The name *Bradley* originates from the Anglo-Saxon terms *brad* and *leah* and means "a broad (or wide) clearing (or meadow)." As with many given names, *Bradley* started out as a place name. Then, as surnames developed during the Middle Ages, it served to identify someone who lived in or near the local meadow or clearing. After the surname was established, *Bradley* began to be used as a first name.

Initially, it was probably given to children as a way to carry on the maternal line or to honor a maternal relative.

When and how often *Bradley* has been used as a first name is the subject of some dispute. Some names historians believe that it was first used as a given name in the United States, but while Americans have a particular fondness for the practice of giving their children surnames as first names, *Bradley* can be found in England as early as the 1850s, if not long before.

The development of the name is much easier to trace in the twentieth century. It can probably be directly connected to the popularity of General Omar Nelson Bradley (1893–1981). Called "the soldiers' general" because of his concern for the men under his command and his dislike for military ceremony, Bradley brilliantly commanded various army divisions during World War II, including the Twelfth Army Group. Many of the soldiers under his command had powerful reasons to name their sons after their former general.

Use of the name only grew after World War II, and by the 1980s, *Bradley* was among the top 50 boys' names in the United States among white families. The name has always been slightly less popular among minority families. Its use has since dropped off slightly. The name's diminutive, *Brad,* has become increasingly common as an independent name, sparked by such personalities as actor Brad Pitt.

◎ Number

Four. In many cultures, four is tied to order and stability. Fours seldom form deep friendships, but when they do they are devoted and loyal friends for life.

☾ Astrological sign

Sagittarius. Many born under the sign of the hunter make excellent strategists in war or peace. They aren't afraid to try new ideas or follow their hunches.

Color

Viridian. The lush green of pastures in springtime restores health and peace.

Stone

Bowenite. This translucent blue or blue-green gem is a type of serpentine. According to gem lore, serpentine was used in travelers' protection amulets, particularly for itinerant traders or sailors. Ancient Africans made bartering beads from serpentine. Today, carvings and jewelry from this gem are highly valued throughout the world. Serpentine got its name from its structure, which resembles snakeskin. Bowenite makes beautiful jewelry and can be found in New Zealand, China, South Africa, and the United States.

 ## Element

Magnesium, which is found in serpentine.

Herb

Meadowsweet *(Filipendula).* Common in damp European meadows and the eastern United States, meadowsweet has a creeping rootstock with yellow-white or reddish flowers. The entire plant has medicinal use and was once considered to be helpful for flu, respiratory problems, arthritis, and fever. Meadowsweet tea was also recommended for kidney troubles. Some healers used a root preparation to cleanse wounds or as a rinse for sore eyes.

♂   BRADNEY: From the root name *Bradley.*

♂   BRAHAM: From the root name *Abraham.*

♂   BRAM: From the root name *Abraham.*

♀   BRANA: From the root name *Brian/Bryan.*

♂ BRAND: From the root name *Brendan*.

♂ BRANDEN: From the root name *Brendan*.

♂ BRANDON: From the root name *Brendan*.

♀ BREANNA: From the root name *Brian/Bryan*.

♀ BREE: From the root name *Brian/Bryan*.

♀ BREN: From the root name *Brenda*.

♥ ♀ **BRENDA** **Bren, Brenna, Brenndah:** The name *Brenda* is probably derived from the Teutonic word *brandr,* meaning "sword." The masculine name *Brand* is still used in Iceland and was found in England up until the twelfth century. Many historians believe *Brenda* to be the feminine form of that name. Among the other theories of *Brenda*'s genesis, names historian Elza Dinwiddie-Boyd stays with the Teutonic root but puts an interesting slant on the name's development from that root when she states that *Brenda* means "firebrand." Historian Alfred Kolatch, on the other hand, is one of the few to completely deviate from the *brandr* root. He traces the name to the Celtic word *bran,* meaning "raven," and states that the name means "dark-haired." In Ireland, Brenda is often taken to be the feminine for *Brendan.* (See also *Brendan.*)

A fairly uncommon name elsewhere, *Brenda* gained its greatest early popularity in Scotland. It was probably Sir Walter Scott who helped the name establish its first firm foothold outside of Scotland when he named one of the heroines of his novel *The Pirate* (1822) Brenda. William Thackeray followed Scott when he included a Brenda among the characters in his book *The Adventures of Philip on His Way Through the World* (1861–1862). By the twentieth century, the name had been brought into use in most English-speaking countries. In the United States, it enjoyed particular popularity in the African American community. By 1950, *Brenda* was among the top 50 girls' names in the United States. Since that time, use of the name has steadily declined.

Number

Eight. Ancient Greek numerologists considered eight to be the most holy of female numbers.

☾ Astrological sign

Leo. The term *firebrand* aptly describes most Leos. They approach life with flaming spirits and shine in the light of their ruling planet, the sun.

☀ Color

Glowing ember. This shade of reddish yellow is related to personal power and self-esteem.

◆ Stone

Yellow fluorite. The name *fluorite* comes from the Latin *fluere,* which means "to flow." When invisible ultraviolet light is shone on fluorite crystals, they seem to emit light. Most often, the fluorescent hue differs from its daylight color. Fluorite is used in steelmaking because it helps liquid steel flow easier and it filters out impurities like sulfur and phosphorus. In New Age practices, fluorite is thought to soften such strong emotions as anger or desperation.

♛ Element

Steel. Metaphysically, steel is thought to have powers of protection against nightmares.

🐉 Herb

Sundew *(Drosera rotundifolia)*. According to herbal lore, sundew was considered helpful for respiratory problems, especially asthma, whooping cough, and bronchitis. Although the herb is mainly used in healing, the plant also has an antibiotic substance that in undiluted form neutralizes strep and staph infections and even the bacteria that causes pneumonia. European medical folklore suggests use of fresh juice from this plant gets rid of warts. Sundew grows in moist areas in North America, Europe, and Asia.

♥ ♂ **BRENDAN** **Brand, Branden, Brandon, Brendon, Brennan:** There are many possible sources for the names *Brendan* and *Brandon*. Some historians trace the origins of the name *Brendan* to the Erse name *Breanainn,* which some say means "stinking" and some say means "prince." Various names historians put forward different theories about the name *Brandon* as well. Leslie Dunkling and William Gosling report that *Brandon,* when used as a place name in England, means "a hill covered with broom." When the name is used as an Irish surname, they say it means a "descendant of Brendan." On the other hand, Elza Dinwiddie-Boyd takes *Brandon* to mean "from the beacon hill." Alfred Kolatch relates *Brandon* back to either the Anglo-Saxon word *brand,* which means "sword," or to the Erse word *bran,* which means "raven." Oddly, it is generally accepted that the female name *Brenda* is from the Teutonic root *brandr,* meaning "sword." The name *Brand*—still used in Iceland—was found in England through the twelfth century, but *Brand* and *Brenda* are seldom, if ever, linked with *Brendan* and *Brandon.* (See also **Brenda.**)

Moving on to firmer historical ground, we find that the earliest known Brendan was Saint Brendan "the Voyager," who lived in the sixth century. Famous for his travels, he is said to have founded monasteries all over the British Isles. The tales of his sea travels were recounted in the eighth century narrative, *Navigatio Brendani*. The *Navigatio* reports that while on one journey, Brendan discovered the "promised land of the saints." Later scholars believed that this land was probably the Canary Islands.

Saint Brendan certainly had many namesakes during the early Middle Ages. In fact, a mountain, called Brandon, is said to be named after him, which may have led to the synonymity of *Brendan* and *Brandon*. However, there are few recorded historic Brendans other than this early saint, and until the twentieth century both *Brendan* and *Brandon* were generally considered surnames or place names.

Brandon began to be more widespread in the United States in the 1930s, especially in African American families. By the 1980s, it was among the top 50 most popular names. *Brendan* was slower to rise to the top, but by 1997, both names were in the top 50.

◉ Number

Five. Fives like to live on the edge and thrive on excitement.

☾ Astrological sign

Scorpio. This sign's element is water, which rules the soul. Many Scorpios have powerful perceptive abilities and analytical minds.

✳ Color

Raven. Like the bird's feathers, this blue-black hue shines with divine power.

◆ Stone

Speckled agate. Agates appear in folk myths as early as the seventh century. Some are striped or speckled; they are often named for where they've been found. Legends expound on the power of this gem that was thought to keep its owner from harm. Speckled agates were considered especially helpful to travelers on or over water. Agates are found in many parts of the world, including Italy, Egypt, and Scotland.

Element

Plutonium, the metal most often connected to the sign of Scorpio through its ruling planet, Pluto.

Herb

Hellebore *(Helleborus foetidus).* Commonly called stinking hellebore, this European plant can be found on the Alps' rocky slopes. The herb and rootstock were used by healers of the past. It is the most potent of the hellebores and was sometimes used as a heart stimulant and for treatment of depression, mania, and epilepsy. It should never be used without proper medical supervision. It has bell-shaped flowers that bloom from March to May.

♂   BRENDON: From the root name *Brendan.*

♀   BRENNA: From the root name *Brenda.*

♂   BRENNAN: From the root name *Brendan.*

♀   BRENNDAH: From the root name *Brenda.*

♥ ♂ **BRENT** **Brentan, Brentyn:** There are several probable origins for the name *Brent.* It was a Celtic place name that meant "high place" or "hill," and it was also the name of a river in England. The name for the River Brent was derived from the same source as the name *Bridget.* (See also *Brittany.*) As with many names that are currently popular, from the place name—hill or river—the name then developed into a surname. Therefore, *Brent* could have meant "someone who lives on or near the hill" or "someone who lives near the River Brent." However, there is another interesting possibility for the development of the surname. It might also have been taken from the word *burnt*. This has led names historians to variously describe the surname as "an outlaw who has been burnt (or branded)" or as "a person who lives near a burnt ground."

Found initially in the United States, the given name *Brent* attained that status rather late for most surnames that became first names. The first popular literary work to use the name for a main character was Sinclair Lewis's *Dodsworth* (1929). Seven years later, Margaret Mitchell gave the name a further boost when she named one of the Tarleton twins Brent. By 1940, the name was beginning to travel across the ocean to England.

The name never became particularly widespread in either the United States or England, though it did have a burst of popularity in Canada during the 1970s. *Brenton* and *Brentton* are two modern African American variations.

Number

Five. Fives are curious and have the energy to explore answers to deep questions. The quicker they find what they're looking for, the better, for then they can be off to something new.

Astrological sign

Capricorn. Although they are never the first up the hill, Capricorns will not fall off while scaling the heights in pursuit of answers to their questions. People of this earthy sign are as steadfast as the nimble mountain goat.

Color

Terre verte. Brown and green bring a sense of safety and warmth to tremulous souls who have climbed too high and must find the way back down.

◆ Stone

Axinite. Although brown is the most common color of axinite, it is sometimes found in a honey color or deep plum. Its name comes from its axhead-shaped crystals. The stone is hard but sometimes too brittle for gem cutting. However, it's still highly prized by collectors. Darker axinite is sometimes confused with smoky quartz. Axinite is found in New Jersey (honey yellow variety); Mexico; Cornwall, England; and France.

Element

Iron, which gives axinite its rich brown color.

 Herb

Water avens *(Geum rivale)*. Water avens, also called chocolate root, is found mostly in North America, Europe, and Asia. The plant has various medical uses. Herbal lore suggests the rootstock makes a pleasant-tasting, strong remedy for dysentery when mixed with milk and sugar. Some Native American tribes used the plant to help fight respiratory congestion and upset stomachs.

♂ BRENTAN: From the root name *Brent*.

♂ BRENTYN: From the root name *Brent*.

♂ BRET: From the root name *Brett*.

♥ ♀♂ **BRETT**   **Bret, Brette, Bretton, Britt:** *Brett* was initially a surname and is variously described as being from Celtic, Latin, and Old French. Suffice it to say that all three languages had a term meaning "a person of Britanny," "a Breton," or "a Briton." Members of the tribe of Bretons migrated from France to Ireland and Scotland during the pre-Christian era. Therefore, the surname has probably existed in England for well over 1,000 years—or at least as long as surnames have been used.

The first historic person who used the surname as a first name didn't appear until the nineteenth century: writer and poet Bret Harte (1836–1902), born Francis Brett Harte, known for his stories about the American frontier. It is not too surprising, then, that the next famous Bret is also connected to the American frontier. Bret Maverick was a television character—played by James Garner from 1957 through 1962—in the hit series *Maverick,* which ran from 1957 through 1962. The popularity of the show coincides with a rise in use of the name Bret. The name enjoyed a new boost during the 1990s, possibly thanks to the popularity of several baseball players: Brett Butler, Bret Saberhagen, and George Brett.

Though it is still considered by names historians to be a masculine name, *Brett* has appeared off and on as a girl's name in the United States since Ernest Hemingway, in his novel *The Sun Also Rises,* named one of his most interesting female characters Lady Brett Ashley.

◉ Number

Two. Modern numerology credits people of this number with diplomacy. They enjoy people and are friendly mixers in any group.

☾ Astrological sign
Aquarius. Most Aquarians are kind and strong-willed. They are faithful but need plenty of breathing room to remain at peace.

☀ Color
Albescent. White is a positive shade and signifies attainment.

◆ Stone
Gypsum. Several types of gypsum are used for decorative stones or jewelry. Most are white or beige. Alabaster is the most important variety and is usually found in various pastel shades. Decorated alabaster columns have been discovered dating back nearly 2,000 years. Satin spar gypsum is favored by some collectors for its cat's-eye effect when cut and polished. Gypsum deposits are found in England, Italy, Mexico, the United States, and Chile.

☘ Element
Uranium, which represents Uranus, one of Aquarius's ruling planets.

☙ Herb
Milkwort *(Polygala vulgaris).* A plant native to Europe, milkwort fares well in the dry parts of meadows or sunny, rocky slopes with limestone soils. The entire plant was found to have healing properties. It was commonly used for coughs, bronchitis, and some chronic lung problems. Rootstock preparations were made to stimulate appetite. It also increased milk in nursing mothers. Milkwort's flowers are usually pale rose or white.

♀♂   BRETTE: From the root name *Brett*.

♂   BRETTON: From the root name *Brett*.

♀   BRIA: From the root name *Brian/Bryan*.

♥ ♂ **BRIAN/BRYAN** Brana, Breanna, Bree, Bria, Brianna, Brianne, Briano, Briant, Brina, Briny, Bryant, Brynn, Brynne: The name *Brian* has a wonderfully confusing background, and there are a variety of interesting possible meanings to choose from when interpreting the name.

The name might be a variation of the ancient Celtic name *Bran*, which means "raven." An important name in ancient Britain and Ireland, in Celtic mythology Bran was the god of the underworld. Another Bran shows us more clearly the possible connection between *Bran* and *Brian*. The famous tale *Imram Brain* is the Celtic name for *The Voyage of Bran*. In the story, Bran and his cohorts travel to the magical Land of Women. After a year they return home; on their arrival, they learn that the voyage actually lasted centuries and that they were remembered only through ancient stories.

Charlotte Yonge is one names historian who relates *Brian* to *Bran*. Strangely, however, even though she lists the name *Bran* as meaning "raven," when she discusses *Brian,* she moves from *Brian* to *Bran* to *brig(h),* which means "force" or "strength." In this way, she defines *Brian* as meaning "strong." It seems that many names historians have followed Yonge's lead, listing the name *Brian* as meaning "strong." (*Brig[h]* is also the root source for *Bridget,* and possibly *Brett* and *Brittany*.)

Other names historians trace the development of *Brian* from a completely different root, the Celtic word *bre,* meaning "hill." Still other interpretations include "virtuous," "fortunate," "nobly born" and "eloquent," but these are probably attributes derived from later personalities who carried the name *Brian*.

Brian has been found in Brittany from the ninth century onward, as well as in Ireland (though it is not known when the name first appeared there). It was probably brought to

England in 1066 with the Bretons, who fought for William the Conqueror during the Norman Conquest. However, it is from the Irish—and before the Norman Conquest—that we get the most important historical Brian: Brian Boru—or Boromhe—who lived from 926 until 1014. In 1002, Boru became the chief king of a united Ireland. A great warrior, he defeated the Danish invaders in 25 battles before being killed at Clontarf. Both Boru and his final battle have been the subject of many epic Irish poems, and he is still one of the country's foremost heroes.

After the Norman Conquest, the name *Brian* was almost as widespread in England as it was in Ireland. Its use declined severely in the seventeenth and eighteenth centuries, and it came to be considered an Irish name. Rare in Colonial America, *Brian* probably came to the United States with the Irish immigrants in the mid-nineteenth century. It was fairly widespread from the 1920s through the 1970s, when use of the name began to drop off. In the 1990s, the name experienced another revival and is again one of the most favored boys' names in the United States. Perhaps not entirely coincidentally, there was a burgeoning fascination with Irish culture in the United States during the 1990s.

The variant spelling *Bryan* has probably been in use for centuries, but its most famous early use was in William Thackeray's *History of Henry Esmond* (1852). After a decline starting in the 1920s, *Bryan* has reasserted itself and is now among the top 100 boys' names.

There are many female variations on the name *Brian*. The earliest for which there is a record seems to be *Briana*, a name found in the second book of Edmund Spenser's *Faerie Queene* (1590). Previously rare, *Briana* and its variations (*Brianna, Brianne,* and *Breana*) started to become more common in the 1980s.

☉ Number

Eight. It's not wise to cross people of this number. When it comes to a battle of wills, an eight usually wins.

☽ Astrological sign

Gemini, a "voice" sign; a large number of entertainers are born under this zodiac sign.

✳ Color

Black. *Dhu* means "black" in Celtic and represents Bran, ancient god of the underworld.

◆ Stone

Schorl. This gem is a black tourmaline with opaque prism-like crystals that can appear in veins several yards long. During the Victorian Age, black tourmaline was used for funeral jewelry. However, schorl is no longer considered a gem of sorrow. Today, tourmaline is thought to attract love and money. Modern metaphysical practices use schorl as an aid during astral projection. It is believed to act as a homing device for spiritual travelers when they are returning to their physical bodies. It is also believed to absorb negative energy.

♕ Element

Quicksilver represents Gemini's ruling planet of Mercury.

⚘ Herb

Bryony *(Bryonia alba).* Bryony is a cultivated climbing plant, but it also grows wild in moist soil and vineyards in Europe. Traditionally, the dried rootstock has been used by healers for such chest ailments as whooping cough. Its pea-size black berries are highly poisonous.

♀ BRIANNA: From the root name *Brian/Bryan*.

♀ BRIANNE: From the root name *Brian/Bryan*.

♂ BRIANO: From the root name *Brian/Bryan*.

♂ BRIANT: From the root name *Brian/Bryan*.

♀ BRIDGET: From the root name *Brittany*.

♀ BRINA: From the root name *Brian/Bryan*.

♀ BRINY: From the root name *Brian/Bryan*.

♀ BRITNEY: From the root name *Brittany*.

♀♂ BRITT: From the root name *Brett* and *Brittany*.

♀ BRITTA: From the root name *Brittany*.

♥ ♀ **BRITTANY** **Bridget, Britney, Britt, Britta:** *Brittany* is among the top 100 girls' names in the United States. The name itself is a modern one, though it has very ancient roots. Most historians connect the name to *Britain* and say that *Brittany* comes from the Latin *Brittania,* meaning "from England." From the eighteenth century onward, girls in England have occasionally been named Brittania, the female personification of British rule. The most famous use of the term is in the patriotic anthem, "Rule Brittania," and it is possible that some parents were directly influenced by the song.

Brittany is also, of course, a region of France. Taken from the same root as *Britain, Britanny* is associated with an ancient Celtic tribe, the Britons, found in Ireland, Wales, and Scotland from early pre-Christian times. Some historians believe that the tribe migrated to the British Isles from what is now France. Around the year 500, the Britons were driven out of England by the Anglo-Saxons. They repopulated the area in France now known as Britanny.

There are other possible ways to interpret the name. *Brita* (or *Britta*) is a pet form of *Bridget* (or the Irish *Brighid*), which some historians relate to the Celtic word *brigh,* meaning "strength." Other historians relate *Bridget* to a pre-Christian Irish goddess and say the name means "high one." In addition, *Brita* is the Swedish variation of *Brighit* or *Birgitta,* which is also related to *Bridget.* (See also **Brett.**)

Number

One. In modern numerology, one represents the here and now, yet it also represents foundation and the genesis of life.

Astrological sign

Virgo. This earth sign symbolizes fertility. Virgos often have high ideals and devote their lives to living up to them.

Color

National blue. According to an ancient form of medieval mysticism, blue is one of the 10 globes of luminous color on the sefirot tree of the Cabala. It represents mercy. This shade is found on both French and British flags.

Stone

Lazulite. Colors of lazulite vary from pale to dark blue. Some stones are transparent, but most are semitranslucent or opaque. The ancient Egyptians believed that lazulite prevented children from having nightmares.

Element

Silver. In India, lazulite beads are strung on silver wire and given to children to promote healthy growth.

ꙮ Herb

Blue flag *(Iris versicolor)*. Also called fleur-de-lis, blue flag grows mainly in the wetlands of eastern North America. It is exported from there to Europe for cultivation. It has a creeping rootstock that produces sword-shaped leaves and large blue or purplish blue flowers. Blue flag's rootstock is believed to help nausea, heartburn, liver and gallbladder problems; and sinus troubles. It's been recommended for migraines. Native Americans used the leaves for burns.

♂ BROCK

Brockley: *Brock* is an unusual name that was first used as a surname. Most names historians say that the name derives from either Anglo-Saxon or Gaelic and means "badger." For a different—and slightly more pleasant—interpretation one might want to look to historian Charlotte Yonge. Though it is probably a stretch at the very least, Yonge relates the Celtic name *Brieuc* to the root word *brigh,* which means "strength." From this initial interpretation, she defines the name *Brockwell* as "strong champion." Unfortunately, Yonge's definition of the name is not confirmed by other names historians.

Perhaps the most famous historical Brock was Sir Isaac Brock, a British general during the war of 1812. He led the British in their conquest of Detroit but was killed not long after in the battle of Queenston. The Canadian city of Brockville, Ontario, was named after him.

꩜ Number

Four. Fours are dependable and self-disciplined.

☾ Astrological sign

Capricorn, represented by the sure-footed goat. Such terms as *reliable* and *cautious* are often associated with Capricorns.

✳ Color
Brown madder. Shades of brown are tied to Capricorn. Dark brown is also one of the colors in a badger's fur.

◆ Stone
Bottle diopside. Gem-quality diopside ranges from light to dark brownish green. Bottle diopside is a deep green owing to its iron content. Some bottle diopside is mistaken for tourmaline or olivine because of the crystalline form and luster when polished. The larger pieces are made into beaded jewelry and the transparent crystals cut well into baguette (rectangular) gemstones. Although this delicate gem occurs mainly in Brazil and Burma, fine crystals are found in Switzerland and New York.

♛ Element
Iron. In ancient magic lore, iron was held to be an ore of strength and protection. In China, dragons were believed to fear iron.

⚘ Herb
Yellow goatsbeard *(Tragopogon pratensis)*. Found in pastures and fields in Europe and southern Canada, yellow goatsbeard has a fleshy taproot and light green succulent stem. The stem contains a milky juice and produces a single yellow flower head with ray flowers that open in the morning and close in the heat of the day. The root was once used in remedies for heartburn, lack of appetite and other digestive ills.

♂   BROCKLEY: From the root name *Brock*.

 ♀♂ **BROOK**   Brooke, Brookes, Brookie, Brooks: *Brook* was originally an English surname. As with many surnames, it began as a way to identify people by where they lived. Therefore, Brook was probably "someone who lives next to the stream or brook." When the name became a first name, it was probably used as a way to keep a maternal ancestor's surname in the family. In this way, the name might be taken to mean "one's ancestor lived near a brook."

The use of *Brook* as a first name for a boy has either been so rare or so recent that many names historians, such as Charlotte Yonge, Ernest Weekley, and George Stewart, make no mention of it in their books on given names. However, from the late nineteenth into the twentieth centuries it was slightly more widespread in the African American community.

The feminine, *Brooke*, has much the same history as *Brook*, though it probably came into use later, and recently it has far surpassed the masculine.

 ## Number

Three. You'll never find a three in last place. They were born to be out front or at the top. They have the ability and will to succeed.

 ## Astrological sign

Gemini. The sign of the twins represents spontaneity and intelligence. Geminis are usually on the go and in the know.

Color

Champagne. This golden hue is perfect for a Gemini. Yellow is a color of communication and elation.

Stone

Amblygonite. Our earth is filled with gems, and amblygonite is one of the rare ones. Its colors include white, pink, green, and blue. However, it is most often golden yellow. Amblygonite can be found in large transparent or translucent crystals, but because it is relatively soft by gem standards, it is cut only for collectors. Brazil is the main source of gem-quality stones, but some have been found in the United States. A pale mauve type has been discovered to occur only in Namibia.

Element

Brass, considered a metal of the sun with positive energy. It has been used in healing rituals.

Herb

Brooklime *(Veronica beccabunga)*. The herb part of the brooklime plant has been found to have medicinal properties. In older herbal remedies, the fresh juice was recommended for intestinal troubles and anemia. It was used extensively for these purposes, but it is largely ignored by modern herbalists.

♀♂ BROOKE: From the root name *Brook.*

♀♂ BROOKES: From the root name *Brook.*

♀♂ BROOKIE: From the root name *Brook.*

♀♂ BROOKS: From the root name *Brook.*

♂ BROSE: From the root name *Amber.*

♂ BRUCE Brucie, Brucina, Brucine: *Bruce* has only recently been adopted as a first name, but as a family or clan name it has a long and powerful history. Originally derived from a Norman place name that is spelled variously *Brieux, Bruis,* and *Braose,* it means either a "thicket or wood" or "someone who lives in a thicket or wood." The name came to Britain during the Norman Conquest with the first Robert de Braose. He established the powerful family line that had branches throughout Britain.

The most famous Bruce was Robert the Bruce (1274–1329) who is sometimes called "the liberator." He became king of a unified Scotland in 1306. One of the most celebrated anecdotes about Robert the Bruce takes place at a particularly bad time in his fight against the English: From watching a spider weaving a web, he is said to have gained the patience and perseverance to beat back his enemy.

As with most noble surnames that became first names, no particular date can be established for the use of *Bruce* as a given name. But in the United States it has always been primarily considered to be a first name. Most historians do agree that it did not really develop as such until the twentieth century. In the United States, by 1950 *Bruce* was among the top 50 boys' names in the country, but by 1970 it had dropped out of use again. Consequently, though many men over the age of 40 or 50 are named Bruce, the name is fairly rare among younger men and boys.

Number
Four. A large number of fours are drawn to social causes. They are patient and persistent.

Astrological sign
Taurus. Earthy Taureans aren't afraid to dig in and stand up for what they believe is right.

Color
Braveheart blue. Blue is tied to the sign of Taurus and promotes healing energy.

Stone

Petrified wood. This organic gem is wood that evolved to stone over thousands of years. Some petrified wood is from trees that lived a million years ago. Found everywhere in North America, petrified wood was used by Native American medicine men as talismans for protection against infections and injury. Many tribes also used this revered stone in their jewelry and as ceremonial rubbing stones to call on earthly elemental spirits. Metaphysically, the stone was thought to bring security, prevent stress and restore physical energy.

Element

Iron. Pure iron is rarely found except in meteorites. The earliest iron came from these mysterious rocks that the ancients saw fall from the sky.

Herb

Woodruff *(Asperula odorata)*. Found in thickets throughout Europe, Asia, and North Africa, woodruff is also called master-of-the-wood. The herb part of the plant was used to alleviate jaundice. It was also used to help migraine headaches and as a calming agent for restlessness, insomnia, and hysteria. Woodruff tea was used to reduce stomach pains and was thought to regulate heart activity.

♀♂ BRUCIE: From the root name *Bruce*.

♀   BRUCINA: From the root name *Bruce*.

♀   BRUCINE: From the root name *Bruce*.

♂   BRYANT: From the root name *Brian/Bryan*.

♂   BRYNN: From the root name *Brian/Bryan*.

♀ BRYNNE: From the root name *Brian/Bryan*.

♀ BUFFY: From the root names *Beverly* and *Elizabeth*.

♂ BUIRON: From the root name *Byron*.

♀ BUNNIE: From the root name *Bonnie*.

♂ BURNARD: From the root name *Bernard*.

♂ BYRAN: From the root name *Byron*.

♂ BYROM: From the root name *Byron*.

♥ ♂ **BYRON   Beyren, Biron, Buiron, Byran, Byrom:**
The name *Byron* most likely is derived from the Teutonic
word *byre,* which meant "a barn or cow shed." First a place
name, the surname may have developed to identify the local
cowherd. Of course, as with many names, not all names historians agree that *Byron*'s origin is "cow shed." Alfred
Kolatch, for example, writes that if one traces *Byron* from a
Germanic root, it might mean "cottage." If one traces it
from the Old English, he says, the name means "bear."
Names historian Linda Wolfe Keister splits the difference
when she notes that the name might mean either "barn for
cows" or "cottage," but she traces the origin of the name to
the Old French. Martin Kelly also traces the name to the Old
French but does not go beyond saying that it means "of
Biron." If the name comes from the Old French, it probably
traveled with the Norman invasion into England. If it has an
Anglo-Saxon or Old English basis, it has existed in the
British Isles since at least A.D. 500.

Wherever or whenever Byron first arose, it achieved its
greatest fame in the early nineteenth century with the poet
George Gordon Noel, Lord Byron. Lord Byron was known
not only for his beautiful poetry but also for his physical
beauty, his clubfoot, and his profligate lifestyle. He could
easily be considered the most romantic figure in English lit-

erature, even today. The use of Byron as a given name probably started after his death.

In the United States, the name can be found in the white community, but it attained its most widespread use in the African American community.

🌀 Number

Two. This number represents both sides—heads or tails, up or down, and in or out. Perhaps this is why twos can always find the heart of a matter and keep the peace.

🌙 Astrological sign

Taurus. Although Taurus is a sign of the earth, it is also tied to the planet Venus that rules the heart. The love of a Taurus is firmly grounded and has the strength of a bull.

✳ Color

Carnation. Pink was once believed to be ruled by the goddess Venus. Sometimes ancients used pink stones to strengthen a romance or instigate a new one.

◆ Stone

Thulite. A member of the zoisite family, thulite's pinkish red color comes from the presence of manganese. Polished thulite is used for beads, ornaments, and decorative work. Zoisite was discovered by Baron S. Zois von Edelstein in the Austrian Sau-Alp mountain range. He named it saualpite, but gemologists later changed the name to honor him.

👑 Element

Lead, considered to be an earth element. In eleventh-century India, charms to help conception or promote fertile crops were engraved on lead tablets.

✿ Herb

Cowslip *(Primula veris)*. Usually found in wet areas, cowslip grows wild in the northeastern United States and Europe. The dried or powdered herb aids healing of wounds, sores or rashes. Leaves harvested in the spring were sometimes eaten as greens. However, modern herbalists have found that cowslip irritates some people when it is fresh, so it must be cooked or dried.

♂   CAELAN: From the root name *Nicholas*.

♀   CAIT: From the root name *Katherine*.

♀   CAITLIN: From the root name *Katherine*.

♂   CAL: From the root name *Caleb*.

♂   CALE: From the root name *Caleb*.

♂ **CALEB   Cal, Cale, Kaleb:** *Caleb* (originally, *Kaleb* or *Kalev*) is an ancient name. If derived from the Hebrew, it means "dog." Many people relate this to the dog's reputed devotion to people and interpret "dog" to mean "having devotion to God." The "dog" definition may also have an earlier pre-Judaic interpretation as a tribal totem. The name also has Arabic origins, where it means "bold" or "brave," and it can be found in the Assyrian language, where it means "messenger" or "priest."

The earliest historical Caleb is the biblical Kalev ben Yefuneh who, with Joshua, was sent by Moses to spy in the Promised Land. After Moses died, Joshua became the leader of the Israelites. The name appears again in historical records after the Reformation in England when biblical names were fashionable among the Puritans. It traveled to America with the Puritans, where it remained extremely popular until the early nineteenth century.

Though the name did not disappear in the nineteenth century, it was somewhat less widespread than it had earlier been. However, writers of the eighteenth, nineteenth, and twentieth centuries remained quite fond of the name. Characters named Caleb can be found in novels as diverse as *The Adventures of Caleb Williams* (1794) by William Godwin, *Oldtown Folks* (1869) by Harriet Beecher Stowe, *Middlemarch* (1871) by George Eliot, and *A Shepherd's Life* (1910) by W. H. Hudson. Historian Eric Partridge writes that during the eighteenth century, *Caleb* was "a fairly general 'Christian' [name], free of cynical association and almost free of Puritan memories." Charlotte Yonge, on the other hand, writing in the mid-nineteenth century, seems to disagree when she states that the name is "seldom copied except by the Puritan taste."

By the 1920s, use of the name dropped significantly, and it revived slightly during the late 1960s, when the first wave of baby boomers became parents and it became fashionable to give "old-fashioned" names, such as *Noah, Joshua,* and *Caleb.* It is also possible that the success of the film *East of Eden,* which featured James Dean as a character named Caleb, influenced parents. It is as yet unclear why *Caleb* had a burst of popularity in the 1990s, though the decade saw another general revival of older names for both boys and girls.

꩜ Number

Five. Numerologists say fives are usually flexible and tolerant. The pentagram is a five-sided figure that, when pointing up, represents the forces of light, spiritual achievement, and education.

☾ Astrological sign

Aries. Dedication and bravery are qualities of most Ariens. Many are superior leaders and courageous in the face of danger. Aries is tied to Mars, the ancient god of war.

Color

Cinnabar. Red is the color of fire and often associated with Mars. This vibrant shade continues to be considered sacred in many cultures.

 Stone

Red zircon. This gem was one of the 12 stones found on the breastplates of ancient high priests. Red zircon was believed to guard against injuries and give energy in times of stress. Worn next to the skin, it supposedly drew pain out of the body. Zircons were believed to promote luck and wisdom and to bring nobility to the heart. Early healers believed zircons cured nervousness, restored appetite, and even increased physical health. Zircons were thought to protect from enemies and natural dangers, especially lightning.

 Element

Gold, which stimulates the power of the red zircon and is referred to as a fire metal.

 Herb

Dogwood *(Cornus florida)*. The dogwood tree is native to the United States and grows to heights of nearly 40 feet. Its bark has been used by native healers to reduce the fevers from ague and malaria. Dogwood trees have white or pink blossoms and red glossy berries.

♂♀ CAM: From the root name *Cameron.*

♥ ♂♀ **CAMERON** Cam, Camron: The name *Cameron* either is derived from the Gaelic word *camshron*, which means "crooked or hook nose," or is a place name that means "crooked stream." It became a Scottish clan name, then developed into a surname. Relatively recently, *Cameron* has been widely adopted as a first name.

Two of the most famous Camerons lived at approximately the same time. Sir Ewan Cameron, the chieftain of Lochiel (1629–1719), was a fierce warrior loyal to both Charles I and Charles II. The best known story about Ewan Cameron is that he once killed a man by biting his neck. Sir Walter Scott appropriated this story for his description of the battle between Roderick Dhu and FitzJames (*The Lady of the Lake,* canto V). Richard Cameron (1648–1680), however, was very much the opposite of Ewan Cameron: He was a scholar and teacher, not a soldier. He was also against the Catholic reign of Charles II. A Covenanter, he founded a religious sect called the Cameronians. They fought a few battles; they were always outnumbered and always lost.

It is possible that these two men influenced some parents to name their children Cameron, but it can't be said that they influenced the name's popularity to a great extent. It is far more likely that parents adopted the name to honor a relative or to maintain the matrilineal name. It was not until the 1950s that the name was used often enough make it onto the "most popular" lists, but since then it has appeared among the top 100 boys' names. Actress Cameron Diaz may have inspired its recent popularity among girls as well.

☺ . Number

Six. Many sixes find their destiny as spiritual leaders.

☾ Astrological sign

Pisces. Forever tied to water, Pisceans know how to go with the flow. But if the flow should become a flood, they know how to swim and ride the waves.

Color

Marine. The blue-green color of the sea brings tranquillity to the soul.

 Stone

Blue celestine. Celestine is a fragile crystalline gem. It is more of a collector's item and museum piece because it's too brittle for cutting and faceting. Ancient mystics believed it possessed healing powers. Blue celestine was worn or carried by priests and pilgrims to promote empathy for all earthly creatures. Although the stone is not plentiful, it has been found in Namibia, Madagascar, and Italy.

 Element

Gold, which promotes acceptance and enhances the power of any gem it touches.

 Herb

Milfoil (Achillea millefolium). This plant has many names, including nosebleed, soldier's woundwort; and yarrow. It is found throughout the world in fields and meadows. The plant's herb part was once made into a medicinal tea for appetite stimulation, stomach cramps, and liver problems. It was found to stop hemorrhaging in the lungs and helped save lives during bouts of pneumonia. It was also used to stop nosebleeds and, as a cold tea, to help cleanse sores, wounds, and chapped hands. Prolonged use of milfoil can make skin light sensitive.

♂   CAMRON: From the root name *Cameron*.

♀   CAMRON: From the root name *Cameron*.

♀   CARALEEN: From the root name *Charles*.

♀   CAREN: From the root name *Katherine*.

♀   CAREY: From the root name *Charles*.

♀   CARI: From the root name *Katherine*.

♂   CARL: From the root name *Charles*.

♀   CARLA: From the root name *Charles*.

♀   CARLENE: From the root name *Charles*.

♀   CARLIE: From the root name *Charles*.

♀   CARLIN: From the root name *Charles*.

♂   CARLOS: From the root name *Charles*.

♀   CARLOTTA: From the root name *Charles*.

♀   CARLY: From the root name *Charles*.

♀   CARMA: From the root name *Carmen*.

♀   CARMELIA: From the root name *Carmen*.

♀   CARMELITA: From the root name *Carmen*.

♀   CARMELLA: From the root name *Carmen*.

♥ ♂♀ **CARMEN** **Carma, Carmelia, Carmelita, Carmella, Carmencita, Carmina, Carmine, Carmita, Carmyna, Charmaine, Karmen, Karmina, Lita, Mina:** The name *Carmen* comes from two sources. The older source is the Hebrew word *carmel,* which means "vineyard," "fruitful orchard," or "garden." The more recent source is the Latin word *carmen,* meaning "song."

It is unknown whether *Carmel* was used as a given name among the early Jews, though historians agree that it seems unlikely. It is also unknown whether the Romans used the Latin-derived *Carmen* as a first name. For this reason, when names historians wish to trace the historical development of the name, many begin with Mount Carmel in Palestine. In the twelfth century, Saint Berthold founded a convent and a church on Mount Carmel because legend had it that the Virgin Mary visited the area with the baby Jesus. His order of nuns, the Carmelites, spread throughout the Christian world and took the name *Carmel* with them. Variations of the name became fairly widespread in Roman Catholic countries, particularly Spain and Italy. The Spanish variation of the name is *Carmen*.

In the mid-nineteenth century, *Carmen* became known worldwide owing, in part at least, to French writer Prosper Mérimée's novel about a Spanish gypsy, *Carmen* (1845). Composer Georges Bizet brought the name even greater international attention when, in 1875, he adapted Mérimée's novel into an opera. Carmen is among the most universally intriguing operatic heroines ever created, and *Carmen* remains one of the most frequently performed operas in the world. It is almost certainly the widespread popularity of the opera that prompted the use of the name among Protestant English speakers.

It is unknown whether Mérimée knew about *Carmen*'s original meaning; he probably chose the name because it was a fairly common Spanish name. The late nineteenth century, however, produced a Carmen who can be directly linked to the Latin interpretation of the name. Carmen Silva was Queen Elizabeth of Romania's pen name. It is said that she chose the name because of her two great loves: singing and the woods.

Though many fascinating American women have borne the name and it is fairly widespread, *Carmen* has still never become a ubiquitous name for American girls. With the rise in population among Latinos in America, *Carmen* and its many Spanish-influenced variations—*Carmencita, Carmina, Carmine, Carmella*—may be heard more often than in the past.

 Number

Nine, which represents purpose and will. The color red is tied to this number.

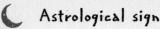 Astrological sign

Aquarius. Independence and originality are prominent characteristics of many born under this sign.

 Color

Carmine. Bright with energy, this vivid red shade signifies courage. In times past, red was linked to religious devotion.

◆ Stone

Garnet. This deep red gem's name comes from the Latin *granatus,* meaning "like seeds" because garnets "grow" in different types of rocks. Although the comparison to a seed may bring small size to mind, some garnets discovered have been as large as cantaloupes. One garnet from India was carved into a water jar. Garnets have inspired many legends, but all the legends agree that the stone had strong healing power. The most famous story was of Noah suspending garnets inside the ark to release the positive energy they absorbed from the sun before the rains came.

♛ Element

Brass. Considered to be a sun metal, brass has been used by both modern and ancient healers for its ability to stimulate curative energy.

🦎 Herb

Garden raspberry *(Rubus idaeus).* A cousin of the North American wild raspberry, this plant is cultivated mainly in Europe for its leaves and fruit. Garden raspberry makes pleasant-tasting tea and aids intestinal woes. Other uses included as a mouthwash and a rinse for skin wounds, sores, and rashes.

♀   CARMENCITA: From the root name *Carmen*.

♀   CARMINA: From the root name *Carmen*.

♀♂ CARMINE: From the root name *Carmen*.

♀   CARMITA: From the root name *Carmen*.

♀   CARMYNA: From the root name *Carmen*.

♀   CAROL: From the root name *Charles*.

♀   CAROLINE: From the root name *Charles*.

♂   CAROLUS: From the root name *Charles*.

♀   CAROLYNN: From the root name *Charles*.

♀   CARRIE: From the root name *Charles*.

♂   CARROLL: From the root name *Charles*.

♂   CARY: From the root name *Charles*.

♀   CASANDERA: From the root name *Cassandra*.

♀   CASS: From the root names *Cassandra* and *Katherine*.

♥ ♀ **CASSANDRA** **Casandera, Cass, Cassandry, Cassie, Kassandra, Sandera, Sandy, Saundra, Sohndra, Zandra:** There is some debate as to the original meaning of the name *Cassandra*. The ancient Greeks used it as a feminine version of *Alexander*. Taken in this sense, the name would translate as "defender of humanity." But some scholars say *Cassandra* isn't a Greek name at all, and they offer a derivation from the Sanskrit. In that ancient tongue, the root *kash* means "to shine," thus defining *Cassandra* as the feminine version of "radiant man."

    Cassandra has become associated with someone who predicts the future but whose warnings are ignored, usually with tragic consequences. History's most famous Cassandra was the daughter of Priam, king of Troy. According to legend, the god Apollo fell in love with Cassandra. She was not interested in his suit, so Apollo "upped the ante" by giving her the gift of prophecy in exchange for her promise to become his lover. When Cassandra reneged on her part of the bargain, Apollo let her keep the supernatural gift but added a curse to ensure that no one would ever believe her prophecies.

Consequently, when she warned her compatriots that the Trojan Horse would bring about their downfall, they refused to listen. In the ensuing battle, Cassandra became the captive of Agamemnon, leader of the opposing army. The playwright Aeschylus in the sixth century B.C. described Cassandra's dread at being led into Agamemnon's banquet hall, for she knew that his unfaithful wife was waiting there to murder Agamemnon and everyone else in his party.

Cassandra reached the height of its popularity in the thirteenth and fourteenth centuries when tales of the Trojan War were all the rage in the form of stories, poems, and ballads. For the next 200 years, though, the name was used only occasionally. A new translation of the medieval ballad "Cassandre" published in the seventeenth century revitalized the name tremendously. Jane Austen's sister, born at the end of the eighteenth century, was christened Cassandra; the name's use in her mother's family could be traced back nearly 100 years.

During the nineteenth century, many writers employed a stock female character called Cassandra to represent a stereotypical rural American. It has continued to enjoy popularity among African Americans, and it is now experiencing a comeback among the general population. Almost all girls named *Cassandra* go through life being called by the diminutive *Cassie*.

⦿ Number

Three. Three is sometimes tied to Pluto, god of the underworld. Threes can face many challenges in their lives, but they have the strength to overcome anything.

Astrological sign

Pisces. Since Pisces is a water sign, it represents the soul. Pisceans have strong intuitive gifts and are often clairvoyant. A Piscean's warning should never be ignored.

Color

Cobalt green. A blend of blue and green unites heaven and sea to bring spiritual peace.

Stone

Malachite. According to gemological lore, malachite was worn by mystics and priests to enhance visionary powers. This intense green opaque stone has lighter green eye-shaped formations or bands. Malachite's rich color comes from its high iron content. Malachite "eye stones" were used to ward off negativity and evil. Even today, malachite is revered for its uncanny ability to warn its owner of impending danger by breaking into two pieces. Ancient Egyptian healers used malachite powder for blood problems and the wealthy wore it as an eye shadow, not only for its brilliance but also for its ability to promote insight.

Element

Tin. Cassiterite is the principal ore component of tin. The name comes from the Greek word *kassiteros,* meaning "tin."

Herb

Senna *(Cassia acutifolia).* The leaflets and fruit of this shrub are always combined with other herbs to make it palatable and temper its potency. Senna was used in preparations for chronic intestinal trouble. It has grayish green leaflets and the fruit is an oblong pod. This variety of senna grows in northern Africa.

♀   CASSANDRY: From the root name *Cassandra*.

♀   CASSIE: From the root names *Cassandra* and *Katherine*.

♀   CAT: From the root name *Katherine*.

♀   CATALINA: From the root name *Katherine*.

♀   CATHARINE: From the root name *Katherine*.

♀   CATHERINE: From the root name *Katherine*.

♀   CATHLEEN: From the root name *Katherine*.

♀   CATHY: From the root name *Katherine*.

♀   CATY: From the root name *Katherine*.

♀   CECE: From the root name *Cecilia*.

♀   CECELY: From the root name *Cecilia*.

♀♂   CECIL: From the root name *Cecilia*.

♀   CECILE: From the root name *Cecilia*.

♥ ♀ CECILIA   Cece, Cecely, Cecil, Cecile, Cecilius, Cecily, Cele, Celio, Cilla, Cissie, Kikelia, Sacilia, Seelie, Sissela, Sissy: Most names historians trace *Cecilia* from the Latin word *caecus*, meaning "blind." The name was first a Roman clan name—*Caecilii* or *Caecilius*. Names historian Charlotte Yonge says that the clan name came from the word *coecilia*, meaning "a slowworm," which was a blind reptile. Alfred Kolatch, on the other hand, says the founder of the family *Caecilii* was blind. Whatever its origin, the surname *Caecilius* was common in Rome throughout the early Christian era.

Both the masculine and feminine first names developed from this clan name. It is interesting to note, however, that historians credit the development of the first names differently. Some historians insist that *Cecilia* is the feminine of *Cecil*, which grew out of the Latin *Cecilius*. Others state the opposite: that *Cecil* is the masculine derivation of *Cecilia*. It seems most likely that the masculine and feminine developed equally and independently from the clan name.

However, it is the feminine form that has had the longest and most widespread history. The earliest female historical character with the clan name was Tanaquil, whose real name was said to be Caia Caecilia. Charlotte Yonge writes that she was "the model Roman matron and patroness of all other married dames." Tanaquil may have helped to establish *Caecilia* as a first name for Roman girls.

The most famous early figure with the first name *Caecilia* was an aristocratic Roman Christian woman from the third century who purportedly vowed to remain a virgin, refused to consummate her marriage, and was martyred. According to the Benedictines, Saint Caecilia was killed by steam in her own bathroom for her devotion to God and her determination to remain pure. It is said that she sang hymns up until the point of her death, and for this reason she has become the patron saint of music and poetry. One of her symbols is the organ, and she is often (incorrectly) credited with having invented the instrument. She was a popular saint throughout the Middle Ages; both Philip I of France and William I of England named one of their daughters Cecile.

It was through William, his daughter, and the Norman Conquest that the name came to England. The English transformed the name into *Cicely,* which was soon widespread among both the aristocracy and common people. Its popularity lasted until the Reformation, when nonbiblical saints fell from grace in England. Even then, however, the name remained in use and it has never fallen completely out of favor.

After the Reformation, *Cicely* became associated with commoners and even, for a time, became the generic term for milkmaid, as in the oft-quoted phrase "When Tom came home from labour and Cis from milking rose." During this period, some aristocratic women with the name *Cicely* are said to have changed it to *Cecilia.*

The literature of the late eighteenth and early nineteenth centuries shows that among writers at least, both variations remained popular. *Cecilia* is the name of the title character in *Cecilia* (1782), by Fanny Burney, and is used in *Nicholas Nickleby* (1837–1838), by Charles Dickens. Sir Walter Scott employs the "common" *Cicely* in his novel *Kenilworth* (1821). The class consciousness associated with the names and their diminutives can best be summed up by a line from Charles Dickens's *Hard Times* (1854). When reporting that her name is Sissy, a child is given this response: "Sissy is not a name. Don't call yourself Sissy. Call yourself Cecilia."

As a nonbiblical saint's name, *Cecilia* and its variations were not common in the Puritan American colonies. The variation *Cecily* is found, however, among free black women in the eighteenth century. By the late nineteenth century both *Cecilia* and *Cicely* had become fairly well established in the United States. At the same time, both names were reaching a new level of popularity in England.

Surprisingly, after a period of widespread use of the names, their popularity began to decline. By the 1920s both names had become fairly rare, and they were not revived for the remainder of the century. When it is used, girls are often called by the diminutives Cece (pronounced *seesee*), *Sis,* or *Sissy* (as is actress Sissy Spacek).

Finally, many names historians connect the name *Cecilia* with the name *Celia* and its variation *Sheila*. Because *Cecilia* and *Celia* come from different roots, they are dealt with separately in this book. However, they are close enough that at some point in history the names were probably confused with each other or used interchangeably.

◎ Number

Six. In modern numerology, six represents marriage and musical harmony.

Astrological sign

Virgo. Ancient myths consider Virgo to be the daughter of Themis and Jupiter and call her the goddess of justice. Many Virgos have analytical minds.

 ## Color

Milk-rose. Shades of pink soothe the heart and soul like soft music and poetry.

 ## Stone

Crocidolite. A member of the "eye stone" group, crocidolite is one of the most powerful in its class. The Assyrians believed that eye stones gave the power of invisibility to their owners. Anyone lucky enough to own one was looked on with awe and perhaps fear. Crocidolite has a fine grain and is silky to the touch when cut and polished. Anyone who put this "eye" on could see clearly, both physically and mentally. Many healers also believed that these stones cured diseases of the eye.

 ## Element

Silver. Silver acts as a stabilizer, securing the power of this lustrous gemstone to increase self-esteem and good health.

 ## Herb

Smooth sweet cicely *(Osmorhiza longistylis)*. The root of smooth sweet cicely was used for congestion, indigestion, and weak appetites. Recognizable by its licorice-like scent, this plant grows in the woodlands of Canada, Alaska, and Colorado. It reaches heights of about three feet and has white flowers that bloom during May and June.

♂ CECILIUS: From the root name *Cecilia*.

♀ CECILY: From the root name *Cecilia*.

♀ CELE: From the root name *Cecilia*.

♀ CELENE: From the root name *Selina*.

♀ CELIA: From the root name *Sheila*.

♀ CELIE: From the root names *Selina* and *Sheila*.

♀ CELINE: From the root name *Selina*.

♂ CELIO: From the root name *Cecilia*.

♀ CELYNA: From the root name *Selina*.

♀ CESYA: From the root name *Alexander*.

♂ CHAD: From the root name *Charles*.

♀ CHARIN: From the root name *Sharon*.

♀ CHARLAYNE: From the root name *Charles*.

♀ CHARLENE: From the root name *Charles*.

♥ ♂ CHARLES Arlo, Caraleen, Carey, Carl, Carla, Carlene, Carlie, Carlin, Carlos, Carlotta, Carly, Carol, Caroline, Carolus, Carolynn, Carrie, Carroll, Cary, Chad, Charlayne, Charlene, Charlie, Charlotta, Charlotte, Charlton, Charmaine, Chas, Cheri, Cheryl, Chick, Chip, Chuck, Costa, Ina, Karel, Kari, Karl, Karoline, Karoly, Lena, Lina, Lola, Lolita, Roline, Sharel, Sharleen, Sharmain, Sheri, Sheryl: The name *Charles* and all of its many variations originated with *karl*, the Teutonic word for "man." The variation *Charles* is probably French and may have come from both the Teutonic *Karl* and the Latin variation *Carolus*. The most famous early Charles was, of course, the Frankish king Charlemagne, or Charles the Great (A.D. 742–814). In 800 he became the first emperor of the Holy Roman Empire. Though *Charles* was already a popular name, Charlemagne's power and fame spread use of the name throughout Europe. There have been kings named Charles (or some other variation of *Karl*) in most European countries, including Spain, Portugal, Sweden, Romania, Italy, and Hungary.

Normandy was not one of the places where *Charles* became a popular name. At the time of the Norman Conquest, in the eleventh century, France was composed of a group of warring kingdoms, and *Charles* was a name associated with Normandy's enemies. So although a few *Charles*es did sneak by and enter the English lists by the twelfth century, the name was not at all common.

Charles didn't begin its transformation into a quintessentially English name until the seventeenth century when Charles I ascended the throne of Britain, and it was not until his son Charles II became king that the name was ensured a long and dignified history. The prejudice against the name can be seen in Charles I's father, King James I of England. His birth name was actually *Charles,* and *James* was his middle name. As a diplomatic move, he called himself by his second name because *James* was considered to be more British and more Protestant than *Charles*. It is unknown why he named his second son Charles, but it is possible that he never expected this son to ascend to the throne.

Charles did not initially travel well to the New England colonies. After all, it was the Puritan Oliver Cromwell who beheaded Charles I. The name fared better in the southern colonies, at least officially. By the late seventeenth century when Charles II had recaptured the British crown and the Restoration had begun, one of the most important southern cities was named for him, Charles Town (later Charleston), and both North and South Carolina were named for the feminine derivative of *Charles*.

By the late eighteenth century, Puritan prejudices had decreased and *Charles* was one of the top 10 names in the country. It has remained at the top throughout the two centuries since.

It is easy to trace the progress of the most common feminine variations of *Charles*. *Caroline* became popular in England after George II married a German princess, Caroline Brandenburg-Ansbach. *Charlotte* (spelled *Charlet* at the time) could be found in England before the end of the seventeenth century, but not commonly. It was a second German princess, George III's wife, Charlotte Sophia of Mecklenburg-Strelitz, who sparked the widespread English use of that variation. Both *Charlotte* and *Caroline* have remained consistently popular in the United States as well as in England.

The variation *Carol* (or *Carole*) was originally a masculine name and is probably derived from the original *Karl* via the Dutch *Carolus* or *Karel*. It began its American ascent in the late nineteenth century. By the early twentieth century, *Carol(e)* was firmly established as a feminine name.

In the 1990s, many of the variations of the original *Karl* remained popular. *Charles* is still among the top 100 boys' names, as is the Spanish variation *Carlos*. The Germanic-based *Carl* has dropped out of favor in recent years, as have *Charlotte* and *Carol*. The feminine *Caroline* is back among the top 100 after losing popularity around mid-century.

The masculine variation *Carroll* is still found among older men in English-speaking countries, though it is rare in younger men and in boys. Among girls, *Charleen, Charlene,* and *Charlayne* are not obsolete, but they are more rare than they once were. *Carolyn* is still commonly found among women and girls. *Charlie* and *Chuck* are common diminutives for boys named *Charles*. *Carrie, Lena,* and *Lina* are nicknames for girls named *Caroline* and *Carol,* though all are used as independent names as well.

◉ Number

Three. In numerological circles, three represents Jupiter. Some threes are proud and dislike being under obligation to anyone.

☾ Astrological sign

Sagittarius. This sign is ruled by Jupiter, whose influence inspires the fulfillment of destiny.

✳ Color

Royal blue. A rich shade often connected with nobility, royal blue also indicates honorable intentions when seen in a person's aural emanation.

◆ Stone

Sapphire. There is much lore associated with the sapphire. The Greeks tied it to Apollo. They also believed it awoke the "third eye" and expanded psychic ability. Sapphires were considered guardians of love and fidelity by many cultures. Cornflower blue sapphires come from India, whereas dark blue varieties are found in Thailand or Australia. A beautiful metallic shade comes from Montana.

♔ Element

Gold. Considered a metal of destiny, gold is the perfect setting for a sapphire.

⚘ Herb

Carline thistle *(Carlina acaulis)*. A legend from the Middle Ages tells that an angel showed Charlemagne how to use this plant to stop an epidemic that was killing his soldiers. Another tale relates that anyone carrying this thistle could draw energy from other people and animals. Still another story says that eating the cooked thistle would bring the strength and virility of a young stallion. Today, Carline thistle's use is much less earthshaking, with its rootstock preparation being used mainly for removing minor scars.

♀♂ CHARLIE: From the root name *Charles*.

♀ CHARLOTTA: From the root name *Charles*.

♀ CHARLOTTE: From the root name *Charles*.

♂ CHARLTON: From the root name *Charles*.

♀♂ CHARMAINE: From the root names *Carmen* and *Charles*.

♂ CHAS: From the root name *Charles*.

♂ CHE: From the root name *Joseph*.

♀ CHELLIE: From the root name *Chelsea*.

♥ ♀ CHELSEA Chellie, Chelsey, Chessie: *Chelsea* is a uniquely English name. The Old English phrase *cealc hyth* refers to a site on a river that is used for the import of chalk or limestone, hence the meaning "chalk port" for *Chelsea*. It is a port in London and is also a place name in Australia and in other English-speaking countries. According to names historians William Gosling and Leslie Dunkling, the word was first used as a name for a child in Australia.

In the late 1960s, the internationally famous folk singer Joni Mitchell recorded a pleasant song she titled "Chelsea Morning," and there is every likelihood that the popularity of that song inspired parents to name their daughters Chelsea. It was once considered something of a counterculture name. But when one famous couple, Hillary and Bill Clinton, announced that they named their daughter Chelsea because of their fondness for the song, it probably dispelled the counterculture association for many people. In 1994, the year after Bill Clinton took office as president of the United States, *Chelsea* ranked forty-sixth among the most popular names given to baby girls.

There are several alternative spellings for *Chelsea,* mostly phonetic, such as *Chelsi* or *Chelsy.* Nicknames include *Chellie* and *Chessie.*

Number

Eight. Eights can be cool in manner, but they have warm souls and deep emotions.

Astrological sign

Pisces. Most Pisceans feel a strong pull toward water and find peace living by lakes, rivers, or oceans.

Color

Aurora australis. This blue-green luminous phenomenon occurs in Southern Hemisphere skies and is also called the southern lights or southern dawn.

Stone

Angel's-skin coral. Coral has had an exalted place in magical and religious rituals for centuries, especially in native tribes of the Pacific Islands. Ancient people left coral on grave sites to protect the deceased. In Mediterranean lore, coral was revered as a stone that held the essence of the Mother Goddess, who lived in a coral "tree" under the sea. Angel's-skin coral is a rare pinkish white variety found only in the Mediterranean.

Element

Silver. This metal is associated with the element of water, making it a perfect setting for angel's-skin coral.

✿ Herb

Sea sedge *(Carex arenaria)*. The roots of the sea sedge herb were once used to make remedies for various stomach and intestinal ills. Traditional healers also made soothing gargles for hoarseness and sore throats. For some with mild cases of tuberculosis, the silicic acid from the rootstock was found to be useful in stabilizing damaged lungs. Sea sedge has tiny green flowers.

♀ CHELSEY: From the root name *Chelsea.*

♀ CHERI: From the root name *Charles.*

♀ CHERYL: From the root name *Charles.*

♀ CHESSIE: From the root name *Chelsea.*

♀ CHIARA: From the root name *Clara.*

♂ CHICK: From the root name *Charles.*

♂ CHICO: From the root name *Francis.*

♂ CHIP: From the root name *Charles.*

♀♂ CHRIS: From the root name *Christopher.*

♀ CHRISSA: From the root name *Christopher.*

♀ CHRISSY: From the root name *Christopher.*

♀ CHRISTA: From the root name *Christopher.*

♀ CHRISTAL: From the root name *Crystal.*

♀ CHRISTAN: From the root name *Christopher.*

♂ CHRISTIAN: From the root name *Christopher.*

♀ CHRISTIANA: From the root name *Christopher.*

♀ CHRISTIE: From the root name *Christopher.*

♀ CHRISTINA: From the root name *Christopher.*

♀ CHRISTINE: From the root name *Christopher.*

♂ CHRISTOFFER: From the root name *Christopher.*

♂ CHRISTOFORO: From the root name *Christopher.*

♂ CHRISTOPHE: From the root name *Christopher.*

♂ CHRISTOPHER Chris, Chrissa, Chrissy, Christa, Christan, Christian, Christiana, Christie, Christina, Christine, Christoffer, Christoforo, Christophe, Christophoros, Christos, Christy, Kirsten, Kirsty, Kit, Kris, Krista, Kristen, Kristo, Kristofer, Kristos, Kristy, Krystle, Stina, Teena, Tina, Tino, Tiny: The Latin term *Christus* means "anointed one." The term *Christian*—and hence the name—comes from the Latin word *Christianus,* which means "follower of Christ." The feminine *Christina* is thought to have been the feminine diminutive of *Christus.*

The name *Christopher* has a slightly different origin. It is derived from the Greek and means, literally, "one who carries the anointed one." The interpretation of this is "one who carries Christ in his heart." Originally, the word was not a name, but a term Christians used when referring to themselves. It is believed that the literal meaning of the name *Christopher* caused the legend to develop that Saint Christopher carried the Christ child across a river. The actual Saint Christopher was a third-century martyr. Today, he remains one of Christianity's most popular saints; his fame has been responsible for the widespread use of the name throughout the world. He is the patron saint of travelers, particularly sailors.

Variants of *Christian, Christiana,* and *Christopher* traveled throughout the world as Christianity itself spread. In England, the name *Christen* entered the language around 1200. *Christian* began to be used after 1600. However, these two male variations were never as common as the feminine *Christiana.* Slowly, the variation *Christina* took over from *Christiana.* Some historians believe that the name came from France or Germany, found its early British foothold in Scotland, and was only slowly adopted in England. Other historians believe that *Christina* came to Britain directly from Italy and was immediately popular everywhere. *Christina* was also a royal name in both Sweden and Spain. The variations

Kristen and *Kirsten* are both generally considered Scandinavian, though *Kirsten* was also used in Scotland.

Christopher was adopted by the English in the fifteenth century and became widespread by the seventeenth century. The name traveled to America with the first colonists and remained popular with Puritans and non-Puritans alike. Interestingly, although *Christopher* seems to be a perpetually ubiquitous name, it did suffer a decline in the nineteenth century and did not return to popularity until the mid-twentieth century. Christopher Robin of A. A. Milne's famous Pooh stories is probably the figure most responsible for the name's return to favor.

Surprisingly, *Christian* was not an overly popular name with the Puritans and probably came to America with German and Dutch colonists. *Christina*—and its close variation *Christine*—have both consistently been common American girls' names. *Kristen* and *Kirsten* are much later additions to the American lists. Though they probably entered the United States with Scandinavian (and in the case of *Kirsten*, Scottish) immigrants, the names did not enter the broader population until the 1950s. In the 1990s, many of the variations of "follower of Christ" have held on to their long-standing popularity. *Christopher, Christian, Christina,* and *Kristen* all are among the most popular names given to boys or girls.

The common diminutive for boys named *Christopher* and *Christian* is, of course, *Chris.* Girls named *Christina, Christine, Kirsten,* or *Kristin* usually go by *Chris, Chrissy, Kris, Christy, Kristy,* or *Kirsty* at some point during their lives. *Tina* is also a common nickname for girls named *Christina.*

◎ Number

Four. According to numerologists, fours often champion social reform and do their best to ensure justice for those who cannot defend themselves. Because of their beliefs and the willingness to stand behind them, fours can make powerful enemies.

🌙 Astrological sign
Capricorn. For people of this earth sign, life is rarely carefree. However, Capricorns are strong-willed and reliable.

☀ Color
Yew. The deep green hue of yew leaves heals troubled souls. Yew trees symbolize immortality in many cultures.

◆ Stone
Imperial jasper. Jasper is a member of the chalcedony family. Its history is ancient and varied. Many believed it possessed powers of the gods, including the ability to protect against physical and mental harm. Imperial jasper is a combination of red, green, and brown, making it especially potent through the combined power of three colors. Red adds protection, green boosts health, and brown centers psychic balance. Imperial jasper was also an identity gemstone for one of the 12 tribes of Israel. Mystics believed that if one dreamed of the gemstone jasper, it signified the return of love or loved ones.

👑 Element
Electrum, a mixture of metals—usually gold, silver, and platinum—used to make a metaphysically charged alloy.

🌿 Herb
Saint Christopher's herb *(Osmunda regalis).* Also called herb Christopher, this perennial plant is of the fern family. It grows mostly in moist meadows. A rootstock preparation was used to soothe coughs. The herb was also considered helpful in making ointments for wounds.

♂ CHRISTOPHOROS: From the root name *Christopher*.

♂ CHRISTOS: From the root name *Christopher*.

♀♂ CHRISTY: From the root name *Christopher*.

♀ CHRYSTEL: From the root name *Crystal*.

♂ CHUCK: From the root name *Charles*.

♀ CILLA: From the root name *Cecilia*.

♀ CINDA: From the root name *Cynthia*.

♀ CINDY: From the root name *Cynthia*.

♀ CINNY: From the root name *Cynthia*.

♀ CINTIA: From the root name *Cynthia*.

♀ CISSIE: From the root name *Cecilia*.

♂ CLAAS: From the root name *Nicholas*.

♀ CLAIR: From the root name *Clara*.

♀ CLAIRE: From the root name *Clara*.

♥ ♀ CLARA Chiara, Clair, Claire, Clarabel, Clare, Clarence, Clarice, Clarissa, Clarisse, Klaire, Klarance, Klaretta, Klaryce, Sinclair: *Clara* is the feminine form of the Latin word *clarus*, meaning "bright" or "clear." The earliest figure recorded in history with the name was Saint Clarus (A.D. 280), the first bishop of Nantes in Brittany. The French were later responsible for transforming the name into *Clair*. A seventh-century Norman saint inspired the naming of two towns in that region of France.

The Normans brought the name to England after the invasion of 1066, usually as the surname *de Clair*, meaning "of the town of Clair." The English and Irish sometimes changed the spelling of the name, leading to the naming of County Clare in Ireland (from a land grant given by Edward I to a Norman from Saint Clair) as well as of the town of Clare in Suffolk, England. The town seems to have given rise to the noble title the Duke of Clarence, which eventually gave rise to the given name. The surname *Sinclair* is a more direct transformation of *Saint Clair*.

The earliest known feminine reference to the name is in Spanish ballads that tell of a daughter of Charlemagne named Clara. But certainly the most famous Clare in Christendom is the disciple of Saint Francis, Saint Clare of Assisi (1194–1253). Saint Clare founded the order of nuns called the Order of the Poor Ladies or Poor Clares, according to the rule of the followers of Francis. With Saint Clare's popularity, the already existing variations of the name became firmly identified as feminine names.

Two variations of *Clare*—*Clarisse* and *Clarice*—were first used in France and Italy, though a *Clarice* is recorded in England as early as 1199. *Clarice* became much more widespread throughout Europe after it appeared in Torquato Tasso's sixteenth-century romance as the name for the wife of Rinaldo and sister of Huon of Bordeaux. Clarissa is the title character's name in *Clarissa Harlowe* (1747–1748) by Samuel Richardson, who seems to have created the variation ending in *a*. Perhaps owing to the popularity of Richardson's book, *Clarissa* was also a popular name for free African American women in the 1700s. Clara Barton's parents were obviously fond of the name. The famous founder of the American Red Cross was born Clarissa Harlowe Barton. Other writers adopted the variation as well. A character in *David Copperfield* (1849–1850) is named Clarissa (another character is named Clara), as is the central character in Virginia Woolf's *Mrs. Dalloway*.

In both Great Britain and the United States during the Romantic period and throughout the nineteenth century, *Clara* virtually replaced the English variation *Clare*. By the 1920s, however, *Clara*—along with *Clarisse, Clarice,* and *Clarissa*—was on the wane, and the French *Claire* was becoming the more common variation. By the 1950s, it had became the accepted American variation. *Claire*'s rise in popularity may have been influenced by the actresses Clare Booth Luce (1903–1987) and Claire Bloom (1931–). The name became less popular during the 1970s and has never fully recovered its former stature.

◉ Number
Three. This number has great significance in numerology and is symbolic of the never-ending circle. Threes usually accomplish what they set out to do.

☾ Astrological sign
Aquarius. The planet Uranus rules Aquarius and its influence instills a deep love of humankind for those born under this sign.

✳ Color
French blue, a bright, clear blue that elicits visions of health and pure water.

◆ Stone
Blue lace agate. There are numerous varieties of agates and they all belong to the chalcedony family. Mystics of the past wore or carried blue lace agates for peace and healthy minds. Some ancient healers believed that the blue lace agate helped balance the body's fluids and prevented dehydration during illness.

♛ Element
Copper. Well known today as an electrical conductor, copper was used by shamans to stimulate healing. When copper was combined with a blue lace agate, positive and negative energies were balanced to restore health.

🌿 Herb

Comfrey *(Symphytum officinale).* Commonly found in the moist meadows of Europe and North America, comfrey is called the heal-all herb. Rootstock preparations made a healthy gargle, and taken internally, it helped digestive ailments. Powdered rootstock was mixed with other herbs for wound poultices, bruises, sores and insect bites. Hot rootstock pulp made excellent chest plasters for bronchitis and pleurisy. It also eased pain from injured tendons. And if all that weren't enough, women added rootstock to their bathwater as a skin softener.

♀ CLARABEL: From the root name *Clara.*

♀ CLARE: From the root name *Clara.*

♂ CLARENCE: From the root name *Clara.*

♀ CLARICE: From the root name *Clara.*

♀ CLARISSA: From the root name *Clara.*

♀ CLARISSE: From the root name *Clara.*

♥ ♂ **CLARK** Clarke, Clerc, Clerk: It is not difficult to realize that *Clark* is an occupational name deriving from the British word *clerk,* meaning someone who worked as a recordskeeper. But the origin of the name is ancient, and the story is more interesting than it first appears.

According to the Old Testament, each of the 12 tribes of Israel received an allotment of land to call its own—each, that is, except for the Levites. The Levites instead received the hereditary duty of working as assistants in the temple. Consequently, it was said of the Levites that "their only inheritance was the Lord." The ancient Greeks called the Levites *klerikos,* meaning "inheritors."

Being a temple attendant was a noble profession. Because the *klerikos* were required to interpret Scripture, they were a literate minority in the ancient world. They served as scribes, lawyers, teachers, and judges. Aging fathers passed the job along to their young sons.

During the medieval period in Britian, religious workers were still among the few who could read and write. Scribes serving in monasteries and churches were called *clereks,* a corruption of the earlier *klerikos.* This connection between literacy and religious service is the reason that matters pertaining to the church are called clerical—as are things pertaining to writing and recordkeeping.

Like other occupational names during the Middle Ages (such as *Taylor* and *Hunter*), *Clerk* became a surname and was applied to succeeding generations along with the occupation itself. The appellation probably became *Clark* as the written word grew more prevalent. (In Great Britain, of course, the word *clerk* is pronounced "clark.")

Names experts believe *Clark* flourished as a surname and eventually as a first name largely because it is easy to spell and to say. Public adoration of the American actor Clark Gable boosted its use in the first half of the twentieth century. The advent of the Superman comic series, which had Superman disguised as the bumbling reporter Clark Kent, no doubt inspired parents to name their boys Clark in the 1940s and 1950s. By 1990, though, the United States Census Bureau ranked Clark as only the four hundred and sixth most common of all male names.

☉ Number

Nine. Some numerologists tie nine to strength of purpose and tradition.

☾ Astrological sign

Virgo. Virgo's ruling planet of Mercury adds a dimension of mental quickness to those born under this sign.

Color

Ciba. In many cultures, the color blue represents trust.

 ## Stone

Sugalite. This stone ranges in color from deep blue to almost sky-colored. Sugalite is usually opaque but some exquisite 12–sided crystals have been discovered in the volcanic lava from Mount Vesuvius in Italy. Once carved for ornamental purposes and amulets, sugalite is now used for beaded jewelry. A cabochon cut (half-moon shape) is favored to bring out its color. In ancient times, it was revered as a stone to clear out such negative emotions as envy, hate, and even cowardice. Early Egyptians believed sugalite brought inner peace by creating a bond between spirit and body.

Element

Copper, which complements the serene vibrations of sugalite.

Herb

Inkberry *(Phytolacca americana).* The roots, leaves, and fruit of this native North American plant, which is also known as pokeweed, were used to aid intestinal problems. A dried root poultice was also thought to help reduce inflammation from arthritis or rheumatism. The purple berries produce a crimson juice that was used to treat skin cancers and as ink or dyes. The fresh plant, roots, and berries are toxic and must be cooked or thoroughly dried before use.

♂   CLARKE: From the root name *Clark*.

♂   CLAUDE: From the root name *Claudia*.

♀   CLAUDETTA: From the root name *Claude*.

♀   CLAUDETTE: From the root name *Claudia*.

♥ ♀ CLAUDIA Claude, Claudetta, Claudette, Claudine, Claudius, Claudy, Klaudio: *Claudia* derives from the ancient Roman tribe called *claudus*. Most scholars translate *claudus* as *lame*, surmising a distinguishing characteristic of an original tribal elder. But names expert Charlotte Yonge alone links *claudus* to an earlier sound-alike root meaning "I am known for," or "of renown." Given the features of Roman history, it seems more likely the powerful tribe identified themselves as "famous" rather than "lame."

Variants of the venerable clan name were common throughout the Roman Empire. They took root in Britain as well when Emperor Claudius conquered the territory in A.D. 51. The invasion also led to history's first known Christian named Claudia. After their defeat, the British king and his family were brought to Rome as captives. But instead of killing them, Claudius set them free. Impressed by the monarch's kindness, one of the princesses adopted the name *Claudia* and converted to Christianity. Saint Paul immortalized her in his second letter to Timothy (2 Timothy 4:21).

Claudia flourished in early Christian households because of the story of the British convert-princess—probably because the old Roman name could be honored along with the new religion. *Claude* and *Claudius* escalated in popularity at this time as well. Besides various Roman politicians named *Claudius,* there were several Saint Claudias and a French Archbishop Claude, all of whom helped propagate use of the names.

Around the time of the Middle Ages, the French started using *Claude* for girls as well as boys. It became especially fashionable when Louis XII gave his daughter the name. Likewise, though *Claude, Claudius,* and *Claudia* had long been common in Britain, they all received a boost in the 1500s. It happened when a prominent family with ties to France baptized their son Claude. In the ensuing years, Shakespeare and other writers made frequent use of *Claude* and its variants. The popularity of *Claude* and *Claudius* sustained *Claudia* in Great Britain and France through the centuries.

In the United States, hit films starring actress Claudette Colbert (1905–1996) spurred use of her name after 1930, and thereafter *Claudette* and *Claudine* became favored over *Claudia*.

 Number

Six. People of this number are more determined than any others to carry out their plans. Although sometimes unyielding, they are always kind and fair.

 Astrological sign

Virgo. Those born under this sign face adversity with a level gaze and calm demeanor. They have a high degree of family devotion. Claudette Colbert was a Virgo.

 Color

Steel gray. Gray is a mixture of black and white and symbolizes fairness as well as self-control.

 Stone

Harlequin opal. Harlequin opals are gray or bluish black in color, owing to their formation in volcanic rocks or silicate hot springs. The legends about this gemstone center around power and material wealth. Ancient dream interpreters believed that visions of opals meant that the dreamer would soon have good fortune.

 Element

Gold, the metal of monarchs and divine appointees.

🦎 **Herb**

Roman plant *(Myrrhis odorata)*. The aromatic Roman plant is native to Europe. The leaves can be eaten as salad greens, and the roots and seeds are edible once boiled. A tonic made from the roots of the Roman plant was once used to quell coughs and as a digestive aid.

♀ CLAUDINE: From the root name *Claude*.

♂ CLAUDIUS: From the root name *Claudia*.

♀♂ CLAUDY: From the root name *Claudia*.

♂ CLERC: From the root name *Clark*.

♂ CLERK: From the root name *Clark*.

♂ CLIFF: From the root name *Clifford*.

♥ ♂ **CLIFFORD Cliff, Clive, Clyfford:** Like so many names, *Clifford* was originally a place name, which then became a surname, and then finally a given name. Its meaning is just what it would seem—"a ford near a cliff" (or vice versa, if you prefer.) In England, *Clifford* is the name of several small villages as well as a name that has had aristocratic connections for generations. Shakespeare's English history plays are full of aristocratic Cliffords. However, the name did not surface as a common English first name until early in the twentieth century.

Clifford's American debut occurred somewhat sooner, at the end of the nineteenth century. A character named Clifford in Nathaniel Hawthorne's classic novel *The House of the Seven Gables* (1851) may take some credit for spreading the name's popularity. Among the most famous twentieth-century Cliffords are actor-playwright Clifford Odets (1906–1963), who helped found the famous Group Theatre, and the first African American secretary of the army (appointed by President Jimmy Carter), Clifford Alexander. In the second half of the twentieth century—probably as part of a larger trend and not influenced unduly by Secretary Alexander—*Clifford* has been particularly popular in the African American community.

Boys and men named *Clifford* almost inevitably are nicknamed *Cliff*. But *Cliff* has frequently been given to boys as an independent name. (It can also be a diminutive of *Clive* or *Clifton*.) *Cliff* has actually had more widespread success than *Clifford*, at least in terms of famous bearers. Among the most well-known *Cliffs* are rock musician Cliff Richard (1940– ; originally Harry Webb), the actor Cliff Robertson, and the character from the television show *Cheers*, Cliff Clavin.

 ## Number

One. According to numerologists, ones like to be in control and usually accomplish what they set out to do.

Astrological sign

Virgo. Those born under this sign are known for their superb reasoning powers. Actor Cliff Robertson is a Virgo.

Color

Dover white. White stands for kether, or the crown of the mystical sefirot tree of the Cabala. The famed cliffs of Dover on Great Britain's coast are white.

Stone

Rosolite. As a member of the garnet family, rosolite has an ancient history tied to healing. Early physicians believed that garnets stopped bleeding and could promote vitality in the healthy. Rosolite is usually light red and can occur in hues from pale pink to dark rose.

♛ Element

Mercury. A metal linked to Virgo, mercury is tied to two elements—water and earth. Its molten silver appearance and unusual properties made it attractive to ancient magicians as an ore of power.

🐉 Herb

Hydrangea *(Hydrangea arborescens)*. Also called seven barks, this native North American shrub is usually found on dry slopes, wooded areas, or near stream banks. Stems are covered with thin layers of multicolored bark. Hydrangea roots are still used by some herbalists to prevent kidney stones.

♂   CLIVE: From the root name *Clifford*.

♂   CLOVIS: From the root name *Louis*.

♂   CLYFFORD: From the root name *Clifford*.

♂   COB: From the root name *Jacob/James*.

♂   COBY: From the root name *Jacob/James*.

♂   COLAS: From the root name *Nicholas*.

♂   COLE: From the root name *Nicholas*.

♂   COLEMAN: From the root name *Nicholas*.

♀   COLETTE: From the root name *Nicholas*.

♂   COLIN: From the root name *Nicholas*.

♥ ♀ **COLLEEN**   **Collie, Colline, Kolleen:** The name *Colleen* is from the Irish term *cailin,* which means "girl." It is also frequently and, most names historians say, incorrectly, thought to be the feminine of the name *Colin. Colin* itself is thought to come from two different possible sources. It can be considered a one-time diminutive of *Nicholas* that later became a popular independent name. It can also be seen as an Anglicization of the Scottish-Irish Gaelic name *Cailean*, which means "youth," "whelp," or "puppy." The similarities between *cailin* and *Cailean* are quite intriguing, and it is strange that names historians do not seem to link the two.

Colleen is a fairly new creation and has become popular only since the 1940s. Ironically, the name has never been embraced in Ireland. *Colleen* peaked in the United States in the early 1960s. At that time, when "traditional" names and names reflecting one's ethnic heritage were becoming extremely fashionable, *Colleen* became particularly popular among families of Irish descent. Among the most famous bearers of the name are Australian novelist Colleen McCullough, who wrote *The Thorn Birds* (1977), and the brilliant actress Colleen Dewhurst (1926–1991), whose last appearance was as Avery Brown on the television show *Murphy Brown*.

⊚ Number

Three. Some numerologists consider three to be the number of creativity and inspiration.

☾ Astrological sign

Gemini. Many Geminis are found in the entertainment field. They are playful people and sparkling conversationalists. Colleen Dewhurst was a Gemini.

☀ Color

Daffodil. Bright yellow cheers the spirit and heightens the intellect.

◆ Stone

Sinhalite. In the early 1950s, gemologists discovered this new mineral, named for the island of Sri Lanka. Sinhalite ranges in hue from pale yellow to dark greenish brown. When it is cut and polished, it displays different shades depending on the angle from which it is viewed.

🌾 Element

Aluminum, a mineral found in sinhalite. Since it has been mass-produced for only just over a century, it seems the perfect complement for this relatively unique, new gem.

🐉 Herb

Youthwort *(Drosera rotundifolia).* Traditional herbal lore considers youthwort to be helpful for respiratory problems, especially asthma, whooping cough, and bronchitis. Although the herb is mainly used in healing, the plant also has an antibiotic substance that in undiluted form neutralizes strep and staph infections as well as pneumonia bacteria.

♀ COLLIE: From the root name *Colleen.*

♀ COLLINE: From the root name *Colleen.*

♀♂ CON: From the root names *Connor, Conrad,* and *Constance.*

♀♂ CONNIE: From the root names *Conrad* and *Constance.*

♥ ♂ **CONNOR** Con, Conor: The original meaning of the name *Connor,* or *Conor,* is a matter of debate among names scholars. It is probably a modern Irish form of the very old and powerful Celtic name *Conchobair*, which means either "strong help," or "high desire." Another possibility, if one traces the origin of *Connor* back to the name *Connaire*, is that it means "hound of slaughter." Alone, *Conn* means "wisdom" in the ancient Celtic tongue, and names that include the root *conn* usually have something to do with wisdom, strength, or courage.

Whatever its origins, the name has noble connotations, since Irish history boasts a long line of kings who bear the name *Connor*, and later, *O'Connor*. Among the earliest is King Conchobar mac Nessa, the subject of many legendary tales, and uncle to Cucullain, the great ancient Irish hero. Conchobar is said to have lived in the first century B.C., and stories about him were transmitted orally until the eleventh century when they were collected into a volume called *The Ulster Cycle*. By the twelfth century, the O'Connors were great kings of the Connaught region of Ireland. The most famous of these Connaught kings were Turloch O'Connor and his son, Rory. Turloch gained enough power to rule over all of Ireland, and Rory is said to have been the last Irish king before the Anglo-Norman invasion. Even though they later lost the larger kingdom, O'Connors continued, for a time, to reign in Connaught.

The surname *O'Connor* came to America with Irish immigrants, but it has been only since the 1970s that *Connor* gained popularity here as a first name. In 1990, it hadn't yet appeared among the top 40 in lists of fashionable names, but by the end of the 1990s, it was among the nation's most popular boys' names.

◉ Number

Seven. Independence and military prowess are often associated with seven in numerology. Many sevens have a keen desire to travel and explore.

☾ Astrological sign

Leo. This fire sign goes well with the name *Connor* and its noble history. Leos are known for their passion and generosity.

☀ Color

Erse green. The color of Irish moss helps cool the heels of a Leo who needs rest after a long journey. It is also a color in Ireland's flag.

◆ Stone

Red moss agate. Thought to be stones of strong energy, agates were commonly used in ancient healing amulets dating back to Babylon. The red moss agate in particular was used to promote the healing of battle wounds. The stone was also believed to help warriors triumph over their enemies.

♔ Element

Brass. Ancient physicians used brass bracelets to speed the healing of bones.

♨ Herb

Hound's-tongue *(Cynoglossum officinale)*. Also called gypsy flower, hound's-tongue is a type of weed found in rocky soil and along roadsides throughout Europe and North America. Among early herbalists, the roots and herb were used to treat burns, bruises, and wounds, although in some people it caused allergic reactions.

♂   CONOR: From the root name *Connor*.

♥ ♂ **CONRAD**   Con, Connie, Conrade, Conrado, Cort, **Curt, Konrad, Kurt:** The names *Conrad* and *Kurt* both come from the same Teutonic words: *kuon,* meaning "bold" or "able," and *rad,* meaning "speech" or "council." The most famous Conrad was King Conradin (1252–1268), who was also known as "little Conrad." The king of Sicily and Jerusalem, he was overthrown and executed by Charles of Anjou. After his death, *Conradin's* popularity spread, particularly in Germany, where variations of his name became common, and one of them, *Kunz,* was often used for cats.

Conrad can be found in England by the mid-eighteenth century as a character name used by writers and poets. *Conrad*s appear in *The Castle of Otranto* (1764) by Horace Walpole and in Lord Byron's poem *The Corsair* (1814), among other works of English literature. However, the name didn't come into use among the general populace until the mid-nineteenth century. No one really knows what sparked the name's adoption by English-speaking parents at that time.

In the 1930s and 1940s, *Conrad* had a minor American surge in use. *Conrad's* diminutive, *Kurt,* has had more success among Americans, though it also could never be considered a common American name.

Diminutives for *Conrad* include *Con, Conn, Conni, Connie,* and *Cort.* It is known in France as *Conrade* and in Italy, Spain, and Portugal as *Conrado.*

Number
One. People of this number are born with the ability to make things happen. Determination is a key trait of most ones.

Astrological sign
Pisces. The myth of Pisces says that when Venus and Cupid were frightened by the giant Typhon, they threw themselves into the Euphrates River and became fishes. Minerva marked the event of their transformation by placing the fishes constellation in heaven.

✳ Color
Bice green. The color of cat's eyes brings harmony to a discordant soul.

◆ Stone
Green zircon. Zirconium and uranium are the main minerals that comprise a zircon. This gemstone reflects light brilliantly, both absorbing and emitting powerful energy. Green zircons were used by ancient magicians to attract wealth. Zircons were believed to have magical qualities. Their healing reputation comes from centuries past when they were used to restore physical and emotional balance. Some mystics believed that zircons increased vocal projection. Priests and statesmen wore them for this purpose.

♛ Element
Platinum. Platinum enhances the power of the mighty zircon.

♘ Herb
Catnip *(Nepeta cataria)*. Commonly named catmint or catswort, catnip is a member of the mint family. The leaves of the plant were used to brew tea for upset stomachs, colic and heartburn. European herbal lore also suggests use for chronic bronchitis.

♂   CONRADE: From the root name *Conrad*.

♂   CONRADO: From the root name *Conrad*.

♥ ♀ CONSTANCE   Con, Connie, Constancia, Constant, Constanta, Constantine, Constanz, Constanza, Costa,

Konstance, Konstantija, Konstantin, Konstantina, Konstanz, Kosta, Tina: The name *Constance* comes from the Latin word *constans,* which means "firm," "loyal" or "constant." The most famous bearer of the masculine variation is the Emperor Constantine who, in the third century, gave Christians Roman citizenship. Because he was so popular, his name spread throughout Christian Europe, particularly in Russia, where it became *Konstantin* or *Kostja.* Its popularity in Britain may have been connected to the widespread use of the word *con* (meaning "hound" or "wisdom") as the beginning of many names.

The earliest record of a feminine variation, *Constancia,* was used often among Christians during the late Roman period, and different variations remained popular throughout continental Europe. The name came to England via the Provençal region of France, where it was a royal name. William the Conqueror named one of his daughters Constance. John of Gaunt's wife was a Spanish woman named Constanza, and she probably also helped to popularize use of the name in England.

The English variation was initially *Custance,* which Chaucer used in his "Man of Law's Tale" of *The Canterbury Tales.* Later, the English altered the spelling to *Constance.* Shakespeare used the name for King John's mother in his play *King John* (c.1596) and Oliver Goldsmith used the name for one of the characters in his play *She Stoops to Conquer* (1773). Beyond writers and playwrights, the name was widespread among the general populace.

Though its use fell off after the English Reformation, the name came back into style by the seventeenth century. There are two opposite theories for the name's resurgence at that time. Some names historians feel that *Constance* returned because it held an aristocratic sensibility for many people. Others point to the name's popularity among Puritans and report that *Constance* was considered a "moral name." Both of these theories are probably true, and the Puritan influence cannot be denied, particularly with the name's development in the early American colonies. By the mid-eighteenth century, with the fading popularity of Puritanism, *Constance* was heard less often. For no known reason, there was a slight resurgence between 1900 and 1925. After this period, though, the name never regained widespread use.

Connie is a diminutive of *Constance,* though it has also been given as an independent name.

⊚ Number
Four. This is a number of sensibility and stability. Fours can be counted on through thick and thin.

☾ Astrological sign
Leo. Constant and loyal, people born under Leo make good allies and mates. Their sunny outlook will brighten the world for others, too.

✳ Color
Sunset. Any shade of orange projects warmth and stimulates positive energy.

◆ Stone
Cherry-orange amber. One of nature's precious biological gems, amber is tied metaphysically to the sun. It is probably the oldest mineral used for jewelry. Amber adornments have been found in northern European burial sites dating back

8,000 years. Since amber is a fossil, its lore is connected to longevity. Ancient mystics also believed amber was part of akasha (fifth element), which united the other four elements of earth, air, fire and water.

 Element

Gold, a sun ore that is tied to Leo.

Herb

Alder dogwood *(Rhamnus frangula)*. Usually referred to as buckthorn, this shrub grows in swamps and damp areas throughout North America and Europe. It was a helpful remedy for liver and gallbladder problems. Powdered or dried bark was mixed with other herbs for intestinal troubles. Buckthorn tea was thought to relieve colic. However, fresh bark and unripe fruit cause symptoms of poisoning and must always be heated to be safe. Medical supervision is required.

♀   CONSTANCIA: From the root name *Constance.*

♂   CONSTANT: From the root name *Constance.*

♀   CONSTANTA: From the root name *Constance.*

♂   CONSTANTINE: From the root name *Constance.*

♀   CONSTANZ: From the root name *Constance.*

♀   CONSTANZA: From the root name *Constance.*

♥ ♀♂ **COREY**   Corri, Cory, Curry, Korry: *Corey* has only recently begun to be used as a first name. Each names historian seems to have his or her own interpretation of *Corey*'s original meaning. These interpretations range from a Latin derivation from the word *helmet* to an Anglo-Saxon derivation from the phrase "the chosen one." Most historians, however, do seem to think that the name derives from a Celtic root. Yet even when this parentage can be agreed upon, the actual interpretation of the name's original Celtic meaning varies from "ravine" to "hollow" to "a hollow (or misty) pool."

Corey was almost certainly a place name first, and if one continues to trace its development from a Scottish or Irish place name to a surname, then its meaning becomes "a person who lives by a pool (or a ravine, or a hollow)."

Widespread use of the name in the United States seems to have begun in the 1960s in the African American community and it has since become popular among other American culture groups.

Number

Three. Threes like to be in touch with their physical environment. They respect nature in all its glory.

Astrological sign

Scorpio. People of this sign harbor strong beliefs and pursue life with zest. Although their passion can make waves for those around them, Scorpios aren't afraid to follow the truth. Picasso was a Scorpio.

Color

Water mist. This pale blue shade refreshes like a kiss of mist from a mountain pool.

Stone

Hauyne. Ancient volcanoes of Germany and Morocco are the best sources for this beautiful blue or lilac gemstone. It is related to lapis lazuli and is sometimes found in the same deposit. Like lapis, this stone was worn to bring protection from curses or negative forces of black magic. It's considered a durable stone and doesn't show normal wear. Today, this gem is rarely found, perhaps because of the overmining of its sister gem, lapis.

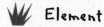 **Element**

Copper. Water rules copper. This metal has long been linked to divine attention.

Herb

Coriander *(Coriandrum sativum)*. This annual plant has been cultivated for thousands of years. It grows in Europe, the Mediterranean area, and North and South America. Coriander seeds were once used for stomach distress and as an appetite stimulant. Some early herbalists used it in poultices for rheumatism and other types of joint pain. Coriander also improves the flavor of other remedies. Modern cooks use it as a spice.

♀   CORRI: From the root name *Corey.*

♂   CORT: From the root name *Conrad.*

♀   CORTNEE: From the root name *Courtney.*

♀   CORY: From the root name *Corey.*

♀   COSETTE: From the root name *Nicholas.*

♂   COSTA: From the root names *Charles* and *Constance.*

♀♂   COURTENAY: From the root name *Courtney.*

♀   COURTLAND: From the root name *Courtney.*

♀   COURTNEE: From the root name *Courtney.*

♥ ♀♂ **COURTNEY** Cortnee, Courtenay, Courtland, Courtnee, Curt, Kourtney: *Courtney* is a relatively new first name that traveled the much-worn path from place name to surname to given name. The name is generally taken to be from the French and is said to mean "one who lives at court" or "one who frequents the court." In modern French, *Courtney* is very close to *court,* meaning "short," and *nez,* meaning "nose," but it is doubtful that this was the original derivation of the name.

The name's English use seems to have come from a town in France, spelled *Courtenay.* When an aristocratic family of that town migrated to England (probably with William the Conqueror), the place name traveled with them. From there it developed into an aristocratic English surname. It is unknown when the name began to be adopted as a masculine first name in England, but the spelling remained *Courtenay* until the middle to late nineteenth century, when the more modern spelling, *Courtney,* came into use. At approximately the same time, the name came into use in the United States, where it found particular popularity in the African American community.

In the early 1960s, there was a significant decrease in the use of more traditional "American" names, such as Bob and Mary, and a variety of ethnic names became increasingly popular. At the same time, it became popular to use surnames as first names, particularly for girls. It was during this period that *Courtney* began to be considered a feminine name, though it is still used occasionally for a boy. By 1987, it was more popular than either *Lisa* or *Mary.* It seems to be losing ground now, though not rapidly.

☺ Number

Four. Whether in the presence of royalty or commoners, fours have no trouble being themselves. They are unimpressed by material wealth and prefer necessities over luxury.

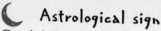

Astrological sign

Gemini. People of this sign are like a breath of fresh air. They enjoy freedom in their relationships and careers. Geminis are usually sparkling conversationalists.

Color

Amethyst. A favorite color of royalty, purple represents dignity and spiritual grace.

Stone

Sillimanite. Discovered by Yale University Professor Benjamin Silliman, this crystalline-like stone occurs naturally in long slender prisms. Violet and blue stones are mined in Myanmar (formerly known as Burma), whereas greenish gray stones come from Sri Lanka. Another variety called fibrolite is found in Idaho and sometimes Italy, Germany, India, and Brazil. When cut and polished, sillimanite has a reflective sparkle that would enhance the jewelry of any courtier.

Element

Brass. Any gem set in brass will support one's physical energy. Brass has a high iron content and brings out the rich color of the gemstone it holds.

Herb

Queen's delight *(Stillingia sylvatica)*. This plant is found in sandy soils and scrub pine forests. Queen's delight (also called stillingia) grows wild in the southern United States and can be cultivated around the world. A rootstock preparation was used by early herbalists for serious and stubborn skin problems. Because of this plant's potency, only small amounts should be used—only under supervision of an herb specialist.

♥ ♂ **CRAIG:** The name *Craig* comes from the Gaelic language group and can be traced to similar words in both the Scottish and Welsh subgroups—*creag* and *craig,* which both mean "rock" or "crag." In Scotland and Wales today, there are many places named Craig, including Ailsa Craig, a rocky islet in the Firth of Clyde, Scotland, and Craig-y-Llyn Peak in the county of Mid Glamorgan, Wales.

Following the traditional pattern of place names becoming surnames, *Craig* came to mean a person who "is from a rocky place" or "lives near the crag." The name seems to have become a first name in the mid-nineteenth century, though there is disagreement among historians as to whether the trend started in Great Britain or in the United States.

Number

Two. When a two has a hunch, it is usually the right hunch. Twos who listen to their inner voices will make it to the top of whatever pinnacle they are striving for.

Astrological sign

Capricorn. Although some Capricorns may come across as cantankerous and stubborn, they are simply trying to take the safest route through life. Advice from a Capricorn should be heeded.

Color

Breen. This earthy mixture of brown and green soothes even the crankiest souls.

Stone

Epidote. Dark green or brown epidote is found in the Austrian and French Alps. Although rarely cut into jewelry because of its fragile nature, epidote is a lovely crystal-like gemstone. However, this delicate stone can be polished by the tumbler method (silicate sands and water) and displayed for its beauty. Yellow epidote can be found on the island of Elba (off the Italian coast), Mozambique, and Mexico.

♛ Element

Iron, one of the components of epidote. Iron has a magical reputation for defensive power that dates back to the earliest civilizations.

☙ Herb

Goat's rue *(Galega officinalis)*. Goat's rue grows wild in southern Europe and western Asia. Its spreading root system anchors it in rocky or shalelike soils. Traditional herbal lore suggests that goat's rue was useful in reducing fevers and cleansing bites from poisonous animals. Because the fresh plant can be harmful if not properly used, goat's rue is not used by modern herbalists.

♀   CRISTAL: From the root name *Crystal.*

♀   CRYSTA: From the root name *Crystal.*

♥ ♀ **CRYSTAL Christal, Chrystel, Cristal, Crysta, Kristle, Krystal:** The 1980 *Oxford American Dictionary* defines the noun *crystal* as "a clear transparent colorless mineral" or "a very clear glass of high quality." At various times and in various cultures, crystals have been valued as sources of healing and spiritual powers. In recent years in the United States and elsewhere, so-called New Age philosophers and healers have tapped their spiritual powers again, making crystals popular gemstones once more. The word itself comes from the Greek noun *krystallos,* which means "ice."

Oddly enough, the earliest use of the name *Crystal* comes from a completely different source. In the Middle Ages, Crystal was a man's name. Either derived from or used as a diminutive of *Christopher*, *Crystal* (and its variant spelling *Chrystal*) could be found in Scotland and northern England. By the time of the Reformation, however, the name had completely dropped from use.

Historians disagree as to when *Crystal* began to reappear. Some have found references to the name at the beginning of the nineteenth century. Others say that the name did not come back into popular use until the end of the nineteenth century. However, there is no dispute over the fact that when *Crystal* did reappear, it was as a feminine name whose lineage could be traced directly to the gemstone. By the end of the nineteenth century, the use of the names for gemstones as girls' names had become something of a fad. It was during this period that *Ruby, Amber,* and *Beryl,* in addition to *Crystal,* all came into general use.

In the United States, *Crystal* has become increasingly popular since the 1950s, particularly in the African American community. In the 1980s, the name gained popularity with characters in movies and on television and began to show up even more frequently on birth records. By the late 1980s, *Crystal* was among the top 20 girls' names in the United States. By the early 1990s, its popularity had dropped off somewhat, but it has since returned to the top 100.

◎ Number

Eight. Many numerologists credit people of this number with subconscious sensitivity to others' emotions. Eights' innate ability to read the feelings of those around them aids them in both business and personal relationships.

☾ Astrological sign

Taurus. Lucky are those who know the love of a Taurus. Although they can be heel-dragging stubborn, they are wonderful companions and protectors.

Color

Blue ice. This color represents clarity of mind and depth of spirit.

Stone

Benitoite. The blue crystals of benitoite were discovered in 1906 by a prospector who mistook them for sapphires. Benitoite crystals are shaped like flattened pyramids and have brilliant reflective power similar to that of a diamond. The stone can appear colorless when viewed from different angles. The only known source of this gem is San Benito County, California, for which it was named.

Element

Lead, which is ruled by the element of earth.

Herb

Iceland moss *(Cetraria islandica)*. Iceland moss is actually a type of lichen found in cool, damp areas of Europe, Iceland, North America, and Asia. Tea brewed from Iceland moss can be used for respiratory troubles, anemia, and certain gastric ailments, such as acid stomach and heartburn. Native healers used the tea for coughs, hoarseness, and bronchitis and as a remedy for tuberculosis. The plant makes nourishing food but must be boiled for a lengthy period to make it palatable.

♂   CURCIO: From the root name *Curtis*.

♂   CURRY: From the root name *Corey*.

♂   CURT: From the root names *Conrad, Courtney,* and *Curtis*.

♥ ♂ **CURTIS** **Curcio, Curt, Kurt, Kurtis:** *Curtis* was probably originally a surname that later came into use as a first name. Interestingly, though, there is one theory that it was a nickname first, and then became a surname. Some historians derive the name quite literally and believe that it comes from the Middle English word *curthose* meaning "short hose," but most relate the name to the French word for "courteous"— *courtois*. Both the English and French words for "courteous" derive from the word *court*. Therefore, *Curtis* could mean anything from "courteous" to "court-bred" to "fit for court life" to "someone who lived in or near the royal court."

Like many English names with a French basis, *Curtis* probably traveled to England after the Norman Conquest, but no one knows for certain when the name arrived as a surname in England. The start of its use as a first name is generally fixed at the early nineteenth century, both in England and the United States. Its true popularity in the United States didn't begin until the 1950s. Since then, the name has remained in frequent use, particularly in the African American community. According to the 1990 census, *Curtis* was the one hundred twelfth most popular name among living American males. The short form *Curt* is a common nickname for boys named *Curtis*. *Kurt,* however, is usually associated with the name *Conrad*.

◉ Number

Nine. Some numerologists believe that nines are destined to have difficult childhoods but that through experience nines develop iron wills and ultimately learn how to overcome adversity.

☾ Astrological sign

Gemini. Astrologers often link creatures to zodiacal signs. Butterflies and exotic birds are tied to Gemini—quite appropriate for a sign whose element is air. Singer Curtis Mayfield (1942–) is a Gemini.

Color
Auramine. This butter-yellow shade nourishes the soul with cheerful light.

◆ Stone
Tektite. Normally black or brown, this variety of natural glass stone is usually translucent. In its natural state, tektite is rough and has a spiky or pocked surface due to its volcanic or meteoric origin. Tektite is not of a crystalline structure like obsidian but has bubbles or honeycomb-like swirls. Tektite found in Thailand is carved for decorative items, medallions, and amulets. Many once believed wearing tektite protected them from evil.

👑 Element
Quicksilver, also called mercury, a mysterious substance that is sometimes defined as a liquid ore. It is tied to Gemini's ruling planet, Mercury.

🌿 Herb
Chervil *(Anthriscus cerefolium)*. This annual plant has been cultivated worldwide for centuries. Its main use continues to be as a kitchen spice; however, juice from the flowering herb was believed to help eczema, abscesses, and other less serious skin problems. Some early European healers used the flower juice to help lower blood pressure.

♀ CYBELE: From the root name *Sibyl*.
♀ CYBIL: From the root name *Sibyl*.

♀   CYN: From the root name *Cynthia*.

♀   CYNDA: From the root name *Cynthia*.

♥ ♀ CYNTHIA Cinda, Cindy, Cinny, Cintia, Cyn, Cynda, Kynthia, Sindy, Synda, Synthia: *Cynthia* (or *kynthia*) is a Greek word meaning "of Cynthus" and was a title given to the Greek goddess Artemis because she was born on the island of Cynthus. Among the earliest references to the name is one by the Roman poet Sextus Propertius, who in the first century B.C. dedicated his love poems to a woman he called Cynthia, though *Hostia* was her real name.

Although very popular among poets and novelists, *Cynthia* was a name rarely given to children. It sometimes appeared in the late Middle Ages in England, but many historians believe that this is because scribes, in attempting to spell the Spanish name *Sanchia,* would mistakenly spell it *Cynthia.* In the sixteenth century, however, both Ben Johnson and Edmund Spencer used the name when referring to Queen Elizabeth I. In those instances, there is no doubt that they were linking the queen with the famed virgin moon goddess.

By the mid-nineteenth century, the name was still popular among writers and poets but not among parents. Elizabeth Gaskell included a Cynthia among the pivotal people in her novel *Wives and Daughters* (1866). In the same book, she also explained the name's situation very clearly when she had another character comment that *Cynthia* is ". . . an out-of-the-way-name, only fit for poetry, not for daily use."

In the United States, on the other hand, *Cynthia* appeared earlier and more often as a given name. It was fairly common among enslaved African women. Names historians Leslie Dunkling and William Gosling report that plantation wives gave the name as part of a general trend toward using classical names for slaves.

Toward the end of the nineteenth century, in both England and the United States, the name came to be used more widely among the white population. Again, there is no known reason for this sudden upsurge. Perhaps Gaskell's novel had an effect and perhaps there was a growing affection for classical figures and Romantic poetry, but no one really knows for sure.

By 1950, *Cynthia* was among the top 20 most frequently used girls' names in the United States. By 1974, the name was in the top five. The name lost popularity in the 1980s but returned to the top 50 in the 1990s. The diminutive *Cindy* (which is also used as a diminutive for *Lucinda*) came into use as an independent name around 1956 and became relatively common for a short period after the song "Cindy Lou" became popular.

Number

Eight. Those whose number is eight are strong individuals with compassion for the unloved. Shades of dark gray, blue, or black are associated with the number eight.

Astrological sign

Virgo. Many Virgos have superb reasoning powers. They are often fond of the arts and love to read.

Color

Moon mist. This iridescent glow of moonrise on water relaxes the body and refreshes the spirit.

Stone

Exotic gray pearl. Pearls are one of the four precious organic gems. Their biological origins are part of the reason for the mystical lore surrounding them. They were considered a gift of love from the sea and treasured for their ability to stimulate romance. Although many pearls used for modern jewelry are cultured to be perfect spheres, natural pearls are prized for their irregular shape and variety of color and size. Gray pearls are rare and valued for this reason. They have been harvested mainly in the Persian Gulf and the Red Sea.

Element

Quicksilver, or mercury, represents the planet Mercury, which rules Virgo.

Herb

Wormwood *(Artemisia absinthium).* The leaves and flowering tops of this silky plant were used for medicinal purposes by ancient herbal healers. Wormwood, also known as absinthe, was a popular remedy for stomach problems, including indigestion, cramps, and heartburn. Midwives used wormwood tea for pain relief during childbirth. Caution is advised for any use of pure wormwood oil, which causes poisoning.

♂   DAEMON: From the root name *Damian*.

♂   DAFYDD: From the root name *David*.

♂   DAI: From the root name *David*.

♀   DAILE: From the root name *Dale*.

♀   DAISEE: From the root name *Daisy*.

♥ ♀ **DAISY** **Daisee, Dasie:** *Daisy* can be traced both to the flower and to a pet form of the name *Margaret*. The name came into use in England around 1860. At that time, the French version of *Margaret—Marguerite—*started to become more widespread. (*Marguerite* means *daisy* in French.) At the same time that parents began naming their daughters *Marguerite*, flower names in general were becoming a British fad, and *Daisy*, along with *Rose, Iris, Holly, Fleur,* and *Flora,* became popular.

In the mid-1800s, the common noun *daisy* came to be used as an adjective with the slang connotation of "good" or "fine," as in "She's a daisy girl." This usage probably influenced the increasing popularity of the name. As a noun, *daisy* comes from the Anglo-Saxon root *daeges eage,* which means "day's eye," reflecting both the look of the flower itself and the fact that it opens in the sun.

The most famous early Daisies were literary and musical figures. Henry James helped the name's viability with his book *Daisy Miller* (1879), and of course there is the famous

1892 song "Bicycle Built for Two" (or "Daisy Bell") with the line "Daisy, Daisy, give me your answer, do." As with most names derived from flowers, by 1930 the name had begun to fall out of fashion.

However, *Daisy* is back among the most popular girls' names in the United States. No one really can point to a specific character or person who may have sparked the resurgence of the name, but it may reflect a general tendency for parents to choose names that sound old-fashioned, including many of the flower names that were popular in the nineteenth century.

Number
Four. This number is sometimes attributed to those of a rebellious nature. Four is ruled by Aquarius.

Astrological sign
Aquarius. People of this sign are anything but conventional. Although most have peaceful natures, they are true free spirits and must have room to maneuver in their careers and personal relationships to be happy.

Color
Apricot. This airy shade of orange dispels negative energy.

Stone
Carnelian. One of the most popular agates, carnelian has a rich and varied gemological history. In the Middle Ages, alchemists used carnelian as a boiling stone to stimulate the metaphysical energy of other agates. They believed its power could enhance the properties of a weaker stone or one that had been "drained" either through negative use or evil attack. Carnelian is a translucent stone with color ranges of red-orange to dark brown, with each color symbolizing a

different power. Orange carnelian was often used to improve appetite in convalescents.

♆ Element
Uranium, the ore tied to Aquarius.

♋ Herb
Oxeye daisy *(Chrysanthemum leucanthemum)*. This flower is a common sight in fields and meadows. An old European legend connected it to the thunder god, whereas other ancients dedicated it to Artemis, goddess of women. The herb and flowers were collected and dried for use in tonics and teas. Daisy herbs were also used for whooping cough and asthma medication as well as in lotions for wounds and bruises.

♀ DALANNA: From the root name *Madeleine.*

♀♂ DALE Daile, Dalen, Daley, Dallan, Dallana, Dayle: The name *Dale* comes from either Old English or Old Norse and means "a hollow" or a "small valley." The name was first used as a surname to identify someone living in or near a dale. It came into use as a first name only in the nineteenth century, and the most famous early bearer of the name was Dale Carnegie (1888–1955). The author of the wildly famous book *How to Win Friends and Influence People,* Carnegie was probably the figure most responsible for *Dale*'s entry into general use in the United States in the 1930s.

The second most famous figure to bear the name is Dale Evans (1912–) who was born Frances Octavia Smith. As the wife and partner of Roy Rogers, Dale Evans was one of the most beloved figures in the United States in the 1950s. In the 1960s, *Dale* as a girl's name experienced a slight rise in popularity, perhaps because of Dale Evans's influence. The name became even more popular—this time for boys—in the 1980s, though by the 1990s its use had declined.

Though it is considered both a feminine and a masculine name, *Dale* is used far more frequently as a man's name. As of the 1990 census, it was the one hundred ninth most common name among living American men. It was only six hundred ninety-sixth among American women.

⊚ Number

Four. Among the many traits of a four, honesty ranks high. Fours often find attraction to matters that involve the public, either through social justice or oration.

☾ Astrological sign

Cancer. Although people born under the sign of Cancer may have a reputation for crusty temperaments like their symbolic crab, inside they are gentle and loving.

✳ Color

Ultramarine. This blue shade represented several ancient gods of India, linking their origin to the ocean.

◆ Stone

Blue druzy quartz. All types of quartz are known for their innate energy to stimulate communication, whether it be for modern technology or the metaphysical practices of past civilizations. Druzy comes in several colors and is composed of small bubbles of quartz that resemble sea foam. The energy produced within this beautiful gem depends on the mineral associated with each color. Blue druzy was once used to calm the mind and influence peace and clear thinking.

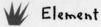

Element

Silver, which is well known as a "moon" metal and acts as a stabilizing influence for any gem it holds.

Herb

Hedge mustard *(Sisymbrium officinale)*. Commonly referred to as English watercress, this plant is found in fields and valleys throughout Europe and North America. The plant is still used by herbalists, especially those in Europe, for colds, coughs, sore throats, hoarseness, bronchitis, and chest congestion.

♂   DALEN: From the root name *Dale*.

♂   DALEY: From the root name *Dale*.

♂   DALLAN: From the root name *Dale*.

♀   DALLANA: From the root name *Dale*.

♀   DAMIA: From the root name *Damian*.

♥ ♂ **DAMIAN**   Daemon, Damia, Damiano, Damien, Damienne, Damion, Damon, Damya, Damyon: The name *Damian* comes from the Greek name *Damianos*, which means "to tame" or "to subdue." This meaning was later interpreted as "tamer of men" or "divinely powerful." There have been four saints in Christian history named Damian. The most famous lived in the third century. Damian and his twin brother were thrown into the sea because they were Christians, and an angel is said to have saved them. Then they were stoned and burned, but these attempts also did not succeed in killing them. They finally died when they were beheaded. Saint Damian later became a patron saint of physicians.

Throughout the Middle Ages, *Damian* was used almost solely as an ecclesiastical name. After the Reformation it largely dropped from use and came to be considered exclusively a "Catholic name." Even among Catholics, however, the name was not widely used.

There is no known reason why *Damian* finally began to be adopted by a broader population in the twentieth century, but its use still could not be called widespread. The name's greatest growth happened in the 1970s, but since then it has again dropped off.

The name *Damon* is closely linked to *Damian*. Many historians believe that the former is a variant of the latter. Other historians believe that *Damon* was a surname that came to be used as a first name. What no one disagrees about is that the earliest reference to the name is in the Greek story of Damon and Pythias. Because of the myth, *Damon* has become linked to the idea of perfect friendship, which is exhibited in the story.

Like *Damian, Damon* did not come into general use until fairly recently. By the late nineteenth century, it was becoming slightly more common, and this might be due in part to a character who bears the name in Thomas Hardy's classic novel *Return of the Native* (1878). *Damon* is a more common name in the United States, generally, than is *Damian*. According to the 1990 census, *Damon* is the three hundred fifty-seventh most common name among living American men. Interestingly, the French variation, *Damien*, is the next to be found on the list—at five hundred seventy-eighth. The English spelling *Damian* is so unusual that it is not even among the top 1,000.

🌀 Number

Six. Most sixes have a strong social conscience. Many pursue scholarly work and make excellent spiritual or intellectual mentors.

☾ Astrological sign

Scorpio. The sign of the scorpion is ruled by water and the planets of Pluto and Mars. Piety and the ability to forge strong wills are common traits of Scorpios.

✳ Color

Cardinal. For millennia, red was used to symbolize divinity. It was associated with numerous deities, including the god of war, Mars.

◆ Stone

Black opal. Precious black opals are the rarest types of opal. Opals are a "water-formed" stone and can crack when not immersed periodically in water. They were considered a mysterious gem because each one appears different from another, even when similar in color. However, the more rainbow fire the gem emits, the more it is valued. The ancients believed that as a health aid, opals increased the body's ability to digest and use proteins.

♔ Element

Platinum. This element is at the top of the metallurgic pyramid and is considered to be the strongest energy enhancer of all ores.

♘ Herb

Damiana *(Turnera aphrodisiaca).* Also called Mexican damiana by some herbalists, this plant is a small shrub found in dry places, such as Texas, Baja, California, and parts of northern Mexico. The leaves are used by some healers to make tonics to help boost positive energy in those who feel depressed. It is also reputed to have aphrodisiac properties.

♂ DAMIANO: From the root name *Damian*.

♂ DAMIEN: From the root name *Damian*.

♀ DAMIENNE: From the root name *Damian*.

♂ DAMION: From the root name *Damian*.

♂ DAMON: From the root name *Damian*.

♀ DAMYA: From the root name *Damian*.

♂ DAMYON: From the root name *Damian*.

♂ DAN: From the root name *Daniel*.

♥ ♀♂ **DANA** **Danay, Dane, Danet, Danica, Danie, Dayna:** The name *Dana* has a variety of different possible origins. Some people consider it to be a diminutive of *Daniel* or *Daniella*. Others believe that it derives from a surname of unknown origin. Perhaps the most interesting theories describe *Dana*'s Scandinavian history. One is the "invasion theory," which posits that *Dana* is an Americanization of the name *Dane*. *Dane* became a surname in Britain during the ninth through eleventh centuries when the Viking (Danish) raiders invaded areas throughout the British Isles. The second Scandinavian theory is that despite the fact that *Dana* was used first for boys, the name relates directly to the name of the mother of the gods in Danish mythology, *Dana*. Names historians Leslie Dunkling and William Gosling suggest that *Dana* was unknown in England and that it is a purely American variation of either the first name *Daniel* or the surname *Dane*.

Whatever its origins, *Dana* did not come into general English-speaking usage until the nineteenth century and was not a common name until at least the 1940s, when the film actor Dana Andrews (born Carver Daniel Andrews) became famous. Not long after mid-century, *Dana* was virtually taken over by girls. By the 1980s, *Dana* could be found at least as frequently in the African American community as among white Americans. A particularly popular variation in the African American community, *Danica,* is from a Scandinavian root and means "morning star." As of the 1990 census, *Dana* was the one hundred seventy-ninth most common female name among living American women. It was the three hundred fourteenth most common American male name. Today, it is considered primarily a girl's name and it is rare to find a young boy with the name. However, it is not unusual to meet a man named *Dana.*

Number

Two. Twos have genial natures and love to be around people. Although they may not be the life of the party, they usually have many friends.

☾ Astrological sign

Aries. Anyone under this fire sign has the potential for greatness. However, success comes from hard work and a courageous spirit.

✳ Color

Scarlet madder. This divine shade of deep red is linked to the mother of the gods. Madder is a southwestern Asian plant used by ancient tribes for making red dyes.

◆ Stone

Red jadeite. Although most associate the color of green with jadeite, it's found in several colors. Red jadeite, one of the rarer hues, comes from Japan and California. Its color is due to traces of iron or aluminum. Jadeite is used for jewelry, but it's also a favored stone for decorative items. For generations, Far Eastern artisans have used jadeite to make thin-walled vases, cups, and even chains with individual links made from a single gem.

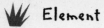 **Element**

Gold, long considered a noble metal, goes well with red jadeite.

Herb

Star grass *(Aletris farinosa).* Also called starwort and star root, this grass is native to eastern North America. Its thick rootstock is used in preparations for colic and a variety of stomach troubles. Native Americans used the leaves to make a tea for relief from digestive ailments.

♂ DANAL: From the root name *Daniel.*

♀ DANAY: From the root name *Dana.*

♂ DANDIE: From the root name *Andrew.*

♀♂ DANE: From the root names *Dana* and *Daniel.*

♀ DANEAL: From the root name *Daniel.*

♀ DANELLA: From the root name *Daniel.*

♀ DANET: From the root name *Dana.*

♀ DANETTA: From the root name *Daniel.*

♀ DANETTE: From the root name *Daniel.*

♀ DANI: From the root name *Daniel.*

♀ DANICA: From the root names *Dana* and *Daniel.*

♀ DANICE: From the root name *Daniel.*

♂ DANIE: From the root name *Dana.*

♥ ♂ **DANIEL** **Dan, Danal, Dane, Daneal, Danella, Danetta, Danette, Dani, Danica, Danice, Danielle, Danika, Danill, Danise, Danit, Danita, Danitza, Danna, Dannon, Danny, Dannyce, Danya, Danyal, Danyele:** *Daniel* is an ancient Hebrew name and comes from the words *dan,* meaning "judge" and *el*, meaning "God." Hence, it is translated "God is my judge." (However, some names historians have interpreted the name as meaning "the judging God.") *Dan*, now considered a diminutive of *Daniel*, can be found as an independent name in the Bible as the son of Jacob and Bilha, Rachel's servant. This Dan is an ancestor to a founder of one of the 12 tribes of Israel.

The first known figure with the name *Daniel* is the prophet of the Old Testament book of Daniel. He was held captive by the Babylonian king Nebuchadnezzar and became a favorite of the king because of his ability to interpret dreams. After he refused to deny his religion, Daniel was thrown into a lion's den. He was saved from certain death by God's protection and emerged from the lion's den unharmed.

Daniel has been known in England since the early Middle Ages. However, prior to the Norman Conquest the name was a purely ecclesiastical one, reserved for monks and bishops. The Normans brought with them the secular use of the name, and by the twelfth century *Daniel* had become fairly common. By the fourteenth century, it was in widespread use. The popularity of the name may be linked to its similarities to the old Welsh name *Deiniol* and the old Irish name *Donnal* (or *Domhnall*), which is also Anglicized to *Donald*. *Daniel* became less popular in England in the fifteenth and sixteenth centuries, but the English Reformation and Puritanism brought the name back in the seventeenth century.

As with many popular names among English Puritans, *Daniel* traveled early to the New World. It was among New England's most popular names throughout the eighteenth century. Two of the most famous figures in American history are statesman Daniel Webster and woodsman Daniel Boone. *Daniel* started to lose its hold on parents in both the United States and England by the mid-nineteenth century, thanks, perhaps, to the decline of the Puritan ethic and the rise of Romanticism. It is also possible that, like many Old Testament names, Daniel came to be considered primarily a Jewish name during the same period. (In 1876, George Eliot had published the novel *Daniel Deronda,* which had a Jewish title character.) Although it is true that *Daniel* is a perennial favorite name with Jewish parents, it has also remained consistently popular among Catholics and Protestants.

Whatever the reason, the name did not return to widespread use until the twentieth century. By 1955, it was again one of the favorite names of Americans. This surge in popularity coincided with a revival of Daniel Boone lore in popular music, movies, television, and books of the period.

Danielle is the French feminine of *Daniel.* It did not appear commonly in English-speaking countries until the 1940s. Since then, it has become steadily more popular. *Daniel* and *Danielle* are now both among the top 100 baby names in the United States. The diminutive *Danny* is used for both boys and girls.

◉ Number
Nine. Most numerologists agree that nine represents virtue and courage.

☾ Astrological sign
Leo. The sign of the fearless lion seems particularly appropriate for the name *Daniel.*

☀ Color
Justic. This shade of golden yellow enhances mental powers.

◆ Stone
Danburite. Although generally colorless, danburite crystals are also found in white, yellow, or pale pink. They form in

an unusual structure of wedge-shaped prisms resembling topaz. Because danburite does not cut well, most stones find their way into gemologists' collections. However, if handled carefully, danburite can be faceted into beautiful gem-quality stones for jewelry. This stone was first discovered in the nineteenth century in Danbury, Connecticut. Other localities with gem-quality deposits include Myanmar (the former Burma; yellow danburite), Mexico, Switzerland, Italy, and Japan.

 Element

Gold. In metallurgic lore, gold was used to harness solar energy for rites of worship and healing. Legends tell of the Druids collecting mistletoe with golden sickles and of herbalists of the Middle Ages using golden harvesting implements to increase the power of the plants they gathered.

 Herb

Lion's-foot *(Prenanthes alba)*. The entire lion's foot plant has healing potential. Herbalists from the past used a root preparation for dysentery. They also had their patients drink the plant's milky juice to neutralize poisonous snakebites. A leaf poultice was made to apply directly on other snake and insect bites. Lion's-foot grows in wooded areas of the United States and Canada.

♀   DANIELLE: From the root name *Daniel*.

♀   DANIKA: From the root name *Daniel*.

♀   DANILL: From the root name *Daniel*.

♀   DANISE: From the root name *Daniel*.

♂   DANIT: From the root name *Daniel*.

♀   DANITA: From the root name *Daniel*.

♀   DANITZA: From the root name *Daniel*.

♀   DANNA: From the root name *Daniel*.

♀   DANNE: From the root name *Diana*.

♂   DANNON: From the root name *Daniel*.

♀♂   DANNY: From the root name *Daniel*.

♀   DANNYCE: From the root name *Daniel*.

♀   DANYA: From the root name *Daniel*.

♂   DANYAL: From the root name *Daniel*.

♀   DANYELE: From the root name *Daniel*.

♂   DARAN: From the root name *Darren*.

♀   DAREL: From the root name *Darryl*.

♂   DAREN: From the root name *Darren*.

♂   DARIN: From the root name *Darren*.

♂   DARIO: From the root name *Darren*.

♂   DARON: From the root name *Darren*.

♂   DARREL: From the root name *Darryl*.

♂   DARRELL: From the root name *Darryl*.

♥ ♂ **DARREN** **Daran, Daren, Darin, Dario, Daron, Darrin, Darrion, Darron, Daryn, Derron, Deryn:** The name *Darren* has a variety of valid definitions—all of them interesting—that span the globe. Some names historians have related the name to the Greek and say it might mean "wealth." The variant spelling *Daren* is a Nigerian word (of the Hausa language) meaning "born at night." Historically, however, most forms of *Darren* in the English-speaking world are probably related to the surname, which derives from an Irish-Gaelic root and means "small, great one."

Like many surnames that later became first names, *Darren* didn't come into common use until quite recently. Its popularity peaked in the 1960s, perhaps during the run of the successful television series *Bewitched* (1964–1972) and its succession of *Darren*s. It is also possible that the popularity of pop singers James Darrin and Bobby Darin gave the name a further boost as did the use, at the same time, of such similar-sounding names as *Sharon* and *Karen*. Since the 1960s the use of the name has plummeted. As of the 1990 census, Darren was the two hundred forty-third most common name for American men.

Number

Six. People of this number have a wealth of magnetism and can attract a multitude to their cause.

☾ Astrological sign

Taurus. Taureans are bullish in mind and heart. They are strong in love and practical in matters of life.

✳ Color

Midnight. A deep shade of blue shows noble spirit in a person's aura.

◆ Stone

Blue moonstone. Many legends are attached to this pearly feldspar. The ancients considered it a hopeful gem, and because of its uplifting reputation, moonstones were popular in amulets. Other lore ties the gift of extrasensory perception with moonstones, claiming they clear the mind and allow the bearer to make wise decisions. All stories agree that moonstones enhance sensitivity and are especially powerful at night during certain phases of the moon.

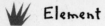 **Element**

Gold, the best ore for conducting any form of energy. It's also durable and doesn't tarnish. Most ancient talismans of power were made from gold.

Herb

Evening primrose *(Oenothera biennis)*. European herbal lore refers to this plant as king's cure-all or night willow-herb. It grows in European dry meadows and east of the Rocky Mountains in North America. The plant was once used to make cough soothers and sometimes as a tonic for mental depression. Some healers made ointments to relieve the itch of rashes or other irritations. The whole plant is edible.

♂ DARRICK: From the root name *Derek*.

♂ DARRIN: From the root name *Darren*.

♂ DARRION: From the root name *Darren*.

♂ DARROL: From the root name *Darryl*.

♂ DARRON: From the root name *Darren*.

♥ ♀♂ **DARRYL** **Darel, Darrel, Darrell, Darrol, Darrylene, Daryl, Darylin, Derril, Deryll:** *Darryl* probably comes from the Old French and means "little, sweet, or loved." However, it may also be the English corruption of a Norman place name, *D'Airel*. It is most likely that it traveled to England after the Norman Conquest in 1066 as *Darrel* and was used as a place name. The first recorded use of *Darrel* as a given name was in 1866 in England.

The modern variation, *Darryl*, which enjoyed widespread use in the mid-twentieth century in the United States, can be linked fairly directly to the famous film producer

Darryl Zanuck. For more than 20 years, millions of parents saw the name appear on movie screens in darkened theaters across America. *Darryl*'s popularity has dropped off in recent years. According to the 1990 census, *Darrell* was the one hundred sixty-fifth most common male name among American men. The more modern spelling—*Darryl*—was two hundred thirty-second and the variation *Daryl* was two hundred eighty-first.

 ## Number

Six. Modern numerologists sometimes link the number six to marriage or commitment.

 ## Astrological sign

Virgo. Often shy when promoting themselves, Virgoans are, however, fiercely devoted to their families and have no problem expounding on a loved one's attributes.

 ## Color

Beloved, an endearing shade of pink that has the power to unite lovers.

 ## Stone

Tugtupite. This unusual deep pink-and-white stone was first discovered in Tugtup, Greenland. The name means "reindeer stone." Tugtupite ranges from dark red to bright pink with some shades of orange. When the stone is left in the dark, the pink pales to white, but as soon as the stone is exposed to light, the color returns. Tugtupite is used for jewelry or carvings and is found in massive opaque veins. Tugtupite was recently discovered in the northern parts of the former Soviet Union.

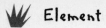 **Element**

Aluminum, a mineral found in tugtupite.

Herb

Wild strawberry *(Fragaria vesca)*. This perennial plant grows in forests, fields, and shady areas throughout Europe, northern Asia, and eastern North America. The entire plant has medicinal properties, including as a tonic and fluid reducer. Strawberry tea was once used for a variety of kidney problems. Externally, the cold tea was thought to be effective against eczema and acne. Fresh strawberry juice was used to help reduce fevers and the leaf tea was used to help children recuperate from illness.

♀ DARRYLENE: From the root name *Darryl*.

♂ DARYL: From the root name *Darryl*.

♀ DARYLIN: From the root name *Darryl*.

♂ DARYN: From the root name *Darren*.

♀ DASHA: From the root name *Dorothy*.

♀ DASIE: From the root name *Daisy*.

♂ DAVE: From the root name *David*.

♂ DAVEY: From the root name *David*.

♥ ♂ **DAVID** **Dafydd, Dai, Dave, Davey, Davida, Davide, Davidson, Davies, Davin, Davina, Davis, Davita, Davon, Davy, Divina:** *David* ranks near the top of the list of favorite names American parents have chosen for their boys in almost every generation. Although it is one of the most ancient names to have survived into modern times, there have been few spectacular changes to its spelling, and it has relatively few diminutives. Its tenaciousness attests to the name's rock-solid foundation in Judeo-Christian history. The dramatic biblical story of David's defeat of Goliath and his subsequent rise to power as the second king of Israel underpins much of Western and Eastern religious faith. With his genius for architecture and engineering, David left such a mark on Jerusalem that it is to this day referred to as the City of David. This same David is believed to be the author of the Psalms, and as such, his name has been repeated by people of faith on a daily basis for 3,000 years. The name in Hebrew means "beloved of God."

In the Middle East, where there are many Arab Christians, the name *Daoud* is still widely used and has been since the rise of Christianity 2,000 years ago. In fact, until relatively recently, Christians in the Middle East were more likely to use the name for their boys than were Jews, in spite of the Hebrew origin of the name. Since the turn of the century, however, *David* has been heard more frequently among Jews both in the Diaspora and in Israel. *Davida* is the female form of the name and is often used in Israel today. When the state of Israel formed in 1948, it took as its national symbol the six-pointed Star of David.

David traveled west with the spread of Christianity. It landed most famously in Wales and from there began to circulate in Scotland. Several Celtic names, such as *Dahi* and *Dathi,* were in wide use during the fifth century and were close enough in pronunciation to be easily subsumed by *Dafydd.*

The name gained tremendous admiration when the sixth-century bishop of Menevia, whose name was David, took up residence in Wales. A man of stature both physically and spiritually, he was, by all accounts, beloved of all people who knew of him, and, at six feet four inches tall, he must have cut quite a figure among his flock. His fame as a spiritually gifted leader spread to Scotland, and he is credited both with popularizing the name *David* there and extending the influence of Christianity. He was eventually canonized Saint David, which further guaranteed the proliferation of the name. His cathedral, known since his death as Saint David's, is still a popular pilgrimage focus and tourist stop.

In the United States, *David* has never waned in popularity. One reason may be that it is considered by parents to be a "low-risk" name. That is, whatever else he does to bring shame and dishonor upon himself, a *David* runs little risk of being ridiculed on account of his name. *David*, *Davy*, and *Dave* don't rhyme, for example, with any derisive, pejorative, or ridiculous word. It is not a name likely to go out of style, and hence parents can be sure that whatever his occupation, their son David will not be handicapped by an antiquated name or one that was popular at the time of his birth but came quickly to seem eccentric. The diminutive *Davy*, which is almost the only pet name derived from *David*, is easily shed by adolescents wishing to leave their childhood behind. Even so, Davy Crockett, the most famous American to keep the diminutive as an adult, used it with great success even as he entered Congress in the early nineteenth century. Presumably, the folksiness of *Davy* fit perfectly with the image of a country bumpkin that Crockett liked to project as a way of disarming his political opponents. *Dave* is a recent short form of the name and is popular among adult men.

☉ Number
Four. When it comes to issues of social concern, fours are drawn to them like magnets to metal. Some modern numerologists connect the image of a blue star to this number.

☾ Astrological sign
Libra. Libra is an air sign, signifying intellectual prowess.

Color

Dahlia. This brilliant blue can inspire the imagination and soothe the soul.

 ## Stone

Star sapphire. The star sapphire is valued for its color and rarity. It is a clear, deep blue and has a six-pointed white star that appears when cut in a cabochon (half-moon) shape. A star sapphire's iron or titanium content gives the gem strength as well as exquisite color. The most famous star sapphire is the Star of India. Throughout history, sapphires have been called the ultimate soul gem—one that ties all religions together like an ecumenical synod. In the Old Testament, sapphires were frequently mentioned in connection with wisdom and divine favor. It was revered as a prophetic gem and often referred to as a philosopher's stone.

 ## Element

Gold, the metal of nobility and divinity.

Herb

Houseleek *(Sempervivum tectorum).* This perennial European plant likes dry, stony soils. Its rootstock produces a rosette of fleshy leaves and starlike, rose-colored flowers. Fresh crushed leaves were once applied to the forehead to reduce fever. Ancient warriors carried leek leaves for protection. In the sixth century, Saint David directed Welshmen to wear leeks in their caps to identify themselves during the fight against Saxon invaders. To honor their victory, the leek became the national emblem of Wales.

♂   DAVIDE: From the root name *David*.

♂   DAVIDSON: From the root name *David*.

♂ DAVIES: From the root name *David*.

♂ DAVIN: From the root name *David*.

♀ DAVINA: From the root name *David*.

♂ DAVIS: From the root name *David*.

♀ DAVITA: From the root name *David*.

♂ DAVON: From the root name *David*.

♀ DAVRAT: From the root name *Deborah*.

♂ DAVY: From the root name *David*.

♀ DAYANN: From the root name *Diana*.

♀♂ DAYLE: From the root name *Dale*.

♀ DAYNA: From the root name *Dana*.

♥ ♂ **DEAN** **Deanna, Deanne, Deen, Deyn, Dino:** The name *Dean* has several possible meanings, and probably, at some point, it followed the surname-to-first name pattern. However, *Dean* does not offer a particularly neat history of its development for us to follow. Some historians connect the name to a word that means "valley." If this is in fact the case, then the surname developed to identify a person living in a valley, and the first name possibly developed to keep a matrilineal name in the family.

On the other hand, it is also possible that the Latin term *decanus*, which means "leader of 10," informed the earliest use of the name. In the Christian church, this term came to refer to a person who was in charge of several priests. In English, the term used for the parish leader is, of course, *dean*.

Lest things become too clear or simple, there is a variation within this interpretation of the name. In the United States, where the first name *Dean* has been most popular, the word *dean* is more closely linked to the academic world. Some historians believe that this connection to the collegiate term implied a certain importance and status on the bearer and that this more "academic" history is the genesis at least of the name's popularity, if not of the name itself.

Dean also bears a close resemblance to *Dan* and *Don*, the diminutives of two other names, which became popular independent names. To sum up, *Dean* can be taken to mean "a person who lives in (or near) a valley" or "a church leader" or "an academic leader."

Though the name is not as popular today, many famous and historic figures of the twentieth century in the United States have borne the name *Dean*, including statesmen Dean Acheson (1893–1971) and Dean Rusk (1909–1974); actors Dean Jagger (1903–), Dean Martin (originally Dino Crocetti; 1917–1995), and Dean Stockwell (1936–), and the novelist Dean Koontz (1945–).

Number

Six. Some numerologists believe six rules the balance of opposites. Sixes often bring peace to their environments through love, compassion, and truth.

Astrological sign

Taurus. The number six rules the sign of Taurus. Terms like *down to earth* and *logical* are usually associated with this sign, but Taureans have a sensitive, caring side that would put even a passionate Scorpio to shame.

Color

Meadow. The color of a lush green valley represents life and nature's health.

◆ Stone

Microcline. This form of feldspar comes in several colors, but the most common is green or greenish blue. The striking green color comes from the presence of lead. In its natural state, the stone has a lustrous surface that resembles cracked marble. It was once used to decorate buildings and temples but now appears mainly in jewelry. It can be found in a few locations around the world, including the United States and Canada.

♛ Element

Lead, which is found in microcline. The ancients considered it an earth elemental ore and used it in defensive or protective magic rites.

♗ Herb

Smartweed *(Polygonum hydropiper)*. Sometimes called knotweed or water pepper, the flowering herb of this plant was once used for coughs and colds. The freshly crushed herb was often substituted for a mustard plaster to help relieve pain from tumors. Ancient herbalists also made a mouthwash or gargle from this plant for toothaches and larynx problems.

♀ DEANNA: From the root names *Dean* and *Diana*.

♀ DEANNE: From the root name *Dean*.

♀ DEB: From the root name *Deborah*.

♀ DEBBIE: From the root name *Deborah*.

♀ DEBERA: From the root name *Deborah*.

♀ DEBORA: From the root name *Deborah*.

♥ ♀ DEBORAH   Davrat, Deb, Debbie, Debera, Debora, Debra, Deva, Devora, Devorah, Devorit, Dobra, Dvora, Dvoshke: The name *Deborah* (sometimes spelled *Devorah*) literally means "bee" in Hebrew (as does the name *Melissa* in Greek). From the literal translation, the name has taken on the meaning "the buzzing sound that bees make." From that association the name came to mean "eloquence" or "speaking kindly." It is also sometimes associated with the industriousness of bees.

The first historical Deborahs are all biblical figures. The first is Rebekah's nurse, whose death, as names historian Charlotte Yonge says, "was so lamented that the tree she was buried beneath was known as the oak of weeping." The second Deborah is even more famous. She was a prophetess and judge who, in 1150 B.C., led the Israelites in revolt against the Canaanite king. The "Song of Deborah," one of the oldest extant Hebrew poems, is the celebration of her triumph. The third biblical Deborah is the least well known and was the mother of Ananiel. Because of these biblical Deborahs, the name has come to be associated with wisdom, leadership, and the feminine ideal.

While *Deborah* and its variations have been consistently popular among Jews, Christians were slow to embrace it. The name did not appear with any frequency until the late seventeenth century when the Puritans finally began to use it. The name appears to have maintained a slight vogue through the early eighteenth century, but with the decline of Puritanism it again became fairly rare.

There was one famous eighteenth-century American named Deborah who may be said to have followed in the courageous steps of her namesake. Deborah Sampson, disguised as a man, served as a Continental soldier in the American Revolution. After her death, Congress voted to give her heirs a full military pension. It is believed that she is the first woman to be so rewarded. Unfortunately, it is doubtful that she influenced the popularity of the name.

Despite its lack of acceptance among most parents, writers of the eighteenth and nineteenth centuries seemed fond of the name. There are characters named *Deborah* in the novels *The Adventures of Peregrine Pickle* (1751) by Tobias Smolett, *The Vicar of Wakefield* (1766) by Oliver Goldsmith, and *Cranford* (1851–1853) by Elizabeth Gaskell. In fact, Charlotte Yonge lays some of the blame for the name's lack of popularity at the feet of the literary world. In her classic book *History of Christian Names,* she writes that the name "has acquired a certain amount of absurdity from various literary associations, which prevent 'Deb' from being used except by the peasantry."

Finally in the 1950s, however, the name rose to become among the most popular, at least in the United States. Two famous actresses of the period, Deborah Kerr (b. 1921) and Debbie Reynolds, who was originally Mary Frances Reynolds (b. 1932) may have influenced its use. Debbie Reynolds helped the diminutive *Debbie* (or *Debby*) to become more widespread as an independent name. The variation *Debra* also came into use in the 1950s. Still common in 1970, *Deborah* dropped out of the top fifty girls' names by 1980. It remains popular in Jewish families with many variants and diminutives, including *Dvora, Davrat, Deva, Devera, Devorit, Devra,* and *Dvoshke* (Yiddish).

⑨ Number

Eight. Modern numerology often ties images and concepts to numbers. Some believe eight represents blindfolded justice and great trees, including the oak.

☾ Astrological sign

Libra. For a Libran, life is always a question of balance. However, their innate ability to judge well between pro and con leads them to harmony.

Color

Maroon. An aura of dark purplish red signifies the balance of spirit and body.

 ## Stone

Violet sapphire. Folklore connects the sapphire with heavenly favor. It was considered a hard-working stone that brought mental clarity to those fortunate enough to possess one. Ancient Buddhists believed that sapphires enhanced spiritual enlightenment. Violet sapphires, also called "oriental amethyst," were used to support and encourage good judgment. While violet sapphires are uncommon, some have been found in Thailand and Myanmar (Burma).

 ## Element

Gold has a rich metaphysical history. Many believed it improved inner wisdom.

Herb

English oak *(Quercus robur).* There's no argument that an oak tree is majestic. Legends revere their longevity—some have existed for over a thousand years. Ancient Hebrews considered it a blessed tree because Abraham supposedly provided aid to God and two of his angels disguised as travelers under an oak. In literature the oak is associated with strength and stability. Oak bark was brewed into teas and given as a restorative tonic for exhaustion. Ground acorns were sometimes substituted for coffee.

♀   DEBRA: From the root name *Deborah*.

♀   DEDE: From the root name *Diana*.

♂   DEEN: From the root name *Dean*.

♀ DEENA: From the root name *Gerald*.

♂ DEMENICO: From the root name *Dominic*.

♂ DEMINGO: From the root name *Dominic*.

♀♂ DEN: From the root name *Dennis*.

♀ DENISE: From the root name *Dennis*.

♂ DENNET: From the root name *Dennis*.

♥ ♂ **DENNIS Den, Denise, Dennet, Dennison, Denny, Denys, Deon, Dinny, Dion, Dionysia, Dionysius, Diot, Tennyson:** The name *Dennis* is a tribute to a mysterious figure called "The Deity from Nysa"—better known as the Greek god Dionysius. The illegitimate son of Zeus, Dionysius grew up in the region of Nysa. He became the god of wine, revelry, and immortality. The Greeks loved Dionysius. They conferred his name so often upon their children that scholars think he may have been an actual person.

The New Testament contains the first record of the name in a Christian context. Preaching about immortality to a crowd of skeptics, Saint Paul succeeded in converting the Athenian senator Dionysius.

Several saints bore the name in the following centuries. The Italian bishop Denys is the most notable. He traveled to France to convert the Gauls. Successful, beloved, beheaded, and canonized, he was chosen by the French to be one of their patron saints. Worshipers kept his bones in a church near Paris. Six hundred years later, officials of that church forged a manuscript that identified their own Saint Denys with Dionysius, the contemporary of Saint Paul. The outcome was spectacular, and the saint became a star. As a result, the name *Denys*, along with the variations *Dion* and *Diot*, grew hugely popular.

The French Normans brought *Denys*, *Dion*, and *Diot* to England when they conquered that country in the eleventh century. The British dedicated no fewer than forty-one church-es to saints bearing forms of the name Denys. By the end of the twelfth century *Denys* was more often spelled *Denis*. *Dion* spawned several surnames, including *Dennison* and *Tennyson*. Parents chose *Denis* and *Diot* for their daughters as well. In fact, the female names were among the most common in England for at least half a millennium. (*Diot* would even-tually be transformed to the masculine name *Dwight*.)

In Ireland, the masculine *Denis* acquired another *n*. Scholars attribute the new spelling—and the speed with which *Dennis* took root—to the popularity of the already established Celtic name *Donnchadh*. *Dennis* has flourished steadily in Ireland ever since.

The English, however, used *Denis* sporadically over the next few hundred years. Nearly extinct in one century, fash-ionable in the next, the name proved to be as hardy as the vine it commemorates. It experienced a revival in the early 1900s. After 1920, trend-setting Americans employed the French spelling and pronunciation, *Denise,* for girls. Up until the 1960s, the preferred spelling for sons was *Denis,* with *Dennis* and *Denys* listed as common alternatives. Since the 1920s, *Dennis* and *Denise* have waxed and waned, but have always remained among the most popular names. The 1990 United States Census listed *Dennis* as the fortieth most common name for all American males. Now, however, at the end of the twentieth century, it might experience a lull.

 Number

Two. A number two is a genial soul who loves to be around people.

☾ Astrological sign

Taurus. Taureans are kind-hearted and as earthy as their ele-ment.

Color

Mulberry. This reddish purple shade joins devotion with spirituality. It is also a type of table wine.

 ### Stone

Dendritic agate. A dendritic agate resembles the coloring of the fur of the beloved Dalmatian breed with dark blue or brownish black starlike spots on a milky background. All forms of agates were believed to have abilities to boost strength, offer protection from various evils and support emotional or mental well-being. Different types of agates had special "powers" associated with them. Dendritic agates were thought of as powerful protective stones for travelers, whether they journeyed on land or sea. It was thought to stabilize energy levels to keep travelers alert to avoid accidents or unseen dangers.

Element

Silver. Silver supports the safeguarding power of a dendritic agate, especially when traveling at night and under a bright moon.

 ### Herb

Blazing star *(Liatris spicata)*. Also called dense button snakeroot, this native North American plant prefers dry clearings and fields. It has dense spikes of blue-purple flowers that bloom from May to September. The crushed root was applied on poisonous snakebite wounds. A preparation added to milk was taken internally for the same purpose.

♂ DENNISON: From the root name *Dennis*.

♀♂ DENNY: From the root name *Dennis*.

♀ DENYS: From the root name *Dennis*.

♂ DEON: From the root name *Dennis*.

♥ ♂ **DEREK** **Darrick, Deric, Derk, Derrick, Deryk, Dirk:**
The name *Derek* comes from an ancient Teutonic name, *Theodoric,* which is said to mean variously "people's rule," "ruler of people," or "people's wealth." (Names historian Alfred Kolatch gives a slightly different source, the Teutonic name *Hrodrich,* which he reports means "famous ruler.") Theodoric was a famous king of the Teutonic tribe, the Ostrogoths. He ruled in Eastern Europe from 475 until 526, and his main city was Verona. It is thought that he was named after a mythic figure named Theuderik.

Known for his wisdom, and for his skill as a diplomat and leader, Theodoric developed into one of the greatest heroes of early Germanic literature. Not only is he the hero of his own cycle of romances, but he is included in the German epics the Nibelungenlied, and the Book of Heroes, where he is called Dietrich of Bern (Bern being a variation of Verona). Both these books relate different versions of Dietrich's encounters with a faithless, dangerous lady named Kriemhild. As his fame spread throughout Continental Europe, each area developed its own *Dietrich* story. The Dane's have a story of King Tichrich's battle with a dragon, and the Dutch developed a mythic king named Dirk-mit-den-Beer (Dietrich with the beard).

During the early Middle Ages, variations of *Dietrich/Derek* became common among many of the Teutonic tribes, including the Anglo-Saxon, the Visigoth, the Frank, and the German. Though this would seem to indicate that the name existed in England from the early Middle Ages, many historians report that it traveled to England later, with the Dutch. An early English variation, *Tedric,* can be found in the medieval census, The Domesday Book. *The Oxford Dictionary of Christian Names* reports that the variations *Dederick, Dyryke,* and *Deryk* existed in England in the fifteenth century, "borrowed, no doubt, from the Low Countries" (i.e., Holland). In 1605, historian William

Camden recorded *Derric* as the English form of the name and *Terry* as the French.

After an auspicious history throughout the Middle Ages and into the Renaissance, the name became rare in the seventeenth, eighteenth, and nineteenth centuries. Only the German *Dietrich* and Dutch *Dirk* continued to be common. *Dietrich, Dirk,* and *Dieterick* probably came to the early American colonies with the Dutch and German settlers, but they did not spread throughout the rest of the populace.

No one knows why, but the name revived as the variation *Derek* in the late nineteenth century. Never particularly common in the United States, it virtually disappeared in the 1930s. Throughout the century the variation *Derrick* could be found in the African American community. In 1970, this variation was listed among the fifty most popular boys' names in the country. It stayed among the top fifty through the early 1980s, and during the 1990s, the variation *Derek* made it to the top twenty boys' names in the country.

🌀 Number

Seven. Seven is thought to be symbolic of the hope of things yet to be. Sevens often use their intellect to catapult their ideas into action.

🌙 Astrological sign

Leo. Leos are natural born rulers. Many are courageous with souls of fire and light.

✳ Color

Snapdragon. Bright as the sun, this yellow hue signifies keen intelligence.

Stone

Dravite. This member of the tourmaline family ranges from dark golden brown to orange-brown. Tourmalines often look like spiked crystals, but have stronger magnetic properties than the highly charged quartz. While tourmalines were unknown to ancient magic practitioners, they are respected in modern lore as an aid for energy and courage. Dravite's color comes from its rich magnesium content and its name from Drave, Austria, where it was first discovered. It has also been found in parts of North and South America.

 ## Element

Platinum. Any gem set in platinum must have high enough energy to cope with the power of this silver-white metal. Dravite meets this challenge brilliantly.

 ## Herb

Arum *(Arum dracontium).* Arum, also called dragonroot, grows mainly in shady moist places. The plant's rootstock was used medicinally by mixing a preparation with honey for bronchitis, asthma, and symptoms of rheumatism. It also made a healing salve for skin sores. While the tuberlike rootstock is poisonous when fresh, it's edible if dried or cooked thoroughly.

♂ DERIC: From the root name *Derek.*

♂ DERK: From the root name *Derek.*

♂ DERRICK: From the root name *Derek.*

♂ DERRIL: From the root name *Darryl.*

♂ DERRON: From the root name *Darren.*

♂ DERYK: From the root name *Derek.*

♂ DERYLL: From the root name *Darryl.*

♂ DERYN: From the root name *Darren*.

♀ DEVA: From the root name *Deborah*.

♀ DEVORA: From the root name *Deborah*.

♀ DEVORAH: From the root name *Deborah*.

♀ DEVORIT: From the root name *Deborah*.

♂ DEWITT: From the root name *Dwight*.

♂ DEYN: From the root name *Dean*.

♀ DI: From the root name *Diana*.

♀ DIAHANNE: From the root name *Diana*.

♥ ♀ DIANA Danne, Dayann, Deanna, Dede, Di, Diahanne, Diandra, Diane, Dyanne: *Diana* and its French variation *Diane* are both derived from the Latin root *diva*, which means "goddess" (or the masculine, *divus*, which means "divine"). *Diana*'s antecedent may be either the Latin word *diviana*, which means "belonging to *Divia*," or more directly, Diva Jana, an early variation of the feminine divinity who represents the night and the moon. The name was bestowed on Diana, goddess of the moon and the hunt, who is the Roman version of the Greek goddess Artemis. *Diana* was certainly popular in the pre-Christian Roman era and survived into the Christian period, for there are early Christian inscriptions that bear the name *Diania*.

This fondness for the name did not last, however, and as the Christian church sought to separate itself from its pagan past, the name largely dropped out of use. *Diana* did not revive until the sixteenth century, when the late Renaissance and early chivalric poetry reintroduced a love of the classical period. Jorge de Montemayor is said to have started it all when he wrote *The Seven Books of the Diana* (c.1559). During the same period, the French variation, *Diane*, gives us another important figure in the name's resurgence. Diane de Poitiers was a widow and the mistress to a French king: Henry II. It is said that Henry wore her colors when he competed in tournaments. Their romantic love affair inspired parents all over France to name their daughters *Diane*.

England was also influenced by the return to the classics and Diana is the name of a character in *All's Well that Ends Well* (c. 1604), by William Shakespeare. However, it was the court of Charles II sixty years later that provided the real breakthrough for the name in England. Exiled to France after the beheading of Charles I, the Cavalier court, as they were known, soon adopted the popular French name. When Charles II returned to the throne in England, his court brought the name with them. They reasserted the Latin *a*, and *Diana* became a thoroughly English name. By the nineteenth century, it had become a favorite of writers. Novels as diverse as *Rob Roy* (1818) by Walter Scott, *Jane Eyre* (1847) by Charlotte Brontë, and *Diana of the Crossways* (1885) by George Meredith all had characters with the name.

In the United States, the variant spelling *Dianna* was used by free African women during the eighteenth century, and many other variations of the name have remained popular among African Americans ever since. On the other hand, while *Diana* could be found in the white population, it wasn't an extremely common name until the twentieth century. Then, it was the French variation, *Diane,* which achieved prominence first.

Diana reasserted itself in the 1950s, although it did not overtake *Diane* in popularity. In the decades following the 1950s *Diana* gradually gained ascendancy, and since the advent of Diana, Princess of Wales, in the 1980s, there has been a sharp rise in the use of the name. Her fame, culminating in her death in 1997, will almost certainly ensure that the name remains a favorite for many years to come.

Spelling variants for *Diana* include *Deanna, Deana, Dianna, Dyanne, Dyan, Diahann,* and the diminutive, *Di.*

☺ Number

Two. This number rules Cancer. Most twos are sensitive and sentimental.

☾ Astrological sign

Cancer. Some born under this moon-ruled sign are timid or reclusive, yet beneath this shy exterior lies a soul filled with hope and love. The late Princess Diana was a Cancer.

☀ Color

Janus green. A color directly related to the goddess Diana signifying nature's bounty and fertility.

◆ Stone

Green moonstone. Moonstones are a variety of feldspar and prized for their pearl-like sheen. While most people think of moonstones as white, there are several colors, including the rare green, which is found mainly in Canada and Kenya. Since recorded history, moonstones have been tied to magic, with its power being the strongest during the full moon. The Romans revered this stone for they believed it carried the essence of their beloved moon goddess, Diana. To possess a moonstone meant that Diana would bestow love, wealth, and wisdom on the owner.

♛ Element

Selenite. Selenite is a mineral named for another moon goddess, Selene.

⚘ Herb

Pitcher plant *(Sarracenia purpurea)*. Commonly called hunter's cup, this unusual plant is carnivorous. It catches flies in its pitcherlike leaves that are sticky inside. Its rootstock is believed to have some homeopathic qualities and Native Americans used it as a root tonic against smallpox, both as a disease preventative and to relieve the symptoms of it. Controversy arose when nineteenth-century doctors rejected its usefulness. However, they never proved that it didn't work.

♀ DIANDRA: From the root name *Diana*.

♀ DIANE: From the root name *Diana*.

♂ DICK: From the root name *Richard*.

♂ DIEGO: From the root name *Jacob/James*.

♀ DINNY: From the root name *Dennis*.

♂ DINO: From the root name *Dean*.

♂ DION: From the root name *Dennis*.

♀ DIONYSIA: From the root name *Dennis*.

♂ DIONYSIUS: From the root name *Dennis*.

♂ DIOT: From the root name *Dennis*.

♂ DIRK: From the root name *Derek*.

♀ DITA: From the root name *Judith*.

♀ DIVINA: From the root name *David*.

♀ DOBRA: From the root name *Deborah*.

♀ DODIE: From the root name *Dorothy*.

♀ DODO: From the root name *Dorothy*.

♀ DOLLY: From the root name *Dorothy*.

♂ DOLPH: From the root name *Randolph*.

♂ DOM: From the root name *Dominic*.

♀ DOMENICA: From the root name *Dominic*.

♂ DOMENICO: From the root name *Dominic*.

♀ DOMINA: From the root name *Donna*.

♀   DOMINCA: From the root name *Dominic*.

♀   DOMINGA: From the root name *Dominic*.

♂   DOMINGO: From the root name *Dominic*.

♂   DOMINI: From the root name *Dominic*.

♥ ♂ **DOMINIC** **Demenico, Demingo, Dom, Domenica, Domenico, Dominca, Dominga, Domingo, Domini, Dominique, Dominizia, Domitia, Mika, Nick, Nicky:** The name *Dominic* is the English variation of the Latin word for lord, *dominicus,* and can be derived two ways, either as "belonging to the Lord," or as "born on the Lord's day" (from the Latin *dies dominica*). *Dominicus* and its variations have frequently been given to children who were born on Sunday.

The name has been used throughout Europe from early Christian times. Both *Dominicus* and the feminine *Dominica* can be found fairly frequently among Christian inscriptions of the Roman Empire. In England during the Anglo-Saxon period, *Dominic* (or *Dominick*) was a common monk's name.

The first canonized *Dominic* was Saint Dominic of the Cuirass. A penitent, he mortified himself and died in 1024. The second Saint Dominic (1170–1221) is by far the more famous bearer of the name, and probably is the figure more responsible for its continued use through the centuries. The founder of the famous monastic order, the Dominicans, Saint Dominic was seen in a vision by the pope as one of the pillars of the Catholic church. This second Saint Dominic inspired English parents to name their sons after him, and the name ceased to be a purely monastic one. It never became wildly fashionable, however.

In the sixteenth century, the Reformation virtually ended British use of the name because *Dominic* was considered a

Roman Catholic name. For the same reason the name did not travel well to early America. It was not until the late nineteenth century that *Dominic* gained prominence in the United States, and that was almost entirely thanks to the wave of Italian immigrants who reached the country during that time. Throughout the first half of the twentieth century, the name and its variations remained largely within the French, Hispanic, and Italian-American communities.

By the 1950s the name, and its French variation, *Dominique* (often used for girls), began being used by a broader spectrum of Americans. Particularly popular in the African American community, both versions of the name are among the top one hundred boys' and girls' names in the country.

Number

Four. Fours are often drawn to social reforms and the plight of the underdog.

Astrological sign

Scorpio. Many Scorpios find happiness through spiritual pursuits. Historically, the constellation Scorpius is considered one of the oldest, with details of its existence dating back to 5000 B.C.

Color

Sunday yellow. Some ancient civilizations associated colors with days of the week. Yellow was for Sunday to honor God's light.

Stone

Golden topaz. Although topaz comes in several colors, a golden hue has the highest market value. Ancient Egyptians believed that a golden topaz symbolized the sun god, Ra, and honored it for its fiery energy. Golden topaz was also worn on the breastplates of Jewish high priests. Topaz is thought to bestow warmth and hope.

👑 Element

Platinum. Platinum is a high-energy metal that complements the vitality of the powerful topaz.

🦎 Herb

Friar's cowl *(Arum maculatum).* There are nearly a thousand species of arum. Most are found in tropical climates with marshy soil conditions. This plant's tuberous roots can be roasted or baked and eaten like potatoes. The starchy juice was used to stiffen lace ruffles in Elizabethan times and a powdered starch was used for skin cosmetics, including the bleaching of freckles. The rootstock was used in medicinal preparations for digestion and respiratory problems.

♀   DOMINIQUE: From the root name *Dominic.*

♀   DOMINIZIA: From the root name *Dominic.*

♀   DOMITIA: From the root name *Dominic.*

♂   DON: From the root name *Donald.*

♀   DONA: From the root name *Donald.*

♥ ♂ **DONALD**   **Don, Dona, Donalda, Donaldina, Donaleen, Donall, Donalt, Donaugh, Donella, Donette, Donita, Donnell, Donnelle, Donny:** The name *Donald* is probably an Anglicization of a Gaelic name, *Domhnall.* The most ancient derivation of the name seems to be two primitive Celtic words, *dubno,* which means "world" and *walos,* which means "might." Another theory on the name's origin and meaning is that it is an Anglicization of the name *Donghal* and it means "brown stranger." Lexicographer Eric Partridge writes that the name's meaning has been "glossed [over] by many Irish scholars" who have said that it means "proved chieftain."

For centuries *Donald* has been an extremely common name in Scotland, and historian Charlotte Yonge reports that it was the name of the first Christian king of that country. It is certainly the name of many later Scottish kings. There is also a clan named *Donald,* and of course the surname that means "the son of Donald" has become known all over the world as a fast food restaurant, McDonald's. One of the earliest records of the name's use in England is in the medieval census The Domesday Book, where a man named *Doneuuald* is recorded. In Ireland the variation is *Donal,* which, strangely, is often taken as the Irish equivalent to the name *Daniel.*

While *Donald* certainly appeared in the American colonies, it did not become at all common until the middle of the nineteenth century. This increase in use may have been in part due to the popularity of Sir Walter Scott's novels, since he used the name *Donald* frequently. The influx of Scots immigrants certainly had an impact on the number of boys given the name in the United States. However, despite an increase in American use in the nineteenth century, the name cannot be said to have become widespread outside of Scotland until the early twentieth century. From 1900 to 1950 it was fashionable in both England and the United States, though there is no specific source that anyone can identify which would explain its popularity during this period. By the 1950s, use of the name began to diminish. Some scholars have linked the name's decline to the animated character Donald Duck, but this is an unsupported theory and seems rather hard on the duck.

Boys named *Donald* will certainly be called *Don* by their friends as they grow older. They may be called *Donny* as a diminutive by parents and teachers when they are young.

Variations: *Donal, Donnal* (masculine), *Dona, Donaldina, Donalda, Donaleen, Donella, Donnelle, Donette, Donita* (all feminine).

Number

Five. Some numerologists believe fives are impulsive. They seem to have no middle ground, but are usually unerringly positive in outlook.

Astrological sign

Aries. Those born under the sign of the ram have much drive and initiative. Ariens are natural leaders.

Color

Umber. This deep shade of reddish brown promotes vitality and stability.

Stone

Plume agate. Plume agates normally occur in the southwestern U.S. This gem is brilliant red with grasslike plumage that looks like a fiery sunburst. Agates were once used as part of magical or healing rituals for bravery, longevity, and the enhancement of physical strength. The Romans wore red agates to protect themselves from insect bites and to heal illnesses of the blood.

Element

Leadhillite. Leadhillite was named for its place of origin—Leadhills, Scotland.

Herb

Mandrake *(Podophyllum peltatum).* Also called duck's foot, mandrake was used in magic rituals by many ancient cultures because of its resemblance to the human body. The dark brown fibrous rootstock was used by Native Americans to get rid of warts.

♀   DONALDA: From the root name *Donald*.

♀   DONALDINA: From the root name *Donald*.

♀   DONALEEN: From the root name *Donald*.

♂   DONALL: From the root name *Donald*.

♂   DONALT: From the root name *Donald*.

♂   DONAUGH: From the root name *Donald*.

♀   DONELLA: From the root names *Donald* and *Donna*.

♀   DONELLE: From the root name *Donna*.

♀   DONETTE: From the root name *Donald*.

♀   DONIA: From the root name *Donna*.

♀   DONICA: From the root name *Donna*.

♀   DONITA: From the root names *Donald* and *Donna*.

♥ ♀ **DONNA** **Domina, Donella, Donelle, Donia, Donica, Donita, Donnell, Donni, Ladonna, Madonna:** The name *Donna* comes from the Italian term *donna*, which in turn comes from the Latin term *domina* or *domna*. *Domina* means "lady" or, more literally, "mistress of the house." All these terms are derived from the Latin word *domus*, which means "house." Sometimes *Domina* has been used as a given name as well. The word *Madonna* (literally, "my lady") has become a universal designation for the Virgin Mary. After the Romans brought the term *domina* to England, it was adopted as the title given to a woman who held a barony.

Interestingly, while the word *donna* is an extremely common term of respect in Italy, it never came into use there as a given name. *Donna* seems to have first appeared, though rarely, in English-speaking countries in the 1920s. By the 1940s it started to become more popular, and with the advent of the actress Donna Reed, who starred in her own television series in the 1950s, the name became widespread. Donna Reed came to epitomize the perfect American mother, and the 1950s was an era when that image was desirable for many parents naming their baby daughters. (Remember the vision of Donna Reed vacuuming in high heels?)

Other famous women to bear the name and who might have influenced parents are the singer Donna Summer, the actress Donna Mills, the fashion designer Donna Karan, and even the singer Madonna. *Donna* is also used in combination with other names. The most common combination has traditionally been *Donna-Marie*.

◉ Number
Three. Threes are reliable people who thrive in harmonious environments. They often pursue artistic or literary careers.

☾ Astrological sign
Cancer. Most Cancers are nurturing parents. Cancers prefer their own hearths and rarely travel far from home.

✳ Color
Turquoise. Hues of blue and green enhance spiritual serenity and physical relaxation.

◆ Stone
Moonstone. The moonstone resembles the moon—smooth and luminescent, with a slightly bluish sheen. The gem was believed to influence the body's magnetic field. It was used to reduce anxiety, and in powdered form, to treat childhood ailments like fevers, coughs, and colds. The moonstone was

also given by lovers as a sign of devotion—on a moonlit night, of course!

♛ Element

Silver. According to folklore, silver induces strong positive emotions. Silver is also the ore linked to Cancer.

🦁 Herb

Lady's nightcap *(Convolvulus sepium).* This perennial is an herbaceous vine that can be cultivated, but also grows wild in the eastern United States and parts of Europe. Powdered preparations of the flowering plant and rootstock were once used to reduce inflammation from sinus-related problems.

♀♂ DONNELL: From the root names *Donald* and *Donna.*

♀ DONNELLE: From the root name *Donald.*

♀ DONNETTE: From the root name *Donald.*

♀ DONNI: From the root name *Donna.*

♂ DONNY: From the root name *Donald.*

♀ DOORTJE: From the root name *Dorothy.*

♀ DORA: From the root names *Dorothy* and *Theodore.*

♀ DORAT: From the root name *Dorothy.*

♀ DORETTA: From the root name *Dorothy.*

♀ DORI: From the root name *Dorothy.*

♀ DORIKA: From the root name *Dorothy.*

♀ DORINDA: From the root name *Dorothy.*

♀ DORLISSA: From the root name *Dorothy.*

♀ DORO: From the root name *Dorothy.*

♀ DOROTA: From the root name *Dorothy.*

♀ DOROTHEA: From the root name *Dorothy.*

♥ ♀ DOROTHY   Dasha, Dodie, Dodo, Dolly, Doortje, Dora, Dorat, Doretta, Dori, Dorika, Dorinda, Dorlissa, Doro, Dorota, Dorothea, Dorrit, Dory, Dosha, Dot, Dotty, Tea, Thea: Like the name *Theodore, Dorothy* is Greek for "God's gift." Scholars surmise that *Dorothy* began as *Theodora*, and that both names were coined by Christians during the first century A.D. The theory goes that *Theodora* was simply flip-flopped on a whim of fashion.

Legends of the third century martyr Saint Dorothy of Cappadocia (modern-day Turkey) did much to establish the name in Italy and Germany. It took longer for her fame to spread to England. But by the fifteenth century, Saint Dorothy was the subject of stained glass windows and other religious art in that country. England was full of girls named *Dorothy* by the end of the sixteenth century, and the name was pronounced "Dorotee."

Dorothy generated the nicknames *Dorat, Dotty, Doll,* and *Dolly* (the latter two because of a linguistic tendency to change "r" to "l"). Doll was so popular that nearly every little girl called her make-believe baby "Doll"—and "doll" passed into the English language as a generic term for what used to be called a puppet or poppet. But *Doll* had also become synonymous with a woman of low moral repute, due largely to William Shakespeare's character Doll Tearsheet. Dorothy disappeared as a given name for the first half of the eighteenth century, possibly because of these associations.

Dorothy made a comeback among members of the next generation, perhaps as new mothers began naming babies after their grandmothers. New variations were *Dorothea, Dot, Dora,* and *Dodo. Dorothy* disappeared again from 1800 to 1880, but *Dora* became an independent name. In the early years of the twentieth century, Germans began to use *Dorothea* and *Dorlisa*. The French chose *Dorothée, Dorette,* and *Doralise. Dorinda* was very common in Ireland.

Dorothy—now pronounced with the "h"—was a huge success in the United States from 1880 to 1900. *The Wizard of Oz* was one of many turn-of-the-century novels that featured a character named Dorothy. And a song called "Goodbye Dolly Gray" was so popular that names scholars believe it may have contributed to the name's demise. By the early 1900s, *Dorothy, Doll,* and *Dolly* had been literally played out. *Dora* was still frequently chosen, though.

By 1930, however, *Dorothy* was the third most popular name for baby girls, and *Dotty* or *Dot* was the chosen nickname. Ten years later it still ranked high (fifteenth). In 1950 it dropped to thirty-third. During the 1990s, Dorothy has not placed in the top one hundred lists of popular baby names. But due to its previous high profile, the 1990 United States Census lists *Dorothy* as tenth most common name of all American women and girls.

🌀 Number

Six. Modern numerologists connect six to musical harmony. Many sixes find their destiny in spiritual endeavors.

🌙 Astrological sign

Capricorn. An Eastern myth says that Capricornus was nurse to the young sun god, Ra. Singer Dolly Parton is a Capricorn.

✳ Color

Emerald. Shades of green inspire creativity and curiosity, and promote healing.

◆ Stone

Green fluorite. Fluorite crystals are transparent, and occur in colors ranging from clear to black. The rare green fluorite is found in Peru, Norway, England, and Germany. Many New

Agers use the stone to strengthen their powers of learning, concentration, and analysis.

⚜ Element

Lead. Lead is an earth element and is linked to the sign of Capricorn. Lead was used to frame pieces of stained glass for religious images in cathedral windows.

🦎 Herb

Dolloff *(Seiraca ulmaria)*. This plant thrives in damp areas of the eastern U.S. and Europe. The dolloff had many medicinal uses. Dolloff tea is used to treat the flu, respiratory problems, arthritis, fever, and kidney troubles. Some herbalists made a root preparation to cleanse wounds or to be used as an eye rinse.

♀   DORRIT: From the root name *Dorothy*.

♀   DORY: From the root name *Dorothy*.

♀   DOSHA: From the root name *Dorothy*.

♀   DOT: From the root name *Dorothy*.

♀   DOTTY: From the root name *Dorothy*.

♂   DOUG: From the root name *Douglas*.

♥ ♂ **DOUGLAS**   **Doug, Doyle, Dugaid:** *Douglas,* whose origin is in the word *dubhghlas,* is a Gaelic name meaning "dark water." The surname evolved as a designation for families living near rivers in Scotland, and that country's most powerful family carried the name into the mainstream. Members of the Douglas clan (whose slogan is "never behind") were instrumental in fighting Scotland's fourteenth-century war of independence from England. Interestingly, when *Douglas* first began to be used as a given name, Scots parents named their daughters *Douglas*. By the end of the seventeenth century, though, only boys had the name.

Douglas traveled to England as a first name during the seventeenth century and became fairly widespread, but did not make it to the United States until the mid-1800s with the first wave of Scottish immigrants. It has remained in continuous use ever since, and is no longer confined to families of Scottish ancestry. The 1990 census record reports that, among living American men and boys, *Douglas* ranks forty-fifth in popularity. It is not currently rated among the top one hundred names for boys in the United States, but *Douglas* is one of those solid names for boys that will wax and wane, but will never fully lose its fashionability.

Number

Seven. In some numerological circles, seven is linked to people of formidable military skills. Douglas MacArthur was a brilliant American general.

Astrological sign

Pisces. Many Pisceans have a strong attachment to water and find peace living by lakes, rivers, or the ocean.

Color

Deep blue. Dark blue indicates a noble spirit when seen in someone's aural emanation.

Stone

Cairngorm quartz. Ancient mystics thought of quartz as solid water and used it in religious or shamanistic rites for thousands of years. Its connection to water gave quartz value as a rainmaking tool in many regions of the Pacific including Australia and New Guinea. Cairngorm quartz is smoky brown and is found in the Cairngorm Mountains of Scotland. Smoky quartz was thought to alter moods and was worn to dispel depression, despair and other harmful negative emotions.

⚜ Element

Iron. Iron was considered a protective ore. Small pieces were hidden in homes or buried around property borders to repel evil or hexes.

🦎 Herb

Water flag *(Iris versicolor)*. Water flag is a variety of iris native to eastern North America. Today, bulbs are exported to Europe for herbal and floral cultivation. Its sword-shaped leaves and bluish purple flowers grow from a thick rootstock. Herbalists use the rootstock to make remedies for heartburn and sinus inflammations. Some recommended potions of water flag for migraines and the nausea associated with this once mysterious condition.

♂ **DOYLE:** From the root name *Douglas*.

♀ **DREENA:** From the root name *Andrew*.

♀♂ **DREW:** From the root name *Andrew*.

♂ **DRUD:** From the root name *Andrew*.

♂ **DRUGI:** From the root name *Andrew*.

♂ **DUGAID:** From the root name *Douglas*.

♥ ♂ **DUNCAN Dunn:** *Duncan* is from the Gaelic and was originally *Dunecan,* which in turn seems to be derived from *Donn-chaddh*—*donn* meaning "dark" and *cath* meaning "battle." The name has been interpreted to mean either "dark-haired (or dark-skinned) warrior." More simply, it can be interpreted as "brown warrior," though some names historians simply list the meaning of the name as "brown head." Strangely, *Donn-chaddh* was not Anglicized to *Duncan*, but rather it became *Denis*. There seems to be some disagreement about the possibility that *Duncan* is not Scottish in its ultimate origin, since some names historians list the name's etymology as "Old Irish," despite its Scottish history.

There was one saint named Duncan—in the seventh century—and there were two Scottish kings, Duncan I and Duncan II—in the eleventh century. The most famous of the kings, Duncan I, was immortalized in Shakespeare's *Macbeth* (1606). The name also appears in the famous medieval Icelandic saga *Burnt Njal*. Unlike many other Scottish names, *Duncan* did not become particularly widespread in England, perhaps because of its royal Scottish connotations. One man named Donecan is recorded in the medieval census The Domesday Book as having lived in Somerset, but the name remained almost exclusively Scottish until the twentieth century. Even in the United States, with its large number of Scottish immigrants, few named their sons *Duncan*. In the nineteenth century, James Fenimore Cooper introduced the name to American literature when he included a character named Major Duncan Heyward in his novel *The Last of the Mohicans* (1826). However, there is no known reason why the name gained popularity outside of Scotland during the twentieth century, nor is there an obvious reason for the name's decline in use since the 1960s.

 Number

Three. Most numerologists agree that threes are usually inspired by life and in turn, inspire others.

Astrological sign

Aries. When a sign is ruled by the planet Mars, chances are anyone born under it will have the spirit of a warrior.

✳ Color

Russet. This rich shade of reddish brown tempers the power of fire with the stability of earth to keep a valiant hero from seeking vengeance instead of justice.

◆ Stone

Iceland spar. This is a transparent, colorless calcite crystal that usually appears in a rhomboid shape. It has been used for decoration and carving. Because of its soft nature (by gem-cutting standards), it is only faceted for collectors. Calcite was used by mystics for its purported power to purify, heal, and bring peace. Iceland spar, like other calcites, has unique optical qualities that refract light, making a double image. Shamans used it during magic rituals to double the power of the spell they were making.

⚜ Element

Cinnabar. Cinnabar is a mineral found with calcite.

☙ Herb

Woundwort *(Solidago virgaurea)*. This herb has many names, including brownwort and selfheal. The herb of woundwort was used to make tea for internal wounds. Used as a wash, the cold tea cleansed external injuries. Some early physicians used it as an herb preparation for a gargle to relieve throat irritations and laryngitis. Others believed it ended fits, convulsions, and expelled the demon that caused such afflictions.

♂ DUNN: From the root name *Duncan*.

♀ DVORA: From the root name *Deborah*.

♀ DVOSHKE: From the root name *Deborah*.

♥ ♂ **DWIGHT** **DeWitt, Witt:** There are several different theories as to the origin of the name *Dwight*. However, all historians seem to agree that the name started out as a surname and then was adopted as a first name. Many believe that *Dwight* derives from the Greek, and that it means "white," "blond," or "fair." They trace the name from the Greek god Dionysius, and say that the diminutive of *Dionisia*—a variation of the name *Dionysius*—is *Diot*. It is unclear how *Diot* became *Dwight,* but as with many names, it certainly transformed in its travels through Europe. A far more prosaic (and less common) interpretation of the name *Dwight* is that it derives from the French and was originally *de Wight,* meaning "From the Isle of Wight."

As a first name, *Dwight* is almost entirely American. The Dwight family was an early and extremely prominent family in colonial New England. The first Dwight in America was John Dwight. Originally from Dedham, England, he immigrated to America in 1635. Among his descendants is the famous early nineteenth-century president of Yale University, Timothy Dwight. It is said that the most famous Dwight in American history, President and General Dwight D. Eisenhower, was named after Timothy Dwight.

Despite the influence of figures such as Eisenhower, the nineteenth-century evangelist Dwight Lyman Moody, and Dwight F. Davis (the founder of the Davis Cup tennis tournament), *Dwight* is no longer a very fashionable name among American parents. The name probably reached its peak in the 1870s, and possibly had another rise during World War II and Eisenhower's presidency. Though it is still used, it cannot be considered widespread. According to the 1990 census, *Dwight* was the two hundred fifty-seventh most common name for living American men.

⊙ Number

Eight. An eight has the inborn power to play a major role on life's stage. Their abilities to focus on a goal and draw in others to help them contribute to their success.

☾ Astrological sign

Libra. This September/October sign is represented by balanced scales to remind humankind that there should be justice for all. Dwight Eisenhower was a Libra.

☀ Color

White blond. The Greeks, Druids and Confucianists revered white as a symbol of ultimate divinity.

◆ Stone

Datolite. Datolite comes from the Greek and means "to divide." It is normally colorless and faceted only for gem collectors. Small prismatic crystals occur in white or pale tints of yellow, green and red. Most often, datolite is found in massive pieces and used commercially to extract the mineral, boron. Datolite is found in Germany, Norway, and Italy. Beautiful gemstone specimens have been discovered in the Lake Superior area of the United States.

♛ Element

Copper. Copper is the metal associated with Venus, Libra's ruling planet. It is sometimes also found in datolite.

⚘ Herb

Pleurisy root *(Asclepias tuberosa)*. This native North American plant grows in dry areas such as fields and sandy soils along the east coast and westward to Arizona. Also called white root in Native American herbal lore, the fleshy root was widely used for cough remedies in the late nine-teenth century. Some Native American tribes chewed the dried root or made tea by boiling the root for treatments of pneumonia and bronchitis.

♀ DYANNE: From the root name *Diana*.

♥ ♀♂ **DYLAN** **Dylana, Dylane:** *Dylan* has a wonder-ful, if somewhat sparse, story. It is also one of the few names whose modern ascent to popularity we can trace directly to two historical figures, one still living. They are the Welsh poet Dylan Thomas and the American songwriter Bob Dylan.

To begin at *Dylan*'s genesis: the name is generally taken to mean either "of the sea," "son of the waves," or "born near the sea." The first Dylan was the Welsh god of the sea. He had a twin brother, Lleu Llaw Gyffes (which translates as "Lleu of the Dexterous Hand"). Dylan and Lleu's parents were brother and sister. Their father, Gwydion, was a magi-cian, poet, musician, and warrior. Their mother, Aranrhod, was the goddess of the sky, who also symbolized fertility. Gwydion and Aranrhod's father was Don. Don was the head of one of the two great mythic families of Welsh gods. These two warring families are thought to either represent the powers of darkness and light (Don and his family were light), or the gods of the Welsh (Don and his family again) versus the gods of an invading tribe.

From an American perspective, the advent of *Dylan*'s popularity began in the mid-twentieth century with the Welsh poet Dylan Thomas. Thomas cut a romantic figure in the literary world and was extremely popular in the United States. It is certainly possible that he influenced some parents to give their sons the name. Dylan Thomas so impressed a young folk musician, Robert Zimmerman, that Zimmerman adopted the poet's name. Bob Dylan's influence on American culture is hard to estimate. Through his new name, Dylan certainly inspired both a renewed interest in the poet Dylan Thomas as well as the current popularity of *Dylan* as a first name.

Number

Two. In modern numerology two represents sensitivity and deep emotions. Many twos are artists, poets, and writers.

Astrological sign

Scorpio. This sign is ruled by the element of water that signifies the soul. Dylan Thomas was born under the sign of the scorpion.

Color

Claret. Deep red shades fuel passion in poetic souls, especially if they're Scorpios.

Stone

Blue pearl. A pearl is a mysterious creation of the sea. Much lore surrounds this organic gem. One legend claims that the pearl has the power to relax minds and free positive energy for balanced love relationships. The Hindus believed that the pearl reflected and captured the moon's influence on earth, protecting it from calamitous weather. Blue pearls are hard to find and vary in color, but most are a pale shade. Many of the world's sea pearls are harvested in the waters around Sri Lanka.

Element

Silver. Silver is tied to the element of water and goes well to support the precious energy of a pearl.

🌿 **Herb**

Lustwort *(Drosera rotundifolia).* Lustwort is an insectivorous (traps insects for food) plant found in moist areas of North America, Europe, and Asia. The plant's herb was used to make preparations for chest problems including asthma, whooping cough and bronchitis. It was also found to be helpful against nausea and other types of stomach distress.

♀   DYLANA: From the root name *Dylan.*
♀   DYLANE: From the root name *Dylan.*

♂ EAMON: From the root name *Edmund*.

♂ EAN: From the root name *John*.

♀ EBA: From the root name *Eve*.

♂ EBERMAN: From the root name *Abraham*.

♂ ED: From the root names *Edmund* and *Edward*.

♂ EDAN: From the root name *Aidan*.

♂ EDDIE: From the root names *Edmund* and *Edward*.

♂ EDEN: From the root name *Aidan*.

♂ EDIK: From the root name *Edward*.

♀ EDMA: From the root name *Edmund*.

♀ EDMÉE: From the root name *Edmund*.

♀ EDMONDA: From the root name *Edmund*.

♂ EDMONDE: From the root name *Edmund*.

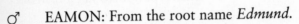 ♂ **EDMUND** **Eamon, Ed, Eddie, Edma, Edmée, Edmonda, Edmonde, Edmunda, Edmundo, Ned, Ted, Teddie:** As Jane Austen wrote in her novel *Mansfield Park*, "There is nobleness in the name of Edmund. It is the name of heroism and renown; of kings, princes, and knights; and seems to breathe the spirit of chivalry and warm affections." Though the name is not as popular now as it once was, Edmund has a proud history.

The name can be traced back to the old English words

"ead," meaning "rich" and "mund," meaning "protection." It is interpreted as "fortunate warrior" or "rich protector."

The earliest Edmund of note was the king of East Anglia, who lived at the end of the ninth century. According to local legend, he was the first to die at the hands of the Danish invaders, leading to his canonization. Later, he became the patron saint of the town, Bury Saint Edmunds, in Suffolk, England. Two English kings were named Edmund: Edmund the Magnificent (c.922–946 A.D.) and Edmund Ironside (c.993–1016 A.D.). Another Saint Edmund was Archbishop of Canterbury in the thirteenth century.

The name probably traveled to France after the Norman Conquest in 1066, and the spelling changed to *Edmond*. From France the name moved throughout the rest of Europe, but it never became particularly common except in Italy, where it became *Edmondo*. It gained its greatest popularity in Ireland, with the Celtic version *Eamon*.

England's Henry III (ruling from 1216–1272) helped maintain the popularity of *Edmund* when he christened one of his two sons with the name (the other was called Edward). Thereafter the name remained fashionable among British royalty and nobility, as well as among commoners. Later English heroes who bore the name were the royal astronomer Edmund Halley—after whom the comet is named (1656–1742)—and the English poet, Edmund Spenser (1552–1599). Among the fictive *Edmund*s, the most famous is probably Edmund in Shakespeare's *King Lear*. Testifying to the repute of the name in the nineteenth century, the Romantic poet John Keats mentioned in a letter to his sister that "if my name had been Edmund, I should have been more fortunate."

Edmund came to America with the earliest settlers, many of whom were from Suffolk. It has gone in and out of style over the past few decades, but has never completely dropped from use.

Number

Eight. In cosmic awareness, the number eight represents the subconscious mind. Eights are often misunderstood and can be the tool of fate for others without realizing it.

Astrological sign

Cancer. In various lands and different times, many names have been given to the stars that form the constellation of Cancer. The Egyptians called it the Scarab.

Color

Glacier ice. This breathtaking shade of blue is rarely seen except in photographs or by mountain climbers. It brings refreshment to mind and soul.

Stone

Indicolite. A form of tourmaline, indicolite is dark blue and also referred to as indigolite. Tourmalines have potent energy-producing properties and are used in industry because of their shatterproof durability when high frequencies pass through them. Indicolite is a marvelous gem to wear for reducing stress. It is found most often in Brazil. Well-known for its intuitive enriching power, silver goes especially well with the blue energy of indicolite.

Element

Silver. Silver is associated with many different celestial bodies, including comets.

Herb

Silvery cinquefoil *(Potentilla anserina).* A plant of many names, cinquefoil has been called silverweed by ancient herbalists. The leaves are dark green and have silvery hairs on the underside. The herb part of the plant was used to make tea for relief of dysentery, an affliction that knights of yore contracted when traveling to war or on quests. Left untreated, dysentery killed many. Silvery cinquefoil is found in fields or pastures and marshy areas in North America and Europe.

♀   EDMUNDA: From the root name *Edmund*.

♂   EDMUNDO: From the root name *Edmund*.

♂   EDOUARD: From the root name *Edward*.

♂   EDUARDO: From the root name *Edward*.

♂   EDVARD: From the root name *Edward*.

♥ ♂ **EDWARD** **Ed, Eddie, Edik, Edouard, Eduardo, Edvard, Edwarda, Edwardine, Ewart, Lalo, Ned, Neda, Ted, Teddie:** The name *Edward* is from the Anglo-Saxon *ead* meaning "rich" or "happy," and *vard* or "weard" meaning "guardian" or "ward." Popular interpretations of the name include "happy guardian" or "rich protector." The first recorded English royal so-named was Alfred the Great's son, Edward the Elder, who reigned over the Anglo-Saxon south in the early tenth century. The second Anglo-Saxon King Edward, "the Martyr," was also the first Saint Edward. He ascended the throne in 975 A.D. when he was twelve years old, but only reigned for three years before he was murdered by a rival faction.

The Edward who made the name truly famous, however, was the eleventh-century English king and saint Edward "the Confessor." Considered by the Anglo-Saxons to be the last native king of England, he was also believed by the Norman invaders to be their direct blood link to the English throne. Edward the Confessor wasn't a particularly effective ruler, but because of his mythic piety, he became a popular historic figure who ultimately became the patron saint of England. In 1605, Camden wrote "the Christian humility of King Edward the Confessor brought such credit to the name that since that time it has been most used in all estates."

Henry III became quite a follower of Edward the Confessor and brought the name into Norman England by christening one of his sons Edward. (Edward I reigned from 1272–1307.) The name survived the establishment of the Church of England and the Protestant Reformation, largely because Saint Edward the Confessor was a non-biblical saint. In fact, one of England's earliest Protestant kings was Edward VI.

Edward is one of the few Anglo-Saxon names to become popular in Europe. Due to a royal marriage, it traveled to Portugal, where Edward I's granddaughter named her son Duarte. The name then became popular throughout the Continent. The French version is *Edouard,* the German is *Eduard,* and the Italian is *Eduardo.*

Despite its popularity in Europe, *Edward* had a hard time becoming established in the early American colonies. This may have been because new parents did not want to honor a non-biblical saint (at least not in Puritan New England), or to pay homage to a line of British kings. Though many of the Jamestown and Raleigh colonists were named Edward, they did not give the name to their children. Consequently, it did not take off in the United States until the late 1700s.

Since that time, though, *Edward* has consistently been one of the most common names in the country. Nicknames for *Edward* include *Ned, Neddy, Ed* and *Eddie. Ted* or *Teddy* are also diminutives of *Edward,* but that form is now used only rarely, being more frequently associated with *Theodore.* European versions of *Edward* have gained in popularity as various waves of immigrants traveled to the United States. Lately the Italian derivation, *Eduardo,* has ranked among the most popular names in the country.

◉ Number

One. Some of the world's outstanding leaders were ones, including four English kings and five American presidents. Ones command respect from those around them, and usually get it.

☾ Astrological sign

Cancer. Many Cancers seem passive, yet they are deeply emotional and as restless as the ocean tides.

✳ Color

Steel blue. Silver and blue are colors tied to Cancer and both signify serenity of spirit.

◆ Stone

Celestine. Also called celestite, this normally colorless crystalline gem does occur in other colors. When the colorless variety is cut and polished it gives off a silvery sheen. Some past cultures believed that celestine had magical qualities and they wore or carried it to promote compassion. It is also tied to the element of water. Most of the gem-quality crystals are found in Namibia or Madagascar, but celestine's also been discovered in Europe.

♔ Element

Gold. Gold has long been connected to kingly wealth, but many feel it to be strongly linked to divinity as well.

♘ Herb

Stone root *(Collinsonia canadensis)*. Stone root, commonly named richweed, is found in damp woods in eastern to midwestern North America. In traditional herbal lore, the fresh rootstock juice of stone root was often suggested for some bladder problems. Fresh stone root leaves were made into poultices to help heal wounds and soothe bruises.

♀ EDWARDA: From the root name *Edward*.

♀ EDWARDINE: From the root name *Edward*.

♂ EGOR: From the root name *George*.

♀ EILEEN: From the root name *Helen*.

♀ EIRE: From the root name *Erin*.

♀ EIRENE: From the root name *Irene*.

♀ EIRYN: From the root name *Erin*.

♀ EKATERINA: From the root name *Katherine*.

♀ ELAINE: From the root name *Helen*.

♀ ELAN: From the root names *Elizabeth* and *Helen*.

♀ ELANA: From the root name *Helen*.

♀ ELEANOR: From the root name *Helen*.

♀ ELENA: From the root name *Helen*.

♥ ♂ **ELI** **Elie, Elliot, Eloi, Eloy, Ely:** *Eli* and its variant spelling *Ely,* are often considered diminutives of the name *Elijah*. In fact, though the names share the letters "el," *Eli* has its own separate and distinct history as a given name. It is also interesting to note that while a few names historians relate the "el" in *Eli* to "God," most believe that *Eli* is an ancient Hebrew word which means "height," or "high." (See also *Elijah*.) The earliest known figure with the name Eli can be found in the Old Testament: the high priest Eli was Samuel's father, mentor, and teacher.

As with *Elijah,* and many other Old Testament names, the name *Eli* came into English-speaking Christian use with the Reformation and the rise of Puritanism. Unlike many Old Testament names, it remained in fairly common use beyond the seventeenth and eighteenth centuries and survived through the nineteenth. Among the most famous

American men with the name Eli are Eli Whitney, the eighteenth century inventor of the cotton gin, Eli Lilly, the pharmaceutical pioneer, and the film actor Eli Wallach. It has been suggested that the name's enduring popularity in previous centuries is probably due to its simplicity. It fell out of favor with parents after the 1930s, and is only now enjoying a small revival. Even so, it is still considered somewhat rare.

 ## Number
Eight. Eights possess the power to accomplish the impossible. Many of this number have an ingenious streak and enjoy inventing ways to make life better.

 ## Astrological sign
Sagittarius. People born under this Jupiter-ruled sign need the highest kind of stimulation to stay happy and productive.

 ## Color
Bishop's purple. This color has ecclesiastical associations and was worn by ancient priests and prophets as a sign of their devotion.

 ## Stone
Violet tanzanite. Tanzanite is usually pale bluish purple, but violet tanzanite is darker and rarer. Tanzanite is a variety of zoisite crystal first discovered high in the mountains of Austria. Beautiful cameos have been carved from tanzanite.

 ## Element
Tin. Tin is tied to Jupiter, the ruling planet of Sagittarius. In metallurgic lore, it's considered a lucky metal.

White oak *(Quercus alba).* The name *Elon,* a variation of *Eli,* means eternal oak. There are several varieties of oak and its bark has healing properties. Oak bark tea was used to stop internal bleeding and reduce fevers. Throughout history, the oak has been revered by many cultures. Northern Europeans believed it was the tree of life and sacred to Thor, the god of thunder. They also used a cluster of oak leaves as a sign of victory or heroics. This symbol is still used in American military decorations.

♂ ELIAS: From the root name *Elijah.*

♂ ELIE: From the root name *Eli.*

♂ ELIHU: From the root name *Elijah.*

♥ ♂ **ELIJAH** **Elias, Elihu, Elliot, Ellis:** *Elijah* is an ancient Hebrew name (originally spelled *Eliyahu*) and is most often believed to mean "Jah (Jehovah) is God." It is also interesting to note that while most names historians agree that in the name *Elijah,* El means "God," they say that *Eli* is an ancient Hebrew word which means "height," or "high." The two are not that far apart. Therefore, *Elijah* might be taken to mean, not only "Ja is God" but also that "Ja is highest." (See also *Eli.*)

The earliest known figure with the name was the Old Testament prophet whom names historian Charlotte Yonge called "the noblest prophet of the kingdom of Israel." He stressed monotheism more than any previous figure in history and is known for chastising Ahab and Jezebel, an action for which he was severely punished. The prophet Elijah is recognized by the Christian faith as well as by the Jewish faith and the Islamic faith. At the Jewish Passover Seder a cup of wine is left for Elijah. The tradition says that Elijah will arrive as an unknown guest and will foretell the arrival of the Messiah. Among Christians, John the Baptist, as another great biblical prophet, is sometimes referred to as Elijah.

The Greek variation of the name is *Elias,* and a figure in the New Testament (which was influenced by the Greeks) is known by that name. The European variations based on the Greek *Elias* were particularly popular during the Middle Ages, when the English *Ellis* as well as the French *Elie* came into use. Unlike many English names, *Ellis* probably did not transform out of the French variation after the Norman Conquest, but came via Holland where the Greek variation, *Elias,* was the one used.

Elijah came into English-speaking use after the Reformation and with the rise in Puritanism, when Old Testament names became extremely widespread. As such it entered the Americas with the Puritan colonists. Like many other names that were popular with the early American colonists, *Elijah* did not remain particularly widespread after the decline of Puritanism.

Though popular use of *Elias* and *Elijah* declined in the nineteenth century, the names remained in the public consciousness through the work of many great novelists of the period. Walter Scott, in his novel *The Abbot* (1820) named a character Elias, as did Anthony Trollope in *Phineas Finn* (1869) and Thomas Hardy in *Under the Greenwood Tree* (1872). Charles Dickens preferred the Hebrew variation when he named a character Elijah in his novel *Martin Chuzzlewit* (1843–44).

An exception to *Elijah*'s decline can be found in the African American community. The name has been popular with African American parents from the seventeenth century through to the present day. In the latter part of the twentieth century, the name has been particularly popular among Black Muslims. This popularity can be directly connected to the late leader of the Nation of Islam, Elijah Muhammad.

The recent general popularity of traditional names has led to *Elijah*'s being among the 100 most popular boys' names in America. *Elliot* is also sometimes thought to be a derivation of *Elijah*, via *Elias* and *Ellis*, but others say the name is derived from *Eli*.

 Number

Nine. Ancient Greek mathematician and numerologist Pythagoras chose nine as the ultimate number. He believed it represented those with virtuous hearts and a passion for justice.

 Astrological sign

Aquarius. Although there is no myth associated with this sign, it has been connected with the god Hapi who is usually represented pouring water from two jars into the Nile River.

 Color

Anthracite. The color of coal shines with divine power. It also represents understanding on the Sephiroth Tree of the Cabala.

 Stone

Obsidian. Some gems are connected to planets. Obsidian is tied to Saturn, a ruling planet of Aquarius. It is also linked to the Aztec deity Tezcatlipoca. The Aztecs made flat square mirrors of obsidian to use for divination or contact with their gods. Obsidian is naturally occurring glass created by volcanic heat. The stone is usually black, but can occur in dark red or navy blue.

 Element

Lodestone. The ancient Assyrians as well as many other ancient civilizations held the powers of lodestone in the highest regard.

Herb

Jerusalem sage *(Pulmoniaria officinalis).* Sometimes referred to as lungwort, this plant grows in shady areas of the northern United States and Europe. Tea made from the flowering herb was found to help respiratory problems including coughs and hoarseness. The funnel-shaped flowers turn from rose to blue with both colors occurring at the same time.

♀ ELISA: From the root name *Elizabeth*.

♀ ELISE: From the root name *Elizabeth*.

♀ ELISSA: From the root name *Alice*.

♀ ELIZA: From the root name *Elizabeth*.

♥ ♀ **ELIZABETH** **Babette, Bess, Beth, Betsy, Bette, Bettina, Bettine, Betty, Buffy, Elan, Elisa, Elise, Eliza, Ellspet, Elsa, Elsie, Elspeth, Ilse, Isabelle, Lib, Libby, Lisa, Lisbette, Lise, Lisette, Liz, Liza, Tibbie, Ylisabette, Ysabel:** No other woman's name has as many variations, diminutives, and nicknames as *Elizabeth* does. The advantage of such a name is that parents can choose a charming diminutive by which to call their daughters when they are small, and at the same time provide a sophisticated—some would say regal—name for their daughters to carry into adulthood. Many of the variants have an obvious linguistic connection, but there is speculation that others came about when young bearers of the name tried to pronounce it. It is known, for example, that Queen Elizabeth II was for years affectionately known as Lilibet, because that is the way she pronounced her own name as a child.

The name *Elizabeth* is of Hebrew origin, first noted as *Elisheba,* who was Aaron's wife. Her name meant "God hath sworn," or "oath of God." In modern etymologies *Elizabeth* is often interpreted as "one who worships God," or "God is her oath." John the Baptist's mother was also named Elischeba and was canonized in the Christian Eastern Orthodox religion. The New Testament account of her meeting with her cousin Mary—when Elisabeth's womb "leapt" as Mary, newly pregnant with Jesus, walked into the room—is among the most cherished stories in the Gospels. Her canonization led to the name's popularity throughout Eastern Europe.

The earliest historical figure named for Saint Elischeba appears to be the Muscovite princess Elisavetta, who became immortalized in nineteen songs by the Norwegian king Harald Hardraade. He composed these songs of praise for the beautiful princess and thereby won her hand. Though she died young, these songs established the name in Scandinavia where it appears in ballads and stories as *Elsebin, Lisbet,* and *Helsa.*

Elizabeth is one of the world's best-traveled names. The Greeks changed the pronunciation of *Elisheba* to *Elisabet,* and that led to the Latin *Elisabeth.* The Russians pronounced the name *Lescinska.* The transformation of *Elisabeth* to *Isabelle* began in the twelfth century, when Elizabeth of Hainaut (now in Belgium) married Philippe Auguste of France and, at her husband's request, changed her name to Isabella. Over time, *Isabelle* has become more popular in France than *Elizabeth,* and there is one French saint, Saint Isabel the Virgin, who almost certainly helped foster the widespread use of the name. *Isabelle* has spawned the pet names *Lisette, Gisella, Babette, Babichon, Babet,* and *Babel.* In Spain and Portugal, as well, *Isabel* or *Ysabel* are still the most popular forms of the name. The Germans are responsible for substituting "z" for the "s" in *Elizabeth,* and that is the version of the name that came to the American colonies with both the Raleigh settlers and the Mayflower settlers. *Elizabeth* is the spelling still most common in England and the United States.

Many famous *Elizabeth*s have helped to keep the name alive and thriving. Among the several saints named *Elizabeth*, Saint Elizabeth of Hungary has perhaps the most colorful history. This thirteenth-century daughter of the King of Hungary fed the poor in her palace, built hospitals, and dressed the wounds of the suffering. She married Ludwig, Landgrave of Thuringia at an early age, and when he died she was driven from his palace with her children, thus experiencing the cold and hunger she had sought to alleviate in others. She died at the age of twenty-four, and stories of miracles surrounding her became legion. Other saints were Saint Elizabeth, niece of Elizabeth of Hungary who became Queen of Portugal, and Saint Elizabeth of Sconauge, who died in 1165 and was said to be a great visionary. The English queens Elizabeth I and II, both popular throughout the world during their reigns, are certainly responsible for the continued popularity of the name in English-speaking nations.

Bess was once among the most popular of *Elizabeth*'s many diminutives, and Bess Truman and Bessie Smith were two famous Elizabeths who used the nickname into adulthood. *Bess* is no longer common, but the old-fashioned nickname *Tess* is heard more and more frequently today. *Betsy* has also been on the decline in the last quarter of the twentieth century, though one of our most famous Americans, Betsy Ross, made the name very popular indeed in the colonial and post-colonial periods. In American traditional culture, the term *betsy* crops up as a generic name for the long rifle. Daniel Boone even named his firearm "Old Betsy," and always spoke of her with warm affection. Her deeds and exploits were almost always mentioned in the tales that grew up around his legend. *Betsy* has frequently been given as an independent name, as has *Eliza*.

Such stars as Liza Minnelli and Bette Midler have the same name roots as Elizabeth Taylor. Among the other nicknames drawn from *Elizabeth* that have enjoyed popularity in the past are *Elsie, Lisa, Betty, Beth, Elspeth, Bella, Bell, Tibbie,* and *Libby, Liz, Lizzy, Ilse* (German), *Bettine* (German) or *Bettina* (Italian), *Babbette* (French), *Elise* (French) and *Liza* (English, Servian and Slovak).

Number

Seven. Many sevens have been writers, painters, or poets. They tend to be somewhat eccentric, and have a unique outlook.

Astrological sign

Virgo. Virgos are no shrinking violets. They face hostility in business or love with a level gaze and their heads held high.

Color

Indigo. This deep shade of blue indicates spirituality when seen in a person's aura.

Stone

Lapis lazuli. Also called lazurite, this royal blue stone is flecked with white and yellow, which is calcite, pyrite, and gold. Ancient lore credits lapis lazuli as a stone of wisdom and love. It was once used to boost psychic abilities.

Element

Gold. Gold is the ore most associated with royalty.

Herb

Cornflower *(Centaurea cyanus).* Commonly called bluebonnet or bluebottle, this plant has large blue flowers that appear from June to August. Traditionally, its flowers were used to make tonics for digestive troubles and for eye-washes.

♀   ELLA: From the root names *Alice* and *Helen*.

♀   ELLEN: From the root name *Helen*.

♀   ELLIE: From the root name *Helen*.

♂   ELLIOT: From the root names *Eli* and *Elijah*.

♂   ELLIS: From the root name *Elijah*.

♀   ELLMA: From the root name *William*.

♀   ELLSPET: From the root name *Elizabeth*.

♂   ELOI: From the root name *Eli*.

♀   ELOISE: From the root name *Louis*.

♂   ELOY: From the root name *Eli*.

♀   ELSA: From the root names *Alice* and *Elizabeth*.

♀   ELSIE: From the root name *Elizabeth*.

♀   ELSPETH: From the root name *Elizabeth*.

♂   ELY: From the root name *Eli*.

♀   EM: From the root names *Emily* and *Emma*.

♀   EMALEE: From the root name *Emily*.

♀   EMELDA: From the root name *Emily*.

♀   EMELINA: From the root name *Emma*.

♀   EMELINE: From the root names *Emily* and *Emma*.

♂   EMIL: From the root name *Emily*.

♀   EMILIA: From the root name *Emily*.

♂   EMILIJ: From the root name *Emily*.

♀   EMILIJA: From the root name *Emily*.

♂   EMILIO: From the root name *Emily*.

♥ ♀ EMILY Amalie, Amalina, Amelia, Em, Emalee, Emelda, Emeline, Emil, Emilia, Emilij, Emilija, Emilio, Emmy, Emyln, Mila, Milica, Milka: The root word *amal* ("work" in Hebrew and in the Teutonic languages) and the Latin name *Aemilian* or *Aemelius* ("flattering" or "witty") seem inextricably linked in the formation of the two currently popular names, *Emily* and *Amelia*.

Many Gothic royal names came from *amal* or a form of that root. Ancient queens of Teutonic lands such as Navarre and the Asturias used *Amelina* and *Simena*. In Hebrew *Amelia* is equivalent to *Eishet Hayyil* meaning "woman of valor." Although there are no exact translations of any Hebrew name, this meaning can be linked to King Solomon's observation on the toils of Jewish women found in Proverbs.

After the Norman Conquest in 1066 masculine forms arose in France as *Amelot* and *Amalric,* in Germany as *Amalrich,* and in Spain as *Almerigo*. The English adopted *Almerick,* and the name *Amaury* belonged to a king of Jerusalem.

German ladies favored *Amalie* and northern Italians liked *Amala*. The French and southern Italians took *Aemilia,* and when that Latinate form mingled with the Teutonic, it finally became *Amelia* in England and *Amelie* in France by the 1600s. *Amelia* did well in the American colonies from the beginning.

As it so often happens in the story of names, literature propels a name to popularity. So it was with Henry Fielding's 1751 novel *Amelia*. Throughout the 1800s, *Amelia* saw regular use and was frequently the top girls' names in the United States, England, and Wales well into the early 1900s. Now considered somewhat dated, it is associated with women born before 1930.

Emily, however, is enjoying immense popularity. Though it seems more rooted to the Roman name *Aemelius* than to

Amal, there is no sensible way to untangle the connection between the two source names. Several early saints of the Christian church took variants of *Aemelius,* and its popularity spread to Eastern Europe and Russia as a result. The masculine *Emilij* has been popular in Russia since the early Middle Ages, and there the feminine forms became *Emilija, Milica, Mila* or *Milka.* The figure who led to the name's widespread popularity in Spain and Italy was a Spanish saint, Aemilianus, who is now known as St. Milhan the hermit. Over time *Aemilianus* transformed into *Emilio,* which for centuries has been an extremely common boy's name in Italy and Spain, and it remains in widespread use among Latinos in the United States. In France, *Emile* became common after Rousseau's hero gained popularity.

The feminine version of the name, *Emilia,* gained popularity in fourteenth-century Italy after the poet and author Boccaccio created the heroine of Teseide. As the popularity of Boccaccio's work spread across Europe, so did the name of his character, Emilia. Here may be where the German and Latin names met. The name *Amalie* had long been popular in Germany. With the arrival of Boccaccio's Emilia, the two names seemed to meld and *Amelia* became the common German form. Also in the fourteenth century in England, Geoffrey Chaucer gave *Emily* to one of the characters in his *Canterbury Tales.* Then, in the eighteenth century, *Emily* was made more popular in England by George II, who commonly referred to his daughter as Princess Emily. In recent surveys of frequently chosen names, *Emily* usually takes first or second place.

Amy is considered a nickname of *Amelia* as well as of *Amanda.* But *Amy* is also often chosen as a name for a girl independent of either name. A charming diminutive for *Emily, Emmy,* is also often used as a diminutive for the name *Emma.*

Number

Five. Individuals of this number are usually energetic. They get along well with others and form many new friendships throughout their lives. Care must be taken not to overachieve, lest they exhaust themselves both mentally and physically.

Astrological sign

Virgo. This is a sign often connected with industrious people. Virgo's element is Earth, which represents the body. Its ruling planet of Mercury brings versatility to an earthy Virgo by adding a dimension of quickness on both the physical and mental levels.

Color

Roan. This lustrous reddish-brown shade is found among many breeds of workhorses. The power of red has aggressive energies and aids physical strength, yet the stable earth tone of brown tempers the zealous lest they become overworked.

Stone

Brown topaz. Topaz has been called the "golden stone" or "fire stone." Topaz means "fire" in Sanskrit. Early physicians believed that topaz could calm stress and restore physical vigor.

Element

Quicksilver. Quicksilver represents the planet Mercury and ties in well with the name Amelia.

Herb

Peppermint *(Mentha piperita).* For millennia, this herb was used for colic and other types of digestive distress. It was also thought to calm heart palpitations and cure insomnia.

Oil of peppermint was distilled by medieval apothecaries to alleviate nausea and peppermint tea is still used today as an herbal remedy for nervous stress.

♥ ♀ **EMMA Em, Emelina, Emeline, Emmalyn, Emmet, Emmott, Emmy:** Though *Emma* has never been particularly popular in the United States, it has been rising in popularity during the 1990s. As a measure of how the fortunes of a name can change, the 1990 census ranked *Emma* at one hundred thirty-fourth in popularity among all living women in the United States, but it is now among the top names chosen by parents for baby girls.

From the Old German word *ermin,* which means "all embracing," *Imma* or *Emma* probably migrated to England with the Norman invasion of 1066. It flourished during the Middle Ages and then fell from grace. Although we tend to associate the name with an earlier period, it was rarely used again until the mid-1800s. It is likely that the Puritans did not like the name because it had no biblical associations, and it was not at all common in colonial America.

There is every reason to think that Jane Austen's witty romance *Emma* (1815) had something to do with the name's revival. Since then, novelists and poets have loved the name, and most assuredly have contributed to its popularity. Emma is the main character, for example, in Flaubert's controversial and widely read *Madame Bovary* (1856). *Emma* reached the height of fashion in England in the 1960s, and is now making a steady climb up the charts in the United States. The current revival may reflect a combination of the trend toward using old-fashioned sounding names and the recent cinematic interpretations of Austen's *Emma*.

According to Dunkling and Gosling, the widespread use of *Emma* in the Middle Ages spawned the surname *Emmet,* which subsequently has become a first name for boys. *Emmet* is uncommon—but not unheard of—in the United States today.

🌀 Number

Five. Fives enjoy people and are usually witty and unerringly positive.

🌙 Astrological sign

Cancer. Most born under this sign have affectionate natures and romantic souls. However, they are extremely protective of their loved ones.

✳ Color

Moonlit rose. Silver-pink is created when moonbeams embrace red roses on a summer night.

◆ Stone

Pink pearl. According to ancient Eastern myths, anyone who wears a pearl will enjoy good fortune. In early Saxon religious lore, pearls were thought to be the tears of the goddess Freya, and an ancient Syrian goddess was called the Lady of Pearls. Mystics of yore suggested that dreaming of pearls meant someone had or would soon meet a faithful friend. Ancient Hindu lore believed that the moon was a feminine entity. Red-tinted pearls were believed to stimulate intellect.

👑 Element

Silver. Silver is metaphysically connected to the moon. Since it is found and used in pure form, it was one of the first ores ever used by humans.

Herb

Emetic herb *(Lobelia inflata)*. This indigenous Native American plant has beautiful blue flowers. The plant has medicinal value and was used to treat asthma and whooping cough. External preparations included poultices for bruises, insect bites, sprains, and poison oak or ivy. Caution is advised as overuse of this herb can cause harmful reactions.

♀ EMMALYN: From the root name *Emma*.

♂ EMMET: From the root name *Emma*.

♂ EMMOTT: From the root name *Emma*.

♀ EMMY: From the root names *Emily* and *Emma*.

♀ EMYLN: From the root name *Emily*.

♀ ENGRACIA: From the root name *Grace*.

♀ ENRICHETTA: From the root name *Henry*.

♂ ENRICO: From the root name *Henry*.

♂ ENRIQUE: From the root name *Henry*.

♂ ENZIO: From the root name *Henry*.

♥ ♂ **ERIC** **Airika, Erica, Erich, Erik, Erika, Eryk, Eyrica, Rick, Rickie, Ricky:** Of all the Scandinavian names that traveled to the United States during mass immigration of the nineteenth century, *Eric* has been the one to make its way into the general population and stay there. It has ranked consistently high on all historical lists, and hit the top ten in 1975. It is still among the top fifty names parents choose for their boys.

Eric is Old Norse and means "powerful ruler" or "complete ruler." It is as ancient as the Norse culture, with its most famous bearer being the great Viking conqueror Erik the Red.

Since in the Scandinavian cultures children were given their father's first name as a surname—with the suffix -son or -datter added—Erickson is a common surname wherever Scandinavians have immigrated. As a first name, it entered the United Kingdom from Denmark but languished until 1858 when, all historians agree, the publication of *Eric, or, Little by Little,* by Frederic Farrar boosted it to enormous popularity. The feminine form, *Erica,* has been a continuous favorite since the mid-nineteenth century as well, both in England and the United States. Never quite as widespread as *Eric, Erica* currently is among the top one hundred names for girls.

Eric is frequently spelled *Erik,* and *Erica* is often spelled *Erika.* Boys might eventually acquire the nickname *Rick,* though it is more often associated with *Richard* or *Frederick.* Girls are sometimes called by the diminutive *Rickie.*

Number
Eight. People of this number can accomplish the impossible. Eights usually have strong ideals and the discipline to live up to them.

Astrological sign
Aries. Many Ariens are natural leaders. They are unafraid to explore new ways and ideas. Musician Eric Clapton, writer Erica Jong, and actor Eric Roberts are Ariens.

Color
Royal scarlet. Red symbolizes courage and was worn by ancient warlords and rulers.

Stone
Dichroite. This deep violet-blue gem is sometimes mistaken for a sapphire after it's been cut and polished. Like the sap-

phire, dichroite is a durable gem and makes beautiful jewelry. According to legend, the Vikings used dichroite for navigation. They called it a "sun stone" because it appeared clear when viewed in the direction of the sun, even on cloudy days, therefore providing direction. Gem-quality pebbles come from river deposits in Myanmar and India. Dichroite crystals are found in Norway and Finland.

 ## Element

Magnesium. Magnesium is a light silvery, metallic element found in dichroite.

Herb

Norway spruce *(Picea abies)*. This evergreen is native to central and northern Europe. A lukewarm tea made from the young shoots was helpful against coughs and flu symptoms. Inhaling hot vapors from a boiling tea was a treatment for bronchitis. Norway spruce has scaly reddish brown bark and yellow or red male flowers that bloom in April and May. The female flowers are bright purple.

♀ ERICA: From the root name *Eric*.

♂ ERICH: From the root names *Eric* and *Frederick*.

♂ ERICO: From the root name *Frederick*.

♂ ERIK: From the root name *Eric*.

♀ ERIKA: From the root name *Eric*.

♀♂ **ERIN** **Eire, Eiryn, Erina, Erynn:** What does *Erin* have in common with *Shannon, Kelly,* and *Ryan*? They are all Irish names that are rarely, if ever, used in Ireland. Erin comes from the old Gaelic word *Eireann,* meaning "western island" and from an ancient clan called the Erainn that inhabited modern-day Ireland. *Erin* does appear in Irish poetry as a personification of the country. But it is seldom used as a given name, probably because no queens, saints, or literary figures were ever called *Erin*.

Irish appellations began sweeping the United States beginning about 1980. Name books published in the previous decade rarely contained entries for names such as *Erin* and *Ryan*. But by 1980, *Erin* ranked as the twentieth most popular name given to girls. (*Ryan* was sixteenth for boys.) *Erin* has lost ground since then, but is still considered fashionable. The United States Census counted it as the 160th most popular name for all women and girls in 1990, indicating its steady usage for the previous ten years.

 Number

One. Determination is a characteristic common to most ones.

☾ Astrological sign

Cancer. While gentle-natured, Cancers can be fierce when it comes to their offsprings' protection. Most Cancers find peace by the sea.

✳ Color

Sterling. Any shade of silver is linked to Cancer and its celestial ruler, the moon.

◆ Stone

Silver lace onyx. Onyx appears in different shades and patterns. Silver lace onyx is usually a darker hue and has lacy silver threads running through it. Onyx was believed to be a guardian stone and worn when confronting enemies or conflicts of any kind. In ceremonial magic, the image of the god

Mars or the mighty Hercules was carved on a piece of onyx and either worn or carried for courage. When someone dreamed of an onyx it was supposed to mean a continued happy marriage or the meeting of a faithful future partner.

 Element

Silver. Using silver as a setting for the silver lace onyx gem not only highlights the silver lace, but also offers support for its protective abilities.

🦂 Herb

Eryngo *(Eryngium maritinum).* Sometimes called sea holly, eryngo likes sandy soil. The root has curative properties and was used in various ways. Traditional English herbal lore suggests that if the roots were eaten, liver ailments, cramps, and convulsions would be cured. Also, root preparations worked well against persistent coughs and bronchitis.

♀   ERINA: From the root name *Erin.*

♂   ERYK: From the root name *Eric.*

♀   ERYNN: From the root name *Erin.*

♂   ESTEBAN: From the root name *Stephen.*

♂   ESTEVAN: From the root name *Stephen.*

♂   ETAN: From the root name *Ethan.*

♀   ETANA: From the root name *Ethan.*

♥ ♂ **ETHAN**   **Etan, Etana:** While historians agree that *Ethan* comes from the Hebrew name *Eythan,* there are a few different opinions as to what the name actually means. Most say it means "firm," "perennial," or "constant," but

251

others believe that it means "old" or "ancient." The former definition of the name has led to the belief that it was, first, a word that referred to streams that never go dry—an important source of water in a perpetually dry climate such as is found throughout the Middle East. The latter definition of *Ethan* leads to the theory that it was used as an honorific for an old man. Whatever the name's original meaning, the first record of it is in the Old Testament, where the name appears in the title of Psalm 89. Ethan the Ezrahite is also a periphery character in the Old Testament Book of Kings, where he is mentioned as not being as wise as Solomon.

Like many Old Testament names, *Ethan* was probably brought into use by the Puritans in the seventeenth century, but, surprisingly, it was not among the most popular early American names. Ethan Allen, leader of the Green Mountain Boys during the American Revolution, certainly helped the name's more widespread use in the late eighteenth century, but use of *Ethan* declined in the late nineteenth century.

In spite of the fact that it was never widely used in America, *Ethan* does enjoy the connotation of an "old American name," and, as such, it began to rise in popularity from the 1960s on, along with other traditional and biblical names such as *Caleb, Eli, Joshua,* and *Jesse.*

Number
Three. Some numerologists equate the number three with action. Threes are often at the head of the pack or in a position of honor.

Astrological sign
Virgo. Among Virgo's many positive qualities, unswerving commitment to high ideals ranks highest.

Color

Verdigris. The green blush of a mountainside in spring inspires peace.

 ## Stone

Hiddenite. Emerald-colored hiddenite is a variety of spodumene. Its brilliant color comes from the mineral chromium. This gem is popular with collectors but its fragility makes it difficult to facet. Hiddenite was named after W.E. Hidden, who unearthed the first known specimen in North Carolina in 1879.

 ## Element

Aluminum. Modern mystics use small pieces of aluminum to enhance mental abilities.

Herb

American elder *(Sambucus canadensis)*. There are several varieties of elder. American elder is a shrub that grows in damp areas, particularly in the eastern and central United States. The roots, bark, leaf buds, leaves, and flowers were all used in various healing preparations. Some Native Americans used root-bark tea for headaches, congestion, and to stimulate labor in childbirth. The dried berries were made into tea and believed to help fight cholera. American elder produces a dark purple berry that can be cooked and used in pies or jams. However, all parts of the fresh plant are poisonous and must be cooked or dried before using.

♂   ETIENNE: From the root name *Stephen*.

♀   ETTA: From the root name *Henry*.

♀   ETTY: From the root name *Henry*.

♥ ♂ **EUGENE** **Eugenia, Eugenio, Eugenius, Evennia, Evgeny, Geena, Gene, Gina, Jeena, Jenna, Jennie:** *Eugene* is from the Greek, and means "well born." One of the oldest known bearers of the name was *Eugenes,* the ancient Greek author. The most common ancient Greek spelling, however, was *Eugenios,* which became *Eugenius* when adopted by the Romans.

There were four popes named Eugenius. The first, who died in 657, was canonized and is sometimes called "an African Confessor." There was also a Eugenius who was a bishop of Toledo, Spain in 646. He is thought to have helped the name's popularity in Spain and Italy in the form *Eugenio.*

The popularity of *Eugenio* in Italy led to the naming of Prince Eugene of Savoy (Austria, Holy Roman Empire), who was descended, on his mother's side, from Roman stock. Rumored to be the illegitimate son of Louis XIV—who always denied it—Eugene became a soldier for Leopold I. Later, he fought on behalf of Joseph I and Charles VI. He taught Frederick the Great, and was the only military strategist Napoleon ever considered worth studying. He fought both the Turks and the French from 1697 through 1718.

Through his fame as a great military leader, Eugene did more than any other figure to popularize the name across Europe and England. The Eastern Europeans and Russians became attached to the name—spelled *Jevjenij or Djoulija*—because Eugene held back the Turkish hordes. The French favored the name because he was an admirable foe. The English came to the name largely through Eugene's close friend the Duke of Marlborough, who named a son after him.

Shortly after Prince Eugene brought the name such renown, however, there was a much more notorious Eugene alive in England. It is possible that the negative connotations connected to the noted scholar and murderer Eugene Aram (1704–1759) blunted some of the name's popularity in

England. His exploits were romanticized in a ballad by Thomas Hood and in the novel *Eugene Aram* (1832) by Bulwer-Lytton.

Earlier British references to *Eugene* or *Eugenius* can be somewhat problematic. The early Scottish kings listed as *Eugenius* were probably *Eoghan, Ewan,* or *Evan,* which has no relation to *Eugenius*. In Ireland, *Eugene* came to be considered the English form for the Celtic *Eoin,* which is actually *John*. By the nineteenth century, however, few remembered the original connection.

From the mid-nineteenth century through the early twentieth, *Eugene* developed into quite a popular name in both England and America. (In 1875, it was among the top twenty names in the United States.) Among the famous American *Eugene*s born during that period were Eugene O'Neill and Eugene Debs. By the mid-twentieth century, the diminutive, *Gene,* had come into use as an independent name.

Far less common than either *Eugene* or *Gene* is the feminine form *Eugenia*. There was one Saint Eugenia, a Roman woman who was converted in the third century by Saints Protus and Hyacinthus and became a virgin martyr. There were also a few recorded *Eugenia*s in England in the twelfth and thirteenth centuries. The French form, *Eugénie,* was made famous through Emperor Napoleon III's wife. Some trace the Irish usage of *Eugenia* to *Eughania,* the feminine form of the Erse name *Eoghan*. Dunkling and Gosling, authors of *The Facts on File Dictionary of First Names,* report that *Eugenia* has been "regularly but quietly used in English-speaking countries since the mid-nineteenth century."

◎ Number

Three. Some of the classical gods are associated with the number three, including Mars, the Roman god of war. Many numerologists believe three personifies people of action.

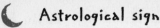 ## Astrological sign

Leo. This leonine sign is the sign of the "well born." In the constellation of Leo there is a star called Regulus and the ancients believed it was the monarch of celestial beings.

Color

Spanish ocher. A hot shade of orange to stoke a Leo when his internal embers are low.

Stone

Titanite. Titanite is referred to as sphene by gemologists. This exquisite transparent stone has strong "fire"—even more than a diamond. However, its fragility makes it a challenge to cut for jewelry and it's more of a serious collector's item. Titanite should not be confused with a synthetic stone called titania that is manufactured to imitate diamonds.

Element

Titanium. Titanium is the best metal to lend strength to the desirable yet delicate titanite stone.

Herb

Cloves (*Eugenia aromatica*). While clove may be most familiar as an aromatic baking spice, it has been used medicinally for centuries. Early dentists discovered clove oil stopped toothaches and its antiseptic ability helped prevent infections. Healers also found a few drops of clove oil in water stopped vomiting and clove tea dispelled nausea. The outside shell of the flower bud turns from yellow to red when dried. This part is either used whole as a spice or ground into powder. Clove trees grow mainly in the Spice Islands.

♀   EUGENIA: From the root name *Eugene*.

♂   EUGENIO: From the root name *Eugene*.

♂   EUGENIUS: From the root name *Eugene*.

♀   EVA: From the root name *Eve*.

♂   EVAN: From the root name *John*.

♥ ♀ **EVE** Aoiffe, Eba, Eva, Evelina, Evelyn, Evetta, Evie, Evika, Evita, Evonne, Evvy, Yvonne: The names *Eve* and *Eva* are from the Hebrew and mean "life" or "life-giving." Originally, the name probably sounded more like "chavva." *Eve* is also, of course, the name ascribed to the first woman in the Old Testament Book of Genesis. She is the only woman in the Bible to bear that name. It is believed that the Jews of Alexandria, while translating earlier versions of the Bible, were the ones who transformed the name into *Eva*. The importance of *Eve* as a Biblical character is the only explanation needed for the name's continued use throughout history. Yet *Eve* has not always traveled lightly over the world.

For many years, parents in Germany and Scandinavia maintained the popular belief that naming a child either *Adam* or *Eva* would help to protect it. Therefore the name became very popular in those countries and in Eastern Europe, as well. In Ireland *Eva* was easily connected to the Erse name *Aioffe,* and thus it prospered. In England, however (where the name became *Eve*), it has always been less popular. This is probably thanks to the negative connotations associated with the biblical Eve and her culpability in man's expulsion from paradise. Despite the namesake's bad reputation, *Eve* did not completely disappear in Britain, and there are even some recorded incidences of male and female twins being christened *Adam* and *Eve*.

Both *Eve* and *Eva* were used rarely in the American

colonies. Unsurprisingly, they do not appear at all among the early Puritans who avoided names associated with bad behavior. *Eva* gained some popularity in the late nineteenth century, after Harriet Beecher Stowe wrote *Uncle Tom's Cabin* and named the novel's heroine "little Eva." In the twentieth century the names have not fared well in either American history or popular culture. To most Americans, the most famous twentieth century *Eva* is Eva Braun, Hitler's mistress—not a happy connotation. In popular culture, the two most famous *Eve*s come from film titles: *The Three Faces of Eve* and *All About Eve*. While the films are both brilliant, neither offers a vision of happy women.

There has been a slight increase in the use of *Eve* and *Eva* in recent years, with the first "e" in *Eva* pronounced variously as a long *e* and as a long *a*. The name has been blended with *Lynn* to form *Evelyn*. Though *Evelyn* is not currently in vogue, it was a favorite in the mid-twentieth century and many women bear the name.

◎ Number
Five. This number represents people who are multifaceted, but can be broody. Fives have no trouble making and keeping friendships, but can't be tied down for long as they become restive.

☾ Astrological sign
Cancer. While the symbol of this sign is a crustacean, most Cancers are empathetic and loving beneath their tough shell. Cancers love their homes and show great respect for their mothers.

✴ Color
Aquagreen. The colors of blue for the sea and green for fertility make this a perfect shade for *Eve, Eva* or *Evelyn*.

Stone

Opal. Some say opals are the oldest gemstones formed from water and crystalline rock. Most are a milky color, but all have a rainbow iridescence. Legends call the opal "Eve of the Gods" or "Cupid Stone," linking it to the ancient deity Cupid. Opals are worn by modern mystics during astral projection and some say this gem's power can help recall someone's past incarnations.

 Element

Silver: This soft whitish metal supports intuition and is a perfect setting for an opal.

Herb

Birthroot *(Trillium pendulum).* This herb has many folk names including coughroot and jew's-harp plant. Among traditional healers, the rootstock of this herb was used for coughs, bronchitis, and even bleeding in the lungs. They also found a salve of birthroot was effective on insect bites and bee stings.

♀   EVELINA: From the root name *Eve*.

♀   EVELYN: From the root names *Eve* and *Lynn*.

♀   EVENNIA: From the root name *Eugene*.

♀   EVETTA: From the root name *Eve*.

♂   EVGENY: From the root name *Eugene*.

♀   EVIE: From the root name *Eve*.

♀   EVIKA: From the root name *Eve*.

♀   EVITA: From the root name *Eve*.

♀   EVONNE: From the root name *Eve*.

♀   EVVY: From the root name *Eve*.

♂   EWART: From the root name *Edward*.

♀   EYRICA: From the root name *Eric*.

♀   FANNIE: From the root name *Francis*.

♀   FARICA: From the root name *Frederick*.

♂   FEDERICO: From the root name *Frederick*.

♂   FEDOR: From the root name *Theodore*.

♀   FEDORA: From the root name *Theodore*.

♀   FELIPA: From the root name *Philip*.

♂   FELIPE: From the root name *Philip*.

♂   FELIPPO: From the root name *Philip*.

♂   FERENC: From the root name *Francis*.

♂   FERI: From the root name *Francis*.

♀   FIFI: From the root name *Joseph*.

♂   FILIP: From the root name *Philip*.

♀♂ FRAN: From the root name *Francis*.

♀   FRANCES: From the root name *Francis*.

♀   FRANCESCA: From the root name *Francis*.

♂   FRANCESCO: From the root name *Francis*.

♀   FRANCETTA: From the root name *Francis*.

♂   FRANCHOT: From the root name *Francis*.

♀   FRANCINE: From the root name *Francis*.

♥ ♀♂ **FRANCIS**   Chico, Fannie, Ferenc, Feri, Fran, Frances, Francesca, Francesco, Francetta, Franchot, Francine,

Francisco, Franco, François, Franio, Frank, Frankie, Franny, Frants, Franz, Frasco, Frascuelo, Pacho, Paco, Pancho, Paquito: Interestingly, the name *Francis* derives from the term "Frank," which of course, later became a nickname for *Francis*. Not originally a name of a person at all, the Franks were a Germanic tribe, which in the ninth century dominated the areas of Western Europe that now include France, Germany, and Italy. Later the tribe's empire was split. The northern area became the former German duchy of Franconia and part of the Holy Roman Empire. The southern area of the empire—peopled by Gallo-Romans who, over time, peacefully regained power—retained at least one element of the Franks, the name of their country, France. The term frank either originally came from the Teutonic for free lord, *frang,* or came from the tribe's own word for javelin, *franca.* All the various versions are now taken to mean "free."

The name of the tribe is the origin for the proper names that then developed throughout Western Europe. Most of the proper names probably started out as a generic term for "Frenchman" or "Frank." Among the different variations, there is *François* (m) and *Françoise* (f) from France, *Francisco* (m) from Spain and Portugal, *Franz* from Germany, and *Francesco* or *Franco* from Italy, as well as the English versions *Francis* (m) and *Frances* (f). Though there were probably people named *Francesco* or *Franciscus* prior to the advent of the Italian Saint Francis of Assisi (1182–1226), he is, historically speaking, the first important person to bear that name. He is still possibly the most famous. Ironically, his baptismal name was Giovanni. His father, in training him to become a merchant, had him learn French, and his proficiency in the language earned him the nickname *il Francesco* (the Frenchman). While a priest, he was known as Francesco, and he was canonized under the name Franciscus. His order of monks quickly became known as the Franciscans.

Though present in France, the name *François* didn't become commonplace there until the reign of François I, who ruled France from 1515 through 1547. Another *François* was the last emperor of the Holy Roman Empire (as François II) as well as the first emperor of Austria (as François I). The name remained popular throughout the history of the Austro-Hungarian Empire down through Emperor Franz Joseph and his unfortunate nephew Franz Ferdinand, whose assassination sparked World War I.

Francis came into use in England after the Norman Conquest in 1066. At first the word was just a nickname meaning "Frenchman." After Saint Francis of Assisi gained fame, it became more popular as a proper name in England. Among the name's more aristocratic bearers were Francis Drake (1540–1596) and Francis Bacon (1561–1626). It traveled with the English colonists (both Puritan and otherwise) to America. However, the name did not survive among the Puritans once they landed and became rare among other English colonists as well.

By the nineteenth century *Francis* was again popular in the United States, but it became used more commonly as a girl's name. By the end of the nineteenth century parents were differentiating between the genders by spelling their daughters' names with an "e" and not an "i." Despite the attempt to differentiate between the masculine and feminine names, public opinion continued to favor the name as feminine, and though some parents continued to name their boys *Francis* and call them *Fran* or *Frank,* more parents began naming their boys *Frank* independent of *Francis.* Even famous men formally named *Francis,* such as Francis Sinatra, went by the more masculine *Frank. Fran* and *Franny* were, for a time, popular diminutives for the feminine name and *Francine* was a popular variation. In Spanish speaking countries, the name *Francesco* took on the nicknames *Paco* and *Pacho,* which evolved into individual names.

◉ Number

Seven. Sevens often have great influence over others. They are also intelligent and succeed through the use of their wits. Many love to read anything about travel and have an avid interest in world civilizations.

☽ Astrological sign

Aquarius. Although the symbol of Aquarius is the water carrier, it is an air sign that represents the mind. Sir Francis Bacon was an Aquarius.

❋ Color

Sienna. This rich brownish red shade promotes stability and vitality, a good color to keep breezy Aquarians going, but not too far above the earth.

◆ Stone

Brown aventurine quartz. This member of the quartz family has small crystals that mirror light and emit various colors. The mineral pyrite found in this particular aventurine quartz gives it a brownish hue. Aventurine quartz gems can be found in the United States, Brazil, India, and Tanzania.

⩊ Element

Pyrite. Commonly called "fools gold," pyrite is a mineral often found near veins of real gold.

⚘ Herb

Frankincense *(Boswellia thurifera).* Frankincense is the hardened honey-brown gum resin of a tree that grows in Saudi Arabia and Somalia. It was one of the four scents used in Jewish ceremonial incense. Early Romans burned it on state occasions, while some of the wealthier citizens used it at home. Kohl, a black powder used by ancient Egyptian women as make-up, was made of charred frankincense.

♂ FRANCISCO: From the root name *Francis*.

♂ FRANCO: From the root name *Francis*.

♂ FRANÇOIS: From the root name *Francis*.

♂ FRANIO: From the root name *Francis*.

♀♂ FRANK: From the root name *Francis*.

♀♂ FRANKIE: From the root name *Francis*.

♀ FRANNY: From the root name *Francis*.

♂ FRANTS: From the root name *Francis*.

♂ FRANZ: From the root name *Francis*.

♂ FRASCO: From the root name *Francis*.

♂ FRASCUELO: From the root name *Francis*.

♀♂ FRED: From the root name *Frederick*.

♀ FREDA: From the root name *Frederick*.

♀ FREDALENA: From the root name *Frederick*.

♀♂ FREDDIE: From the root name *Frederick*.

♀ FREDERICA: From the root name *Frederick*.

♥ ♂ **FREDERICK Erich, Erico, Farica, Federico, Fred, Freda, Fredalena, Freddie, Frederica, Frederico, Fredrika, Fridrick, Frieda, Friedel, Friedrich, Fritz, Fritzchen, Fritzi, Rica, Rick, Ricky:** The name *Frederick* is the English variation of the German name *Friedrich*. *Friedrich*, in turn, is the modern variation of the ancient Teutonic name *Frithuric*, which is derived from two Teutonic words, *frithu*, which means "peace" and *ric* (or *ricju*), which means "ruler." For centuries *Friedrich* was both a royal name and an extremely popular name in Germany, as was its diminutive, *Fritz*.

In England, though it was rare, the Anglo-Saxon variation *Freodhoric* was used. The medieval census, the Domesday Book, reports one *Fredericus*, the Latin variation of the name. The Norman conquerors probably introduced the medieval French variation of the name *Frery* (or *Ferry*) to England in the eleventh century, which was used in England for the next few hundred years.

The true popularity of the British *Frederick*, however, began in the eighteenth century with the importation of the German Hanovarian monarchs to England. King George II's son was Frederick, Prince of Wales. In this way, Frederick became a royal British name and was therefore widely adopted by commoners all over the country.

The Americans, understandably, were less fond of the new British monarchs and *Frederick* did not come into common use in America until after the Revolution. In 1810, the name appears on the lists of Harvard students and by mid-century, after a large German immigration to America, it had reached the top ten among the attendees of that university. By the late nineteenth century, it was among the most popular boys' names in most English-speaking countries.

Though *Frederick* suffered in the United States during the two world wars, it has remained in use. It was the forty-second most popular name in 1925, and its diminutive *Fred* was thirty-fifth. By 1950, *Fred* was no longer in the top fifty, but Frederick had risen to thirty-eighth. By 1970, however, *Frederick* had dropped out of the top fifty boys' names in the United States, and now the name is no longer even among the top one hundred.

Boys and men named *Frederick* are frequently called by the short form *Fred*. The diminutive is *Freddy* or *Freddie*. Occasionally the nickname *Rick* is derived from *Frederick*. A variant for girls and women, *Frieda* (or *Freda*), was sometimes given to American girls up until about 1950, but it has always been rare.

Number
Seven. Sevens often have great influence over others. They find success through the use of their wits.

Astrological sign
Libra. Libras are born peacemakers. True to their symbol of the scales, Librans strive for balance and accord.

Color
Violet hydrangea. Purple is a color of psychic equilibrium. Hydrangeas are one of the flowers tied to Libra.

Stone
Lepidolite. This brilliant lilac stone is also known as the Stone of Peace in gemological lore. It is a lithium-rich gemstone that is exotic-looking and fragile. It can occur in two and three-foot pieces with streaks of pink tourmaline crystals. Lepidolite was believed to soothe anger. New Agers consider it to be a calming stone and use it to relieve stress.

Element
Gold. In Druidic rituals, gold was used to protect the wearer from ill health and dark enchantments.

Herb
German elder *(Sambucus nigra)*. Elder's root, bark, shoots, leaves, flowers, and fruit were all used for various curative

properties. Teas made from the flowers eased cold symptoms and some rheumatic aches. Leaf tea was brewed to treat kidney problems.

♂ FREDERICO: From the root name *Frederick*.

♀ FREDRIKA: From the root name *Frederick*.

♂ FRIDRICK: From the root name *Frederick*.

♀ FRIEDA: From the root name *Frederick*.

♂ FRIEDEL: From the root name *Frederick*.

♂ FRIEDRICH: From the root name *Frederick*.

♂ FRITZ: From the root name *Frederick*.

♂ FRITZCHEN: From the root name *Frederick*.

♂ FRITZI: From the root name *Frederick*.

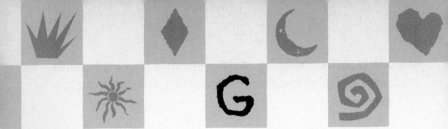

♀♂ GABBY: From the root name *Gabriel*.

♂ GABE: From the root name *Gabriel*.

♥ ♂ **GABRIEL** **Gabby, Gabe, Gabriella, Gabrielle, Gabriello, Gaby, Gavra, Gavriel, Gavrielle, Gavrilo:** *Gabriel* comes from the Hebrew name *Gavri'el* and is said to mean "hero of God" or "God is my strength" or "mighty God." In Arabic the name is *Gibra'il, Jabra'il,* or *Jibril.* The best-known figure to bear the name—the archangel Gabriel—is also responsible for the name's enduring popularity in the Jewish, Christian, and Islamic religious traditions. Gabriel brought messages from God to Daniel, Zacharias, and the Virgin Mary. He is also said to be the one who will blow the trumpet on Judgment Day.

From the fame of, and love for, the archangel grew the adoption of his name throughout Europe, for both boys and girls. *Gabriel* and the feminine variations *Gabrielle* and *Gabriella* were particularly popular in France and Italy. The variations *Gabel* or *Gabell* were used in England during the Middle Ages, though they were never particularly common names.

The name did not join the large number of Old Testament names adopted in the seventeenth century by the Puritans, perhaps because of the angel's connection to the Virgin Mary and *Gabriel*'s popularity among Catholics. Obviously, English-speaking Protestants overcame their prejudice against the name by the eighteenth century when the name became more widespread in the English-speaking world.

During the nineteenth century, various writers, including Walter Scott, Charles Dickens, Wilkie Collins, and Thomas Hardy, kept the name in the public consciousness by including characters named *Gabriel* in their novels. In addition, nineteenth-century free Africans in America were extremely fond of the name. This popularity among African Americans is probably linked not only to a fondness for biblical names in general, but also to the fame of Gabriel Prosser, who in 1800 planned the largest slave revolt in American history. Despite the fact that the revolt was unsuccessful, Prosser became a hero to enslaved and free blacks throughout America.

In the twentieth century *Gabriel* again became rare and it was not until the 1940s that the name had a small revival. The renewed interest in *Gabriel* during this time might be linked to the increase in use of the feminine *Gabrielle*, but there is no known reason for the growth of either name during that period. Similarly, it is unknown why the French form, *Gabriella*, suddenly became more fashionable in English-speaking countries during the 1950s. By the 1990s *Gabriel*, *Gabrielle*, and *Gabriella* were among the most popular children's names in the country. For both boys and girls, the diminutives *Gabe*, *Gabby*, and *Gabey* add to the names' charm.

 Number

Nine. Nines are sometimes linked to strife, but their fight is for justice. A nine will never lack courage to defend the truth.

☾ Astrological sign

Aries. Many Aries are natural leaders. Dedication and bravery are top qualities in those born under this sign.

❋ Color

Platinum. This silvery shade of white symbolizes spiritual grace. Ancient Druids believed white was the high emblem of purity.

◆ Stone

White celestine. Sometimes called celestite, this crystalline gem is beautiful when cut and polished. Ancient mystics believed that celestine had magical qualities and they carried it to promote compassion. Others revered celestine because they felt it possessed the power to heal. While the stone is not common, gem-quality crystals are found in Madagascar.

♛ Element

Brass. Brass is tied to the element of fire and considered a metal of positive energy. It's also used to make musical instruments, including the trumpet.

♘ Herb

High angelica *(Angelica atropurpurea)*. This plant appears in herbal lore as archangel or wild archangel. There are several varieties of angelica, and this type grows in fields and damp areas. The rootstock, roots, and seeds are used in healing preparations for heartburn, colic, and other digestive troubles. Root tea was found to increase appetite. Salves were made for skin lotions and to relieve pain from rheumatism.

♀ GABRIELLA: From the root name *Gabriel*.

♀ GABRIELLE: From the root name *Gabriel*.

♂ GABRIELLO: From the root name *Gabriel*.

♀♂ GABY: From the root name *Gabriel*.

♀ GAIL: From the root name *Abigail*.

♀ GAILA: From the root name *Abigail*.

♀ GALINA: From the root name *Helen*.

♂ GARETH: From the root name *Gerald*.

♂ GARRETT: From the root name *Gerald*.

♂ GARRIN: From the root name *Gerald*.

♂ GARY: From the root name *Gerald*.

♂ GAULTIER: From the root name *Walter*.

♂ GAUTHIER: From the root name *Walter*.

♀ GAVRA: From the root name *Gabriel*.

♂ GAVRIEL: From the root name *Gabriel*.

♀ GAVRIELLE: From the root name *Gabriel*.

♂ GAVRILO: From the root name *Gabriel*.

♀ GAYEL: From the root name *Abigail*.

♀♂ GAYLE: From the root name *Abigail*.

♀ GEENA: From the root name *Eugene*.

♀ GEENIA: From the root name *Virginia*.

♀ GELYA: From the root name *Angela*.

♀ GEMMA: From the root name *Jacob/James*.

♀ GENA: From the root name *Jennifer*.

♀♂ GENE: From the root names *Eugene* and *John*.

♀ GENEVIEVE: From the root name *Jennifer*.

♀ GENNA: From the root name *Jennifer*.

♀ GENNIE: From the root name *Jennifer*.

♀ GENNIFER: From the root name *Jennifer*.

♂ GEOFF: From the root name *Geoffrey*.

♥ ♂ **GEOFFREY** Geoff, Godfrey, Jeff, Jefferies, Jeffers, Jeffrey, Jeoffroi: Names experts agree that the name

Geoffrey (and hence its variant, *Jeffrey*) comes from the Old German, but no one is really sure which of its three possible derivations is the correct one. Medieval records show forms as varied as *Gaudfrid* (meaning "land peace"), *Walafrid* ("traveler's peace"), and *Gisfrid* ("pledge of peace").

But some trace the name back to *Gottfrid* ("God's peace"), which became the French *Godefroi;* then the English *Godfrey;* and eventually, *Geoffrey*. If one traces the development along these lines, then Gottfried of Lorraine— also called Godfrey of Bouillon (1060–1100)—is the man most credited with spreading the name throughout Europe. A leader of the First Crusade, he also became the first European ruler in Palestine upon the defeat of Jerusalem in 1099. Although he was not popular with the other crusaders, he became a legend back in Europe, where he was considered to be a paragon of Christian knighthood. His name spread along with his fame, and numerous variations arose. In Italy he became *Giotto;* in Spain, he was *Godofredo;* and in Poland he was *Godfrid*.

Geoffroi was a very noble name among the French during the Middle Ages. In the eleventh century, Geoffroi of Preully is said to have invented the medieval tournament. In the early twelfth century, Geoffroi de Villehardouin wrote a famous eyewitness account of the Fourth Crusade.

Geoffroi traveled with the Normans to England during the eleventh century and became *Geoffrey* or sometimes *Jeffrey*. The first royal Plantagenet was Geoffrey of Anjou, married to Queen Matilda in the mid-twelfth century, and father of Henry II. However, the name did not become popular among succeeding British royals. Other famous British bearers of the name are Geoffrey of Monmouth (d.1154), who wrote the *History of the Kings of Britain* and Geoffrey Chaucer (c.1342–1400), who wrote *The Canterbury Tales*. From the twelfth through the fifteenth or sixteenth centuries, the name was very common in Britain. After the sixteenth century, however, it became less popular until the late nineteenth century.

Its non-biblical background, in addition to its loss of popularity, meant that Geoffrey did not initially travel well as a first name to the American colonies. However, in the reverse of the usual shift from surname to first name, *Geoffrey*—as its variant *Jeffrey*—had been transformed into various surnames, including *Jefferson, Jeffreys,* and *Jeffers,* during the Middle Ages, and these did make their way across the ocean. The name has had a resurgence of popularity since 1960, and is now one of the top one hundred American boys' names.

 ## Number

Three. People of this number enjoy their freedom. Three is the most divine number in many cultures.

 ## Astrological sign

Pisces. Few Pisceans can stand to be confined to one place for long. They aren't afraid to dive into the stream of life, for most know how to swim in any direction.

 ## Color

Dove gray. For centuries, the dove has been a sign of peace. This soothing bluish gray shade goes well with *Jeffrey*'s history.

Stone

Aquamarine. Once considered a sacred stone, aquamarines are a pale blue transparent crystalline gem with a bright sparkle. The Romans called it "water of the sea" and believed it protected fishermen and brought in good catches.

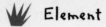 **Element**

Cesium. A soft silvery white to blue-gray metallic element used in photoelectric cells. It is highly electropositive. Cesium is tied in modern numerology and astrology with the planet Neptune.

Herb

White pond lily *(Nymphaea odorata).* This aquatic plant grows in ponds and slow- moving water in eastern North America. It has fragrant, many-petaled white blossoms that bloom above the water for three days, opening before noon. They flower from June to September. Medicinally, a potion of the rootstock was used as an antiseptic for the throat, eyes, and mouth. As a lotion it helped heal sores and soften skin. Both the root and leaves were sometimes used in poultices for wounds.

♂   GEORDIE: From the root name *George*.

♂   GEORG: From the root name *George*.

♥ ♂ **GEORGE**   Egor, Geordie, Georg, Georgeann, Georgeina, Georges, Georgette, Georgia, Georgie, Giorgia, Giorgio, Goran, Gyuri, Igor, Jerzy, Jiri, Jorgan, Jorge, Jorgina, Jurgen, Jurek, Ygor, Yuri, Yurik: *George* is from the Greek word *georgos* meaning "husbandman." The earliest known *Georgos* or *Georgios* was a Roman soldier who was martyred at Nicomedia around A.D. 303 and was later canonized. Constantine is said to have built a church in his honor in Byzantium. This led to the name's popularity in Greece, and through the Orthodox Church, in Russia.

The popularity of Saint George—about whose life very few details are known—grew over time. He was introduced to Europe when the crusaders of the eleventh century brought his story back from their travels. In fact, he became the crusaders' patron saint after he was reported to have appeared at the battle of Antioch in the eleventh century. Soon the legend of "Saint George and the Dragon" developed. Probably a Christian revision of the Greek story of Perseus, the legend has Saint George saving a Libyan princess from a dragon. He kills the monster after the king's subjects promise to convert to Christianity. Already firmly established in the oral tradition of many European countries, it became even more popular after 1265–1266 when Jacob de Voragine published the story as *Legenda aurea.*

Due to the overwhelming popularity of the story, by the end of the Middle Ages there were more chivalric orders of Saint George than of any other kind. During the medieval period, when monarchs honored warriors, they used the phrase "In the name of Saint George and Saint Michael, I dub thee knight." St. George became the patron saint of Venice, and later of Burgundy and Aquitaine. From Burgundy the fame of the saint traveled to Germany, where he became the patron saint for a time. Through Henry II of Burgundy, the name also traveled to Portugal. In Italy, the spelling is *Giorgio,* in Spain and Portugal, *Jorge,* in Germany *Georg* or *Jurgen,* in Poland, *Jerzy,* and in Russia, *Georgij* or *Jurgi.*

The Scottish people adopted their own version of *George, Geordie,* long before the name became popular in England. The source of *Geordie* in Scotland is said to be a Hungarian noble who was in England during the Norman Conquest. A supporter of King Harold, he fled to Scotland and founded the house of Drummond. His descendants kept the name in the family and it spread from there.

In England in 1349 Edward III dedicated the Order of the Garter to Saint George, and George became the country's patron saint. However, it took several centuries for the name to catch on among the populace. While there were English

Georges, including George of Clarence, Edward IV's brother, *George* only gained its enormous popularity after George I—Georg Ludwig—became king of England in 1714.

A similar story holds true in the American colonies, and while some of the earliest settlers bore the name *George,* they did not pass it on to their children. Again, it was George I who popularized the name, though only in the Middle and Southern colonies. The most notable early American bearer of the name is, of course, George Washington. Had the Revolutionary general and first president of the United States not been named George, the name might have died on the vine in America, since it was the hated King George III against whom the Revolution was fought. Instead the name grew steadily in popularity from the founding of the nation onward. In the first half of the twentieth century *George* was so common a name that it became the generic term of address for Pullman porters. Another early twentieth century phrase, "Let George do it," gives further proof that the name had become so widespread that it was a generic term for "guy." In the latter half of the twentieth century, *George* has become slightly less popular, but it is still in the top one hundred. George Clooney is one example of someone keeping the name up there, as he slays many hearts on television and movie screens today.

The feminine versions *Georgia* and *Georgina* have never been so wildly popular. *Georgette,* the French feminine of the name, can be heard, but it also never gained widespread use.

◎ Number

Three. People of this number can be proud and usually dislike being in any position that isn't in the lead. Threes are conscientious in whatever duty they undertake. King George V was a three.

☾ Astrological sign

Leo. This midsummer sign is known for individuals with forceful personalities and a desire for glory. As a rule they are outgoing and fiercely loyal. George Bernard Shaw was a Leo.

☀ Color

Flame red. Often considered a regal color, this shade of red matches the fiery gout of the mythical dragon that Saint George supposedly slew. Long ago, red was thought to ward against fire and lightning.

◆ Stone

Sardonyx. This stone is a blend of onyx and sard (a type of agate) with straight white bands of onyx and stripes of reddish brown sard. This tri-color effect is beautiful and unusual. Sardonyx was worn to enhance courage in battle. On a peaceful level, others used the sardonyx to instill domestic harmony.

☗ Element

Gold. A metal tied metaphysically to fire and one that complements the power of a sardonyx.

☙ Herb

Bistort *(Polygonum bistorta).* Commonly called dragonwort, this herb grows in damp high mountain meadows and along higher elevation streams and creeks. Long ago the rootstock was used in poultices and applied on wounds to stop bleeding. Bistort also has red or rose-colored flowers that bloom through August.

♀   GEORGEANN: From the root name *George.*

♀   GEORGEINA: From the root name *George.*

♂ GEORGES: From the root name *George*.

♀ GEORGETTE: From the root name *George*.

♀ GEORGIA: From the root name *George*.

♀♂ GEORGIE: From the root name *George*.

♥ ♂ **GERALD** Deena, Gareth, Garrett, Garrin, Gary, Geralda, Geraldine, Geraldo, Gerard, Gerhard, Gerianne, Gerri, Gerrick, Jarell, Jerald, Jeraldeen, Jeralee, Jere, Jerrie, Jerrold, Jerry: *Gerald* and *Gerard* come from one of two Teutonic German names: *Gerwald* (or *Gairovald*), which means "spear power," and *Gerhard* (or *Gairhard*), which means "firm spear." Over time, the names have become closely linked, and today, while it is probably most accurate to say that *Gerard* means the latter and *Gerald* the former, it is close to impossible to track their histories separately.

The first known historic figure of importance to bear the root name was an eighth-century Anglo-Saxon saint named *Gerhold*. A great figure in the legends of the Irish saints, *Gerhold* went to Ireland, became a monk, and founded the monastery of the Tempul Gerald. He is best known for putting a curse on a queen of Connaught, which cut off her descendants from any throne in Ireland. The Irish called him *Garalt,* and his name became confused with the Celtic name *Gareth,* who was a knight of King Arthur's Round Table. Due to this confusion, *Gareth* and *Gerald* have since become synonymous.

Despite the appeal of Saint Gerhold's story, his influence on the development of the names seems largely limited to the inclusion of *Gareth* into the mix. The popularity of the names spread throughout Europe as the result of two different Norman variations, *Gerard* and *Girroald*. No one knows when *Gerard* first came to England, but the name was in use prior to the Norman Conquest—the latinizations *Gerardus* and *Girardus* both appear in the medieval census record, the Domesday Book. *Gerald* definitely followed later, arriving with William the Conqueror's soldiers. And, while the Norman invasion didn't bring *Gerard* to Britain, it did ultimately help to make the name more popular.

From England both names then traveled to Ireland and became more widespread there, perhaps because the Irish already had their own Saint Gerhold.

In England, after the thirteenth century, *Gerald* largely disappeared as a first name. It did survive in Kildare, Ireland, as part of the surname *Fitzgerald* (or *Geraldin*). *Gerard* remained popular as a first name up until the seventeenth century, when it became quite rare. However, the variation *Garret*—probably first used as a surname—came in to replace it, especially in Ireland. Though it is unknown when it first came into use, or how, *Garrett* was common enough by the seventeenth century for the names historians Camden and Lyford to include it in their lists of Christian names.

After *Gerald* and *Gerard* fell out of use in England, the names did not reappear again until the nineteenth century and there is no known reason for their return. When they did come back into use, however, *Gerald* became the more popular of the two.

In America, *Gerard* never became fashionable, but *Gerald* certainly did. Its acceptance probably came from two sources: the name's English popularity and the mid-nineteenth century Irish immigration. Some credit for the name's early twentieth century popularity might go to D. H. Lawrence, who created a ruthless but romantic character named Gerald in his famous and controversial novel *Women in Love*. Up until the 1980s, *Gerald* was consistently popular in the African American community, but it had fallen out of use with much of the rest of the United States.

As for *Garrett*, it is unknown when it came to the United States, and it wasn't widely used until recently. However, it is now one of the most popular boys' names in the country. *Garrett*'s diminutive, *Gary*, became more common as a name in its own right in the 1930s, after the actor Gary Cooper (originally Frank James Cooper) became one of the most beloved movie stars in American history. *Jerry* serves both as a nickname for *Gerald* and *Gerard* and as an independent. In recent years, *Gary*'s and *Jerry*'s popularity has dropped off.

The feminine variation, *Geraldine*, came into use in England after the Middle Ages, ironically, at around the same time as *Gerald* fell out of use. The name was probably invented by the Earl of Surrey around 1540. He wrote a poem to the Lady Elizabeth Fitzgerald, which was published in 1597 as "The Lady Geraldine to the Earl of Surrey." In 1800 Coleridge helped the name's popularity by using it in his poem "Christabel." In the U.S., *Geraldine* never became one of the most popular girls' names, though it was often used among families of Irish descent.

Number

Two. Two represents the moon and rules the sign of Cancer. Twos are usually patient and intuitive.

Astrological sign

Cancer. Ancient Egyptians believed people born under the sign of Cancer would create good families. Cancers are fiercely protective of their loved ones and homesteads. Former United States President Gerald Ford is a Cancer.

Color

Ocher. Orange is a projective color sending out emanations of confidence. Some mystics believed it also brought good luck.

Stone

Spessartine. As a member of the garnet family, spessartine was considered by many cultures to be a curative stone. Gem-quality spessartine is rare, making it a collector's item. When pure, it's bright orange, but a higher iron content darkens the stone to deep orange or red. Spessartine was first found in the Spessart district of Bavaria, Germany. Sometimes it may be mistaken for hessonite or yellow topaz.

 ## Element

Copper. Copper strengthens the body's reaction to any gemstone and acts as an extra boost for the healing energy of spessartine.

 ## Herb

Larkspur (*Delphinium consolida*). Sometimes called knight's spur in ancient herbal lore, larkspur is found in dry woods or on rocky slopes. The flowering part of the plant was used by healers for intestinal problems. It is not used much by modern herbalists because the seeds and young plants are dangerous if misused.

♀ GERALDA: From the root name *Gerald*.

♀ GERALDINE: From the root name *Gerald*.

♂ GERALDO: From the root name *Gerald*.

♂ GERARD: From the root name *Gerald*.

♂ GERHARD: From the root name *Gerald*.

♀ GERIANNE: From the root name *Gerald*.

♂ GEROME: From the root name *Jerome*.

♂ GERONIMO: From the root name *Jerome*.

♀ GERRI: From the root name *Gerald*.

♂ GERRICK: From the root name *Gerald*.

♂ GERRY: From the root name *Jerome*.

♂ GIACOMO: From the root name *Jacob/James*.

♂ GIAN: From the root name *John*.

♀ GIANNA: From the root name *John*.

♀ GINA: From the root names *Eugene, Reginald,* and *Virginia*.

♀ GINELLE: From the root name *Virginia*.

♀ GINERVA: From the root name *Jennifer*.

♀ GINETTA: From the root name *Jennifer*.

♀ GINGER: From the root name *Virginia*.

♀ GINIA: From the root name *Virginia*.

♀ GINNY: From the root name *Virginia*.

♂ GIORDANO: From the root name *Jordan*.

♀ GIORGIA: From the root name *George*.

♂ GIORGIO: From the root name *George*.

♂ GIOVANNI: From the root name *John*.

♀ GIUDITTA: From the root name *Judith*.

♀ GIULIA: From the root name *Julian*.

♂ GIULIO: From the root name *Julian*.

♂ GIUSEPPE: From the root name *Joseph*.

♀ GIUSEPPINA: From the root name *Joseph*.

♀ GIUSTINA: From the root name *Justin*.

♂ GIUSTINO: From the root name *Justin*.

♥ ♀♂ GLEN/GLENN Glenda, Glendon, Gleneen, Glenna, Glennie, Glin, Glynis: The name *Glen* derives from the obvious association: a glen or valley. It then follows the familiar pattern that has changed many a common word to a place

282

name, the place name to a surname, and the surname to a first name. *Glen* was probably first used in the British Isles to identify someone who lived in the glen or was somehow connected to a glen. As a surname, *Glenn* is Scottish, but it has close relatives in Wales, including *Glyn,* which is also used as a first name. Owen Glendower (Owain Glyndwr), for example, was a rebel chieftain in the fifteenth century. As with the English word glen, the Welsh word for valley is *glyn.*

As a first name, *Glen* was the earlier version and is said to have appeared in the early nineteenth century. The name continued to be unusual until the 1920s when the variant *Glenn* came into use. Most historians believe that while the actor Glenn Hunter may have introduced the name to the American public, it was either the bandleader Glenn Miller and/or the actor Glenn Ford (originally Gwyllyn Ford) who led to both *Glen* and *Glenn*'s more widespread use. After John Glenn became the first American to orbit Earth, both variations of the name became even more popular. The country singer Glen Campbell also probably influenced a rise in use of the name. The name is not usually used for girls, though actress Glenn Close is a famous exception to this.

Interestingly, the many traditionally feminine names that are similar to *Glen* are sometimes from different roots. The name *Glenda* is from the Welsh and is not simply the feminine of the Scottish name. Its roots are said to be *glan,* which means "clean" (or "pure") and *da,* which means "good." Another figure with a name very similar to *Glenda* may have familiarized many Americans with the name. Glinda, as in "the Good Witch" from *The Wizard of Oz,* seems to be a made-up name, but it sounds so similar to *Glenda* that fans of the movie may have confused the two.

The Welsh name *Glynis* has its roots in the word *glyn,* while the very similar sounding *Glenys* has its root in the word *glan*. While *Glenys* remains extremely rare, the actresses Glynnis O'Connor and Glynis Johns have helped to popularize that name, at least in Britain.

 ## Number

Two. This number is most often linked to the natural world. Twos are usually gentle souls and make friends easily.

 ## Astrological sign

Taurus. It never hurts to have a Taurus on your side. They are kind and sensitive, yet have the strength of their totem symbol, the bull.

 ## Color

Autumn leaf. This mixture of green and brown stimulates health like a walk in the countryside at the turn of the seasons.

 ## Stone

Brown sard. The history of sards is tied to agates and is the common name for all unnamed clear agates. While sards were not as popular with the ancients as the more spectacular multihued or mottled agates, they were revered nonetheless. Brown sards were used as stones of protection. Ancient people carved them into beads and wore them around their necks to ward off attacks of negative energy such as curses or hexes. Sard can be found throughout the world.

 ## Element

Copper. When brown sard is set in copper its energy is enhanced. It encourages well-being and peace for anyone who wears it.

Herb

Fragrant valerian *(Valeriana officinalis)*. This perennial plant was once cultivated but now grows wild in northern areas of the United States and throughout Europe. The brownish yellow rootstock was used in preparations for nervous conditions including migraine headaches and insomnia.

♀ GLENDA: From the root name *Glen/Glenn.*

♂ GLENDON: From the root name *Glen/Glenn.*

♀ GLENEEN: From the root name *Glen/Glenn.*

♀ GLENNA: From the root name *Glen/Glenn.*

♀♂ GLENNIE: From the root name *Glen/Glenn.*

♂ GLIN: From the root name *Glen/Glenn.*

♂ GLYNIS: From the root name *Glen/Glenn.*

♂ GODFREY: From the root name *Geoffrey.*

♂ GORAN: From the root name *George.*

♂ GORDEN: From the root name *Gordon.*

♂ GORDIE: From the root name *Gordon.*

♥ ♂ **GORDON**   **Gorden, Gordie, Gordy:** The name *Gordon* was originally a Scottish surname, probably from the Gaelic, and may mean "big hill," though some historians believe it is from the Old English and means "from the marshes." The Gordons were an important Scottish clan in the border country, and throughout Scottish history, Gordons are reported to have been involved in various frays. Currently, Gordon is the name of a district in Northeastern Scotland. There is also the Gordon setter, a breed of dog named after the seventeenth century Duke of Gordon. Gordon setters are known not only for their beauty but also for their loyalty.

Gordon came into use as a first name in the mid-nineteenth century and is one of the few names where the transition to common first name use can be traced to a specific individual: General Charles George Gordon (1833–1885). General Gordon was enormously popular with the British public during his lifetime and was variously known as "Chinese Gordon"—because of his role in Britain's wars there—and "Gordon of Khartoum"—because he died during the siege of Khartoum, Sudan.

How or why *Gordon* traveled to the U.S. is unknown. It probably came with Scottish immigrants and followed the maternal surname-to-first name route, at least initially. It is doubtful that General Gordon had much influence on American parents, though reports of his exploits certainly crossed the ocean. It is also unknown why *Gordon* reached its peak of popularity in America during the 1920s and 1930s.

Since that time, use of the name declined except in the African-American community. The name's success there may be due in part to the fame of photographer and filmmaker Gordon Parks. With the rise in interest in genealogy since the mid-1970s, *Gordon* has had a modest return to popularity among parents who want to embrace their Scottish ancestry. Boys named *Gordon* are often called by the diminutive *Gordy*.

🌀 Number

Three. There's never too big a hill for a three to climb. People of this number thrive under a challenge. They also have a deep respect for nature and all living creatures.

🌙 Astrological sign

Capricorn. As an earth sign, Capricorn represents the body. Capricorns achieve their goals through a "never say die" attitude.

Color

Marsh brown. Long connected to the earth and stability, this shade is also one of the colors of the famed Gordon setters.

 ## Stone

Enstatite. Belonging to the pyroxene family, enstatite is a magnesium and iron-rich silicate stone. Some enstatite crystals occur in small prisms, but most gem-quality stones are found as rounded pebbles. Colors range from yellowish green to brownish green (Myanmar) and sometimes emerald green. Some varieties are also chatoyant (eye stone effect), but these are found only in Sri Lanka or India. The main deposits of enstatite are in the United States, Greenland, Switzerland, and Scotland. The name comes from the Greek language meaning "opponent" or "contrary."

 ## Element

Iron. Iron is a metal of force. The term "iron will" describes a person's strength of character.

 ## Herb

Swamp tea *(Ledum palustre)*. Also called marsh tea in some herbal lore, this evergreen shrub was used to make remedies for skin problems. Internally, it stimulated the nerves and the stomach. A cold tea was used for rheumatism, gout, and arthritis. Some healers made a syrup to cure coughs and hoarseness.

♂   GORDY: From the root name *Gordon*.

♀   GORGEINA: From the root name *George*.

♥ ♀ **GRACE** Engracia, Gracia, Gracie, Gratia, Gratiana, Grazia, Graziella, Graziosa, Grazyna: In current parlance, the name *Grace* can call to mind a fluidity of movement, or it can call to mind thanksgiving toward a deity, or the blessing of forgiveness and salvation given by the deity to humans. The origin of the name is from the Latin *gratia,* and it implies the second meaning, gratitude. The Greek Charities were known in Roman mythology as the Graces. They were sometimes referred to as the daughters of Zeus, and they were the goddesses of everything that lends beauty to nature or to human life, which helps explain how the word came to stand for physical seemliness.

Not surprisingly, the Puritans prized the name highly, and it remained popular in the United States almost until World War II. Even before the Victorian period, its meaning began to shift toward a secular approach closer to "graciousness." Now, its religious significance is almost always behind the choice of *Grace* for a baby daughter, and it usually signifies the third meaning, as the concept of a gift from God.

Grace Kelly, from Philadelphia, brought the name to international prominence when at the height of her career as a film star in the 1950s, she married Prince Ranier of Monaco and transformed herself into royalty as Princess Grace. Even with her celebrity, *Grace* did not enjoy a revival of its former popularity until recently.

Number

Seven. According to ancient folk beliefs, seven is a number of spirituality. Modern lore connects seven to meditation and transcendentalism as well.

Astrological sign

Gemini. Geminis are free spirits who enjoy being on the move.

☀ Color

Xanthophyll. The goddess Athena wore a robe of this golden color to represent her communication with Zeus in matters of peace.

◆ Stone

Yellow jasper. Much lore surrounds this opaque gemstone dating back to the earliest civilizations. Jasper's connection to divine grace made it a revered stone in many religions. The Bible mentions jasper often. In ancient healers' tomes, jasper was thought to cure problems of a digestive nature and also helped to balance hormones. Yellow jasper was believed to alleviate old fears and festering guilt.

♛ Element

Quicksilver. Quicksilver has a fluid beauty found in no other ore. Metaphysically, it has always been respected for its mysterious composition. It is tied to Gemini's ruling planet, Mercury.

Herb

Herb of Grace *(Verbena hastata).* This aromatic plant is found in Europe, China, and Japan. In European folk medicine, the leaves and flowering heads were used to make remedies to relieve colic in infants. Tonics were concocted to improve appetite and stimulate digestion. Preparations were also used to reduce fevers, ulcers, and pleurisy. Homeopathic practitioners made crushed leaf poultices to cure headaches.

♀   GRACIA: From the root name *Grace.*

♀   GRACIE: From the root name *Grace.*

♂   GRAIG: From the root name *Gregory.*

♀ GRATIA: From the root name *Grace*.

♀ GRATIANA: From the root name *Grace*.

♀ GRAZIA: From the root name *Grace*.

♀ GRAZIELLE: From the root name *Grace*.

♀ GRAZIOSA: From the root name *Grace*.

♀ GRAZYNA: From the root name *Grace*.

♀♂ GREER: From the root name *Gregory*.

♂ GREG: From the root name *Gregory*.

♂ GREGOIRE: From the root name *Gregory*.

♀ GREGORIA: From the root name *Gregory*.

♂ GREGORIO: From the root name *Gregory*.

♥ ♂ **GREGORY Graig, Greer, Greg, Gregoire, Gregoria, Gregorio, Gregos, Grigor, Grigorios, Grzegorz:** *Gregory* is a variation of the Greek name *Gregorios,* which comes from the Greek word *gregoreo* or *gregoros*. It is itself a bastardization of an earlier Greek word, *egeiro,* which probably means "to wake" or "to watch." This led to the name's current interpretation as "watchman." In early Christian times, many bishops used the name because it connoted their role as "watchers of the flock" or "shepherds of the Church." The two earliest famous owners of the name were were Saint Gregorius of Nazianzen (c.330–c.389 A.D), a friend of Saint Basil and Saint Gregorius Thaumaturgos of Nyssa, "the wonder-worker"(c.331–c.395 A.D). They popularized the name in the Eastern Christian world, and spawned the popular Russian variations *Grigorij* or *Grisha.*

In the Western Christian world, the first Pope Gregory, "the Great" (c.540–604 A.D.), made the name popular not only among the papacy—there have been a total of sixteen popes named *Gregory*—but also among the laity. In France, the name became *Gregoire;* In Italy, *Gregorio.* The German variation is *Gregor,* and in Scandinavia, the spelling is *Gregos.* Some also connect the Scandinavian name *Greis* to *Gregory,* while others trace its origin to the Norse word *Grjotgard. Greis* also means "stone" in ancient Norse (Teutonic).

Scandinavia is not the only area where there are conflicting explanations of the name's origins. This holds true for the name's development in the British Isles, especially Scotland. While it is generally believed that *Gregoire* came to England with the French during the Norman Conquest, in Scotland at least, there is a possibility that it descends from the Celtic word *grig* or *gairig,* meaning "fierce." In addition, *Greg,* usually considered the diminutive of *Gregory,* had already been used in Scotland for centuries as an independent name, which might explain the presence of the ancient name *Macgregor.*

Whatever its source, *Gregory* developed into a favorite name throughout Britain. It was most popular in England from the sixteenth through the eighteenth centuries, and did travel to the United States with the early colonists, especially those from Scotland. However, it didn't become truly fashionable here until the 1940s. The reason for the name's dramatic rise in popularity is most credibly traced to the actor Gregory Peck. Now *Gregory* is among the top fifty male baby names. Increasingly, the name's diminutives, *Greg,* or now *Gregg,* are used independently.

 ## Number

Five. Some modern numerologists believe that five represents innovation, rethinking, radicalism, curiosity. Five symbolizes the number of new directions. Others say that fives have innate resiliency and seem to be able to rebound rapidly from life's disappointments.

☾ Astrological sign

Aquarius. Many Aquarians' love of people often lead them to a life of humanitarianism and they find great satisfaction in careers such as social work and counseling.

☀ Color

Ivory. Symbolic of popes and miracles, white is the harmonious blending of all colors.

◆ Stone

Clear zircon. Also called white zircon, this stone was used as a substitute for diamonds in ancient magic and religious rituals. While zircons come in many colors, the white stone was believed to bring clear thinking and connection to one's deity. It was also worn by the chaste as a sign of their celibacy.

♛ Element

Uranium. This natural element is associated with Uranus, a ruling planet of Aquarius.

♌ Herb

Blessed thistle *(Cnicus benedictus)*. Some call this plant holy thistle. It grows wild throughout southern Europe and western Asia and has pentagonal, branched stems with spiny leaves. Its flowers bloom from May to August. In the past, thistle tea was used for stomach troubles, liver problems, headaches, and fever. Blessed thistle's name came from its reputation as a cure for many diseases, including the Black Plague.

♂   GREGOS: From the root name *Gregory*.

♀   GRETA: From the root name *Margaret*.

♀ GRETCHEN: From the root name *Margaret*.

♂ GRIGOR: From the root name *Gregory*.

♂ GRIGORIOS: From the root name *Gregory*.

♂ GRZEGORZ: From the root name *Gregory*.

♂ GUALTERIO: From the root name *Walter*.

♀ GUGLIELMA: From the root name *William*.

♂ GUGLIELMO: From the root name *William*.

♂ GUILLAUME: From the root name *William*.

♀ GUILLELMINA: From the root name *William*.

♂ GUILLERMO: From the root name *William*.

♀ GUINEVERE: From the root name *Jennifer*.

♀♂ GUS: From the root name *Austin*.

♀ GUSTA: From the root name *Austin*.

♀ GWEN: From the root name *Jennifer*.

♀ GWENDOLYN: From the root name *Jennifer*.

♂ GYURI: From the root name *George*.

♀ HADRIA: From the root name *Adrian*.

♂ HADRIAN: From the root name *Adrian*.

♀ HADRIENNE: From the root name *Adrian*.

♂ HAGAN: From the root name *Henry*.

♀ HAILEA: From the root name *Hayley*.

♂ HAL: From the root name *Henry*.

♀♂ HALEIGH: From the root name *Hayley*.

♂ HALEY: From the root name *Hayley*.

♀ HALINA: From the root name *Helen*.

♀ HALLE: From the root name *Holly*.

♀♂ HALLIE: From the root name *Hayley*.

♂ HAMISH: From the root name *Jacob/James*.

♂ HANK: From the root name *Henry*.

♀ HANNA: From the root name *Anna*.

♀ HANNAH: From the root name *Anna*.

♀ HANNELORE: From the root name *Anna*.

♂ HANNES: From the root name *John*.

♂ HANS: From the root name *John*.

♂ HANSCHEN: From the root name *John*.

♂ HANSEL: From the root name *John*.

♂ HAROUN: From the root name *Aaron*.

♂   HARRY: From the root name *Henry*.

♀   HATTIE: From the root name *Henry*.

♀♂   HAYLEIGH: From the root name *Hayley*.

♥ ♀♂ **HAYLEY** **Hailea, Haleigh, Haley, Hallie, Hayleigh:** *Hayley* and its variants are all fairly recent names and are generally thought to be of Irish origin. There is some dispute, however, as to the original meaning of the names. Some describe *Haley* as meaning "ingenious." It also might be related to the surname *Hale,* which means "a remote vale, glen, or valley." However, *Hayley* is sometimes described as an English place name that became a surname. This variation of the name is said to mean "hay meadow."

Until the 1990s all the variations of the name remained fairly rare in the U.S. In particular, the spelling *Hayley* has never found a place in the States. But now variant spellings, such as *Haley* and the even more recent *Haleigh* were both among the most popular girls' names. There is no known reason for their current popularity, though it is possible that the return of Halley's Comet in 1986 helped influence American parents.

The actress Hayley Mills, best known in the United States for the film *The Parent Trap,* in the 1960s, is no doubt responsible for keeping the name in the public eye, particularly in Britain. Her first name comes from her mother, whose maiden surname was *Hayley*.

Interestingly, a name that is similar to *Haley*—*Halle*—has a completely different origin, since it is said to be a variant of *Holly*. The similar looking and sounding name, *Hallie,* is thought by some to be a feminine variation of *Hal,* the pet name for Harold.

⊙ Number

Four. Many fours are young at heart and born to be in the spotlight. However, some numerologists attribute a definite stubborn streak to people of this number.

☾ Astrological sign

Aries. An Arian is fearless when it comes to speaking out. They are often assertive, dynamic, and single-minded when pursuing their goals. Hayley Mills is an Aries.

☀ Color

Xanthin. Yellow stimulates the power of the mind and heightens communication.

◆ Stone

Red flint. Folk names for this opaque quartz variety include thunderstone and elf-arrow. It is tied to Mars, the ruling planet of Aries. Ingenious uses for the stone were discovered by early people of the Stone Age and led to making fire and tools. Later in time, ancient mystics used it in protection and healing rites. The Irish encased flint knives in silver and wore them to guard against impish fairies.

ⱽⱽ Element

Pyrite. Pyrite was once believed to attract money and luck. Even today, superstitious gamblers may carry a piece of the ore in their pocket.

⚘ Herb

Yellow melilot (*Melilotus officinalis*). Commonly known as hay flowers, this plant grows in Eurasia and North America. The flowering herb was used for external salves to treat swellings, boils, and other skin problems. Poultices were also applied to arthritic joints. It has sweet-smelling, golden-yellow flowers that bloom from June to November. Early Europeans sewed the dried plant into herb pillows to freshen beds and linen.

♂   HEATH: From the root name *Heather.*
♂   HEATHCLIFF: From the root name *Heather.*

♥ ♀ **HEATHER   Heath, Heathcliff:** The name *Heather* comes, quite simply, from the shrub that produces beautiful, delicate purple, lavender, pink, or white flowers. The lavender sheen of some bushes is sometimes said to represent beauty, while the white flowers are said to represent protection from danger. The term *heather* is considered by some etymologists to be derived from the word *heath.* Heaths are large tracts of treeless, uncultivated land that cover many areas of Scotland and England. However, the *Oxford English Dictionary* questions this derivation.

As a girl's name, *Heather* came into use in the 1880s when a great many other plant names such as *Iris, Lily, Hazel, Violet,* and the much more unusual *Azalea* were also becoming popular. The Latin term for heather is *erica,* which is also used as a feminine name. But usually *Erica* is considered the feminine of the name *Eric,* and most parents are probably thinking of this derivation when they adopt the name.

The name *Heath* is sometimes used as a male variety of *Heather.* However, it more logically began as a surname and evolved into an independent first name. *Heath* was probably first used in the U.S. to honor the Revolutionary War officer William Heath. The romantic hero of Charlotte Brontë's *Wuthering Heights,* Heathcliff, may have prompted some parents to adopt both *Heathcliff* and *Heath,* but neither have ever been particularly common names. Interestingly, although heather is a very romantic flower, the name has not been used particularly frequently in literature. An exception is Agatha Christie, who used the name for a character in her mystery story *The Mirror Crack'd from Side to Side* (1962).

There is no specific reason anyone can point to that would explain *Heather*'s recent widespread use, though certainly the actress Heather Locklear has brought the name into a broader public consciousness. Whatever the factors, *Heather* has taken off in the past fifteen years, being currently among the top one hundred names for baby girls.

 ## Number

Two. This number is linked to the Moon in numerology. Twos are gentle and romantic.

 ## Astrological sign

Taurus. People born under this springtime sign are logical and earthy, but have sentimental hearts.

 ## Color

Lavender pink. Romance and devotion are represented by any shade of pink.

 ## Stone

Rose quartz. Rose quartz has been revered for more than two thousand years by the ancient Egyptians and by Tibetans and other Asian civilizations. Rose quartz was considered a beauty enhancement that would prevent skin from aging and keep complexions clear. Rose quartz intaglios carved with images of warriors were quite popular in ancient Rome as well.

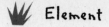 **Element**

White gold. White gold is a powerful setting for rose quartz. Its metaphysical properties are reinforced by the strong conductive energy of this precious metal.

Herb

Heather *(Calluna vulgaris).* Traditional herbalists used the flowering shoots of the heather plant to alleviate insomnia. Flower preparations were made to relieve gout and rheumatic pains as well as stomachaches, coughs, and facial skin problems.

♀   HEDY: From the root name *Heidi*.

♀   HEIDA: From the root name *Heidi*.

♥ ♀ **HEIDI   Adelaide, Hedy, Heida:** The name *Heidi* is most probably a diminutive of the German name *Adelheid*—the English variation is *Adelaide*—which means "noble." Sometimes *Heidi* is also defined as "cheerful" or "kind," but this may have more to do with the personality of the fictional Heidi than the actual etymology of the name. Other theories on the name say that it developed out of *Hedy* or *Heidy,* both diminutives of *Hedwig,* which comes from the Teutonic and means "struggle" or "strife." One historian points to the remote possibility that *Heidi* is related to *Haidee,* which seems to be a made-up name which first appeared in Lord Byron's poem "Don Juan." The variation *Heide* was a name used among free black women of the eighteenth century.

However, most historians believe that *Heidi* became an independent name in late nineteenth-century Germany. They connect this directly to the popularity of the children's classic *Heidi* (1881) by Johanna Spyri. In England and the United States the name came into its most widespread use in the 1960s or 1970s. Its popularity among English-speakers can be traced to two English sequels of the Heidi story: *Heidi Grows Up* and *Heidi's Children,* by Charles Tritten. According to the 1990 census *Heidi* was the two hundred forty-first most popular name for living American women.

Number

Eight. In some numerological circles, eight represents Saturn. This planetary influence can cause eights to be misunderstood. They must take care not to let the intensity of their beliefs outweigh good sense.

Astrological sign

Capricorn. A Capricorn is not daunted by the prospect of strife, especially when they believe they are right. They are not afraid to climb the highest alpine peak if necessary to achieve a goal.

Color

Canary. Like the voice of the gentle songbird, yellow brings cheer to heart and mind.

Stone

Topazolite. This beautiful gem is a yellow variety of andradite garnet. It can vary from pale to dark yellow and comes in small crystals. Topazolite crystals are only found in the Swiss and Italian Alps. Cut and polished topazolite makes beautiful jewelry with high fire and brilliance. Since ancient times, garnets were valued as stones that brought well-being and family harmony.

Element

Iron. Iron is a mineral found in topazolite. It has a magical reputation for defensive power that dates back to the earliest civilizations.

🌿 Herb

Buckwheat *(Polygonum fagopyrum)*. Sometimes referred to as heidekorm or buchweizen, the fruit of this plant was ground up and used in poultices to restore milk flow in nursing mothers. Buckwheat flour is still used in cooking for breads and cakes. Himalayan Hindus ate buckwheat cakes and breads during their special religious holidays and feasts.

♂   HEINDRICK: From the root name *Henry.*

♂   HEINRICH: From the root name *Henry.*

♂   HEINZ: From the root name *Henry.*

♥ ♀ **HELEN**   **Aila, Aileen, Aliana, Alina, Eileen, Elaine, Elan, Elana, Eleanor, Elena, Ella, Ellen, Ellie, Galina, Halina, Helena, Hélène, Hellenor, Ileana, Ilene, Ilona, Jelena, Jelika, Lana, Leanora, Lena, Lenia, Lenore, Leonora, Lina, Nelda, Nell, Nellie, Nonnie, Yelena:** *Helen* and its many variants all come from the Greek root *ele,* meaning "light." The earliest known use of this root in a name can be found in two Greek deities: Helios, the Sun god, and Selene, goddess of the Moon.

One of history's most famous *Helen*s was Helen of Troy. Made notorious by Aeschylus's play *The Trojan Women,* she was a daughter of Zeus, and considered to be the most beautiful woman in the world. While married to the Greek king Menelaus, Helen was carried away by Prince Paris to his home in Troy, which was in Asia Minor (modern-day Turkey). Menelaus convinced his Greek compatriots to join him in a battle for her return, and thus began the Trojan War. It was this legendary episode that inspired playwright Christopher Marlowe to call Helen's visage "the face that launched a thousand ships."

Whether the name *Helen* existed prior to Aeschylus's play is unknown, but the appellation is said to be a female variant of the male name *Helenos.* Aeschylus reportedly used a twist on *Helenos* to create *Helen,* turning it into a pun—for in ancient Greek, *Helen,* as he wrote it, also means "the ship-destroying." The name *Helen* traveled with the saga to Rome, and many aristocratic ladies during that city's Golden Age were called by it. It remained popular in Greece, as well; *Eleni* is still very common there today.

Just as this Destroyer of Ships spent time in Asia Minor, a second, and even more popular Helen sprung from the same land. Experts believe that this next Helen was the real reason for the spread of the name and its survival into the early Christian era and beyond.

She was born in Bithynia in the fourth century, and was the mother of the emperor Constantine, ruler of Byzantium (like Troy, both Bithynia and Byzantium are now part of Turkey). She was noted for her compassion for the poor, and for her pilgrimage to the Holy Land, where she was supposed to have unearthed the Holy Sepulcher and to have found pieces of the true cross. She was canonized upon her death, and became so well loved throughout Europe that veneration of Saint Helen was practically a cult. The British went so far as to claim her as their own, alleging that she was the daughter of Old King Cole, of nursery rhyme fame.

Saint Helena was particularly popular in the British Isles. In Wales the variation of the name became *Elayne,* immortalized as the mother of Sir Galahad in the legends of King Arthur. (This crafty woman magically transformed herself into the likeness of Guinevere, the lover of Lancelot, and thus was able to take advantage of the young knight.) *Elayne* became *Elaine,* popularized after Tennyson published his romantic saga "Idylls of the King" in 1859, which included the story of Lancelot and Elaine (with the new spelling).

Elaine was used regularly in the English-speaking world until the 1950s, when it began to fade.

Neither *Helen* nor *Helena* was popular in England until the Renaissance, when the classics of Greece and Rome were considered an important source of culture. After the Reformation, however, both names lost their appeal, especially among the Puritans, and so they did not travel well, initially, to the American colonies. The name regained its status in both the United States and England during the seventeenth century. At the same time, yet another variation from the original Greek root became popular: *Selina,* from the moon goddess, Selene.

The Scots dropped the *h* when pronouncing *Helen,* and thus *Ellen* became their variant of the name. After the seventeenth century, *Ellen* was used throughout Ireland; in England, it was found mainly among the lower classes. *Lena* was sometimes found as a nickname. *Ellen* probably came to the United States with the non-Puritan colonists, most likely the Scots. By the 1950s, it was beginning to displace *Helen* in popularity. But by the 1980s and 1990s, both names became less common.

The development of the name *Eleanor* is in dispute. Some trace it to *Helen* via the post-Roman Italian *Elena,* saying it transformed into *Alienor* when it traveled to Provençe. However, other sources trace the origin of the name to the Greek word *eleos,* meaning "pity" or "mercy." Still others believe that the name derives from the Latin *Honora* (meaning "reputation").

Whatever its beginnings, *Alienor* came to England as *Eleonore* (or *Eleanor*) in the twelfth century, when the famous duchess of the Aquitaine married Henry II. In northern England the name contracted to *Annora. Eleanor* came to America with the Raleigh colonists in 1587, but the name has never been hugely popular here.

Eleanor of Aquitaine gave her daughter the same name,

and the younger Eleanor took the name to Castille, where it became *Leonor.* That version spread throughout Europe, and its own variations came to the United States with the arriving European immigrants. Though never very common in the United States, the name *Lenore* is inextricably linked to Edgar Allan Poe's poem "The Raven."

That *Eileen* (or *Aileen*) is the Irish variant of *Helen* is also questionable. It may well be derived from the Celtic *Eibhlin,* which is pronounced *eye-leen* in some parts of Ireland, and *ev-leen* in others. It may be a form of *Evelyn,* which derived from *Aveline. Aveline* was introduced by the Normans, and gave rise to *Evelina,* which led to *Evelyn.*

The diminutives and variants of *Helen* are numerous, and many have come to be used as names in their own right. An example is the German diminutive *Lena,* which was sometimes used in England as well. In Eastern Europe, various examples include *Lena, Lenia,* and *Jelika.* Diminutives of *Eleanor, Eleanora,* and *Elinor* can also be *Nora, Nell,* and *Nelly. Nell* and *Nelly* were popular independent names among free black women in the 1700s.

Ellie is usually considered to be a shortened form of *Ellen* or *Eleanor,* and it became popular as such in the 1870s. However, *Ella* has several other possible derivations. *Ella* was common in England after the Norman Conquest; it may be a Norman name, deriving from the Old German *alia,* meaning "all." But some experts believe it comes from the Anglo-Saxon *aella,* meaning "elf-friend," a rather more charming interpretation. And, in past centuries it was linked to *Alice. Ella* went out of style in the seventeenth century, but came back two hundred years later, along with many other medieval names popularized by pre-Raphaelite writers.

Number

Nine. Chosen by Pythagoras as the ultimate number, nine represents righteousness and justice. Nines can sometimes cause strife and may be linked to warfare.

Astrological sign

Gemini. People born under this sign (May 22–June 21) make great entertainers. They love conversation and can be playful.

Color

Sunflower yellow. Any shade of yellow stimulates communication and this sunny shade goes well with the beautiful name of *Helena* and all her variations.

Stone

Heliodor. The name comes from the Greek language and means "gift of the sun." This yellow-green gem is from the beryl family and because it is uncommon, collectors treasure it. The highest quality stones are found in the Ukraine, but heliodor has been discovered in Namibia, Madagascar, and Brazil as well.

Element

Gold. An excellent metal to enhance the sunlight intensity of the rare heliodor.

Herb

Elecampane (*Inula helenium*). This herb can be cultivated, but also grows wild along roadways and in meadows. A colorful plant, it has olive-tinged leaves with white veins and large yellow flowers that bloom from July to September. The fruit and the rootstock are brown. Tea is brewed from the rootstock and was used by early herbalists to control whooping cough, bronchitis and other lung inflammations.

♀ HELENA: From the root name *Helen.*

♀ HÉLÈNE: From the root name *Helen.*

♀ HELLENOR: From the root name *Helen.*

♀ HELMA: From the root name *William.*

♀ HELMINA: From the root name *William.*

♀ HELMINETTE: From the root name *William.*

♀ HELOISE: From the root name *Louise.*

♀ HENDRIKA: From the root name *Henry.*

♂ HENERIK: From the root name *Henry.*

♀ HENIE: From the root name *Henry.*

♀ HENKA: From the root name *Henry.*

♂ HENNING: From the root name *Henry.*

♂ HENRI: From the root name *Henry.*

♀ HENRIETTA: From the root name *Henry.*

♀ HENRIKA: From the root name *Henry.*

♥ ♂ HENRY   Arrigo, Enrichetta, Enrico, Enrique, Enzio, Etta, Etty, Hagan, Hal, Hank, Harry, Hattie, Heindrick, Heinrich, Heinz, Hendrika, Henerik, Henie, Henka, Henning, Henri, Henrietta, Henrika, Rico, Yetta, Yettie: *Henry* has a rather convoluted history of spellings and variants. The name is said to mean "home ruler," and that odd phrase has an interesting history in itself. *Henry* comes from the ancient German name *Heimirich,* which in turn is most likely related to the even more ancient *Heimdall.* In both names, the prefix *heim* means "home." *Heimdall* was the guardian of Valhalla, the mythical realm that the souls of slain Norse warriors called home. According to the legend, *Heimdall* is so alert that he can hear grass grow and wool sprout on the backs of sheep. He carries a sword and a trumpet, to be used when the gods eventually battle with the anti-gods.

It is not known exactly how, when, or where *Heimdall* became *Heimirich,* but by the Middle Ages, the latter was very popular in Germany. Ultimately, six emperors, scores of princes, and even household cats bore versions of the name. With the fame of the German emperors, it spread throughout Europe. Finally, in France, it was rendered a new appellation when an infant prince was christened *Henri.*

It seems obvious that *Henri* would have become *Henry* when it crossed the English Channel, and it did. But, oddly enough, the name first did a stint as *Harry.* This etymological odyssey began after the French Normans vanquished England in the eleventh century. William the Conqueror named his son *Henri,* but it was pronounced in the French way, *Awn-REE.* The *n* sound is all but lost in French diction, and the British eventually dropped it. Then, by sounding the *h* (as they still do in parts of England), they created *Herry* or *Harry* (pronounced as it is today). The many British *Harry*'s, though, were all officially listed as *Henricus,* because legal documents were kept in Latin. Since *Henricus* was pronounced as we would today say *Henry* (and with a *cus* on the end), the modern pronunciation and spelling finally came into being.

So began a long tradition of royal English *Henry*'s, all of whom have gone by the nickname *Harry.* Following the linguistic rule that converts *r* to *l, Hal,* in turn, became a nickname for *Harry.* (Consider *Sarah*'s nickname *Sally,* and *Molly*'s derivation from *Mary.*)

By the 1800s, *Harry* was so ubiquitous that it became part of the famous generic term for any man, as in "every Tom, Dick and Harry."

In the United States, *Henry* did not become very common until 1800. For the remainder of that century and for the first half of the next, its popularity grew. *Harry* was usually not the American choice for a nickname. (In the United States, *Harry* is usually an independent name or a nickname for *Harold*.) The diminutive Americans inexplicably chose for *Henry* is *Hank,* the etymology of which remains a linguistic mystery.

Henry, Hank, and *Harry* all began to decline after the 1950s, but *Harry* is currently being revived for its "down-to-earth" feel, and, perhaps, in response to the Prince and Princess of Wales naming their second son Henry. *Hank* and *Henry,* though, are now rarely given.

Number

Seven. Long associated with the occult, the number seven is linked to people who have remarkable dreams and gifts of high intelligence.

Astrological sign

Aries. Unafraid to speak their mind, Ariens lean toward self-confidence and unbridled honesty. Harry Houdini was an Arien.

Color

Scarlet. Never a bashful color, this shade of red goes well with Henry, and Aries's ruling planet, Mars. While red can indicate anger, it also is a color of courage.

Stone

Red diamond. Always considered the monarch of all gems, the diamond has unrivaled qualities of hardness and prismatic fire when polished. Red-hued diamonds are rare and prized by collectors. Diamonds were once used as a poison by the upper class. The stone was ground into powder and sprinkled in an enemy's food or drink.

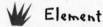 Element

Platinum. Of the three "noble" metals, platinum is the most precious and has a high energy of its own.

Herb

Good King Henry *(Chenopodium bonus henricus)*. Good King Henry, also called goosefoot, now grows wild, having spread from past cultivation as a garden herb. Many still eat it in place of spinach. Leaf poultices were made for skin sores. There is also a variety of red goosefoot that has a reddish stem and grows up to three feet high.

♂ HEW: From the root name *Hugh*.

♂ HIEROME: From the root name *Jerome*.

♂ HILAIRE: From the root name *Hilary*.

♀ HILARIA: From the root name *Hilary*.

♂ HILARIO: From the root name *Hilary*.

♂ HILARIUS: From the root name *Hilary*.

♥ ♀♂ **HILARY** Alaire, Allaire, Hilaire, Hilaria, Hilario, Hilarius, Hilliary, Ilario: *Hilary* is from the Latin name *Hilarius,* which in turn is derived from the Latin word *hilaris,* meaning "cheerful." All told, there are many Christian saints who bear variations of the name *Hilarius.* Though knowledge of accurate spellings can be difficult, names historian Ernest Weekley reports that there were eight saints named *Hilary*, three named *Hilaria*, and two each named *Hilarion* and *Hilarinus*.

The most important of these saints was also an early pope, Hilary (Hilarius) of Poitiers. His fame as defender of the Church led to the name's widespread use in France, where it became *Hilaire*. It is quite possible that the name traveled to England with the Norman Conquest, but that is not certain. What is known is that by the twelfth century, Hilarie was becoming a common name all over Britain. It remained in widespread use until the sixteenth century, when the Reformation sent saints' names into decline.

Throughout much of its early history, the name *Hilary* was used for women as well as men. In the Latin form of the name, *Hilaria* was the feminine. During the twelfth and thirteenth centuries in England, women were named several variations of *Hilary*: the early English version of the name, *Hilarie*, as well as Latin feminine versions *Hilaria* and sometimes *Illaria*. The use of the name for women seems to have declined by the fourteenth century, and was not revived until the twentieth century. The name fell out of fashion for men in the seventeenth century. Though it was in continual use from that time, it could in no way be considered a common name.

There is no known explanation for why *Hilary* revived toward the end of the nineteenth century, but it did. During the twentieth century the name—as both a feminine and masculine—has had important help from various writers. John Galsworthy and J. B. Priestly included male characters named *Hilary* in their novels, and Agatha Christie included a female *Hilary* in one of her mysteries. The great mountaineer and conqueror of Mount Everest, Sir Edmund Hillary, may also have inspired some parents.

While the name has never been as common in the United States as in Britain, when it has been used here, it has been almost exclusively for girls. For many, the variant spelling, *Hillary*, has become the American spelling of the name.

Hilary is still the more common version in Britain. This distinction will probably only be solidified by First Lady Hillary Rodham Clinton, who is the first nationally known American to bear the name. Other variations have included *Hillery* and *Hilarie,* and the obvious diminutives are *Hil* and *Hilly. Alaire* is the masculine variant that is more common today.

 ## Number

One. Ones often lead highly directed lives. Their positive natures can take them to the top of their chosen fields.

 ## Astrological sign

Libra. Living with the ups and downs of a Libran can be difficult, but they're only trying to keep themselves and those around them in balance.

 ## Color

Helianthin. This orange shade mixes the divine power of red with the cheerful hue of yellow to bring joy to the soul.

 ## Stone

Clear fluorite. Formerly known as fluorspar, this gemstone occurs in various colors. When cut and polished correctly, it resembles a diamond. Fluorite's name comes from the Latin *fluere,* which means "to flow." In New Age practices, fluorite is thought to soften strong emotions such as anger. Many believe it strengthens its owner's ability to analyze.

 ## Element

Brass. Brass was sometimes used in place of gold for gem settings and magical spells. Its bright appearance and connection to the sun adds positive energy to a stone or the person wearing it.

🦎 **Herb**

Hillberry *(Gaultheria procumbens)*. Better known as winter-green, this North American evergreen shrub is found from Newfoundland to Georgia and Manitoba to Michigan. Oil obtained from the leaves has pain-relieving effects like aspirin. It was used for relief of headaches and other types of inflammatory aches caused by arthritis and rheumatism. For external use, a leaf tea was cooled, then given as a gargle for sore mouths and throats.

♀   HILLIARY: From the root name *Hilary*.

♀   HOLLIE: From the root name *Holly*.

♀♂ HOLLIS: From the root name *Holly*.

♥ ♀ **HOLLY** Halle, Hollie, Hollis: *Holly* derives from the evergreen shrub originally called *holin* in Middle English and *cuilenn* in Middle Irish. The plant first gave a surname to the English language, when people living near a stand of holly eventually came to be called *Hollis* or *Hollings*.

From 1850 to 1900 naming girls after plants and flowers was at the height of fashion. Of course, girls born during Yuletide were often called *Holly*. People of the Victorian period also developed a taste for names connected to Arthurian romance and legends of old England, and since *Holly* figures prominently in pagan British lore, it was extremely popular.

Though the holly tree is now inextricably associated with Christmas—when "boughs of holly" are brought inside to decorate homes—the use of holly in late winter was once so closely linked to pagan worship that the church fathers tried to ban its use. In pre-Christian times holly was venerated as a symbol of fertility and rebirth. The red berries were associated with blood, and hence holly was also a goddess symbol. The British customs were themselves predated by the ancient Roman Saturnalia, also a celebration of rebirth. During Saturnalia Romans gave holly as a gift, believing it could repel lightning and ward off evil spirits. When the clergy failed centuries later to stop the use of holly, they encouraged an association between the red berries and the blood of Christ, and the holly's spiky leaves as his crown of thorns.

Holly lost favor as a girl's name by the turn of the century but made a comeback in the 1960s, thanks to popular culture. The hit movie *Breakfast at Tiffany's* (1961) featured a charming woman named Holly as the main character. Also at this time John Galsworthy's novel *The Forsyte Saga*, featuring another Holly, was very popular, as was the follow-up television series.

Holly lost favor again after the 1960s, but it is still fairly widely used, and, of course, many living women have the name. Variations on the spelling include *Holli*, *Hollie*, and *Hollee*.

◎ Number

Nine. Some numerologists consider nine to be a number of divine potency because it is the triple of the sacred number three.

☾ Astrological sign

Capricorn. Respect for elders' wisdom and experience is often an inborn trait of Capricorns. They are never out front in a marathon, but like the steady tortoise that overtook the cocky hare, they will eventually triumph.

✳ Color

Evergreen and berry red. The tranquil shade of pine trees and a spark of brilliant red combine to bring body and soul into positively charged harmony.

◆ **Stone**

Rubellite. Rubellite is part of the tourmaline family with color ranges from deep red to violet-red. Darker shades are more valuable for their resemblance to rubies. Rubellite is from Latin meaning "red." Ancient Romans used tourmalines to instill relaxation, particularly for insomniacs. Quality rubellite is found in Siberia, Madagascar, the United States, Brazil, and East Africa.

🌿 **Element**

Platinum. Platinum goes well with all tourmalines and boosts a rubellite's already potent magnetic energy.

🦎 **Herb**

Hollyhock (*Althaea rosea*). Tea made from the flowers of the tall hollyhock plant helped soothe mouth sores and irritated throats of people long ago. Some ancient healers found that leaning over the vapors of a boiling hollyhock brew eased earaches. Today, the multicolored hollyhock flowers are used in various types of cosmetics. Also called rose mallow and althea rose, this plant grows naturally in India and southern Europe.

♀   HONOR: From the root name *Nora*.

♥ ♂ **HOWARD Howie, Ward:** The origin of the name *Howard* is uncertain and may be derived from a few different sources. It is also most often treated as a surname that has only lately come into use as a first name. The name is not included in Charlotte Yonge's *Preeminent History of Christian Names*, proving that in England, in 1884 at least, its use as a first name was so uncommon that it didn't merit her inclusion. However, she does explore the Saxon name

Heorovard or *Hereward,* which are close to *Howard.* From the Saxon *heoru* meaning "sword," and *vard,* meaning "protect," she gives the meaning as "sword-guardian." This fits with other interpretations of *Howard* such as "noble watchman" and "guardian of the army." Another similar word, *hayward,* was the term used in the Feudal period for a manorial officer.

Another possible source with a similar meaning is the Teutonic name, *Huguard,* which comes from *hugu,* meaning "heart" or "soul" and *vardu,* meaning "ward" or "protection" (Withycombe). Strangely, *The Facts on File Dictionary of First Names* says that the name might also mean "shepherd or pigherd," but no etymology for this is given. Just to spice up the stew a bit, *Howard* can also be connected phonetically to the Old French word for osprey, *huard.*

Despite the fact that most sources state that *Howard* was used first as a surname, there are a few cases in the eleventh and twelfth centuries where *Howard, Heward,* and *Hereward* were all used as first names. Those names then dropped from use before reappearing again in England as a last name with distinctly aristocratic connotations.

No one is completely certain why *Howard* developed into such a popular first name, but there were probably several factors working together. In both England and the United States, there has been a long-standing tradition of using surnames as first names in order to carry on a name from the matrilineal line. There is also the possibility that the surname's aristocratic feel led to its popularity among commoners as a first name. *Facts on File* also points to the popularity of Oliver Otis Howard (1830–1909), a Civil War hero and founder of famed Howard University, as a reason for the name's popularity in the United States.

However it occurred, by the 1870s *Howard* was among the top fifty-one names in the United States. Over time, the name's aristocratic origins have largely gone by the wayside, and it has become a standard first name. In the twentieth century, the millionaire Howard Hughes and the film actor Howard Keel, (originally Harold Keel), probably helped to maintain the popularity of the name. It was still among the top fifty names in the 1950s, but has dropped off radically in the decades since. The diminutive most frequently heard is *Howie*.

◎ Number

Six. Sixes have the power to make strong friendships and attract people to themselves and their causes. It has also been called the "number of Man" in accordance with the biblical revelation that God created mankind on the sixth day.

☾ Astrological sign

Sagittarius. This is the sign of the hunter or archer. It is said that those born under the sign of Sagittarius are protected by heaven and follow the path of truth. Many Sagittarians are gifted with wisdom and foresight.

☀ Color

Plum. All shades of purple are tied to the planet Jupiter, which rules Sagittarius.

◆ Stone

Howlite: This soft mineral can be a chalky white color with veins of black or brown. Large quantities of howlite crystals are found in California. Although this is not a hard rock, it polishes well and is used mainly in beads.

� Element

Iron. For ages, iron has been used for weapons and tools. It was also thought to protect against evil and witchcraft.

Herb

Hyssop *(Hyssopus officinalis)*. A member of the evergreen family, this bushy plant has a strong camphorlike scent and purple-blue flowers. Hyssop grows wild in warmer climates and was brought to North America by southern European settlers. Early healers used the herb part of the plant for poultices on bruises or wounds and to make soothing eye-washes to cure eye infections.

♂   HOWIE: From the root name *Howard*.

♀   HUETTE: From the root name *Hugh*.

♂   HUEY: From the root name *Hugh*.

♥ ♂ **HUGH** **Hew, Huette, Huey, Hughes, Hughina, Hugo, Ugo:** There are two seemingly distinct and separate origins for *Hugh*. The origin for the name throughout most of Western Europe is Teutonic. In ancient German, the word *hugr* is said to mean "thought." In German mythology, two ravens sat on Thor's shoulders: Huginn represented thought and Munninn represented memory. Another myth involving Thor describes his trip to Utgard, when Hugi—thought—was the only thing faster and beat him in the race. A relative of the name appears in one of the earliest Anglo-Saxon stories, *Beowulf*. In that story, the sea-king of the Geats is Hygelac, and his name is taken to mean either "the sport of thought" or "the reward of thought." (There is also a connection to the Teutonic German word *hugu,* which means "heart and mind.")

As a basic name with a worthy meaning and mythic antecedents, variations of *Hugh* spread throughout Continental Europe, changing as it entered new regions and languages. Spelled *Hugo* or *Hugur* in northern Germany and Scandinavia, it became *Hugues* or *Hugon* in northern France.

317

By the tenth century the name was already widely used by the Franks. In A.D. 987, it became even more popular when Hugues Capet, the first of fifteen Capetian kings, ascended the throne. Another important Hugues was Saint Hugues, archbishop of Rouen in the eleventh century.

Many sources report that *Hugh* did not appear in England until after the Norman Conquest and was a variation of the northern French *Hugues*. However, the second possible root for the British *Hugh* comes from a very different source. *Hu* is one of the oldest names among the Welsh, and comes from the Welsh—possibly Druidic—sun god, Hu Gadarn. It is also believed that the holy islands, Iona and Mona were, at one time, both called Ynysgwaw Hu. Some believe that the name traveled to Brittany where it became *Hue, Hues, Huon,* and the feminine, *Huette.* Others believe that these southern French names derived from the Teutonic. In Anglicized Welsh, the name was sometimes written as *Huw* or *Hew*. (It is sometimes thought that the Irish name *Aidan*—from the Celtic root *Aodh,* meaning "fire"—is a Celtic version of *Hugh*.)

It makes sense that as the Anglo-Saxon and Welsh cultures influenced each other, the two names, *Hu* and *Hugh,* became synonymous, but most sources do not mention the Welsh connections to the name. However, after the Norman Conquest, the British history of the name becomes clearer. It appears frequently in the Domesday Book and its popularity was increased with the canonization of Saint Hugh (ca. A.D. 1140–1200), especially in the North of England. Later another saint, Little Saint Hugh of Lincoln (A.D. 1245–1255), made the name even more common. Chaucer immortalized his story in The Prioress's Tale. And in Scotland from the fourteenth through the sixteenth centuries, the name appears as *Huchon*. In England, up until the sixteenth century, the name is often spelled *Huon*.

Hugh became less popular after the Protestant Reformation and did not travel with the Puritans to the American colonies. After the Puritan influence dwindled, the name came back into vogue, at least slightly. The diminutive Huey has been made famous by Huey Long, the notorious Louisiana governor and "Huey" the duck of "Huey, Duey, and Louey," a reference that may have, in fact, contributed to the name's decline in the last three decades in the United States.

Number

Eight. Many numerologists link eight to intuition and regeneration. Eights have no middle ground; they are either great successes or total failures.

Astrological sign

Aries. The ram is the first of the twelve signs of the zodiac. Ariens are often self-assertive and fearless in their pursuits. Hugh Hefner is an Aries.

Color

Burnt carmine. While carmine is considered a vivid red, this slightly darker shade adds an element of heated intensity, appropriate for a name connected to a sun god.

Stone

Essonite. A member of the grossular garnet family, essonite ranges from honey-brown to orange-brown. The coloration comes from the presence of manganese and iron in the stone. Gem lore suggests that garnets help balance one's energy. Ancient Greeks and Romans used hessonite to make stunning cameos. Essonite is found mainly in Sri Lanka and Madagascar.

Element

Manganese. This brittle metallic element is used in making alloys of steel. It is number 25 in the periodic table of elements.

Herb

Cinnamon *(Cinnamomum cassia)*. This fragrant reddish brown spice is related to the cassia plant. Ground powder from the dried bark was used in traditional Chinese medicine for treating some kidney conditions. Cinnamon tea was thought to be helpful in dispelling nausea and heartburn. Cinnamon oil is used in modern massage treatments and aromatherapy.

♂ HUGHES: From the root name *Hugh*.

♀ HUGHINA: From the root name *Hugh*.

♂ HUGO: From the root name *Hugh*.

♥ ♂ **HUNTER:** The name *Hunter* is from the Anglo-Saxon and derives, quite simply, from the occupation. It then became a surname and has only recently come into use as a given name. An excellent example of the process by which occupations became surnames can be found in the report of the tragic death of a man in 1246. The death was reported as such: "Thomas, son of Siward the Otterhunter, fell from a horse in Yarrow water and was drowned." As names historian C. M. Matthews notes, had Thomas lived he would either have adopted the surname *Siward,* or an abbreviation of his father's occupation, that is, *Hunter.*

The irony of the success of the name *Hunter* is that after the Norman Conquest, most of the English were in fact forbidden to hunt independently in the huge areas of England that became Norman royal or baronial lands. The English, however, were allowed to hunt as employees of their Norman overlords. Some historians believe that the English continued to use the Anglo-Saxon term, as opposed to the Norman ones, *chasseur* and *veneur,* as a small measure of defiance.

As a first name, *Hunter* was used more often in Scotland, but is rare enough that almost no books on first names even list it. No one knows specifically why the name has become so popular in the United States in recent years. Certainly, the recent fashion for surnames as first names in general has influenced the adoption of the name. Whatever the reason, *Hunter* is consistently among the top one hundred boys' names. One contemporary actress, Hunter Tylo, has recently gained public attention, and in this age of cross-gender naming, she may well inspire some parents to adopt the name for girls as well.

◎ Number

Five. Most fives are quick-witted and think well under pressure. Modern numerologists see five as a number of the innovative and curious. P. T. Barnum was born under the number five.

☾ Astrological sign

Sagittarius. Sagittarians often enjoy sports and love to be outside. This seems fitting for the sign of the symbolic hunter.

✳ Color

Hunter green. This rich shade of green refreshes the spirit and is restful to the eyes.

◆ Stone

Aventurine quartz. Also called "Indian jade," this green quartzite gem is iridescent from its content of fuchite mica. Ancient Tibetans used aventurine on their statues, particularly for the eyes as a symbol of visionary ability. It was also used in pendants and amulets for luck in gambling. Major sources of aventurine are found in Brazil, India, Russia, and Tanzania.

Element

Brass. Brass was once believed to have the power to attract money.

Herb

Coltsfoot *(Tussilago farfara)*. This plant has horse-hoofed shaped leaves and several equine-related common names, including horsefoot. It grows along streamsides and in moist pastures. According to herbal lore, the flowers were used in respiratory remedies for coughs, colds, and vocal hoarseness. Natives found that smoking the leaves helped dry coughs and shortness of breath. Crushed leaves applied to insect bites, skin ulcers, and burns relieved pain and itching.

♂   IACOPO: From the root name *Jacob/James*.

♂   IAGO: From the root name *Jacob/James*.

♂   IAKOB: From the root name *Jacob/James*.

♂   IAN: From the root name *John*.

♂   IBRAHIM: From the root name *Abraham*.

♂   IGOR: From the root name *George*.

♂   IKE: From the root name *Isaac*.

♂   ILARIO: From the root name *Hilary*.

♀   ILEANA: From the root name *Helen*.

♀   ILENE: From the root name *Helen*.

♀   ILONA: From the root name *Helen*.

♀   ILSE: From the root name *Elizabeth*.

♀   ILYSEE: From the root name *Alice*.

♀   ILYSSA: From the root name *Alyssa*.

♀   INA: From the root name *Charles*.

♂   IOANNIS: From the root name *John*.

♂   IOSEP: From the root name *Joseph*.

♀   IRA: From the root name *Irene*.

♀   IRANDA: From the root name *Irene*.

♥ ♀ **IRENE**   **Arina, Eirene, Ira, Iranda, Iriana, Irina, Orina, Reenie, Rena, Rene, Renie, Rennie, Rina, Yarina**: The name *Irene* is a variation of the Greek word *eirene* and means "peace." Eirene was the goddess of peace in Greek mythology, though she is far better known by her Roman name, Pax. Whether it was thanks to the Romans or early Christians, at some point the name eventually transformed into *Irene*. Among the earliest historical *Irene*s of Christendom was the widow who cared for and revived Saint Sebastian after his martyrdom. Another famous *Irene* was one of three sisters, Agape, Irene, and Chionia who supposedly were martyred at Thessalonica around A.D. 303. Altogether, there have been four saints named *Irene*. These holy *Irene*s led to the name's popularity in Greece, and many empresses have been given the name. From Greece, *Irene* traveled to Russia and Eastern Europe where it became one of the most widely used names—*Irina*.

In spite of its long history, *Irene* only began to appear in England and the United States in the late nineteenth century. In England, it is pronounced closer to the Greek pronunciation—with three syllables. Some sources believe that this pronunciation proves that the early use of the name in England was by parents from the upper classes, because they are the ones most likely to have received a classical education, which included the study of Greek.

Irene seems to have traveled to the United States at about the same time a great number of Greek, Eastern European, and Russian citizens immigrated, and it caught on rapidly. By 1900, it was among the top fifty American girls' names. (It didn't become that common in England until the 1920s.) Some historians speculate that, because *Irene* was, from the start, pronounced in the United States with two syllables, it may have entered through literary and intellectual sources rather than on the immigrants' family rosters.

The popular song "Goodnight Irene" as well as the film actress Irene Dunne have both helped maintain the name's popularity. Overall it has become less fashionable in recent decades, but seems to be remaining popular among African American families. *Irene*'s diminutives include *Rene, Renie, Renee, Rena, Rennie*. Though similar, none of these should be confused with the French, *René*.

Number

Six. Some modern numerologists tie this number to devotion and equilibrium.

Astrological sign

Libra. People of this sign dislike being rude, but will find a way to correct an errant situation even if it means pointing out someone else's mistake. True to their symbol of the scales, Librans strive for balance and accord.

Color

Lavender. This soft shade of purple represents peace and meditation. It is also a color of healing, spirituality, and purification.

Stone

Violet fluorite. Once called fluorspar, this gemstone comes in a variety of colors. It can be faceted and polished to a brilliant sheen. Ancient Egyptians used fluorite to decorate statues. Sacred scarabs carved from this gem have been discovered in burial sites. Some of the largest fluorite crystals are found in the United States.

Element

Copper. According to folklore, copper is a lucky metal. It is also tied to the planet Venus and was worn by some to attract love.

🌿 Herb

English lavender *(Lavandula vera).* A tonic made from the flowers and leaves of this Mediterranean shrub were once used as a sedative and for headaches. The lilac-colored flowers have a delicate pleasing scent and were added to bath water by ladies of many cultures. They believed the perfume relaxed the mind and soothed the body. Lavender comes from the Latin word *lavandus,* which means "to be washed."

♀   IRIANA: From the root name *Irene.*

♀   IRINA: From the root name *Irene.*

♂   ISAAK: From the root name *Isaac.*

♀   ISABELLE: From the root name *Elizabeth.*

♂   ISACCO: From the root name *Isaac.*

♂   ISKANDER: From the root name *Alexander.*

♥ ♂ **ISAAC** **Ike, Isaak, Isacco, Itzak, Izak, Yitzhak, Zack, Zak:** Although the original name may have non-Hebrew roots, *Isaac* comes from the Hebrew word *yizchak,* meaning "laughter." It is sometimes said to mean "God may laugh," or "Look kindly upon this person." Many names scholars believe that the Israelites Hebrewized a foreign name that sounded to them like *yizchak* and called it "laughter" in order to link it to the story of Isaac, the son of Abraham and Sarah. When Sarah learned that she was to have a child, she laughed aloud, not only because it was a happy occasion, but because her baby's father was already one hundred years old. According to the Book of Genesis, Sarah realized that others might laugh as well, hence the possible pleading interpretation to "look kindly upon this person" when young Isaac was introduced.

Yizchak is found frequently in the Talmud, and was the name of an influential Palestinian scholar during the third century A.D. Transformed into *Isaac* when it was Latinized, the appellation was quite popular in the early Eastern Orthodox Church as well. A variant, *Isaak,* was favored by Byzantine royals in Constantinople, from where it traveled, through its connection to Eastern Orthodoxy, to Russia.

Isaac appears a few times in medieval English census records. Probably made popular in England through mystery plays—dramas based on the life of Christ—the name was used by both Christians and Jews during that period. In the twelfth century it was possibly the number-one name among English Jews. French Huguenots also bestowed it often, and it spread successfully throughout Europe after the Protestant Reformation.

As an ancient biblical name, *Isaac* was chosen with great regularity by the Puritans of the seventeenth century. It traveled with them to America, and remained in vogue throughout the eighteenth and nineteenth centuries. It has always been popular among blacks in America. (Two black heroes of the American Revolution were named Isaac.) However, it began to lose ground among white Christians in the United States early in the twentieth century. By 1950, it had almost completely disappeared among members of that culture group. Many historians ascribe the loss of the name among Christian whites to the increase of the Jewish population and the associated rise in anti-Semitism, which began just prior to the turn of the century. Increasingly, *Isaac* came to be considered a Jewish name. Among African Americans during the same period, though, the name maintained its longstanding popularity.

In the 1960s *Isaac* surged again in popularity among all Americans, and by the 1990s, it was among the most popular boys' names in the United States. The original Hebrew name became increasingly recognizable as Yitzak Perlman, the violinist, and Yitzak Rabin, Israel's late prime minister, achieved prominence.

Zak, or *Zack,* is a traditional diminutive for *Isaac,* but in modern times that form is more commonly associated with *Zachary. Ike* and *Izzy* are probably the favorite nicknames for *Isaac* today.

⊚ Number

Six. This is a number of the resolute. Sixes are sincere and can excel in scholarly or spiritual pursuits.

☾ Astrological sign

Capricorn. Capricorns are not usually carefree and flashy types, instead they proceed on their life paths like the sturdy mountain goat climbs steep slopes. Sir Isaac Newton and Isaac Asimov were born under this sign.

✳ Color

Apple green. This bright shade signifies joy and laughter. When part of someone's physical aura, green reveals ingenuity and versatility.

◆ Stone

Peridot. These beautiful transparent green gems were prized by Egyptian pharaohs and worn by their priests to ward off envious thoughts about a pharaoh's absolute power. Peridots were also carried for their healing properties. Some lore said that when medicinal tonics were drunk from cups made of peridot, the potion became stronger.

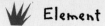 **Element**

Gold. In Druidic rituals gold was used with peridot to protect the wearer from ill health and dark enchantments.

Herb

Desert Tea *(Ephedra spp)*. This herb comes from a broom-like shrub that grows mainly in arid climates. It has grooved bright green stems and some species grow to six feet high. Herbal teas brewed from this plant have a pleasant taste. Several southwestern Native American tribes used the tea as a remedy for kidney pain or fever. The pioneers used desert tea as a blood purifier.

♂   ITZAK: From the root name *Isaac*.

♀   IVA: From the root name *John*.

♂   IVAN: From the root name *John*.

♂   IZAK: From the root name *Isaac*.

♂ JACE: From the root name *Jason*.

♂ JACK: From the root names *Jacob/James* and *John*.

♀ JACKETTE: From the root name *Jacob/James*.

♀♂ JACKIE: From the root names *Jacob/James* and *John*.

♂ JACKO: From the root name *Jacob/James*.

♂ JACKSON: From the root name *Jacob/James*.

♂ JACO: From the root name *Jacob/James*.

♥ ♂ JACOB/JAMES   Cob, Coby, Diego, Gemma, Giacomo, Hamish, Iacopo, Iago, Iakob, Jaco, Jack, Jackette, Jackie, Jacko, Jackson, Jaco, Jacqueline, Jacquenetta, Jacques, Jacqui, Jago, Jaime, Jake, Jameson, Jamie, Jaquith, Jay, Jemma, Jim, Jimmy, Jock, Seamus, Shamus, Yakov: *Jacob* is one of the oldest names in the Western lexicon. It first appears in the Old Testament as the name of Isaac and Rebekah's second son, called Ja'akob, *Akkub,* or most commonly, *Yaakov.* Most scholars believe that the name comes from the Hebrew root *akeb,* meaning "heel." It came to mean "supplanter," because Jacob supplanted his elder brother Esau. Of course, there is also the view that *Yaakov* is actually a far more ancient, pre-biblical name, and that all this interpretation of its meaning was only attached after the biblical Jacob became famous.

The name became common, not only among the Hebrew tribes, but also among the Arabs, where it is transliterated

Yacoub. The name became *Jakobos* among the Greeks and *Jacobus* or *Jacomus* among the Romans. Another biblical Jacob is Akkub of the Book of Nehemiah, who stands up with Ezra to read the law to the people. Both of the Christian Apostles who were called James in English, were originally called *Yaakov* or *Akkub*, (i.e., *Jacob*.)

One of these apostles attained his greatest early fame in Spain, where he reportedly spent some time. There his name became Santo Jaco de Compostella, which ultimately transformed into Santiago de Compostella. Among the Spanish, Santiago was reported to have appeared during their battles with the Moors. He became their champion, and his name became their war cry. Three Spanish orders of knights were named after him, and his shrine in Spain became a place of pilgrimage for Christians all over Europe. In his honor, many Spanish children were christened *Tiago* or *Diego*.

The *m* which transformed the name into the English *James* was found first among the people of Aragon, where *Jaco* became *Jayme* or *Jaime*. The name was then adopted among the royal lines of Aragon, Sicily, and Majorca. Among the Italians, the name became *Giacopo*, *Jacopo*, *Giacomo*, and *Como*, while the Germans returned to *Jakob*. The French transformed the name into *Jacques* and the name grew to be so popular that "Jacques Bonhomme" became a generic French term for the peasantry. The Russians, who also revered the two apostles, transformed the name into *Jakov*, *Jascha*, and *Jaschenka* for boys, and *Zakelina* for girls.

Oddly enough, another form, *Iago*—a name Shakespeare made famous in his play *Othello*—seems to have been used only by the Italians and the Welsh.

The name *James* first appears in England one hundred years after the Norman Conquest, at around the time of the first known English pilgrimage to the Spanish shrine of Santiago de Compostella. Until the seventeenth century, however, it was more common as a surname than as a given name—as in *James, Jameson,* and *FitzJames.*

In Scotland and Ireland, a variation of *James* came into use as a first name far earlier than in England. The Highland Scots transformed the name into *Hamish* and the Irish transformed it into *Seumuis* or *Seamus. James,* itself, became a royal Scottish name that was used for generations. In fact, it is through the Scottish King James—who became James I of England in 1603—that the name really became widespread in England.

The first permanent English colony in America was established as Jamestown in 1607, and *James* was popular among the English settlers. But the later Scottish immigrants made it even more common. It has consistently been one of the most popular names among African Americans. *James* is still on any list of popular boys' names, usually in the top ten. Nicknames for *James* include *Jim, Jimmy,* and *Jamie.*

Jacob, on the other hand, did not gain a popular American foothold until recently. Despite its staunch biblical background, the name was not common among the Puritans, probably because it was connected to two other settler groups—the Germans who settled in Pennsylvania and became known as the "Pennsylvania Dutch," and the Jews who settled in New York and Rhode Island. *Jacob*'s diminutive, *Jake,* was also limited for a long time to those two groups. Only in the past few decades has the name spread in popularity. *Jake,* given as an independent name, is also among the most popular boys' names.

A traditional feminine version of *James* is *Gemma* (or *Jemma*), which began to appear in England during the Middle Ages and remains in use today. However, the French *Jacqueline* and its diminutive, *Jackie,* have been the most consistently popular feminine forms of the name. Another modern feminine variation is *Jamie* (or *Jaime*), which was among the top one hundred girls' names in 1996. *Jaime* is a Spanish version of *James,* and occasionally parents name boys in the United States *Jaime* and pronounce it identically to *Jamie.*

🌀 Number

Four. Four is the ruling number of Aquarius and is also tied to the planets of Saturn and Uranus. Fours often like to rebel against rules and regulations.

🌙 Astrological sign

Aquarius. While most Aquarians are tranquil by nature, many get a secret kick out of defying the conventional. James Dean, James Joyce, and James Michener were all Aquarians.

✴ Color

Turquoise green. A combination of blue and green unites the sky color associated with Aquarians and the lush landscapes of Ireland and Scotland.

♦ Stone

Jadeite. Also called jade, this stone comes in many colors, but the shade most commonly associated with it is green. The ancient Chinese called it "imperial jade" and linked it to wisdom and inspiration of the mind. The Spanish conquistadors wore amulets fashioned from it, copying the art of the natives they enslaved. Jadeite's rich color comes from the mineral chromium.

👑 Element

Copper. For ages, copper has been tied to healing. In Mexico, pennies were laid on a person's navel to prevent motion sickness.

🌿 Herb

Jacob's ladder *(Polemonium cæruleum)*. Often found in wild bushy places and by streams, the plant is bright green and smooth. Jacob's ladder has large blue flowers and is cultivated in Scotland and Ireland for its beauty. The herb of the plant has traditionally been used by healers for nervous conditions, headaches, and hysteria.

♀ JACQUELINE: From the root name *Jacob/James*.

♀ JACQUENETTA: From the root name *Jacob/James*.

♂ JACQUES: From the root name *Jacob/James*.

♀ JACQUI: From the root name *Jacob/James*.

♂ JAGO: From the root name *Jacob/James*.

♂ JAIME: From the root name *Jacob/James*.

♂ JAISEN: From the root name *Jason*.

♂ JAKE: From the root name *Jacob/James*.

♂ JAMESON: From the root name *Jacob/James*.

♀♂ JAMIE: From the root name *Jacob/James*.

♀♂ JAN: From the root name *John*.

♀ JANA: From the root name *John*.

♀ JANE: From the root name *John*.

♂ JANEK: From the root name *John*.

♀ JANET: From the root name *John*.

♀ JANETTE: From the root name *John*.

♀ JANIA: From the root name *John*.

♀ JANICE: From the root name *John*.

♀ JANINE: From the root name *John*.

♀ JANIS: From the root name *John*.

♀ JANNA: From the root name *John*.

♂   JANOS: From the root name *John*.

♀   JAQUITH: From the root name *Jacob/James*.

♂   JARAD: From the root name *Jared*.

♀   JARDENA: From the root name *Jordan*.

♥ ♂ **JARED**   Jarad, Jarrod, Jerrid: *Jared* is an ancient name that is descended from the Arabic word *ward* and from the Hebrew name *Yered* (or *Yared*). It is variously said to mean either "rose" or "to descend." Some believe that it probably came from a much older language and that no one today knows its true meaning. The earliest historical *Jared* is a character in Genesis, who is most notable because he lived to be 962 years old. He is the second oldest man in the Bible and is only outdone by his own grandson, Methuselah, who lived to be 969.

As a first name, *Jared* has been used almost exclusively by Americans since it came into vogue among Puritans in the seventeenth century. An early American *Jared* was Jared Eliot (1685–1763), a colonial minister, physician, and agronomist. Another noted bearer of the name was Jared Sparks (1789–1866) editor of *The North American Review* and president of Harvard College. He also was a prominent historian of the period, but his fondness for cleaning up American history and embellishing the writings of the Founding Fathers have led much of his work to be dismissed among modern historians.

The name has also been passed down in the Ingersoll family. The first two Jared Ingersolls—who were influential in the arena of public affairs—began the tradition in the late 1700s. Also, two American towns have been named for men with the first name *Jared*. In 1808, Mansfield, Ohio, was named for the U.S. surveyor general, Jared Mansfield, and Jared Torrance founded Torrance, California in 1911.

No one really knows why the name emerged again in the mid-1960s, but it did. Oddly enough the initial resurgence occurred in Britain, but now it is among the most popular boys' names in the United States. *Jarrod* is usually thought of as a variant spelling of the name and is particularly popular in African American families.

Number

Two. Most twos are kind-natured. They usually exhibit patience and tolerance under most circumstances.

Astrological sign

Taurus. Astrologers label Taureans as down-to-earth and even stodgy, but being ruled by Venus gives them a romantic soul that rivals the passions of a Scorpio.

Color

Antique ivory. A blending of brown and white represents stability and wisdom.

Stone

Brown amber. This organic gem of ancient tree resin is considered to be as old as time itself. The name comes from the Arabic *anbar,* but the Romans called it *succinum,* which means "tree sap." Its use as sacred jewelry or ornaments dates from the Neolithic era. It is usually a honey-brown to dark brown color and transparent, revealing either plant or animal remains, preserved in perfect detail.

Element

Iron. Iron was once considered a "protective" metal. Some placed iron pieces in every room and buried small bits at the four corners of their property.

Herb

Fringe Tree *(Chionanthus virginica)*. More commonly called "old man's beard" or "gray beard tree," this tree grows in the mid- and southern United States and sometimes New England. It has fragrant white flowers that bloom in May and June with fringelike petals. Its bark was once used to break fevers and aid those with stomach distress or liver or kidney ailments. Bark poultices helped minor wounds and soothed skin irritations.

♂   JARELL: From the root name *Gerald*.

♂   JARROD: From the root name *Jered*.

♂   JASE: From the root name *Jason*.

♀   JASIA: From the root name *John*.

♥ ♂ **JASON** Jace, Jaisen, Jase, Jay, Jayson: The name *Jason* has a somewhat confusing history. *Merriam-Webster's Collegiate Dictionary* defines the name as, "Jason, noun, [Latin Iason, from the Greek Iason]: a legendary Greek hero distinguished for his successful quest of the Golden Fleece."

But Jason—from *Eason* or *Aeson*—is also the Greek form of the Hebrew name *Joshua*. It was adopted by Hellenistic or Greek-speaking Jews. *Joshua*—and therefore Greek-Jewish *Jason*—is said to mean variously "healer" or "the Lord is my salvation." Some sources insist that the two names have nothing to do with each other. But, if we accept all of the above listed derivations of the name, it has a much richer history.

The earliest known *Jason* is the famous figure of Greek mythology who captured the Golden Fleece, married Medea, and then left her in order to marry a king's daughter. For this insult, Medea killed their two children. After the mythic

Jason, the next important Greek with the name is Jason of Pherae. This Jason was a notorious despot who ruled the kingdom of Thessaly from 385 B.C. until he was assassinated in 370 B.C.

A high priest of Jerusalem under Antiochus IV (c.172 B.C.) was, in fact, given the Hebrew name *Joshua,* but because of his Hellenistic loyalties, he was (and still is) more commonly known by his Greek name, *Jason.* Jason and his even more Hellenistic rival, Menelaus, went to war when Antiochus gave Menelaus the position of high priest. Jason succeeded in conquering Jerusalem, which he then ruled for two years before Antiochus retook the city. Jason of Cyrene, a Jewish historian, is said to have compiled a five-volume history that is summarized in II Maccabees. This history covers the same period.

In the New Testament, a Jason is recorded to have hosted Paul when he visited Thessalonica when he went there to establish a Christian community. As his patron, Jason was legally responsible for Paul's actions and was persecuted for this reason.

Despite its rich and interesting history, the name seems to largely disappear in the post-biblical period. Dante uses it in *Canto XIX Inferno,* but it almost seems to be an epithet. In criticizing Pope Clement, Dante writes that Clement is "a shepherd without law, of uglier deed" and a "new Jason."

The name does not reappear in historical records until it began to be used, rarely, in England in the seventeenth century. There are few references to the name in early American history. However, in 1775, the Jason Russell House was the scene of a skirmish between the British and the American colonists, and in 1834 a group of Methodists, headed by Jason Lee, established the first permanent settlement in the Willamette valley of Oregon.

Jason's history gains force again in the twentieth century. In William Faulkner's classic novel *The Sound and the*

Fury (1929), a major character is named Jason. In the 1950s Jason Robards, Jr., began his exceptional theatrical career. Since the 1970s, the name has been among the most popular boys' names in the country. One occasionally hears the nickname *Jace* given to boys named *Jason,* and it is sometimes used as an independent name.

 ## Number

Five. Holding a five back is like trying to control the ocean tides. They are energetic and willing to brave any storm.

 ## Astrological sign

Cancer. People of this sign often want to cling to home base, yet are reluctant to settle down. Because they are ruled by water, Cancers are quite sensitive and will withdraw into their shell when their heart is wounded.

 ## Color

Sea foam. Green is the hue of health and worn by some mystics during healing rituals.

 ## Stone

Argonite. While argonite is normally transparent and colorless or white in its purest form, the presence of trace minerals can add shades of yellow, blue, pink, or green. It appears in various forms including spiked crystals that form in a circle. Argonite is also found in stalactites. Some argonite deposits occur in Turkey, France, Colorado, and Cumbria, England. Due to its delicate nature, it is not faceted, but used instead for beaded jewelry and decoration.

 ## Element

Silver. Silver is a moon metal and is also linked to water. It is believed to boost psychic and healing energy.

❧ Herb

Figwort *(Scrophularia nodosa).* This perennial grows in rich woodlands and thickets in the United States from Maine to Georgia and South Dakota and Kansas. The entire plant was used mainly for skin problems such as eczema, tumors, and many types of rashes. Sometimes the plant was ground and boiled to make ointments for scratches, bruises, and minor scrapes or cuts.

♂ JAY: From the root names *Jacob/James* and *Jason.*

♀ JAYNE: From the root name *John.*

♂ JAYSON: From the root name *Jason.*

♀ JEAN: From the root name *John.*

♀ JEANIE: From the root name *John.*

♀ JEANNETTE: From the root name *John.*

♀ JEANNINE: From the root name *John.*

♀ JEENA: From the root name *Eugene.*

♂ JEFF: From the root name *Geoffrey.*

♂ JEFFERIES: From the root name *Geoffrey.*

♂ JEFFERS: From the root name *Geoffrey.*

♂ JEFFREY: From the root name *Geoffrey.*

♀ JELENA: From the root name *Helen.*

♀ JELIKA: From the root name *Helen.*

♂ JEM: From the root name *Jeremy.*

♀ JEMMA: From the root name *Jacob/James.*

♂ JEMMY: From the root name *Jeremy.*

♀ JEN: From the root name *Jennifer.*

♀ JENELLA: From the root name *Virginia.*

♀ JENELLE: From the root name *John.*

♀ JENI: From the root name *John*.

♀ JENNA: From the root names *Eugene* and *Jennifer*.

♀ JENNIE: From the root name *Eugene*.

♥ ♀ **JENNIFER** **Gena, Genevieve, Genna, Gennie, Gennifer, Ginerva, Ginetta, Guinevere, Gwen, Gwendolyn, Jen, Jenna, Jennie, Jennora, Jenny, Wendy, Winifred:** The name *Jennifer,* more popular in the United States today than ever before, is directly descended from *Guinevere,* a name that has ever been associated with beauty and tragic romance. In most accounts of King Arthur's legend, Arthur's best friend and most loyal knight, Lancelot, falls in love with Arthur's queen, Guinevere, and she with him. Their passion drives them to rebellion, leads to war, and lands Guinevere in a convent where she lives out her days in seclusion. The story has, of course, inspired countless ballads, tales, plays, and poems, all of which have ensured the continual popularity of the name.

Even before the coming of Guinevere to King Arthur's court, there was, according to legend, a heroine there named Gwendolyn who was the daughter of Corineus, the Duke of Cornwall. She was betrothed to one Locryn, son of the Trojan Brutus, who later fell in love with Astrild, the king of Germany's beautiful daughter. Locryn married Gwendolyn because he was afraid of her father, but after Corineus died, he dismissed her and made Astrild his queen. Thereupon the valiant Gwendolyn rallied her father's troops, and they killed the faithless Locryn in battle.

Both *Guinevere* and *Gwendolyn* were names formed from *gwen,* a Welsh word closely related to the Celtic words meaning "white" or "fair." The word *gwen* also means, simply, "woman." In Old Welsh it was common to use the suffix *wen* to feminize masculine names. So one might encounter the name *Cainwen,* the feminine form of *Cain.*

Winifred is also a Welsh name derived from the root *gwen*. It gained a following thanks to Saint Gwenfrewi of Wales, whose name was eventually modernized to *Winifred*. At the turn of the twentieth century, *Winifred* was widely used in England, and enjoyed some popularity in the United States. Though still used in England, *Winifred* has almost completely fallen away here.

The French name *Genevieve* is believed to have come from the English *Gwenhwyfar*, the original form of *Guinevere*. The first time the name was recorded was in A.D. 422, when the venerable Saint Genevieve was born in Nanterre, France. Saint Genevieve distinguished herself by going unarmed before the marauding Franks, delivering supplies to her besieged countrymen and pleading for the lives of prisoners. She became the patron saint of Paris after her death, and throughout France there are to this day many diminutives of the name in use including *Javotte, Genevion,* and *Vevette.*

In Germany there is a beloved folk tale about one Genovefa, whose husband casts her out and drives her into the forest because he wrongly doubts her fidelity to him. While banished to the forest, Genovefa gives birth to an infant who is fed by a white doe. From that point in the story there are innumerable variations, including variants still told in North America among the French-speaking Cajun people of Louisiana and the French Canadian people. Whether the tale originated in the German and migrated to France before the French colonists settled in Canada (and eventually migrated to Louisiana), or whether it originated in the French is unknown. At any rate, in the North American versions of the story, the heroine's name is, predictably, Genevieve.

Jennifer probably first appeared in Cornwall, England, as a corruption of *Guinevere* and *Genevieve*. It remained popular in England, so much so that when Richard Arkwright (1732–1792) invented a machine that automated the process of spinning thread—which helped to spark the industrial revolution—it was commonly called "the spinning jenny."

Jennifer has had even more success in the United States, especially in recent years. *Jenny, Jen, Jenna, Genna,* and *Gena,* are all popular derivatives or nicknames associated with *Jennifer* and, less frequently, *Genevieve. Jenny* appears to be a popular diminutive for other names as well, including *Virginia* (*Ginny*). Many sources trace *Jenny* to an English or Scottish variant of *Johanna* or *Jane,* or even to *Janet. Jenna,* often a nickname for *Jennifer,* has also been used as a variant of *Jeanette. Jenna* has recently become common as an independent name. *Gwendolyn* is heard, but is not fashionable at present. However, the related name, *Wendy,* has had a steady following as an independent in the second half of the twentieth century.

 ## Number

Nine. This number rules the sign of Scorpio. Nines may be impulsive, but have great courage.

 ## Astrological sign

Scorpio. People of this sign might be volatile and are often misunderstood because they prefer to keep their secrets to themselves. Beware of a Scorpio when riled.

 ## Color

White rose. This pale pink shade promotes calmness of the heart and peace in love.

 ## Stone

Pink coral. Some Hindus believe that the ocean is the dwelling place of souls after death. For this reason, they revered coral and used it in protective amulets for their children. White or pink coral supposedly helped a person focus and dispelled inner strife. Ancients felt that coral could balance the body and relax the mind. Most pink coral is found in the warmer waters of the Far East.

⚜ Element

Quicksilver. Mystically, quicksilver (mercury) is a complex metal. It has a dual nature: metal and liquid. This unusual molten material is considered to be ruled by three elements; water (liquidity), earth (density), and air (rapid movement).

⚜ Herb

Shepherd's purse *(Capsella bursa-pastoris)*. Also called mother's heart, this plant is common in fields. It has small white flowers that bloom all year and a heart-shaped fruit. The herb part of the plant was used by medieval healers to help clot blood. It was also used by midwives during childbirth to encourage contractions.

♀ JENNORA: From the root name *Jennifer.*

♀ JENNY: From the root name *Jennifer.*

♂ JEOFFRI: From the root name *Geoffrey.*

♂ JERALD: From the root name *Gerald.*

♀ JERALDEEN: From the root name *Gerald.*

♀ JERALEE: From the root name *Gerald.*

♂ JERAMIE: From the root name *Jeremy.*

♀♂ JERE: From the root names *Gerald* and *Jeremy.*

♀ JEREMIA: From the root name *Jeremy.*

♂ JEREMIAH: From the root name *Jeremy.*

♥ ♂ **JEREMY** Jem, Jemmy, Jeramie, Jere, Jeremia, Jeremiah, Jeri, Jerry: *Jeremy* is from the Hebrew name *Yirmeyahu,* which means "exalted of the Lord" or "God will uplift." The transliteration of the original Hebrew is *Jeremiah.* The Greeks made it *Jeremias.* Jeremiah is one of only six prophets mentioned by name in the Talmud. One of the most interesting biblical figures, Jeremiah was both a prophet and a reformer. However, perhaps because he led a difficult and controversial life, his name is not among the most popular from the Bible. The Lamentations of Jeremiah in the Old Testament is a mournful and poetic catalogue of the reasons for the downfall of the contemporary society.

There are a few minor Eastern saints with the name, and in Russia it was transformed into *Jeremija.* In Switzerland, it became *Meis,* or *Mies.* In France, *Jeremiade* became synonymous with "lamentation," and the Book of Lamentations in the Old Testament is often referred to as "The Jeremiad."

The name *Jeremy* (or *Jeremiah*) was first used among the English in the thirteenth century, but there appears to be no particular reason for its sudden appearance. There is also some disagreement about how the names were adopted. Some say that the early English used *Jeremiah* as the written version of the name, while *Jeremy* was the spoken version. Others believe that *Jeremy* was the English version in both forms.

It is known that the more biblical version of the name, *Jeremiah,* became particularly popular among the Puritans of the seventeenth century and traveled with them to America. It remained the most common form of the name here up until the twentieth century. *Jeremiah* was also used in Ireland and it is sometimes considered the English variation of the Gaelic name *Diarmaid* (or *Dermot*). Both *Jeremiah* and *Diarmaid* have remained popular in Ireland, possibly thanks to the Irish legend that tells of a visit to the country by the prophet *Jeremiah.*

In the twentieth century, the popularity of *Jeremy* grew in Britain, and at the same time, Jeremy also began to take over from *Jeremiah* in the United States. The name received high-profile status with Beatrix Potter's book *The Tale of Jeremy Fisher*. During the 1970s and 1980s, the name became even more common in the United States. It seems to be associated with American traditional names, and has enjoyed the upsurge in popularity of all names in that category.

The diminutive, *Jerry*, which is also the diminutive of *Gerald* and *Jerome*, is rarely heard for children. As an independent name it was made popular in previous decades by both Jerry Lewis (born Joseph Levitch) and the mouse, Jerry, of the "Tom and Jerry" cartoons.

◎ Number
Four. In some numerological circles, fours have a character like none other. While many fours promote social justice, they sometimes have trouble making friends because their opposing viewpoints create enemies.

☾ Astrological sign
Virgo. People of this sign often express their love through unselfish devotion to their families and friends. However, they can be cool and modest.

✳ Color
Cerulean. Dark blue is often associated with the sign of Virgo and deep religious feelings. Cerulean seems an appropriate hue for the name of a prophet.

◆ Stone
Dumortierite quartz. When polished this deep blue stone is lustrous. Some ancient Madagascar artisans carved intricate decorative figurines and bottles from dumortierite. Today, most gem-quality dumortierite is found in Nevada, though

some has been found in France. The name came from French scientist M. E. Dumortier.

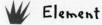 Element

Aluminum. A silvery-white metallic element used to form lightweight, corrosion-resistant alloys. Aluminum is found in dumortierite. Some modern mystics use small pieces of aluminum to enhance mental abilities and imaging.

Herb

Almond *(Prunus amygdalus).* Early herbalists used ground almond kernels for cleansing. Some varieties of almond oil were used for sedatives and to help control coughs. In Christian medieval art, the almond symbolized God's blessing. Almond trees are cultivated in Mediterranean countries, and California.

♀ JERI: From the root name *Jeremy.*

♂ JEROEN: From the root name *Jerome.*

♂ **JEROME** **Gerome, Geronimo, Gerry, Hierome, Jeroen, Jerry:** The name *Jerome* comes from the Greek word *hieros* or *ieros,* meaning "sacred." This root is part of many famous Greek names including those belonging to three kings of Syracuse: *Hieron, Hieracles* (meaning "holy fame") and *Hieronymus* (meaning "with a holy name"). From the Greeks, the name *Hieronymus* traveled to Rome. Among the earliest notable Romans with the name was the scholar Eusebius Hieronymus Sophronius (A.D. 347–420). Sophronius provided the translation of the Bible on which the Vulgate was based. He later became a saint, and the modern Italian tongue changed the initial *h* to a *g*. This is the origin of San Geronimo. The French changed the *g* to a *j* and left out the middle syllable, and voilà, we have *Jerome*.

The Germans, on the other hand, maintained the original Greek and kept *Hieronymus*. Among the most famous Germans to bear the name is the fifteenth-century painter Hieronymus Bosch.

The French version of the name came to England after the Norman Conquest. In 1206, the name is listed in a Latinized version as *Jeronimus,* but the common form remained *Jerome*. (An exception is in Cambria, where *Hieronome* or *Hierome* was, for a time, the form the name took.)

In the sixteenth century *Jerome* was particularly popular and became so again in the nineteenth century. Among the most famous recent *Jerome*s are Jerome K. Jerome, who wrote *Three Men in a Boat,* Jerome Kern, who is sometimes called the father of the American musical, and Jerome Robbins, one of the most exciting and original choreographers of the twentieth century. The Spanish variation, *Geronimo,* is most famous in America as the name of the great Apache chief. *Jerry* is sometimes used as a diminutive for *Jerome*. In recent years, both *Jerry* and *Jerome* have declined in popularity, despite such TV personalities as Jerry Seinfeld and Jerry Springer.

☉ Number

Three. Many numerologists, past and present, believe threes are always among the inspired and artistic.

☾ Astrological sign

Libra. In ancient Babylon, the constellation of Libra was linked with the judgment of the dead and the living. Today, it's considered the sign of balance. Choreographer Jerome Robbins was a Libra.

Color

Cobalt. This vivid shade of blue goes well with the air element of Libra. Blue has often been associated with sacredness.

 ## Stone

Apache tears. These round translucent obsidian pebbles are actually volcanic glass. Tied to the planet Saturn and the element of fire, these shiny black gems are thought to bring luck. The legend behind the name relates how the earth wept when an Apache warrior died. Today, Apache tears are still carried by some as good-luck charms.

 ## Element

Platinum. Ancients believed all metals had potent magic, but today metallurgy and its connection to magic is regarded as superstition. Platinum was thought to have the highest energy, even beyond gold.

Herb

Blue vervain *(Verbena hastata).* A native North American plant, blue vervain is also called Indian hyssop. It has small dark blue or purplish blue flowers. The rootstock and the herb have medicinal value as a tranquilizer and an aid against insomnia. Warm tea brewed from either the rootstock or herb was used for fevers, colds, and chest congestion. Cold blue vervain tea soothes sores and wounds.

♀ JERRID: From the root name *Jared.*

♀ JERRIE: From the root name *Gerald.*

♂ JERROLD: From the root name *Gerald.*

♀♂ JERRY: From the root names *Gerald, Jeremy,* and *Jerome.*

♂ JERZY: From the root name *George.*

♀♂ JESS: From the root names *Jesse, Jessica,* and *John.*

♀ JESSA: From the root name *Jessica.*

♀ JESSALIN: From the root name *Jessica.*

♥ ♀♂ **JESSE** Jess, Jessie: *Jesse* is from the Hebrew name *Yishay* and means "Jehovah exists." Names historian Eric Partridge writes: "Perhaps the first Jesse was a staunch and impressive affirmer of the existence of 'the true God.'" The earliest known *Jesse* was King David's father in the Old Testament.

The name became popular among Christians after the Protestant Reformation when Old Testament names in general had a major resurgence. It seems to have been most widely adopted during the eighteenth century, which is later than many Old Testament names.

Jesse has had its greatest success in the United States where there have been several national heroes (and anti-heroes) who have helped to keep the name alive. Despite his ignominious career, the outlaw Jesse James was an enormously popular figure. While Dunkling and Gosling believe that Jesse James "made the name notorious," it seems equally likely that he increased the name's popularity.

If Jesse James did, in fact, turn parents away from the name, the athlete Jesse Owens (originally James Cleveland Owens) certainly returned them to it, particularly in the African American community. Owens definitively demolished the racial supremacist theories of the Nazis by winning several gold medals at the 1936 Berlin Olympics. More recently, national leader and renowned speaker Reverend Jesse Jackson has kept the name in the public consciousness.

In recent years *Jesse* has consistently ranked among the top one hundred boys' names in the United States.

Boys named *Jesse* are often called by the shortened form, *Jess*. Though many girls are called *Jessie,* it is usually a short form of *Jessica* (see below). Occasionally, however, parents have named their girls *Jesse* or *Jessie* independent of *Jessica*.

 Number

Four. In most cultures the number four is tied to order and evenness like the equal sides of a square. However, some numerologists think of fours as people who follow their own rules, and do so with unwavering discipline.

 Astrological sign

Virgo. Earthly harvest is represented by Virgo and like the farmer reaping his crops, Virgos collect, analyze, and digest many facts to form their life values. The outlaw Jesse James and athlete Jesse Owens were both born under the sign of Virgo.

 Color

Lead gray. A somber shade to some, yet its composition of black and white promote metaphysical receptivity. Gray is a color connected to the sign of Virgo.

 Stone

Hematite. Most hematite is opaque black with metallic luster and displays a blood red color when thinly sliced. Specular hematites appear as black crystals with reflective surfaces and were used by the ancients for mirrors. Another form called iron rose is so named because the stone's formation looks like flower petals. Powdered hematite was once used for paint pigment. Healing lore reveals that some believed hematite jewelry protected blood from disease, hence the name *hema,* which means "blood" in Greek.

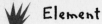 **Element**

Lead. Lead was used to frame pieces of stained glass for sacred images in church windows.

Herb

Loosestrife *(Lythrum salicaria)*. First introduced to North America by European settlers, loosestrife is found in marshes or moist areas. The herb part of loosestrife had traditional medicinal value as an intestinal aid for illnesses like dysentery and typhoid fever, two diseases the Europeans also introduced to North America.

♀ **JESSICA** Jess, Jessa, Jessalin, Jessie: *Jessica* is often considered to be the feminine of *Jesse*. However, Jessica evolved from a different Hebrew name—*Iscah*—which means "Jehovah sees" or "God beholds."

William Shakespeare is thought to have coined the English variation, *Jessica,* when he created a character of that name in his play *The Merchant of Venice* (1596–1598). Because Shakespeare's Jessica is the daughter of Shylock, one of the most famous Jewish characters in English literature, *Jessica* was considered a Jewish name for most of its history. Only recently, particularly in the United States, has the name been adopted by a broader population. There are many famous twentieth-century media stars who may have influenced *Jessica*'s rise in popularity. Like *Jesse* for boys, *Jessica* is one of the top one hundred girls' baby names in the United States. Girls named *Jessica* are very frequently called by the diminutive *Jesse, Jessie,* or *Jess,* which is why the boys' name and the girls' name are often associated with one another.

◉ Number

Three. This number is sacred to countless cultures, both ancient and modern, and represents the eternal circle of beginning, middle, and end.

☾ Astrological sign

Aries. People born under this fire sign usually have adventurous spirits and energetic personalities.

☀ Color

Violet-pink. Any shade of purple promotes sensitivity and pink attracts love. Together they help keep an overzealous Arien from unintentionally stepping on anyone's feelings.

◆ Stone

Kunzite. A gem variety of the mineral spodumene, kunzite is an intense lilac-pink color. When cut and polished its sparkle is eye-catching. The color comes from the presence of manganese and lithium. Although it's a fragile gemstone, it's popular with today's collectors. Kunzite was named after American gemologist G. F. Kunz at the turn of the century. Some of the largest kunzite crystals come from Maine and Connecticut.

♛ Element

Aluminum. Aluminum is a mineral in spodumene, and it is of recent origins. It seems the perfect complement for kunzite.

⚘ Herb

China rose hibiscus *(Hibiscus rosa-sinensis).* There are nearly two hundred species of hibiscus and many have medicinal qualities. The China rose variety is grown mostly for its ornamental beauty, but it was used to reduce swelling in inflamed tissue and soothe irritated skin. The roots were boiled and the cooled mixture used as an eyewash in Malaya. The plant is still admired for its large rose-colored flowers.

♀♂ JESSIE: From the root names *Jesse* and *Jessica*.

♂ JESUS: From the root name *Joshua*.

♂ JIM: From the root name *Jacob/James*.

♂ JIMMY: From the root name *Jacob/James*.

♀ JINIA: From the root name *Virginia*.

♀ JINNA: From the root name *John*.

♀ JINNIE: From the root name *Virginia*.

♂ JIRI: From the root name *George*.

♀ JO: From the root names *John* and *Joseph*.

♀ JOAN: From the root name *John*.

♀ JOANNA: From the root name *John*.

♀ JOANNE: From the root name *John*.

♂ JOCK: From the root names *Jacob/James* and *John*.

♀♂ JODY: From the root names *John, Joseph,* and *Judith*.

♂ JOE: From the root name *Joseph*.

♥ ♂ **JOEL** **Joela, Joelin, Joelle, Joely, Joelynn, Jowella:** *Joel* is the Anglicized version of the ancient Hebrew name *Yoel*, which combines the two Hebrew terms for God, *Ya* and *El*. Therefore, *Joel* means "God is God" or "Jehovah is Lord." The Hebrew *Yoel* later became the Greek *Ioel*. It is from the Greek that the English *Joel* is derived. *Joel* was the second of the twelve biblical prophets and a book of the Old Testament is named for him.

While the name *Joel* appears in medieval English records after the Norman Conquest, it is not derived from the biblical prophet, but from the Breton name *Judicael* (or *Juhel*), who was a hermit saint. The *Joel* of the biblical derivation did not appear until after the Protestant Reformation. Though not as popular as many other biblical names, *Joel* did travel early to the United States. Among the nineteenth-century Americans to bear the name was the author of the Uncle Remus stories, Joel Chandler Harris. In 1876, George Eliot included a character named Joel in her popular novel *Daniel Deronda*.

In the twentieth century, the actor Joel McCrea brought the name national attention, as did the actor Joel Grey, who became famous after his appearance in the film *Cabaret*. Along with many other Old Testament names, *Joel* has become more popular since the 1960s. Now *Joel* is among the top one hundred boys' names in the United States.

⦿ Number
Four. Some numerologists designate four as the number connected to Uranus. As a result of this tie, some believe that fours can be sensitive and easily wounded.

☾ Astrological sign
Scorpio. Although the sign of Scorpio is ruled by Pluto, the planet Uranus influences this sign for seven years as it makes an eighty-four-year trip around the sun. Make no mistake, Scorpios are strong-willed and even more so when shadowed by Uranus.

☀ Color
Ebony. Black is one of Scorpio's colors. Mystically, black is symbolic of quiet authority and protection.

◆ Stone
Black diamond. The saying "diamonds are forever" is not just a line to sell jewelry. This honorable gem is made of pure

carbon, the elemental foundation of earthly organic life. Deep within the earth, diamonds are created under enormous heat and pressure. Gemologists call the black diamond carbonado. Its rarity makes it a highly coveted collector's item.

♛ Element

Titanium. Since titanium is the earth's toughest metal, linking it to the hardest gem seems particularly fitting.

♘ Herb

Cubeb *(Piper cubeba).* Commonly called Java pepper, the unripe fruit of the cubeb vine was considered to have medicinal value by herbalists of yore. Dried cubeb berries look like black pepper nuggets. Cubeb helped indigestion and bronchitis. Cigarettes made from cubeb were smoked to relieve hay fever and asthma. Cubeb vines grow in the forests of Penang, Sumatra, and New Guinea.

♀ JOELA: From the root name *Joel*.

♀ JOELIN: From the root name *Joel*.

♀ JOELLE: From the root name *Joel*.

♀ JOELY: From the root name *Joel*.

♀ JOELYNN: From the root name *Joel*.

♀♂ JOEY: From the root name *Joseph*.

♂ JOHANN: From the root name *John*.

♥ ♂ JOHN Anno, Ean, Evan, Gene, Gian, Gianna, Giovanni, Hannes, Hans, Hanschen, Hansel, Ian, Ioannis, Iva, Ivan, Jack, Jackie, Jan, Jana, Jane, Janek, Janet, Janette, Jania, Janice, Janine, Janis, Janna, Janos, Jasia, Jayne, Jean, Jeanie, Jeannette, Jeannine, Jenelle, Jeni, Jess, Jinna, Jo,

Joan, Joanna, Joanne, Jock, Jody, Johann, Johnny, Jon, Jonathan, Jonelle, Joni, Jovan, Juan, Juanita, Keon, Owen, Seamus, Sean, Shana, Shane, Shanna, Shawn, Shawna, Sheena, Sinead, Vanek, Vanko, Vanya, Yanni, Yochanan, Zane: The name *John* comes from the Hebrew name *Yohanan* and means "God (Jehovah) has favored." The very similar name *Jonathan*, which also comes from Hebrew, means something slightly different: "God (Jehovah) has given." *Yohanan* was a very popular name among Jews, and it is the name of two major figures in the Bible, John the Baptist and John the Evangelist. *Jonathan*'s most famous biblical connection comes from the friend of King David.

There is no other name that matches *John*'s enduring popularity throughout the Christian world over the centuries. The name and its variations have been borne by popes, kings, artists, and heroes. *John* itself came into widespread use in England after the Norman Conquest. Early forms of the name were *Johan, Jean,* and *Jan.* It was used increasingly throughout the Middle Ages and from the sixteenth century through the middle of the twentieth century it was consistently one of the most common names for boys throughout the English-speaking world.

Jonathan, on the other hand, did not become particularly fashionable until the seventeenth century, when the Puritans adopted it with a vengeance. For this reason, *Jonathan* was one of the most popular early American names. During the American Revolution, the British army even used the term "Brother Jonathan" as a generic term for an American. (This is similar to the later use—particularly during World War II—of *Ivan* to denote a Russian. *Ivan* is the Russian variation of *John*.) Many names historians believe that, in reaction to the nickname, *Jonathan* became less popular among parents after the Revolution. The name did not have a significant revival until the 1940s, when parents were choosing alternatives to the ubiquitous *John*.

As with *Jonathan,* the middle of the twentieth century saw the ascendancy of *John*'s other variations in the United States. The Spanish variation, *Juan,* has been among the top fifty boys' names in the United States since the 1940s. The Irish variation *Sean* (and less often *Shawn*) has been among the top 100 since the 1970s. The Anglicized version of *Sean, Shane,* became popular in the 1950s after the movie *Shane* was released. After a short period it began to disappear, but had a resurgence beginning in 1996. *Ian,* the Scottish form of *John,* enjoyed enormous popularity during the 1990s.

Many boys and men named *John* are called by the diminutive *Jack,* which developed out of the combination of an early English form of *John*—*Jan*—with the suffix "kin." The resulting *Jankin* was later shortened to *Jack.* As an independent name, Jack was among the top forty boys' names in 1930 and 1940, possibly due to the popularity of comedian Jack Benny. After him, many *Jacks* rose to prominence in all walks of life, including President Jack Kennedy, golfer Jack Nicklaus, and actor Jack Nicholson.

There are as many feminine variations of the original *Yohanan* as there are male variations, though they currently do not have the same popularity. The first English variations seem to be *Joanne* and *Joan,* which developed out of the French names *Jhone* or *Johanne.* They both grew in popularity from the twelfth through the sixteenth centuries with *Joan* being consistently the more common. In the sixteenth century, *Joan* was the third most common girls' name in England. By that time, however, it had also become so ubiquitous that it had developed a derogatory connotation and the variation *Jane* became more popular. Both *Joanne* and *Joan* came back into style in the early twentieth century. Some historians point to George Bernard Shaw's play *St. Joan* (1924) as a primary reason for the name's return. Other historians believe an earlier work, the film *Joan the Woman* (1916), was far more responsible. Despite luminaries such as

Joan Crawford, Joan Blondell, Joan Fontaine, and Joanne Woodward, both names ceased to be particularly fashionable around 1950 and have never recovered.

Jane originated from the Southern French variation *Jehane*. After overtaking *Joan* in the sixteenth century, it has remained among the most popular girls' names in the centuries since. *Jane*'s use did not begin to decline until the 1950s. Its diminutives include *Janet, Janette,* and *Janice. Janeta* was a common variation during the medieval period. *Janet* became particularly widespread in Scotland. During the twentieth century, *Janet* became more popular in the United States. Use of the name probably increased because of stars such as Janet Gaynor and Janet Leigh. *Janice* seems to have been invented by novelist Paul Ford in 1899. The variation *Janis* followed soon after.

Jean, though spelled the same as the French masculine, is said to be the Scottish variation of the French feminine *Jehane* and is closely related to the modern French *Jeanne.* It, like *Jane* and *Joan,* was in widespread use throughout the medieval period and into the nineteenth century. Toward the end of the nineteenth century, the name began to spread beyond Scotland and by the 1920s was fashionable throughout the English-speaking world. *Jean* reached the peak of its popularity in the 1930s when Jean Arthur was a major movie star, but after that, use of the name began to decline and has not revived.

Other variations include *Johann, Hans, Hansel* (German), *Jonas* (Scandinavian), *Giovanni* (Italian), *Vanya* (Russian), *Evan* (Welsh), and *Juanita* (Spanish, feminine). Diminutives include the popular *Jon* (as in Jon Bon Jovi and Jon Voight), *Johnny, Jock, Jeannie, Joannie,* and *Janey.*

 Number

Two. Many numerologists link strong intuitive natures to the number two.

☾ Astrological sign

Aquarius. While there is no myth for this sign, the God Hapi pouring water from a jar was the ancient symbol of the River Nile. Aquarians of note include John Hancock, Johanes Gutenberg, Jack Benny, Jackie Robinson, and Jack Nicklaus.

✳ Color

Misty sky. All shades of light blue are tied to Aquarius. It represents mercy.

◆ Stone

Blue John fluorite. While most fluorite is transparent, this unusual variety can be opaque. It is dark blue with purple and yellow bands throughout the stone. Ancient Romans believed that drinking alcoholic beverages from a cup carved from Blue John would let them drink as much as they wanted without becoming intoxicated. Blue John fluorite is found in England.

᭝ Element

Gold. Metallurgic lore suggests that wearing gold improved inner wisdom.

⚘ Herb

Saint John's wort *(Hypericum perforatum).* Sometimes called amber, St. John's wort is a shrubby plant found in dry soil and sunny places throughout the world. The herb part of the plant is used to make calming preparations for ailments like insomnia as well as nervous conditions and depression. An oil from the herb can be taken for various types of stomach ills and lung congestion. Oil extract also makes soothing applications for burns, wounds, sores, and other skin problems. A flower tea was helpful for anemia and headaches. For some, this plant can make the skin sensitive to light.

♂   JOHNNY: From the root name *John*.

♀   JOICE: From the root name *Joyce*.

♀   JOLETTE: From the root name *Julian*.

♀   JOLINE: From the root name *Joseph*.

♂   JOLYON: From the root name *Julian*.

♂   JON: From the root name *John*.

❤   ♂ **JONAH** **Jonas:** The names *Jonah* and *Jonas* both come from the ancient Hebrew name *Yonah*, which means "dove" or "pigeon." Sometimes the literal translation of the name is given as "the moaning one." The Greeks transformed the name into *Ionas*. The Latin variation of the name is *Jonas*. *Jonah* is considered the English variation, though both names can be correctly called English variations. Some names historians believe that *Jonas* has been the more common of the two.

The first known historical *Jonah* is, of course, the hero of one of the most well-known Bible stories, that of Jonah and the whale. The Book of Jonah relates the tale of the reluctant prophet Jonah who tried to avoid God's command to save the Assyrian town of Ninevah. He did not wish to save Ninevah because it was a town of Gentiles. Instead, Jonah headed in the opposite direction, and caught a ship to Tarnish. Because of Jonah's disobedience, God created a great tempest. The ship's crew cast lots as to who would appease the tempest by being thrown overboard. Jonah admitted that the tempest was his fault and asked to be thrown overboard instead. The crew obliged. Once in the water, Jonah was swallowed by 'a large fish,' which later came to be the whale of the famous story. Jonah was regurgitated from the whale's belly three days later. He then went to Ninevah and warned the townspeople to repent of their wickedness, which they did. His lesson learned, Jonah spent the remainder of his life speaking out against religious intolerance, saying that Jehovah was the God of both Gentiles and Israelites.

In England, because of Jonah's misfortune (although surviving being eaten by a whale might actually be considered quite fortunate), his name became synonymous with bad luck or a jinx. Historians disagree, however, on whether this led to a decline in use of the name. Whatever the reason, *Jonah* was never among the most popular of Old Testament names, and while both variations have become moderately more popular since the resurgence of Old Testament names in the 1960s, it has never achieved the widespread use of names such as *Joshua* or *Jason*. Jonas Salk, the discoverer of the polio vaccine, is probably the most famous twentieth-century bearer of the name.

 ## Number

Three. In Greek mythology, three is found in connection with deities including the Fates, the Furies, and the Graces. People of this number are proud. They insist on carrying out their own ideas that may lead them astray.

 ## Astrological sign

Scorpio. Passion is a word synonymous with Scorpios. But their passion can be applied to a purpose and when this happens, miracles occur. Dr. Jonas Salk was a Scorpio.

 ## Color

Cayenne. This hot red shade will add spice to any Scorpio in a slump.

Stone

Whalebone ivory. For millennia, ivory has been prized. Some of the finest pieces come from sea mammals, including the sperm whale, walrus, and sea lion. Scrimshaw is the delicate art of whalebone carving practiced by Inuit tribes. Ancient veterinarians and animal handlers believed that carrying ivory protected them from animal injuries. Until recently ivory jewelry and decorative ornaments were quite popular, but with the near extinction of some ivory-bearing elephants, trade has been banned in many countries.

Element

Copper. In metallurgic lore, copper is believed to bring luck—a helpful boost to dispel any superstitious jinx associated with *Jonah*.

Herb

Coral root *(Corallorhiza odontorhiza)*. Coral root is native to the United States and forms around the roots of trees in dry wooded areas from Maine to Minnesota and southeast from Georgia to Missouri. Traditionally, the coral-like rootstock was brewed for teas to reduce fevers. The flowers are reddish with a hint of purple.

♂   JONAS: From the root name *Jonah*.

♂   JONATHAN: From the root name *John*.

♀   JONELLE: From the root name *John*.

♀   JONI: From the root name *John*.

♥ ♀♂ **JORDAN**   Giordano, Jardena, Jordana, Jorie, Jory, **Jourdan:** The name *Jordan* probably comes from the Hebrew word *yardan*, which means "to descend" or "flowing down." It is also the name of the river that flows through Palestine from the Sea of Galilee to the Dead Sea, said to be the river in which Jesus was baptized. For this reason, the crusaders would return to Europe from the Holy Land with vials of water from the River Jordan. The water was used to baptize their children, and those children were named *Jordan*. Unusually, the name was used originally for children of both sexes.

However, as the history of names is rarely simple, there is another possible source for the name *Jordan*; the Teutonic name *Jordanes* is said to be connected to the Old Norse word *jordh,* which means "land." As the name did not appear in England until the twelfth century, no one can be certain what source inspired the first English *Jordan*. There is very little doubt though, that even if the name *Jordan* was introduced into England via the Teutonic name, it stayed alive because of the holy river.

After the name's enormous popularity for both boys and girls in the Middle Ages, by the beginning of the seventeenth century *Jordan* had become an exclusively male name, and even among boys it was fairly rare. While F. Scott Fitzgerald names one of his female characters Jordan in the classic novel *The Great Gatsby* (1925), this did not inspire a major revival of the name. Along with many other traditional names and surnames *Jordan* revived in the late 1960s and early 1970s, and by the 1990s it was among the top American names for both boys and girls. Within the past twelve years, its popularity as a girl's name has grown.

Number

Eight. People of the number eight are often cool in demeanor, but have strong intuition about others' feelings. In mathematics, eight is the cube of two and symbolizes physical matter.

Astrological sign

Aquarius. The mind of an Aquarian doesn't focus on what other people are thinking. While this may give them an air of aloofness, they are not deliberate in their seeming indifference, and are actually friendly free spirits. Athlete Michael Jordan is an Aquarius.

Color

Baptismal blue. Ruled by the planet Neptune, this light blue shade is the color of water in a baptismal font and promotes divine blessing.

Stone

Blue zircon. Sometimes mistaken for diamonds, zircon crystals also appear in several colors. When heated, pale blue zircons turn a brighter blue. Many cultures believed a zircon brought wisdom to its owner along with honor and riches.

Element

Uranium. Uranium is the ore associated with Uranus, the ruling planet of Aquarius. It is also present in some types of zircons.

Herb

Jordan almond *(Prunus amygdalus).* This almond tree can grow to heights of twenty feet and has thorny branches. While the tree grows in some areas of the United States and southern Europe, it prospers best by the Jordan River, giving it the folk name of Jordan almond. Ground almond kernels make wonderful facial cleansers. Some almond varieties produce a bitter oil that has been used as a sedative and in cough remedies. Almond butter is rich in protein.

♀   JORDANA: From the root name *Jordan.*

♂   JORGAN: From the root name *George.*

♂   JORGE: From the root name *George.*

♀   JORGINA: From the root name *George*.

♀   JORIE: From the root name *Jordan*.

♂   JORY: From the root name *Jordan*.

♂   JOSÉ: From the root name *Joseph*.

♥ ♂ JOSEPH   Che, Fifi, Giuseppe, Giuseppina, Iosep, Jo, Jody, Joe, Joey, Joline, José, Josepha, Josephine, Josetta, Josetto, Josip, Josy, Jozef, Osip, Pepe, Pino, Sefa, Sepp, Yosef, Yosepha, Yusuf, Yuszel. The origin of *Joseph* is most often given as the Hebrew name, *Yosef,* meaning either "addition" or "God will add or increase." It might also have an even older origin with an unknown meaning; as *Yussef,* it is among the most common Arab names. The early Greek variation was *Joses.* The earliest known *Joseph* is the biblical patriarch, son of Rachel. One of the most famous *Joseph*s is Mary's husband, Joseph of Nazareth. Other biblical *Joseph*s include the apostle James's brother, Joseph of Arimathaea and Joseph Barnabus. In total there are fourteen saints who bear the name.

In the Roman world the name of a famous Jewish historian and soldier was Flavius Josephus (A.D. c.37–100), who was called, in Hebrew, Yosef ben Matityahu ha-Kohen. In the Middle Ages in Europe it was almost exclusively a Jewish name. However, in 1621 the pope named a day to celebrate Saint Joseph (of Nazareth), and consequently the name became incredibly popular in Roman Catholic Europe, where there have been two German emperors and one Portuguese king named Joseph. In Italy, the variation was *Guiseppe* and in Spain it was *José,* with *Pepe* or *Pepito* or *Che* as the diminutive. In Poland and Germany the spelling was *Josef.* The Slavonians used *Josko* or *Joska* and the Russians used *Joseef* or *Oseep.* In the Tyrol region of Europe, the last part of the name came to be used for the diminutive: *Sepp, Sepperl, Sipp* and *Sippli.*

Legend has it that Joseph of Arimathaea brought the Gospel to England and since the seventeenth century *Joseph* has been a popular name there. Despite its Catholic connections, the name was very popular among the Puritans who brought it with them to the American colonies. Later immigrants, especially Italian and Irish, maintained the popularity of the name when the use of biblical names among Anglo-Saxon Protestants dropped off.

José, the Spanish variation of the name, is also, surprisingly, Aramaic in origin and was popular among Jews from the second through the sixth centuries, (i.e., the Talmudic period). *José* has topped the list of popular American boys' names at least since the 1930s.

The diminutive, *Joe,* became so ubiquitous in the United States that the name of every soldier in World War II became G.I. Joe. In many foreign countries, *Joe* is still the generic term for an American. Joe Louis, who won the World Heavyweight title in 1937, helped the diminutive develop as an independent name, especially in the African American community. By the 1960s, *Joey* also was becoming an increasingly popular independent name among African Americans.

The feminine version of the name is most often *Josepha* or *Josephine. Josephine* didn't come into common use in the English-speaking world until the mid-nineteenth century and only really became popular in Ireland. *Jo* and *Josette* are diminutives for the feminine, as is *Josey.*

 ## Number

One. The number one indicates leadership and resourcefulness.

Astrological sign

Taurus. According to mythology, Taurus was a white bull that Zeus impersonated to court Europa.

Color

Multicolors. As with Joseph's biblical coat of many colors, the entire rainbow spectrum honors *Joseph*.

 Stone

Amethyst. This lavender crystalline quartz has been revered by the Egyptians, Greeks and Romans. Jewish priests wore it to signify godliness and set it as the centerpiece of their breastplates. The Romans thought it gave the wearer power over the will of people. Egyptians employed the amethyst as a healer of fear. The Greeks believed goblets inlaid with amethyst prevented intoxication. Today, Catholic bishops still wear one on the second finger of their right hand.

 Element

Copper. While copper is not considered the best setting for crystals, when combined with amethyst it supports the gem's intuitive power.

 Herb

Joe-pye weed *(Eupatorium purpureum).* Native Americans taught European settlers that Joe-pye weed reduced flu symptoms and broke fevers. It was one of the strongest native remedies for fever. In Rafinesque's "Medical Flora" (1828), he says Joe-pye was an Indian who was famous for curing typhoid. Another story says that one tribe called typhoid fever "jopi" and the herb used to cure it, "jopi weed." It has purplish stems and pale pinkish purple flowers.

♀   JOSEPHA: From the root name *Joseph*.

♀   JOSEPHINE: From the root name *Joseph*.

♀   JOSETTA: From the root name *Joseph*.

♂   JOSETTO: From the root name *Joseph*.

♂   JOSH: From the root name *Joshua*.

♥ ♂ **JOSHUA** Jesus, Josh, Jozua: *Joshua* is from the Hebrew words *Je* (or *Ye*), which means "God" (Jehovah), and *hoshea* (or *hoshua*), and it is most often taken to mean "salvation." Originally the name was *Jehoshea* (or *Yehoshua*). *Hoshea* can also be said to mean "generous" or "helpful." *Joshua* is only one variation of the original name *Jehoshea*. Another variation of the name is *Jeshua*, which later became *Jesus*.

The first known *Joshua* is the biblical figure and hero of the Book of Joshua. Joshua succeeded Moses as the leader of the Israelites. It was he who brought the Jews to the Promised Land after Moses led them out of Egypt. As such an important figure in Jewish history, the name has been fairly consistently popular among Jews throughout the centuries.

The name did not become common among Christian English-speakers until the seventeenth and eighteenth centuries with the advent of the Protestant Reformation. Of particular importance to *Joseph*'s surge in popularity was the Puritan return to Old Testament names. It is also possible that the fame of eighteenth-century British portraitist Joshua Reynolds lent the name a certain aristocratic status.

Joshua was among the earliest names brought to America by the English colonists, and it remained in common use until the mid-nineteenth century. There are many possible reasons why the name fell out of favor at this time, among them the late nineteenth-century return to Romanticism. However, it returned to widespread use nearly a century later, during the 1960s, when traditional names were coming back into vogue.

Joshua is now among the top one hundred boys' names

in the United States. The diminutive, *Josh,* has come into increasing independent use since the 1980s. Although it is rare to find boys named *Jesus* among Anglo-Saxon Protestants or Catholics in the United States, it has always been a popular name among Latinos.

 ## Number

Two. Many twos have an uncanny sense of direction. Medieval alchemists believed two represented the intellectual sphere.

 ## Astrological sign

Scorpio. Many Scorpios take time in their lives to seek spiritual truth. Perhaps this passion for enlightenment comes from Scorpio's ruling element of water, which represents the soul.

 ## Color

Damask. For ages, red has been considered a sacred color. Ancient Egyptians believed that Shu, the god who separated earth from the sky, was red.

 ## Stone

Red carnelian. This stone of the chalcedony family comes in several colors. Red carnelian was worn on the finger by ancient Egyptians to dispel anger, jealousy, and hatred. Even today, mystics believe it promotes harmony. Magicians from the Renaissance period etched swords or the image of a warrior into the stone and used it for amulets to guard against lightning. They also believed it would repel curses and any form of enchantment.

 ## Element

Plutonium. Plutonium is a silvery element and the ore is often tied to Scorpio's ruling planet, Pluto.

❦ Herb

Yerba santa (*Eriodictyon californicum*). Known to herbalists as consumptive's weed or holy herb, yerba santa is an aromatic evergreen shrub. The leaves have medicinal value and were found to be helpful for colds, laryngitis, bronchitis and lung problems. Yerba santa was also considered a blood purifier and used as a remedy for tuberculosis and rheumatism. Native Americans smoked or chewed the leaves to relieve symptoms of asthma.

♂ JOSIP: From the root name *Joseph.*

♀♂ JOSY: From the root name *Joseph.*

♀♂ JOURDAN: From the root name *Jordan.*

♂ JOVAN: From the root name *John.*

♀ JOWELLA: From the root name *Joel.*

♀ JOY: From the root name *Joyce.*

♥ ♀♂ **JOYCE** **Joice, Joy, Joycelyn, Joyous:** A common medieval name, *Joyce* was used for both men and women in a variety of forms, including *Josse, Jos, Joisse,* and *Goce.* It is almost certainly related etymologically to the Latin words for "merry," "joke," and "sportive," but as a name it is of Celtic origin. Its first recorded appearance seems to have been as the name of a seventh-century Breton saint, Jodoc, or Judocus, a hermit of Ponthieu. The name spread with the cult of the saint, throughout northern France, the Low Countries, and southern Germany. In Holland, it became *Joost.*

In England, *Joyce* fell out of favor as a man's name during the fourteenth century, remaining reasonably common only as a surname. It survived as a woman's name but was never one of the most widely used. In the novel *East Lynne*

(1861) by Ellen Price, for example, the character Joyce Hallijohn is greeted with, "Joyce. I never heard such a name. Is it a Christian or surname?"

In the 1890s, *Joyce* became fashionable again, possibly because it was the name of the heroine in the highly popular historical novel *In the Golden Days* by Edna Lyall. Since that time it has been quite widely used as a woman's name in England and the United States, becoming the third most popular in England in 1925. Since that time its popularity has slowly waned, however. While it never really regained its popularity as a man's name, two of the most famous bearers of the name, oddly enough, were men—the poet Joyce Kilmer, author of the widely anthologized and memorized poem "Trees," and the English author Joyce Cary.

A somewhat rare spelling variation for *Joyce* is *Joice*. Its diminutive, *Joy*, is more often given as an independent name today and is a simple adoption of the word meaning "happiness."

Number

Four. As sturdy as an oak and loyal to boot, everyone would do well to have a four on their side.

Astrological sign

Sagittarius. If a sign could be connected to laughter, Sagittarius would be the one. Most Sagittarians are outgoing and jovial. They love to play and enjoy life to its fullest. Joyce Kilmer was a Sagittarian.

Color

Pine. The scent of fresh pine and the sight of a lush forest inspire peace between earth's creatures.

Stone

Green tree agate. Agates come in various types and each has a unique character. Tree agates look as if they have a miniature tree growing within the stone. It's an amazing stone to behold. Many once believed that this gem was touched by the gods. Early healers used many types of natural elements for their arts, including minerals. The green tree agate was believed to reduce fever and eliminate harmful toxins from the body.

 Mineral

Silver. Silver is the perfect metal for the miraculous agate and boosts its power for optimum healing.

 Herb

Red clover *(Trifolium pratense)*. Clover is common in North American and European meadows. Its flowering tops were found to have healing properties. European medical folklore suggests clover be used to help liver and gallbladder problems. It was also recommended as an appetite stimulant for recovering patients. A syruplike flower extraction was used as an external treatment for skin sores, rashes and athlete's foot.

♀   JOYCELYN: From the root name *Joyce*.

♀   JOYOUS: From the root name *Joyce*.

♂   JOZEF: From the root name *Joseph*.

♂   JOZUA: From the root name *Joshua*.

♂   JUAN: From the root name *John*.

♀   JUANITA: From the root name *John*.

♀   JUDITE: From the root name *Judith*.

♥ ♀ JUDITH   Dita, Giuditta, Jody, Judite, Judy, Jutta, Yudi: One of the most widespread feminine names of the twentieth century, *Judith* is an Anglicized form of the Hebrew *Yehudit,* meaning "praise" or "praise of the Lord." It can also mean simply "Jewish woman." In the Bible (Genesis 26:31), Judith is the Hittite wife of Esau. In the Apocrypha, she is, more famously, the "heroine of Bethulia" who risked her life to enter the tent of Holofernes, the general of Nebuchadnezzar, in order to save her native town. This apocryphal Judith boldly cut off the head of the Assyrian, and her townsmen attacked the invaders, defeating them soundly. She has been widely portrayed in painting and sculpture and thus has associated the name with courage, strength, and loyalty.

While *Yehudit* has always been a common name among Hebrew- and Yiddish-speaking Jews worldwide, *Judith* was not popular among non-Jews until relatively recently. Chosen by some parents over the centuries—notably William Shakespeare and Anne Hathaway—*Judith* became briefly fashionable in the eighteenth century and then fell into disfavor until about 1925. Since then, however, it has continued to increase in popularity in all the English-speaking countries. By 1970 in the United States, it was the eighth-ranking name for girls.

This new-found popularity may be in part due to the choice of the name by Frances Gumm when she became the singer and actress Judy Garland, and by another Frances who became the Australian actress Dame Judith Anderson. The popularity of actress Judy Holliday also doubtless helped to gain favor for the name. The name certainly benefitted also from the increasing, post–World War II interest in ethnic identity among Jewish Americans. In more recent years, there have been hundreds of well-known *Judy*s and *Judith*s who have probably influenced the sustained popularity of the name.

Judith provides many charming diminutives for girls, among them *Jodie, Jody, Judi, Judie, Dita,* and *Yudi.* The name *Jody* or *Jodie* has been given to boys, though rarely.

Number

Nine. Some modern numerologists believe that nine stands for transformation. Nines possess great courage and will fight to the death for justice.

Astrological sign

Aquarius. The sign of the water-bearer has been connected to people who believe in the rights of all beings.

Color

Hyacinth. Ancient writings reveal symbolic associations with colors. Amen, the god of life and reproduction, was blue.

Stone

Blue turquoise. This gem's history spans all cultures. Its color ranges from every hue of blue or greenish blue to deep green. The South American Aztec and Inca tribes revered turquoise as a universal stone, believing their minds would connect with the wisdom of the universe when wearing it. Mexican and southwestern-U.S. Native Americans used turquoise to guard sacred burial sites and their priests wore it in ceremonies to call upon the spirits of the sky. Blue turquoise's rich color comes from its copper content.

Element

Copper. Copper connects well with the relaxing energy of blue turquoise.

❧ Herb

Amaranth *(Amaranthus hypochondriacus).* A preparation of amaranth leaves was used to reduce internal hemorrhaging. Herbal lore also suggests that the leaves made a soothing potion for skin problems. The name comes from the Greek word for "unfading." Amaranth's flowers keep their color and shape even after drying. Greek legends considered amaranth to be a symbol of immortality and used it to decorate images of their gods and burial sites. Amaranth is found in literature, symbolizing fidelity and courage.

♀ JUDY: From the root name *Judith.*

♂ JULES: From the root name *Julian.*

♀ JULIA: From the root name *Julian.*

♥ ♂ **JULIAN** **Giulia, Giulio, Jolette, Jolyon, Jules, Julia, Juliana, Julie, Julien, Juliette, Julio, Yulia:** In its meaning, *Julian* is as sweet as it sounds. From the Greek, it means "soft-haired" or "downy-bearded" and symbolically indicates youth. Together with *Julius,* it was quite a popular name in ancient Rome. After the reign of Julius Caesar, its feminine form, *Julia,* became the favorite name of the daughters of Roman emperors. *Julian, Julius,* and *Julianus* were also widely adopted by new citizens of the Empire. In modern Italy, the name became *Julio,* and that version of the name is perennially popular in the United States among Latinos. The love for things classical produced both the French *Jules* and the popularity of *Julian* and *Julius* in England. *Julia* became *Julie* in France and *Giulia* in Italy.

The popularity of *Julian* was certainly increased by the fact that it was the name of ten saints, in addition to a Saint Juliana. The most famous of the Saint Julians was a young man who acted out a variation of the Oedipus legend. It was foretold by a stag that the young man would murder his own parents. In order to escape his fate, he fled to another country. The parents, however, followed after him, and, before he recognized them, he killed them in a fit of jealousy. His penance was to spend the rest of his life ferrying travelers across a river and giving them lodging in his own home. He therefore became the patron saint of travelers. He was also known as a great epicurean and so *Julian* is sometimes associated with the best in food and drink.

In the nineteenth century in the United States, *Julia* came to be associated with the glamour of the theater. No fewer than three of the distinguished Drake family of actors were named Julia, including Samuel Drake's own daughter and two of his granddaughters—Julia Drake and Julia Dean. Julia Dean, especially, added glory to the name, becoming immensely popular in the American West. In the same generation, Julia Arthur became one of the two or three most acclaimed actors of her day. The name continued to be popular among actresses, and therefore also among their admirers, into the twentieth century, when it was then virtually eclipsed by *Julie*. In the second half of the century, that name has been borne by Julie Harris, Julie Andrews, and Julie Christie.

Recently, *Julia* has again become the favored form for girls. Popular variations on the name are *Juliet* and *Juliette*.

Number

Four. Fours are not always the most popular in the crowd because they aren't afraid to go against the majority.

Astrological sign

Libra. Libras need harmony in their lives. They love the arts and find great joy in theater, whether they're behind the stage or on it. Dancer Juliet Prowse, singer/actress Julie Andrews, and Julie London are all Libras.

Color

Deep river blue. Colors emit energy that affect our minds, and water shades encourage healing and relaxation.

Stone

Blue onyx. Onyx is part of the chalcedony quartz family and is usually white with bands of brown and black or black with bands of white. However, a rare variety of blue with white stripes is treasured in collectors' circles. Ancient cultures carved onyx for ornaments, sculptures and beads. Onyx jewelry was thought to protect the wearer from negative influences. Some cultures believed that onyx guaranteed a happy marriage and used it as a wedding gift.

Element

Silver. Silver is ruled by the element of water and boosts the marvelous energy of the rare blue onyx.

 ## Herb

Sweet fennel *(Foeniculum vulgare)*. Fennel grows wild in Asia Minor and the Mediterranean area, but can be cultivated everywhere. It has a long carrot-shaped root with a grooved blue-striped stem. The root and seeds were used in stomach and intestinal preparations. Fennel stimulates appetite and is a tasty addition to many recipes.

♀   JULIANA: From the root name *Julian*.

♀   JULIE: From the root name *Julian*.

♂   JULIEN: From the root name *Julian*.

♀   JULIETTE: From the root name *Julian*.

♂   JULIO: From the root name *Julian*.

♂   JUREK: From the root name *George*.

♂   JURGEN: From the root name *George*.

♥ ♂ **JUSTIN**   **Giustina, Giustino, Justina, Justine, Justinian, Justino, Justinus, Justo, Justus, Justy:** The name *Justin* comes from the Latin term *justus,* which means exactly what it should, "lawful," "right," or "just." It was often used in early Roman times as was the feminine variation, *Justina*. During the Christian period, two Byzantine emperors were named *Justin* and there is one Christian saint with the name, Saint Justin Martyr. A first-century writer and theologian, Saint Justin is important because he helped propagate Christianity by showing how many pagan Greek forms of thought could be combined with Christian philosophy. He is credited with writing two *Apologies* and the *Dialogues with Trypho*. Often considered one of the foremost Christian apologists, he was beheaded in Rome sometime around A.D. 165, after his debate with the cynic Crescens. There are also many other saints with variations of the name *Justin*. In the third century there was a child martyr named Justus of Beauvais. A Welsh saint of the sixth century was named Justinian. He is said to have been St. David's confessor.

The name may have come to Britain with the Romans and there were *Justinus*es listed in census records of the fourteenth century. *Justin* became an especially popular name in Ireland, where it was linked with the Gaelic term *saerbhreathach,* which means "noble judge." The MacCarthy family was particularly fond of the name.

After the Middle Ages, however, *Justin* became less fashionable outside of Ireland. It did not return to widespread use until the 1970s, when it came back into vogue in most English-speaking countries, and particularly in the United States. In the 1990s, Justin became even more popular and has placed among the top ten or twenty boys' names in the United States in the past several years. There is no obvious source, however, which explains why the name has become so fashionable in the last twenty years. Boys named *Justin* are often called by the nickname *Justy.*

The early feminine form of the name, *Justina,* has much the same history as *Justin* and was popular in early Christian Rome. There was a Saint Justina whose dates vary greatly depending upon the source. She lived sometime prior to the seventh century and became the patron saint of the Italian town of Padua, which built a church in her honor. The French form of the name is *Justine,* which has become the most common variation in the United States in the late twentieth century. The popularity of the novel *Justine* (1957) by Lawrence Durrell seems to have been an important influence on the rise in use of the name.

 Number

Three. Modern numerologists consider three to be a number of fulfillment and creativity. It relates to continuity as in yesterday, today, and tomorrow.

 Astrological sign

Libra. Libras revere harmony and are happiest when they achieve this in their family life and career. Most Librans are natural charmers and hate to quarrel.

 Color

Moss. Ruled by Venus, green signifies health and life. It is also the color most often associated with Ireland.

 Stone

Green moss agate. In gem lore, agates are considered to be reliable stones for their slow forming composition and their reputation as a steady source of protective energy. Agates have colored bands, spots, or intricate markings. The green moss agate looks like it has a plant growing within the stone. These gems were used by ancient tribal healers and priests to keep their people's physical and mental health in balance.

 ## Element

Silver. Silver is considered to be the best metal for agates, adding more power to the stone's healing potential.

 ## Herb

Nerve root *(Cypripedium pubescens).* This is an unusual looking plant and has many common names, including Venus shoe. The recognizable flowers are moccasin or shoe-shaped. Its rootstock is fleshy and was traditionally used in herbal tea form as a tranquilizer for nervous headaches, insomnia, and even delirium.

♀ JUSTINA: From the root name *Justin.*

♀ JUSTINE: From the root name *Justin.*

♂ JUSTINIAN: From the root name *Justin.*

♂ JUSTINO: From the root name *Justin.*

♂ JUSTINUS: From the root name *Justin.*

♂ JUSTO: From the root name *Justin.*

♂ JUSTUS: From the root name *Justin.*

♀ JUSTY: From the root name *Justin.*

♀ JUTTA: From the root name *Judith.*

♀ KAATJE: From the root name *Katherine*.

♀ KAITLIN: From the root name *Katherine*.

♂ KALEB: From the root name *Caleb*.

♀ KARA: From the root name *Katherine*.

♂ KAREL: From the root name *Charles*.

♀ KAREN: From the root name *Katherine*.

♀ KARI: From the root name *Charles*.

♀ KARINA: From the root name *Katherine*.

♂ KARL: From the root name *Charles*.

♀♂ KARMEN: From the root name *Carmen*.

♀ KARMINA: From the root name *Carmen*.

♀ KAROLINE: From the root name *Charles*.

♂ KAROLY: From the root name *Charles*.

♀ KASSANDRA: From the root name *Cassandra*.

♀ KATA: From the root name *Katherine*.

♀ KATE: From the root name *Katherine*.

♀ KATHARINE: From the root name *Katherine*.

♀ KATHARYN: From the root name *Katherine*.

♥ ♀ **KATHERINE** **Cait, Caitlin, Caren, Cari, Cass, Cassie, Cat, Catalina, Catherine, Cathleen, Cathy, Caty, Ekaterina, Kaatje, Kaitlin, Kara, Karen, Karina, Kata, Kate, Katharine,**

Katharyn, Kathleen, Kathy, Katie, Katinka, Katja, Katrina, Kay, Kayla, Kaylee, Kitty, Rina, Trina, Trinette, Yekaterin: The name *Katherine* probably comes from the Greek name *Aikaterina* or *Katherina,* and it is derived from the word *katharos,* meaning "pure." Some sources, however, have linked the name to the word *aikia,* meaning "torture."

Both of these translations make sense when you consider the life of the first woman of record to have borne the name: Saint Katherina. Katherina lived in the fourth century in Alexandria, Egypt. A virgin martyr, she was put to death by the Romans for her beliefs. Not much was known about her life, but four hundred years later, many legends sprang up to fill in the gaps. Katherina was said to have successfully debated a legion of philosophers who challenged her on the concepts of Christianity. She refused marriage to the emperor because she was already a bride of Christ. Her oppressors fastened the young girl to a large wheel meant to be an instrument of torture, but due to divine intervention, the machinery that ran the device flew apart, injuring the onlookers. She was finally decapitated, but instead of blood, milk spurted from the wound. The saga concludes with Katherina's body being borne to Mount Sinai by angels, where a monastery in her name was established.

The crusaders learned of Saint Katherina when they entered the Holy Land, and they were evidently moved by her story because they carried news of her back with them to Europe. By the Middle Ages, the extent of her legend was enormous. Ballads were composed in her honor, and she was depicted in plays, paintings, murals, stained glass, and even embroidery. The Spanish began to call their daughters *Catalina,* and the Italians named their daughters *Caterina.* Russian variants were *Ekaterina, Katinka,* and *Katja.* In Slovak lands, the name became *Katrina.* The Danish used *Kathrina* and *Karina,* but the Danish version that is most widely used in the United States is *Karen.*

The name *Katherine* traveled from Europe to England after the first Crusades. Because the English did not originally have the letter *k* in their alphabet, they substituted a *c*, creating *Catherine,* but both spellings were used. The name caught on quickly, as did *Kate,* both as a diminutive and as a given name used in its own right.

Of all the prominent European *Katherines*—the many queens and princesses, and at least six saints—the most powerful and interesting was probably the beloved Russian empress Yekaterina, known today as Catherine the Great. Born in Germany in 1729, Catherine supervised the construction of schools and clinics, advocated religious tolerance, and promoted education for women.

The astonishing popularity of Saint Katherine in England, as elsewhere, was lost on the Puritans, who did not revere nonbiblical saints. Thus *Katherine* did not travel to the American colonies with that venerable group, but did come ashore with other settler cultures. *Kate,* as an independent name, was often found among free black women from 1700 through 1800. As immigration picked up and the United States became more diverse, *Katherine* began to establish itself as a fashionable name, and by the mid-nineteenth century it was quite common. By the early twentieth century, parents chose other forms, such as *Kathleen* and *Karen,* with great regularity, but the actress Katharine Hepburn caused a surge of interest in the original name in the 1940s.

While *Katherine* was slowly becoming established in the United States, it was quickly becoming established in Ireland as *Caitlin.* (Some historians argue that *Caitlin* may also have been influenced by the French *Cateline.*) *Caitlin* was little used outside of Ireland until recent times, but it now ranks among the one hundred most popular names for a girl. Its spellings are various, and include *Kaitlin, Katelyn, Kaitlyn, Catelyn,* and *Caitlyn.*

Kathleen is the English form of *Caitlin*. It reached its height of usage in Britain in the 1920s. From there it came to the United States, for it was at this time that Irish names and those that sounded Irish were favored. Here, *Kathleen* was most popular in the early 1950s.

Karen was probably introduced into the American culture by Scandinavian immigrants. By the 1950s and 1960s, it was among the most popular American girls' names. It is unknown why the name became so common during this period, but some believe that the reason is related to the sound of the name—*Sharon* and *Darren* were fashionable at around the same time. It is also considered to have developed in an unusual pattern because it entered into usage from the bottom up. That is, *Karen*'s initial popularity cannot be traced to the upper classes or to a famous historical figure.

The numerous variations on the name *Katherine* are consistently in the top one hundred American girls' names, including *Katherine* and *Catherine*, *Kathryn*, *Kate*, *Katie*, *Karen*, *Karina*, *Kaitlin*, and *Kaitlyn*. Other variant names, spellings, and diminutives for *Katherine* include, *Kairen*, *Kathy*, *Cathy*, *Cat*, *Kath*, *Kay*, and *Kitty*.

☺ Number

One. In modern numerology, one represents independence and creativity. Metaphysical images include a pillar of fire and the colors of yellow ranging from gold to bronze.

☾ Astrological sign

Pisces. Sensitivity to others is a key trait in most Pisceans. Many feel a strong attachment to water and find peace living by the sea.

Color
Jonquil. A cheerful yellow shade that warms the soul of a sometimes blue Piscean.

 ## Stone
Blue topaz. While the most common topaz is yellow, it comes in many colors. Blue topaz is particularly striking and can range from a pale translucent hue to a rare sky-blue. Early physicians believed that topaz had magnetic energy. It was once thought to prevent tuberculosis.

 ## Element
Gold. This precious metal also comes in different colors including white, yellow, and rose. Used for millennia to make coins, jewelry, and decorations, it's a perfect complement for the high-energy topaz.

Herb
Monk's pepper tree *(Vitex agnus-castus)*. Greek physicians used the seeds of this aromatic tree for spleen problems. Monks were said to sprinkle the ground seeds on their food to reduce sexual desire. This tree's reputation for chastity continued through the Middle Ages and ground pepper was put in the food of young girls to ensure their virginity. Seventh-century herbalists used the seeds and leaves to treat liver problems and found that the berries helped prevent miscarriages and morning sickness.

♀   KATHLEEN: From the root name *Katherine*.

♀   KATHY: From the root name *Katherine*.

♀   KATIE: From the root name *Katherine*.

♀   KATINKA: From the root name *Katherine*.

♀ KATJA: From the root name *Katherine*.

♀ KATRINA: From the root name *Katherine*.

♀ KAY: From the root name *Katherine*.

♀ KAYLA: From the root names *Katherine* and *Michael*.

♀ KAYLEE: From the root names *Katherine* and *Michael*.

♀ KEALY: From the root name *Kelly*.

♀ KEELY: From the root name *Kelly*.

♥ ♂ **KEITH:** Although it has become a fairly common first name in the United States and Britain, *Keith* began life as a surname and continued to be so considered for a very long time. Actually, it would be more accurate to say that it began as a place name, as many Scottish towns are called Keith, based on a word that may have once meant "wood." Families took their surnames from the towns, and only much later did parents begin giving the name to their children as a first name. The most famous owners of the *Keith* surname in Scotland were probably members of the family Keith that gained the title Great Marischal in about 1010. The title, although it meant "Great General" and was given to a warrior member of the family, became hereditary. In later centuries, the Keith family acquired first a lordship and then an earldom, which the members lost for siding with the Stewarts in the early 1700s. Ultimately, Keiths served Scotland as Great Marischals for twenty-eight generations, or about seven hundred years.

Late in the nineteenth century, Scotland, itself, and all things Scottish acquired significant romantic value in the English-speaking world. As a consequence *Keith* became fashionable as a first name. The trend began in Britain and spread quickly to the United States. *Keith*'s popularity reached an all-time high in the 1950s in Britain and in the

1960s in the United States. Though it is still heard, it is no longer fashionable as a name for babies.

◎ Number

Eight. People of this number are credited with great courage and will. They are usually fair-minded and can see through subterfuge. Don't try to fool an eight.

☾ Astrological sign

Leo. Like their sign's totem symbol, Leos have the courage of a mighty lion and the fierceness to punish anyone who would attack their pride.

☀ Color

Vermilion orange. This brilliant mixture of yellow and red represents the essence of sunlight fueled by the power of conviction.

◆ Stone

Cinnamon essonite. This cinnamon-orange colored garnet was used by ancient Romans and Greeks for figurines and jewelry. Essonite's range of color (darker or lighter) depends on its manganese and iron content. It is called the "cinnamon gem" in Madagascar. The garnet's lore dates back for thousands of years. It's been associated with divine events and healing. Some early physicians believed garnets stopped bleeding, eliminated kidney stones, and promoted vitality in their patients.

♛ Element

Iron. Iron is tied to the element of fire and used in defensive or healing magic rituals.

🌿 Herb

Scotch broom *(Cytisus scoparius)*. The young flowering twigs and seeds of this shrub have been used by herbalists of the past for intestinal and stomach troubles. Scotch broom is native to Europe but has been naturalized in North America from seeds brought by European settlers. Modern herbalists advise against use of this plant because of its hallucinogenic properties.

♀   KELCEY: From the root name *Kelsey*.

♀   KELLEE: From the root name *Kelly*.

♀   KELLINA: From the root name *Kelly*.

♥   ♀♂ **KELLY**   **Kealy, Keely, Kellee, Kellina, Kiley:** One of the many surnames that has gained popularity in recent decades as a first name, *Kelly* almost certainly derives from *O'Ceallach*. That family name belonged to the descendants of Ceallach, a celebrated Celtic chief in A.D. 874 The O at the beginning of the name means "son of" and was taken away when the name was Anglicized as *Kelly*. The word *ceallach* means "strife," and, as a name, it was taken to mean "the warlike one." There are other possible derivations, most notably explained by the existence of certain places in Scotland named *Kelly,* perhaps meaning "holly" or "wood." According to most historians, though, the Celtic origin seems most likely.

Although *Kelly* was seldom used as a first name until the past few decades, there was a famous African American scholar and activist who was born in 1863 and named Kelly Miller, and there have been a few other famous *Kelly*s, mostly male. Country singer Kelly Harrell, for example, was born in 1899, and civil rights leader Kelly Alexander was born in 1910 and quite possibly was named after Miller. Then, in the 1960s, the name began suddenly to rise in popularity as a first name, especially for girls. The period was a time when many surnames were adopted as first names and when the Irish in the United States were beginning to assert their ties to their native culture. *Kelly* may simply have been chosen for its Irish associations, but it also may owe some of its popularity to certain celebrities who were highly visible in the 1950s and 1960s, especially Gene Kelly and Grace Kelly. Since the 1960s, *Kelly's* popularity as a girl's name has not waned. Among the variations on *Kelly,* many of which have become independent names, are *Kealy, Keely, Kealey, Kylie, Kiley, Keiley, Keilly, Kellie,* and *Kelley.*

 ## Number

Two. Some numerologists consider two a female number connecting it to goddesses such as Ceres of the harvest or Aphrodite and Venus. Esoterically, two represents the change of spirit into matter.

 ## Astrological sign

Aries. Since Aries is ruled by Mars, the ancient god of war, it's the perfect sign for someone named *Kelly.* Courageous, forthright, and strong are all traits that fit an Arien.

 ## Color

Mars red. "Seeing red" is a term used to describe anger, but in cultures of the past, red was considered a sacred color and a sign of divinity.

 ## Stone

Red aventurine. This quartzlike stone contains crystals of mica that give it a metallic or iridescent quality. Normally found in India and parts of South America, aventurine was used by the ancients as a divining stone to enhance "farseeing" or foretelling of the future. Some shamans used it in rituals to increase intelligence in their leaders, especially if they were preparing for war. Modern metaphysical lore suggests a person use aventurine to increase perception.

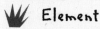 **Element**

Antimony. Antimony is tied to the element of fire and was believed to protect against harm.

Herb

Woody nightshade *(Solanum dulcamara)*. The bark of the roots and the twigs of this plant were used by traditional herbalists for external problems only. Often combined with chamomile, woody nightshade made effective ointments for swellings, bruises, sprains, and even corns.

♀   KELSA: From the root name *Kelsey*.

♀   KELSEIGH: From the root name *Kelsey*.

♥ ♀♂ **KELSEY   Kelcey, Kelsa, Kelseigh, Kelsie:** The name *Kelsey* has ancient Teutonic Anglo-Saxon roots and seems to be connected to water. Beyond this, historians disagree about the name's earliest origins. The name may be a variation of an Old English name, *Ceolsige,* which is said to derive from *ceol,* which means "ship," and *sige,* which means "victory." It also may originally have been a place name and mean "Ceol's island," or "ship's island." Finally, it may mean simply "from the sea, spring, or river." Variations of *Ceol* were fairly popular in Pre-Norman Britain, and include *Ceolwulf, Ceolred, Ceolwald,* and *Ceolnoth.*

Even if a form of the name existed as a first name back in the mists of English history, the modern variation, *Kelsey,* has only developed as a given name fairly recently. To trace the modern *Kelsey,* one should probably follow the standard place name-to-surname-to-first name route. Some historians believe that *Kelsey* as a first name became most common in the southern United States. However, it was certainly used, if rarely, elsewhere. In England, a Kelsey Smith was born in 1871, and in 1917, two creative British parents named their son the variation *Kelsie*.

Today, the name is used for boys far more frequently in the African American community. Among white parents, the name has gained popularity as a girl's name. Whether for boys or girls, the actor Kelsey Grammer of the contemporary television show "Frasier" has certainly brought the name a great deal of publicity.

Spelling variations include *Kelcey, Kelsie,* and *Kelsa* (feminine).

 Number

Five. In planetary connections, five is tied to Mercury. Some fives like to speculate in life and love. Because they do so with great energy, they must temper their enthusiasm lest they exhaust their internal reserves and end up on empty.

 Astrological sign

Pisces. Of all the signs, Pisces seems the most vulnerable to outside pressure. Their sensitivity can sometimes lead them to sorrow.

 Color

Aquamarine. This shade of sea and sky is purifying and promotes victory over ill health.

 Stone

Blue coral. Coral comes in several colors and is valued as an organic gem by many cultures. Dating back to the dynasties of Egypt, coral was favored as a healer stone and thought to protect travelers on either land or sea. Blue coral (*Heliopora coerulea*) is a striking hue and found in the waters around the Philippines.

♛ Element

Calcite. Calcite is the main mineral found in coral's composition and is the organic backbone of this revered sea gem.

♘ Herb

Irish moss (*Chondrus crispus*). Irish moss is a seaweed that lives on or under submerged rocks along the Atlantic coast of France, and of course, Ireland. The living plant has greenish leaves shaped like palm fronds that change to purple when harvested and dried. All of the plant is considered to have homeopathic properties and was used as a remedy for coughs, bronchitis, and even tuberculosis.

♀ KELSIE: From the root name *Kelsey*.

♂ KEN: From the root name *Kenneth*.

♀ KENA: From the root name *Kenneth*.

♀ KENDRA: From the root name *Kenneth*.

♀ KENIA: From the root name *Kenneth*.

♀ KENNA: From the root name *Kenneth*.

♂ KENNET: From the root name *Kenneth*.

♥ ♂ **KENNETH** **Ken, Kena, Kendra, Kenia, Kenna, Kennet, Kennice, Kenny, Kent, Kenton, Kenyon, Kenza:** Although it was the name of an early Irish saint, until the 1870s *Kenneth* was almost entirely a Scottish name. Derived from *Coinneach,* meaning "fair one," and *Cinead,* meaning "fire-sprung," it was the name of the founder and first king of Scotland, Kenneth MacAlpin (A.D. 839–858). Leader of the Scots of Dalriada, Kenneth McAlpin gathered together the ancient Celtic peoples, the Picts, with the Britons of Strathclyde and the Angles of Lothian to form a country that resembled, even at that time, the Scotland of today. Kenneth II ruled Scotland from 971 to 995, warring against the English and thereby gaining great popularity in his own country. For almost a millennium, *Kenneth* was an honored and often-used name in Scotland, and it was little known elsewhere.

In the second half of the nineteenth century, *Kenneth* began to foray into other countries, notably in England. At the beginning of the twentieth century, it became especially fashionable in that country before it peaked in the 1920s and 1930s. In the United States, the name was most popular in the 1950s and 1960s, though it seems to have always been somewhat overshadowed by *Ken* and *Kenny*, which began as diminutives but now function as independent names.

The female counterparts of *Kenneth* are not particularly common. They include *Kennice, Kenia, Kena,* and *Kenza.* The name *Kendra* may be a blend of *Kenneth* and either *Alexandra* or *Sandra* and is more popular than the others. Male names that may be variations of *Kenneth* include *Kent, Kenton,* and *Kenyon. Kent* is used considerably more frequently than the other variations. All three of those names, however, have other possible origins.

⊚ Number
One. Most numerologists tie this number to the sun. Ones are usually positively charged people who are natural leaders.

☾ Astrological sign
Leo. This late summer sign is also thought to be the sign of innate leaders.

Color

Vermeil copper. A gilded shade of yellow and red shines with the power of sunlight to warm the spirit.

 Stone

Golden beryl. The gemstone beryl is connected to several deities including Poseidon, Neptune, and Mara. In fifth-century Ireland, Druids used beryl crystals to scry future events. Other ancients used the beryl in rain-bringing rituals. It was also worn by sixteenth-century magicians to win arguments and debates. They believed it helped the bearer to gain understanding from others and make them seem amenable and well-meaning. Golden beryl ranges in hue from canary yellow to deep gold. The best gems come from Brazil.

 Element

Gold. Gold is the metal of kings and tied to Leo's celestial ruler, the sun.

 Herb

King's fern *(Osmunda regalis)*. There are many varieties of fern. King's fern grows mostly in European or African meadows. The rootstock has medicinal value and some early herbalists used preparations for coughs. If used quickly enough, it also cured jaundice. When mixed with brandy it made soothing backache rubs or ointments for sprains and bruises.

♀   KENNICE: From the root name *Kenneth*.

♂   KENNY: From the root name *Kenneth*.

♂   KENT: From the root name *Kenneth*.

♂   KENTON: From the root name *Kenneth*.

♂   KENYON: From the root name *Kenneth*.

♀   KENZA: From the root name *Kenneth*.

♀♂   KENZIE: From the root name *Mackenzie*.

♂   KEON: From the root name *John*.

♥ ♂ **KEVIN** Kevina, Kevon, Kevyn: Closely related in meaning to *Kenneth, Kevin* was for centuries primarily an Irish name. Indeed, until the 1920s, this name, meaning "handsome at birth," was bestowed exclusively on the children of Eire, in honor of Saint Kevin, or Caomhin, which was the original Gaelic name. This dedicated celibate was so fierce in his resolution that he moved to an island on which, he declared, no woman should ever land. However, he had an equally dedicated wooer in one Kathleen, who loved him and found his hermitage. She did manage to step onto the island, but Saint Kevin flung her from a rock into the water below. She died, but, according to legend, her ghost rose from the tide, smiling at the stalwart saint, and never left the place until he died. This story of doomed love was the subject of a poem by Thomas Moore, in *Irish Melodies*.

Kevin's appeal for parents was probably not based on that saint's determined defense of his virtue, but on his accomplishments after he was persuaded to abandon his solitude. A friend of Irish kings, he was said to have lived to be 120 years old and is credited with a number of extraordinary miracles. His feast day is June 3.

In the early part of this century, the name *Kevin* traveled to England, where it steadily increased in popularity for decades. By 1945, it was highly fashionable in all of Britain and was gaining adherents in the United States, along with other names of Irish descent. The use of the name seems to have peaked in the 1960s, but even so it was still one of the more commonly used names in the United States. In the 1990s, the popularity again began to rise, perhaps, in part, because of the enormous popularity of film stars Kevin Costner, Kevin Bacon, Kevin Kline, and Kevin Spacey.

◎ Number

Seven. Traditionally, seven represents keen intellect. Many sevens are entrepreneurs employing their intellect to achieve success in whatever career they undertake. Seven is linked to spirituality by some modern numerologists.

☾ Astrological sign

Libra. Most Librans love people but are not comfortable in crowds. Because they can't stand discord, they use their logic or laughter to keep the peace.

☀ Color

Irish green. Ruled by Venus (Libra's planet), green is a color of health. Honorary Druids wore green robes or accents.

◆ Stone

Chrysoberyl. This beautiful greenish yellow or green gem is usually found in V-shaped twin crystals. Its hardness makes it favorable for gem cutting. Chrysoberyl's name comes from the Greek language with *chryso* meaning "golden" and *beryllos* referring to the mineral beryllium (which adds the green hue). Chrysoberyl has appeared in Asian gem lore for thousands of years and was revered for its protective power against evil influences. Most often found in the Ural Mountains, this gemstone also comes from Sri Lanka, Rhodesia, Brazil, and Italy.

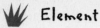 **Element**

Copper. Copper is ruled by water and is the metal associated with the sign of Libra.

Herb

Holy thistle *(Carbenia benedicta)*. Thistle has been cultivated for centuries for its medicinal qualities. However, this variety grows wild in rocky soils of Southern Europe as well. Healers used the herb for several ailments including migraine headaches, plague-related sores, and even as food with bread and butter like watercress.

♀   KEVINA: From the root name *Kevin*.

♂   KEVON: From the root name *Kevin*.

♂   KEVYN: From the root name *Kevin*.

♀   KEVYN: From the root name *Kevin*.

♀   KIKELIA: From the root name *Cecilia*.

♀   KILAN: From the root name *Kyle*.

♂   KILEN: From the root name *Kyle*.

♀♂ KILEY: From the root names *Kelly* and *Kyle*.

♀♂ KIM: From the root name *Kimberly*.

♀   KIMBA: From the root name *Kimberly*.

♂   KIMBALL: From the root name *Kimberly*.

♀♂ KIMBERLEIGH: From the root name *Kimberly*.

♥ **♀♂ KIMBERLY Kim, Kimba, Kimball, Kimberleigh, Kimberlyn, Kimette, Kimiko, Kimmie, Kym:** Tracing a winding course through history, we find that *Kimberley*, meaning "belonging to Cyneburg," was the ancient English town from which John Wodehouse, Earl of Kimberley, derived his titular name. In turn, Lord Kimberley gave that name to a town in South Africa. It is as an extension of the South African town that *Kimberley* became a first name, given exclusively to boys. During the Boer War, the English rushed to the aid of their South African compatriots to defend Kimberley. In a show of patriotism, British parents then named their sons after the place where so many young men died. In addition, Kimberley was an important center for diamond mining and therefore carried with it associations with wealth and value as well as patriotism.

After about 1905, however, the name fell into disuse. Then, in the 1940s, it reemerged—in the United States—as a girl's name. At some point in the process of moving from South Africa to the United States—and in its gender conversion—it lost its second *e*. By the 1960s and 1970s, *Kimberly* was one of the most popular girls' names in the United States and Canada. It remains a common name in the 1990s.

Paralleling the development of the name *Kimberly* is that of its short form, Kim. Although it was used as the diminutive for the man's name Kimball in Rudyard Kipling's *Kim,* the diminutive did not catch on immediately. It was the character Kim Ravenal, the beautiful actress in Edna Ferber's novel *Show Boat* (1926) that inspired parents around the United States to name their daughters *Kim* as an independent name or to call their daughters by the diminutive for *Kimberly*. Ultimately the novel was made into three separate films, and is currently being successfully revived on Broadway. Ferber's character Kim Ravenal has most certainly been an influence on parents. As it happens, many other real-life beautiful actresses in the twentieth century have been named *Kim* or have taken the name as a stage name.

Variations that have been used over the years include *Kimberlee, Kimberely, Kimberlei, Kimba Lee, Kimber, Kimba,* and *Kimberlyn*. Popular diminutives include *Kimmie, Kimmy, Kimette,* and *Kimiko.*

◉ Number

Five. Fives are normally bursting with energy. Most enjoy the company of others and have strong, long-lasting friendships throughout their lives. They are known to have a positive outlook on life.

☾ Astrological sign

Sagittarius. People of this sign know how to have fun. They're often the life of the party and lighten the hearts of all who know them.

☀ Color

Flax. In some ancient cultures, yellow represented Hek, the god of magic. They believed he had yellow skin.

◆ Stone

Cerussite. While cerussite is normally colorless and confused with a diamond by the untrained eye, it's a soft stone and only cut for collectors. This crystalline stone has wonderful luster when polished. White, gray, and black cerussite have turned up, but these colors are rare. Cerussite is found around lead ore. Large, transparent crystals have been discovered in Tsumeb, while smaller crystals appear in Austria, Australia, the United States, Germany, and Scotland.

♔ Element

Gold. Gold adds beauty to cerussite. *Kim* means "golden ore" in Vietnamese.

⚘ Herb

African ginger *(Zingiber officinale).* Ginger is indigenous to tropical Asia but can be grown in greenhouses. Its aromatic buff-colored rootstock has healing properties. Hot ginger tea was used to produce sweating to help rid the body of fever. Traditional herbalists gave it to their patients at the first signs of a cold to ease the symptoms and speed recovery. Rootstock preparations also aided sore throats.

♀ KIMBERLYN: From the root name *Kimberly*.

♀ KIMETTE: From the root name *Kimberly*.

♀ KIMIKO: From the root name *Kimberly*.

♀ KIMMIE: From the root name *Kimberly*.

♀ KIRSTEN: From the root name *Christopher*.

♀ KIRSTY: From the root name *Christopher*.

♀♂ KIT: From the root name *Christopher*.

♀ KITTY: From the root name *Katherine*.

♀ KLAIRE: From the root name *Clara*.

♂ KLARANCE: From the root name *Clara*.

♀ KLARETTA: From the root name *Clara*.

♀ KLARYCE: From the root name *Clara*.

♂ KLAUDIO: From the root name *Claudia*.

♂ KLAUS: From the root name *Nicholas*.

♀ KOLLEEN: From the root name *Colleen*.

♂ KONRAD: From the root name *Conrad*.

♀ KONSTANCE: From the root name *Constance*.

♀ KONSTANTIJA: From the root name *Constance*.

♂ KONSTANTIN: From the root name *Constance*.

♀ KONSTANTINA: From the root name *Constance*.

♂ KONSTANZ: From the root name *Constance*.

♀ KORRY: From the root name *Corey*.

♀ KOSTA: From the root name *Constance*.

♀♂ KOURTNEY: From the root name *Courtney*.

♀♂ KRIS: From the root name *Christopher*.

♀ KRISTA: From the root name *Christopher*.

♀ KRISTEN: From the root name *Christopher*.

♀ KRISTLE: From the root name *Crystal*.

♂ KRISTO: From the root name *Christopher*.

♂ KRISTOFER: From the root name *Christopher*.

♂ KRISTOS: From the root name *Christopher*.

♀♂ KRISTY: From the root name *Christopher*.

♀ KRYSTAL: From the root name *Crystal*.

♀ KRYSTLE: From the root name *Christopher*.

♂ KURT: From the root names *Conrad* and *Curtiso*.

♂ KURTIS: From the root name *Curtis*.

♥ ♀♂ **KYLE Kilan, Kilen, Kiley:** The pattern that has names transfer from place name to surname to first name is familiar during times when parents look to surnames to find interesting and/or unusual first names for their children. *Kyle* is the result of just such a development. Beginning as a Gaelic word meaning "a strait" or "a narrow piece of land," it became a common Scottish place name. The next step was its adoption as a Scottish surname. (Some have suggested a link to Old King Cole.) Then it became an Irish surname. Finally, it was adopted as a first name for boys and introduced to the United States in the late 1940s. Even then, however, its popularity grew slowly. It was not until the late 1950s and early 1960s that it began to catch on. In recent years, Kyle has become quite commonly used—for both boys and girls. Why there has been a sudden surge in popularity is unknown, though a number of celebrities have carried the name into prominence.

A similar name, with a very different derivation, is *Kylie*. It comes from the language of the aborigines of Western Australia and is defined as a "curl, curled stick, or boomerang." In 1975, it was the third most popular name for girls in Australia. It has never neared that level of popularity in any other country.

 Number

Eight. In dream interpretations, the number eight represents the cube, which stands for construction or the foundation of life.

 Astrological sign

Virgo. Virgo's element is earth, which also represents the physical body. People born under this sign (August 24–September 23) are usually excellent analysts.

 Color

Syenite. Deep blue shades such as this are considered colors of Virgo. In ancient Druid orders, blue was worn to signify harmony and truth.

 Stone

Kyanite. Jewel-quality kyanite crystals are usually pale to deep blue. It has also been found in white, gray, and green. Kyanite is formed under high pressure and heat like diamonds and is mined from metamorphic rocks. However, it has also been discovered in river bed sediments. The most valuable kyanite crystals are found in Myanmar, Brazil, Kenya, and the European Alps. Alluvial (water) deposits are rare and have been found in India and Australia.

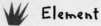 **Element**

Quicksilver. Quicksilver is the metal of Virgo's ruling planet Mercury.

Herb

Curled dock *(Rumex crispus)*. Also called yellow dock, this plant fares well in the wilds of Europe, the United States, and southern Canada. Dock has been considered a medicinal plant since ancient times. In the nineteenth century, healers called it a blood purifier to help cleanse the blood of the ill and prevent infectious diseases from spreading. An ointment was made from the root for itchy skin, sores, and boils.

♀♂ KYM: From the root name *Kimberly*.

♀ KYNTHIA: From the root name *Cynthia*.

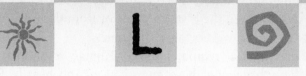

♀ LADONNA: From the root name *Donna*.

♂ LALO: From the root name *Edward*.

♀ LANA: From the root names *Alan/Allen* and *Helen*.

♀ LARA: From the root name *Laurence*.

♂ LAREN: From the root name *Laurence*.

♀ LARIN: From the root name *Laurence*.

♀ LARISSA: From the root name *Laurence*.

♂ LARRANCE: From the root name *Laurence*.

♂ LARRY: From the root name *Laurence*.

♂ LARS: From the root name *Laurence*.

♀ LAURA: From the root name *Laurence*.

♀ LAUREEN: From the root name *Laurence*.

♀ LAUREL: From the root name *Laurence*.

♀ LAUREN: From the root name *Laurence*.

♥ ♀♂ LAURENCE Lara, Laren, Larin, Larissa, Larrance, Larry, Lars, Laura, Laureen, Laurel, Lauren, Laurette, Laurie, Laurus, Lawrence, Lenci, Lon, Lonny, Lora, Loreen, Lorenzo, Loretta, Lori, Lorin, Loritz, Lorna, Lorne, Lory: The name *Laurence* ultimately derives from the laurel plant, though names historian Charlotte Yonge traces it back even further to Roman mythology and custom, saying that a *lares* was a guardian spirit of the hearth. In later Roman mythology, a human woman named Laurentia (or Acca Larentia) is said to have been the foster mother of Romulus and Remus, the twin brothers who founded Rome.

There was a nymph, Lara, in Roman mythology who may have been one these guardians of the hearth. She is described as having lost her tongue, either because she betrayed Jupiter to Juno in the Roman story, or, according to the Greeks, because she talked too much.

The most likely source for *Laurence* is in the ancient city near Rome that was called Laurentium because of the laurels that grew there. The name *Laurentius* means "from Laurentium" in Latin. It was a favorite name among early Christians and also the name of a martyred third-century saint who died by being broiled on a gridiron.

While *Laurence* existed in England as a monk's name before the Norman Conquest, its use as a secular name came with the invaders. Widespread use of the name continued in England until the Reformation, when its popularity declined. There is no clear explanation for why the American variation of *Laurence, Lawrence,* suddenly came into vogue in the late nineteenth century. The major twentieth-century influence on the name must have been the great actor Sir Laurence Olivier. In the United States, the diminutive *Larry* has come into independent use even more frequently.

The feminine name *Laura* derives from the same root as *Laurence,* the laurel, though some names historians believe it is the feminine variation of *Laurus,* a popular name during the Roman period. However, *Laura* did not appear until much later. There was a ninth-century Saint Laura whose martyrdom matches Saint Laurence's in gruesomeness: She was boiled to death in a caldron of molten lead. By far more famous, and ultimately responsible for the enduring popularity of the name, was the woman named Laura who was the subject of Petrarch's famous sonnets in the fourteenth century. Thereafter, the name was fashionable with the numerous poets influenced by Petrarch. By the sixteenth century, the variation *Lora* was being well used in Britain.

After virtually disappearing in the eighteenth century, the name reappeared in the nineteenth century in both Britain and the United States. In the United States, *Laura* has the distinction of having remained among the top fifty most popular girls' names throughout the twentieth century.

The variation *Lauren* became very fashionable when Lauren Bacall (originally Betty Joan Perske) became a movie star. Just as Lauren Bacall's allure has not faded over the years, so the name *Lauren* has remained constantly in use. *Laurel* may or may not be associated directly with *Laurence,* though it is directly connected to the source—the laurel bush. It became fashionable during the turn of the century when girls were frequently given flower names. Unlike most of those names, however, *Laurel* has grown in popularity during the late twentieth century and is currently widely used.

Laurie originally developed as a nickname for boys named *Laurence.* However, as the feminine *Laura* became increasingly widespread, *Laurie* became a variation of the feminine and is now used almost exclusively as an independent girl's name. Never as popular as *Laura, Laurie* and its own variation *Lori* have both remained viable alternatives to the more common *Laura.*

Loretta either was an Italian diminutive of *Laura,* or it came from the French diminutive *Laurette.* A third possibility is that the name is derived from the holy site Loreto in Italy. In England the name can be found as *Lauretta* as early as 1775 when Sheridan wrote in his play *Saint Patrick's Day:* "Lauretta! I never knew any good come of giving girls these heathen Christian names. I always knew Lauretta was a runaway name." The new spelling of *Loretta* seems to have appeared around 1870, but the figure who gave it popular appeal was the actress Loretta Young, who began her film career in the late 1920s. Country singer Loretta Lynn has kept the name in the public consciousness since the 1960s, though it is not now widely used.

British variations include, for boys, *Lorne* and *Lorin*. For girls, parents in the British Isles choose *Laureen, Laurel, Laurena, Lorena, Lora,* and *Lorna. Lars* is a Scandinavian variant, and *Lorenzo* is common among Italian, Spanish, and Latino families. Diminutives for boys include *Lon, Lonnie,* and *Lorrie.*

 Number

Seven. Sometimes associated with the occult and mythology, the number seven often represents people who have prophetic visions and sharp intellect.

☾ Astrological sign

Gemini. All signs are tied to a part of the body. Gemini is called the "voice" sign. Most Geminis love to talk and choose careers where they use their vocal skills. Sir Laurence Olivier was a Gemini.

✹ Color

Golden amber. Yellow hues stimulate intelligent conversations and encourage positive communication.

◆ Stone

Fire agate. Any agates were believed to increase physical endurance, but the fire agate also ensured protection from high energy (lightning) or heat. They were used in amulets and charms dating back to Babylonian times. Fire agates are a deep yellowish or reddish brown with high iridescence. This rainbow effect is enhanced when the stone is cut *en cabochon* (half-moon shape). Fire agates are found in Arizona and parts of Mexico.

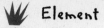 **Element**

Silver. Silver is a perfect ore for a fire agate, supporting its protective abilities and iridescent beauty.

Herb

Laurel *(Laurus nobilis).* Also called Roman laurel or bay laurel, this evergreen bush or tree grows wild in the Mediterranean Sea area. Both the leaves and fruit were used to stimulate digestive health. Bay oil, obtained by pressing the berries and leaves, was used as a liniment for arthritis, bruises, and sprains. A fruit or leaves tonic mixed with honey made chest plasters to alleviate lung congestion and other respiratory problems.

♀ LAURETTE: From the root name *Laurence.*

♀ LAURIE: From the root name *Laurence.*

♂ LAURUS: From the root name *Laurence.*

♂ LAWRENCE: From the root name *Laurence.*

♀ LEA: From the root names *Leah* and *Lee.*

♥ ♀ **LEAH** Lea, Leia: The name *Leah* has several possible meanings. In Hebrew, it may come from *le'ah* and mean "wild cow" or "gazelle." It may also come from the Hebrew word *lawah* and mean "dependence" or "weariness." In Assyrian, it is said to mean "mistress." The most common interpretation of the name is "weariness," and this meaning is connected to the earliest known figure with the name, the Old Testament Leah, who was the wife of Jacob. Some names historians also believe that the biblical Leah has lent the name an additional implication, "forsaken."

The story of Leah and Jacob is an interesting one. Jacob

had worked for Leah's father and intended to marry Leah's sister Rachel, but Leah's father surreptitiously put the bridal veil on Leah. Names historian Helena Swan describes Leah as ". . . Laban's eldest daughter, whom he palmed off on Jacob after his first seven years of service." Names historian Charlotte Yonge gives *Leah* a more attractive heritage. She reports that the poet Dante uses the biblical Leah (or in Italian, *Lia*) to represent "active and fruitful" love, as opposed to her sister Rachel, who represents meditative love.

The name was uncommon among Christians until the Puritan vogue for Old Testament names made it popular. As such, it traveled early and successfully to the American colonies. In addition, unlike many other Old Testament names, *Leah* remained in use throughout the eighteenth and nineteenth centuries. Historians disagree, though, as to whether *Leah* began to decline in the late nineteenth century or the 1930s. From the beginning of the nineteenth century until emancipation, *Leah* was among the top fifty names for free black women in the United States.

Why the name *Leah* has returned to popularity in the 1990s is unknown, though one might speculate on the influence of the character Princess Leia, in the cinema's *Star Wars* trilogy. The name *Lea,* which is often used today as a variation of *Leah,* is in fact a feminine variation of the ancient Roman name *Leo.* Today, however, despite their very different roots, *Leah* and *Lea* are used interchangeably. The actress Lea Thompson is a recent well-known bearer of this variation and may well have helped popularize both *Lea* and *Leah.* The name *Lee* is also from a different source, though it is frequently used as a short form for girls named *Leah.* Ironically, *Lee*'s source is spelled the exact same way as *Leah,* though pronounced differently. The Anglo-Saxon term *leah* means "clearing" or "meadow." (See also **Lee.**)

🌀 Number

Eight. In cosmic lore, eight signifies intensity of thought or deed. It also symbolizes a never-ending cycle: turned on its side, it becomes the glyph that stands for infinity.

🌙 Astrological sign

Gemini. The sign Gemini is tied to duality, with its symbolic figure of the Twins. Geminis are quick-witted. Lea Thompson is a Gemini.

✳ Color

Buttercup. This shade of yellow livens weary souls and stimulates fruitful communication.

◆ Stone

Rainbow obsidian. Obsidian has explosive origins. It is actually volcanic glass, formed when superheated lava cools and fractures. Obsidian is usually black, but rainbow obsidian displays iridescent flashes of red, blue, and green. Many ancient cultures used ceremonial objects carved of obsidian.

👑 Element

Quicksilver. Quicksilver represents Gemini's ruling planet, Mercury.

🦎 Herb

Meadowbloom *(Ranunculus acris).* Traditional herbalists used the shiny yellow flowers of fresh meadowbloom in homeopathic preparations to treat skin diseases, rheumatism, and arthritis.

♀ LEANNE: From the root name *Lee*.

♀ LEANORA: From the root name *Helen*.

♥ ♀♂ **LEE Lea, Leanne, Leigh:** In English, there are a great many place names that include the element "lee," meaning "meadow" or "clearing." From that element came the surname *Lee,* possessed by a number of notables, including, in the United States, General Robert E. Lee of the Confederacy. It was probably to honor the general that parents in the American South first began conferring the name on their sons in the second half of the nineteenth century. Use of the name grew in the first half of the twentieth century. Later, the name got a boost from actor Lee Marvin, peaking in popularity in the 1950s in the United States and Canada. Popular female actors Lee Grant, Lee Remick, and Lee Meriwether have probably all contributed to the name's use for girls in the United States.

Lee has long been useful as a second name for girls, and, unlike most middle names, it is often combined with the first name as a matter of course when addressing the name's owner. Think of Annabel Lee, heroine of Edgar Allan Poe's poem of the same name, and the contemporary actor Jamie Lee Curtis. When used as a first name for a girl, it is often followed by a second name, such as Ann, and that has given rise to the name *Leanne* or *Leeanne* being used as an independent name. Since the 1950s, the variant *Leigh* has gained some popularity—as witness the actor Leigh Taylor-Young—perhaps because of the influence of actors Vivien Leigh and Janet Leigh. *Leigh* is more often used for a girl than a boy, but any form of *Lee,* according to names historian C. V. Appleton, is used for either gender.

The name seems to have peaked in popularity in the early 1980s and become somewhat less popular since then, except as a second name. It has by no means, however, become rare.

✪ Number

Four. Among the numerous qualities attributed to fours, honesty ranks near the top of the list. They also like to help others less fortunate than themselves.

☾ Astrological sign

Sagittarius. The sign of the hunter goes well with a name whose roots come from nature. Sagittarians respect their environment. Cathy Lee Crosby, Lee J. Cobb and Lee Remick are Sagittarians as well as golfer Lee Trevino and singer Brenda Lee.

✳ Color

Mallow. Purple is the color of Sagittarius. It was also worn by ancients who sought to contact divine forces.

◆ Stone

Violet apatite. This collector's gem comes in a variety of colors. When cut on the correct angle it has brilliance and strong color. Apatite is usually found in prismatic crystals. Gem-quality stones are found in a few locations, including Brazil and Myanmar.

♛ Element

Lodestone. Also called magnetite, lodestone is actually an ore with a history from ages past. It was thought to have many powers including healing and the ability to strengthen resolve.

♖ Herb

Meadow sorrel *(Rumex acetosa).* Sorrel is mostly found in damp European or Asian meadows and shorelines. Healers of yore used the entire plant for various remedies. Root preparations helped stop bleeding while a tea brewed from leaves aided those with kidney stones or gallstones. Flower teas were used for mouth and throat ulcers.

♀ LEENA: From the root name *Helen*.

♀ LEESE: From the root name *Alice*.

♀ LEIA: From the root name *Leah*.

♀♂ LEIGH: From the root name *Lee*.

♂ LEN: From the root name *Leonard*.

♀ LENA: From the root names *Alan/Allen, Charles, Helen,* and *Madeleine*.

♂ LENCI: From the root name *Laurence*.

♀ LENDA: From the root name *Leonard*.

♀ LENEEN: From the root name *Leonard*.

♀ LENETTE: From the root name *Leonard*.

♀ LENIA: From the root name *Helen*.

♀ LENNA: From the root name *Leonard*.

♂ LENNARD: From the root name *Leonard*.

♀ LENNETTE: From the root name *Leonard*.

♂ LENNY: From the root name *Leonard*.

♀ LENORE: From the root name *Helen*.

♂ LEO: From the root name *Leonard*.

♂ LEON: From the root name *Leonard*.

♀ LEONA: From the root name *Leonard*.

♥ ♂ **LEONARD** **Len, Lenda, Leneen, Lenette, Lenna, Lennard, Lennette, Lenny, Leo, Leon, Leona, Leonarda, Leonardo, Leonie, Lon, Lonny:** Richard I of England may have gone down in history as "The Lionhearted," but his name meant "strong ruler." The real lion is *Leonard*. In the Old German, *Leonhard* meant "strong as a lion." The name was adapted by the French as *Leonard* and was popularized by a fifth-century saint whose widespread cult made of him the patron saint of pregnant women and prisoners of war. This French form came into use in English-speaking countries, probably during the eighteenth century. The Italian form *Leonardo* graced the most famous of the name's bearers, Leonardo da Vinci. The painter of "The Last Supper" and the "Mona Lisa" was also one of the most original and prescient scientists who ever lived, and thanks to him, the name carries associations of intelligence and creativity.

Leonard saw substantial but not extensive usage until the early twentieth century, when it began to grow in popularity. It peaked in the 1930s and has remained solid ever since. Composer Leonard Bernstein and actor Leonard Nimoy, of *Star Trek* fame, may have helped its popularity. But the name gained phenomenally with the meteoric popularity of actor Leonardo Di Caprio, who "strongly rules" millions of teenage hearts around the world.

An infrequently-used variant spelling of *Leonard* is *Lennard*. The common diminutives—*Leo, Lennie,* and *Lenny*—have passed into independent usage. There is no commonly accepted feminine form of *Leonard*. *Leona* and *Leonie* are both forms of *Leon*. There are, however, feminine variations on *Lenny,* including *Lenda, Leneen, Lenette,* and *Lenna*.

 Number

Six. Numerologists sometimes vary in their interpretations of number characteristics, but many agree that sixes have great passion for their loved ones and their work.

☾ Astrological sign

Aries. An Arien can't fathom the meaning of impossible. They are determined to find answers and usually do.

☀ Color

Leonine gold. This tawny color matches a lion's mane. In Hindu scriptures there are many references to gold as the supreme color of truth.

◆ Stone

Leopard skin jasper. This unusual looking type of jasper resembles a leopard coat both in color and the shape of the animal's spots. Jasper has been used in magic rituals since the beginning of recorded time. Perfectly carved jasper arrowheads were valued in war and thought to bring luck or protection to the owner.

♛ Element

Bronze. Many antique jewelry settings were made from bronze to bring out the color and power of the gems it supported.

☙ Herb

Dandelion *(Taraxacum officinale)*. Folk medical journals also call this plant lion's tooth. Dandelion can be found anywhere. The entire plant is used for healing purposes. Herbalists credit dandelion with the ability to remove toxins from the body and to act as a stimulating tonic. While the root juice is used, the preferred preparation is as tea. Lukewarm tea helps insomnia and fever. Dandelion greens are healthy salad greens, especially when they are fresh.

♀   LEONARDA: From the root name *Leonard*.

♂   LEONARDO: From the root name *Leonard*.

♀ LEONIE: From the root name *Leonard*.

♀ LEONORA: From the root name *Helen*.

♂ LEROY: From the root name *Roy*.

♀♂ LES: From the root name *Leslie*.

♀♂ LESLEA: From the root name *Leslie*.

♀♂ LESLEY: From the root name *Leslie*.

♥ ♀♂ **LESLIE** Les, Leslea, Lesley, Lezley: A number of "name-your-baby" books assert confidently that *Leslie* means this or that, but the fact is, they're all guessing. What we know is that *Leslie* follows the place name-surname-first name pattern. It began as a place name in Scotland. It was then adopted as a surname, in which capacity it served for centuries before becoming a first name. What the original place name meant is a matter for pure speculation. One expert says that it is "probably to be distantly connected with Latin *laetitia*, 'gladness.'" Another gives us "between the less lee [lea] and the mair [greater]," with lea meaning "meadow or clearing." Another states boldly that the name is Anglo-Saxon for "meadowlands," but it is doubtful this is so. The safest thing to say is that *Leslie* is Scottish.

The name first appears in English-speaking countries in the eighteenth century as a woman's name, spelled *Lesley*. It was probably introduced into widespread use by the poem "Bonnie Lesley," written by Robert Burns. The name was particularly popular in the twentieth century, during the 1950s and 1960s, possibly given a boost by the teenaged singer Lesley Gore in the United States. Another young woman not only inspired namesakes, but changed the spelling of the name.

The spelling *Leslie* was for centuries used exclusively for men. As a male name, *Leslie* peaked in popularity in the late 1920s and then declined, in spite of the later success of actor

Leslie Howard. In 1951 a charming young French dancer named Leslie Caron won Gene Kelly's heart in the film *An American in Paris*. She followed up her spectacular debut with enormously popular appearances in such films as *Daddy Long Legs* (1955) and *Gigi* (1958). In all of these films, she was the embodiment of loveliness, innocence, and charm. The combination was a potent one, and the public frankly adored her. Since the 1950s, the female version of this durable name has been spelled *Leslie*.

 ## Number

Eight. An eight is not daunted by a challenge. Early Greeks believed eight was the most sacred female number which symbolized Gaea or the Holy Mother.

 ## Astrological sign

Gemini. The sign of the Twins is considered positive and guarded by the planet of Mercury. Like their symbolic metal quicksilver, Geminis are normally fast-thinking and vivacious.

 ## Color

Tartrazine. Yellow is a color of happiness and found in many Scottish clan tartans.

 ## Stone

Yellow celestine. Some ancient civilizations credited celestine with mysterious powers including the ability to give its owner eloquence and persuasion through oration. While celestine comes in several colors, its yellow shade was thought to bring gladness to those who looked upon it. While the gem is no longer in demand because its brittle nature makes it hard to facet for jewelry, it is still mined in Italy.

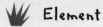 **Element**

Gold. Ancient mystics and priests believed all metals were potent tools of magic and gold was believed to be one of the most powerful.

Herb

Scotch barley *(Hordeum vulgare)*. Barley is cultivated as a food grain and is an excellent source of nutrition. The seeds were brought to North America by Scottish settlers. A mixture of barley and milk makes a calming tonic for irritated stomachs. A paste of cooked barley was once used as external plaster for sores and tumors.

♂ LEW: From the root name *Louis*.

♂ LEWIS: From the root name *Louis*.

♂ LEX: From the root name *Alexander*.

♀ LEXIE: From the root name *Alexander*.

♀♂ LEZLEY: From the root name *Leslie*.

♂ LIAM: From the root name *William*.

♀ LIB: From the root name *Elizabeth*.

♀ LIBBY: From the root name *Elizabeth*.

♀ LICHA: From the root name *Alice*.

♀ LIDIJA: From the root name *Lydia*.

♂ LIEB: From the root name *Ariel*.

♀ LIN: From the root names *Linda* and *Lynn*.

♀ LINA: From the root names *Charles* and *Helen*.

♀♂ LIND: From the root name *Lindsey*.

♥ ♀ **LINDA** Belinda, Belle, Lin, Lindy, Lynne, Melinda, Rosalinda: To anyone who grew up in the 1950s, *Linda* seems as common as Jane or Mary. Every school classroom had two or three *Linda*s, and it appeared that everyone had at least one cousin with the name. And yet, *Linda* has only been in use among English speakers since the nineteenth century. You won't find a single *Linda* among the wives of Henry VIII, in the annals of the Salem witch trials, or among Jane Austen's heroines. As late as 1925, the name did not appear among the top fifty-one names for girls. Then, by 1950, it was second on the list.

It is as difficult to account for the name's sudden and spectacular rise as it is to trace its origins. There are two major theories. The first is that *Linda* is a diminutive for the far older names such as *Melinda, Belinda,* and *Rosalinda.* One source, from the 1930s, states categorically "LINDA; familiarly LINDY. An abbreviation of Melinda." Others are more general, stressing only the Old German origin name element *lind,* meaning "serpent." While this now seems an odd thing to name a young woman, the snake was at one time considered a sacred animal with associations of wisdom and shrewdness. *Belinda,* therefore, means "beautiful snake." *Melinda* means "honey-like snake." *Rosalinda,* oddly, means "horse serpent," which explains why many names books deprive it of its German origin and insist that it comes from the Spanish. In that language, its separate elements would mean "rose" and "pretty," a derivation that is much more appealing. In North America, *Rosalinda* gave rise to *Rosalind*.

It is the Spanish meaning of *linda* that gives rise to the second theory about the derivation of the name. That meaning is, simply, "pretty." This theory has the advantage of simplicity and attractiveness, but is probably not as likely as the other. Unfortunately, early usage does not clear up the issue. One of the earliest recorded *Linda*s was English writer

Linda Villari, who was born in 1836. Since her mother's maiden name was Lind, it seems probable that her naming falls outside the two theories altogether. However, in choosing the name today, a parent can choose any derivation that appeals. There is even a third interpretation. The Italian meaning is "neat, tidy."

In both the United States and the United Kingdom, *Linda* began to lose popularity in the 1960s. Its heyday, however, had flooded the cast lists of films and television shows, as well as the pop music charts, with such names as Linda Crystal, Linda Gray, Linda Evans, Linda Blair, and Linda Ronstadt. An analysis of 1990 census figures places it, still, the third most common name for living women in the United States.

 ## Number
Four. A number four will never be boring. Their views of life and liberty may not be the same as most, but they are dedicated to bringing aid to those who might need it.

 ## Astrological sign
Libra. Anyone who knows a Libra understands their constant ups and downs. While this seesaw trait may drive close friends crazy, Libras are actually cheerful, gentle souls. Snakes and lizards are the animals tied to Libra.

 ## Color
Rose. Delicate as the softest rose petal, this pink shade is packed with loving vibrations.

 ## Stone
Rhodonite. This beautiful pink mineral is found mainly in ores that produce silver and manganese. Rhodonite is common in the southwestern United States with deposits located

near silver mines. It may contain black lead or zinc sparkles or tiny veins of gold or silver. On a metaphysical level this gem has outstanding positive energy. Ancients used it to rebuild physical strength especially if a person had experienced severe emotional trauma.

⚜ Element
Silver. Silver supports the energy of any gem it holds.

⚘ Herb
Horseradish (*Armoracia lapathifolia*). Horseradish is native to southeastern Europe and western Asia. The tapering white root is used both in medicinal and food preparations. Fresh horseradish root is useful for gout, rheumatic troubles, and bladder infections. For lung problems, coughs, and asthma, ancient herbalists combined the root with honey and raw sugar. However, all lore advises not to take too much at once.

♀♂ LINDSAY: From the root name *Lindsey*.

♥ ♀♂ LINDSEY Lind, Lindsay, Lindzy, Linzy: It is possible that the name *Lindsey* means "linden tree grove," but it is far more likely that it is a modern variation of the Scottish surname, *Lindsay*. The earls of Crawford, for example, bore the surname *Lindsay*. The name's Norman antecedents can be seen in the first English form of the name, *de Lindsay*. Some historians believe that the name's Norman origin is De Limesay, Pays de Caux, which is north of Rouen. It is also possible that the earliest variation of the name comes from a part of Lincolnshire, England, now called Lindsey. The Anglo-Saxon Chronicle refers to the area as Lindisse in A.D. 627, as Lindissi in A.D. 678, as Lindesse in A.D. 838, and as Lindesige in A.D. 993. The surname has had even more spelling variations than the place name. Names historian George F. Black reports at least two hundred. Not surprisingly, the malleability of the place name and surname has continued on as *Lindsay* began to be used as a first name. (See the list of variations below.)

While the Scots used the name for both boys and girls, when it started to become popular elsewhere, in the nineteenth century, it was as a boy's name. However, for no known reason, by the 1930s, *Lindsay* was being used predominantly as a girl's name. A famous female bearer of the name is the actress Lindsay Crouse. A prominent male bearer of the name was the British film director Lindsay Anderson. However, it is the actress Lindsay Wagner, famous for the television show "The Bionic Woman," who is probably most responsible for the recent popularity of *Lindsay* and *Lindsey* among women who were named during that period and among women who watched the show as children and are now naming their own girls.

Among the many variant spellings are *Lynsey, Lyndsey, Linsey, Linzi, Linsay, Lindsy,* and *Linzey.*

 Number

Seven. Seven is often linked to the healing arts.

 Astrological sign

Capricorn. As an earth sign, Capricorn represents the body. Capricorns pursue their goals with fortitude and careful planning.

 Color

Linden flower. This greenish yellow hue promotes health and mental stability.

◆　**Stone**

Green druzy quartz. Ancient mystics believed that green druzy could enhance their powers of clairvoyance. The stone was also given to children to ward off nightmares. Druzy quartz is easily identified by the appearance of small bubbles resembling sea foam trapped within the crystal.

♛　**Element**

Leadhillite. Leadhillite is a mineral produced by the oxidation of lead. Its name comes from the place of its discovery—Leadhills, Scotland.

🐉　**Herb**

Linden tree *(Tilia americana)*. This variety of Linden tree, also called basswood, is native to the eastern United States and Canada. Linden flowers and leaves were used in homeopathic remedies to relieve symptoms of colds and the flu. The inner bark can be rendered as a salve to treat rashes, skin irritations, and minor burns.

♀　LINDY: From the root name *Linda*.

♀　LINDZY: From the root name *Lindsey*.

♀　LINELL: From the root name *Lynn*.

♀　LINZY: From the root name *Lindsey*.

♀　LIOA: From the root name *Oliver*.

♀　LISA: From the root name *Elizabeth*.

♀　LISBETTE: From the root name *Elizabeth*.

♀　LISE: From the root name *Elizabeth*.

♀　LISETTE: From the root name *Elizabeth*.

♀　LISSA: From the root names *Alyssa* and *Melissa*.

♀ LISSANDRE: From the root name *Alexander*.

♀ LITA: From the root name *Carmen*.

♀ LIV: From the root name *Oliver*.

♀ LIVVIE: From the root name *Oliver*.

♀ LIZ: From the root name *Elizabeth*.

♀ LIZA: From the root name *Elizabeth*.

♂ LODOVICO: From the root name *Louis*.

♀ LOIS: From the root name *Louis*.

♀ LOLA: From the root names *Charles* and *Louis*.

♀ LOLITA: From the root names *Charles* and *Louis*.

♂ LON: From the root names *Laurence* and *Leonard*.

♂ LONNY: From the root names *Laurence* and *Leonard*.

♀ LORA: From the root name *Laurence*.

♀ LOREEN: From the root name *Laurence*.

♂ LORENZO: From the root name *Laurence*.

♀ LORETTA: From the root name *Laurence*.

♀ LORI: From the root name *Laurence*.

♀ LORIN: From the root name *Laurence*.

♂ LORITZ: From the root name *Laurence*.

♀ LORNA: From the root name *Laurence*.

♂ LORNE: From the root name *Laurence*.

♀♂ LORY: From the root name *Laurence*.

♂ LOTHAIR: From the root name *Luther*.

♂ LOTHAR: From the root name *Luther*.

♂ LOTHARIO: From the root name *Luther*.

♂ LOU: From the root name *Louis*.

♂ LOUIE: From the root name *Louis*.

♥ ♂ **LOUIS** **Aloysia, Aloysius, Clovis, Eloise, Heloise, Lew, Lewis, Lodovico, Lois, Lola, Lolita, Lou, Louie, Louisa, Louise, Lu, Lucho, Ludovic, Ludovica, Ludwig, Ludwiga, Luigi, Luís, Luisa, Lulu:** The names *Louis, Lewis,* and *Luis* all come from the same Teutonic roots, but there is some dispute as to what those roots are or what they mean. Some historians report that the original components of the name were *hlud,* which means "fame," and *wig,* which means "warrior." Other historians say that the roots are *hloda* which came from *hlu,* meaning "to hear," and *viga,* which means "to fight." The earliest form of the name is German or Frankish and is variously said to be *Hlodwig* (or *Hlutwig*) or *Chlodovech.* Whichever of these gave rise to the name, it eventually became *Ludwig.* The most famous bearer known to modern English-speakers is probably the composer Ludwig van Beethoven.

If we follow the *Chlodovech* route in the name's development, the next step makes sense. *Chlodovech* became *Chlodoiwig,* which was Latinized into *Clovis.* The other possibility is that *Hlodwig* was Latinized to *Ludovicus,* which then became *Clovis,* then *Louis.* Whatever the details of the origin of his name, Clovis was the sixth century king who overthrew the Romans in Gaul and started a long French tradition of royalty bearing the name. The first royal Louis arrived three centuries after Clovis. He was Charlemagne's son and ruled over the Holy Roman Empire in the ninth century. The most popular *Louis* may have been Louis IX, who led a crusade in the thirteenth century and was ultimately canonized. His descendant Louis XIV could not have been more different, as he has come down in history as one of the more flamboyant leaders in history. Ultimately, sixteen kings of France were named *Louis.*

Most historians believe that *Louis* came to England during the Norman Conquest and was Anglicized to *Lewis.* While the name became, and stayed, popular in

England, it did not travel well to America. It began to gain ground in North America after the American Revolution. Since the French were the allies of the Americans in that conflict, it may explain why *Louis,* the French version of the name, has always been as popular, if not more popular, in the United States. However, neither version became common until *Louis* had a surge in the 1870s. Taken together, both variations of the name (with *Louis* in the lead) were among the top ten names for boys in the early twentieth century. Since that time use of the name has dropped off.

The Spanish variation, *Luís,* like all other variations of *Louis* throughout Europe, has been popular for centuries in Spain and in Central and South America. It began to gain acceptance among a broader American public during the 1950s, and use of the name has been growing steadily since then as the Latino population grows.

The feminine variants of *Louis*—*Louise, Louisa, Lois, Heloise,* and *Eloise*—were fashionable through the nineteenth century in the United States, and *Louise* and *Louisa* remained popular well into the twentieth century. These names have all become somewhat old-fashioned at the turn of the twenty-first century, though they are by no means obsolete. The diminutive, *Lou,* is still heard both as a first name and as the second half of a double name, as in *Cathy Lou*. It has occasionally been given as an independent name to both girls and boys. *Luisa* remains high on the list of popular names among the Latino population in the United States.

 Number

Four. Some schools of numerological thought believe fours are not the most popular in the crowd because they aren't afraid to contradict the majority.

☾ Astrological sign

Sagittarius. Jupiter's influence leads many Sagittarians to greatness. Ludwig van Beethoven and Louisa May Alcott were Sagittarians.

❋ Color

Burgundy. Reddish purple melds the fire of courage and the power of spirituality. Burgundy is also a former province of France.

◆ Stone

Violet corundum. Gems of the corundum family are some of the hardest on earth and include rubies and sapphires. In mystic healing lore, violet gemstones were thought to act as germicides to help the body create antibodies to fight off infections. It also was used to elevate body heat during chills.

♕ Element

Brass. Brass is tied to the element of fire as is the zodiacal sign of Sagittarius. Brass is considered a metal of positive energy. It's also used to make musical instruments, such as the trumpet.

♘ Herb

Neckweed *(Veronica beccabunga).* This succulent type plant grows in wet or moist areas. The herb portion of neckweed was found to have medicinal properties. In older herbal remedies, fresh herb juice was recommended for intestinal ills. Neckweed potions were thought to be especially helpful for anemia caused by massive blood loss. It was used mainly for this purpose, but is now largely ignored in modern homeopathic remedies.

♀   LOUISA: From the root name *Louis*.

♀   LOUISE: From the root name *Louis*.

♂   LOUKAS: From the root name *Lucas*.

♀   LU: From the root name *Louis*.

♂   LUC: From the root name *Lucas*.

♂   LUCA: From the root name *Lucas*.

♥ ♂ **LUCAS** **Loukas, Luc, Luca, Lucien, Lucio, Lucius, Lucky, Luka, Luke, Luken:** The names *Luke* and *Lucas* are most often said to derive from a Greek name of the post-classical period, *Loucas,* which means "man from Lucania." (Lucania is an area of Southern Italy.) However, some names historians have said that *Loucas* may also mean "wolf." At the same time, *Luke* is said to mean "light" or "bringer of light," perhaps from the Latin term *lux,* meaning "light," which produced *Lucius*—a Roman name that survived well into the Christian era. There have been three popes named Lucius and two characters in the New Testament, one in Acts, another in Romans.

The consistent popularity of *Loucas* and its variations throughout the Christian era is directly linked to Saint Luke the Evangelist. A doctor who was converted by Saint Paul, Luke is the author of the Gospel which bears his name and of the Acts of the Apostles. The variation *Lucas* was the Latin form of the name and was often the form used during the Middle Ages. *Luce* and *Lucien* are the French variations of the name.

Lucien came to England with the Normans, and became the Anglicized *Luke*. The name was fairly common during the Middle Ages. It is not clear when or why it declined in use, but it was long dormant until the late twentieth century in the United States, when many such homespun-sounding names enjoyed a comeback. Whatever the reason, both *Luke* and *Lucas* are now high on the list of popular names for boys in the United States.

Number

Four. Many qualities are attributed to fours. Honesty places high on the list. Fours strive to assist others who cannot help themselves.

Astrological sign

Aquarius. Ruled by mysterious Uranus and infused with the wisdom of Saturn, many Aquarians find their destiny in acts of humanitarianism.

Color

Light blue. Soft as the dawn sky, this shade of blue lifts the soul.

Stone

Blue amber. In centuries past, amber was used for carvings, sacred ornamentation, and mostly for its curative powers. Many wore it directly on the body to protect themselves from infectious illnesses. Some early healers used it in powdered form to relieve patients' headaches, dental pains, lung ailments, and arthritis. Blue amber is one of the rarest colors of this precious organic gem. In fact, blue amber was thought to have the most powerful healing ability by some ancient Greek physicians.

Element

Platinum. Platinum is a high energy ore and enhances the potency of sacred blue amber.

♘ **Herb**

Wolfsbane *(Aconitum vulparia)*. Wolfsbane is the common name for the arnica plant found in the mountains of Canada, the northern United States and Europe. The medicinal parts of the plant are the flowers and rootstock. Arnica preparations are mainly for external use and were made into tinctures or unguents to aid healing of wounds, bruises, sprains, and skin irritations. The plant can have up to nine large yellow, daisy-like flowers. This plant should only be used with proper medical supervision.

♂   LUCHO: From the root name *Louis*.

♂   LUCIEN: From the root name *Lucas*.

♂   LUCIO: From the root name *Lucas*.

♂   LUCIUS: From the root name *Lucas*.

♂   LUCKY: From the root name *Lucas*.

♂   LUDOVIC: From the root name *Louis*.

♀   LUDOVICA: From the root name *Louis*.

♂   LUDWIG: From the root name *Louis*.

♀   LUDWIGA: From the root name *Louis*.

♂   LUIGI: From the root name *Louis*.

♂   LUIS: From the root name *Louis*.

♀   LUISA: From the root name *Louis*.

♀   LUKA: From the root name *Lucas*.

♂   LUKE: From the root name *Lucas*.

♂   LUKEN: From the root name *Lucas*.

♀   LULU: From the root name *Louis*.

♂   LUTERO: From the root name *Luther*.

♥ ♂ **LUTHER** Lothair, Lothar, Lothario, Lutero: The origin of *Luther* as a first name is one of those rare, obvious cases. It can be traced directly to Martin Luther, who began the great Protestant Reformation in the sixteenth century. Still, the original meaning of the surname is in some dispute. Some historians believe that *Luther* derives from the word *lathair,* which in turn is a variation of the Frankish word *lothar,* which means "famous warrior" or "famous in battle." Other historians say that the names *Louis, Clovis,* and *Ludwig* mean "famous warrior" and that *Lothar* (or *Liuther*) means either "people + army" or "people + famous." A particularly lyrical interpretation of the name *Luther* has its meaning as "lute-player," though it is hard to imagine that Martin Luther may have been descended from medieval bards.

The name was rarely used in England and probably came to America with the early German settlers. It was certainly particularly popular among members of the Lutheran Church in the mid-Atlantic American colonies. Since the seventeenth century, *Luther* has remained in use, but it could never be said to be common among Anglo-Saxon Americans.

However, throughout the twentieth century, *Luther* has been very popular in the African American community. There is no doubt that in the 1950s, 1960s, and 1970s, more parents were inspired to name their boys *Luther* in honor of civil rights leader Martin Luther King Jr.

Number

Three. Most numerologists agree that threes know how to get things done and are conscientious in whatever task they undertake. Three is also connected to art and inspiration.

☾ Astrological sign

Capricorn. A Capricorn is not deterred by the possibility of conflict, especially when they believe they are right. Martin Luther King Jr. was a Capricorn.

✳ Color

Hazel. Combining the earth shades of green and brown melds the power of two colors. Hazel represents connection to the earth and steadfastness.

◆ Stone

Chrysocolla. This distinctive bright green and brown gem was once called eilat stone and reputedly came from King Solomon's mines. It's usually found near copper deposits. Ancient mystics believed it to be a stone of peace and used it to soothe distress and to ward off hysterical fear or illusions. Chrysocolla's legend seems to have originated in the Far East, where it was thought to stimulate the mind and dissolve emotional confusion in order to enhance intuitive powers.

♕ Element

Copper. Copper elevates a person's reaction to a gem and acts as an extra boost for chrysocolla.

⚘ Herb

King's cure *(Chimaphila umbellata)*. Some herbal lore refers to this plant as pipsissewa. It is an evergreen that prefers dry woods in northern temperate climates. Doses of leaf tea were used to dissolve painful kidney and bladder stones. Root preparations were suggested for rheumatic problems.

♥ ♀ **LYDIA** **Lidija, Lydie:** *Lydia* is said to have developed as a slave name in ancient Greece. The Greeks often named their slaves for the land of their origin, and Lydia was the name of a country in Asia Minor. The name remained in use in Roman times and was popular with Roman poets, among them the poet Cato. One of his two extant poems is entitled "Lydia." Lydia was also the name of an early Christian woman who was converted by Saint Paul. She is remembered for her hospitality to the saint. Lesser known, but still important, is the biblical character Lydia of Thyatira, whom apocryphal texts say was Joseph of Nazareth's daughter.

This combination of Roman and biblical antecedents almost certainly helped secure *Lydia*'s enduring popularity over the centuries. English poets, novelists, and playwrights from the sixteenth through the eighteenth centuries were fond of the name. Lydias appeared in literary works such as *The Expedition of Humphry Clinker* (1771), a novel by Tobias Smollett, as well as in *The Rivals* (1775), a play by Richard Brinsley Sheridan, and in *Pride and Prejudice* (1813) by Jane Austen.

The name came to America with the early Puritan colonists and did not lag in popularity over the next three centuries. It eventually became one of the most common names among free African American women in the seventeenth and eighteenth centuries, and one of the United States' greatest white abolitionists was named Lydia Maria Child. Although it is still chosen as a name for girls, *Lydia* is not as widespread among young girls as among older women. According to the 1990, census *Lydia* is the two hundred forty-third most common name for living American women.

◎ **Number**

Six. To achieve their full potential, a six would be wise to follow their heart. If they do, humankind will benefit as well.

☾ Astrological sign

Virgo. While basically shy in nature, Virgos hold firm in their beliefs and do not compromise their standards.

✳ Color

Pearl gray. Gray is a color tied to Virgo and represents self-control. It also enhances a person's power to remain focused.

◆ Stone

Blue amblygonite. Mother Earth harbors rare and beautiful gems. Blue amblygonite is one of them. Amblygonite can be found in large translucent crystals, but because it's relatively soft, it's usually only cut for collectors. Currently, Brazil seems to be the main source of gem-quality stones, but some have been found in the United States.

☿ Element

Mercury. Mercury, the metal linked to Virgo, is also tied to two elements—water and earth. Its molten silver appearance attracted use by ancient magicians, but its properties made exposure over prolonged periods lethal.

♋ Herb

Bloodroot *(Sanguinaria canadensis).* Sometimes called pauson, this small perennial plant grows in shady rich soils in the northeastern United States. The rootstock has curative properties, but is potent and used in small doses. Herbalists of yore used bloodroot for sedative potions. Depending on what it is mixed with, bloodroot can also act as a stimulating tonic for someone lacking energy or appetite. External applications were used for sores, eczema, and itchy skin.

♀ LYDIE: From the root name *Lydia*.

♀ LYNDEL: From the root name *Lynn*.

♀ LYNELLE: From the root name *Lynn*.

♀ LYNETTE: From the root name *Lynn*.

♥ ♀ **LYNN** Evelyn, Lin, Linell, Lyndel, Lynelle, Lynette, **Lynne:** *Lynn* is a latecomer in the name game, at least as a woman's name, having come into widespread use only in the twentieth century. Since its advent, it has become very popular as a second name and as a suffix. As a surname, *Lynn* has a much longer history, beginning as a Celtic word for "pool." From that beginning as place name, it made the usual jump to surname. Then, in the nineteenth century, *Lynn* began to be used as a boy's first name. It was never one of the most widely used male names, and when it did rise in popularity in the twentieth century, it shifted over to a name for girls.

There are two theories about *Lynn* as a woman's name. The first is that it is simply a shortened form of *Linda*. The problem with this theory is that *Linda* is almost as late an entry into naming as *Lynn* itself. The second theory seems more probable. That is, the feminine *Lynn* probably is connected to the French suffix *-ine*. In the name *Caroline*, for example, it seems likely that Americans adopted the ending sound as *-line* or *-lyn*. At the beginning of the twentieth century, when Americans were experimenting with variations on traditional names, the suffix *-lyn* was added to any number of names. Thus, *Caroline* became *Carolyn* and was joined by *Marilyn, Jacquelyn,* and less felicitous hybrids such as *Kathalyn* and *Doralyn*. With a slight shift in another direction, they also added *-leen* or *-lene* to the usual names, male as well as female. The result was *Charlene* and *Laureen,* as well as *Harlene* and *Earlene*.

In the midst of all this daring name blending, *Lynn,* as an independent name, made its way into the birth records with some regularity. While it has never attained the popularity of *Mary* or *Linda,* as a second name, *Lynn* is rivaled only by *Ann, Lee,* and *Lou.*

Number
Two. Twos are kind souls. This number rules Cancer and in turn is guided by the celestial body of the moon.

Astrological sign
Cancer. Most Cancers feel a strong affinity with water—they should, it is their element. Water also represents the soul.

Color
Robin's egg blue. In ancient Tibetan lore human moods had mystical connections to color. Dark blue suggested a fierce nature, yet a paler shade was celestial.

Stone
Blue calcite. This mineral is the main component of limestone (including stalactites and stalagmites) and marble. However, calcite comes in large transparent prismatic crystals in a variety of pale colors. Because of its softness (by gem-cutting standards), this lustrous stone makes wonderful carvings, decorative items, and beaded jewelry.

Element
Aluminum. While aluminum is a "modern" metal with no past history in metallurgic lore, it is often recommended as a substitute for mercury in image enhancement therapy for low self-esteem.

❦ Herb

Water mint *(Mentha aquatica)*. Water mint is found in wet, damp areas, mainly in the northern hemisphere. It has a squared purplish stem that can grow up to three feet tall. Mint teas or oil can be taken for nerves, insomnia, headaches and a variety of gastric ills such as poor digestion and abdominal pains.

♀   LYNNE: From the root names *Linda, Lynn,* and *Madeleine.*

♀   LYSSA: From the root name *Alyssa.*

♂   MAC: From the root names *Mackenzie*, *Malcolm*, and *Maximilian*.

♂   MACK: From the root names *Mackenzie*, *Malcolm*, and *Maximilian*.

♥ ♀♂ **MACKENZIE**   Mac, Mack, McKenzie, Kenzie: As a first name *Mackenzie* is traditionally so unusual that it is not listed in most books exploring the etymology of given names. Even when it does appear, it is as a male name. However, *Mackenzie* has begun to scale the heights of popularity as a girl's name.

Mackenzie is originally a Scottish (or, when *McKenzie*, an Irish) surname. A possible early form of the name is *MacCoinnich* or *MacChoinnich*. The ancient Gaelic pronunciation of this spelling would have been *Mackaingye*. The name is said to mean "son of Coinneach." *Coinneach* is sometimes spelled *Cannechusm*, which is said to be an adjective formed from the word *cann*, which means "fair" or "bright." Mackenzie has also been said to mean "son of the wise ruler" or " son of the favored one."

One of the earliest variations of *Mackenzie* was Kenzocht M'Kenzocht, recorded in the charters of the Priory Beauly in 1491. In 1513, a man named Gilcrist Makkingze was arrested on the charge of "forethought felony."

The name certainly traveled to the United States with the Scottish immigrants. It was probably initially used as a first name to honor an ancestor or to keep a mother's maiden name in the family. In the early nineteenth century a man named Donald Mackenzie gained some fame as the governor of the Hudson Bay Company. The writer Washington Irving wrote about Mackenzie in his book *Astoria,* describing him as ". . . over 300 pounds, but so active that he was called 'perpetual motion.'"

There are not many famous *Mackenzies* in American history, and the reason for the recent, widespread use of the name for girls is still something of a mystery. Whether or not she inspired parents to name their daughters after her, the actress Mackenzie Phillips, who rose to fame appearing on the 1970s television sitcom *One Day at a Time,* certainly helped bring the name a great deal of publicity.

It is still not uncommon to hear *Mackenzie* chosen as a boy's name. Boys are often called by the nickname *Mack* or *Mac.* Children sometimes have their name shortened to *Kenzie.*

 ## Number

Six. Sixes are well known for their passionate souls and magnetic personalities.

 ## Astrological sign

Leo. Leos were born to rule and are in their element at the helm of their families or careers. Leos are as fiery as the sun, their ruling celestial body.

 ## Color

Summer light. Shades of yellow and gold are tied to Leo and to personal power.

Stone

Goldstone. This gem is reddish brown, brownish orange, or ocher. It has golden spots that glitter with sparkling iridescence. Ancient Hindus called it "the star stone." Goldstone was used for jewelry and decoration.

Element

Copper. Goldstone set in copper promotes a sense of well being and high energy for anyone who wears it.

Herb

Macleaya *(Bocconia cordata).* Macleaya is cultivated throughout the world. Juice from the leaf stems and root was used on insect bites, both to relieve the itch and to neutralize any venom left under the skin. Macleaya produces large flowers that can range in hue from a soft cream all the way to brown.

♀ MADA: From the root name *Madeleine.*

♀ MADDIE: From the root name *Madeleine.*

♀ MADEL: From the root name *Madeleine.*

♥ ♀ MADELEINE Dalanna, Lena, Lynne, Mada, Maddie, Madel, Madelena, Madge, Madlen, Magdalena, Maida, Maighdlin, Mala, Malena, Marleih, Marlene: There are few names with as many romantic associations as *Madeleine,* or *Madeline.* It derives from the name *Magdalena,* which was the title given to Mary—from Magdala—in the New Testament. Magdalena, or Mary Magdalene, as she was also known, was said to have been "possessed by seven devils" before she met Jesus, but she later became a true saint.

Magdalena has never been widely used since it refers, confusingly, both to a colorful and flagrant sinner and a saint. In England, however, the Greek-influenced *Magdalen,* or *Magdalene,* had some limited popularity in the later Middle Ages. The former spelling is used for a college at Oxford University and the latter for a college at Cambridge. In France, *Madeleine* was the more popular form, and the name has had considerably more currency in that country.

An additional dose of romance was added to the name in the middle of the nineteenth century by the notorious Madeleine Smith murder case. A lovely, young, upper-class woman in Glasgow was accused of murdering her declassé French lover after becoming engaged to a wealthier and more respectable man. Her trial ended in the peculiarly Scottish verdict of "Not Proven" and entered the annals of "Great Unsolved Mysteries." She was a highly sympathetic character and, indeed, probably was not guilty. The case became the subject of articles, books, novels, plays, and, in the early 1950s, a film starring the beautiful and popular Anne Todd.

Between Mary Magdalene and Madeleine Smith, the name acquired a provocative quality that it never lost. It has been adopted as a pseudonym by writers, actresses, and designers and has been given to their daughters by parents with a flair for the romantic. Adding to this aura was its use as the name of a sweet, light sponge cake that is baked in a scallop-shell mold. The cake was immortalized by Marcel Proust in his *Remembrance of Things Past* trilogy. "I raised to my lips a spoonful of the cake . . . a shudder ran through my whole body and I stopped, intent upon the extraordinary changes that were taking place." Delicious as the cake may be, Proust's reaction was due to its triggering in him a memory from his childhood, a continuing theme in his enormously long, sensually meticulous, and greatly admired work. Since its appearance at the end of the nineteenth century, *Madeleine* has carried this romantic scent as well.

Then, in 1939, Ludwig Bemelmans presented the world with the first of his children's books about the intrepid Madeline and her convent-school cronies. Since then, the books have sold more than fifteen million copies and have captivated uncounted nine-year-old hearts. It is impossible to ignore the influence of this classic of children's literature on parents who grew up in the baby-boomer generation.

The diminutive *Maddie* is used for girls named *Madeline* or *Madeleine*. It is also used, however, with the increasingly popular *Madison,* for girls.

⊚ Number

Nine. In karmic terms, nine is the number that signifies a time of reward for actions of previous lives.

☾ Astrological sign

Libra. Many Librans find themselves acting as peacemakers. They are also ruled by the planet Venus, which gives them romantic souls and loving hearts.

☀ Color

Shocking pink. All shades of pink are tied to Venus, the goddess of love. This bright hue would give courage to even the shyest to come forth with what's hidden in their heart.

◆ Stone

Pink druzy quartz. In mystic terms quartz is symbolic of the spirit and human intellect. Druzy quartz is found in several hues. The color of this sparkling gem depends on the mineral present within it. Pink comes from magnesium. Pink druzy was used to stimulate love and open closed hearts. Some ancients also believed it promoted peace and fidelity in marriage.

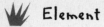 **Element**

Gold. Gold goes well with quartz. It lends strength to an already highly energetic stone.

Herb

Seven barks *(Hydrangea arborescens).* This native North American shrub is usually found on dry slopes, wooded areas, or sometimes near stream banks. Stems can grow up to ten feet high and are covered with thin layers of multicolored bark. The root of the seven barks plant is still used by herbalists as an aid to help remove or prevent kidney and bladder stones.

♀   MADELENA: From the root name *Madeleine.*

♀   MADGE: From the root names *Madeleine* and *Margaret.*

♂   MADISON: From the root name *Matthew.*

♀   MADLEN: From the root name *Madeleine.*

♀   MADONNA: From the root name *Donna.*

♀   MAEGAN: From the root name *Megan/Meghan.*

♀   MAG: From the root name *Margaret.*

♀   MAGDALENA: From the root name *Madeleine.*

♀   MAGGIE: From the root name *Margaret.*

♀   MAIDA: From the root name *Madeleine.*

♀   MAIGHDLIN: From the root name *Madeleine.*

♀   MAIGHREAD: From the root name *Margaret.*

♀   MAIRA: From the root name *Mary.*

♀   MAIRE: From the root name *Mary.*

♀   MAISIE: From the root name *Margaret.*

♂   MAKS: From the root name *Maximilian.*

♀   MALA: From the root name *Madeleine.*

♥ ♂ MALCOLM   Mac, Mack, Malcolum, Malkolm: This primarily Scottish name began as *Maolcolm* and was used to refer to any disciple of the sixth-century saint Columba. A dynamic Irish priest, Saint Columba was born into the Clan O'Donnell in the year A.D. 521 and was a descendant of kings. His baptismal name was Colum, later Latinized to Columba, and he was said to have founded one hundred monasteries in Ireland. In fact, he was responsible for the founding of a number of monasteries, but then, according to legend, he lent his prayers to an army that was about to be engaged in a battle. When those he had prayed against were defeated, three thousand men lay dead on the battlefield.

Devastated by what he had done, Columba went to his confessor for penance. He was told he must leave Ireland and preach the Gospel elsewhere, gaining for God as many souls as there were men who lost their lives in the battle. Columba went to Scotland, where he became known as the Apostle of Caledonia by converting the Northern Picts to Christianity, against the opposition of the Druids.

In the centuries that followed, in honor of Saint Columba, *Malcolm* became an important name for Scottish rulers. Malcolm III, son of Duncan I, is featured in William Shakespeare's play *Macbeth,* becoming king after Macbeth is killed. The name was little used outside Scotland—except by those with Scottish connections—until the first half of the twentieth century, when all things Scottish became the fashion rage. Use of the name began to wane in England after the 1950s, but it is still not an uncommon choice in that country.

Malcolm began to be used in the United States in about 1800 and remained steadily, but not wildly, popular until the 1960s. When, however, the black activist Malcolm X came to national prominence, the name gained considerable currency among African Americans. Others who may have contributed to a mild revival of the name among all Americans include writer Malcolm Lowry, author of the cult novel *Under the Volcano,* and actor Malcolm McDowell, whose electrifying performance in the film *A Clockwork Orange* made him an icon of the rebellious early seventies.

Closely related to the name *Malcolm* are, of course, *Colum* and *Colin,* which are also forms of *Columba.* (*Colin,* a popular independent name, can also be considered to have a French origin, as a diminutive of *Nicole,* which is derived from *Nicholas.*) Many men and boys named *Malcolm* are called by the nickname *Mac* or *Mack.*

 ## Number

Three. This number is often connected to people of success. However, threes can be overambitious and may lean heavily toward perfection.

 ## Astrological sign

Leo. Most Leos are propelled by the fire in their souls.

 ## Color

Cadmium. When orange appears in a person's aura it reveals pride and ambition.

 ## Stone

Cat's eye. An old saying, "eyes are the window to the soul," is connected to this legendary gemstone. Cat's eye is of the star chrysoberyl variety and highly valued both for its honey-brown color and its purported power to bring luck and wisdom. Of all the eye stones, cat's eye was considered the strongest. Romanian folklore tells of a Princess Vrina who became destitute when her land succumbed to famine. She sold everything but her lizard pendant with cat's eyes. When she was at her greatest despair, a lizard showed her a dry riverbed where she discovered a vast deposit of cat's eye gems, thus restoring prosperity to her kingdom.

👑 Element
Silver. A cat's eye set in silver ensures strong mental health and unbeatable good fortune.

🦎 Herb
Skullcap *(Scutellaria lateriflora)*. Skullcap is native to North America. It has a fibrous, yellow rootstock and pale purple or blue flowers. Native Americans used it for convulsions from fevers or nervous conditions. Many believed it was effective against rabies.

♂ MALCOLUM: From the root name *Malcolm*.

♀ MALENA: From the root name *Madeleine*.

♀ MALGORZATA: From the root name *Margaret*.

♂ MALKOLM: From the root name *Malcolm*.

♀ MALLIE: From the root name *Mary*.

♀ MAMIE: From the root names *Margaret* and *Mary*.

♀ MANDA: From the root name *Amanda*.

♀ MANDI: From the root names *Amanda* and *Miranda*.

♀ MANON: From the root name *Mary*.

♀ MARA: From the root name *Mary*.

♀ MARABELLE: From the root name *Mary*.

♂ MARC: From the root name *Mark*.

♂ MARCEL: From the root name *Mark*.

♀ MARCENE: From the root name *Mark*.

♀ MARCIA: From the root name *Mark*.

♀   MARCILLE: From the root name *Mark*.

♂   MARCO: From the root name *Mark*.

♂   MARCOS: From the root name *Mark*.

♂   MARCUS: From the root name *Mark*.

♀   MARCY: From the root name *Mark*.

♀   MAREN: From the root name *Mary*.

♀   MARETTA: From the root name *Mary*.

♀   MARGA: From the root name *Margaret*.

♥ ♀ MARGARET   Greta, Gretchen, Madge, Mag, Maggie, Maighread, Maisie, Malgorzata, Mamie, Marga, Marge, Margery, Margit, Margo, Margot, Marguerita, Marguerite, Marjorie, Maude, Meg, Peg, Peggy, Rita: The classic name *Margaret* is of Persian origin. Some historians say that the original Persian word was *murwari* and meant "pearl." The same word may also mean "child of light." Historian Helena Swan relates a beautiful story on the origin of pearls. Among the ancient Persians, she says, it was thought that oysters worshiped the moon. Every evening they would rise from the bottom of the sea and open their shells. A drop of dew from a moonbeam would then fall into them. This drop would then harden and become a pearl.

When the Greeks adopted the term, it became *Margarites*. The Latin variation is *Magarita,* and the French variation is *Marguerite*. One of the earliest well-known *Margaret*s is probably also the woman most responsible for the popularity of the name. Nothing much was known of Saint Margaret of Antioch until myths began to grow up around her after her death. She is thought to have lived and been martyred in the third century. One of the most famous stories about her is that she, like Saint George, slew a drag-on. In Margaret's case however, the story is slightly less warriorlike. Margaret was swallowed by the dragon. She then killed the monster because the power of her Christian faith split it in two. She was one of the most popular medieval saints and, along with Leonard, is a patron saint of women in childbirth. Later, the name became linked with royalty throughout Europe, which only increased popularity.

While some historians say that Saint Margaret's fame had spread to the British Isles before the Norman Conquest, it seems that common use of the name arrived in Scotland in the eleventh century, probably via the French. One of the first recorded *Margaret*s there was Saint Margaret, wife of King Malcolm III. The name ultimately became so popular among the Scots that it was considered by some to be the national female name. It also became popular in England and has given rise to an astounding number of variations and diminutives.

Like many saints' names, *Margaret* became less popular after the English Reformation and therefore did not travel well to the American colonies. There is one notable exception, Margaret Corbin, who was a legendary heroine of the American Revolution. She did not seem to inspire many namesakes, however, and *Margaret* did not become fashionable in the United States until the twentieth century.

One of the most influential American Margarets in the first half of the twentieth century must be the anthropologist Margaret Mead. Margaret Mitchell, who wrote the novel *Gone With the Wind*, probably also influenced some parents, as did the British Princess Margaret, Queen Elizabeth's sister.

Many of the diminutives and variants for *Margaret* have been widely used as independent names. They include *Margot, Meg, Meghan* (see also a separate entry for **Meghan**), *Rita* (from *Margarita*), *Peggy, Maggie, Maude, Marge, Greta,* and *Maisie*. The name *Gretchen*, which has had periods of popularity in the United States, is a German variant for *Margaret,* and *Marjorie* (or *Margery*) is an English variant.

Number

Two. In ancient magic lore, two symbolized the High Priestess of Light. The colors of cream and white have been tied to this number.

☾ Astrological sign

Cancer. Most Cancers are empathetic and caring beneath their tough exteriors. This soul sign is ruled by the number two.

☀ Color

Moon glow. White represents wisdom and understanding in some ancient cultures.

◆ Stone

Cream pearl. Pearls are organic gems from either salt or fresh-water mollusks. In most folklore, pearls are tied to femininity. Some parents gave pearls to young daughters to help them grow in beauty and spirit. Pearls are sensitive gems and can lose luster when the owner is ill or surrounded by negative energy. Pearls are also harmed by soap and perfumes. Cream pearls are valued by all cultures for their luminous sheen and soft milky glow.

♛ Element

Silver. Silver is a noble metal metaphysically tied to the moon and the sign of Cancer. It supports the beauty and mystic power of this precious gem.

🐉 Herb

Dragon root *(Arisaema triphyllum)*. Dragon root is the folk name for the Indian turnip that grows in moist wooded areas. Its turnip-shaped rootstock was used to make remedies for asthma, rheumatism, and whooping cough in American homeopathic medicine during the nineteenth century. The Pawnee sprinkled powdered root on the head to cure migraines and the Hopi mixed it with water to induce temporary or permanent sterility. The root must be partially dried to be safe. Medical supervision is advised.

♀ MARGE: From the root name *Margaret*.

♀ MARGERY: From the root name *Margaret*.

♀ MARGIT: From the root name *Margaret*.

♀ MARGO: From the root name *Margaret*.

♀ MARGOT: From the root name *Margaret*.

♀ MARGUERITA: From the root name *Margaret*.

♀ MARGUERITE: From the root name *Margaret*.

♀ MARIA: From the root name *Mary*.

♀ MARIAH: From the root name *Mary*.

♀ MARIAN: From the root name *Mary*.

♀ MARIANNE: From the root name *Mary*.

♀ MARIE: From the root name *Mary*.

♀ MARIEL: From the root name *Mary*.

♀ MARIET: From the root name *Martha*.

♀ MARILYN: From the root name *Mary*.

♀ MARINA: From the root name *Mary*.

♂ MARINOS: From the root name *Martin*.

♂ MARIO: From the root name *Mark*.

♀♂ MARION: From the root name *Mary*.

♀   MARISSA: From the root name *Mary*.

♂   MARIUS: From the root name *Mark*.

♀   MARJORIE: From the root name *Margaret*.

♥ ♂ **MARK**   **Marc, Marcel, Marcene, Marcia, Marcille, Marco, Marcos, Marcus, Marcy, Mario, Marius, Marquita, Marsha:** *Mark* derives, quite simply, from *Marcus,* an ancient Roman name. Some historians believe that the name grew out of the name for the Roman god of war, Mars, and therefore they interpret it to mean "warlike." There are numerous famous Romans named *Marcus,* including Marcus Brutus, who helped murder Julius Caesar. Marcus Antonius, better known as Marc Antony, was Caesar's friend and Cleopatra's paramour.

These legendary Roman figures did not influence parents in the Christian era, however. It was the author of the Gospel, the evangelist known as Mark, who helped keep the name alive through the centuries. Interestingly, Mark seems to have been the evangelist's surname. His first name is said to have been John. Despite this discrepancy, early Christians seem to have equated the surname *Mark* with the given name *Marcus,* because variations of *Marcus* were particularly popular among them.

The English name *Mark* probably came from the French version of the name, *Marc*. While the name did appear in England during the Middle Ages it was not very common. There is some disagreement as to whether the name had a burst of popularity in the seventeenth and eighteenth centuries, or whether it became more acceptable in the nineteenth. Historians do agree, however, that unlike *John* or *Luke, Mark* did not become really widespread until the twentieth century, despite the name's biblical heritage. The most famous nineteenth-century American figure with the name, Mark Twain, did not get it from the Bible. He derived his name from Mississippi boatmen who would call out "mark twain" to indicate water that was two fathoms deep.

No one is certain why *Mark* became a huge success in the twentieth century, particularly after 1950. The twentieth-century popularity of the original Latin name *Marcus* is much easier to trace. The name has always been more popular in the African American community where there has been a long-standing tradition of giving children Roman names such as *Cynthia* or *Caesar*. The use of the name in the twentieth century can also be linked with the influence of the black consciousness leader Marcus Garvey. More recently, *Marcus* has begun to cross the color line. This may be due in part to the popularity of the name *Mark* and the current trend to use variants of common names.

The most common feminine variation of *Mark*, *Marcia* (or *Marsha*), is derived from the name *Marcius*, which was in turn derived from *Marcus*. Until recently *Marcia* has followed the path of *Marcus* and *Mark* in its usage. It also was popular among early Christians and then virtually disappeared until the mid-twentieth century, when it burst back upon the scene. Now both *Mark* and *Marcus* are among the top one hundred boys' names in the country. *Marcia*, however, has inexplicably fallen onto harder times.

The name appears across Europe as *Marcel* and *Marceau* in France, *Marco* in Italy, *Markus* in Germany and the Scandinavian countries, and *Marcos* in Spain. Another feminine form crops up with fair frequency in the United States as *Marcy*.

◉ Number

Three. Many who bear three as their name number are inspired by life. They are not content to watch from the sidelines and are often found in a position of honor.

 Astrological sign

Aries. Bravery in the face of peril is a characteristic found in most Ariens. This sign is tied to the god Mars. The actress Marsha Mason is an Aries.

☀ Color

Rubine. Red symbolizes many things in different cultures but most relate it to courage or divine dedication.

◆ Stone

Red quartz. There are many types and colors in the quartz family. It's considered the highest energy-conducting mineral on earth; however, only quartz crystals are used for gems. They are prismatic, usually transparent, and polish to a brilliant sparkle. Red gems were prized for their ancient association with the god Mars. Many considered red stones to be protective and used them to strengthen the body, boost willpower, and promote courage. Some of the largest quartz crystals are found in the French and Swiss Alps.

🜂 Element

Antimony. Antimony is considered to be a fire element and was believed to protect soldiers against mortal injury in battle.

⚘ Herb

Marcory *(Stillingia sylvatica)*. This perennial is native to sandy soils in the southern United States. Its rootstock was used for external preparations to treat skin ulcers, boils, and other hard to cure skin troubles. Internal use is not advised as the fresh plant produces a substance that can cause stomach distress and symptoms of poisoning.

♀ MARLA: From the root name *Mary*.

♀ MARLEIH: From the root name *Madeleine*.

♀ MARLENE: From the root names *Madeleine* and *Mary*.

♀ MARLINA: From the root name *Mary*.

♀ MARLO: From the root name *Mary*.

♀ MARQUITA: From the root name *Mark*.

♀ MARSHA: From the root name *Mark*.

♀♂ MART: From the root name *Martha*.

♀ MARTA: From the root name *Martha*.

♂ MARTELL: From the root name *Martin*.

♀ MARTELLA: From the root name *Martha*.

♥ ♂ MARTHA   Mariet, Mart, Marta, Martella, Marthe, Marthena, Marti, Martina, Marty, Mattie, Pat, Pattie, Tina, Tine: The name *Martha* began with the simple meaning, "woman" or "lady," in the speech of New Testament Palestine, which was Aramaic. However, one of its bearers modified that meaning forever, becoming a lasting symbol of exaggerated devotion to housewifely duties. During a sojourn in Bethany, Jesus stayed at the home of Mary, Martha, and their brother, Lazarus. As he spoke of the spiritual things of this world, Mary sat quietly at his feet, absorbing his wisdom. Martha, on the other hand, bustled about making preparations for supper and providing refreshment for Jesus and his disciples. When she complained that Mary was not helping her, Jesus chided her, saying that Mary's was the better part. Martha later became the name of the patron saint of good housewives.

Understandably, many parents found themselves able to get past Jesus' rebuke, and *Martha* became a popular name in Britain after the Reformation and in the United States in the eighteenth century. It was widely used in the Puritan colonies, as well as in the South. The ascendance of Martha Washington to the position of first lady ensured its popularity, and it remained a highly favored name in this country into the 1950s. In the 1960s it began to lose favor. Recently, however, it has begun to regain popularity, as have several other simple biblical names.

There have been a number of famous *Marthas,* besides Mrs. Washington, but the one most likely to have boosted the use of the name in this country is the great dancer/choreographer Martha Graham. The French *Marthe* is occasionally used in the United States, and the pet name *Marty* (or *Martie*) is sometimes chosen as an independent name.

Number

Seven. Many historic sevens have been linked to the arts.

Astrological sign

Leo. Leos are known for their spirited enthusiasm in whatever task they tackle. Craft maven and home decorator Martha Stewart is a Leo.

Color

Tangerine. Yellow and red are both colors tied to Leo. They symbolize the sun's power. Ancient healers used gems of this color to increase appetite in finicky children.

Stone

Orange almandine. Members of the garnet family vary in shape, size, and color depending on where they come from. Mystics, both past and present, revere the garnet for its protective energies. Some thought the gem held strong medicinal qualities and used them to reduce harmful toxins in the blood. Other healers used garnets to heal emotional problems by placing one under a patient's pillow to ward off depression. Orange almandine was believed to boost failing appetites in ill or recovering patients.

♛ Element
White gold. When set in white gold, an orange almandine's power is reinforced by the strong conductive energy of this precious metal.

🦎 Herb
Ladies' fingers *(Anthyllis vulneraria)*. Sometimes called kidney vetch, this plant's flowering tops were used medicinally. A warm liquid preparation cleansed wounds and a poultice soaked in the same solution was applied afterward. Flower teas settled upset stomachs. Ladies' fingers can be found in Europe. Its yellow flowers bloom from May to September.

♀ MARTHE: From the root name *Martha*.

♀ MARTHENA: From the root name *Martha*.

♀ MARTI: From the root name *Martha*.

♂ MARTIJN: From the root name *Martin*.

♥ ♂ MARTIN Marinos, Mart, Martell, Martijn, Martino, Marty: The name *Martin* derives from the Roman name *Martinus,* which in turn finds its origins in the Roman god of war, Mars. The name survived into Christian Europe largely because of one man, Saint Martin of Tours. Saint Martin was a Roman soldier of the fourth century who became an influential figure in the Church hierarchy. He was not only the Bishop of Tours but was also known as the apostle of Gaul. He is best known and loved, however, for the story that has him dividing his cloak in two in order to give one half to a beggar. This story became a favorite subject for medieval artists. Saint Martin was so popular in England, in fact, that today there are 170 churches named after him. With such a generous (and powerful) antecedent, it is not surprising that five popes were named *Martin*.

Ironically, the next historically important *Martin* was the great challenger of the Catholic Church, Martin Luther. Surprisingly, many historians point to a decline in the use of the name after Martin Luther initiated the great Protestant Reformation. Obviously, the memory of the Catholic Saint Martin was more prominent in people's minds than the reformer Martin. However, Martin Luther certainly influenced some Protestant parents to adopt the name. He also influenced eighteenth-century satirists, such as Samuel Johnson and Jonathan Swift, who used the name "Martin" to represent the Protestant Church.

Martin certainly came to America with the colonists, but it has historically been uncommon here. President Martin Van Buren may have brought it back into fashion to some degree, but it did not become truly widespread until the 1950s. Civil rights leader Martin Luther King Jr. is certainly the single most influential *Martin* in modern times, and the name has enjoyed a degree of popularity among African Americans as well as among white Americans. However, since the 1980s, use of the name has dropped off considerably.

🌀 Number

Three. There's never too big a challenge for a three to face. People of this number know how to achieve. Three is also connected to art and inspiration.

Astrological sign

Scorpio. This water sign signifies passion of the soul. Martin Luther and film director Martin Scorsese were both born under the sign of Scorpio.

 ## Color

Venetian red. Like the passionate history of the great city of Venice, this ruby shade signifies high energy and religious devotion.

 ## Stone

Rubicelle. This is a reddish-orange variety of spinel. Its color comes from the presence of chromium and iron. Higher iron content makes a deeper red hue. Rubicelle was believed to boost physical strength during times of exhaustion or illness. Its name comes from a resemblance to rubies. Quality spinel is found in Afghanistan, Italy, Pakistan, and the United States.

 ## Element

White gold. White gold is a metaphysically energetic ore used to enhance the power of any gem. Gold has long been connected to kings, gods and the element of fire.

 ## Herb

Roman chamomile *(Anthemis nobilis)*. The flowers of Roman chamomile have curative capabilities and were used to make tea for colic, stomachache, and fever in children. It was helpful as a cleansing wash for open sores, boils, and wounds. Chamomile oil can also relieve stomach cramps. Flower extracts were made into rubbing oils and applied on swellings, calluses and inflamed or sprained joints.

♀   MARTINA: From the root name *Martha*.

♂   MARTINO: From the root name *Martin*.

♀♂   MARTY: From the root names *Martha* and *Martin*.

♥ ♀ **MARY**   **Amara, Maira, Maire, Mallie, Mamie, Manon, Mara, Marabelle, Maren, Maretta, Maria, Mariah, Marian, Marianne, Marie, Mariel, Marilyn, Marina, Marion, Marissa, Marla, Marlene, Marlina, Marylin, Maura, Maureen, May, Mimi, Minnie, Miriam, Mitzi, Moira, Molly, Muriel, Polly:** *Mary* (along with all its variations) is one of the most famous and well-used names in the Western world because it was the name of the mother of Jesus. Probably the second most important figure in Christianity, the Blessed Virgin has been the main inspiration for the name throughout the centuries.

Mary itself is the English variation of the Latin variation (*Maria*), which in turn came from the Greek variation (*Mariam*) of the biblical name *Mrym* (or *Miriam*). The New Testament, remember, was written in Greek, and therefore many traditional Hebrew names found their new variations in that source. The original meaning of the name *Miriam* is unknown, but there are a great many possibilities. Some historians connect the name to the Hebrew word *marah*, which means "bitterness." Other historians believe the name means "rebellious." In the past, people were fond of thinking that some element of the name meant "sea." Finally, names historian E. G. Withycombe felt it meant "wished-for child."

Interestingly, early Christians determined that the name was too sacred to be adopted as a child's name. It did not come into secular use until the twelfth century, when the cult of the Virgin rose to prominence. When the various versions of *Mary* were finally adopted, they became an immediate hit. By the sixteenth century in England, *Mary* was rivaled only by the names *Margaret* and *Ann*. During the sixteenth century, however, the name suffered a decline thanks to the unpopularity of the two Catholic queens, "Bloody" Mary of England and Mary, Queen of Scots. All was forgiven (or forgotten) by the seventeenth century, however, and *Mary* returned to its former popularity.

Outside of England during this same period, the love affair with the variations *Marie* and *Maria* had continued unabated. Names historian Charlotte Yonge relates the name's popularity through a common saying: "to seek Maria in Ravenna." This saying was the equivalent of "looking for a needle in a haystack."

Mary traveled well to the early American colonies. Despite its use among Catholics and more secular Protestants, the name was as popular in Puritan New England as in the middle and southern colonies. It has been frequently blended with other girls' names to produce new independent names, most notably *Marian* (sometimes spelled *Marion*), *Marilyn,* and *Marissa*. The diminutive *Polly* has had waves of popularity as an independent name, as has *Molly*. Other diminutives include *May, Mamie,* and *Minnie* (coming back into the spotlight with the actress Minnie Driver).

Mary remained among the most used American girls' names until the 1950s, when parents went looking for more unusual names. In the case of a name as popular as *Mary*, however, it was still usually at the top of the list, though it was no longer number one. For example, by 1970, *Mary* had dropped all the way down to fifteenth, and in 1981, it was thirty-first.

Now *Mary* has dropped even further. *Maria*, however, is gaining in use, and *Mariah* has been extremely popular in recent years (especially with the arrival of singer Mariah Carey on the scene). *Marie,* the French variation, does not seem to have become particularly widespread at all.

✺ Number

Three. In many cultures, three is considered a holy number. It is also linked with the ambitious and strong-willed.

☾ Astrological sign

Leo. Leo is sun-ruled and considered a noble sign. Scientist Marie Curie was a Leo, as are folk singer Mary Travers and newscaster Maria Shriver.

✳ Color

Marigold. Orange signifies beauty and glory on the mystic sefirot tree of the Cabala.

◆ Stone

Pink ruby. A ruby represented the sun in most ancient cultures. Some believed it held the bloodline of humanity within its heart. Rubies range from crimson to pink or deep violet-red. Legends abound about this gem including tales of it changing color to warn its owner of danger. It was worn to protect against misfortune or ill health. Mystics thought when a person dreamed of a ruby it meant that they would soon have unexpected guests. Others believed ruby dreams indicated sudden wealth.

♨ Element

Gold. Gold is a metal of the sun and fuels the fire of the precious ruby.

♌ Herb

Milk thistle (*Carduus marianus*). More commonly known as St. Mary's thistle, this plant grows well in rocky, dry soil. Healers brewed a tonic from its leaves that was used to treat stomachaches. The seeds were helpful for liver and spleen ailments and for jaundice.

♀   MARYLIN: From the root name *Mary*.

♂   MASSIMO: From the root name *Maximilian*.

♂   MAT: From the root name *Matthew*.

♂   MATEO: From the root name *Matthew*.

♂   MATHIAS: From the root name *Matthew*.

♂   MATS: From the root name *Matthew*.

♂   MATT: From the root name *Matthew*.

♀   MATTEA: From the root name *Matthew*.

♂   MATTHAUS: From the root name *Matthew*.

♀   MATTHEA: From the root name *Matthew*.

♥ ♂ **MATTHEW** **Madison, Mat, Mateo, Mathias, Mats, Matt, Mattea, Matthaus, Matthea, Matthias, Mattia, Mattie, Matvey, Matz:** *Matthew* is the English variation of the Hebrew name *Mattathia,* which means "gift of God." Saint Matthew was one of the four evangelists and author of the Gospel that bears his name. This Matthew was first a tax collector and a despised civil servant within the Roman government. In asking him to join the other disciples, Jesus provided a powerful lesson about forgiveness and redemption. The Greek and Latin form of the name is *Matthias.* In the Bible Matthias was the apostle chosen to replace Judas. *Matthias* is now the German variation of the name.

The French variation of the name is *Matheu.* The Normans brought that variation to England where it first became *Mathew,* and later *Matthew.* The name was extremely popular throughout England during the Middle Ages, as demonstrated by the number of surnames related to it, such as *Matthews, Mayhew* and *Matheson.* (From *Matheson* comes the surname *Madison,* which has become a popular name for girls in recent years.) It also, unlike many

New Testament names, seems to have survived the Reformation. Among the more famous post-medieval *Matthew*s was Matthew Arnold, the poet and critic.

There is no reasonable explanation available for why *Matthew* became much less popular in the nineteenth century. It had almost completely disappeared by the 1940s when it began a meteoric rise. After a brief decline in popularity in the 1980s, *Matthew* rose again to become the most popular boys' name by 1996. Boys with the given name *Matthew* almost invariably adopt the diminutive, *Matt*.

 Number

Nine. Ancient numerologists equated nine with people of purpose and iron wills. Some modern believers feel that nine stands for transformation or great changes in a person's later years.

 Astrological sign

Libra. Since Libra is ruled by Venus, people of this sign often have poetic souls and loving hearts. Many are theologians or artisans.

 Color

Aurora borealis. The colors of the luminous streamers in the far northern night skies vary in shades of lavender, blues, and greens—all colors tied to Libra.

◆ Stone

Blue-gray jasper. The divine connection to jasper dates back centuries. A passage in Revelations provides a description of God as to be "in appearance like a jasper stone." Another use of jasper was to wear or carry it to aid mental concentration or restrain unhealthy emotions that could lead to illness or danger. Jasper is found throughout the world with quality gems coming from France, Germany, and the United States.

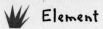 **Element**

Gold. Gold has been used for millennia to make coins, jewelry and decorations. Its link to deities and divine power make it a fine complement for the sacred jasper.

Herb

Venus shoe *(Cypripedium pubescens).* This unusual looking plant has easily identifiable yellow and purple flowers that are moccasin- or shoe-shaped. Its rootstock is fleshy and was traditionally used in herbal teas as a tranquilizer for tremors, headaches, and insomnia. Caution is advised as large doses can cause hallucinations.

♂   MATTHIAS: From the root name *Matthew.*

♀   MATTIA: From the root name *Matthew.*

♀♂ MATTIE: From the root names *Martha* and *Matthew.*

♂   MATVEY: From the root name *Matthew.*

♂   MATZ: From the root name *Matthew.*

♀   MAUDE: From the root name *Margaret.*

♀   MAURA: From the root name *Mary.*

♀   MAUREEN: From the root name *Mary.*

♂   MAX: From the root name *Maximilian.*

♀   MAXANNE: From the root name *Maximilian.*

♀♂ MAXIE: From the root name *Maximilian.*

♂   MAXIM: From the root name *Maximilian.*

♥ ♀♂ **MAXIMILIAN** Mac, Mack, Maks, Massimo, Max, Maxanne, Maxie, Maxim, Maxine, Maxwell: Seldom do we know who actually created a name. Most are so old that we scarcely know when or where they originated, much less by whose agency. Other names that have sprung into being in the relatively recent past can be traced only to their approximate date and location. *Maximilian* is different. According to the great English historian William Camden, it was "first devised by Frederic, the third Emperor who, doubting what name to give his son and heire, composed this name of two worthy Romans, whom he most admired, Q. Fabius Maximus, and Scipio Aemillianus, with hope that his son would imitate their vertues. . . . "

This invention occurred in 1459. It is unclear whether Frederick III would have judged that his son lived up to his name, since he kept the Holy Roman Empire at war most of the time during his rule. He did manage to add to the Hapsburg land holdings considerably, and appears to have gained the approval of his subjects, if names are anything to judge by. The name *Maximilian* became, and remains, one of the most popular German male names, especially in the shortened form *Max*.

In about the 1880s, *Max* began to gain currency in England, possibly because of the Emperor Maximilian of Mexico. It remained fashionable into the 1930s, no doubt helped by the fame and great popularity of the satirical writer and artist Max Beerbohm. In the United States, it was given a nudge by heavyweight boxing champion Max Baer, who reigned in the ring in the middle 1930s, and possibly by cosmetics magnate Max Factor.

Maxwell has been more widely used in the United States than *Maximilian,* probably because it sounds more Anglo-Saxon. It originated as a Scottish place name, becoming later a surname and then first name. It does not share even an ancient root with the other *Max* names, deriving not from the Latin for "great," but from "Maccus's well." Probably the most famous American to bear the name was playwright Maxwell Anderson, whose fame was great enough in the 1920s and 1930s to have influenced the spread of the name.

Interestingly, given the origin of *Maximilian*, the female name *Maxine* was also specifically coined. The actress Maxine Elliott was born Jessie C. Dermot in Maine. However, when she went to New York to make her way in the theater in 1890, she and playwright-director Dion Boucicault created the name *Maxine* to give her a more sophisticated, glamorous image. Elliott was quite adamant about taking credit for the name, and there is certainly no other contender. One names historian writes of another, for example, "Miss Withycombe makes the rather extraordinary statement that Maxine is 'a favorite modern French girl's name.' In fact the name will not be found in any French name dictionary, and French people consider it to be an English name."

 Number

Six. Strength of resolution is a trait in many sixes. Numerologists credit people of this number with strong powers of attraction.

 Astrological sign

Cancer. Most Cancers are drawn to water—this makes sense for this element rules their sign. Water also represents the soul, giving people under this sign sensitive natures.

 Color

Seawater. Shades of blue and green ebb and flow within this color to bring tranquillity.

 Stone

Green calcite. This stone is one of the most common minerals of the earth's crust. It's one of the principal compositions of sea plankton, mollusks, and the skeletons of fish and mammals. It also occurs in huge prismatic crystals in several pale, transparent colors. Beautiful specimens are found in Germany. Other localities for calcite crystals include England, Canada, the United States, and Mexico.

Element

Silver. Silver is considered an ore of the moon, planetary ruler of Cancer.

Herb

Agave *(Agave americana)*. Agave sap has disinfectant capabilities and was used in preparations to stop harmful stomach bacteria that caused ulcers and intestinal trauma. Also called the century plant, agave is considered to be the Tree of Life and Abundance by Mexican natives. Many still use it for food, paper, soap, roofing, dyes, and fodder. It was once believed that the plant flowered every hundred years, but it actually blooms after eight to ten years.

♀ MAXINE: From the root name *Maximilian*.

♂ MAXWELL: From the root name *Maximilian*.

♀ MAY: From the root name *Mary*.

♂ MAZO: From the root name *Thomas*.

♀♂ MCKENZIE: From the root name *Mackenzie*.

♀ MEG: From the root names *Margaret* and *Megan/Meghan*.

♥ ♀ **MEGAN/MEGHAN** **Maegan, Meg, Meggie, Megh-anne:** The Welsh name *Megan* derives, step by step, from the very popular name *Margaret* and its pet name *Meg*. While it seems logical to assume that the name *Meg* began as a diminutive of *Megan*, in fact, it is the other way around. *Meg* came into common use in Scotland in the nineteenth century and soon gave rise to *Meggie*, an even more informal form of *Margaret*. In Wales, those Scottish variations were modified to become *Megan* sometime during the second half of the nineteenth century. In the early twentieth century, Welsh-born David Lloyd George became Prime Minister of England, and the use of *Megan* outside Wales is traced to the celebrity of his daughter Lady Megan Lloyd George, who was born in 1902.

In the second half of the twentieth century, *Megan* has been widely used in the United States, often under the mistaken idea that it is a traditional Irish name. In fact, it has even been given an "Irish" spelling, in the form of *Meghan*. It is also sometimes spelled *Meagan*. Bringing the genesis of the name full circle, many parents shorten the name *Megan* to *Meg* or *Meggie* when calling their young daughters by name.

Number
Four. While fours may seem cool and collected on the outside, they are sensitive and vulnerable.

Astrological sign
Scorpio. Scorpio is ruled by two planets, Pluto and Uranus. Such a powerful combination can't help but give Scorpios passionate souls.

Color
Midnight ink. Black as the heavens at night, this color was worn during ancient magic spells of protection.

◆ Stone

Black pearl. This sea gem was one of the most valuable in antiquity and still is today. A pearl's organic composition is part of the reason for the mystical lore surrounding it. Eastern Indians believed that anyone wearing a pearl would be blessed by Lakshmi (the goddess of prosperity). They also thought pearls helped lengthen life, absolved sins, increased vitality, and brought wisdom. Black pearls are rare and found mainly in the Persian Gulf.

♔ Element

Silver. Silver is ruled by the element of water and the perfect complement for this gem of the sea.

♕ Herb

White weed *(Chrysanthemum leucanthemum)*. Some herbalists call this plant, herb Margaret. Its leaves and flowers had various healing purposes. It was used to promote sweating to break fevers and to treat kidney troubles. Ancient physicians also used a preparation for lung problems such as congestion and asthma. Medieval healers believed a poultice of the leaves and flowers would get rid of warts.

♀   MEGGIE: From the root name *Megan/Meghan*.

♀   MEGHANNE: From the root name *Megan/Meghan*.

♀   MEL: From the root names *Melanie* and *Melissa*.

♀   MELANIA: From the root name *Melanie*.

♥ ♀ **MELANIE**   Mel, Melania, Melantha, Mella, Melly, **Melonie, Milena:** You might think that the woman who won Ashley Wilkes from Scarlett O'Hara would lend a name enough sex appeal to boost it into the upper reaches of name stardom, but for some reason it was not to be. *Gone With the Wind*'s virtuous victor was singularly unglamorous, and her name remained, after both book and film, almost as little used as it had been for centuries before. *Melanie,* which ultimately comes from the Greek *melaina* meaning "black" or "having dark eyes, skin, or complexion," is the French form of the Latin name *Melania*. It was probably taken to England by French Huguenot refugees in the seventeenth century, appearing first in Devon and Cornwall. It later was used sparingly around the United Kingdom.

The name of two saints, *Melani* has been chosen only rarely by parents for their daughters over the years. It did not become fashionable in the United States until the late 1960s. A singer named Melanie Safka, who, like Cher and Madonna, used only her first name, gained widespread recognition for her sweet, ethereal voice. The name was then quite widely used well into the 1970s, but has since dropped into the background of popular names.

 ## Number
Five. Fives are quick-tempered when their liberty is challenged. If they don't have the freedom to explore life's byways, they can turn restless and moody.

 ## Astrological sign
Virgo. Mercury's rule of this sign stimulates versatility, giving Virgos the ability to think and act quickly. Virgo's element is earth, which represents the body.

 ## Color
Indigo ink. Dark blue is a color tied to Virgo. It signifies truth when seen in a person's personal aura.

◆ **Stone**

Melanite. This black or dark red gem is a member of the andradite garnet family. The Greeks and Romans believed that by wearing a garnet for a long time, a person would gain a wealthy inheritance. Melanite crystals have a metallic luster and are usually opaque. It is found in metamorphic rocks and volcanic lava. Fine-quality crystals are found on the island of Elba off the Italian coast and in France and Germany.

〰 **Element**

Titanium. Titanium is considered to be the earth's strongest ore. It is also found in melanite.

🐉 **Herb**

Fenugreek *(Trigonella foenum-graecum).* Herbal lore refers to this plant as Greek hayseed. A widely cultivated annual, fenugreek is used for culinary and medicinal purposes. It is one of the oldest medicinal plants, dating back to the ancient Egyptians and Hippocrates. Its seeds were used in preparations to restore strength to tuberculosis sufferers. Pulverized seed poultices were used for gout, swollen glands, tumors, sores, and skin irritations.

♀ MELANTHA: From the root name *Melanie.*

♀ MELINDA: From the root name *Linda.*

♀ MELISENDA: From the root name *Melissa.*

♥ ♀ **MELISSA** **Lissa, Mel, Melisenda, Melita, Mellicent, Melly, Melosa, Millie, Misha, Missy:** At the very beginning of the saga of Zeus in Greek mythology, Melissa was described as a nymph who cared for him when he was an infant being hidden from his father. She stole honey from beehives to feed the baby god. When her complicity in the plot to protect Zeus from his father's anger was discovered, she was turned into an earthworm. Given that ignominious beginning, it is unlikely that anyone would ever have chosen the name for a daughter had not Zeus stepped in some years later and turned the earthworm, Melissa, into a honeybee.

Melissa, which means "honeybee" in Greek, was used as a first name in early Greece and occasionally during the Roman Empire. It appears in the poetry of sixteenth-century Italy and again in the literature of nineteenth-century England. Melissa was the good witch in Ariosto's *Orlando Furioso* in 1516, and the name is found in Edmund Spenser's *The Faerie Queene,* written in the early 1590s. Charles Dickens used Melissa in *The Old Curiosity Shop* in 1841 and Alfred, Lord Tennyson used it in his poem "The Princess" in 1847. It was also the name of a character in Gilbert and Sullivan's *Princess Ida* in 1884. In spite of all this celebrity, however, *Melissa* remained largely a literary name, about as likely to be used as *Philomena* or *Hebe.*

Then, in the 1970s, *Melissa* suddenly became one of the United States' most popular names for girls, and it has remained in the top ranks ever since. Indeed, the name has been so widely used in the past couple of decades that it has begun to catch up with traditionally popular names like *Sharon, Laura,* and *Deborah.*

The pet name *Lissa* is very often used for girls properly named *Melissa.* Occasionally *Lissa* is given as an independent name.

 Number

Six. Sixes can have a strong romantic streak. They have the power to attract others and when they become attached they will be deeply devoted forever.

 Astrological sign

Gemini. The element of air rules Gemini. People of this sign are free spirits who enjoy being on the move. They are not ones to remain idle for long.

☀ Color

Pollen. This golden yellow is the color metaphysically associated with high energy.

◆ Stone

Prehnite. Sometimes prehnite is light green, but most often it ranges from pale yellow to yellowish brown and occurs in small rounded pebbles or barrel-shaped crystals. The yellowish brown variety can be fibrous enough to be cut in a cabochon (half-moon shape) to show a cat's eye effect. Prehnite deposits are found around volcanic rocks. Beautiful crystalline prehnite is found in France. Prehnite is named after Colonel von Prehn, who first introduced the gem to Europe.

₩ Element

Aluminum. Aluminum is a silvery white metallic element. It's also found in prehnite.

₷ Herb

Beeflower (*Cherranthus cheiri*). Old European herbal manuals laud this member of the cabbage family as a favorite for relaxing stiff and sore muscles. It has a fragrant scent and pretty yellowish orange flowers. Stems and flowers were used to make rubbing oils and diluted for perfumes. The flowers were held and carried to traditional festivals in ancient Europe, giving the plant the common name of handflower. The Greek form is *Zoe,* pronounced like "joy."

♀ MELITA: From the root name *Melissa*.

♀ MELLA: From the root name *Melanie*.

♀ MELLICENT: From the root name *Melissa*.

♀ MELLY: From the root names *Melanie* and *Melissa*.

♀ MELONIE: From the root name *Melanie*.

♀ MELOSA: From the root name *Melissa*.

♥ ♀♂ **MEREDITH Meredyth, Merridie, Merry:** There are a great many theories on the source and meaning of the name *Meredith*. Virtually the only point that names historians agree upon is that it was initially a masculine Welsh name. The most likely theory is that *Meredith* probably comes from *Maredudd,* which is thought to be a combination of two ancient Welsh words, *mawredd,* which means "greatness" and *iudd,* which means "chief." Therefore the name has come to mean "great chief."

Another possible meaning for the name is "sea protector." This theory proposes that the name derives from the Welsh word *mur,* which is the same as the Gaelic word *muir* and is connected to the modern French word *mer.* All these words mean "sea" or "water." When *Meredith* is derived in this way, it is said to be related to the names *Murphy* and *Murdoch.* A final theory on the meaning of *Meredith* at least proves that the name is very old. In *The True Interpretation of Christian Names* (1655), Edward Lyford describes *Meredith* as coming from the Latin term *mere ductus.* He writes ". . . *Mere ductus* for Mereducius [i.e.], brought together without mixing." As names historian E. G. Withycombe notes, this etymology seems rather "fanciful."

For many centuries—not surprisingly, considering its most probable source—*Meredith* has been popular in Wales. By the early twentieth century it had spread to other English-speaking countries. At the same time as the name spread outside Wales as a masculine name, it also began to be adopted as a girl's name. Most names historians believe that the name became attractive to parents of girl children because of its diminutive *Merry,* which had long been used as an independent feminine name.

The name was used for a girl in 1935 when Enid Bagnold published her classic novel *National Velvet.* She named the sister of the novel's heroine Meredith (called Merry) Brown. The name only gained additional prominence when the novel became a movie starring Elizabeth Taylor and Mickey Rooney. In the 1960s, Margaret Forster named a female character Meredith in her novel *Georgy Girl.* Forster describes the character of the name beautifully when she writes: "Meredith's real name was Mary, but she wasn't having any of that. She needed something much more original and pretty, so she chose Meredith and it sounded suitably soft and caressing on the lips of her numerous boyfriends."

 Number

One. Ones have independent natures and chafe at restraints of any kind.

 Astrological sign

Pisces. Pisces is ruled by Neptune and Jupiter and its element is water. In cosmic connections, water represents the soul.

 Color

Ocean. Blue and green enhance contentment of the heart and tranquillity of the soul.

 Stone

White pearl. Pearls were once believed to bring peace of mind and well-being to their owners. According to Hindu legends, pearls can be formed by the gods of air, earth, water, or fire—but the pearl formed by the water god was gleaming white like a heavenly star and considered the most precious. In medical lore, seed pearls (tiny, high-quality gems) were ground into powder for remedies against asthma, tuberculosis, eye troubles, and weak hearts. In modern mystical beliefs, pearls are believed to increase patience and tolerance.

Element

Silver. Silver enhances the power of the pearl.

🦁 Herb

Great burnet *(Sanguisorba officinalis)*. Great burnet is a perennial that thrives in damp meadows, peat bogs, and coastal areas of the United States and Europe. The plant was used mainly to clot blood and stop hemorrhaging. Some healers used it for inflammation of the blood vessels and varicose veins.

♂ MEREDYTH: From the root name *Meredith*.

♀ MERRIDIE: From the root name *Meredith*.

♀ MERRY: From the root name *Meredith*.

♀ MIA: From the root name *Michael*.

♂ MICAH: From the root name *Michael*.

♥ ♀♂ MICHAEL Kayla, Kaylee, Mia, Micah, Michaela, Michel, Micheline, Michelle, Mick, Micky, Miguel, Miguela, Mihail, Mikayla, Mike, Mikey, Mikhail, Mikhayla, Mikhos, Mikkel, Mikko, Misha, Mitch, Mitchell, Mykell: The name *Michael* is from the Hebrew name *Micah*, which means "who is like the Lord." In the Bible, *Michael* is mentioned several times. The archangel Michael is one of the most important saints of the Catholic Church. During the Middle Ages, Saint Michael was believed to be the leader of the heavenly host. For this reason he became the patron saint of soldiers and his name was adopted by military leaders throughout the Christian world.

Michael probably existed in England before the Norman Conquest, but it certainly was more common afterward. The pronunciation of the French *Michel* led the English to the name *Mitchell,* which was used as both a first name and last name. *Mitch,* of course, is a common diminutive for *Mitchell*. There is some disagreement as to when *Michael* went out of vogue with English parents. Some historians say that the Reformation dealt a blow to the name among Protestants, but others feel it did not become less popular until the early nineteenth century.

Upper-class New Englanders almost never chose *Michael* for their sons in the early days of American settlement, but it was used among the lower classes of all regions. This differentiation may be connected to an early Irish presence, as the Irish have had a long-standing affection for the name. Certainly the use of *Michael* increased in the United States during the great Irish immigration of the mid-nineteenth century. By the early twentieth century, both the Irish and the name were more established, and for the remainder of the century *Michael* became one of the most mainstream names in the United States. In 1950, *Michael* was the fifth most popular name for boys. By 1960, it was the second most popular name. In 1970, 1980, and 1990, according to the United States Census it was the most popular boys' name, and it remains so to this day.

The variants and pet names for *Michael* are many. Not only does every European language have its variation, but each variation also has many diminutives. There are also numerous feminine variations and their diminutives. In the

1990s in the United States, a few of these variations have become almost as popular as *Michael* itself. Recently, however, the Spanish and Portuguese version, *Miguel,* has turned up in lists of the top one hundred boys' names in the United States.

Among the feminine variations, in the 1990s *Michelle* and *Mikayla* (or *Michaela*) have been the two most popular. *Michelle* is the English variation of the French name *Michele* and certainly was boosted by the popularity of the 1968 Beatles song "Michelle."

Mikayla is a modern spelling of the feminine for *Michael, Michaela.* This spelling is also probably influenced by various European spellings of *Michael.* For example, the Russian spelling of *Michael* is *Mikhail,* the Finnish is *Mikko,* and the Norwegian is *Mikkel* or *Mikael.* The name *Kayla,* which is currently among the top girls' names, is probably a shortened version of *Mikayla,* though it may also have been influenced by the popular *Kaylee* (which is said to come from *Kay* (*Katherine*), *Keely, Kyle*—or all three.)

Among the many diminutives and pet names for *Michael* and its variants are *Mike, Mikey, Mickie, Mick, Mitch, Mia,* and *Chelle* (feminine).

◉ Number

Six. Individual numerologists vary in their interpretations of number traits, but most agree sixes have great passion for their work. Artistic genius Michelangelo was born under this number.

☾ Astrological sign

Leo. People of this sign often possess spirits of pure light and have positive natures. The term "firebrand" aptly describes many Leos.

Color

Angel's light. In medieval art, the aura surrounding heavenly messengers was depicted as golden white. This hue symbolizes celestial favor or purity in ancient folklore.

 Stone

Emerald. The emerald is the most famous gem of the beryl family. Its name comes from the Persian word for green. Emeralds have always been surrounded by mystery. Asians believed it strengthened memory and imparted the power to foresee monumental events. The Incas worshiped the emerald as a god gem. Jewish high priests used it on their breastplates for a direct connection to God. This rich green jewel has been called the gem of hope, love, and faith. It was also considered a symbol of immortality. Modern lore credits the emerald with the ability to open the mind and increase universal sight. To achieve ultimate creativity, some suggest that artists, writers, and others who use imagination in their work, wear or carry an emerald at all times.

 Element

Electrum. Electrum is a metaphysically-powerful mixture of gold, silver, and platinum.

 Herb

Wild angelica (*Angelica sylvestris*). Wild angelica is found mostly in Europe. Its thick rootstock and root system were used to prepare remedies for colic, cramps, and mild stomach upsets. It has tiny white flowers and should not be confused with European water hemlock, which is highly poisonous.

♀   MICHAELA: From the root name *Michael*.

♂   MICHEL: From the root name *Michael*.

♀ MICHELINE: From the root name *Michael*.

♀ MICHELLE: From the root name *Michael*.

♂ MICK: From the root name *Michael*.

♀♂ MICKY: From the root name *Michael*.

♂ MIGUEL: From the root name *Michael*.

♀ MIGUELA: From the root name *Michael*.

♂ MIHAIL: From the root name *Michael*.

♀ MIKA: From the root name *Dominic*.

♀ MIKAYLA: From the root name *Michael*.

♂ MIKE: From the root name *Michael*.

♂ MIKEY: From the root name *Michael*.

♂ MIKHAIL: From the root name *Michael*.

♀ MIKHAYLA: From the root name *Michael*.

♂ MIKHOS: From the root name *Michael*.

♂ MIKKEL: From the root name *Michael*.

♀ MIKKO: From the root name *Michael*.

♀ MILA: From the root name *Emily*.

♀ MILENA: From the root name *Melanie*.

♥ ♂ **MILES Milo, Myles:** There are two equally probable theories on the derivation of *Miles,* and each of them has
an appeal of its own. It is possible that the name finds its origin in the Slavonic root word *mil,* meaning "dear." Or it may
be that the name is an English form of the Latin name *Milo,*
which comes from the Latin word *miles,* meaning soldier. In
the latter case, it is related to the name *Michael.* Whatever
its derivation, *Miles* has been used in England and America
since the eighteenth century. The military leader of the
Pilgrims, for example, was named Myles Standish, who was
immortalized by Henry Wadsworth Longfellow's 1858 poem

"The Courtship of Miles Standish." Nathaniel Hawthorne used the name Miles Coverdale in his autobiographical novel *The Blithedale Romance,* stealing it from the sixteenth-century first translator of the Bible into English. Another well-known literary Miles is one of the two children in Henry James's macabre story *The Turn of the Screw,* which was published to wide acclaim in 1898.

In the United States, *Miles* had a small burst of popularity in the 1960s, possibly because of jazz trumpeter Miles Davis. In the 1990s, it enjoyed a return to favor. Still, it has never been one of the most commonly used men's names in the United States. On the list of names for the general population derived from the 1990 U. S. Census, it ranks five hundred nineteenth. It remains a name for discriminating parents who appreciate the echoes of our Puritan heritage.

 Number

Four. Many fours are drawn to social issues, some of them unpopular. Their inborn sense of honesty compels them to defend their beliefs with vigor.

 Astrological sign

Aries. People of this sign are not the least bit hesitant to offer opinions. They are fearless in the face of adversity. Woe to those who stand in the path of a righteous Arien.

 Color

Scarlet ocher. A quiet color this is not! This brilliant red hue shouts of conviction when pulsing in one's aural spectrum.

 Stone

Red microcline. This member of the feldspar group comes in several colors, including an unusual shade of red. In its natural state, microcline resembles cracked marble. It is usually found in triclinic (asymmetrical) crystals that can be prismatic. Once used for decorative purposes, microcline is now cut and polished for jewelry. Gem-quality crystals are found in Brazil, Colorado, and Virginia.

♕ Element
Iron. Iron represents the planet Mars, Aries's ruling celestial body. For ages, it has been used for weapons or tools and was believed to protect against witchcraft.

♘ Herb
Trumpet weed *(Eupatorium purpureum)*. A native North American plant, trumpet weed is found in damp wooded areas or meadows. The rootstock and flowering herb were considered to have medical value by many Native American tribes. They used it for kidney problems and rheumatic aches. Some shamans felt it worked well as an aphrodisiac.

♀   MILICA: From the root name *Emily.*

♀   MILKA: From the root name *Emily.*

♀   MILLIE: From the root name *Melissa.*

♂   MILO: From the root name *Miles.*

♀   MIMI: From the root name *Mary.*

♀   MIN: From the root name *William.*

♀   MINA: From the root names *Adam, Carmen,* and *William.*

♂   MINCHO: From the root name *Benjamin.*

♀   MINNIE: From the root names *Mary* and *William.*

♀   MIRA: From the root name *Miranda.*

♥ ♀ **MIRANDA Mandi, Mira, Myra, Randi:** The name *Miranda* comes from the Latin word *miranda,* which means "fit to be admired." The infinitive form of the word is *mirare,* which means "to wonder at." William Shakespeare was the first literary figure to use *Miranda* when he gave the name to the appealing ingenue of his play *The Tempest.* In the play, the hero Ferdinand meets the young Miranda and asks for her name. After learning it, the young man responds with a quintessentially Shakespearean pun, saying "Admir'd Miranda / Indeed the top of admiration."

The character's attributes certainly give prospective parents good reason to choose it. In *The Tempest,* Miranda is beautiful, sweet, and obedient and loyal to her father. She is also completely innocent of men. *Miranda,* like other names made desirable by Shakespearean heroines—such as *Juliet, Cordelia* and *Imogen*—have never been among the top names, but neither have they ever gone completely out of style. *Miranda*'s fortunes are on the upswing, however.

Until recently *Miranda* has always been more common in Britain. But it is now among the top one hundred girls' names in the United States. The success of actress Miranda Richardson has probably been a factor in the recent American popularity of the name. Girls named *Miranda* might be called by the nicknames *Randi (Randy), Mandi (Mandy),* or even *Mira,* newly popularized by the actress Mira Sorvino.

 Number

Six. Sixes often have many admirers.

Astrological sign

Aquarius. Aquarians must be free as the wind to be happy. Although they may inspire love from those around them, they can not be tied down for long.

Color

Isamine. Shades of light blue lift the soul and are associated with the sign of Aquarius.

 ## Stone

Rainbow quartz. Quartz was revered among Native American shamans, Eastern mystics, and ancient Egyptians as a way to enhance physical endurance. New Age gemologists today regard the quartz as a highly positive, energy-producing gem. When a rainbow quartz is cut and polished it displays a wonderful rainbow effect.

 ## Element

Gold. Gold comes in different colors, including white, yellow, green, and rose. Any shade is an appropriate setting for rainbow quartz.

 ## Herb

Lad's love *(Artemisia abrotanum)*. The leaves and flowering tops of this silky-textured plant were used for medicinal purposes by ancient herbalists. Lad's love is native to Europe but has been naturalized in North America. It was a popular remedy for stomach problems, including indigestion, cramps, and heartburn. It was also an effective treatment for fever, coughs, lung congestion, and severe bronchitis.

♀   MIRIAM: From the root name *Mary*.

♀♂ MISHA: From the root names *Melissa* and *Michael*.

♀   MISSY: From the root name *Melissa*.

♂   MITCH: From the root name *Michael*.

♂   MITCHELL: From the root name *Michael*.

♀   MITZI: From the root name *Mary*.

♀ MOIRA: From the root name *Mary*.

♀ MOLLY: From the root name *Mary*.

♀ MONA: From the root names *Monica* and *Raymond*.

♥ ♀ **MONICA Mona, Monique:** No one really knows the origin of the name *Monica*. In Greek, *monos* means "alone." In Latin, *monere* means "to advise or warn," and *nonna* means "nun." These sources have been suggested for *Monica*, but they are not considered reliable. The first recorded user of the name was Saint Monica—the mother of Saint Augustine—who was born in the fourth century in what is now Algeria. Therefore, it seems likely that *Monica* derives from Arabic or another language spoken there at the time.

Saint Monica became a devout Christian after overcoming alcoholism, but she suffered an abusive husband and a shrewish mother-in-law. To make matters worse, her teenaged son, Augustine, was wayward, willful, and given to debauchery. Pious and determined, Monica made Christian converts of her husband and his mother and then threw Augustine out of the house. Augustine begged for forgiveness, and then ran away to Rome.

Monica followed her son and eventually tracked him to Milan, where she and the city's bishop made a concerted effort to reform him. They were successful—so much so, in fact, that Augustine spurned the marriage Monica had arranged for him and took a vow of celibacy.

Monica's death on the journey back to North Africa inspired some of the most fervent passages in her son's famous *Confessions*. The Church eventually canonized her, and members of her cult transported her bones from church to church throughout Italy and France over the next few centuries. Miracles occurred all along the journey, according to folklore, and as each new story spread, more and more baby girls were named *Monica*.

Writing in 1884, names scholar Charlotte Yonge cites the name's frequent usage among French peasants. Parisian women formed the Association of Christian Mothers in 1850 (the purpose of which was to pray for miscreant husbands and sons) and chose Monica as their patron saint. Chapters of the association quickly spread to Catholic countries around the globe, again lending the name a vehicle for circulation.

The name *Monica* has been used more during the twentieth century than at any other time in the past. Until the 1920s, Roman Catholic parents chose the name most frequently; then it came into more general use. *Monica* was at the height of fashion in the 1950s in Britain and a few years later in the United States. Also in the 1950s, the German *Monika* and the French *Monique* began to appear both in the United States and in Britain. The foreign derivations may have been an attempt to soften a former association as a tomboy name by giving it an exotic sound and spelling.

◎ Number

One. Pythagoras, the Greek mathematician, named the numeral one "monad" and considered it the prime cause of all other numbers.

☾ Astrological sign

Sagittarius. Sagittarians need challenges to keep from hitting the doldrums later in their lives. Whether it's for a career or a social cause, they pursue their goals with optimism. Many enjoy physical exercise.

Color

White fire. White fires up psychic energy. It burns away all that is not pure.

◆ **Stone**

Crystal. Rock crystal is a variety of quartz. Although crystals are found worldwide, most quality gems come from Brazil or the Swiss and French Alps. Since medieval times, crystal balls were used to foretell the future. Legends tell of secret rituals where ancient priests used crystals to summon sacred fire by focusing sunlight on wood to ignite it. Other cultures believed that crystals captured the power of a rainbow when light passed through them.

♔ **Element**

Brass. Like copper, brass strengthens the body's physical reaction to a gem.

♌ **Herb**

Monarda *(Monarda punctata).* The leaves and flowering tops of the monarda plant were used in natural medicine for years. Native Americans used brews of the flowers or leaves to combat fever and chills. One tribe supposedly drank a cold extract of the leaves for backaches and another used it to increase heart action.

♀   MONIQUE: From the root name *Monica.*

♥ ♀♂ **MORGAN** **Morgana, Morgance, Morganne, Morgen:** *Morgan* has been both a surname and a first name for centuries. Some experts tie it to the Welsh words *mawr,* meaning "great" and *can,* meaning "brightness." Other experts consider the word to mean "circling sea." As a given name, it has had a respectable following for boys in the United States, especially since it is a common surname and is often conveyed as a first name for boys whose mothers' maiden name is *Morgan.* Even so, it has not been listed among the top one hundred names for boys.

The literary world's most famous *Morgan* was a woman—Morgan Le Fay, the headstrong sister of King Arthur. Morgan Le Fay was a sorceress, and, according to legend, was jealous of King Arthur. With the help of the powerful sorceress Queen Maab, Morgan disguised herself and seduced Arthur. Their illegitimate son, Mordred, was ultimately responsible for toppling Arthur's government and destroying his vision of Camelot. The tale of Morgan Le Fay's treachery has been rendered in dozens of books and plays. One of the best books to treat the Arthurian legend— *The Mists of Avalon* by Marion Zimmer Bradley—takes the point of view of Morgan, and presents her in a more sympathetic light.

Historically *Morgan* has not been widely used for girls, but like the name *Taylor,* however, it has recently jumped genders. It appears consistently among the top fifty names for girls in the late 1990s.

⊚ Number
Five. People of this number can be impulsive. Some fives like to live on the edge.

☾ Astrological sign
Pisces. The Piscean totem is the Fishes, a perfect symbol for a water-ruled sign. Jupiter's influence gives some Pisceans an optimistic outlook.

Color

Sea blue. The color of the ocean encourages harmony and truth.

 ## Stone

Morganite. This pink, peach, or mauve gem is a member of the beryl clan. Its color depends on the manganese content. Some yellow or orange morganite turns pink when subjected to heat. Morganite forms in short prisms, and when polished shows a sparkling, fiery brilliance. The first documented morganite specimen was a pale rose-colored piece discovered in California. Today, some of the finest morganite comes from Madagascar. Brazilian morganite occurs in pink crystals and can sometimes contain aquamarine in the same stone. Other localities of quality gems include Italy, Mozambique, Namibia, Zimbabwe, and most recently Pakistan. Morganite is named after banker and gem collector, J. Pierpont Morgan.

 ## Element

Beryllium. Beryllium is corrosion-resistant metallic element and is also found in morganite.

 ## Herb

Enchanter's plant *(Verbena officinalis)*. Native to the Mediterranean region, enchanter's herb makes external preparations for eczema and other skin irritations. Internally, it's useful for whooping cough, jaundice, and ailments of the kidney and liver. For the Druids, this plant was considered holy food and eaten during ritual ceremonies.

♀   MORGANA: From the root name *Morgan*.
♀   MORGANCE: From the root name *Morgan*.

♀   MORGANNE: From the root name *Morgan*.

♀♂   MORGEN: From the root name *Morgan*.

♀   MURIEL: From the root name *Mary*.

♀   MYKELL: From the root name *Michael*.

♀♂   MYLES: From the root name *Miles*.

♀   MYRA: From the root name *Miranda*.

♂ NALDO: From the root name *Reginald*.

♀ NAN: From the root name *Anna*.

♀ NANCY: From the root name *Anna*.

♀ NANETTE: From the root name *Anna*.

♀ NANI: From the root name *Anna*.

♀ NANON: From the root name *Anna*.

♀ NAOMA: From the root name *Naomi*.

♥ ♀ **NAOMI** Naoma, Navitt, Nomi: *Naomi* comes from the Hebrew word meaning "pleasant." The first recorded use of the name is in the Old Testament Book of Ruth. In one of the best known and most beloved stories in the Bible, famine drives Naomi's family from Judea to Moab, across the Jordan valley. Her sons take wives there, but when her husband and sons perish, Naomi decides to return home, and she instructs her daughters-in-law to return to their own homes.

Naomi must have been "pleasant" indeed, because her daughter-in-law Ruth refused to be separated from her—even though it meant taking up residence in a foreign country. It is Ruth who utters the oft-quoted phrase, "Wither thou goest, I will go." During the journey to Judea Naomi encounters an old friend, who asks, "Pleasant One, is that you?" She replies, "I am not Naomi [the pleasant one] but Mara [the bitter one]," referring to the devastating losses she has suffered.

Naomi's story has a happy ending. Ruth eventually remarries and gives birth to a son. Naomi cares for the child as if it were her own, and the new life revitalizes Naomi.

Perhaps because of her life of suffering, Naomi's name never became as popular as Ruth's. This was true even during periods when biblical names were in vogue. The Puritans picked *Naomi* occasionally, but chose *Ruth* more often. *Naomi* held its own during the 1700s in Britain and the American colonies. Writers of the 1800s created a few literary *Naomi*s, but none so compelling as to spur the name's usage. *Naomi* experienced a surge in Britain in 1970, but has otherwise remained in modest, though steady use.

Number

Seven. Sevens are resilient and have the ability to overcome life's obstacles.

Astrological sign

Gemini. Not much can keep a Gemini down for long. The influence of their ruling planet Mercury helps them move on when life deals them an unfavorable hand.

Color

Golden pheasant. The striking color of pheasant feathers inspires motivation.

Stone

Orange zircon. Zircons have been part of gemological lore for ages. This diamondlike stone was once thought to bestow wisdom and wealth upon its owner. If a zircon lost its luster, it was an omen of impending danger. Woe be to the one who ignored the mighty zircon's warning. Zircons were revered for their clarity and different colors. Orange zircon, named jacinth by early mystics, was worn by some to increase beauty and end jealousy. When carried during travel, it protected against injury. If kept at home, zircons guarded against theft.

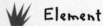

Element
Gold. Gold is the perfect complement for the orange zircon. The ancients believed that when it was set in gold, orange zircon's powers doubled.

Herb
Bittersweet *(Solanum dulcamara)*. Also known as bittersweet nightshade, this woody vine prefers moist areas around houses, hedges, and thickets. It has purple, star-shaped cluster flowers and scarlet bitter berries. Bittersweet is a weak poison, but, like arsenic, when used properly is beneficial. However, most herbalists prefer to use this plant for external problems. It was mostly made into poultices for gout, sores, and skin ulcers.

♀♂ NAT: From the root name *Natalie* and *Nathaniel*.

♀ NATA: From the root name *Natalie*.

♀ NATALIA: From the root name *Natalie*.

♥ ♀ **NATALIE** **Nat, Nata, Natalia, Nataline, Natasha, Nathalie, Natividad, Nattie, Nettie, Tasha:** *Natalie* comes from the name *Natalia*, which is in turn derived from a Latin term *natale domini* meaning "birthday of God." Because of the name's meaning it has been used most frequently for girls born on or near Christmas. Early Christians were fond of *Natalia* and there is one saint with the name. The wife of Saint Adrian, St. Natalia (sometimes called "the Devout") lived in the fourth century.

Natalia has been maintained as a name among Russian parents.

The French transformed *Natalia* into their own *Nathalie* (when pronouncing the name, the *h* is silent) which then traveled to England, where it seems to have first appeared in the 1860s. In the 1880s, English-speakers invented their own variation, *Natalie*. However, neither form of the name was particularly widespread in Britain or the United States until the 1960s. The reason for the sudden rise in use of the name is almost entirely due to the popularity of the actress Natalie Wood, whose original name was Natasha Gurdin.

Natasha has its own rather interesting history in England. A Russian diminutive of *Natalia,* which became an independent name, *Natasha* has been immensely popular in that country for centuries. In England, when *Natalie*'s fortunes began to rise in the 1960s, so did *Natasha*'s. It is most likely that *Natasha*'s short period of popularity can be connected with an English television production of Tolstoy's classic novel *War and Peace,* which featured a character named *Natasha*. The name *Tasha* is a nickname associated with *Natasha*.

Famous contemporary figures with the names *Natasha* and *Natalie* are the singer Natalie Cole and the actress Natasha Richardson. There is no clear explanation why *Natalie* has again risen in the public's estimation, but it has become quite fashionable. *Natasha,* on the other hand, has not been as popular since its slight surge during the 1960s.

◎ Number

Eight. Eights have deep convictions and great strength of character.

☾ Astrological sign

Pisces. Pisces's ruling planet of Neptune gives many Pisceans strong powers of intuition.

Color

Baby blue. Gently soothing, this color inspires health and harmony.

 Stone

White coral. Coral is classified as one of the few precious organic gems. Ancient mystics believed coral dispelled inner strife. Coral can grow to several feet in height and was used by past cultures to make sculptures of honored deities. Coral's color depends on the depth in which it is found—the deeper the water, the lighter the color.

Element

Copper. The Mesopotamians associated copper with the Queen of Heaven, who was also the goddess of love. For this reason, they used copper in love charms and amulets.

Herb

Birthwort *(Aristolochia clematitis)*. Healers as far back as the ancient Egyptians used birthwort to cure snakebites. Early herbalists also used preparations of birthwort to promote contractions for childbirth. Birthwort has dark green, kidney-shaped leaves and greenish yellow cluster flowers that bloom in early spring.

♀   NATALINE: From the root name *Natalie*.

♀   NATASHA: From the root name *Natalie*.

♂   NATE: From the root name *Nathaniel*.

♀   NATHALIE: From the root name *Natalie*.

♂   NATHAN: From the root name *Nathaniel*.

♀   NATHANIA: From the root name *Nathaniel*.

♥ ♂ **NATHANIEL** Nat, Nate, Nathan, Nathania, Thaniel: The names *Nathan* and *Nathaniel* both come from the same root word that means "gift" or "he gave." The first known Nathan was the biblical prophet who relayed God's reprimand to David. Oddly, *Nathan* has sometimes been considered by various Christian communities to be a "Jewish name," while *Nathaniel* (or *Nathanael*) has not had the same association attached to it.

The name *Nathaniel means* "gift of God." The word comes to English via the Greek and Latin name *Nathanael*. The apostle Bartholomew (Bartholomaios) was actually named Nathanael Bartholomaios, but he is referred to and remembered for his last name, not his first. *Nathanael* was used, albeit rarely, during the Middle Ages, and came into great popularity among Christians after the Reformation. Shakespeare was among the first in the English literary world to use the name when he gave it to a character in his play *Love's Labour's Lost* (1595). His use of the name coincides with the growth of Puritanism in England when biblical names began to be used more frequently. *Nathan* also became more common during this period.

Traveling with the Puritan colonists, *Nathaniel* and *Nathan* were among the earliest and most common American colonial names. There were many famous eighteenth and nineteenth century Americans who helped maintain the popularity of the names. They include the Revolutionary War hero Nathan Hale, the generals Nathan Bedford Forrest and Nathanael Greene, the writer Nathaniel Hawthorne as well as the character Natty Bumpo in James Fenimore Cooper's novel *The Deerslayer*. It was not until the Civil War that use of the names began to decline.

Nathan and *Nathaniel* found a home after the Civil War among the freed slaves. (The diminutives *Nat* and *Nate* had been popular since colonial times.) There is an obvious historical reason for African Americans embracing the names.

In 1831, Nat Turner led the only successful sustained slave rebellion in American history. It is certain that among free (and when possible, enslaved) blacks, many boys were named in honor of Nat Turner.

Some historians believe that the name *Nathan* has lost popularity in the African American community in the past two decades, while it has gained popularity in the white community. *Nathaniel,* on the other hand, has increased in popularity in all communities.

✪ Number

Four. Fours often like to be at the top of the ladder. Although they may be embroiled in controversy or conflict, they are always trustworthy souls. Nathaniel Hawthorne was born under this number.

☾ Astrological sign

Pisces. The sign of the Fishes is a water element that symbolizes the soul. Pisceans are gifted with compassionate natures. Legendary singer Nat King Cole was a Pisces.

☀ Color

Azure green. The color of sunlit ocean restores peace to a blue Piscean.

◆ Stone

Blue opal. Some ancients believed opals could be used to create invisibility spells. They wrapped the gem in fresh bay leaves and carried it with them. Opals, still favored by some mystics to boost psychic powers, are worn continuously as jewelry that touches the skin. Others wear opals to enhance inner beauty. The deity Cupid was associated with this stone in ancient gem lore. While opals come in several colors, blue ones are rare. Opals were mined in an area of former

Czechoslovakia from Roman times until the nineteenth century. Now quality opals come from Australia.

 Element

Copper. Copper's ruling element is water and goes well with an opal.

Herb

American gentian *(Gentiana catesbaei).* Also called blue gentian, this native North American plant grows in damp areas from Virginia to Florida. It has large blue flowers. Gentian roots and leaves were used to aid digestion and improve appetite. Fresh leaves added to water makes soothing footbaths.

♀   NATIVIDAD: From the root name *Natalie.*

♀   NATTIE: From the root name *Natalie.*

♀   NAVITT: From the root name *Naomi.*

♂   NEALE: From the root name *Neil.*

♂   NED: From the root names *Edmund* and *Edward.*

♀   NEDA: From the root name *Edward.*

♥ ♂ **NEIL**   **Neale, Nels, Nelson, Nigel, Niles, Nils, Nyle:** *Neil* is an Anglicized version of the Gaelic name *Niall,* which is thought to mean any number of things including "cloud," "passionate" or "champion." *Neil* was widely used in the British Isles during the Middle Ages, particularly in Ireland and in the border regions between England and Scotland. By the nineteenth century, the name had become almost exclusively Scottish.

Nigel is another form of the name that became popular among the English during the Middle Ages and has remained in use. *Nigel* is derived from the Latinized form of *Neil, Nigellus*. In the past, *Nigellus* (and therefore *Nigel*) was mistakenly related to the Latin word *niger* meaning "black."

Neil did not travel particularly well to the United States (though it traveled better than *Nigel*, which has become a stereotypical English name), and it remained fairly unusual until 1969 when Neil Armstrong became the first man to walk on the moon. At the same time, singer Neil Diamond and playwright Neil Simon made the name even more prominent in the public's consciousness.

The name *Nelson* was originally a surname that derived from *Neil*. That is, it was used to designate the boys in a family whose father was named *Neil* (*Neil*'s son). The earliest most famous *Nelson* was Admiral Nelson, who defeated the French at the Battle of Trafalgar. While never among the top boys' names, as a first name *Nelson* has always had more success in the United States than in England. Such great American figures as writer Nelson Algren, industrialist Nelson Rockefeller, and singer Nelson Eddie have certainly influenced some American parents. More recently, Nelson Mandela has been responsible for a new surge in the use of the name, particularly among African Americans.

◉ Number

Four. Fours have no difficulty being themselves in any crowd. They are unimpressed by wealth and are often drawn to causes that promote social justice.

☾ Astrological sign

Leo. For those born between July 23 and August 23 no challenge is too big to face. Leo is the sign of noble champions. Neil Armstrong is a Leo.

Color

Sunset clouds. Red, yellow, and orange are the colors of a summer sunset. Many cultures equate these shades with motivation and organization.

 Stone

Yellow onyx. Magicians and spiritualists of yore used onyx to protect themselves during certain rites and rituals. They also believed it would protect against evil and negative spells cast by witches. Ancient Egyptians thought that if onyx was worn around the neck or near the heart, it could cool the passions of love and invoke discord that would eventually separate lovers—an interesting way to end an unwanted relationship. Yellow onyx is rare and sometimes striped with bands of black or white.

 Element

Brass. Brass is a sun metal and goes well with yellow onyx.

 Herb

Passion flower (*Passiflora incarnata*). The passion flower plant is a woody climbing vine that grows wild in the southern United States. It can also be cultivated in cooler climates. The white flowers have purple, blue, or pink fringes and the fruit (maypop) is edible. The flowers were traditionally used for treatment of insomnia, restlessness, and nervous headaches.

♀   NELDA: From the root name *Helen*.

♀   NELL: From the root name *Helen*.

♀   NELLIE: From the root name *Helen*.

♂   NELS: From the root names *Neil* and *Nicholas*.

♂   NELSON: From the root name *Neil*.

♀ NESSA: From the root name *Vanessa*.

♀ NESSIE: From the root name *Vanessa*.

♀ NETTA: From the root name *Anthony*.

♀ NETTIE: From the root names *Anna, Anthony,* and *Natalie*.

♂ NICHOL: From the root name *Nicholas*.

♥ ♂ **NICHOLAS   Caelan, Claas, Colas, Cole, Coleman, Colette, Colin, Cosette, Klaus, Nels, Nichol, Nick, Nicky, Nicole, Nicolette, Nicolo, Nikita, Nikki, Nikolai, Nikolia, Nikos, Niles, Nilos:** *Nicholas* is derived from the word that has, coincidentally, become one of the most familiar icons in American popular culture. The Greek word *nike* means "victory." It is first and foremost a feminine word, and in ancient Greece it was used as a suffix for many women's names such as *Stratonike* (army victory), and *Pherenike* (bringing victory). Some believe the popular English name *Veronica* is a form of *Pherenike*.

When the word *nike* was used in men's names, it became a prefix rather than a suffix. The Greek forms *Nikon, Niklias, Nikodemos,* and *Nikolaos* (victory of the people) all come from that source.

Ever since the Bishop of Myra (in Asia Minor) was canonized Saint Nicholas during the fifth century, his feast day has been celebrated at Christmas time. Among the stories that led to his canonization, the one that catapulted him to near universal fame involves his gift to three poor sisters who had no hope of marriage because they had no dowry. He left the money, it is said, in their window during the night. His generosity was later celebrated most ardently in Flanders and Holland, where the Dutch form of *Nicholas, Klaus,* was used to name the saint who filled children's shoes or stockings with surprises at Christmas. Saint Nicholas is also known as the patron saint of schoolboys and sailors because he was believed to have raised three boys from the dead and to have the power to calm storms at sea.

Until recently the name "Old Nick" was recognized everywhere as a synonym for the Devil. There is, however, (heaven forbid!) no connection between "Old Nick" and St. Nick. Rather, traditional German culture produced a demon named Nix, and it is from his nefarious deeds that the Devil got his nickname. (The word *nickname,* by the way, is not related to the name *Nicholas* either. It is from the Middle English *ekename,* meaning "an additional name.")

The name *Nicolas* came to England by way of the Norman Conquest in 1066, and became popularized as *Nicol,* the French form of the name. The female form, *Nicole,* was also widely used both in France and England. Some scholars think the *h* was added to *Nicolas* in England during the seventeenth century. The fictional Nicholas Nickleby from the novel by Charles Dickens, and Nick Bottom (the weaver) of Shakespeare's *A Midsummer Night's Dream,* are among the most famous English-language literary representations of the name.

Nicholas has traveled the world over as *Nicol, Nicole,* and *Colin* in France; *Nicolo* and *Cola* in Italy; *Nikolai* and *Kolya* in Russia; *Klaus, Niklas,* and *Nikolaus* in Germany; *Niklaas, Klasse, Nils,* and *Niles* in Scandinavia; and *Mikolei* in Poland. Pet names derived from *Nicholas* include *Nickie* or *Nicky* (used for both boys and girls) and, less often, *Nicco.* In addition, the United States has added the variant *Cole* to the list (Cole Porter). The popularity of the name has been enhanced in recent years by celebrities such as Nick Nolte and Nicolas Cage, and as a female ideal, Nicole Kidman.

◎ Number

Nine. A nine never lacks courage to seek or defend the truth. Nine is also tied to the art of healing in modern numerological lore.

☾ Astrological sign

Aquarius. This sign is ruled by the planet Uranus, which exerts its influence by instilling a deep love of mankind in the Aquarian soul. Sixteenth-century astronomer Nicolaus Copernicus was an Aquarian, as is twentieth-century actor Nick Nolte.

✳ Color

Nickel. On the sefirot tree of the Cabala, gray or silver represents chokmah (wisdom).

◆ Stone

Green sapphire. While most sapphires are blue, the green variety is prized for its rarity. It is only found in Australia, Sri Lanka, and Montana. The bright green comes from fine alternating stripes of yellow and blue sapphire. The ancients called it the "oriental emerald" for its brilliant green color.

♔ Element

Platinum. Platinum makes a high energy setting for the green sapphire.

☘ Herb

Masterwort *(Heracleum lanatum)*. The rootstock and seeds of the masterwort plant were used to make remedies for colds and asthma, and for some digestive troubles such as cramps and colic.

♂   NICK: From the root names *Dominic* and *Nicholas*.

♂   NICKY: From the root names *Dominic* and *Nicholas*.

♀   NICOLE: From the root name *Nicholas*.

♀   NICOLETTE: From the root name *Nicholas*.

♂   NICOLO: From the root name *Nicholas*.

♂   NIGEL: From the root name *Neil*.

♂   NIKITA: From the root name *Nicholas*.

♀♂   NIKKI: From the root name *Nicholas*.

♂   NIKOLAI: From the root name *Nicholas*.

♀   NIKOLIA: From the root name *Nicholas*.

♂   NIKOS: From the root name *Nicholas*.

♂   NILES: From the root names *Neil* and *Nicholas*.

♂   NILOS: From the root name *Nicholas*.

♂   NILS: From the root name *Neil*.

♀   NINA: From the root name *Anna*.

♂   NOACH: From the root name *Noah*.

♥ ♂ **NOAH** Noach, Noak, Noé: The use of *Noah* as a name for boy babies was almost nonexistent through the twentieth century in the United States. However, in the 1990s, it became one of the top fifty most popular names, demonstrating how quickly the pendulum swings in terms of the popularity of names, and how far the trend for old and even ancient names has taken us.

Though the source for the name is uncertain, it means "long lived" in Hebrew. The biblical Noah, the famous builder of the ark, lived for 950 years. Except for him and the great American intellectual Noah Webster (1758–1843), there have been few *Noah*s on the national or international scene that have gained fame to help spread the name. It was a favorite among Puritans in seventeenth century England, and it was used in colonial America. Since then it has always cropped up in every generation, but not until now has it enjoyed a degree of popularity.

☺ Number

Two. Modern numerology credits twos with traits of patience and tolerance.

☾ Astrological sign

Capricorn. Capricorns have charitable natures and are willing to aid others in need. They have the internal stability to weather any storm.

✳ Color

Driftwood. Brown is a color of security and longevity.

◆ Stone

Uvarovite garnet. Although the color red is usually associated with garnets, this variety is bright green. The brilliant shade is due to its chromium content. Uvarovite garnets are highly prized by collectors. They are often found with serpentine deposits and the best clear crystals occur in the Ural Mountains of the former Soviet Union. Uvarovite was recently discovered in Finland, Turkey, and Italy. An ancient legend connects the garnet to the biblical Noah. It was said that he hung garnets inside the ark to boost morale throughout the long confinement during the flood. In ancient Hindu texts, garnets were revered for healing powers and called *tamda*.

⚡ Element

Gold. The power of gold adds strength and beauty to any garnet, especially the rare and precious uvarovite.

🦎 **Herb**

Noah's ark *(Cypripedium pubescens).* Some herbalists refer to this plant as nerve root. A tea brewed from the fleshy rootstock made strong medicine for nervous headaches, sleeplessness, and hyperactivity. It was also useful for cramps associated with delirium-induced muscle spasms or convulsions. Overdoses cause hallucinations and allergic skin reactions in some.

♂ NOAK: From the root name *Noah.*

♂ NOÉ: From the root name *Noah.*

♂ NOLL: From the root name *Oliver.*

♀ NOMI: From the root name *Naomi.*

♀ NONA: From the root name *Anna.*

♀ NONIE: From the root name *Anna.*

♀ NONNIE: From the root name *Helen.*

♥ ♀ **NORA** **Honor, Norah, Noreen, Norina:** *Nora* is most often considered an Irish diminutive of the name *Honora,* which was a Norman name brought to England and Ireland after the Norman Conquest. However, *Nora* also may have been used as a diminutive of *Eleanora* and *Leonora* on occasion, in which case it means, "mercy" or "pity."

Honora finds its origins in the Latin word *honor,* which means "reputation" or "beauty." Saint Honoria was a companion of Saint Ursula. There was also a saint named Honorata. In the Middle Ages it was written as *Honora,* *Onora,* and *Annora,* with *Annora* being the most widespread. The Puritans became fond of *Honor* (or *Honour*) for both boy and girl children, but the name declined as Puritanism faded out and it is now quite rare.

While *Honor* was popular among the Puritans and came to America with them, *Nora* certainly came in the mid-nineteenth century with the major Irish immigration. Norwegian playwright Henrik Ibsen may have influenced some parents in Europe and North America when he named the main character and heroine Nora in his play *A Doll's House* (1879). There are also two famous Irish plays with characters named Nora: George Bernard Shaw's *John Bull's Other Island* (1904) and Sean O'Casey's *The Plough and the Stars* (1926).

In the twentieth century popular singer and star Nora Bayes (originally Dora Goldberg) may have influenced some parents, but in the late twentieth century, the only nationally known American figure with the name is the novelist and screenwriter Nora Ephron. Although girls continue to be named *Nora,* the name is not among the most popular names of the last decade.

Variations include *Norah, Noreen, Norine, Norita, Norina,* and *Norette.*

Number
Three. A person who bears three as their number will often be found in a position of trust or responsibility.

Astrological sign
Libra. Libras are usually good-natured, but they can turn sulky and balk at taking orders. They love to converse at length, yet are good listeners.

Color
Damson. This shade of purple enhances rest and signifies honor in many cultures.

Stone

Tanzanite. Tanzanite is a variety of violet-blue zoisite. When cut and polished it can be confused with a sapphire because of its color. It is found almost exclusively in Tanzania. However, overmining of tanzanite has nearly exhausted the deposit there. Because it is rarely available on the market, it is in high demand by collectors.

 Element

Copper. In ancient Mesopotamia copper was tied to the Queen of Heaven as well as goddesses connected to Libra's ruling planet Venus. For this reason, copper was believed to bring love.

 Herb

Acacia *(Acacia senegal)*. This small shrub or spiny tree prospers best in sandy soil in tropical Africa. The resinous gum has medicinal value and can only be collected after the rainy season from December to June. Healers of the past dissolved the gum in water and used it as a treatment for respiratory inflammations including typhoid fever. According to Hebrew legends, Moses built the Ark of the Covenant from acacia wood with instructions from God.

♀   NORAH: From the root name *Nora*.

♀   NOREEN: From the root name *Nora*.

♀   NORINA: From the root name *Nora*.

♂   NYLE: From the root name *Neil*.

♀ OHNDREA: From the root name *Andrew*.

♀ OLIVE: From the root name *Oliver*.

♥ ♂ OLIVER Lioa, Liv, Livvie, Noll, Olive, Oliverio, Olivette, Olivia, Olivier, Olivine, Ollie, Olva: Does *Oliver* come to us courtesy of the olive tree? Yes, say some experts, pointing out that *Olivarius* is the Latin word for "olive tree." Others argue that this association came later, and that the name originated in Scandinavia when *Anleifr*, a name meaning "ancestor" and "remains," was bestowed on sons in the hope that they would be inspired to carry on family traditions. *Anleifr* evolved into *Olaf* or *Olave,* and in all the Germanic languages, means "ancestor's relic." Some believe that the English *Oliver* is a variation of the French version of *Olaf, Olivier.* Although their exact origins are debatable, *Oliver* and its feminine version, *Olivia,* have long been cele-brated in legend and history.

In Scandinavia, Saint Olaf is credited with bringing Christianity to Norway, and the name *Olaf* is still used among Danish royals and commoners alike. Two London churches dedicated to Saint Olaf are reminders of Danish settlements in England, but for the most part, *Olaf* was replaced by *Oliver* after the Norman Conquest.

Oliver, a paladin or knight in Charlemagne's retinue, was an important supporting character in the Roland romance poems of the Middle Ages. (Most likely, the actual eighth-century Oliver was called Olafur by his contemporaries.) According to these tales, Oliver and Roland challenged each other to a series of duels. When neither could vanquish the other after five days, they became fast friends. These hot-headed heroes prompted the expression, "to give a Roland for an Oliver," which, in England, means to give as good as you get; to return blow for blow. In various versions of the *Song of Roland,* Oliver is either a wise friend urging the proud Roland to blow his famous horn to summon the help they need when they and their comrades are fatally ambushed, or he is an equally proud knight too confident that together they can rout any enemy.

The name *Oliver* is listed in the Domesday Book survey of English lands, circa 1086, and other references to *Oliver* or *Holiver* appear in records until the mid-seventeenth century. The Puritan leader Oliver Cromwell may have produced some namesakes during his rule as Lord Protector of England (1653–1658), but, given that association, after the Restoration of the royal family in 1660, *Oliver* was understandably rare in aristocratic circles. The name persisted in less-threatened classes, though, and *Oliver* had its reputation somewhat redeemed when historian Thomas Carlyle (1795–1881) published a more favorable reappraisal of Oliver Cromwell.

In Puritan and democratic America, *Oliver* was an accepted, but not overly popular, choice. The two Oliver Wendell Holmeses, father (1809–1894) and son (1841–1935), garnered many admirers in literary and legal circles, but brought *Oliver* only limited attention.

Olivia has a shorter history than *Oliver,* but it may have a brighter future. From the Latin for the Italian *olive,* it was the name of a Shakespearean heroine (*Twelfth Night,* 1601) as well as a character in both a play and a novel by Oliver Goldsmith (1730–1774). We can guess why this Oliver liked the name. *Olivia* became more accepted generally in the eighteenth century. A variant, *Olive*, appeared around the mid-nineteenth century, and it eclipsed *Olivia* in the 1920s. The pendulum has swung again, however, and *Olivia* is by far the more common name now. It has been, in fact, among the top forty names for girls in the 1990s.

Variants for *Oliver* include *Oliverio, Olivero, Olivier, Olliver,* and *Ollivor*. Nicknames are *Noll, Ol, Olley,* and *Ollie*. Infrequently used variants for *Olivia* include *Lioa, Lioia, Liv, Olia, Oliva, Olive, Olivet, Olivette, Olivine, Ollie,* and *Olva*. Nicknames include *Liv, Livvie,* and *Ollie*.

Number

Nine. Pythagoras personified nines as those who are born with virtuous hearts and a passion for equity. The legendary wizard Merlin has sometimes been tied to this number.

Astrological sign

Libra. Sometimes known as the peacemaker sign, Librans are often at the center of a quest for justice. They are also drawn to the arts.

Color

Scandinavian sunset. Shades of lavender and pink dispel strife and disharmony.

Stone

Olivine. This gem is closely related to the peridot, but is a darker green. The ancients wore it to protect against negative spells or curses. Olivine was also considered a love-attracting stone. Early mystics believed olivine came to earth via a distant sun's explosion. While its earthly origins are volcanic, it was recently discovered in meteorites. Olivine can be found in Norway.

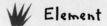 Element

Gold. When set in gold, olivine's power was reputed to be formidable. Olivine, set in rings and golden necklaces as protective charms, was worn directly on the skin.

 Herb

Olive *(Olea europaea)*. The olive tree is native to the Mediterranean area but also grows in tropical areas. Traditionally the leaves, bark, and fruit have been used in herbal medicines. Healers of yore made preparations of the leaves and bark for fever and nervous tension. Olive oil applied on burns, bruises, and insect bites relieved pain and itching. The tree produces fragrant white flowers and shiny black fruit.

♂ OLIVERIO: From the root name *Oliver*.

♀ OLIVETTE: From the root name *Oliver*.

♀ OLIVIA: From the root name *Oliver*.

♂ OLIVIER: From the root name *Oliver*.

♀ OLIVINE: From the root name *Oliver*.

♀♂ OLLIE: From the root name *Oliver*.

♀ OLVA: From the root name *Oliver*.

♀ ORINA: From the root name *Irene*.

♂ OSIP: From the root name *Joseph*.

♂ OSTYNN: From the root name *Austin*.

♂ OWEN: From the root name *John*.

♂ PAAVO: From the root name *Paul*.

♂ PABLO: From the root name *Paul*.

♂ PACHO: From the root name *Francis*.

♂ PACO: From the root name *Francis*.

♂ PADDIE: From the root name *Patrick*.

♂ PADHRAIG: From the root name *Patrick*.

♀ PAM: From the root name *Pamela*.

♥ ♀ **PAMELA** **Pam, Pamelina, Pamilla, Pammie:** Most historians believe that the writer Sir Philip Sidney invented the name *Pamela* in 1590. He used the name for a character in his novel *Arcadia*. No one knows Sidney's original intention in creating the name, but the most popular theory is that it is derived from the Greek term *pan meli,* which means, literally, "all honey." "All honey" is then interpreted to mean "all sweetness." Though the name was used after Sidney's book was published, it remained rare.

One hundred and fifty years later, however, the author Samuel Richardson wrote a bestseller called *Pamela, or Virtue Rewarded* (1740). As the heroine of the book, Pamela Andrews, was a servant the novel probably didn't move the aristocracy to adopt the name, but there is evidence that it influenced use of the name among the less fortunate members of British society. Over two centuries after

Pamela was published, names historian Charlotte Yonge writes that *Pamela* was "still not uncommon among the lower classes."

Pamela also sparked an interesting literary battle. When Richardson published his novel, he wrote that it was designed to cultivate the principles of virtue and religion in both sexes. His contemporary Henry Fielding then wrote a novel in response to this lofty goal. About the "rude and ungenerous" brother of Pamela, the novel *Joseph Andrews* (1742) only gave the name more publicity.

Fielding's novel also pointed out another interesting issue with *Pamela,* its pronunciation. When Sidney first coined the name, it was pronounced *Pam"ee"la*. By the mid-eighteenth century, the pronunciation was in doubt. In *Joseph Andrews,* Fielding writes: "She told me that they had a daughter of a very strange name, Pamel(l)a or Pame(e)la; some pronounce it one way, and some the other."

With an unknown pronunciation, *Pamela* first appeared on record in the United States in 1812, but it did not become particularly widespread until the 1920s. By this time the accent on the *e* was fairly well established as short. Use of the name peaked in the 1950s and 1960s. There is no reliable explanation for the reason *Pamela* became more popular during this period or why it then went into decline.

◉ Number

Three. Threes are nature lovers, and have an affinity for ecology.

☾ Astrological sign

Gemini. Ancient Egyptians used twins to symbolize Gemini because of the double stars of the Gemini constellation. The twins represent versatility.

Color

Honeycomb. Warm as the sun, the golden yellow color of a honeycomb comforts and cheers.

 Stone

Orange amber. In India, yoga adepts wear an amber necklace to keep their mind and body in balance. Amber has magnetic properties and produces electricity when rubbed. Some believe that its magnetic power works on the body's electromagnetic field, enhancing mental stability and physical health. Amber has a sweet scent that is extracted for high-priced perfumes. A number of medical cures were once tied to amber, but today the stone is used mainly as jewelry. Mystics believed dreams of amber meant the dreamer would take a long journey.

 Element

Gold. Amber is a gem of the sun, and gold's energy enhances amber's fiery power.

 Herb

Sweet magnolia *(Magnolia glauca)*. The magnolia is an evergreen tree found on the Atlantic and Gulf coasts of the United States. It has glossy green leaves and large cream-colored flowers. Magnolia bark was used for stomach troubles, dysentery, fever, and some skin diseases. It has been suggested that smokers can break the habit by drinking magnolia bark tea.

♀　PAMELINA: From the root name *Pamela*.

♀　PAMILLA: From the root name *Pamela*.

♀　PAMMIE: From the root name *Pamela*.

♂　PANCHO: From the root name *Francis*.

♀   PAOLA: From the root name *Paul*.

♂   PAOLO: From the root name *Paul*.

♂   PAQUITO: From the root name *Francis*.

♀♂ PAT: From the root names *Martha* and *Patrick*.

♀   PATRICE: From the root name *Patrick*.

♀   PATRICIA: From the root name *Patrick*.

♂   PATRICIO: From the root name *Patrick*.

♥ ♂ **PATRICK   Paddie, Padhraig, Pat, Patrice, Patricia, Patricio, Patricka, Patrik, Patrizius, Patsy, Pattie, Patton, Tricia, Trisha:** From the Latin *patricius,* or "nobleman," *Patrick* is truly a legendary name in Ireland. But before Patricius was renowned as the "great and glorious Saint Patrick," he was the humble and heartbroken slave Succat. The son of a Roman official in Wales or Scotland, fifteen-year-old Succat (meaning "warrior") was kidnapped by pirates and sold to a pagan Irish chieftain sometime around A.D. 400. Beaten often by his master, he was fed alongside the sheep and swine he tended.

On those rugged, lonely hills in northeast Ireland, Succat turned to his Christian faith with a fervor he had never felt in his father's comfortable villa. Patrick's own written accounts—and Irish folklore—speak of miraculous interventions and a daring escape six years after his capture. Scholars agree that Succat did return to Britain and studied for the priesthood. About twenty years later, he set sail for Ireland, bearing a new name, Patricius, and vowing to convert the people who had enslaved him.

Contrary to common belief, Patricius, or Patrick, was not the first Christian missionary to Ireland—but he was the most successful. Traveling with a band of priests, workers, and artisans who could build a church from start to finish, and carefully selecting sites in lands controlled by strong rulers, the practical and politically savvy missionary left a legacy of nearly three hundred churches and many dramatic legends. One story—how Patrick (or Phadraig, as he was known in Ireland) rid the region of snakes—may have stemmed from a misconception about his name, since the word for "toad" in the Norse language was *paud*. Hearing other tales about this Phadraig's miracles, the Norsemen may have assumed he deserved credit for Ireland's remarkable absence of snakes, too.

At first Patrick's followers revered him so much that they hesitated to call themselves after him, using instead *Mael-Patraic,* "the pupil of Patrick," or *Giolla-Patraic,* "the servant of Patrick," which later evolved into the surnames *Gilpatrick* and *Kilpatrick*. Such reticence eventually evaporated, and *Phadraig* in Ireland and *Patrick* in Scotland became common. *Paddy* and *Pat* were such ubiquitous nicknames in Ireland (and, later, among the Irish in the United States) that they became synonymous with Irishmen. (*Pate* and *Patie* were the Scottish nicknames.) Medieval pilgrims to Saint Patrick's Purgatory, a cave-shrine in Ireland, may have brought *Patrice* to France, *Patrizio* to Italy, and *Patricio* to Spain. *Patrikij* is even found in Russia.

Scots-Irish settlers transported *Patrick* with them to America during colonial times. Indeed, in one Pennsylvanian regiment in 1776, *Patrick* was the fourth most frequent name. The influx of native Irish immigrants around the mid-nineteenth century gave *Patrick* a steady popularity, which continues to this date, just as other ethnic Irish names such as *Brian, Kevin,* and *Ryan* have remained fashionable.

Patricia hasn't fared as well. Some say the Scots created *Patricia* as a feminine version of *Patrick,* others argue that *Patricia* existed still earlier as the Latin term for "noble woman." Whatever its origin, *Patricia* was relatively infrequent until the 1880s. Then, perhaps because one of Queen

Victoria's granddaughters was christened Princess Patricia, it enjoyed a sudden and enormous popularity in England and the United States that lasted until the 1970s. But, unlike its brother name, *Patricia* has waned as other Irish names for girls, such as *Kelly, Megan,* and *Kaitlyn,* have advanced.

Variants of *Patrick* include *Paddey, Paddie, Patrice, Patrik, Patrizius,* and *Patryk.* Many boys and men with the name come eventually to be called by the diminutive *Pat.* Variants of *Patricia* include *Patreece, Patreice, Patria, Patric, Patrica, Patrice, Patricka,* and *Patrizia. Patricia* provides many diminutives, including *Patsy, Patti, Pattie, Patty, Tricia, Trish, Trisha.*

 ## Number
Six. Many numerologists believe sixes are at their best as spiritual leaders.

 ## Astrological sign
Gemini. Being born under the sign of the Twins allows a Gemini to see both sides of a situation clearly. American patriot Patrick Henry was a Gemini.

 ## Color
Shamrock. This bright green shade inspires healing and peace.

 ## Stone
Jade. Since the beginning of recorded history, the Chinese have linked jade with wisdom. They also believed it had extensive healing abilities and would ensure long life and a peaceful death. It's still the most popular stone for Chinese jewelry and carvings. The Greeks used jade for eye ailments by placing the gem directly on the eyelids or using it in an eyewash. Some Greek healers ground jade into a powder and used it as an antidote for snakebites.

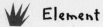 **Element**

Gold. Gold has the power to boost the mystic capabilities of jade.

Herb

Clover *(Melilotus alba).* Clover is a member of the melilot family and grows in shady areas throughout North America and Europe. The plant's herb was used to make tonics for heartburn and digestive ills. As one of the first plants cultivated by man, it is still highly regarded by modern herbalists. It's also the national flower of Ireland. Legends say that the three-leaf clover was planted by St. Patrick. In the Middle Ages clover was used to make charms against witches.

♀ PATRICKA: From the root name *Patrick.*

♂ PATRIK: From the root name *Patrick.*

♂ PATRIZIUS: From the root name *Patrick.*

♀ PATSY: From the root name *Patrick.*

♀ PATTIE: From the root names *Martha* and *Patrick.*

♂ PATTON: From the root name *Patrick.*

♥ ♂ PAUL Paavo, Pablo, Paola, Paolo, Paula, Paule, Paulette, Paulin, Pauline, Paulus, Pauly, Pavel, Pavia, Pavla, Pol, Polly, Poul: Considering the great influence of its most famous bearer, *Paul* has a surprisingly humble meaning. It comes from the Roman name, *aullus,* or *aulus,* a contraction of *auxillus,* which means "small." Despite traditions suggesting that the rabbi-tentmaker Saul of Tarsus chose to call himself Paul in humility after his conversion to Christianity, most likely he was given the name many years before. Tarsus was in the Roman province of Cilicia (today's Turkey), and his parents probably chose Paullus when they enrolled their son as a Roman citizen—perhaps because its sound resembled his Hebrew name Saul (which means "he who is asked for").

Known as the Apostle to the Gentiles, Paul preached the Gospel in Asia Minor and Europe (reaching, some say, as far as Spain and England) before his martyrdom. His influence on Christians in the West and East, of course, continued after his death because the epistles he wrote to fledgling church communities form a large part of the New Testament. Missionaries spread Paul's fame, then, as well as Christ's when they preached from the Bible. That is why *Pablo* is found in Spain; *Pol, Paul,* or *Paulot* in France; *Paolo* in Italy; *Paulo* in Portugal; *Paul* in Germany; *Paultje* in Denmark; and *Pavel* in Russia. Feminine forms include the German *Paula,* the Italian *Paola,* and the French *Pauline.*

In England, *Paul,* or *Powle,* suffered some in its usual second-place association with *Peter,* the other great church leader. Churches dedicated to both apostles, who share the same feast day, were often called "Saint Peter's." (Of course, London's famous St. Paul's Cathedral stands alone.) The two saints' names were often combined, as with the painter Sir Peter Paul Rubens (1577–1640), again with *Paul* in second place. After the Reformation, *Peter* lost some of its favor, however, because *Peter,* as the first bishop of Rome, was closely associated with the papacy. Meanwhile, *Paul* became the accepted spelling and pronunciation (although it remained *Pawl* in Wales).

In 1853, the play *Paul Pry* introduced a new phrase for a meddlesome busybody into the British vernacular, perhaps dimming some of *Paul*'s appeal. Around that same time, Henry Wadsworth Longfellow's poem, "Paul Revere's Ride," which described the midnight heroics of the Revolutionary War patriot and silversmith, might have added to *Paul*'s status in the United States. Another American folk hero, Paul Bunyan, also captured the public's imagination.

Paul remained in steady usage throughout the nineteenth century, becoming very popular in the mid-twentieth century. Was it the influence of Pope Paul VI, Pope John Paul II, or Paul McCartney, songwriter and ex-Beatle? In the past decade, though, *Paul* has fallen from grace somewhat. Both *Paula* and *Pauline* were popular girls' names in the United States around the turn of the twentieth century, and they remained fashionable into the second half of the century. Now, at the turn of the twenty-first century, though there are still many women from the baby-boom generation carrying the names, neither ranks among the top one hundred names for babies.

 Number

Five. Fives have boundless energy and often dedicate themselves to their beliefs.

 Astrological sign

Capricorn. Capricorns scale life's mountain one small step at a time, but they always reach the top. Paul Revere and artist Paul Cezanne were both Capricorns.

 Color

Pewter. Gray and blue represent wisdom and mercy on the sefirot tree of the Cabala.

 Stone

Silver topaz. Ancient gemological lore ties great healing powers to the topaz. Early physicians believed it had the ability to control anger and balance or cure emotional disorders like schizophrenia and dementia. In late eighteenth-century Europe, jewelry was made with gems whose first letters formed a motto when combined. Topaz was sometimes used to spell "dearest." While golden Brazilian topaz is the most famous, this silver-hued gem is found more plentifully in Africa.

Element

Platinum. Platinum, the highest ore on the noble metal pyramid, is the supreme complement for the magnificent topaz.

Herb

Paul's betony *(Veronica chamaedrys).* Also called "eye of Christ" and "angels' eyes," this plant grows by riverbanks, in pastures, and shaded woods. Traditional healers believed potions made from the flowering herbs purified the blood and cured many skin diseases. Others used it as a remedy for smallpox and measles. It also relieved skin irritations associated with both these illnesses. Betony was useful in reducing fevers, coughs, and symptoms of asthma.

♀   PAULA: From the root name *Paul.*

♀   PAULE: From the root name *Paul.*

♀   PAULETTE: From the root name *Paul.*

♀   PAULIN: From the root name *Paul.*

♀   PAULINE: From the root name *Paul.*

♂   PAULUS: From the root name *Paul.*

♀♂   PAULY: From the root name *Paul.*

♂   PAVEL: From the root name *Paul.*

♀   PAVIA: From the root name *Paul.*

♀   PAVLA: From the root name *Paul.*

♂   PEADAR: From the root name *Peter.*

♂   PEDRO: From the root name *Peter.*

♀   PEG: From the root name *Margaret.*

♀ PEGGY: From the root name *Margaret*.

♂ PEPE: From the root name *Joseph*.

♂ PERRIN: From the root name *Peter*.

♀ PERRINE: From the root name *Peter*.

♂ PERRY: From the root name *Peter*.

♀ PET: From the root name *Peter*.

♂ PETE: From the root name *Peter*.

♥ ♂ **PETER   Peadar, Pedro, Perrin, Perrine, Perry, Pet, Pete, Peterina, Petra, Petronella, Petronija, Petrova, Pierce, Pierette, Piero, Pierre, Piers, Pietra, Pietro, Pyotr:** According to the Bible, Christ himself gave his apostle Simon the nickname *Petrus,* in a sense making *Peter* the very first Christian name. The text reads, "Thou art Petros [stone] and upon this petra [rock], I will build my Church." Most likely, Christ used the Aramaic word *cephas,* which means "rock" or "stone," but biblical writers chose the Greek *petros* or the Latin *petrus.*

As the apostles' leader, Petrus later became the first Bishop of Rome—the first pope. As Christianity grew, so did the use of *Petrus* as a baptismal name, becoming *Pietro, Piero, Pier,* and *Pietruccio* in Italy; *Pedro* in Spain; *Peder* in Denmark; *Per* in Sweden, and *Pierre, Pierrot, Perrin,* or *Peire* in France.

When William the Conqueror ordered the compilation of The Domesday Book (1086), a survey of England, a Petrus was listed as a landholder. The English used *Piers,* a borrowing of the French *Pierre,* in everyday speech. They also borrowed *Pierce* from the French, and that name was translated into Irish as *Feories. Pedr,* similar to the Spanish *Pedro,* is the Welsh version of *Peter.*

Other versions and spellings of *Peter* found in medieval England were *Petur, Petyr, Pers,* and *Pearse;* you can see traces of these variants in modern day British surnames such as *Person, Pears, Pearson,* and *Perkins.* The modern spelling of *Peter,* however, didn't appear until the fourteenth century.

Peter the Great (1672–1725) may have given *Petr* aristocratic connotations in Russia, but, by this time in England, *Peter* had fallen from favor. Even though it is a biblical name, *Peter*'s close associations with the Roman Catholic Church made it unpopular among the upper classes after the Reformation. The much disliked—and formerly compulsory—annual collection for papal expenses was called "Peter's pence." But *Peter* remained in steady use among ordinary people. In fact, it became somewhat synonymous with country folk and their simpler ways, as in the nursery rhyme "Peter, Peter, Pumpkin Eater," and the prickly country squire Sir Peter Teazle in Richard Sheridan's farce *The School for Scandal* (1777).

Peter was rare among New England settlers in America, though it had some currency among Dutch and German settlers—and their descendants—in New York and Pennsylvania. It became very popular in the early decades of the twentieth century in England and the United States, reflecting perhaps some of the attention given to the magical orphan who refused to grow up in J. M. Barrie's hit play, *Peter Pan* (1904).

Although the prevalence of *Peter* has slipped in recent decades, its long history gives it a strong following among parents looking for a distinctive, but traditional choice. The usual nickname is *Pete* or *Petey.* Other variants include *Pearce, Pearson, Petro, Pierson, Pieter,* and *Pietro.* Although not widely used in the United States, *Petra* is sometimes recorded as a feminine variation.

⟲ Number

One. Some modern numerologists feel that one represents the foundation of life. Ones are usually positively charged people and natural leaders.

☾ Astrological sign

Taurus. Many born under this earth sign have music in their soul. Taureans of note include composer Peter Tchaikovsky and musicians Peter Frampton, Pete Seeger, and Pete Townshend.

✳ Color

Prussian blue. All shades of blue are tied to Taurus. Blue also represents mercy.

◆ Stone

Green jasper. In gemological history jasper is connected to divine occurrences. It is a variety of chalcedony (a cousin of quartz) and appears in several colors. Green jasper has been used in healing magic for centuries. It is tied to Venus and is an earth element, both representing Taurus. Amulets of green jasper were worn to ward off ill health and prevent nightmares or fever dreams to promote healing sleep. A piece of green jasper engraved with the image of a dragon surrounded by sun rays was worn by an ancient Egyptian king, Nechepsus, to strengthen his digestive tract.

♔ Element

Gold. Gold is often related to wealth, but the ancients felt it was a strong link to their deities.

⚘ Herb

Rock brake *(Polypodium vulgare).* There are many types of fern and this variety grows in shaded areas around rocks or old tree stumps. Its rootstock was used for cough remedies, throat irritations, and respiratory problems. Some Native Americans used a boiled concoction to cleanse minor wounds to prevent infection.

♀ PETERINA: From the root name *Peter*.

♀ PETRA: From the root name *Peter*.

♀ PETRONELLA: From the root name *Peter*.

♀ PETRONIJA: From the root name *Peter*.

♀ PETROVA: From the root name *Peter*.

♂ PHIL: From the root name *Philip*.

♥ ♂ **PHILIP** **Felipa, Felipe, Felippo, Filip, Phil, Philippa, Phillippine, Philly, Pippa, Pippo:** The name *Philip* comes from the Greek name *Philippos* and means "lover of horses." *Philippos* in turn is derived from two words—*philein*, which means "to love," and *hippos*, which means "horse." A more accurate interpretation of the name might be "horseman." Among the earliest known figures with the name was Alexander the Great's father, who lived in the fourth century B.C. The name is found in the Bible on several occasions. The most famous biblical character with the name is the Apostle Philip. The name then remained common throughout the early Christian period.

During the Middle Ages *Philip* was a royal name in France and no less than six French kings bore it. No one is certain when the name came to England but it was commonly used during the Middle Ages and is the basis for many common surnames such as *Phipps, Philps,* and *Phillips.* In addition and somewhat unusually, the name only increased in popularity after the Protestant Reformation, in England at least, and since the sixteenth century it has been one of the most common boys' names there. During the nineteenth century (the name's greatest period of English decline), two classic Philips appeared in the literature. William Makepeace Thackeray named his hero Philip in *The Adventures of Philip* (1861–1862) and Philip Pirrip (best known as Pip) is the hero of Charles Dickens's timeless novel *Great Expectations* (1860–1861).

Historians disagree, however, on the name's success in the United States. For example, names historian George Stewart reports that *Philip* "never became extremely common, and has a slight English or 'learned' suggestion, possibly because of its 'ph' spelling." This seems to be contradicted by other historians, and though the name did not do well in Puritan New England, it does seem to have found a foothold in the more secular middle and southern colonies. In one Virginia regiment of the Continental Army, *Philip* was the ninth most common name. Further, Stewart's assertion is belied by Dunkling and Gosling. They list *Philip* as among the top fifty most popular boys' names in 1925, 1950, 1970, and 1982. (The variation *Phillip,* they note, was the popular choice in the latter year among African Americans.)

Philip does seem to have suffered a decline in the 1990s, however. The most famous current bearer of the name is probably Prince Philip, Queen Elizabeth of England's husband.

Boys are typically called *Phil* by their friends, if not by their families. The girl's name *Philipa* is not uncommon in Britain. The diminutive *Pippa* is often used for girls. Other variations include *Phillip* (English), *Phillipa, Phillippa, Phillipina* (English, feminine) and *Philipe, Phillipe, Phillippe* (French).

 Number

Seven. Sevens succeed through use of their intellect. Many love to read and travel.

Astrological sign

Sagittarius. According to myth, Sagittarius was a centaur who raised Jason, Achilles, and Aeneas. Talk show host Phil Donohue is a Sagittarius.

 ## Color

Purple narcissus. This flower is linked to Sagittarius. Purple is the color of royalty.

 ## Stone

Green turquoise. Turquoise has been revered in many civilizations, including the Egyptians, Tibetans and Native Americans. Turquoise was used by the Navajos as a horseman's talisman. Even today, some riders wear turquoise to protect themselves from falls, and attach a piece to the bridle to protect their horses.

 ## Element

Iron. Iron horseshoes and the nails used to secure them were ancient tools of magic. A horseshoe hung over the front entrance of a home offered safety and good luck. The shoe had to be hung with the points upward to keep the guardian magic intact.

 ## Herb

Prince's feather *(Amaranthus hypochondriacus).* This herb is cultivated worldwide and grows wild in central North America. A leaf preparation was used to stanch hemorrhaging. Herbal lore also suggests that the leaves made a soothing gargle for mouth and throat irritations. The leaves are pointed and have a large purplish red spot on each one.

♀ PHILIPPA: From the root name *Philip*.

♀ PHILLIPPINE: From the root name *Philip*.

♀♂ PHILLY: From the root name *Philip*.

♂ PIERCE: From the root name *Peter*.

♀ PIERETTE: From the root name *Peter*.

♀ PIERO: From the root name *Peter*.

♂ PIERRE: From the root name *Peter*.

♂ PIERS: From the root name *Peter*.

♀ PIETRA: From the root name *Peter*.

♂ PIETRO: From the root name *Peter*.

♂ PINO: From the root name *Joseph*.

♂ PIPPA: From the root name *Philip*.

♀ PIPPO: From the root name *Philip*.

♂ POL: From the root name *Paul*.

♀ POLLY: From the root names *Mary* and *Paul*.

♂ POUL: From the root name *Paul*.

♂ PYOTR: From the root name *Peter*.

♂ RAB: From the root name *Robert*.

♥ ♀ RACHEL Rachelle, Rae, Raquel, Rashelle, Rochelle, Shelley: The name *Rachel* is said to mean "ewe" and is the English variation of the Hebrew name *Rahel*. It is unknown whether *Rahel* is from an older language and has another earlier meaning. The most famous *Rachel* is a biblical character who was Jacob's favorite wife. Probably because of both the meaning "ewe" and the biblical Rachel's character, the name has come to connote "gentleness."

Rachel has remained consistently popular among Jews, and it did not become a favorite among Christians until the sixteenth and seventeenth centuries when Puritans began adopting a variety of Old Testament names. Even then, it did not become nearly as popular as the Old Testament name *Rebecca*. However, like *Rebecca,* and unlike many other Old Testament names, *Rachel* remained in use, though somewhat rarely, after Puritanism went into decline.

In the mid-nineteenth century, the name received publicity when a French-Jewish actress named Rachel became a famous tragedienne. Like many of the characters she played, Rachel died young, in 1858, which only increased her romantic aura. Her fame grew even further when Matthew Arnold wrote a poem about her death. During the same period, George Eliot included a character named Rachel in her popular novel *Adam Bede* (1859). In the late nineteenth century, Charles Dickens helped to keep the name in the public's consciousness when he included a character named Rachel in his novel *Hard Times*.

Like most Puritan names, *Rachel* came to America early, often spelled as *Rachell*. It was also an early name among African Americans, both enslaved and free, and can be found in *Black Names in America*, which is based on Newbell Puckett's groundbreaking research. In *Black Names in America*, *Rachel* appears in the list entitled "In the beginning 1619–1799." However, the high number of teenagers and women currently named *Rachel* can be traced to the 1960s, when Americans of all backgrounds were returning to traditional names. It was widely used in the 1970s and early 1980s, when its popularity seems to have peaked. *Rachel* is still very common. Variations on the spelling include *Rachael*, *Rachelle*, *Rachele*, and *Rachell*.

Number

Two. Twos are genial and sensitive. They make friends easily, but some prefer to be in the background rather than out front.

Astrological sign

Aries. The sign of the ram goes well with *Rachel*'s roots. As the first sign of the zodiac, Aries represents birth.

Color

Cerise. This vibrant red matches the inner fire of an Arien. Red is a sacred color to many cultures signifying both life and death.

Stone

Star ruby. Star rubies are one of the most prized gems in history. A six-rayed crystalline star across the face of this blood-red gem gives it its name. Collectors consider it to be one of the world's few perfect gems. In ancient Egypt, rubies were worn to enhance wealth. In some Eastern civilizations, the ruby was honored as a spiritual stone that showed a soul's beauty. It was exalted by ancient astrologers and some believed that when worn by an Arien it gave intelligence, honor, and progeny. While the finest rubies come from Myanmar, they are also found in North Carolina.

Element

Platinum. Since platinum is considered to be the top of the metal pyramid, it is the perfect choice for the precious star ruby.

Herb

Mother of thyme *(Thymus serpyllum)*. There are several species of the thyme plant. Mother of thyme is smaller than the garden variety and grows wild in thickets. It was brought to North America from Europe. Herbal lore details the plant's usefulness as a respiratory aid for congestion.

♀   RACHELLE: From the root name *Rachel*.

♀   RAE: From the root name *Rachel*.

♂   RAEMOND: From the root name *Raymond*.

♂   RAIMONDO: From the root name *Raymond*.

♂   RAIMUND: From the root name *Raymond*.

♂   RAINAULT: From the root name *Reginald*.

♀   RAISA: From the root name *Rose*.

♂   RAMON: From the root name *Raymond*.

♀   RAMONA: From the root name *Raymond*.

♀   RANA: From the root name *Veroncia*.

♂   RANDALL: From the root name *Randolph*.

♀   RANDI: From the root name *Miranda*.

♂   RANDOLF: From the root name *Randolph*.

♥ ♂ **RANDOLPH   Dolph, Randall, Randolf, Randy:** The name *Randolph* comes from an Old English name, *Randwulf,* which means "shield-wolf." The name can be interpreted to mean "strong protector" or "home protector." Over time, *Randwulf* became *Ranulf* and then *Randal.* In common use prior to 1066, the variations on *Randwulf* became even more popular in Britain after the Norman Conquest. This is because the Normans used a name that was quite similar, *Randulfr,* but which was derived from the Old Norse language. *Randal* remained an extremely common first name until the fourteenth or fifteenth century when it began to decline.

During the Middle Ages, when written and spoken forms of names were often different, *Ranulf* and *Randal* were the spoken variations of the original *Randwulf,* while the written variations were *Ranulphus* and *Randulphus.* These written variations led to the modern name *Randolph,* which appeared in the eighteenth century. At that time, scholars misinterpreted the name as found in medieval texts. While they knew that the name *Randal* existed, for some unknown reason, the written variation was deemed the more correct version of the name, and *Randolph,* both in spelling and pronunciation, was created.

Having been derived from an Old English name of pagan origins, *Randall* was not used by the Puritans. Therefore, as a first name at least, *Randall* did not travel to America in the first wave of immigrants. By the nineteenth century, however, the United States was far less Puritan and generally more open to English cultural influence. Walter Scott's use of *Randal* as a character's name in his novel *The Fortunes of*

Nigel (1822) may have helped bring the name a modest increase of use, as may have, a century later, George Bernard Shaw's use of the variant spelling *Randall* in his play *Heartbreak House* (1919). Certainly the Churchill family brought fame and favor to the name *Randolph*. Both Winston Churchill's father and his son were named *Randolph*. The actor Randolph Scott also helped to bring the name a wider public awareness.

The diminutive, *Randy,* is frequently given as a name for boys independent of either *Randolph* or *Randall*. While the diminutive's idiomatic meaning as "promiscuous" or "lecherous" seems to have deterred its use in Britain, in the United States today there are a number of famous *Randy*s, including the composer Randy Newman and the country singer Randy Travis. Another diminutive for *Randolph—Dolph—* is sometimes used for boys and men.

While *Randal* is very similar to the name *Ralph,* they are slightly different. Some names historians, however, incorrectly connect the two. In fact, *Ralph* comes from *Raedwulf* and means "wolf counsel."

◎ Number
Seven. Numerologists consider seven to be the number of intellect. Many sevens are excellent writers.

☾ Astrological sign
Taurus. Most Taureans are considered to be practical, patient, and successful. Publishing magnate William Randolph Hearst was a Taurus.

☀ Color
Silver wolf. This shade of blue-gray calms and matches the luxuriant fur of a timber wolf.

Stone

Bardiglio marble. English castle builders of yore would have given anything to use Bardiglio marble in their structures. The richest deposits of this ashy blue stone are found in the Apuan Alps near Tuscany, Italy. Marble was used for exterior architecture and statues. Magically, marble enhanced protective spells and altars made from it were thought to intensify power. Today this type of marble is used in polished slabs, expensive furnishings, and monuments.

 ## Element

Pyrite. One of the minerals found in marble is pyrite and its presence helps produce luster when polished.

 ## Herb

Club moss *(Lycopodium clavatum)*. In club moss, also called wolf claw, only the spores have homeopathic value. This low growing plant is found in dry acid soils throughout the world and the spores come from clublike spikes that grow from the plant. Native Americans and even early Europeans used powdered club moss spores to stanch nosebleeds and hemorrhaging wounds. While the plant itself is poisonous if eaten, the spores have proven their worth for centuries.

♂ RANDY: From the root name *Randolph*.

♀ RAQUEL: From the root name *Rachel*.

♀ RASHELLE: From the root name *Rachel*.

♀ RASIA: From the root name *Rose*.

♂ RAY: From the root name *Raymond*.

♂ RAYMENT: From the root name *Raymond*.

♥ ♂ **RAYMOND** Mona, Raemond, Raimondo, Raimund, Ramon, Ramona, Ray, Rayment, Raymonde, Raymundo, Romonde: The name *Raymond* comes from a Frankish Teutonic name, *Raginmund. Raginmund* comes from the word *ragan* (or *raen*), which means "counsel" (though it may also mean "might" or "wise") and the word *mund,* which means "protection." There are three saints named *Raymund.* The name (spelled *Raimund, Raimond,* or *Reimund*) became widespread in France in the early Middle Ages. At that time it had a distinctly chivalric connotation and was considered a knight's name. A number of variations came to England with the Norman invasion and were transformed into the English variation, *Raymond.* While the name was brought to England as a given name, its early use in England was more common as a surname.

As a first name, *Raymond* did not come into widespread use until the 1840s. There is no known reason why it suddenly became more popular as a first name at that time, but it did, especially in the United States. In fact, by the early 1900s, it was among the twenty most popular boys' names in the country. In the 1930s, the actor Raymond Massey and the writer Raymond Chandler certainly influenced use of the name, as did the actor Raymond Burr in the 1950s.

Like *Randy*—the popular independently used diminutive of *Randall* and *Randolph*—*Ray,* the diminutive of *Raymond,* has had great success as an independent name. Among the many influential *Ray*s are the actors Ray Bolger, Ray Milland, and Ray Liotta, the singers Ray Price and Ray Charles, the boxers Sugar Ray Robinson and Sugar Ray Leonard, and the writer Ray Bradbury.

Variations include *Ramon* (Spanish), *Raimondo* (Italian), *Raymonde* (French, feminine), and *Raimund* (German).

🌀 Number

Nine. Nines are "scrappers" during their lives and gain success through grit and sheer will. In Hebrew writings it is taught that God descended to earth nine times.

☾ Astrological sign

Scorpio. Ancient mysteries fascinate Scorpios and many have a passionate empathy for humankind.

✳ Color

Sable. This shade of black is red-tinged and carries ancient ties to mystical magic and divine power.

◆ Stone

Red beryl. Red beryl is an extremely rare member of this crystalline rock family that also includes emeralds. The ruby-red color is due to the presence of manganese-iron oxide. Because of its rich color and rarity, it is a coveted gem and on every collector's most wanted list. To date, it's only been found in the mountains of Utah and New Mexico. Red beryl is also referred to as bixbite, but shouldn't be confused with bixbyite, which has no gemological worth.

👑 Element

Manganese. Manganese is of high commercial value for its use as an alloy to strengthen softer metals.

🦎 Herb

Storksbill *(Erodium cicutarium)*. Also called the red-stem filaree, storksbill is native to the Mediterranean region and through human migration now grows in dry sandy soils on both United States coasts and several southwestern states. It has geraniumlike flowers that bloom from early spring to late autumn. Midwives used this plant to prevent and stop hemorrhaging.

♂   RAYMONDE: From the root name *Raymond*.

♂   RAYMUNDO: From the root name *Raymond*.

♀   RAYNA: From the root name *Reginald*.

♀   REBA: From the root name *Rebecca*.

♀   REBBIE: From the root name *Rebecca*.

♥ ♀ **REBECCA** **Becca, Becky, Becs, Reba, Rebbie, Rebekah, Rheba, Riva, Rivi**: *Rebecca* is from the Hebrew name *Ribqah* (or *Ribka*) and is of uncertain origin. Sometimes the name is said to be a variation of the Hebrew word *biqrah,* which means "heifer," but most often it is said to come from the word *rabak,* which means "to bind." Following this derivation, *Ribqah* is said to mean "noose" or "noosed cord." This definition is often said to connote a strong marriage bond and/or a fierce loyalty to family. This definition probably grew out of the first famous character to bear the name, the biblical Rebekah, wife of Isaac and mother of Jacob and Esau.

Rebekah (or the New Testament variation, *Rebecca*) has consistently been a popular name among Jewish people. It made the transition to the Christian population along with many other Old Testament names after the Protestant Reformation. Particularly common among the Puritans, *Rebecca* was among the earliest names in the American colonies. However, there is some dispute as to when *Rebecca* lost its popularity. Some names historians believe that, like many Old Testament names, it declined in use with the decline of Puritanism. Others believe it remained popular until the late nineteenth century.

Whether or not the name was popular among the general population after the late seventeenth century, many writers were fond of the name. Among the earliest, Sir Walter Scott does not seem to have inspired an increased use of *Rebecca*, even though he used the name for a beautiful romantic character in his novel *Ivanhoe* (1819). Half a century later, William Makepeace Thackeray may have influenced parents when he named his central character Rebecca (Becky) Sharp in the novel *Vanity Fair* (1847–1848). At the end of the century, Henrik Ibsen influenced at least one person with the character of Rebecca West in his play *Rosmersholm* (1886). The novelist Rebecca West (originally Cicily Fairfield) chose her pen name based on Ibsen's character. In 1903, a character appeared who certainly influenced parents. Kate Wiggin created a children's classic when she wrote *Rebecca of Sunnybrook Farm*. There is very little doubt that the spirited little girl she created moved many parents to adopt the name.

In 1938, however, a *Rebecca* arrived on the literary scene who was destined to bring the name back into the popular imagination: Rebecca De Winter, wife of Max De Winter in Daphne Du Maurier's novel *Rebecca*. The film version of the novel, released two years later, brought the name into even more widespread use. It stayed popular until the 1960s. Ironically, while many other Old Testament names were becoming popular, *Rebecca* went into decline, at least in the United States. However, it could never be said to be completely out of style, and it is still quite a common name.

Girls named *Rebecca* or *Rebekkah* are often called by the diminutives *Becka, Becky, Rebbie, Reba,* and *Becs. Becky* has occasionally been given as an independent name.

 Number

One. Ones like to control their own destinies. Most have the innate ability to do so.

Astrological sign

Gemini. Ancient Egyptians called the bright twin stars of the constellation Gemini, Castor and Pollux. From that association people born under the sign of Gemini were considered to be versatile and adaptable.

 ## Color

Sunnybrook yellow. Any shade of yellow stimulates higher brain functions and joy.

 ## Stone

Yellow sapphire. Sapphires are of the corundum family and the hardest gemstone behind the diamond. Blue is the color of most sapphires and is quite rare. The most valuable shade is a lemon yellow, which is caused by its iron content. Eastern mystics believed a yellow sapphire talisman brought courage, health, wisdom, and wealth. It was thought to protect the wearer from evil, accidents, and even schizophrenia. Maidens from wealthy families wore a yellow sapphire to find suitable mates.

 ## Element

Iron. Iron may not be thought of as a pretty metal, but it is a good match for a strong-willed *Rebecca*.

 ## Herb

Poplar *(Populus tremuloides)*. The bark and buds of this stately tree have been used for ages by traditional healers. The sticky winter buds were made into teas for coughs and soothing salves for wounds and burns. A biblical story ties the poplar to Rebecca's son, Jacob, and says that his father-in-law had promised him all the striped or mottled goats born to his herd, thinking to cheat Jacob. But Jacob (supposedly with God's help) placed striped rods from the poplar tree before the breeding animals that resulted in a large number of the offspring.

♀   REBEKAH: From the root name *Rebecca*.

♀   REENIE: From the root name *Irene*.

♂   REG: From the root name *Reginald*.

♂   REGGIE: From the root name *Reginald*.

♀   REGINA: From the root name *Reginald*.

♥ ♂ REGINALD   Gina, Naldo, Rainault, Rayna, Reg, Reggie, Regina, Reginalt, Reinhold, Reinwald, Renata, Renault, Rene, Rex, Reyna, Reynaldo, Reynolds, Rinaldo, Ron, Ronald, Ronnie, Ronny: *Reginald* may seem the epitome of British formality now, but it traces its roots back to a free-wheeling, high-spirited French hero. Legends say that Renaud, or Regnault, was a knight during Charlemagne's reign (around A.D. 768–814) who became an outlaw when, enraged by an insult during a chess game, he struck—and killed—his opponent, the emperor's nephew, with a gold chess board. Forced to flee, Regnault and his brothers became known as the daring *Quatre Fils d'Aymon* (four sons of Aymon), stealing what they needed to live. After many adventures, Regnault made his peace with the emperor and God. His work building the Cologne Cathedral was cut short when he was murdered by disgruntled workmen.

Something was added in the translation when *Renaud* became *Rinaldo* in Italian ballads. Reckless and bold, Rinaldo had many more romantic escapades, though as with Regnault, his best friend remained his faithful warrior-horse (Bayard in France, and Bajardo in Italy). Spanish ballads also chronicle the exploits of a Don Reynaldos, another soldier adventurer.

Reginald, from the Old English, *regn* ("power") and *weald* ("force"), was rarely used among the Anglo-Saxons. But the Normans, changing the Old Norse *Raganwald* or *Rognwald* to *Reinald,* introduced several forms, including *Reynold,* from the French *Regnault* or *Reynault.* The Domesday Book listed *Ragenald, Reynald,* and *Rainald;* from these names come *Reginald* (as well as the English surname *Reynolds,* which is sometimes used as a first name for boys.). The Scots used the northern form, *Rognvald,* which led to *Ronald.*

One Scottish Ronald, the earl of Orkney, was a noted medieval poet. Another Ronald, a chieftain from Orkney, built the cathedral of Saint Magnus at Kirkwall. Murdered by rebels in 1158, he was considered a Christian martyr.

Reginald Pole, Archbishop of Canterbury during Mary Tudor's reign (1553–1558), was known in speech as Reynold; *Reginald* was his official name, usually written as *Reginaldus.* By the sixteenth century, *Reginald* became the preferred use in both speech and writing.

But *Reginald* was relatively rare until the mid-nineteenth century. Its greatest popularity seems to have been in the mid-1920s, when the nickname *Reggie* was in vogue in the United Kingdom. *Rex,* another name closely associated with *Reginald,* perhaps because of its kingly or powerful associations, was briefly popular in the years following the coronation of Edward VII (1901). Again, perception is different in the United States, where *Rex* is popular as a dog's name, and only rarely given to boys.

Ronald could be considered *Reginald*'s more down-to-earth American cousin. Though popular in the United Kingdom in the 1920s, it declined there, only to be embraced by Americans in the 1930s and 1940s. *Ronald* remained high on lists of popular names for boys until 1980, but usage has dropped off since.

Diminutives of *Reginald* include *Reg, Reggie,* and *Rex.* Variants of *Ronald* include *Ron, Ronn, Ronney, Ronni, Ronnie,* and *Ronny.*

 Number

Seven. Seven is connected to military prowess by some numerologists. Others tie it to spirituality. Shades of blue are good colors for sevens.

 Astrological sign

Aquarius. Many Aquarians are free-spirited, but find satisfaction in careers where they make a difference for humanity. Ronald Reagan is an Aquarian.

 Color

Bleu d'azur. Sky blue is the color of Aquarius and represents peace.

 Stone

Blue spinel. Spinel is a crystalline gem that comes in a variety of colors. Blue spinel is considered a noble gem and ranges from light violet-blue to deep blue-gray. Rare specimens are a bright blue and are often mistaken for sapphires. Like a sapphire, it is hard and facets well for fine jewelry. Blue spinel is found in Sri Lanka, but some has been discovered in Burma. *Spina* is Latin for "little thorn" and describes the sharp points of the raw gem.

 Element

Titanium. Titanium is the earth's toughest metal—a perfect match for blue spinel.

 Herb

Fleur-de-lis *(Iris versicolor).* Sometimes called wild iris, this perennial plant is native to eastern North America, but is exported to Europe for herbal and floral cultivation. Sword-shaped leaves and bluish purple flowers grow from the thick creeping rootstock. Herbalists use the rootstock to make preparations to help nausea, heartburn, and sinus troubles. Some believe it to be an effective remedy for migraines and the stomach upset often associated with this painful condition.

♂ REGINALT: From the root name *Reginald*.

♂ REINHOLD: From the root name *Reginald*.

♂ REINWALD: From the root name *Reginald*.

♀ RENA: From the root names *Andrew* and *Irene*.

♀ RENATA: From the root name *Reginald*.

♂ RENAULT: From the root name *Reginald*.

♀♂ RENE: From the root names *Irene* and *Reginald*.

♀ RENIE: From the root name *Irene*.

♀ RENNIE: From the root name *Irene*.

♂ REX: From the root name *Reginald*.

♂ REY: From the root name *Roy*.

♀ REYNA: From the root name *Reginald*.

♂ REYNALDO: From the root name *Reginald*.

♂ REYNOLDS: From the root name *Reginald*.

♀ RHEBA: From the root name *Rebecca*.

♀ RHODA: From the root name *Rose*.

♀ RICA: From the root name *Frederick*.

♀ RICARDA: From the root name *Richard*.

♂ RICARDO: From the root name *Richard*.

♂ RICCIARDETTO: From the root name *Richard*.

♂ RICH: From the root name *Richard*.

♥ ♂ **RICHARD** Dick, Ricarda, Ricardo, Ricciardetto, **Rich, Richelle, Richia, Rick, Rickie, Ricky, Riik, Rikkert, Ritchie, Ritshard, Ryszard:** In meaning alone, *Richard* is a name truly fit for a king. Its first syllable harkens back to the old German word *rich*—"ruler" or "king"—and its second syllable recalls *hart*—"hardy" or "strong." Often translated as "powerful ruler," the name has long been associated with nobility in legends.

In one early story, Richard, or Richardet, a French paladin (knight) in Charlemagne's reign (c. A.D 772) becomes an outlaw when his brother, Renaud, enraged at an insult during a chess match, strikes and kills the emperor's nephew with a gold chess board. (In some versions, Richard strikes the blow.) Joined by their other two brothers, the four become the famous *Quatre Fils d'Aymon,* living like Robin Hood's merry men by stealing what they need.

The popularity of the name *Richard* in England may stem originally from the renowned Ricehard, an Anglo-Saxon king in Kent, who gave up his throne to enter the monastery at Lucca. Many believed miracles resulted from his intercession.

By the time of the Norman Conquest, *Richard* had a firm hold among the nobility. The first King Richard—*Richard Coeur de Lion* (Richard the Lion-Hearted)—reigned from 1189–1199. According to legend, while he fought nobly in the Crusades, his craven brother John taxed the people excessively, forcing the noble-born Robin Hood from his lands and into a life of stealing from the rich to feed the poor until the return of "good King Richard."

During the Middle Ages, only about twenty names for men and boys were in common use. Most, like *Richard,* were Norman names. *Richard* was always among the top six. Pet names or nicknames such as *Rick, Hick, Dick, Rich, Hitch,* and *Higg* emerged to help distinguish one *Richard* from another. In fact, when surnames later developed from

Richard, these nicknames were well represented in the English names *Ricketts, Hicks, Dickens, Richards, Hitchcock,* and *Higgins.*

Richard's continuing popularity was assured when Richard of Chichester (1197–1253), a simple-living, pious bishop, widely admired for his generosity to the people during times of famine, was canonized Saint Richard in 1262. His tomb at Chichester Cathedral attracted many pilgrims.

The brief reign of King Richard III (1483–1485) gave Richard notoriety of another sort. A century later, William Shakespeare shaped the whispers surrounding the mysterious deaths of Richard III's two young nephews—the rightful, but underage, heirs to the throne—into one of the stage's most complex and enduring villains.

Perhaps as a result of Richard III's alleged infamy, British royalty dropped the name, but *Richard*—and especially the nicknames associated with it—persisted. Indeed, *Dick* was such a prevalent nickname that the phrase "any Tom, Dick, or Harry" became shorthand for the common man. Popular nicknames today include *Dicky, Dickie, Rick, Ricky, Rickie, Rich,* and *Richie.*

In colonial America, *Richard*'s everyman associations rose as its kingly associations declined. After all, when Ben Franklin published his famous maxims, it was in *Poor Richard's Almanac* (1732–1758). *Richard* was in thirty-ninth place in popularity in 1875. The twentieth century saw an upswing. *Richard* was number five in popularity in 1930, and the name held steady through the century. The much talked-about birth of "little Ricky," on the popular "I Love Lucy" television show in the mid-1950s, may have partly accounted for *Richard*'s steady hold in the top ten popular names through the sixties. The name has undergone a decline since 1970, but it is still among the top one hundred names for boys.

Whether king or commoner, *Richard* remains *Richard* in

France but is *Ricardo* in Portugal; *Riccardo, Ricciardo,* and *Ricciardetto* in Italy; *Ryszard* in Poland; and *Rikkert, Riikard,* or *Riik* in the Netherlands.

 ## Number
Seven. Most numerologists link seven to people with high intelligence and a hunger for knowledge that often leads them to travel. Seven is also tied to military prowess.

 ## Astrological sign
Scorpio. Mysteries fascinate Scorpios and they use their analytical powers to solve them. Piety can also be a Scorpio trait. But beware—the sting of a scorpion can be fatal.

 ## Color
Jet. Black is connected with divinity in many cultures. It signifies understanding on the symbolic sefirot tree of the Cabala created by Middle Ages mystics.

 ## Stone
Red coral. Many ancients revered coral as a gift from sea deities. Red coral was considered powerful enough to destroy negative energy. The Romans used it to protect or heal children from respiratory diseases. Some healers rubbed red coral on babies' gums to end teething pain. If worn around the neck, legends say red coral will pale when the wearer is ill, and then regain its bright color when health returns. Red coral was worn by newlyweds to protect against sterility.

 ## Element
Gold. Gold is a metal of nobility and worthy of kings. It honors the precious red coral.

🜪 **Herb**

Lion's tail *(Leonurus cardiaca)*. The flowering tops and leaves of this plant were used in preparations to help nervous heart problems and stomach cramps. Lion's tail is found in the northern parts of the United States and throughout Europe.

♀ RICHELLE: From the root name *Richard*.

♀ RICHIA: From the root name *Richard*.

♂ RICK: From the root names *Eric, Frederick,* and *Richard*.

♀ RICKIE: From the root names *Eric* and *Frederick*.

♂ RICKY: From the root names *Eric, Frederick,* and *Richard*.

♂ RICO: From the root name *Henry*.

♂ RIIK: From the root name *Richard*.

♂ RIKKERT: From the root name *Richard*.

♀ RINA: From the root names *Irene, Katherine,* and *Reginald*.

♂ RINALDO: From the root name *Reginald*.

♂ RIOBARD: From the root name *Robert*.

♂ RIP: From the root name *Robert*.

♀ RITA: From the root name *Margaret*.

♂ RITCHIE: From the root name *Richard*.

♂ RITSHARD: From the root name *Richard*.

♀ RIVA: From the root name *Rebecca*.

♀ RIVI: From the root name *Rebecca*.

♂ ROB: From the root name *Robert*.

♀♂ ROBBY: From the root name *Robert*.

♥ ♂ **ROBERT** Berta, Bertie, Bo, Bob, Bobby, Bobette, Bobinette, Rab, Riobard, Rip, Rob, Robby, Roberta, Robertene, Robin, Robinson, Rory, Rupert, Ruperta: One of the fundamental names in the English language, *Robert* is a French name of Germanic origin, from the Old German *Hrodebert* or *Hruadperaht,* a combination of *hrothi* "fame" and *berhta* "bright" or "famous". The name of two Dukes of Normandy—the father of William the Conqueror and his eldest son—*Robert* arrived in England via the Norman Conquest (1066). It then became so popular that six short English forms and two Scottish dialect versions were created. Eventually, the Norman-French form *Robert* predominated.

Through the ages, *Robert* has been the name of one famous man after another. Hruadperaht was a bishop who founded the first Christian church at Wurms around A.D. 700. (The name later became *Ruprecht* in Germany and *Robert* in France.) Like Saint Nicholas, the German Ruprecht sometimes doled out Christmas gifts, but more often, he secretly supervised naughty children.

In the Middle Ages, there was a relatively small store of Christian names—about two dozen for each sex. Around 1086, the form *Robertus* appears in the Domesday Book, a survey of English lands ordered by William the Conqueror. From 1372–1376, John of Gaunt's *Register of English Names* lists *Robert* over and over, along with *John, William, Richard,* and *Thomas.* In the *Dictionary of National Biography, Robert* is featured prominently in a list of celebrities who died before 1750.

In France, *Robert* was a royal name in the Middle Ages and was also popular among commoners. In Scotland, the name gained recognition when Robert Bruce was King of Scotland from 1306–1329. The eighth man in his family to be named Robert, he freed Scotland from English domination. The name is still popular there and in all English-speaking countries.

Other notable *Robert*s include: Robert Boyle, the English founder of modern chemistry (1627–1691); Robert Louis Stevenson, the English author (1850–1894); Robert Burns, the Scottish poet (1759–1796); and General Robert E. Lee, the American commander-in-chief of the Confederate army during the Civil War (1807–1870).

Robert is also the name of seven saints. Sir Robert of Molesme founded the French Cistercian Order in 1098, under Benedictine rule. Saint Robert of Newminster, a Yorkshire priest, died 1159. Saint Robert Bellarmine was a sixteenth-century Jesuit priest, scholar, and cathedral pulpit preacher who later became a cardinal, archbishop, and contender for pope.

In literature, *Robert* and its variations have long been associated with romance and adventure, for example: Robin Hood, Robinson Crusoe, Swiss Family Robinson, and Rob Roy.

The name has accumulated many variations and nicknames, probably because so many men were named *Robert* in any given time and place. *Hob* and *Dob*—common in the Middle Ages but obsolete now—produced surnames like *Dobson, Hobbs, Hopkins,* and *Roberts.* Modern-day nicknames include: *Rob, Robbie, Robby, Bob, Bobbie,* and *Bobby.*

Feminine forms include *Roberta* and *Robin,* which is also still a name given with fair frequency to boys. *Robin* is usually an independent name; that is, it is probably not associated with *Robert* by the parents who give the name to their children. *Roberta* is infrequently given to girls at the present time, but many women named *Roberta* go by the nickname *Bobbie.*

 Number

Six. People of this number are charismatic. Many sixes find their destiny as spiritual leaders.

☾ Astrological sign

Leo. Leos approach life with fiery determination and shine brightly in their professions. Legendary actors Robert De Niro, Robert Mitchum and Robert Redford are Leos.

☀ Color

Phosphine. A color as bright as the sun opens hearts and minds. Phosphoros is Greek for "light-bearing."

◆ Stone

Yellow zircon. Because of its brilliance, zircon has become the most popular substitute for diamonds in modern jewelry. It occurs in many colors. The ancients had a different name for each hue. The Persians called yellow gems *zargun* "gold-colored." Different powers were attributed to each color. In the Middle Ages yellow zircons were called *ligure,* and were used to increase satisfaction of physical desires. In the eighteenth century, when gems were set to spell out certain mottoes or sentiments, zircon was used for *Zes,* which is Greek for "mayest thou live."

♛ Element

Gold. Gold is the metal of royalty, divinity, and also tied to Leo's celestial ruler, the sun.

☙ Herb

Herb Robert *(Geranium robertianum).* The herb of this plant can be used for various remedies to relieve many forms of stomach distress. It was also helpful in reducing the pain and inflammation of gout when the fresh herb was crushed and applied in a salve. Hot poultices of boiled leaves aided healing in bruises and persistent skin problems. Herb Robert tea was used as a rinse for mouth sores. Diluted tea made a soothing eyewash.

♀ ROBERTA: From the root name *Robert*.

♀ ROBERTENE: From the root name *Roberta*.

♀♂ ROBIN: From the root name *Robert*.

♂ ROBINSON: From the root name *Robert*.

♀ ROCHELLE: From the root name *Rachel*.

♂ RODGE: From the root name *Roger*.

♂ RODGER: From the root name *Roger*.

♂ ROG: From the root name *Roger*.

♂ ROGELIO: From the root name *Roger*.

♥ ♂ ROGER **Rodge, Rodger, Rog, Rogelio, Rogers, Rogiero, Ruggiero, Rutger:** The name *Roger* derives from the Teutonic roots *hrod* (or *hrothi*), which means "fame," and *gairu* (or *ger*), which means "spear." The Old English form of the name was *Hrothgar,* and the Old German form was *Hrodgar.* The variation *Roger* is French and was brought to England by the Normans in the eleventh century. The Latin variation, *Rogerus,* is common in the medieval census, the Domesday Book, and *Roger* became an increasingly common name throughout the Middle Ages.

During the eleventh and twelfth centuries there were two kings of Sicily named *Roger*. Roger I took Sicily from the Arabs. His son, Roger II, built the Sicilian court into one renowned for its grandeur and support of the arts. Among the most famous late medieval *Roger*s was Roger Mortimer. Mortimer was Queen Isabella's lover; Isabella was the wife of Edward II of England. Together the two lovers forced Edward's abdication. They are also thought to be responsible for his murder. After Edward's abdication and death, Mortimer then became the de facto king of England. His rule lasted only three years, however. In 1330 he was hanged by Edward III.

The name became less common starting in the sixteenth century. Many historians believe that it ceased to be used during this period because it had become associated with the peasantry. Throughout the Middle Ages, a nickname for *Roger, Hodge,* was used as a generic term for farm laborers, and led to the surname *Hodges.* By the sixteenth century, the name may also have developed an association with unemployed laborers, vagabonds, and rogues. Though no one is really certain where the term "Jolly Roger" came from, it may be connected to the pirates being "a crew of rogues." By the early nineteenth century, the name had become quite rare.

Initially, *Roger* did not travel well to the American colonies. There are two probable reasons to explain the name's lack of colonial popularity. First, it was losing popularity generally in England. Second, the name had no biblical connotations and was therefore not a favorite among the Puritans. Nonetheless, there are several important men named *Roger* in early American history. Roger Williams was the founder of Rhode Island and a champion of religious freedom, and Roger Sherman was a member of the Constitutional Convention of 1787. His idea for representation of the small and large states prevented a dangerous deadlock.

For reasons that are not apparent, *Roger* came back into common use in the 1840s in both England and the United States. It has remained fairly popular into the twentieth century. The radio term "roger" points to the popularity of the name in the twentieth century. "Roger" means "received and understood." Though it is not currently one of the most popular boys' names in the United States, *Roger* is still considered a standard American name.

 Number

Nine. In some numerological circles, nines are linked to strife, but their fight is usually for the benefit of humankind.

Astrological sign
Sagittarius. People born under Sagittarius, the sign of the hunter, enjoy being outside. Sagittarians strive to go all the way in pursuit of their quarry, whether it's a career or an ideal.

 ## Color
Providence purple. This color stimulates spiritual reflection and is tied to intuitive thinking in ancient metaphysical lore.

 ## Stone
Flint. This black opaque member of the quartz family has many folk names, including adderstone. It was first used by Stone Age people, leading them to make better tools for hunting and gathering. Continued contact with flint helped them to discover how to make fire. Later in history, shamans and priests wielded it during healing or religious ceremonies. Flint is used in modern-day Brazil by mystics who divine for gold, water, gems, and other buried treasures.

 ## Element
Tin. Tin is the metal tied to Jupiter, Sagittarius's ruling planet. It was believed to aid seers in predicting the future.

 ## Herb
Spikenard (Aralia racemosa). Spikenard is found in rich woodlands in eastern and southeastern North America. Its fleshy rootstock and long roots are dried and ground into powder for rheumatism, asthma and coughs. Externally, powdered remedies treated skin diseases and blisters. Native Americans used spikenard for backaches, wounds, bruises, inflammations, and chest pains. Root pulp made poultices and wound dressings.

♂ ROGERS: From the root name *Roger*.

♂ ROGIERO: From the root name *Roger*.

♂ ROI: From the root name *Roy*.

♀ ROLINE: From the root name *Charles*.

♀ ROMONDE: From the root name *Raymond*.

♀♂ RON: From the root names *Aaron, Reginald,* and *Veronica*.

♂ RONALD: From the root name *Reginald*.

♀ RONICA: From the root name *Veronica*.

♀ RONNIE: From the root names *Reginald* and *Veronica*.

♂ RONNY: From the root names *Aaron* and *Reginald*.

♀♂ RORY: From the root name *Robert*.

♀ ROSA: From the root name *Rose*.

♀ ROSALIND: From the root names *Linda* and *Rose*.

♀ ROSALINDA: From the root name *Rose*.

♀ ROSALYN: From the root name *Rose*.

♥ ♀ ROSE Rasia, Rhoda, Rosa, Rosalind, Rosalinda, Rosalyn, Roseann, Roselind, Roseline, Rosella, Rosemarie, Rosemary, Rosetta, Rosie, Rosita, Roslyn, Roze, Rozele, Rozsi, Zita: The oldest and perennially the most popular of the flower names, *Rose* surfaced in biblical days and was used throughout the Middle Ages. Most people assume that *Rose* comes from the Latin word *rosa*. But it may also have Germanic roots.

Besides its botanical connection, the name *Rose* has always had religious significance. The rose has been used as an emblem of the Virgin Mary, as the root for the rosary, and in sacred art and church architecture.

In the Bible, a servant girl named Rhoda (a form of *Rose*) answered the door to Saint Peter after the angel of the Lord helped him to escape from prison. Since biblical times, the name *Rose* has endured around the world, with almost every country using the same word to represent the flower and the color.

Several saints have been named *Rose* or variations of *Rose*. Saint Rosalia of Sicily, who died in 1160, lived as a hermit in a mountain grotto. Saint Rosa of Viterbo (1235–1252) is said to have seen a vision of Christ on the cross. Saint Rosaline (1263–1329) defied her father by filling her apron with food for the poor. When he asked what she was carrying, she answered "Only roses," and showed him an apron miraculously filled with flowers.

Rose of Lima, the Peruvian saint born in 1586, was christened Isabel. But she was such a beautiful baby that everyone called her Rose. Afraid that her beauty might tempt someone, she rubbed her face with pepper until it was red and blistered.

Saint Rose Philipine Duchesne was born in France and came to the United States in 1769. She founded a boarding school for daughters of pioneers and a school for Indians, who called her "the woman who is always praying."

Rose and its variations have also been immensely popular names in literature. For example, Rosa was a character in Charles Dickens's book *Bleak House,* and Rosalind was used in Shakespeare's *As You Like It* and in Edmund Spenser's love poem, *The Shepheardes Calender.*

Rose was well-used in the nineteenth century, reaching its pinnacle in English-speaking countries around 1900. Then its popularity began to wane. However, with today's trend toward traditional and family names, *Rose* is regaining popularity in the United States. It will be interesting to see whether the recent use of *Rose* for the main character in the most successful film of all time, *Titanic,* has an impact on the name's popularity in the near future.

In its simplicity, *Rose* lends itself to combination with other names to form, notably, *Roseann, Roselind, Rosella, Rosemarie, Rosemary,* and *Rosalyn.* The most common nickname is *Rosie,* made quite popular again by the actress and comedian Rosie O'Donnell.

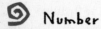 Number

Three. Threes are in tune with their environment. They respect nature in all its glory.

Astrological sign

Libra. Libra is ruled by Venus, the planet of love. Although Librans are tough in their fight for equality, they are tender-hearted. Roses are one of Libra's flowers.

Color

Rosa mundi. Shades of pink attract love and devotion. Rosa mundi is a type of pink and white striped rose.

Stone

Rhodochrosite. This rose-red or pink translucent stone has milky, lacelike designs. Legends call it Rosa del Inca or Inca rose. Rhodochrosite was originally discovered by the Incas in remote areas of Argentina and prized as a pink rosette pearl. The name comes from the Greek words *rhodo,* for "rose" and *cros,* which means "color." Today, Colorado pink rhodochrosite is popular and expensive.

Element

Copper. Copper is found in rhodochrosite and was used for healing by the Incas.

♈ Herb

Rosemary *(Rosmarinus officinalis)*. Preparations of the leaves and flowering tops of the rosemary shrub helped liver function, digestion, and could be used to improve circulation. The name comes from the Latin *rosmarinus*, meaning "dew of the sea." Rosemary is beloved in herbal lore. Ancient Greek students wore garlands around their neck to enhance memory and it was also used as a wedding flower in Europe from the time of Charlemagne. In the seventeenth and eighteenth centuries it was used as a funeral flower to symbolize the memory of loved ones.

♀ ROSEANN: From the root name *Rose*.

♀ ROSELIND: From the root name *Rose*.

♀ ROSELINE: From the root name *Rose*.

♀ ROSELLA: From the root name *Rose*.

♀ ROSEMARIE: From the root name *Rose*.

♀ ROSEMARY: From the root name *Rose*.

♀ ROSETTA: From the root name *Rose*.

♀ ROSIE: From the root name *Rose*.

♀ ROSITA: From the root name *Rose*.

♀ ROSLYN: From the root name *Rose*.

♂ **ROSS** **Rosse, Rossell, Rosslyn:** The name *Ross* began as a place name derived from the Gaelic word *ros*, which means "headland" or "peninsula." Of course, as with many names, there are other interpretations as to its origin, including the belief that the name comes from Anglo-Saxon and means "woods" or "meadow." Another theory agrees that

Ross means "headland," but asserts that its root is Old Norse. Finally, some believe that the name may have derived from Latin and means "rose" or Gaelic and mean "red." This, however, seems to be the most unlikely theory put forward.

Originally a Scottish place name (and then surname), *Ross* began to be used widely as a given name in the 1840s. Two famous *Ross*es may have contributed to its dissemination as a given name. The first Sir James Ross was a famous Antarctic explorer of the early nineteenth century. In fact, there is a seal named the Ross seal, a sea in Antarctica called the Ross Sea, and an island in Antarctica called Ross Island. The second is one of America's most famous figures, Betsy Ross, who is said to have sewn the first United States flag. While a respectable number of men have the name, it is not among the most popular names in the United States. Combined with *Lynn, Ross* forms the once-popular girl's name *Rosslyn*.

Number

Eight. In some numerological lore, eight represents Saturn, the ruling planet of Capricorn. Eights pursue their beliefs with spirit and conviction.

Astrological sign

Capricorn. This sign has an earth element that represents the body. Some Capricorns' reserved demeanor hides their bright wit. Betsy Ross was a Capricorn.

Color

Seal. The union of brown and red represents earthly energy and physical vitality. It is also the color of the Ross seal.

Stone

Brown tourmaline. This tourmaline family member ranges from dark golden brown to orange-brown. Its color varies with magnesium and aluminum content. It forms in long, three-sided prismatic crystals. Some mystics believe that if a tourmaline appears in a dream, it's a warning of an impending accident. In late eighteenth-century jewelry making, it was popular to express a sentiment by using stones whose first letters spelled out a message. Tourmaline was used to create the word charity. Brown tourmaline is plentiful in North and South America.

Element

Aluminum. Aluminum is present in tourmaline. Modern mystics use this silver-white element as an aid to enhance concentration.

Herb

Headsman *(Plantago major)*. Common plantain can be found throughout North America and Europe. The plant has medicinal value in remedies for bladder troubles and certain kinds of ulcers. Some Native Americans chewed on the roots to relieve toothaches. Its greenish white and brown flowers bloom from May to October.

♂ ROSSE: From the root name *Ross*.

♂ ROSSELL: From the root name *Ross*.

♀ ROSSLYN: From the root name *Ross*.

♂ ROUSELL: From the root name *Russell*.

 ♂ **ROY** **Leroy, Rey, Roi, Ruy:** *Roy* is from the Gaelic word *rhu* (or *ruadh*) which means "red." Found in Scotland, the name was often given to male children with red hair. Since red hair was a frequent occurrence among the Gaels, it became a fairly common name. The most famous early Roy is the Scottish character Rob Roy, an eighteenth-century outlaw. Originally named Robert MacGregor, he became known as Robert the Red, hence Rob Roy. Sir Walter Scott made the character even more famous when he wrote his novel *Rob Roy* in 1818.

There is another possible original meaning for *Roy*. It may be more closely associated in some parts of the world with the French word *roi,* meaning "king." There was even one man named Le Roy in the Continental Army of Virginia. This surname undoubtedly gave rise to the name *Leroy,* once fairly common in the United States, but currently not considered fashionable.

Roy did not become common as a first name in the United States, however, until the 1870s. It reached its height around 1900. One of the earliest *Roy*s recorded in American history was the legendary frontier justice, Judge Roy Bean. While some names historians believe that *Roy* began go out of vogue in the 1920s, others say that it was still popular in the 1950s. This would coincide with the rise to fame of one of the most famous *Roy*s in history, the "singing cowboy" Roy Rogers (originally, Leonard Slye), who reached his peak of popularity in the 1940s and 1950s. *Roy* has been dropping in use since the 1960s, though there are still many men who bear the name.

Number
Four. Some fours rebel against regulations, preferring to devise a set of their own. This number is sometimes tied to the sun.

Astrological sign
Leo. The king of signs seems appropriate for the name *Roy*. Leo's element is fire, which represents the spirit.

Color

Desert mesa sunset. Gold and orange are linked to royalty and positive energy.

 Stone

Taaffeite. This rare gem is unique in that it wasn't recognized as a new mineral species until it had been cut and faceted for jewelry. The first specimen was found by Count Taaffe in a jeweler's box of loose stones. It looked like spinel, but had a mauve tinge and was discovered to be a new double refractive gem (rather than single refractive like spinel). Since then, more gems have surfaced with colors ranging from red to blue or even colorless. Taaffeite has only been found in Sri Lanka, China, and the former Soviet Union.

 Element

Beryllium. Beryllium is a corrosion-resistant metallic element found in taaffeite.

♔ Herb

Bean herb *(Satureia hortensis)*. Called savory in many herbal circles, this plant grows wild in the Mediterranean area and is cultivated worldwide as a kitchen herb. The herb has been used by herbalists of the past and present. Savory tea is a gentle and safe remedy for most stomach and intestinal troubles including cramps, nausea, indigestion, and poor appetite. The tea also works well as a sore throat gargle. The entire plant has a strong aroma and its flowers bloom from July through October.

♀   ROZE: From the root name *Rose*.
♀   ROZELE: From the root name *Rose*.

♀   ROZSI: From the root name *Rose*.

♂   RUGGIERO: From the root name *Roger*.

♂   RUPERT: From the root name *Robert*.

♀   RUPERTA: From the root name *Robert*.

♂   RUSH: From the root name *Russell*.

♂   RUSS: From the root name *Russell*.

♂   RUSSEL: From the root name *Russell*.

♥ ♂ **RUSSELL   Roussell, Rush, Russ, Russel, Rusty:**
Russell was originally a surname that developed from a French
pet name, *Rousel*, which means "little red one." *Rousel* is itself
a diminutive of the French term *rous*, which is a variation of
the Latin word *russus*. Both mean "red." In England during the
Middle Ages, a red fox was sometimes called a russel. Names
historian Alfred Kolatch throws an unusual origin into the mix
when he asserts that *Russell* may also be derived from the
Anglo-Saxon, and mean "horse." However, this theory is not
supported by other names historians.

The name seems to have begun its history as a first name
in America in the seventeenth century. It is believed that it
was given to American children in honor of Lord William
Russell. Russell, who was beheaded, was considered a
republican martyr during the reign of Charles II.

Russell did not come into really widespread use as a first
name until the early twentieth century. Some historians
believe that many parents during this period named their
children Russell in honor of the philosopher Bertrand
Russell, who championed pacifism, free love, and nuclear
disarmament. On the other hand, it is also possible that the
popular use of *Russell* as a first name in the early twentieth
century was part of a more widespread and longer term
trend. At the same time as *Russell* came into more common

use as a given name, many other well-known surnames, such as *Howard, Sidney,* and *Mortimer,* were making the same transformation.

In England, the use of surnames as first names was largely confined within the aristocracy until the nineteenth century. Then the trend seemed to reverse itself and the commoners began to adopt famous surnames, while the aristocrats began to focus on first names of noble origin, such as *John, Henry,* and *Charles.* This change in the use of surnames-as-first names happened as well in the United States, though to a lesser degree. Therefore it is the broader habits of the population that may be responsible for the increased adoption of the given name *Russell.*

The name continued to be widely used until the 1980s when it became less popular, but it can still be considered a fashionable name. Boys named *Russell* often acquire the nicknames *Russ* or *Rusty. Rusty* is especially appropriate as a diminutive for boys with strawberry blond or red hair, and is sometimes given as an independent name.

◎ Number

Seven. Throughout history a large number of sevens have been writers, painters or poets, finding unique ways to show different views on life.

☾ Astrological sign

Scorpio. Many Scorpios find great fascination in human history and become philosophers. Their passions can sometimes lead them into dangerous waters.

☀ Color

French russet. This reddish brown hue exudes an aura of stability and warmth.

◆ Stone

Red fluorite. While fluorite is common, with many variations in color, it was initially used by the ancients for decoration and sculptures. It was particularly favored by Asian artisans whose work emphasized the beauty and delicacy of this crystalline gem. In ancient gemological lore it was suggested that fluorite was best used in tandem with other gems. It was considered a booster for the healing or protective effects of other stones. Beautiful red fluorite comes from Brazil and Madagascar.

♛ Element

Bronze was used for many antique jewelry settings. The rich luster of bronze brings out the color and power of red fluorite.

♕ Herb

Foxtail *(Lycopodium clavatum)*. Only the spores from the club-shaped spikes of this low growing plant have medicinal properties. Foxtail grows throughout the world. Native Americans and early Europeans used powdered foxtail spores for nosebleeds and other types of hemorrhaging. While foxtail is poisonous if eaten, the spores have aided many throughout the centuries.

♂   RUSTY: From the root name *Russell*.

♂   RUTGER: From the root name *Roger*.

♂   RUY: From the root name *Roy*.

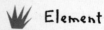 ♂ **RYAN** *Ryon, Ryun: Ryan* is an Irish surname whose origin is in doubt. Names historian Evelyn Wells reports that the name means "the laughing" and says that it comes from the Latin. Elza Dinwiddie-Boyd, on the other hand, says that

the name means "kingly" and is fundamentally Irish. Neither writer gives a source for interpretation, though Dinwiddie-Boyd is probably closer, since the Gaelic word for king is *ri*. Most of the classic names dictionaries don't even list *Ryan*.

The few names historians who do discuss *Ryan* believe that the transition from surname to first name did not start in Ireland, but in England. The name continued to be used occasionally through the 1960s in both England and the United States. After 1970, however, *Ryan*'s true popularity as a given name was in the United States, where parents of Irish descent seem to have adopted it. The actor Ryan O'Neal and his appearance in the film *Love Story* (1970) gave the name an enormous boost. It is also possible that the television soap opera "Ryan's Hope" inspired some parents. Whatever the reasons, *Ryan*'s popularity has only continued to grow.

 Number

Four. The number four is connected to the sun by some numerologists. Fours may tend toward melancholy and should strive for stability in love.

 Astrological sign

Aries. Those born from mid-March to mid-April fall under this sign. They are usually energetic and love the arts.

 Color

Erin green. Cooling verdant tones relieve stress and anxiety.

 Stone

Chrome diopside. Some diopside crystals are colorless, but most range from a light or bottle green to a darker brownish green shade. The name comes from the Greek *dis* and *opsis* meaning "double-vision." Gem-quality chrome diopside resembles an emerald in color and is found in South Africa and Finland.

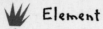 **Element**

Chromium. Chromium makes this variety of diopside crystal a brilliant green, increasing its value for jewelry and gem collecting.

Herb

Bedstraw *(Galium aparine).* Commonly called loveman or sweethearts, bedstraw grows in moist grassy areas along streams or rivers. It has small greenish white flowers and fruit with a bristlelike covering. The herb of this plant was used mainly for skin problems; however, a tea or fresh plant juice was thought to help stomach problems as well. Salves were also made by mixing fresh juice with butter. In medieval Europe, crushed leaves were applied directly to wounds or sores to speed healing.

♂ RYON: From the root name *Ryan*.

♂ RYSZARD: From the root name *Richard*.

♂ RYUN: From the root name *Ryan*.

♀ SABILLA: From the root name *Sibyl*.

♂ SACHA: From the root name *Alexander*.

♀ SACILIA: From the root name *Cecilia*.

♀ SADIE: From the root name *Sarah*.

♀ SAFFI: From the root name *Sophia*.

♀ SAL: From the root name *Sarah*.

♀ SALEENA: From the root name *Selina*.

♀ SALLY: From the root name *Sarah*.

♀♂ SAM: From the root names *Samantha* and *Samuel*.

♥ ♀ **SAMANTHA Sam, Sammie, Semanntha, Simantha, Symantha:** The origin of the name *Samantha* is the subject of great dispute, but the fascinating theories within those disputes help to make it one of the more interesting feminine names. Many historians believe *Samantha* is a feminine variation of the name *Samuel,* which means "heard of God" or "name of God" (see also **Samuel**). Quite possibly *Samantha* is a combination of *Samuel*'s diminutive form, *Sam,* and of the feminine names *Ianthe* or *Anthea. Ianthe* was a sea nymph found in Greek mythology. Both *Ianthe* and *Anthea* are thought to mean "flower," "flowery," or "lady of the flowers." If this theory of the name's origin is correct, then it was invented in the southern United States in the seventeenth or eighteenth century. In the South there has been a long-standing tradition of giving children highly individual names. Names historian Heller notes in his book, *Black Names in America,* that *Samantha* is found in lists of unconventional names adopted by both African Americans and whites.

Two names historians who report a completely different origin for *Samantha* are Sue Browder and Martin Kelly. They suggest that the name means "one who listens" and is of Aramaic origin. Kelly writes that ". . . this is one of the few names whose origin is traced to a language spoken in the Middle East around the time of Jesus."

Whether *Samantha* was invented in the southern United States in the seventeenth century or is two thousand years old, it has remained a fairly unusual name. It can, however, be found among given names in New England in the eighteenth century. Next, it appears on a series of books written by Marietta Holley, who wrote under the pen name Samantha Allen in the 1880s. The subsequent important historical *Samantha* does not appear until 1956 when the film musical *High Society* was released. In the movie, Grace Kelly plays a woman named Tracy Samantha Lord. Cole Porter wrote a song for the movie called "I Love You, Samantha."

Then, in the early sixties, *Samantha* got its greatest boost. Not only did actress Samantha Eggar begin appearing in films in 1962, but also the television series "Bewitched" premiered in 1964. As played by Elizabeth Montgomery, the lead character Samantha the Witch was enormously popular. Whether because of the reruns of "Bewitched" or because of the name's increased use in the 1960s, *Samantha* now ranks among the top one hundred girls' names in the country.

Girls named *Samantha* are often called by the diminutives *Sam* and *Sammie* or *Sammy.*

🌀 Number
Five. Many fives find joy in their faith and dedicate themselves to their beliefs. English diarist Samuel Pepys (1633–1703) was born under this number.

🌙 Astrological sign
Virgo. The bounty of earthly harvest is represented by Virgo, mythical goddess of justice.

✳ Color
Bewitching blue. Blue was considered a color of strong medicine and used by early mystics during healing rituals.

◆ Stone
Gray sard. Many ancient cultures revered the sard. The grayish blue sard was most often used as a protective stone to ward off evil curses and hexes. Gemological folklore credits sards as enhancements for the healing power of many different types of agates. In particular, sards were recorded as having the ability to reduce or relax physical spasms and infant colic when placed on or held over the abdominal area. Only sards in cool colors, such as gray, were thought to be effective in this way.

〰 Element
Quicksilver. Quicksilver is a mysterious substance that is defined as a liquid ore. It is tied to Virgo's ruling planet, Mercury.

🦎 Herb
Flower-of-an-hour *(Hibiscus trionum)*. Another variety of the hibiscus group, flower-of-an-hour is originally from central Africa but now grows wild throughout North America. The entire plant has medicinal value and has been used in

various preparations for coughs and bronchial problems. It was also used to make skin softening lotions for calluses and eczema.

♀   SAMMIE: From the root name *Samantha*.

♂   SAMMY: From the root name *Samuel*.

♥ ♂ **SAMUEL   Sam, Sammy, Samuela, Samuello, Shem:** An Old Testament biblical name, *Samuel* comes from the Hebrew words *schama* and *El* ("hear" and "God"). Its most obvious meaning is "heard of God," referring to the words of Hannah, the biblical Samuel's mother, whose prayers for a son were answered by God. Other possible meanings include "asked of God," "offering of God," and "appointed by God."

Two books in the Old Testament are named after Samuel. In one of the most famous bible passages, Hannah presents the infant Samuel to Eli the Priest saying, "For his whole life he will be given over to the Lord." The promise is fulfilled, and as an adult, Samuel becomes a Hebrew judge, prophet, and the virtual ruler of Israel in the eleventh century B.C., until he appointed first Saul, and then David, as successive kings.

During the Middle Ages, *Samuel* was a rare name in England and Scotland, except among Jews, where it has always been widely used. Then, in the mid-sixteenth century, the Reformation spurred interest in old biblical names. English Puritans, who were no longer compelled to name their children after Roman Catholic saints, chose names from the Old Testament. Among these, *Samuel* was clearly the favorite.

By the seventeenth century, *Samuel* was a common name in England, where it remained popular until the beginning of the twentieth century. In the United States, the name was one of the top fifty for boys one hundred years ago, was well used until the late 1920s, and then declined slowly. Although *Samuel* has had its popularity peaks and valleys, it continues to be used consistently in all English-speaking countries. Now, as the twentieth century comes to an end, *Samuel* is quite fashionable in the United States where traditional names are certainly in vogue.

With a name as perennially popular as *Samuel,* there is no use pointing to one or two famous carriers of the name who might have fostered its fashionableness in any given era. Certainly it is a name that has been handed down from father to son over the course of generations.

Fictional *Samuel*s and *Sam*s abound across the British and American literary landscape. Samuel Pickwick and his servant Sam Weller are characters in Charles Dickens's *Pickwick Papers*. In the United States the name connotes an old-fashioned can-do spirit to the point that the personification of the nation is the bearded character dressed in red, white, and blue: Uncle Sam. The name came from the original initials for the United States: U.S.A.M. The nicknames for *Samuel* are *Sam* or *Sammy*. *Samantha* may have derived from *Samuel,* but there are other theories about that name's history. (See above.) Variations are *Sammel, Shem,* and *Sem* in English; *Shemuel* in Hebrew; *Samouel* in Greek; and *Samuele* in Italian.

Number
Eight. Eights are known to be courageous and fair-minded.

Astrological sign
Libra. Libras do their best to keep the world in balance. Their vigilance for justice is often tempered by their heart. Samuel Taylor Coleridge was a Libra.

Color

Orchid. Red, white, and blue mixed together can make lavender, a color tied to Libra.

 Stone

Orbicular jasper. Jasper is a fine-grained opaque member of the chalcedony clan. The orbicular variety is one of jasper's most unusual types. It can be found in any shade of brown, grayish blue, red, yellow, green, or mixture thereof with white or gray eye-shaped patterns. It was thought to protect against blindness and eye disease. Some ancients believed it could prevent drought when used in certain rituals. All lore attributes divine connections to jasper. It has been found in religious artifacts and holy relics. Ancient artisans once carved jasper into royal seals and engraved bases and handles for gold items such as statuettes, goblets, and utensils for noble patrons. Today, orbicular jasper is found mainly in California.

 Element

Platinum. Platinum, the highest energy metal on the metaphysical scale, is perfect for orbicular jasper.

Herb

Echinacea *(Echinacea angustifolia)*. Also called Sampson root, this perennial is native to the United States and grows in the prairie states northward to Pennsylvania. Rootstock tonics were used to purify the blood from infections, promote digestion, and as a remedy for typhoid fever. It has purple flowers that bloom through October.

♀   SAMUELA: From the root name *Samuel*.

♂   SAMUELLO: From the root name *Samuel*.

♀ SANDERA: From the root name *Cassandra*.

♂ SANDERS: From the root name *Alexander*.

♂ SANDOR: From the root name *Alexander*.

♀ SANDRA: From the root name *Alexander*.

♀♂ SANDY: From the root names *Alexander* and *Cassandra*.

♀ SARA: From the root name *Sarah*.

♥ ♀ **SARAH** **Sadie, Sal, Sally, Sara, Sarena, Sari, Sarine, Sarita, Sasa, Shara, Shari, Sorcha, Sydel, Zahra, Zara, Zarita:** The name *Sarah,* and its variant spelling *Sara,* both mean "princess," and have their origins in the biblical character of *Sarah,* Abraham's wife and Isaac's mother. She was originally named *Sarai,* which may mean either "contentious" or "contrition." Genesis, chapter 17, verse 15 describes the name change: "And God said unto Abraham, As for Sarai thy wife, thou shalt not call her name Sarai, but Sarah shall her name be." *Sara* comes from the Greek adaptation and is found in the New Testament.

A consistently popular name among Jews, the name came into widespread Christian use in the sixteenth century after the Protestant Reformation. Though the name—written *Sarra*—was used occasionally in England during the Middle Ages, it was Puritanism, with its attachment to Old Testament names, which gave it a particular boost. (Oddly, some historians say that the name did not become popular in England until the Restoration period, but this seems somewhat unlikely.) In the late seventeenth and early eighteenth centuries, Sarah Churchill, Duchess of Malborough, was a figure famed for her influence over the English Queen Anne. A few decades later, the actress Sarah Siddons certainly helped to maintain the widespread use of the name, as did the nineteenth-century actress Sarah Bernhardt.

Like many names that became popular after the English Reformation and the rise of Puritanism, *Sarah* traveled early and often to the American colonies. It remained a popular name in the United States through the eighteenth and well into the nineteenth centuries. By the end of the nineteenth century, it had begun to be considered rather old-fashioned, and the name's diminutive *Sally* (or *Sallie*) began to gain in independent use. With the return to traditional names over the last thirty years, *Sarah* has regained its previous popularity.

Several diminutives for *Sarah* have become independent names, as well. In English they are *Sally,* of course, *Sarina, Sari,* and *Sadie*. The charming *Sarita* is a Spanish variant.

Number

Two. Many twos have strong psychic abilities and should heed their visions.

Astrological sign

Leo. Leo is a perfect sign for a name that means "princess." Like the mighty lioness, a Leo woman is protective of her family pride.

Color

Goldenrod. This color is often tied to Leo. When seen in a person's aura, yellow indicates great intelligence.

Stone

Oregon sunstone. Sunstones are a type of feldspar also called noble orthoclase. They have reflective red, yellow, or green crystals that give it a metallic sparkle, but the Oregon variety is translucent orange. This gem is tied to the element of fire and was used by ancient magicians for defensive magic. During the Renaissance period this gem was associated with the sun due to its glittering orange-gold colors. It was always set in gold and worn to call on the sun's power during magical or religious rites. Sunstone is found in Norway, the United States, and Canada.

 Element

Gold. Gold settings stimulate a sunstone's energy and charge its owner with radiant power.

Herb

Sarsaparilla *(Smilax officinalis)*. The tuberous rootstock of the sarsaparilla plant was considered an excellent remedy for gout and rheumatism. It was also useful in treating colds and fevers as well as some minor stomach upsets. Sarsaparilla tea made a soothing external wash for many types of skin problems. Herbal literature also classified it as a blood purifier and a "spring tonic" to aid listlessness and lack of energy.

♀ SARENA: From the root name *Sarah*.

♀ SARI: From the root name *Sarah*.

♀ SARINE: From the root name *Sarah*.

♀ SARITA: From the root name *Sarah*.

♀ SASA: From the root name *Sarah*.

♂ SASCHA: From the root name *Alexander*.

♂ SASHI: From the root name *Alexander*.

♂ SAUNDER: From the root name *Alexander*.

♀ SAUNDRA: From the root names *Alexander* and *Cassandra*.

♂ SCOT: From the root name *Scott*.

♥ ♂ **SCOTT** **Scot, Scottie, Scotto:** The name *Scott* follows the familiar pattern of place name–to–surname–to–first name. In this case the place name is a country. *Scot* or *Scott* was sometimes used in foreign countries as a surname to indicate a person of Scottish heritage. Ironically, the tribe named "Scots" originally came to Scotland from Ireland. Some names historians believe that the term *Scot* originally meant "tattooed one."

Scott was used as a given name in Scotland and England during the Middle Ages, but it was never particularly widely used. By the time of the Reformation, the name was considered a surname. The twentieth-century use of the name as a given name came from the surname and not from its medieval use as a first name. Among the more famous people with the surname or middle name *Scott* were the novelist Sir Walter Scott and the composer of the American national anthem, Francis Scott Key.

The figure who is said to have been the greatest influence on the use of *Scott* as a first name was in turn named after Francis Scott Key. Francis Scott Key Fitzgerald became famous as the novelist F. Scott Fitzgerald. His rise to fame in the 1930s coincides with the name's first real spurt of widespread popularity. Other possible American influences might be the ragtime composer Scott Joplin and the slave who sued for his freedom, Dred Scott.

As with many surnames, *Scott* became far more popular as a given name in the United States than in Britain. In the 1950s, the actor Scott Brady (originally Gerald Tierney) helped to keep the name alive in the public consciousness. More recent influences in the naming of children might be the astronaut Scott Carpenter, the actor Scott Glenn, and the figure skater Scott Hamilton. The nickname *Scotty* has become an integral part of American popular culture. Mr. Scott was the name of the chief engineer of the 1960s cult television show "Star Trek." (Of course, he was from

Scotland.) His nickname, *Scotty,* led to the now famous phrase, "Beam me up, Scotty. There's no intelligent life on this planet," which has since become a mainstay of American graffiti culture.

 ## Number
Five. Modern numerologists see five as a number of the innovative and curious.

 ## Astrological sign
Libra. Libra's symbolic balanced scales mean more than seeking fairness; they also signify harmony. F. Scott Fitzgerald was a Libran.

 ## Color
Butterscotch. This warm yellow shade symbolizes happiness and clear thinking.

 ## Stone
Banded agate. This type of agate can be any color. It is characterized by bright bands or stripes of different colors depending on where the agate is found and the minerals in the area. They can be parallel bands and patterns of alternating colors almost as if the stone is tattooed with the design. Banded agates were thought to be powerfully protective stones and emotional reinforcers for the overly sensitive or chronically nervous. Early healers recommended them for someone who might need extra energy or courage. Many forms of agates are found in Scotland.

 ## Element
Copper. Copper is the official metal of the sign Libra and has been considered a healing ore throughout the ages.

🜲 Herb

Ragwort *(Senecio aureus)*. The ragwort plant grows in marshy areas and along stream banks in mideastern Canada and the United States. It has a brown-streaked stem and golden-yellow rayed flower heads with brown disks. Ragwort preparations were often recommended for kidney stones. The plant contains toxic alkaloids that have poisoned livestock and proper medical supervision is needed to use this plant.

♂   SCOTTIE: From the root name *Scott*.

♂   SCOTTO: From the root name *Scott*.

♂   SEAMUS: From the root names *Jacob/James* and *John*.

♂   SEAN: From the root name *John*.

♂   SEB: From the root name *Sebastian*.

♥ ♂ SEBASTIAN Bastian, Seb, Sebastiana, Sebastiane, Sebastiano, Sebo: *Sebastia* (or *Sebastos*) was the Greek name of a city in Asia Minor and probably means "venerable." Among Byzantine emperors the term *sebastos* was synonymous with the Latin term *augustus*. The Greeks and then the Romans turned the place name into the first name. The Latin variation is *Sebastianus*. In the third century A.D., Saint Sebastian helped to spread use of the name and it became quite common among early Christians. Saint Sebastian was one of the many Christian martyrs during the reign of Emperor Diocletian. He was a Roman soldier who was martyred when his fellow officers shot him full of arrows. He later became a particularly popular subject for artists of the Middle Ages. This inevitably helped in spreading the name throughout Europe, particularly in Spain and France.

The use of *Sebastian* declined along with many other saints' names after the Protestant Reformation, particularly in England. The literary masters Shakespeare, Dryden, and Fletcher all had well-known characters named *Sebastian,* but their use of the name actually gave it a foreign connotation. In his play *Twelfth Night,* for example, Shakespeare gave the name to the traveler who was Viola's twin brother. Another difficulty with *Sebastian* is that it provides no diminutive or nickname.

By the nineteenth century the name was quite rare, even in England, and it didn't come back into vogue until the 1940s. More recently, the British athlete Sebastian Coe has brought the name some publicity, as has the character named *Sebastian* in the wildly popular television adaptation of Evelyn Waugh's novel *Brideshead Revisited.* However, to many Americans, the name still has a distinctly English quality, and it has never been widely used in the United States.

 Number

Nine. In ancient numerological lore, nine is the number of force, volatile energy, and warfare. It represents iron, the metal linked to Mars, the god of war.

 Astrological sign

Aries. Most Arians are energetic and have the drive to get things done. They are courageous and have pioneering spirits.

 Color

Autumn dogwood. In eras past, this bright scarlet shade represented deities and religious reverence.

 Stone

Sienna carnelian. This reddish brown member of the chalcedony family is translucent and was once thought to calm anger and quiet the blood. Carnelian was thought to increase the body's energy levels and was worn or carried by some early physicians as a healing aid. Quality carnelian comes from India and changes from brown to red when placed in direct sunlight.

♛ Element

Iron. Iron is linked to Aries. Long ago, Romans drove iron nails into their doorways and windows to prevent the plague from entering their homes.

♗ Herb

Wahoo *(Euonymus atropurpureus)*. Commonly known as arrow-wood, Indian arrow, or burning bush, wahoo is a shrub or small tree that can reach twenty-five feet. It prefers moist soil near rivers or forests. During the nineteenth century wahoo bark was recommended for chest and lung congestion, indigestion, and fever. In the early twentieth century it was discovered to have a digitalislike effect on the heart and became widely used as a cardiac drug. It has scarlet fruit that can cause symptoms of poisoning such as nausea and cold sweats.

♀   SEBASTIANA: From the root name *Sebastian*.

♀   SEBASTIANE: From the root name *Sebastian*.

♂   SEBASTIANO: From the root name *Sebastian*.

♂   SEBO: From the root name *Sebastian*.

♀   SEELIE: From the root name *Cecilia*.

♀   SEFA: From the root name *Joseph*.

♀   SEILA: From the root name *Sheila*.

♀   SELENE: From the root name *Selina*.

♀   SELIA: From the root name *Selina*.

♥ ♀ SELINA   Celene, Celie, Celine, Celyna, Saleena, Selene, Selia, Selinda, Sena: No one is quite certain where the name *Selina* (sometimes spelled *Selena*) came from, but there are two major theories to choose from. The first is that *Selina* is a variation on the name of the Greek goddess of the moon, Selene. The root of the name is from the Greek *ele*, which means "heat" or "light." (Interestingly, this root is the same as the Teutonic root *hell*, which means "bright" or "light.") The second theory is that the name is a variation of the French name *Celine*, derived from the Latin name *Coelina*, which grew out of the Latin term *caelum*, meaning "heaven." *Celine* was a fifth-century saint who is best known as the mother of Saint Remy. *Celia* is a more common variation of *Celine*.

As a variation on *Selene*, *Selina* seems to have been created in the early seventeenth century in England, and the name became fashionable under numerous spellings. There was at least one woman named *Zelina* who lived in the seventeenth century. In 1687, the spelling *Selinah* was recorded, as was, ten years later, the spelling *Sillina*. Around 1680, a noblewoman of the Finch family appears whose name is spelled both *Celina* and *Selina* (a common occurrence at the time). This woman's daughter was called Selina Shirley (there seems to be no confusion on the spelling of her name). Since that time, the name *Selina* has been particularly popular in both these noble families.

Selina Shirley also helped to spread the name to a broader population. The Countess of Huntingdon, Selina Shirley was a committed and devout Methodist. By the time of her death in 1791, she had spent most of her money and her time on promoting the religion. She must certainly have inspired namesakes among devout Methodists.

While *Selina* and *Selena* are beautiful names, they have never been particularly widespread. In England, *Selina* has come into vogue in the past twenty years largely because of the popularity of the newscaster Selina Scott, but the name's popularity does not seem to have transferred to the United States from England. However, among the Latino population *Selena* has been widely used, and it has recently been in the spotlight following the murder of the Latina singer who went simply by the name Selena, and whose life was portrayed in a successful 1997 movie by the same name. Of course, the most famous personality tracing her roots to this name today is the unsinkably popular singer Celine Dion.

 ## Number

Six. Some modern numerologists suggest that six is a number of tolerance, perfection, and harmony.

 ## Astrological sign

Cancer. Many Cancers are protective and have strong parental instincts. This sign is a water sign and ruled by the moon.

 ## Color

Lunar luster. The pale luminescence of moonlight restores peace and love.

 ## Stone

Selenite. This mineral can be clear or a milky color. It was named for the moon goddess, Selene, and given to lovers as a token of forgiveness or reconciliation after a disagreement. This stone was also worn by early priestesses to bring moon energy to their bodies, thus keeping them divinely connected with their deity. Selenite was a favorite of female mystics to invoke prophetic dreams.

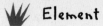 **Element**

Silver. Silver has always been connected with lunar powers and manifestations of the Great Mother, the eternal goddess. Female mystics of the past honored her by wearing necklaces with a silver crescent.

Herb

Moonseed *(Menispermum canadense).* Moonseed is the folk name for yellow parilla, a perennial vine found in moist woods or hedges near streams and rivers in eastern North America. It has greenish white flowers that bloom in July. Its woody, yellow rootstock and roots make a bitter concoction that was used as a tonic for lack of energy. It was sometimes used as a remedy for colds, fevers, and minor stomach problems. Medical supervision is advised when using this plant.

♀   SELINDA: From the root name *Selina.*

♀   SEMANNTHA: From the root name *Samantha.*

♀   SENA: From the root name *Selina.*

♂   SEPP: From the root name *Joseph.*

♂ **SETH:** *Seth,* from the Hebrew name *Sheth,* is one of the earliest names in the Bible, that of Adam and Eve's third son. It is variously described as meaning "to put" (or "to set") or as meaning "compensation" (or "substitute"), or finally, as meaning "the appointed." This latter interpretation comes directly from a translation of the Bible where Eve says, "God has appointed for me another child." The second definition of the name listed above, "compensation," or "substitute," is most likely also taken from the same biblical scene. Eve's new son, Seth, was compensation (or a substitute) for the son she lost, Abel.

There is one recorded instance of a *Seth* in pre-Reformation England. Seth Denwall was a mason who lived in the early sixteenth century. However, like many other Old Testament names, Seth became truly popular among Christians after the Protestant Reformation, particularly in the eighteenth century. It was probably often used in reflection of Eve's story, for a child who was born after an older sibling died. The name remained fashionable well into the nineteenth century. In 1843–1844, Charles Dickens included a character named Seth Pecksniff in his novel *Martin Chuzzlewit*. The character, though, is not a sympathetic one and cannot be responsible for the name's singular spurt of popularity around 1850. In 1859 the writer George Eliot named the title character's brother *Seth* in her novel *Adam Bede*.

In England by the end of the nineteenth century, use of *Seth* had dropped off dramatically. Americans may have held on to the name slightly longer but it too dropped off in use, and by the mid-twentieth century was fairly uncommon. It had a slight revival in the 1970s, but in the 1990s, among American parents, *Seth* definitely returned from obscurity. Though by no means as ubiquitous as *Thomas* or *Michael*, *Seth* is back among the top boys' names in the United States.

 Number

Seven. In numerological lore, sevens are linked to divine appointment.

 Astrological sign

Aquarius. Aquarians are anything but conventional. A true Aquarian has a calm soul and a freedom-loving spirit.

Color

Evening twilight. Blue indicates spiritual devotion when seen in a person's auras. The deeper the color, the stronger the conviction.

 Stone

Leucosapphire. A sapphire's color comes from trace elements. Clear or white sapphires are free of impurities. Leucosapphires are rare, and are usually only found in Sri Lanka. Sapphires have been called gems of destiny and wisdom. They hold a place of honor in many of the world's religions. Mystics believe them to be guardians of love.

 Element

Titanium. Titanium is the earth's toughest ore—a perfect match for one of nature's hardest gems.

Herb

Ginseng *(Panax schinseng)*. The root of the ginseng plant has been used medicinally for thousands of years. It was considered valuable for fever and inflammatory illnesses and for blood diseases. It was thought to promote mental and physical health. The name comes from the Chinese for "likeness of Man" because its roots can resemble a human figure.

♂   SHAMUS: From the root name *Jacob/James*.

♀   SHANA: From the root names *John* and *Shannon*.

♂   SHANAN: From the root name *Shannon*.

♀♂   SHANE: From the root names *John* and *Shannon*.

♀   SHANI: From the root name *Shannon*.

♀   SHANNA: From the root names *John* and *Shannon*.

♀♂   SHANNEN: From the root name *Shannon*.

♥ ♀♂ **SHANNON** **Shana, Shanan, Shane, Shani, Shanna, Shannen:** As the name of Ireland's most famous river, *Shannon* is said to mean, literally, "old one," which is the term for an ancient divinity. It is also sometimes said to mean "slow waters," but this is probably a misinterpretation influenced by the river and not an accurate derivation. It is a ubiquitous surname in Ireland. Some names historians believe that whatever the Irish meaning of the place and surname, the given name *Shannon* comes from a very different source. They propose that it is, in fact, a combination of the names *Shane* and *Sharon*.

Shannon was first used as a given name in the United States in the 1930s, but no one can really trace a specific influence that may have sparked its adoption. Though the *Shane/Sharon* theory may be correct, its main problem is that the name *Shane* did not itself become particularly popular until after the movie *Shane* had been released in 1953.

Shannon did travel to Britain in the late 1940s, but it never really caught on there, and it has remained a predominantly American name. Whatever its original inspiration or derivation, *Shannon* had caught the public's imagination. It continued to be used in increasing numbers throughout the 1980s. In the African American community, the name also became popular for boys as well as girls. Still in widespread use in the 1990s, the name has since gone into a decline.

◎ **Number**

Four. Numerologists attribute the quality of dependability to the number four.

☾ Astrological sign

Capricorn. A Capricorn is never reckless. Capricorns respect the wisdom and experience of their elders.

✳ Color

Clover. Green is a color of hope and life. It is also associated with both Capricorn and Ireland.

◆ Stone

Serpentine. This green gem is usually banded or grained with an appearance like reptile scales. It was a choice stone for carving both for its softness and exquisite patterns. It ranges in shade from light green to gray or dark olive. Roman travelers wore it as a nighttime amulet to guard against unseen dangers. Some Native Americans carved serpentine into prayer sticks and inlaid it in burial pots. Serpentine is linked to the planet Saturn, Capricorn's ruling planet. Ancient Assyrians carried seals carved from serpentine so that gods and goddesses would bestow blessings upon them.

☥ Element

Magnesium. Magnesium is one of the minerals found in serpentine.

☙ Herb

White balsam *(Gnaphalium polycephalum).* Also referred to as old field balsam, this fragrant plant is found in open pine woods. The herb was used to make tea for lung and intestinal problems. External uses included preparations for skin troubles and for some kinds of arthritis. Dried flowers were sometimes put in pillows to aid against insomnia.

♀ SHARA: From the root names *Sarah* and *Sharon*.

♀ SHAREL: From the root name *Charles*.

♀ SHARI: From the root names *Sarah* and *Sharon*.

♀ SHARIA: From the root name *Sharon*.

♀ SHARLA: From the root name *Sharon*.

♀ SHARLEEN: From the root name *Charles*.

♀ SHARMAIN: From the root name *Charles*.

♀ SHAROLYN: From the root name *Sharon*.

♥ ♀ **SHARON** **Charin, Shara, Shari, Sharla, Sharolyn, Sharona, Sharonda, Sheran, Sherry:** The use of the term *Sharon* as a personal name is a relatively recent innovation in naming history, but it hails from a very old source. The place, Sharon, is a fertile plain between Mount Carmel and Jaffa in the Holy Land. The "rose of Sharon" was a beautiful shepherdess made eternally famous in the biblical "Song of Solomon," where it is written: "I am the rose of Sharon, and the lily of the valley." It would probably be most accurate to say that the modern name *Sharon* means "fertile plain," but as it has evolved from this biblical verse to a first name, it has come to mean "beloved."

After agreeing that the Song of Solomon inspired the use of the personal name *Sharon*, history takes the name on two divergent paths. The first is the Puritan adoption of the name. Some historians believe that the English Puritans were the first to use *Sharon* as a given name, and that the Puritans then brought the name to the American colonies. However, among the Puritans, *Sharon* was considered a masculine name, and it seems to have dropped from use long before the late nineteenth century saw the advent of *Sharon* as a feminine name.

Other names historians make no mention of the masculine (or Puritan) use of the name. They follow the development of *Sharon* through the feminine name *Rose-of-Sharon*. This poetic variation was inevitably, and quite understandably, shortened to *Rosasharn*, a name John Steinbeck introduced to an enormous public when he used it for an unforgettable character in his classic novel, *The Grapes of Wrath*. The novelist Sinclair Lewis is the first known writer to give a character the name of Sharon. In his novel *Elmer Gantry* (1927), a character named Katie Jonas changes her name to Sharon Falconer. The subsequent rise in popularity of the name *Sharon* is linked with the fame of the novel, and during the 1950s, *Sharon* was among the top girls' names in the United States. There is no verifiable explanation for its decline since then, but it is still fairly well used and could in no way be considered an uncommon name.

Number

Three. This number is connected to a goddess in Celtic mythology who appears as three aspects: a maiden, the mother who births mankind, and the old wise woman who cares for the dead. She is referred to as *Cerridwen* and *Brigid* and *Rhiannon*.

Astrological sign

Taurus. Most people of this sign are thought to be practical. But Taurus is also ruled by Venus, which adds warmth and romance to their natures.

Color

Viridian. Green as the fertile plains of Sharon, this color symbolizes hope.

Stone

Rose microcline. Fine microcline crystals are prismatic in shape and have a fine network of lacy veins that give it a spider-webbed appearance. This type of feldspar comes in several colors with rose or pink being the rarest. Pink stones were worn by the ancients to promote peace. When cut and polished, microcline can have a silky luster. It is found in Madagascar and Italy.

⚜ Element

Copper. Copper is a metal of Venus. It was also worn to attract love and increase fertility.

🜳 Herb

Shepherd's heart *(Capsella bursa-pastoris)*. This common annual plant grows wild in meadows and fields around the world. The plant produces a heart-shaped fruit and its white flowers bloom all year. The plant's herb was traditionally used as a blood clotter by early surgeons and midwives. It was effective during childbirth to stimulate contractions. Shepherd's heart was helpful in regulating heart action and blood pressure, acting as a stabilizer.

♀ SHARONA: From the root name *Sharon*.

♀ SHARONDA: From the root name *Sharon*.

♂ SHAWN: From the root name *John*.

♀ SHAWNA: From the root name *John*.

♀ SHAYLA: From the root name *Sheila*.

♀ SHEELA: From the root name *Sheila*.

♀ SHEENA: From the root name *John*.

♥ ♀ **SHEILA** **Celia, Celie, Seila, Shayla, Sheela, Sheilagh, Sile:** Tourists in Australia might be surprised at just how often *Sheila* crops up in conversation there. Y'see, mate, that's because *sheila* is Australian slang for a generic girl or woman. Perhaps the many Irish immigrants and their descendants Down Under prompted this colloquial use of *Sheila*, which is the English phonetic spelling for the Irish name, *Sile*.

The name has a distinguished history. *Sile* (pronounced *Sheela*), is the Irish form of *Celia*, an English name based on the Latin name *Caelia*, which is in turn derived from *Caelius*, the name of an ancient Roman clan. Most likely it was a prominent family: After all, *Caelius* comes from *caelum*, meaning "heavens," and the Caelian Hill in Rome is said to be named in honor of a long-ago member of the clan.

Before the eighteenth century, *Caelia* was found as often as *Celia*, but *Celia* gradually became the normal spelling. Perhaps conscious of its heavenly associations, sixteenth- and seventeenth-century English authors used the name as a symbol of idealized womanhood. For instance, *Celia* was a romantic young heroine in Shakespeare's *As You Like It*. And Ben Jonson famously implored, "Drink to me only with thine eyes," in his lyric poem "To Celia."

Celia, like its cousin, the similar-sounding *Cecilia*, and other non-biblical names, fared poorly after the Reformation, and rebounded only somewhat in the eighteenth century. In France at about this time, poets were singing the praises of the French version, *Celie*, in their pastoral poems, and the name became very fashionable. In the United Kingdom, the Irish version *Sile*, or *Sheila*, had similar success; it peaked there during the 1930s but has declined since then. In the United States, *Sheila* had a modest—and brief—popularity during the 1960s.

Variant spellings, such as *Shelagh* and *Sheelagh*, appeared early in the twentieth century.

✆ Number

Nine. Some modern numerologists hold to the belief that nine symbolizes completion in the karmic cycle.

☾ Astrological sign

Libra. Many Librans revere harmony. They are natural charmers and hate to quarrel or see others in strife.

☀ Color

Heavenly blue. The color of clear skies inspires serenity of mind and spirit.

◆ Stone

Star diopside. Delicate diopside crystals range from light to dark green; the higher the iron content, the darker the color. A rare form of this sparkling gemstone is called star diopside and is usually dark green to black. It has a four-rayed star that shows when the gem is cut *en cabochon* (half-moon shape that is flat on one side). Two of the rays are straight while the others appear slightly wavy. Most star gemstones have six rays. Star diopsides have been found weighing several carats, but this is unusual. Currently, star diopside comes only from southern India.

♛ Element

Iron. The earliest iron came from meteorites, which the ancients called heavenly rocks when they witnessed them falling from the sky.

♕ Herb

Ladysmock *(Arum maculatum).* This perennial plant grows mostly in shady damp areas. Its tuberous rootstock is used internally for asthma or rheumatic remedies, and externally as an ointment for skin sores or blisters. The fresh rootstock is poisonous but medicinal, and even edible, after it's dried or boiled thoroughly.

♀   SHEILAGH: From the root name *Sheila*.

♀   SHELLY: From the root name *Rachel*.

♂   SHEM: From the root name *Samuel*.

♀   SHERI: From the root name *Charles*.

♀   SHERON: From the root name *Sharon*.

♀   SHERRY: From the root name *Sharon*.

♀   SHERYL: From the root name *Charles*.

♂   SHIMON: From the root name *Simon*.

♀   SHOSHANA: From the root name *Susannah*.

♂   SI: From the root name *Simon*.

♀   SIB: From the root name *Sibyl*.

♀   SIBBIE: From the root name *Sibyl*.

♀   SIBELLA: From the root name *Sibyl*.

♥ ♀ SIBYL   Cybele, Cybil, Sabilla, Sib, Sibbie, Sibella, Sybille: Meaning "seer" or "prophetess," *Sybil* connotes the future. Yet its roots are firmly in the past where stories of sibyls, or prophetesses, abound in the ancient worlds of Babylonia, Egypt, Greece, and Italy.

In one Greek myth, Sibylla is a young maiden seduced by Apollo, who, in his gratitude, gives her the gifts of prophecy and long life. These twin gifts also play a part in Roman mythology, which portrays the far-seeing sibyls as half divine, half mortal. The cave-dwelling Sibyl of Cumae safely guides the great Trojan hero Aeneas through dark Hades so that he can seek counsel from his dead father, Anchises. She wisely warns him that to enter Hades is easy, but, "To retrace the path, to come up to the sweet air of heaven,/ That is labor indeed." With her help, Aeneas reaches his father in the peaceful Elysian Fields and learns of a new people, the Romans, the future rulers of the world. The Sibyl then leads

Aeneas back to earth, where he sets sail for his promised new home.

Many, many years later, this same Sibyl offers several books of prophecy to the Roman king Tarquinius Priscus, who reigned from 616 to 578 B.C. Each time he refuses them, the Sybil takes the books back, destroys one, and returns, asking a higher price for the remaining books. Finally, when only one book is left, Tarquinius agrees to buy it. According to the legend, this last book contains prophecies that later prove to be true, including the prediction of a rule of peace that came to be known as the Pax Romana.

Because of the Sibyl's link to this prediction, Christian Romans came to view sybils as pagan prophets of the coming of Christ. (That is why sibyls are included in Michelangelo's Sistine Chapel.) In time, *Sibilla* or *Sibila* became a favored Christian name. For those familiar with Norse mythology, it also may have brought to mind *Sippia*, *Sib*, or *Sif*, the wife of Thor, whose golden hair suggests the harvest. Whether or not that connection strengthened the name's appeal, *Sibila* was found among Norman nobility, and *Sibille* made its way to France and England.

Sibella, *Sibyl*, or *Sibbie* also became popular in Ireland and Scotland, though these names may have stronger roots in the Gaelic *Selbflaith* (which means "lady of possessions"). In the United States, *Sibyl* has become inextricably linked to the best-selling book and movie of the same name, which told the true story of a woman beset with multiple personalities. Spelling variants include *Sybil*, *Sibbell*, *Sibel*, *Sibella*, *Sibilley*, *Sybelle*, *Sybill*, *Sybilla*, *Sylbille*, and *Sybyl*.

๑ Number

Four. Numerologists equate the ability to get to the heart of any situation with number four people. This vision can make them seem harsh, but they are only telling what they see.

Astrological sign

Pisces. With Neptune as their ruling planet, many Pisceans are gifted with strong intuition. This distant planet also influences spirituality.

 ## Color

Harvest gold. The color of autumn wheat is tied to the goddess Ceres, the harvest deity.

 ## Stone

Tiger's eye. The most famous of the eye gems is the mysterious golden brown tiger's eye. It's a star chrysoberyl and when light hits it at a slant, the gem appears to have an iris. The Egyptians used tiger's eyes for the eyes of a god's statue to symbolize divine vision. Healers used tiger's eyes to reduce headaches and nerve spasms from severe emotional trauma. Ancient mystics believed that dreaming of an eye-stone was a warning of impending treachery. Even today, modern mystics wear tiger's eyes as a talisman to increase psychic ability.

 ## Element

White gold. White gold is a metaphysically powerful metal. It boosts the awesome energy of the tiger's eye.

 ## Herb

Roman laurel *(Laurus nobilis)*. Oil pressed from the leaves and fruit of this evergreen can be used in liniment for rheumatism, bruises, and skin problems. Both fruit and leaves also aid those with digestive troubles. Some herbalists make a leaf or fruit paste mixed with honey as a chest plaster for colds and other lung ailments.

♀♂ SID: From the root name *Sydney*.

♀♂ SIDNEY: From the root name *Sydney*.

♂ SIDON: From the root name *Sydney*.

♂ SIDONIO: From the root name *Sydney*.

♂ SIKANDER: From the root name *Alexander*.

♀ SILE: From the root name *Sheila*.

♂ SIM: From the root name *Simon*.

♀ SIMANTHA: From the root name *Samantha*.

♂ SIMEON: From the root name *Simon*.

♂ SIMMONS: From the root name *Simon*.

♂ SIMMY: From the root name *Simon*.

♥ ♂ **SIMON** **Shimon, Si, Sim, Simeon, Simmons, Simmy, Simona, Simone, Simonetta, Simpson, Symms, Symon, Symone, Szymon, Ximenes:** From biblical times on, *Simon* has been linked with great men, saints, sinners, and fools. One of patriarch Jacob's twelve sons was Simeon, or *Schimeon,* from the Hebrew word "schama," meaning, "to hear." That the New Testament mentions five *Simeon*s, including the apostles Simon Peter and Simon the Zealot, shows the strength of the name among the Jews. The biblical writers, however, translated *Simeon* as the Greek word *Simon* (which also means "snub-nosed"), and a new name was born. (A new sin, too: From Simon Magus, the magician who tried to buy the power to perform miracles from the apostles, comes simony, the sin of selling church positions or blessings.)

The British monk Saint Simon Stock reinvigorated the Whitefriars or Carmelites in the thirteenth century, but anti-royalist Simon de Montfort, who set up the first Parliament in 1265, may have done more for the name's popularity in

England. *Simon* thrived in England throughout the medieval period. In France, peasants adopted *Simon* and the feminine version, *Simonette*. In Italy, *Simone* was fairly common and produced the surname *Simoncelli*. In Portugal, *Sima* appeared; in Spain, *Ximon;* in Poland, *Szymon*.

Simon declined after the Reformation because of its link with Saint Peter. Yet it remained strong among the common folks as the nursery rhyme, "Simple Simon" attests. The expression, "simon pure," or "genuine" (as in the American phrase, "the real McCoy") comes from an early eighteenth-century play *A Bold Stroke for a Wife*, which describes the complications that arise when someone impersonates the straightforward Simon Pure. Another literary character, the urbane Simon Templar ("The Saint") in Leslie Charteris's popular novels, may have influenced an upswing in British *Simon*s during the 1960s and 1970s.

In the United States, *Simon* appeared with some regularity until about 1850. Then it dropped into obscurity until very recently. There is every likelihood that the publication of *Uncle Tom's Cabin* in 1852 had something to do with the decline of the name. The name Simon Legree, which Harriet Beecher Stowe gave to the villainous plantation owner in her novel, has since been used as a synonym for an evil, oppressive man who wields dubious power over his underlings.

Conversely, in South America, *Simon* became widespread as parents sought to honor the hero Simón Bolívar (1783–1830), who liberated Venezuela, Colombia, and Bolivia from Spain. Hence the name is widely used in Latin America and among Latinos in the United States. Variants include *Simeon, Simion, Simm, Simms, Simone, Symms,* and *Symon*. The usual nicknames are *Si, Sim,* or *Simmy*.

◉ Number

Seven. Modern numerologists associate transcendentalism and intuition with this number. Some also link military expertise to sevens.

☾ Astrological sign

Cancer. Cancers are soulful people, sentimental and fiercely protective of loved ones. Many express their sensitivity through careers in the arts.

✳ Color

Azurite. Blue-green hues signify purity of the soul and peace of mind.

◆ Stone

Green amber. Amber is the fossilized resin of ancient conifer trees. Its color is usually golden yellow to orange, but it also occurs in other shades such as green. A famous Chinese ear ornament worked into the shape of a panda bear is a valuable piece in one gemologist's collection. Ancient medicine men ground amber to make healing elixirs for everything—except a broken heart. They mixed it with honey or oils and also made salves for injuries. When worn on the body, amber supposedly relieved headaches, toothaches, infections, and even rheumatism. Sicilian amber is called simetite.

♔ Element

Brass. Any gem set in brass will be supported by fiery energy. Brass highlights green amber's unusual color.

⚘ Herb

Simpler's joy (Verbena officinalis). This plant is native to the Mediterranean region. The entire plant has medicinal value.

Herbalists found it useful as a tonic to stimulate energy in recovering patients as well as remedies for whooping cough, jaundice, and kidney troubles. Preparations were also made into cleansing washes for wounds.

♀ SIMONA: From the root name *Simon*.

♀ SIMONE: From the root name *Simon*.

♀ SIMONETTA: From the root name *Simon*.

♂ SIMPSON: From the root name *Simon*.

♂ SINCLAIR: From the root name *Clara*.

♀ SINDY: From the root name *Cynthia*.

♀ SINEAD: From the root name *John*.

♀ SIOUX: From the root name *Susannah*.

♀ SISSELA: From the root name *Cecilia*.

♀ SISSY: From the root name *Cecilia*.

♀ SOFIE: From the root name *Sophia*.

♀ SOHNDRA: From the root name *Cassandra*.

♀ SONDRA: From the root name *Alexander*.

♀ SONIA: From the root name *Sophia*.

♀ SONJA: From the root name *Sophia*.

♀ SONNIE: From the root name *Sophia*.

♀ SONYA: From the root name *Sophia*.

♀ SOOSANNA: From the root name *Susannah*.

♥ ♀ SOPHIA Saffi, Sofie, Sonia, Sonja, Sonnie, Sonya, Sophie, Zofi, Zofia, Zsofe, Zsofia: The internationally fashionable name *Sophia*—or the somewhat more popular *Sophie*—projects a worldly sophistication at odds with its original associations with God's holy wisdom.

From the Greek word for wisdom, *Sophia* is similar to latter-day names like *Patience* and *Prudence,* in that it commemorates a spiritual virtue, not a saint. Yet early Christian tradition does mention a holy woman named *Sophia*. In one story, the Roman emperor Hadrian (who reigned from A.D. 117–138) imprisons Sophia's three young daughters. When the oldest daughter, Faith, a girl of twelve, refuses to renounce her Christian beliefs, Hadrian has her scourged and doused with boiling water. Her younger sisters, Hope and Charity, also refuse and are placed in a fiery furnace. When all three girls remain unscathed, Hadrian has them beheaded. Three days later, their mother Sophia dies while praying at their graves.

Pointing out that the Bible speaks of Wisdom as "the mother of Love and Hope and holy Fear," scholars now interpret this dramatic story as an allegory about Divine Wisdom, from which springs Faith, Hope, and Charity. Indeed, the inspiration for the famous Church of Saint Sophia supports this view. Built in Constantinople by the Byzantine Emperor Justinian (who reigned from A.D. 527–56), this magnificent structure venerates the *hagia sophia*—Holy Wisdom, Christ as the Incarnate Word.

Perhaps as a compliment to his recently completed church, the niece of Justinian's empress was baptized Sophia. When this niece married Justinian's nephew and successor, Sophia became fashionable among the elite of Constantinople. From there, it spread to other Eastern or Slavic nations. The marriage of the Hungarian princess Sophia to Magnus of Saxony (Northwestern Germany) in 1074 introduced the name to the Germanic tribes. Traveling to all Saxony's neighbors, *Sophia* eventually found a regal home in Denmark as a favorite choice among the Danish royals.

Sophia appeared in English-speaking countries around the seventeenth century. Two classic novels of the eighteenth century, Henry Fielding's *Tom Jones* (1749) and

Oliver Goldsmith's *The Vicar of Wakefield* (1766), featured romantic heroines named *Sophia*. Although less popular for most of the nineteenth and twentieth centuries, *Sophia*, its variant *Sophie*, and the Russian diminutive *Sonia* have become increasingly favored as the twenty-first century approaches.

Among *Sophia*'s many other variants are the Italian *Sofia*, the Polish *Zofia* and *Zosia*, and the Hungarian *Zsofia* and *Zsofe*. Variants for *Sonia* include *Sonja* and *Sonya*.

☺ Number
Five. Fives often find joy in their faith. Modern numerologists tie the forces of light, spiritual achievement, and education to this number.

☾ Astrological sign
Capricorn. People of this earth sign are often wise and serious-minded. They are charitable souls and willing to help those who might need a steady hand on life's rocky path.

☀ Color
Conifer. The deep color of a mountain forest is considered to be an emotional soother as well as a shade to promote healing.

◆ Stone
Green topaz. The name *topaz* may have come from the Sanskrit word *tapas*, meaning "fire." Ancient mystics who interpreted dreams said that visions of a topaz meant no harm would come to them. In late eighteenth-century France and England, jewelry was often set with gems whose first letters, when combined, formed a motto. Topaz was used to spell out both "faith" and "charity." Green topaz is beautiful and uncommon. A 21,005–carat green

topaz called "The Brazilian Princess" was once the largest gem ever faceted.

⚜ Element
Gold. Gold's fire energy heightens the power of the magnificent topaz. Ancients believed topaz was especially powerful when worn on the left arm and set in gold.

🦎 Herb
Danewort *(Sambucus ebulus)*. This plant is a variety of dwarf elder and is an herbaceous shrub found in eastern and central Europe and the United States. The rootstock has curative abilities and was used to make ointments or salves to treat burns.

♀   SOPHIE: From the root name *Sophia*.

♀   SORCHA: From the root name *Sarah*.

♂   SPENCE: From the root name *Spencer*.

♥ ♂ **SPENCER** **Spence, Spenser:** *Spencer* is now climbing up in the ranks of popular names for boys, but it began quite simply as a job description. Many English surnames evolved from the work performed in villages during the Middle Ages. In Northern English dialect, a "spence" is a pantry. A "spencer," then, is someone who stores and dispenses food and supplies, most likely in a lord's castle or manor house. In that class-bound society, if your father was a spencer, so were you, and your son would be, too, so it made sense that eventually, your descendants would be known as the *Spencer* or *Spenser* family.

    Hugh Le Spenser gave this family name added status as the Chief Justice for Henry III, who reigned from

1216–1272, and Edmund Spenser (1552–1599), author of *The Faerie Queene,* later added to its distinction.

But *Spencer,* not *Spenser,* became the more typical spelling by the seventeenth century. Perhaps it was a case of "money talks." Before his death in 1627, Robert Spencer had amassed the greatest fortune in England. After John Churchill, the renowned general, died in 1722, Charles Spencer became the second duke of Marlborough. He was a trend-setter to the degree that "spencer" became slang for the type of wig he favored. Another Spencer, English politician G. J. Spencer (1758–1834), first popularized what became known in fashion circles as a "spencer"—a close-fitting man's jacket sporting lapels and reaching right below the waist.

Spencer was often given as a personal name to those connected through marriage to the family in order to keep the matrilineal name in circulation. One example was Prime Minister Spencer Perceval, who was assassinated in 1812. Another *Spencer* connection, the famous Sir Winston Leonard Spencer Churchill, had far better luck in that high office.

During the nineteenth century, *Spencer* had some limited usage in England and the United States. Herbert Spencer (1820–1903), the British thinker who held that biological and social evolution equals progress, may have earned some converts for his name, if not his optimistic philosophy. In the first half of the twentieth century, the well-respected actor, Spencer Tracy (1900–1967), might have inspired some namesakes.

The recent death of Lady Diana Spencer, Princess of Wales, and the well-publicized eulogy delivered by her handsome brother, Earl Spencer—may carry *Spencer* to even greater popularity into the next century. The diminutive, *Spence,* very often becomes the primary name by which boys named *Spencer* are called in the United States.

🌀 Number

Eight. In modern numerology, eight represents good fortune and prosperity.

🌙 Astrological sign

Cancer. People of this sign enjoy being the host. Their home is their castle and those who enter are treated like royalty.

✹ Color

Silver leaf. This color is tied to Cancer and represents *chokmah* (wisdom) on the sacred Sefirot tree of the Cabala.

◆ Stone

Spessartite garnet. Garnets are high in magnesium and aluminum and believed to possess healing abilities. Ancient mystics believed that if a person dreamed of a garnet, it meant that the solution of a mystery was imminent. This particular member of the vast garnet family is usually an orange shade—a color associated with appetite stimulation and digestion. Spessartite often has thin featherlike streaks throughout the stone giving it a lacy appearance. It is found mainly in the United States (Virginia and California), Mexico, and Madagascar.

🔥 Element

Magnesium. Magnesium is a light silvery, metallic element that burns with a brilliant white flame. It is also an essential mineral for good health.

🌿 Herb

Cheese plant *(Malva rotundifolia)*. This member of the mallow plant group is a low growing perennial found along roadways and cultivated throughout North America. The plant's herb makes healing teas for coughs, bronchitis, and tonsillitis. It has trumpet-shaped flowers that bloom from May to November.

♂ SPENSER: From the root name *Spencer.*

♂ STAFFAN: From the root name *Stephen.*

♀ STEFA: From the root name *Stephen.*

♂ STEFAN: From the root name *Stephen.*

♂ STEFANO: From the root name *Stephen.*

♂ STEFFEL: From the root name *Stephen.*

♀ STEFFI: From the root name *Stephen.*

♂ STEPHAN: From the root name *Stephen.*

♀ STEPHANA: From the root name *Stephen.*

♀ STEPHANIE: From the root name *Stephen.*

♂ STEPHANOS: From the root name *Stephen.*

♂ STEPHANUS: From the root name *Stephen.*

♥ ♂ STEPHEN Esteban, Estevan, Etienne, Staffen, Stefa, Stefan, Stefano, Steffel, Steffi, Stephan, Stephana, Stephanie, Stephanos, Stephanus, Stephine, Stevana, Steve, Steven, Stevenson, Stevie, Tiennot: The name *Stephen* comes from the Greek *Stephanos,* meaning "garland" or "crown," and probably refers to the wreath of leaves given to winners of Greek games. No famous men in ancient Greece had the name; rather, it gained fame because of Saint Stephen, the first Christian martyr.

The story of Saint Stephen is told in the New Testament Book of Acts. He was one of seven deacons chosen by the apostles to distribute food to the needy, but he went far beyond the call of duty and became a powerful preacher, winning many people over to Christianity. Angry and jealous, the Jewish leaders tried to argue with Stephen, but they couldn't compete. So they persuaded some men to lie about him, saying that he'd spoken words of blasphemy against Moses and God. Stephen denied this by summarizing Old Testament teachings. The Bible says he faced the crowds without fear, and that his face looked like an angel's. But the Jewish leaders were so angry that they dragged him out of the city and stoned him to death. His feast day is December 26, one day after Christ's.

Saint Stephen's fame made the name a favorite among early Christians. In the Middle Ages, *Stephen* was widely used in the rest of Europe, but it was rare in England before the Norman Conquest (1066). Although *Stephen* wasn't recorded in the Domesday Book (a recorded survey of English lands ordered by William the Conqueror around 1086), *Stefanus* was. The fact that nine early popes, eight saints, and several kings were named Stephen attests to the name's popularity. The first King Stephen of Hungary founded the Hungarian monarchy and later became a saint. In England the name was popularized by King Stephen of Blois, who ruled from 1135–1154, and by Stephen Langton, the theologian, historian, and poet who became Archbishop of Canterbury and died in 1228.

By the fourteenth century, the name had inspired several surnames, including *Stevenson, Stevens,* and *Steen.* Because *Stevyn* and *Steven* were popular forms then, most surnames are, even now, spelled with a *v.*

After the Reformation in the sixteenth century, *Stephen* continued to be used, even though Protestants were discarding saints' names. The name remained very popular in the English-speaking world until the end of the eighteenth century, held its own throughout the nineteenth century, and then bottomed out in the 1920s. Since then, it has moved up and down the popularity charts, coming on strong from the

1940s to the 1960s, then fading out in the United States in the 1970s. It remained the most popular boy's name in England until 1975, but by the 1980s it was showing signs of wear and tear in both countries. However, *Stephen* and its alternative spelling, *Steven,* are both in the top one hundred names for boys, and the female form, *Stephanie,* is one of the top one hundred names for girls.

Stefan and *Stephan* are foreign forms of *Stephen* used in English-speaking countries. *Steffen* is another English form of the name. In Greece, the name is *Stephanos;* in Italy, *Stefano;* in Spain, *Estevan* and *Esteban;* in France, *Etienne* and *Tiennot;* and in Germany, *Stephan* and *Steffel.* Nicknames are *Steve* and *Stevie.*

◉ Number

Six. Sixes often pursue scholarly work and make excellent mentors. Many sixes find destiny as spiritual leaders.

☾ Astrological sign

Leo. This is the crown jewel of astrological signs. The star Regulus, found in the Leo constellation, was believed by ancients to be the king of celestial lights.

✺ Color

Solar corona. The color of the sun's luminous outer atmosphere represents the crown (white) on the Sefirot tree of the Cabala, an esoteric symbol of God.

◆ Stone

Diamond. A diamond's creation comes from superheated earthly fire and intense pressure. The pure crystal that survives this process is so powerful that it is the only gem known to man that has the ability to absorb all energy. For example, when a diamond is placed in warm milk, the milk cools and the diamond warms. Diamonds were considered a stone of high energy and prized by the ancients for their prismatic brilliance. Clear diamonds are still the most highly treasured gems today. Referred to as the sovereign of gems, diamonds carry a price tag that reflect this moniker.

♛ Element

Stephanite. Stephanite is a form of silver antimony used to protect warriors in battle.

🦎 Herb

Crowfoot (*Geranium maculatum*). This plant is also called spotted cranebill and is common in woodlands throughout North America. Its thick, horizontal rootstock was used to make remedies to prevent hemorrhage. It made a cleansing mouthwash and sore throat gargle. It has rose-purple flowers that bloom into the summer months.

♀　STEPHINE: From the root name *Stephen*.

♀　STEVANA: From the root name *Stephen*.

♂　STEVE: From the root name *Stephen*.

♂　STEVEN: From the root name *Stephen*.

♂　STEVENSON: From the root name *Stephen*.

♀♂　STEVIE: From the root name *Stephen*.

♂　STEWARD: From the root name *Stuart*.

♂　STEWART: From the root name *Stuart*.

♀　STINA: From the root name *Christopher*.

♂　STU: From the root name *Stuart*.

♥ ♂ **STUART**　**Steward, Stewart, Stu:** The surname of Scotland's kings and queens, *Stuart* traces its roots to a much humbler position. *Stuart,* or its variant *Stewart,* derives from the Old English words for "sty ward"—a phrase used to describe someone who watched over animals intended for meat. The lord's steward was a prestigious position in medieval England, and naturally, as properties (and the villages associated with them) grew in size and importance, so did the role of stewards.

The rigid class structure of the time meant that certain families inherited particular occupations. When surnames evolved, these families became identified by their work—as did the *Stewards* or *Stewarts* (the Scots version), who managed the estates of the Counts Dol in Britanny during the eleventh century.

In the early twelfth century, the Stewarts arrived in England. Later, Walter, son of the fourth steward of Dol, became the steward of David I, King of Scots. In 1157, King Malcom IV made the stewardship a hereditary position. When Walter, the High Steward of Scotland, married Marjorie, the daughter of King Robert the Bruce, in 1315, a royal dynasty was formed. Then, in 1371, their son, Robert II, became the first Stewart king of Scotland.

The male Stewart line ended with James V in 1542. His daughter, Mary, who was raised in France, adopted the *Stuart* spelling (sometimes seen as *Steuart*), because there was no letter *w* in the French alphabet. The change in spelling seemed to bring the dynasty better luck—Mary's son, James VI, not only ruled in Scotland, but in 1603, through the twists and turns of British royal succession, he also inherited the English throne as James I. But years of turmoil followed. Stuarts reigned off-and-on in England, until the Act of Settlement (1701) denied the English throne to any Roman Catholic, effectively excluding the Catholic Stuarts. William III and Mary I (who reigned in 1689–1702), however, were descendants of the Stuarts. This royal couple was childless, and after the death of Mary's sister, Queen

Anne (1702–1714), the monarchy changed into the hands of the Hanover dynasty.

Some lingering affection for the last royal Stuarts may have led to *Stuart*'s wider use as a first name in the early nineteenth century in the United Kingdom, especially in Scotland, and it became even more popular in the last half of the twentieth century in the United Kingdom.

In the United States, Stuart was sometimes found among those of Scottish descent, but the Civil War cavalry officer Jeb Stuart (1833–1864) may have inspired even more namesakes among his Confederate admirers. *Stuart*'s popularity declined since the 1980s. Parents have occasionally named sons with the variant spellings. Boys named *Stewart* or *Stuart* often go by the diminutive *Stew* or *Stu*.

 ## Number

Nine. Nines are sometimes linked to conflict because they courageously defend justice and truth.

 ## Astrological sign

Taurus. Since Taurus is an earth sign, many born under this sign find happiness in caring for land and animals. Taureans are reliable. Film star Jimmy Stewart was a Taurus.

 ## Color

Plaid. The royal tartan of the Stuart clan is red, royal blue, white, and green.

 ## Stone

Ivory. Animal breeders and ancient veterinarians believed that ivory protected them from injuries while handling livestock. Ivory has been used for carving and facial and neck jewelry for centuries. Highly prized ivory netsukes were carved into animal or human forms and hung from Buddhist monks' belts to represent their belief in human virtues. Ivory prayer beads were used by Western religions as rosaries. Ivory's sheen increases when rubbed. While ivory necklaces carved in India and China are the finest in the world, the near extinction of some ivory-bearing elephants has caused ivory trade to be banned in most nations.

Element
Copper. Copper is reputed to have healing qualities and is the metal associated with the sign of Taurus.

♆ Herb
Scotch quelch *(Agropyrum repens)*. Also called couch-grass, this plant is abundant in fields in Britain and throughout continental Europe. The name "couch" comes from the Anglo-Saxon *civice,* which means "vivacious." The rhizome (underground stem) was collected in the spring and used for kidney troubles, especially to help dissolve kidney stones. Rhizome preparations were also recommended for gout and rheumatism.

♀ SUE: From the root name *Susannah.*

♀ SUKI: From the root name *Susannah.*

♀ SUSAN: From the root name *Susannah.*

♀ SUSANETTA: From the root name *Susannah.*

♀ SUSANNAGH: From the root name *Susannah.*

♥ ♀ SUSANNAH Shoshana, Sioux, Soosanna, Sue, Suki, Susan, Susanetta, Susannagh, Suschen, Susette, Susie, Suzanne, Suzette, Suzy, Zanna, Zsa Zsa, Zusa, Zuza: *Susannah* comes from the Hebrew word, *schuschannah,* or "lily." Although some biblical scholars, notably Saint

Jerome, questioned its validity, the story of Daniel's defense of Susannah proved too good a story to ignore. Its combination of a damsel-in-distress theme with suspenseful courtroom drama—not to mention a bath scene—made Susannah's story an appealing subject for many medieval ballads, tapestries, and paintings.

According to the biblical story, Susannah is the beautiful and faithful wife of Joachim. Two evil judges, taken with her loveliness, take to spying upon her. Catching her bathing alone in her garden, the judges pressure her to have intercourse with them, threatening to accuse her of adultery—a crime punishable by death—if she won't. When Susannah steadfastly refuses, the angry judges condemn her to death, saying they surprised her and a young man in her garden. As Susannah is being led to execution, young Daniel steps forward to expose the evil judges by interrogating them separately. One judge claims he saw Susannah and the young man lying under a mastic tree; the other, under an oak.

Other *Susannah*s also suffered because of their faithfulness to their beliefs. The Church of Saint Susanna, which still stands in Rome, attests to the fidelity of an early Christian martyr. Another *Susanna* reputedly was martyred because she refused to marry the pagan son of the emperor Diocletian; still another, the wife of a soldier in a military unit commanded by Saint Meletius, was martyred in second-century Galatia.

Later-day associations with *Susannah,* including the famous Stephen Foster tune, "Oh, Susannah" (1848), are far cheerier. Popular in France (*Susanne, Suzette, Suzon*) and Switzerland (*Susanne, Zosa, Zosel, Zosel*), *Susannah* appears in English-speaking countries in the sixteenth century. Its shortened version, *Susan,* appears in the eighteenth century, and by the twentieth century, *Susan* has eclipsed the longer form.

During the 1950s and 1960s, *Susan* was among the top ten names for the baby-boom generation. *Susan*'s diminutives *Susie*, *Susy*, and *Suzy* shared in that popularity, as did the diminutive *Sue*—by itself or as second name (e.g., *Peggy Sue, Bobby Sue*). Today, *Susan* is less widespread, but its many variants may help it regain some of its former glory. These include *Sukie, Suky, Susann, Susanna, Susannah, Susanne, Suschen, Suse, Susetta, Susette, Susi, Susie, Suzanne, Suzetta, Suzette, Suzi, Suzie, Suzy, Zsa Zsa, Zusa,* and *Zuza*.

 ## Number

Two. In modern numerology, two symbolizes the conscious mind. Twos are rarely completely satisfied, but they are sympathetic souls and deeply protective of loved ones.

 ## Astrological sign

Aquarius. The planet Uranus rules Aquarius and its influence instills a deep love of mankind in many Aquarians. Most choose careers as teachers, social workers, and writers. Susan B. Anthony was an Aquarian.

 ## Color

Sky sapphire. Blue signifies the air in ancient Judaic writings. It was also considered the color of truth by ancient Greeks.

 ## Stone

Blue jadeite. Jadeite is a variety of jade. It can be semitransparent, depending on the hue and where it is found. Green is the color commonly associated with jade, but it occurs in several hues. Blue shades range from pale to gray-blue. Much lore is attached to this gem and some called it a love-attracting stone. In ancient China, a bride-to-be would give her prospective husband jade to bind their engagement. The Chinese also believed this gem could prolong life. Currently, most jadeite comes from Myanmar.

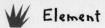 **Element**

White gold. White gold honors the beauty of blue jadeite.

Herb

Lily-of-the-valley *(Convallaria majalis).* While this perennial plant is native to Europe, it is cultivated in gardens in the United States and Canada. The plant was used to make ointments for headache plasters and for gout or rheumatic pains. In some homeopathic remedies, it is suggested for use as a cardiac drug. This plant is easily identifiable by its white, bell-shaped flowers.

♀   SUSCHEN: From the root name *Susannah.*

♀   SUSETTE: From the root name *Susannah.*

♀   SUSIE: From the root name *Susannah.*

♀   SUZANNE: From the root name *Susannah.*

♀   SUZETTE: From the root name *Susannah.*

♀   SUZY: From the root name *Susannah.*

♀   SYBILLE: From the root name *Sibyl.*

♂   SYD: From the root name *Sydney.*

♀   SYDEL: From the root name *Sarah.*

♀   SYDELLE: From the root name *Sydney.*

♥   ♀♂ **SYDNEY** **Sidm, Siddie, Sidney, Sidon, Sidonio, Syd, Sydelle, Sydnie:** During the reign of the first Plantagenet king, Henry II (1154–1189), a prominent family emigrated from Anjou to England. In various documents the family's surname was recorded as *de Sancto Dionysio* or "of Saint Denis," most likely the name of their home in Anjou. Over time, the British tradition of contracting saints' names, as in

Tobin (Saint Aubyn), turned Saint Dennis into *Sidney*. (Because early typesetters used *i* and *y* interchangeably, *Sidney* and *Sydney* developed simultaneously.) Among aristocratic families such as the *Sidney*s, many parents honored the mother's family by giving a son her maiden name as a first or middle name.

Aside from family pride, some national pride may have fostered *Sydney*'s use as a personal name among the English. Sir Philip Sidney (1554–1586), poet, diplomat, and soldier, was considered among the best and brightest at the court of Elizabeth I. He also won acclaim as the author of the very successful pastoral romance *Arcadia*. Later, while fighting in the Netherlands, he was said to have nobly given his only cup of water to a dying soldier. When *Sidney* himself died in battle at age thirty-two, a national month of mourning followed.

At first *Sydney* might have seemed too aristocratic for democratic America. But the support of the English statesman Thomas Townshend, Viscount Sydney, for the American cause during the Revolutionary War may have changed that image somewhat. (Sydney, Australia, also is named after him.) Throughout the nineteenth century, *Sidney* steadily rose in popularity, with a notable upturn in 1870 to 1890. Charles Dickens's classic *A Tale of Two Cities* first appeared in 1859. This novel of the French Revolution tells the dramatic story of Sydney Carton, a ne'er-do-well who undergoes the guillotine to save the husband of the woman he loves. Was that romantic sacrifice behind *Sydney*'s position as one of the top fifty names for boys in 1900?

During the twentieth century, *Sydney* as a boy's name has declined, despite such personalities as Sidney Poitier, the well-known stage and screen star. It may have declined because, since the nineteenth century, it has been used more often as a girl's name. Some argue that the feminine *Sydney* comes from the Irish girl's name *Sidony*, based on the Roman Catholic Feast of the Sindon, which commemorates the "winding-sheet" or Shroud of Turin. Also, the French *Sidonie* or *Sidony*, from the Latin *Sidonia* (woman of Sidon), might have influenced *Sydney*'s gender transformation. Others argue as persuasively that *Sydney*, just like *Shirley* or *Beverly*, demonstrates how a surname, once given as a personal name to the boys, then the girls in a particular family, can eventually evolve into a feminine name among the wider population.

Whatever its origin, the feminine *Sydney* is definitely on the upswing. Just as its brother name was in the top fifty names for boys nearly a century ago, *Sydney* holds that position now for girls.

Masculine nicknames for *Sidney* include *Sid*, *Siddie*, *Sidon*, *Sidonio*, and *Syd*. Feminine variant spellings include *Sydne*, *Sydnie*, and *Sydny*.

 ## Number

Two. Geniality and sentimentality are traits of many twos. Modern numerology credits people of this number with diplomacy. Pope Leo XIII and Pope Pius X were both born under the number two.

 ## Astrological sign

Capricorn. Although many Capricorns can be stubborn and relentless in their persistence, they are also steadfast and loyal. Sydney Greenstreet was a Capricorn.

 ## Color

English pink. The color of romance and devotion stimulates heart and soul.

 ## Stone

Green flint. Most color associations with flint are black, yet it occurs in several colors. It is a type of microcrystalline quartz found in small, slightly flattened masses. It is a strong and durable mineral. Flint was often used in religious and magical rituals throughout the world. Native Americans used it in religious and curative rites. Cherokee shamans handled flint during their incantations to prepare for healing treatments.

 Element

Silver. Silver is an ore connected to flint and provides vital support for its healing energy.

Herb

Soldier's herb *(Plantago lanceolata)*. This herb is a member of the plantain group. It's a perennial plant found in meadows in eastern and Pacific U.S. coastal states as well as Canada and Europe. Soldier's herb was used as a cough remedy and other ailments of the lungs. A special preparation of the dried leaves was found to encourage clotting and was used for battle wounds.

♀   SYDNIE: From the root name *Sydney*.

♀   SYMANTHA: From the root name *Samantha*.

♂   SYMMS: From the root name *Simon*.

♂   SYMON: From the root name *Simon*.

♀   SYMONE: From the root name *Simon*.

♀   SYNDA: From the root name *Cynthia*.

♀   SYNTHIA: From the root name *Cynthia*.

♂   SZYMON: From the root name *Simon*.

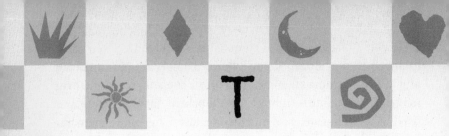

♂ TAILER: From the root name *Taylor.*

♀♂ TAILOR: From the root name *Taylor.*

♂ TAMEK: From the root name *Thomas.*

♀ TAMMIE: From the root name *Thomas.*

♂ TAMSIN: From the root name *Thomas.*

♂ TANDIE: From the root name *Andrew.*

♥ ♀ **TARA Tarah, Tarra, Taryn:** The name *Tara* comes from the Gaelic word *temair,* which may have originally meant "a high place with a good view" or "a sacred place." *Tara* is usually translated as "a hill." Many hilly places in Ireland are called *Tara,* but the most famous is in County Meath. County Meath is home to the ruins of the prehistoric political/religious/ceremonial complex known for thousands of years as Tara. It was reputed to be home to Ireland's gods and goddesses, kings and heroes. Many medieval Irish texts—sagas, histories, legal documents, and religious works—contain references to Tara. As early as the seventh century A.D. these texts called it the "capital of Ireland." Some of Tara's residents were only mythical, but many were actual historical figures.

Tara has only been used as a given name in recent times. Margaret Mitchell's 1936 novel, *Gone With the Wind,* featured a cast of charismatic characters, and much of the action took place on Scarlett O'Hara's childhood plantation home, which was called, unforgettably, Tara. Soon after the novel's release, *Tara* leaped in popularity as a given name for girls. The appearance of the blockbuster movie a few years later only added sheen to the name. At the same time the names *Ashley, Scarlett* and *Rhett* made brief appearances on baby names lists. Like *Ashley, Tara* remained in the names lexicon over the next few decades, but it was not among the most popular. The late 1960s saw a surge of popularity for *Tara* in Britain and Ireland, possibly thanks to the character Tara King on the hit show "The Avengers." Until the 1980s, *Tara* was often chosen by new parents in the United Kingdom. Then, while the name declined abroad, *Tara* and other Irish names became fashionable in the United States. While never hugely popular, *Tara* is fairly common today.

 ## Number
Four. Fours are known for being resourceful, ambitious, and tenacious.

 ## Astrological sign
Capricorn. Those born under this sign are not intimidated by conflict, especially when they believe they are right.

 ## Color
Terra-verde. Deep green is tied to Capricorn, and also inspires visions of rolling Irish hills.

 ## Stone
Massive green zoisite. Almost always used for ornamental purposes, this crystalline type of green zoisite has ruby spots. The bright green color makes a striking contrast to the ruby crystals distributed throughout the stone. Green zoisite is cut, sculpted, and polished into items such as boxes, bowls, and

other decorative items. Green zoisite comes from Tanzania and is still highly prized by artisans and collectors alike.

☿ Element

Aluminum. Aluminum is found in zoisite. Modern mystics use pieces of aluminum to boost concentration when meditating.

☿ Herb

Tarragon *(Artemisia dracunculus)*. This shrub grows in sunny, dry areas of the western United States and southern Asia, and is cultivated in Europe. The flowering plant was a popular remedy for digestive ills and kidney troubles. A flower tea helped promote healthy appetites, especially during recuperation. Tarragon has greenish white or yellow flowers.

♀   TARAH: From the root name *Tara.*

♀   TARESA: From the root name *Theresa.*

♀   TARRA: From the root name *Tara.*

♂   TARRANCE: From the root name *Terrence.*

♀   TARYN: From the root name *Tara.*

♀   TASHA: From the root name *Natalie.*

♀♂   TAYLER: From the root name *Taylor.*

♥ ♀♂ **TAYLOR** Tailer, Tailor, Tayler: Falling, of course, into the category of occupational names, *Taylor* is from the French infinitive *taillier,* which means "to cut." It entered England and the English language during the Norman Conquest of 1066 and eventually became one of the more common surnames in both England and the United

States. As a surname, it is sometimes spelled *Tailor.* As a boy's first name, *Taylor* enjoyed a heyday in the nineteenth century in England, though it was not popular in the United States.

The most fascinating story of *Taylor* began unfolding in the early 1990s. As a boy's name it was the 422nd most popular name borne by American boys and men in 1990. But by 1994, it ranked 39th among names given to boy babies that year. Even more startling is the skyrocketing popularity of Taylor as a girl's name. The 1990 census listed it 805th in terms of usage among women and girls. Four years later, in 1994, it was the sixth most popular name given to girl babies, and it is still going strong.

Taylor is a very common surname, and since practice of fashioning a child's first name from the mother's maiden name is once more on the upswing, it is easy to understand the recent surge in popularity in the name for boys. Since—at the same time—it has become acceptable to assign girls with names that have been traditionally reserved for boys (e.g., *Alex, Avery, Morgan, Tyler,* and the like), it seems inevitable that *Taylor* would have found its way into one of the top spots in terms of popular girls' names.

⑨ Number
One. This number represents beginnings. Ones are always creative.

☽ Astrological sign
Taurus. Taureans are not afraid to work for what they want and usually succeed in whatever field they choose.

☀ Color
Madder blue. A dye made from the madder plant was used to color cloth. Blue is tied to the sign of Taurus.

Stone

Rutilated quartz. This quartz variety can have different hues, but all specimens have needlelike rutile crystals throughout the stone. Colors can be red, black, or brassy yellow and all have a metallic sheen. The rutile needles can be gold, sliver, gray or black. The ancients called rutilated quartz Venus-hair stone or sagenite because of these unusual inclusions. They also used the stone as a positive energy strengthener. Rutilated quartz is found throughout the world with the quality gems coming from Madagascar, Brazil, India, Germany, and Switzerland.

 Element

Steel. Steel was once believed to safeguard against mischief by fairies and pixies. It is also used to make high-quality cutting shears.

 Herb

Tailed pepper *(Piper cubeba)*. Also known as tailed cubeb in some herbal manuals, the unripe fruit of this vinelike plant was considered to have medicinal properties. Dried tailed pepper berries look like ordinary peppercorn. These nuggets were ground into powder and made into preparations for indigestion. Powdered tailed pepper was sometimes smoked to relieve respiratory problems.

♀   TEA: From the root name *Dorothy*.

♂   TEADOR: From the root name *Theodore*.

♂   TED: From the root names *Edmund, Edward,* and *Theodore*.

♀♂ TEDDIE: From the root names *Edmund, Edward,* and *Theodore*.

♀ TEDRA: From the root name *Theodore*.

♂ TEEMOFE: From the root name *Timothy*.

♀ TEENA: From the root name *Christopher*.

♂ TENNYSON: From the root name *Dennis*.

♂ TENTON: From the root name *Anthony*.

♂ TEODOOR: From the root name *Theodore*.

♀ TERA: From the root name *Theresa*.

♂ TEREN: From the root name *Terrence*.

♀ TERENA: From the root name *Terrence*.

♥ ♂ **TERENCE** **Tarrance, Teren, Terena, Terencio, Terry, Teryna:** Although *Terence* has been in use from ancient times, the name is in the process of being eclipsed by its short form, *Terry*. Those boys and girls—and men and women—named *Terry* probably are unaware that their name comes from a Latin clan name, *Terentius,* meaning "to rub," "to wear out," or "to use up." Ironically, the clan received its greatest fame when one of its slaves, Publius Terentius Afer, originally from North Africa, took his master's name after being freed. This Terentius became the comic Roman playwright known by English-speaking students of the classics as Terence.

In early Christian times, another *Terence* earned fame of a different kind as a martyr. Some conjecture that he was the "Tertius" who wrote out Saint Paul's epistle to the Romans. This martyr and bishop, as well as other saints called *Terence* by the English, gave the Irish a suitable Christian replacement for the decidedly unsuitable Irish name *Turlough*. A relic of Ireland's Viking past, *Turlough* means "like Thor" (the Viking god).

Though it was used rarely in England until the twentieth century, *Terence* thrived in Ireland. One famous bearer of the name was the Lord Mayor of Cork, Terence McSwiney, who starved himself to death in protest of British rule while imprisoned in 1920.

In the United States, Irish immigrants and their descendants kept *Terence* in steady use throughout the nineteenth and first half of the twentieth centuries. In the 1950s and 1960s, its diminutive *Terry* ranked in the top forty names for boys. Some historians point out that *Terry* was originally an independent name, a variant of *Derek,* and as such, *Terye* appears as early as 1629. But *Terry*'s close association with *Terence* probably best explains why *Terence*'s star has faded as *Terry*'s has risen.

Complicating the picture is the emergence of *Terry* as a name for girls. Beginning in the late 1930s, *Terry* was given both as an independent name to girls, or used as a diminutive for *Theresa* or *Teresa*.

Variant spellings for *Terence* include *Tarrance, Terencio, Terrance,* and *Terrence.*

Number

Seven. Sevens are thought to have psychic powers and gifts related to the healing arts. Through their abilities, sevens influence others and present unique views of life for the world to contemplate.

☾ Astrological sign

Libra. Libras can be wise and kind, and are always champions for justice. They have gentle, loving spirits.

☀ Color

Emeraude. Green is the color of Venus, Libra's ruling celestial body. It is also a color in the national flag of Ireland.

Stone

Thunder eggs. These gem rocks are also called geodes, but their association with Thor, the god of thunder, gave rise to the term *thunder eggs*. Geodes occur as stone balls with crystal, topaz or amethyst centers. When cut open the crystal creation inside is revealed. The crystalline core can have agate or jasper bands. Thunder eggs vary greatly in size and color. They are found when two land masses have joined and the water between the masses was unable to escape. Friction or rubbing during the joining formed a stone ball like an oyster creates a pearl and the thunder egg was ejected. Because of their supposed creation by an elemental god, thunder eggs were used for prophetic readings by ancient tribes. Thunder eggs are abundant in Mexico and the southwestern United States.

 ## Element

Silver. Silver enhances psychic ability.

 ## Herb

Corkwood *(Hibiscus tiliaceus)*. Hibiscus identifies a genus with about two hundred species, but only a few have medicinal value. Corkwood is a shrub or tree found in tropical areas and warmer climates. The inner bark was used in cough remedies and lotions to soothe and soften skin.

♂ TERENCIO: From the root name *Terrence*.

♀ TERESA: From the root name *Theresa*.

♀ TERESITA: From the root name *Theresa*.

♀ TEREZINHA: From the root name *Theresa*.

♀ TERI: From the root name *Theresa*.

♀♂ TERRY: From the root names *Terrence* and *Theresa*.

♀ TERYNA: From the root name *Terrence*.

♀ TESS: From the root name *Theresa*.

♀ TESSA: From the root name *Theresa*.

♂ THANIEL: From the root name *Nathaniel*.

♀ THEA: From the root names *Dorothy* and *Timothy*.

♂ THEO: From the root name *Theodore*.

♂ THEODOR: From the root name *Theodore*.

♀ THEODORA: From the root name *Theodore*.

♥ ♂ THEODORE   Dora, Fedor, Fedora, Teador, Ted, Teddie, Tedra, Teodoor, Theo, Theodor, Theodora, Theodorus, Theodosia, Theodosios, Tudor: During its long history, *Theodore* has been the name of saints, popes, kings, and presidents—and, a disco-singing chipmunk. The legends surrounding an early Christian martyr named Theodoros or Theodorus (from the Greek, "God's gift") include tales of gruesome torture and a fiery death. One story described him as "Theodorus the Recruit," while another promoted him to "Theodorus the General," linking him to that other great soldier-saint, Saint George. Indeed, in one version, Theodorus is credited with the dragon-slaying talent later attributed to the more famous Saint George. The Venetians designated *Teodoro* as a patron saint of their beautiful city. The Spanish called him *Teodor;* the French, *Theodore;* the Germans, *Theodor* or *Pheodor. Theodore* became *Feodor* or *Fyodor* in Russia and Poland.

For the English, the accomplishments of Pope Theodore I (642–649) and Theodore II (897) may have meant less than those of the humble Greek monk, Theodore of Tarsus, who became their Archbishop of Canterbury in 667. Theodore presided over the first synod, or meeting, of the Anglo-Saxon church, and set up the diocesan system of church organization in England.

The Welsh form of *Theodore*, *Tewdwr*, gradually evolved into the surname *Tudor*, which reached the English throne in 1485 and remained the last name in royalty until 1603.

Given the United States' more democratic notions, it is not surprising that the aristocratic-sounding *Theodore* gave way to *Teddy*, as the press wrote about the exploits of Theodore Roosevelt and his Rough Riders. When a story circulated during his presidency (1901–1909) that Roosevelt had spared a bear cub while hunting big game, the perennially adored "teddy bear" stuffed toy was born.

Theodore was among the top fifty names for boys in 1940, but it has never cracked the top ten most popular names. Perhaps that's why the creators of the 1960s TV show featuring an animated chipmunk named Alvin selected Theodore as a distinctive name for his pudgy brother. A new style in music during the late 1970s and early 1980s prompted the show's return: The chipmunks' high-pitched vocals were perfect for disco tunes.

But the status of another, more recent television show may be the force behind the emergence of a *Theodore* variant. "The Cosby Show" entertained millions with the warm home life of the attractive Huxtable family, which included a decidedly cool teenage son named Theo. Other variants include *Teador, Ted, Tedd, Teddey, Teddie,* and *Tedor*.

 Number

Nine. Pythagoras attributed heroics and fearlessness to this number.

 Astrological sign

Scorpio. Scorpios pursue life with zest and aren't afraid to follow the truth wherever it leads them. Theodore Roosevelt was a Scorpio.

Color

Dragon's blood. Red and black are linked to Scorpio. These two colors were also worn by ancient priests when asking for divine intervention.

 Stone

Water sapphire. Lore abounds around the mighty sapphire. It has been called the gem of fate and is the toughest natural stone next to a diamond. Water sapphires are also called cordierite and range in color from a deep to light or grayish blue. Variations in color depend on the iron or titanium content. Water sapphires come mainly from Sri Lanka, but some are found in the United States. They occur as medium-sized pebbles, with the largest being a couple of carats in size. Ancient mystics believed that dreams of a sapphire meant escape from danger. Buddhists thought sapphires inspired spiritual enlightenment.

 Element

Red gold. Red gold was connected to kingly wealth, but metallurgic lore also links it to divinity. Gold heightens the energy of a water sapphire.

 Herb

Cacao *(Theobroma cacao).* Cacao trees are cultivated in South America, Ceylon, Java, and other tropical areas of the world. The seeds are ground into powder or pressed to extract oil for lotions and cosmetics. The seed oil is also used to make fine chocolates. *Theobroma* is Latin for "food of the gods."

♂ THEODORUS: From the root name *Theodore.*

♀ THEODOSIA: From the root name *Theodore.*

♂   THEODOSIOS: From the root name *Theodore*.

♀   THEOPHANIE: From the root name *Tiffany*.

♥ ♀ **THERESA** **Taresa, Tera, Teresa, Teresita, Terezinha, Teri, Terry, Tess, Tessa, Thérèse, Theresina, Theresita, Tracy, Tresha, Tressa, Tressie, Zita:** During its long history, *Theresa* (or *Teresa*) has been associated with women who were noble, either by birth or in spirit. *Theresa* may come from the Greek word for "reaper" or may refer to "a lady from Therasia," which encompasses two islands near Greece. Yet its first known use was in Spain. In the early sixth century, a Spanish lady named Theresa and her Roman husband, Paulinus, corresponded with Saint Jerome, who translated the Bible into Latin. A Spanish noblewoman Teresa was crowned queen in Leon in the tenth century, yet the name did not become frequent outside Spain until the devotional writings of Teresa of Avila (1515–1582) brought her fame throughout Catholic Europe.

Marie Therese (1638–1683), queen of France and daughter of Philip of Spain, helped popularize the name in France. Unlike her daughter—Marie Antoinette of France—the much-admired Austrian Empress Maria Theresa (1740–1780) inspired great loyalty among her subjects, and *Theresa* flourished there.

In Protestant England, *Theresa* was little known until the eighteenth century; its variant, *Tracy* (or *Tracey*), had more success. The old name *Treasa* ("strength") took on new life as the Irish equivalent of *Theresa*.

The attention given to the 1925 canonization of another Saint Theresa, the humble "little flower" of France, Therese of Lisieux (1873–1897), may have helped boost *Theresa*'s popularity in the United States. By 1960, both *Teresa* and *Theresa* were among the top forty names given to girls.

Perhaps the recent death of Mother Teresa, respected throughout the world for her work with the poor, will prompt a new generation of *Theresas*.

Variants of *Theresa* include *Teresina, Teresita, Teressa, Terrasa, Terrise, Terazon, Terezija,* and *Therese.* Popular diminutives include *Teri, Terrey, Terry, Tess, Tessa,* and *Tessie.*

One variation, *Tracy,* shared *Theresa*'s popularity in the second half of the twentieth century and emerged as a name in its own right. Some credit Hollywood, suggesting that either screen icon Spencer Tracy, or Samantha Tracy Lord, the heroine of the 1956 movie *High Society* (played by the elegant actress Grace Kelly), sparked the interest. *Tracy* was number ten in popularity in 1970, though its luster has faded since. Variant spellings include *Tracey, Trace, Tracie,* and *Traci.*

 Number

Four. Most fours are not swayed by material wealth and prefer necessities over luxury. A large number of fours are drawn to social causes.

 Astrological sign

Virgo. This sign is symbolized by a virgin bearing earthly harvest. Virgos often express their love through unselfish devotion. Mother Teresa was a Virgo.

 Color

Autumn harvest. Golden as the setting sun, this color sates a hungry soul.

 Stone

Indian agate. Much folklore surrounds the Indian agate, especially those with an "eye" marking. This gemstone was used as a ward against evil in many early cultures. Major

Middle Eastern and African civilizations credit Indian agates with safety and the prevention of injury or harm from negative influences. These people also used Indian agates as an offering to appease their elemental gods when asking for protection of their harvests from droughts, floods, or insect destruction. Agates were popular as rosary beads and necklaces among Sufi saints and Indian and Persian Hindus.

Element

Silver. Silver is an excellent metal to support the mystic power of the Indian agate.

Herb

French rose *(Rosa gallica)*. French rose is found growing wild in Europe and West Asia where its seeds escaped from cultivated gardens and traveled across continents. Preparations of the dried petals were used to make cleansing rinses for minor wounds and eyewashes. Other uses included tonics for headaches and dizziness. Red roses are considered the best for medical use.

♀ THÈRÉSE: From the root name *Theresa*.

♀ THERESINA: From the root name *Theresa*.

♀ THERESITA: From the root name *Theresa*.

♂ THOM: From the root name *Thomas*.

♀ THOMA: From the root name *Thomas*.

♥ ♂ **THOMAS** Mazo, Tamek, Tammie, Tamsin, Thom, Thoma, Thomasina, Thomazine, Thompson, Thumas, Tom, Toma, Tomaso, Tomasz, Tome, Tomek, Tomlin, Tommie: *Thomas* comes from the Hebrew word meaning "twin." In the New Testament, Thomas was one of Jesus' twelve apostles, but his name may have originally been Judas, and he may have been called *Thomas* to distinguish him from Judas Iscariot and Judas, the son of James. The Greek version of *Thomas* is *Didymus,* which some authorities translate as "twin" and others as "double-minded."

The second translation hints at the biblical Thomas's doubting tendencies and sets the stage for one of the best-loved Bible stories. A passionately inquisitive man, Thomas was dubbed "Thomas the Doubter" because of his reluctance to accept the other apostles' story that they had seen the risen Christ three days after he was crucified. Eight days later, the New Testament says that Christ returned from the dead and Thomas finally saw him, put his hands in his wounds, and believed. That is when Christ said, "Because you have seen me, you have believed; blessed are those who have not seen and yet have believed."

Not much is known of Doubting Thomas after this time. The New Testament records his presence at another scene after the resurrection of Jesus—when a miraculous catch of fish occurred on Lake Tiberias. He is later thought to have been martyred in India while preaching on the Malabar coast. A large native population there still call themselves "Christians of Saint Thomas," and his shrine still stands near Madras.

Thomas's humanity in admitting his doubt has appealed to Christian preachers and lay people through the years, and this may partly explain why the name *Thomas* has remained popular. It was used by priests in England before the Norman Conquest (1066), but was not recorded as an English baptismal name before that invasion. *Thomas* became famous in the English-speaking world because of Thomas à Becket (1118–1170), the Archbishop of Canterbury, who was murdered in his cathedral because his beliefs clashed with those of Henry II. Afterward, Thomas was declared a martyr and a saint. Four hundred years later, Henry VIII tried to discredit Saint Thomas by holding a mock trial convicting him of high treason. Today, Christians still make pilgrimages to the Canterbury Cathedral.

Other saints named Thomas include Saint Thomas More, chancellor under Henry VIII, who was beheaded for refusing to let royals interfere in Church affairs. Saint Thomas Aquinas, the thirteenth-century Sicilian theologian and philosopher was the greatest thinker of the Middle Ages. His teachings—called Thomism—are basic to the Roman Catholic faith.

For centuries, *Thomas* has been one of the most widely used names in English-speaking countries, and is also well known among Spanish speakers as *Tomás*. Although its use declined in England after the 1920s, it enjoyed a revival there in the 1980s. In the United States, the name remains in wide use, consistently appearing on lists of the one hundred most popular boys' names. With film stars Tom Cruise and Tom Hanks around, the name is bound to stay popular.

Literature and folklore abound with the name *Thomas* and its nicknames *Tom* and *Tommy*. We have the nursery rhyme characters "Tom, the Piper's Son" and "Little Tommy Tucker." The expression "peeping Tom" comes from a character blinded for watching Lady Godiva ride naked around town. *Tom Jones* (1749) by Henry Fielding satirized English priggishness. *Uncle Tom's Cabin* (1852) was written by the abolitionist author Harriet Beecher Stowe, and *The Adventures of Tom Sawyer* (1876) is one of Mark Twain's best-known novels.

Surnames derived from *Thomas* include *Thompson, Thomson,* and *Tomson,* and, of course, *Thomas* itself is also used as a surname. English variants include *Thom* and *Tomas;* in Italy, *Thomaso, Maso,* or *Masuccio;* in Spain, *Tomás, Tome,* or *Mazo;* in France, *Thomas* or *Thumas;* and in Germany, *Thoma*. The feminine forms, *Thomasina* and

Thomasine, have enjoyed widespread use in Britain, but they have rarely been used in the United States.

🌀 Number

Four. Some fours consistently take the opposite view of those around them. They are not being contrary, only trying to satisfy an insatiable curiosity.

🌙 Astrological sign

Aquarius. Aquarians are ruled by the number four and are anything but conventional. Thomas Paine and Thomas Edison were Aquarians.

☀ Color

True blue. Associated with loyalty, this hue shows conviction in one's aural emanation.

◆ Stone

Blue diamond. Blue diamonds are rare and prized by collectors. They are blue-white or can be as bright as a bluejay. All emit a delicate blue radiance. Once called *vajraneel* in Hindu lore, blue diamonds were the favorite of Indra, the king of subgods. Many stories surround the diamond, perhaps stemming from the fact that it is nature's hardest gemstone. An old Eastern legend reveals that if a diamond is placed in the mouth of one who stutters, their speech affliction will be cured. The most famous diamonds in ancient times came from India. One called the "Great Mogul" was 787.5 carats.

👑 Element

Pyrite. Pyrite was used to divine the future. Ancient shamans believed it awakened psychic awareness.

❧ Herb

Twin leaf *(Jeffersonia diphylla)*. Twin leaf is a perennial found in limestone soils and wooded areas near rivers. Its horizontal rootstock and fibrous roots made preparations that were beneficial for chronic rheumatism. Used as a gargle it was helpful for throat infections. Some used it to make poultices to relieve pain from external causes.

♀   THOMASINA: From the root name *Thomas*.

♀   THOMAZINE: From the root name *Thomas*.

♂   THOMPSON: From the root name *Thomas*.

♂   THUMAS: From the root name *Thomas*.

♀   TIBBIE: From the root name *Elizabeth*.

♂   TIENNOT: From the root name *Stephen*.

♥ ♀ **TIFFANY** **Theophanie, Tiffenie, Tiffie, Tiffney:** *Tiffany* has a mystical background and meaning that has become somewhat lost in recent years. It comes from the Greek name *Theophania*, composed of the roots "theo" and "phania." *Theo* is God. *Phania* is "manifestation" or "revelation," or "fantasy"—as in the appearance of images in the mind. The name *Theophania,* then, means "appearance of God" and was used to refer to the first time the Magi saw Christ, an event called the Day of Epiphany. But the appellation also implies the spiritual vision the Magi received as they placed their gifts before the infant Christ.

Christians celebrate the Epiphany on January 6. Traditionally, girls born during the twelve days of Christmas—that is, between December 26 and January 6—were given some variant of the name.

Romans in the early years of Christianity used the name

Epifana often, as myths and miracles connected with the Day of Epiphany were thriving at that time. Byzantine emperors continued the tradition by frequently bestowing *Theophano* on their newborn daughters, and commoners imitated royalty. Epiphany legends abounded, including the unlikely tale that a Tifaine was the mother of the Magi," odd because the Magi were not known to be brothers. In A.D. 972 the Byzantine Princess Theophano married a German emperor and carried the name to Western Europe.

The medieval French rendered *Theophania* as *Tifaina* and *Tifaine*. The English picked it up from the French, using both *Tifaine* and *Epiphany* until the seventeenth century. Subsequently those names were not uncommon, but by the nineteenth century they had become rare. *Tiffany* burst on the scene again in the middle of the twentieth century—in 1961, to be exact. This time though, it carried a very different association. People linked the name to wealth and glamour thanks to the hit movie *Breakfast at Tiffany's*. By the 1970s, little girls were named *Tiffany* with increasing regularity, especially in the African American community. In 1980 *Tiffany* ranked eighteenth among names given to girls. It was used so frequently during the 1980s that by the time of the 1990 U.S. Census, it was the one hundred tenth most common name for all American females. Since then, though, the pendulum has swung again, and *Tiffany* has lost ground.

Number

Nine. The ancient numerologist, Pythagoras, chose nine as the number of righteousness.

Astrological sign

Capricorn. People born under this earth sign (December 22–January 20) take life seriously. They are strong-willed and reliable.

☀ Color

Absinthe. Green is the color of new life. It also represents Mo-li Ch'ing, the guardian of the east in Chinese legends.

◆ Stone

Nephrite jade. Ancient musicians used jade to make instruments such as gongs, wind chimes and xylophones. When jade is rapped it produces a beautifully resonant tone. These instruments were used in ceremonies by ancient Chinese, Africans, and the Hopi Indians. In New Zealand the people of the Maori tribe carve nephrite jade into images of their sacred ancestral figures with mother-of-pearl eyes. They call these figurines *hei tiki* and wear them as amulets during ceremonial occasions. Legends about nephrite call it a stone of good fortune. Some mystics believed that jade had the power to control weather. It was cast into water by shamans or holy men to bring mist, rain, or snow. Nephrite ranges in color from dark green to cream-white.

♛ Element

Gold. Gemological lore recommends that jade always be set in gold to achieve its greatest power potential.

Herb

Sacred bark *(Rhamnus purshiana).* Sacred bark is the folk name of cascara sagrada, a deciduous tree native to the mountains of North America. Its reddish brown bark made strong remedies for intestinal ills and gallstones or liver ailments.

♀   TIFFENIE: From the root name *Tiffany*.

♀   TIFFIE: From the root name *Tiffany*.

♀ TIFFNEY: From the root name *Tiffany*.

♂ TILAR: From the root name *Tyler*.

♂ TIM: From the root name *Timothy*.

♀♂ TIMMIE: From the root name *Timothy*.

♂ TIMO: From the root name *Timothy*.

♂ TIMOFEI: From the root name *Timothy*.

♂ TIMOSCHA: From the root name *Timothy*.

♂ TIMOTEO: From the root name *Timothy*.

♀ TIMOTHEA: From the root name *Timothy*.

♂ TIMOTHEE: From the root name *Timothy*.

♂ TIMOTHEO: From the root name *Timothy*.

♂ TIMOTHEUS: From the root name *Timothy*.

♥ ♂ **TIMOTHY** Teemofe, Thea, Tim, Timmie, Timo, **Timofei, Timoscha, Timoteo, Timothea, Timothee, Timotheo, Timotheus, Timoty, Tymon, Tymoteusz:** *Timothy* might be called "the comeback kid" of boys' names. Throughout its long history, it has suffered periods of neglect, but has never failed to resurface. *Timotheus* (from the Greek, meaning "to honor God") was the name of Alexander the Great's lyre player some three hundred years before the birth of Christ. Centuries later, Saint Paul influenced another Timotheus to convert to Christianity, and he eventually became bishop of Ephesus. He was the recipient of two of Paul's letters to the Ephesians found in the New Testament.

As Christianity spread throughout Europe, so did the name *Timotheus*. It received variant spellings in different cultures: *Timofei, Timoscha,* and *Teemofe* in Russia; *Timothee* in France; *Timoteo* in Italy; *Tymoteusz* in Poland; and *Timoty* in Slavic countries. The Irish adopted the

English form, *Timothy*, with the diminutive *Tim* as a Christian equivalent to their own *Tadgh* ("a bard").

In sixteenth-century England, the revival of interest in the classics—and classical names—boosted *Timothy*'s popularity, as did the Reformation's renewed emphasis on the Bible and on Bible-based, non-saints, names. *Timothy* remained in steady if not spectacular use throughout the seventeenth and eighteenth centuries in the United Kingdom.

Among the settlers of New England, *Timothy* was not an unusual name, but neither was it popular. To pun lovers, it might have seemed as common as grass: American farmer Timothy Hanson introduced timothy grass—a coarse grass used for fodder—in the United States around 1730–1740. *Timothy* was briefly popular in the United States around 1800, then became relatively rare in the second half of the nineteenth century. Timothy Michael Healy (1855–1931), who became the Governor-General of Ireland, probably helped influence the widespread use of the name—and especially of the nickname *Tim*—among the Irish immigrants in the United States.

During the last half of the twentieth century, *Timothy* enjoyed a wave of genuine popularity. In 1960, it peaked as the fifteenth name most commonly given to boys. It has slowly moved down the list since then but is still among the top fifty names given to boys.

⊚ Number

Two. Twos are tender-hearted and follow the path of true love until they find their soul mates. Once they do, they are devoted forever. Many pursue careers in music.

☾ Astrological sign

Scorpio. Piety and resolution are characteristics of Scorpios. Many find happiness and fulfillment through their spiritual quests.

Color

Crimson madder. Robes of deep red were worn by ancient priests to symbolize devotion to their faith.

 ## Stone

Red lace agate. Belonging to the huge variegated chalcedony clan, agates were used in ritual to cleanse both body and spirit. In particular, ancient healers believed that red lace agates would purify the blood. It was felt that agates could enhance strength during recovery. While most agates were thought to be protective stones, lace agates were used to alter attitudes, especially despair or depression. Although agates are found everywhere, some of the most beautiful gems come from the southwestern United States.

Element

Brass. Agates set in brass boost mental energy. Brass's high iron content also highlights any red gem it supports.

 ## Herb

Grass burdock *(Arctium lappa)*. Burdock grows wild in the northern United States and in Europe. Its roots, seeds and leaves have curative ability and were used in a variety of herbal remedies. The root made tea and tinctures to help stomach distress. Fresh leaves were used for liver problems and in treatments of poison oak or ivy. The seeds produce an oil that should only be used under proper medical supervision.

♂ TIMOTY: From the root name *Timothy*.

♀ TINA: From the root names *Austin, Christopher, Constance,* and *Martha*.

♀   TINE: From the root name *Martha*.

♂   TINO: From the root name *Christopher*.

♀   TINY: From the root name *Christopher*.

♀♂   TOBE: From the root name *Toby*.

♂   TOBIAH: From the root name *Toby*.

♂   TOBIAS: From the root name *Toby*.

♂   TOBIN: From the root name *Toby*.

♂   TOBIT: From the root name *Toby*.

♥ ♀♂ **TOBY** **Tobe, Tobiah, Tobias, Tobin, Tobit, Tova:**
Toby is the short form for *Tobias,* which means "God is good" in Hebrew. The name comes from a character in one of the Bible's most dramatic stories, the Book of Tobit.

The story begins with Tobit, the father of Tobias. After the destruction of the Northern Kingdom of Israel (in the eighth century, B.C.), he is forced to live in exile in Ninevah. For many years he prospers. But when he bravely buries Jewish victims of the new, oppressive King Sennacherib, all his property is confiscated and he and his family must flee. Their joy at being able to return after Sennacherib's death is cut short when Tobit is blinded by cataracts.

After praying for death, Tobit asks his son Tobias to travel to Media to recover funds he left with a kinsman there years before—those funds will be Tobias's only legacy. Before setting out on his journey, Tobias unknowingly hires the angel Raphael as a guide. When Tobias stops to bathe, a large fish tries to swallow his foot. Raphael advises him to grab the fish and not let go. Then, after ordering him to cut out and keep the fish's gall, heart, and liver, Raphael promises a doubting Tobias that these will make useful medicines.

Tobias finds out just how useful when he and Raphael arrive at the house of Raguel, another kinsman. Raguel offers Tobias his daughter Sarah as a bride. But there's a complication: Each of Sarah's seven previous husbands were killed by a jealous demon on their wedding night. Not to worry, Raphael tells the understandably nervous Tobias: Remember the fish's liver and heart? Burn them like incense in the bedroom. Repelled by the smell, Sarah's demon-lover flees—never to return.

Tobias and Sarah, still accompanied by Raphael, retrieve Tobit's funds from his kinsman and return to Ninevah. Raphael reminds Tobias that he still has the fish's gall and instructs him to smear it on Tobit's eyes. Again, the foul-smelling but heaven-sent medicine works: The cataracts peel away, and Tobit's eyesight returns. During the celebrations that follow, Raphael finally reveals his angelic nature.

Though some questioned the Book of Tobit's validity, its larger than life elements made Tobias's story a frequent theme in the art of the late Middle Ages, and thus spread the popularity of the name. *Tobias* became *Tewes* in Germany, *Tobia* in Italy, and *Tobie* in France.

In later centuries, the short form *Toby* enjoyed a more down-to-earth life of its own—whether as the name of the dog in Punch and Judy puppet shows, as nineteenth-century slang for cheap cigars or as a collector's term for those prized mugs in the shape of a stout old gentleman with a cigar. *Toby Tyler* (1881), the classic children's book about a boy who runs away to join a circus—and the subsequent movie versions of that book—may have helped popularize *Toby* in the United States.

Recently, the name has undergone some gender jumping, as more and more parents choose to name their daughters *Toby* or one of several variants: *Tobe, Tobee, Tobey, Tobi, Tobie.*

⊙ Number

Three. This number is tied to Pluto, god of the underworld. Threes face many challenges in their lives and have the ability to meet and beat them all.

☾ Astrological sign

Pisces. Pisces's symbol of two fish swimming in opposite directions represents Venus and Cupid, who threw themselves into the Euphrates River to escape danger. Like fish, a Piscean finds peace in or around water.

☀ Color

Persian blue. A deep rich shade of blue promotes divine blessing and healing energy.

◆ Stone

Azurite. Ancient Romans and Egyptians believed that azurite gave its owner great insight. Ancient seers used it to enhance their visionary powers. Some healers employed it as a stone to induce hypnosis before treating wounds or performing surgery. Many mystics used it to help them relax and dispel inner turmoil. Azurite is a dark blue gem laced with greenish blue or bright green malachite. Azurite occurs near copper deposits.

♛ Element

Copper. Copper is the perfect enhancer for the healing powers of azurite. Today, copper is used as an electrical conductor.

🦎 Herb

Eye root *(Hydrastis canadensis)*. This small plant is usually cultivated but still grows wild in shaded woods or damp meadows. It has a knotty yellow root that has external and internal uses. A tea can be applied with a toothbrush for sore gums or used as antiseptic gargle or mouthwash. It also makes soothing eyewashes when combined with boric acid.

♂   TOD: From the root name *Todd*.

♥ ♂ **TODD** Tod: Most scholars list as the meaning for *Todd,* "fox-hunter." In Old English, *todde* means "fox," and the words are still used interchangeably in some parts of Britain. The theory is that *Todd* became an occupational surname for men who made their living hunting fox. Then, of course, it followed the usual progression, becoming a first name when mothers whose maiden names were *Todd* gave the name to their sons.

All that sounds logical enough, but it is just as likely that *Todd,* with its association to the fox, originally designated someone who was shrewd and crafty. While many names can be traced to vocations, a significant number derive from nicknames. Nicknames were fashionable in Europe during the Middle Ages because surnames were not yet established. Many nicknames came from nature since most of the population made a living by hunting and farming. In addition, legends about animals abounded in ballads and folklore. A work called *Physiologus*—a not-quite-scientific compendium of animals that included commentaries on their moral character—was almost as widely read and quoted as the Bible. The fox, or *todd,* was a prominent character in *Physiologus* and in a vast number of songs and fables. Thus, if someone's neighbor exhibited the foxlike traits known from popular lore, he became known as *le fox* or "the *todd.*"

Medieval documents list several families called *le Fox* throughout the British Isles. *Le Tod* and *Todd* were found as well, although more frequently in northern England and Scotland.

As a first name, *Todd* was rare in the United States until the late 1930s. Its popularity increased steadily and reached an apex in 1970. *Todd* declined sharply after that. It has, however, endured. It remains a common surname in the United States and in England.

 ## Number
Seven. Most sevens have an innate ability to clear life's hurdles with shrewd use of their intuitive gifts.

 ## Astrological sign
Gemini. Being ruled by Mercury helps Geminis to be adaptable and resourceful.

 ## Color
Maize. Shades of yellow enhance psychic awareness and confidence.

 ## Stone
Yellow tourmaline. Tourmalines appear in a vast assortment of colors. Tourmalines were believed to be able to transfer energy between two people who are important to each other. Yellow tourmaline was especially powerful in matters of communication on an intellectual level. Gemological lore ties yellow stones with the planet Mercury, which also rules Gemini.

 ## Element
Pyrite. Pyrite is also called "fool's gold" because it is found near veins of real gold. Ancient magicians believed it aided in spells of disguise created to avoid evil or an enemy's curse.

🦎 Herb

Slippery root *(Symphytum officinale)*. Rootstock preparations of slippery root made healthy mouthwashes and throat gargles. Taken internally, the preparation helped digestive ailments. Powdered rootstock was mixed with other herbs for wound poultices, bruises, sores, and insect bites. Hot rootstock pulp made healing chest plasters for pleurisy.

♀ TOINETTE: From the root name *Anthony*.

♂ TOM: From the root name *Thomas*.

♀ TOMA: From the root name *Thomas*.

♂ TOMASO: From the root name *Thomas*.

♂ TOMASZ: From the root name *Thomas*.

♂ TOME: From the root name *Thomas*.

♂ TOMEK: From the root name *Thomas*.

♂ TOMLIN: From the root name *Thomas*.

♀♂ TOMMIE: From the root name *Thomas*.

♂ TONETTO: From the root name *Anthony*.

♀♂ TONI: From the root name *Anthony*.

♀ TONIA: From the root name *Anthony*.

♂ TONIO: From the root name *Anthony*.

♀♂ TONY: From the root name *Anthony*.

♀ TONYE: From the root name *Anthony*.

♀ TOVA: From the root name *Toby*.

♀ TRACY: From the root name *Theresa*.

♂ TRAVER: From the root name *Travis*.

♂ TRAVERS: From the root name *Travis*.

♥ ♂ **TRAVIS** Traver, Travers, Travys: *Travis* was originally a surname and came from the French word *travers,* which means "crossing place." England acquired the term from the Norman conquerors, and it was most often used to denote a ford or bridge where tolls were paid. In this way the surname came to mean "toll collector." *Travis* came into use as a first name chiefly in the United States, though no one is exactly certain when it made the transition from surname to first name.

As a surname, *Travis* is common, though not prominent in American history. Probably the most important American *Travis* is Colonel William B. Travis, who was a leader in the ill-fated attempt to hold the Alamo. Another, lesser known *Travis* is Walter J. Travis. Many consider him to be the first great U.S. golfer. He won both the U.S. Amateur and the British Amateur titles early in the twentieth century. Ironically, the next important American golfer had a surname from the same source as *Travis*. A few years after Walter Travis won his titles, Jerome D. Travers won both the U.S. Amateur Championship and the U.S. Open title.

There is one *Travis* who, in terms of name recognition, outshines all the others. Travis Bickle is the hero (or anti-hero, if you prefer) of Martin Scorsese's film *Taxi Driver.* As played by Robert De Niro, Travis Bickle uttered the now famous line: "You talkin' to me?" Considering that in the film Travis Bickle tries to assassinate a politician, it is doubtful that his character moved many parents to adopt the name. Nonetheless, whatever their inspiration, parents have become increasingly fond of *Travis*.

 Number

Eight. Eights have the will to drive themselves to greatness.

☾ Astrological sign

Sagittarius. Sagittarians often view life as a series of cross-roads. They are inspired by continual challenge.

☀ Color

Alamo twilight. Shades of purple signify honor in many cultures.

◆ Stone

Staurolite. One of staurolite's folk names is "cross stone." Legends of good fortune surround this unique stone, and American presidents Roosevelt, Wilson, and Harding carried pieces of it for luck. Staurolite occurs in twinned crystals that form equal-armed crosses. In ancient Brittany, peasants believed staurolite fell from the skies, and many carried a piece as a charm. European magicians used staurolite to represent the four elements.

♛ Element

Tin. Tin is linked with Jupiter, Sagittarius's ruling planet. In metallurgic lore, tin is considered to be a lucky metal.

⚘ Herb

Traveler's joy *(Verbena hastata).* This native North American plant has small dark blue or purplish blue flowers. The rootstock and the herb have medicinal value as a tranquilizer. Warm tea brewed from either the rootstock or herb was used for fevers, colds, and chest congestion. A cold tea was used to treat festering sores and wounds.

♂   TRAVYS: From the root name *Travis.*

♂   TREFOR: From the root name *Trevor.*

♀   TRESHA: From the root name *Theresa*.

♀   TRESSA: From the root name *Theresa*.

♀   TRESSIE: From the root name *Theresa*.

♂   TREVAR: From the root name *Trevor*.

♥ ♂ **TREVOR** **Trefor, Trevar:** *Trevor* is the English version of *Trefor,* which is a combination of the Welsh words *tref,* meaning "homestead," and *mawr,* meaning "great." Towns called *Trefor* appear in various places on a map of Wales. *Trevor* most likely developed as a surname in Wales in response to the question newcomers anywhere are asked most often, "So, where are you from?"

Trefor appears as the middle name of several prominent Welshmen of the Middle Ages, including two bishops of Llandaff and the tenth-century chieftain, Tudor Trefor ap Ynyr. Because the *Trefor*s, as their name suggests, were most likely landholders, they could in a sense afford a place-name surname at a time when most poor Welsh had none at all. Up until the nineteenth century, many were known by their lineage alone, which led to long, awkward constructions, such as *Owen* ap (son of) *Gryffydd ap Rhys.*

In the mid-nineteenth century, *Trevor* began appearing as a given name, perhaps in tribute to a mother's side of the family. It had its greatest popularity in the first half of the twentieth century, and by 1950, it was twenty-nine in a ranking of boys' names in the United Kingdom. Was that influenced by the distinguished British film actor Trevor Howard (1916–1988)? Perhaps so. By 1965—just about the time Trevor Howard made the transition from romantic lead to character actor—Trevor dropped to forty-two in the ranking, and it has declined since then.

Not seen as a first name in the United States until the twentieth century, Trevor is less a name with a past here—

and more a name with a future. Names experts point out that British-born surnames (*Tyler, Travis*) are very popular as given names for boys now. *Trevor* fits that pattern to a *T*, ranking among the top one hundred names for boys in the late 1990s. Though unusual in the United States yet, several spelling variants exist including *Trev, Trevar, Trever,* and *Trevis*.

 ## Number

Eight. In mathematics eight is the cube of two and some numerologists link eights to the adage "salt of the Earth," as this mineral crystallizes into cubes.

Astrological sign

Virgo. Most Virgos are practical as is befitting of their earth element. But since this sign is also ruled by the unpredictable planet of Mercury, Virgos can be versatile and restless.

Color

Valley harvest. The earth tones of healthy vegetation and soil represent health and plentiful life.

 ## Stone

Brown druzy quartz. All types of quartz are known for their high energy and ability to enhance communication. Druzy comes in several colors and is composed of small bubbles of quartz that resemble sea foam. The energy within this transparent gem depends on the mineral associated with each color. Brown was used to strengthen the physical body as well as the mind. Quartz was supposedly used in the secretive Eleusinian rituals to evoke sacred fire from the sun.

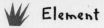

Element

Gold. Gold is a high energy ore and will boost the power of quartz to its highest power level.

Herb

Walewort *(Sambucus ebulus).* A type of dwarf elder, walewort is a perennial shrub that grows in clusters in the United States and Europe. Its creeping rootstock was used in homeopathic preparations for intestinal ailments. The black, four-seeded berries are poisonous and should never be used.

♀ TRICIA: From the root name *Patrick.*

♀ TRINA: From the root name *Katherine.*

♀ TRINETTE: From the root name *Katherine.*

♂ TRIS: From the root name *Tristan.*

♀ TRISHA: From the root name *Patrick.*

♂ TRISTAM: From the root name *Tristan.*

♂ TRISTRAM: From the root name *Tristan.*

♥ ♂ **TRISTAN** Tris, Tristam, Tristram, Trystan: *Tristan* has a complex and romantic history. Although the Celtic meaning is "a herald," the name also has roots in the French word *triste* and the Latin word *tristus,* both meaning "sorrowful." Legend has it that when Tristan's mother realized she was dying just after he was born, she asked her handmaiden to christen the baby Tristan, meaning "a sorrowful birth."

A better known medieval legend is the tragic love story of *Tristan and Isolde.* In one representative version, Sir Tristan of Lyonesse is the bravest knight in King Arthur's court. He is sent to Ireland by his uncle, King Mark of

Cornwall, to bring home the king's betrothed, Princess Isolde the Fair. Before the voyage, Isolde's mother gives Isolde's maid a love potion to be drunk by the bride and groom on their wedding day. But on the way home, a storm arises at sea, and the maid becomes confused and gives the love potion to Tristan and Isolde, hoping it will calm them. It has quite the opposite effect, and they fall desperately in love.

When Isolde marries King Mark, a heartbroken Tristan leaves Cornwall to fight for King Howel of Brittany. When Tristan is critically wounded in battle, he sends for Isolde, hoping her love will cure him. But he's already dead when she arrives, and so she dies of grief beside his coffin.

Historically, folk legends have been written to make names conform to a recognizable word, and this is probably what happened with Tristan—linking the name to the French and Latin words for sadness. But at the same time, Sir Tristan of Lyonesse was a real Arthurian hero immortalized in Malory's *Morte d'Arthur* and Swinburne's *Tristram of Lyonesse*. His tomb in England bears the name *Drustagni*, an early form of *Tristan*.

Today, *Tristan* is gaining in popularity in the United States. In 1977, it was ranked the fifty-first most popular boys' name. Still associated with romance and glamour, *Tristan* is often put into the category of "New Age" names—masculine yet sensitive—with just enough panache to have true star quality.

Variations in spelling include *Trystan* (mainly Welsh) and *Tristram* (English), which was a rather common name during the Middle Ages. *Tristram* was made famous in Laurence Sterne's eighteenth-century novel *Tristram Shandy*. In a well-known passage in that book, the narrator comments that first names have a lasting effect on people's characters and then calls *Tristram* the worst name in the universe.

⊚ Number

Two. In most numerological lore, twos are considered great romantics. However, they will become melancholy when love does not go the way they want it to.

☾ Astrological sign

Cancer. This sign is ruled by the moon and the number two—a combination that makes Cancers vulnerable to matters of the heart.

☀ Color

Sea green. This blending of blue and green calms a troubled mind and elates the soul.

◆ Stone

Conch shell. The bright pink and white interior layers of conch shells are often carved into intricate cameos or other decorative pieces. Shells make beautiful organic jewelry and were used for centuries to create images that honored sea gods. Early Romans built their cities by the sea and made fans, earrings, hair accessories, and even plates or utensils from shells. Folklore equates shells with physical strength and power.

♛ Element

Silver. Silver is considered a moon metal because of its tie to the sign of Cancer. It also acts as a stabilizing energy for any gem it holds.

♘ Herb

Heartweed (*Polygonum persicaria*). In European folk medical lore, this plant's herb was used to make remedies for arthritis, lung problems, jaundice, and eczema. Juice pressed from the herb was applied to wounds, bruises, and cuts. Some may be sensitive to this plant and herbalists used it with care. It has spikes of greenish, magenta, or pink flowers.

♂   TRISTRAM: From the root name *Tristan*.

♂   TROI: From the root name *Troy*.

♥ ♂ **TROY** **Troi, Troye:** Substituting surnames and place names for first names is all the rage now, but *Troy* probably made that leap centuries ago. It probably comes from Troyes, a city in France, and means "water" or "foot soldier." But when we hear it, we usually think of the ancient city of Troy in Asia Minor, described in Homer's *Iliad*.

The Trojan War may have been based on an actual conflict in twelve-fifty B.C. In the legend, Greece went to war against Troy because Paris, a Trojan, abducted Helen, the wife of Menelaus of Sparta. The Greek army attacked Troy for ten years, then pretended to withdraw. But they left behind an enormous wooden horse, which the Trojans dragged through the city gates. That night, Greek soldiers hidden inside the horse opened the gates and let in the Greek army, killing most of the Trojans and burning the city. Medieval legend says that a few Trojans survived and later founded Rome and Great Britain.

As a first name in the United States, *Troy* reached its peak in the late 1950s and early 1960s when the actor Troy Donahue was popular, and stars and singing idols had names like *Chad*, *Dean*, and *Rick*, which seem associated with the era when *Troy* was widespread. Now, after several years in relative obscurity, *Troy* is coming back into fashion, perhaps because of the general upsurge of place names–to–given names (*Dakota*, *Montana*, and *Chelsea*) and surnames–to–given names, such as *Avery*, *Murphy*, and *Forrest*.

Number

Six. A six can draw multitudes to their cause—whether it's for right or wrong. When roused by anger or jealousy they will fight to the death for the person or purpose they support. Napoleon was born under the number six.

Astrological sign

Sagittarius. Jupiter influences people born under this sign to seek the best from life. A Sagittarian will pursue his goal with lust and the spirit of the hunt.

Color

Mauve. Purple is the color most often connected to Sagittarius. It is thought to help boost spiritual and physical strength.

Stone

Violet spinel. Spinel comes in a large range of hues. Color is determined by the presence of other minerals. A violet or pinkish mauve tint comes from magnesium and aluminum. Ancient gemologists referred to violet spinel as Balas ruby for the Balascia region of Afghanistan where they occur. Spinel can be cut in a variety of shapes and makes exquisite jewelry.

Element

Gold. Gold is considered the metal of lovers. Its high energy, fueled by its fire element, makes a perfect setting for violet spinel.

Herb

Soldier's herb (*Plantago lanceolata*). Soldier's herb belongs to the plantain family and grows throughout North America and Europe. The entire plant has curative uses including preparations for bladder troubles and various kinds of ulcers. Herbal lore cites that chewing the rootstock will relieve toothaches. It once was thought that a plant juice concoction increased virility.

♂ TROYE: From the root name *Troy*.

♂ TRYSTAN: From the root name *Tristan*.

♂ TUDOR: From the root name *Theodore*.

♂ TY: From the root name *Tyler*.

♂ TYLAR: From the root name *Tyler*.

♥ ♂ **TYLER** Tilar, Ty, Tylar: *Tyler* comes from the Old English word *tiler,* a medieval designation for someone who either made or worked with tiles. *Tiler* derives from *tigl,* an even older, almost prehistoric word that ancient Germanic tribes used to designate anything covering the tops of their dwellings.

In medieval Britain, homes and churches were roofed with straw. Families hired skilled thatchers and reeders to perform the work. (These men's families eventually took the surnames *Thatcher* and *Reed*.) But straw roofs were so prone to catching fire that more and more hamlets outlawed their use. Tilers increased in importance as the Middle Ages progressed, and the name became more frequent and widespread.

Tyler as a surname traveled to the United States during the early Colonial period. A William Tyler was among Virginia's first governors. The governor named his son John, and John Tyler, of course, served as U.S. President from 1841 to 1845.

The previous centuries had seen some migration of last names to first names (such as *Todd* and *Clark*). But the custom of baptizing children with family names was not yet common—at least it was not as fashionable as it would later become in the South, especially for daughters. (Although parents had begun to call their sons *Washington* after the first president, there is no evidence that *Tyler* enjoyed the same honor.) Well-to-do Protestant parents began to use *Tyler* as a boy's given name starting around the 1940s. Nearly half a century later it was still so rare that it was almost always excluded from baby-naming books. Beginning around 1990 though, English occupational surnames took the maternity wards by storm. *Tyler* was the twenty-fourth most popular boys' name in 1990. It remained among the top twenty-five names most commonly given to baby boys throughout the 1990s.

 ## Number

Eight. The number eight is tied to Capricorn and its ruling planet, Saturn. Eights may hide their true feelings, but have warm hearts nonetheless.

 ## Astrological sign

Capricorn. Terms such as reliable, careful and prudent are often associated with Capricorns. Actress Mary Tyler Moore is a Capricorn.

 ## Color

Terra cotta. Tile and pottery are often made from this reddish brown clay. Metaphysically, a combination of red and brown stimulates earthly energy.

 ## Stone

Marbled breccia. Marble is a metamorphic rock that forms slowly over a long period of time. The final result is beautiful and worth the wait. Marbled breccia comes from the Apuan Alps outside Tuscany, Italy. It is a light-colored gray or off-white background with rust-colored veins running through the matrix. Quite lustrous when polished, it's highly valued for expensive interior flooring.

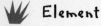 **Element**

Calcite. Calcite is one of the minerals that compose brecciated marble.

Herb

American linden *(Tilia americana)*. Also called a basswood tree, the American linden grows mainly in the eastern United States and Canada. Some reach heights of 120 feet. Medicinal parts of the tree include its flowers, leaves and bark. Traditionally, the leaves and flowers were used as a home remedy for relief of cold symptoms. The inner bark was used by Native Americans to make salves for irritated skin and burns.

♂   TYMON: From the root name *Timothy*.

♂   TYMOTEUSZ: From the root name *Timothy*.

♂   UGO: From the root name *Hugh*.

♀♂ VAL: From the root name *Valerie*.

♀ VALARIA: From the root name *Valerie*.

♀ VALE: From the root name *Valerie*.

♀ VALERIA: From the root name *Valerie*.

♂ VALERIAN: From the root name *Valerie*.

♥ ♀ VALERIE   Val, Valaria, Vale, Valeria, Valerian, Valerio, Valery, Vallie, Valorie, Valry: *Valerie* derives from the Latin clan name *Valerius*, which means "strong" or "healthy." Like many of the ancient Roman family names, it was frequently chosen by Christian parents.

There were at least three saints named *Valerie* or *Valeria* by the time of the Middle Ages, and in their honor many parents named their daughters by variants of the names. The worship of Saint Valerie was particularly strong in France and Italy, and to this day *Valerie* is popular in France and *Valeria* in Italy. In Britain, *Valeria* was found until the 1890s. After that, foreign names came into vogue and the French *Valerie* was adopted and replaced the earlier form. To name a daughter *Valerie* was considered the height of fashion in Britain from the 1930s to 1960s. It took a little longer to catch on in the United States, and while it was not uncommon here, Americans did not favor *Valerie* to the same degree. *Valerie* became even less frequent here in the 1970s, and has not been a strong name since then, though it is still in use.

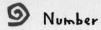 ## Number

Nine. Some nines may be impulsive. They have courage and a sense of justice.

Astrological sign

Leo. People born under this summer sign are known for their strong personalities. Actress Valerie Harper is a Leo.

Color

Sunrise. The colors of a summer sunrise inspire healthy spirits and happiness.

Stone

Orange calcite. Transparent calcite crystals are prismatic, and come in pastel colors. Orange calcite is actually closer to a light peach color. Twinned crystals are common. Gem mystics believed that orange stones boosted personal power and attracted luck or success.

Element

Gold. Gold's fiery energy is perfect for orange calcite. Ancient shamans believed all metals were potent tools of magic, but gold was believed to be one of the strongest because of its tie to the sun.

Herb

Fragrant valerian *(Valeriana officinalis)*. This plant is common in the eastern United States and throughout Europe. Its yellowish brown tuberous rootstock was useful for numerous types of nervous ailments such as insomnia, hyperactivity, and migraine headaches. Taken as a tea, it also helped fatigue and stomach cramps.

♂ VALERIO: From the root name *Valerie*.

♀♂ VALERY: From the root name *Valerie*.

♀ VALLIE: From the root name *Valerie*.

♀ VALORIE: From the root name *Valerie*.

♀ VALRY: From the root name *Valerie*.

♂ VALTHER: From the root name *Walter*.

♀ VAN: From the root name *Vanessa*.

♂ VANEK: From the root name *John*.

♥ ♀ **VANESSA** **Nessa, Nessie, Van, Vanetta, Vanija, Vanna, Vanya, Venetta:** There are at least two possibilities for the origin of *Vanessa*. The Greek word *phanes* means "butterfly," and one of the Greek mystic divinities was named *Phanessa*. Obviously, *Vanessa* may have evolved forthwith.

There is another theory, however, that the name was the invention of Jonathan Swift (1667–1745), the Anglo-Irish author of *Gulliver's Travels*. Extravagantly feminine names first came into fashion during the Restoration period in England (1660–1688). During this era of literary and scientific accomplishment, playwrights wrote ribald, satirical comedies and made up names for their heroines that had Latin endings, like *Pamela, Amanda, Belinda,* and *Hortensia*. The first recorded English use of *Vanessa* appears in Swift's "Cadenus and Vanessa," a poem about a man who refuses a marriage proposal from a young lady called Esther Vanhomrigh. In fact, Esther Vanhomrigh was one of Swift's loves. In this case, *Vanessa* is apparently a combination of *Van,* the first syllable of her Dutch surname, and the suffix *essa,* which is similar to the first syllable of her given name.

A pretty, soft-sounding name, *Vanessa* is just as much in style today as it was in Swift's time. It does not lend itself to nicknames, but *Nessa* is a popular diminutive.

⊚ Number

Nine. Nine is sometimes tied to the art of healing in modern numerological lore.

☾ Astrological sign

Gemini. Some astrologers link animals or insects to the zodiacal signs. Butterflies are connected to Gemini.

❋ Color

Monarch wings. Like the soft orange, black, and yellow hues of the monarch butterfly, this combination of colors allows the mind to soar, taking heart and soul with it.

◆ Stone

Yellow apatite. This transparent crystalline stone is relatively soft, making it difficult to facet. However, when cut correctly the gem has strong color and bright sparkle. It's a favorite of many collectors. Yellow apatite is found in Brazil and Mexico.

♕ Element

Lodestone. Metallurgic lore tells of the lodestone's power to attract love. An old Roman legend says that when a lodestone statue of Venus and an iron image of Mars were placed in a temple, somehow Venus moved Mars next to her.

♘ Herb

Butter rose *(Primula officinalis)*. A variety of primrose, butter rose is common in Great Britain and Europe. Several parts of the plant have medicinal value including the flowers, herb, and rootstock. A flower potion helps migraines, insomnia, and various nervous conditions. Flower tea was recommended for rheumatic symptoms. Rootstock made strong remedies for coughs and bronchitis. Butter rose's yellow funnel-shaped flowers bloom during April and May.

♀ VANETTA: From the root name *Vanessa*.

♀ VANIJA: From the root name *Vanessa*.

♂ VANKO: From the root name *John*.

♀ VANNA: From the root name *Vanessa*.

♀ VANYA: From the root names *John* and *Vanessa*.

♀ VARINA: From the root name *Barbara*.

♀ VARVARA: From the root name *Barbara*.

♀ VEERA: From the root name *Veronica*.

♀ VELMA: From the root name *William*.

♀ VENETTA: From the root name *Vanessa*.

♀ VERA: From the root name *Veronica*.

♀ VERLEE: From the root name *Beverly*.

♀ VERLYE: From the root name *Beverly*.

♀ VEROHNICCA: From the root name *Veronica*.

♥ ♀ **VERONICA** **Rana, Ron, Ronica, Ronnie, Veera, Vera, Verohnicca, Veronice, Veronika, Veronike, Veronique, Vonnie:** *Veronica,* which is among the top one hundred girls' names, has roots in the first days of Christianity. The name is a hybrid of the Latin word *vera,* "true," and the Greek word *eikon,* "image." *Veronica* owes its longevity to the power of a biblical legend about how Jesus cured a nameless woman.

In this legend, a woman had been sick for twelve years with "an issue of blood" that no doctor could cure. She was present the day Jesus was crucified and struggled through the crowd to touch the hem of his garment. Miraculously, she was healed on the spot. She then walked with Jesus as he carried the cross to Calvary, wiping the blood and sweat from his face with her handkerchief. Later, she found his image imprinted on the cloth. Called "Veronica's Handkerchief," the cloth is now a sacred relic in Rome.

During the ensuing years, face cloths called "Veronicas" were used by Christians living in the Roman catacombs. These cloths ostensibly held the imprint of Christ's features. No one knows which came first—the face cloths called Veronicas or the use of *Veronica* as a personal name. In fact, *Veronica* may actually have been redefined to mean "true image" in order to fit it to the biblical story.

In the eighteenth century, Veronica of Milan, a fifteenth-century monastic nun, was canonized a saint. The fact that this Saint Veronica started out as a poor working girl undoubtedly added to the popularity of this name among the common populace.

Beginning in the seventeenth century, Roman Catholics in Scotland began using the name *Veronica*. They were certainly influenced by the saint, but the Veronica is also a flower prevalent in Scotland. It is a brilliant blue color that might be said to reflect the image of the heavens. In the nineteenth century, many French peasant parents named their daughters *Veronica* or *Veronique,* and the name came into wider use. It enjoyed moderate popularity in the 1920s and 1930s, then had a revival in the 1950s, perhaps because of the sultry actress Veronica Lake. Since the 1980s, the name has rarely cropped up in Great Britain. However, *Veronica* is holding its own in the United States, especially among African American parents, who often spell it *Veronice* or *Veronique.*

Veronica is popular in France as *Veronique,* in Germany as *Veronike,* and in Scandinavia as *Veronika.* In the United States, the pet name for girls named *Veronica* is *Ronnie* or *Roni.*

⊚ Number

Six. In numerology, six is tied to the planet Venus, Taurus's ruling celestial body. Sixes are determined and often possess an obstinate streak.

☾ Astrological sign

Taurus. Earthy Taureans are loyal and steadfast in matters of the heart and spirit.

☀ Color

Red bud blossom. This delicate shade of lavender appears on the spring-rejuvenated red bud tree. Purple represents spiritual devotion in many cultures.

◆ Stone

Heliotrope. Dark green and red-spotted heliotrope is from the chalcedony family. The red spots or blotches are from the presence of iron oxides. These distinct marks resemble blood, hence the gem's nickname of plasma. Middle Ages mystics connected special powers to heliotrope including the ability to heal. Many also wore it to calm fears, increase courage or dispel anger. Other legends tell of longer life for anyone who owned this mysterious gem. Some ancients believed that dreaming of a heliotrope meant that distressing news would soon be delivered.

☗ Element

Gold. Gold has a rich metaphysical history. Some metallurgists believed it enhanced the power of any gem it touched.

☖ Herb

Speedwell *(Veronica officinalis)*. Speedwell is a small plant that grows in dry fields and meadows. The flowering herb has many uses. European herbal lore suggests speedwell can be used to heal everything. However, most herbalists use it for respiratory problems and headaches. It has light blue flowers with violet streaks.

♀ VERONICE: From the root name *Veronica*.

♀ VERONIKA: From the root name *Veronica*.

♀ VERONIKE: From the root name *Veronica*.

♀ VERONIQUE: From the root name *Veronica*.

♀♂ VIC: From the root name *Victor*.

♀ VICENTA: From the root name *Vincent*.

♂ VICENTE: From the root name *Vincent*.

♀ VICENTIA: From the root name *Vincent*.

♀ VICENTINE: From the root name *Vincent*.

♂ VICENZIO: From the root name *Vincent*.

♀♂ VICKIE: From the root name *Victor*.

♥ ♂ VICTOR   Vic, Vickie, Victoria, Victorien, Victorina, Victorine, Vidor, Viktor, Viktorija, Vittore, Vittoria, Vittorio, Vittorios: The names *Victor* and *Victoria* come from the Latin and mean "conqueror" and "victory" respectively. *Victor* and *Victoria* were commonly found in Christian inscriptions of the Roman Empire. The names signify the deep faith of the early Christians and were conferred on many men and women who were martyred for their religion.

Because of its popularity among early Christians, several saints and popes were designated *Victor*. Saint Victorinus and Saint Victor were third-century martyrs during the reign of King Decius of Rome. The king had them tortured on racks and whipped. Victorinus was then tossed into a huge marble mortar and pounded to death. Witnessing his friend's faith and courage, Victor was inspired to say: "In that is salvation and true felicity prepared for me." This inspired the king to also have Victor tossed into the mortar and pounded to death.

Other religious figures who add to the glory and popularity of the name are Saint Victor de Plancy, a French hermit who had heavenly visions, and Saint Victor of Damascus, who was thrown into a fiery furnace and stayed there for three days without being burned.

Vittore became a favorite Italian name when an early pope and several martyrs shared it, and *Victor* became fashionable in France during the French Revolution in the eighteenth century. It was seldom used in English-speaking countries until the 1850s. It reached its peak in Great Britain from 1900–1935, and in the United States in the late 1950s.

Victor is a solid-sounding, manly name that's never been truly in or out. In Germany, Scandinavia, Poland, and Czechoslovakia, the name is spelled *Viktor*. The nickname is *Vic*.

A favorite name today, *Victoria*'s most famous progenitor was the Roman goddess of victory. However, the first *Victoria* in recorded history was a third-century Roman virgin who was stabbed to death when she refused to marry a heathen husband or worship a heathen idol.

In Great Britain, the form *Victory* was popular as a girl's name in the sixteenth century, but *Victoria* was rarely used until the start of the nineteenth century. The name gained some popularity with the accession in 1837 of Queen Victoria, who acquired the name from her German mother, Mary Louise Victoria. Although the nation was entranced by the young Queen Victoria, her name wasn't widely used until around the turn of the twentieth century, after her death in 1901. It was then that *Victor* simultaneously started becoming popular. *Victoria* became wildly popular in Great Britian beginning in the 1940s, reaching a peak in the 1970s. It caught on in the United States in the 1950s, 1960s, and 1970s and is still widely used today.

Victoria is popular in Germany and Scandinavia as *Viktoria,* and in Italy as *Vittoria.* The French forms are *Victoire* and *Victorine.* Pet names for *Victoria* are *Viccy, Vicky, Vikki, Vickie, Vicki* (most popular in the United States), and recently, *Tory* or *Torrie.*

Number

Six. Sixes have the drive to conquer the world if they so desire. England's Queen Victoria was born under this number.

Astrological sign

Sagittarius. This sign is ruled by the element of fire, which fuels a Sagittarian's inspiration to fulfill their destiny.

Color

Gridelin. All shades of purple are tied to Sagittarius. This color also signifies victory in some ancient cultures.

Stone

Violet diamond. Ancients were awed by the exceptional hardness of diamonds, but because they were only found in India during early history, it became a gem of kings or the wealthy. By the eighteenth century diamond mining began in Brazil, and later in South Africa. Currently, Australia is the main producer of diamonds. Sophisticated methods of faceting bring out the fiery brilliance that make diamonds the highest valued gem for modern jewelry. Diamonds with definite colors are rare, yet they do occur in several shades. Violet is one of the rarest.

⚜ Element

Platinum. In metallurgic lore, platinum has the highest energy—a perfect fit for the coveted diamond.

⚘ Herb

Holy herb *(Siegesbeckia orientalis)*. This small plant or shrub grows in hot climates. The juice, leaves, and sometimes the whole plant are used in herbal medicines. The West Indian Creoles used a salve made from the leaves for a protective covering for wounds and burns. When the juice is applied to the skin it leaves a light, clear coating that soothes mild sunburns. In China it was used as a fever remedy.

♀ VICTORIA: From the root name *Victor*.

♂ VICTORIEN: From the root name *Victor*.

♀ VICTORINA: From the root name *Victor*.

♀ VICTORINE: From the root name *Victor*.

♂ VIDOR: From the root name *Victor*.

♂ VIKTOR: From the root name *Victor*.

♀ VIKTORIJA: From the root name *Victor*.

♂ VILHELM: From the root name *William*.

♀ VILMA: From the root name *William*.

♂ VIN: From the root name *Vincent*.

♂ VINCE: From the root name *Vincent*.

♥ ♂ **VINCENT** Vicenta, Vicente, Vicentia, Vicenzio, Vin, Vince, Vincentine, Vicents, Vincenzio, Vincien, Vinny, Vinzenz: A companion name to *Victor*, *Vincent* also means "to conquer" and comes from the Latin word *vincere*, whose first syllable resembles the English word "win." Although this name has been dormant for several years, revival seems imminent now that ancestral names are becoming popular. Search your family tree, and you may find a *Vincent* there.

The first recorded use of *Vincent* was in the second or third century, when three early Christians—all of whom were martyred under the Roman emperor Diocletian (284–305) shared the name. Several other early saints also bore the name, including Saint Vincent of Lerins, the fifth-century French author.

During the Middle Ages, *Vincent* became popular in France and also in England, when Shakespeare named one of his characters *Vincentio*. Saints continued to popularize the name, including the fourteenth-century Dominican friar Vincent Ferrer. But the saint who really put *Vincent* on the map was Saint Vincent de Paul (1581–1660), one of the first social workers. This noble, gentle man established layman's societies to care for the poor and also founded the Vincentian Fathers and the Sisters of Charity.

Vincent is a name known around the world. In Italy, the name is *Vincente, Vincenzo,* or *Vicenzo.* In Spain, it is *Vicente;* in German, *Vinzenz;* and in Hungarian, *Vince.* Common diminutives in the United States are *Vince* and *Vinnie.*

◉ Number

Six. Numerologists attribute sincerity and magnetism to sixes. Shades of red go well with this number.

☽ Astrological sign

Aries. Nothing conquers the passion of an Aries, especially when they are fighting for what they believe is right. Artist Vincent van Gogh was an Aries.

Color

Vermilion. Red is a shade tied to courage. It has been a sacred color since early in recorded history.

♦ Stone

Almandine. This gem is a member of the vast garnet family. Its deep red color can appear to be black in certain light. While it is usually opaque, almandine can be transparent with a high luster. When cut and polished they make exquisite gems for fine jewelry. Some rare almandines have four-rayed stars. The ancients believed that garnets could cure melancholy and warm the heart.

 Element

Gold. Gold's element of fire acts as a perfect energizer for the almandine. It stokes up the healing vibrations in this precious gem.

🦎 Herb

Scarlet pimpernel *(Anagallis arvensis).* Also called poor man's weatherglass, this low-growing annual is cultivated around the world. Its starlike red flowers close up in bad weather, hence its common name. A tincture of the plant was used by early European herbalists for skin problems and sores. Used properly, small amounts of a tonic made from the rootstock helped some nervous conditions. Medical supervision is advised.

♀   VINCENTINE: From the root name *Vincent.*

♂   VINCENTS: From the root name *Vincent.*

♂   VINCENZIO: From the root name *Vincent.*

♂   VINCIEN: From the root name *Vincent.*

♂ VINNY: From the root name *Vincent*.

♂ VINZENZ: From the root name *Vincent*.

♀ VIRGE: From the root name *Virginia*.

♀ VIRGIE: From the root name *Virginia*.

♥ ♀ **VIRGINIA** **Geenia, Gina, Ginelle, Ginger, Ginia, Ginny, Jenella, Jinia, Jinnie, Virge, Virgie, Virginie:** No, *Virginia,* your name isn't derived from the Latin word *virgo,* meaning "virgin." It actually comes from the Latin *ver,* which means "spring" or "flourishing." The name was originally spelled *Verginia* in ancient Rome, where it was a common family name used by common folk, or plebeians.

The Romans liked a good story, and they told one about a corrupt ruler, Appius Claudius, who wanted to sleep with a young girl, Virginia. So he got one of his subordinates to claim that Virginia was his slave. When the girl's father realized the terrible fate awaiting his daughter, he killed her, rather than have her lead a life of disgrace. The theme of this story became a common one in European tragedies like Frances Brooke's *Virginia, a Tragedy.*

Romantic legends aside, *Virginia*'s origin as a modern name can be traced to 1587, when Sir Walter Raleigh founded the first American colony and named it Virginia, in honor of England's Elizabeth I, the Virgin Queen. The first child born in the colony was also named Virginia. Thus it is among the rare names that became popular in America before it appeared in other countries.

Two centuries later, *Virginia* became a sentimental favorite in France, England, and Germany when the romance *Paul et Virginie* was written by French author Bernardin de Saint-Pierre (1737–1814).

Although *Virginia* was a plebeian name in legends, today it has stature, especially now that ancestral names are in vogue. Looked at another way, *Virginia* might be called an early "place name"—joining the ranks of the modern day *Dakota, Montana, Chelsea,* and *Eden.*

The French form of *Virginia* is *Virginie*. Nicknames are *Ginny* or *Jinny*. Note that the nickname *Jenny* is not usually a diminutive of *Virginia*, but of *Jennifer*.

 ## Number

Eight. Ancient Greeks believed eight was a number linked to Gaea (Holy Mother).

 ## Astrological sign

Aquarius. Originality is high on the list of Aquarian attributes. Writer Virginia Woolf was an Aquarius.

 ## Color

Wisteria. Pale blue stimulates imagination and peace of mind.

 ## Stone

Blue lace agate. Lace agates normally have radiating circular designs like a stone dropped into water. Blue lace agates were used by early healers to balance body fluids and reduce toxic levels. They also believed it eliminated stress that could prevent healing. Many ancients wore or carried blue lace agates to maintain inner peace. It remains popular as a "touch stone" to promote emotional serenity. Modern mystics suggest that lace agates help stabilize imagination and inspiration in artistic people.

 ## Element

Silver. Silver shares the same element (water) as the blue lace agate. It offers positive support to this peace-enhancing gemstone.

🦎 Herb

Wild hyssop *(Pycnanthemum virginianum).* Common names for this plant include Virginia mountain mint and Virginia thyme. It grows in dry pastures and hilly areas from Quebec to North Dakota, southward. The whole plant has various medicinal uses and exudes a mintlike fragrance. A hot preparation of hyssop helped colic in babies and a cold tonic was said to be useful as a stimulant for convalescents. Wild hyssop has small white or lilac flowers that bloom from July to September.

♀   VIRGINIE: From the root name *Virginia.*

♂   VITTORE: From the root name *Victor.*

♀   VITTORIA: From the root name *Victor.*

♂   VITTORIO: From the root name *Victor.*

♂   VITTORIOS: From the root name *Victor.*

♀   VONNIE: From the root name *Veronica.*

♂ WAIN: From the root name *Wayne.*

♂ WALDER: From the root name *Walter.*

♂ WALLY: From the root name *Walter.*

♂ WALT: From the root name *Walter.*

♥ ♂ **WALTER Gaultier, Gauthier, Gualterio, Valther, Walder, Wally, Walt, Walther, Wat, Watkins:** *Walter* is a Teutonic name of Old German origin. Teutonic names arose from Anglo-Saxon (Old English), Danish (Old Norse), and Frankish (Old German). These languages were related, so the names they produced were similar, only slightly different in form and sound. Like most Teutonic names, *Walter* is dithematic—made up of two important but grammatically different parts. The origin and meaning of these two parts is where *Walter*'s etymology becomes murky.

Walter may come from the Anglo-Saxon elements *weald,* meaning "rule" or "power," and *here,* meaning "army." Or it may be traced back to an Old German personal name consisting of *wold,* "rule" and *heri* or *hari,* "army" or "warrior." Either way, the resulting name was *Wealdhere.* A third possible origin is from the Anglo-Saxon *Waldher,* composed of the ancient words *wald,* "wood" or "forest" and *heer,* "master." In fact, our modern verb "to wield," having to do with power and influence, comes from the Anglo-Saxon *wealdan,* which is related to *weald,* meaning "forest." So the

678

last possibility does share a common thread with the other two.

Walter went through several stages of evolution before reaching its current form. A first-century monastic saint was named *Walther,* and then two other saints bore the name. Their travels and fame gave this form wide exposure in Europe. During the Norman Conquest (1066) the name *Wealdhere* was replaced in England by continental forms, such as *Waldemar,* in use among the Normans. In about 1086, twenty-eight *Walter*s were listed in The Domesday Book, a survey of England compiled for William the Conqueror.

In medieval Germany, Walther von der Vogelweide (1170–1230) was a famous lyric poet and musician. The name *Walter* was fairly prominent in the thousand-name register of the medieval duke, John of Gaunt (1372–1376), when only fifty or sixty male names were in use. In the sixteenth century, Sir Walter Raleigh was a well-known English adventurer and poet who was executed by King James I. Sir Walter Scott (1771–1832) was a Scottish poet and romantic novelist whose works included the historical novel *Ivanhoe.*

In the seventeenth century, Shakespeare created the character Walter Whitmore in his play *Henry VI, Part Two.* At this time, *Walter* was apparently pronounced "Water," a fact the playwright used to foreshadow the death of another character by water.

Although the name *Walter* has been in constant use since the Middle Ages, it went out of fashion in England in the eighteenth century. By 1850, it had climbed back up to popularity there, reaching its pinnacle in the 1970s and then becoming rare ten years later. In the United States, *Walter* was most popular in the 1930s and 1940s; today, it's being kept in circulation mainly by African American parents.

Modern variants of *Walter* are *Walther* (German), *Valter* (Scandinavian), *Gauthier* and *Gautier* (French), and *Gualtierio*

(Italian). In the old days, nicknames were *Wat* and *Watty*, but today, *Wally* and *Walt* are popular. *Walter* also inspired many surnames, such as *Walters, Watts,* and *Watkins.*

Number

Seven. Many sevens are gifted poets. Sevens are visionaries and enjoy making their dreams come true.

Astrological sign

Sagittarius. Sagittarians are fearless when it comes to trying out new ideas or pursuing a hunch. Walt Disney was a Sagittarius.

Color

Magenta azalea. A brilliant combination of purple and red enhances poetic inspiration and romantic passion.

Stone

Wood opal. Opal's name comes from the Sanskrit *upala,* meaning "precious stone." Opals can be formed in different ways including during the process of silicification of petrified forests. Because of its great antiquity (petrified wood is millions of years old), wood opals were valued as aids to extend life. They were also carried as a protective gem because of their hardness and unique appearance. Some thought wood opals could scare off evil. They can be found in petrified wood throughout North America.

Element

Iron. Iron has been used for weapons and tools for millennia. It was also thought to protect against witchcraft.

Herb

Walnut *(Juglans regia)*. There are several varieties of walnut trees. The English walnut is usually cultivated for its fruit. It can grow to heights of eighty feet. The leaves of the English walnut were used to make a stomach tonic to help promote appetite and good digestion. External uses included cleansing washes or bath additives for rheumatism, gout, acne, dandruff, and even as a mouthwash for gum troubles.

♂   WALTHER: From the root name *Walter*.

♂   WARD: From the root name *Howard*.

♂   WARE: From the root name *Warren*.

♂   WARING: From the root name *Warren*.

♥ ♂ **WARREN   Ware, Waring, Warriner:** *Warren* started as a surname and probably originated from more than one source. It may be a form of the Old German name *Varin*, meaning "to watch or guard." Or, *Warren* may come from a town in Normandy called La Varenne, which literally means "warren," a place for keeping small game. The name may also have been given to a person who lived near a warren or was a warren-keeper.

When the Normans invaded England in 1066, they brought with them the surnames *Warin* and *Guarin*, which became *Warren* in English. (Because there was no *w* in the French language, *gu* took the place of the letter in many old names.) All of these names were recorded in The Domesday Book—a survey of England compiled for William the Conqueror around 1086. *Warin* and *Guarin* were still being used in the thirteenth century, but during the next one hundred years, all forms of the name virtually died out.

In 1655, *Warren* appeared on a list of English surnames. Then, in the 1700s, parents began using *Warren* as a given name—a whole century before this trend really caught on.

Through the ages, many distinguished—and controversial—men in England and the United States have been named *Warren*. Warren Hastings (1732–1818), England's first Governor General of India, is remembered for his involvement in a sensational political trial, which resulted in his resignation and impeachment (although he was later acquitted). *Warren* was his mother's maiden name. Warren G. Harding (1865–1923), the twenty-ninth President of the United States, died after only thirty months in office. During this time, he was embroiled in the infamous Teapot Dome oil reserve scandal, which involved bribes and other high-level corruption.

In the United States, *Warren* became fairly popular during the Depression and World War II years. In England, the name stayed fairly popular until the 1970s, then faded. It has been more popular in the United States than in England, and it is not uncommon to meet a middle-aged man named *Warren*. It is not among the most popular of names given to boys today.

 ## Number

Seven. Seven is sometimes tied to those with talents in the military arts such as strategy and physical strength.

 ## Astrological sign

Virgo. This sign often represents vigilant and industrious people. Virgo's element is earth, which represents the body.

 ## Color

Indanthrene blue. Deep shades of blue signify awareness and commitment when seen as part of a person's electromagnetic aura.

Stone

Tanzanian axinite. This rare form of axinite crystal is deep blue. While most gemological interest in axinite is limited to researchers or collectors, it is an interesting stone. The name comes from the Greek for "axe" and describes its sharp crystalline edges. When held over a flame it turns the fire green due to its boron content. When exposed to ultraviolet light it shows a faint red fluorescence.

 ## Element

Boron. Boron is an element used in warning flares and some metallic alloys. It is also found in Tanzanian axinite.

 ## Herb

Warnera *(Hydrastis canadensis).* Also called golden seal, eye balm or eye root, this plant grows wild in rich, shady woods or damp meadows. Its knotty yellow rootstock has medicinal value. It has been a popular remedy for internal and external problems for centuries. In tea form it helped to heal sore gums and helped to relieve nausea, especially during pregnancy. A preparation of the rootstock mixed with other herbs made a soothing eyewash.

♂ WARRINER: From the root name *Warren.*

♂ WAT: From the root name *Walter.*

♂ WATKINS: From the root name *Walter.*

♂ WAYN: From the root name *Wayne.*

♥ ♂ **WAYNE   Wain, Wayn:** *Wayne* evolved from the Teutonic words *wain* and *waegen,* which mean "cart" or "wagon." First used as an occupational surname, the name originally would have been given to someone who drove or made wagons. It's one of the more popular surnames to be used as a first name.

Wayne probably came into use in the United States during the American Revolution, when the daring general "Mad" Anthony Wayne was winning battles over the British. Even so, *Wayne* is essentially a twentieth-century name. Its popularity in the United States (and possibly elsewhere) was likely inspired by the actor John Wayne, the quintessential western hero, whose film career began in the 1920s and spanned more than four decades. His real name was Marion Morrison, and the surname *Wayne* was suggested by his director, whose hero was—who else?—"Mad" Anthony Wayne.

In the United States, *Wayne* came into regular use as a given name in the 1930s; in England, by 1940. Its popularity peaked with American parents in the 1950s and 1960s, and with English parents, in the early 1970s. When the 1980s rolled around, *Wayne* was waning in popularity, especially in the United States. Occasionally the name has been spelled *Wayn* or *Wain*.

 ## Number
Five. Fives have inborn resiliency and are able to rebound rapidly from life's ruts.

 ## Astrological sign
Taurus. Strong in heart and sturdy in body, Taureans are determined and rarely veer from their chosen path.

 ## Color
Azure violet. This bluish purple shade signifies strength and mercy in ancient cultures. These two colors are also tied to the sign of Taurus.

Stone

Blue apatite. Apatite comes in several colors. Its name is derived from the Greek for "to deceive." It occurs in prismatic crystals with exquisite specimens found in the United States, Morocco and Algeria. Blue apatite is rather rare and ranges from gray-blue to almost colorless. Gem quality blue apatite comes mainly from Myanmar.

 Element

Wavellite. A mineral called wavellite is sometimes found in apatite crystals. It appears in a circular form with fibrous "spokes" that give it the appearance of a wheel. Wavellite is named for its discoverer, Dr. William Wavell of England.

 Herb

Buckthorn *(Rhamnus cathartica)*. Sometimes referred to as waythorn, this shrub is common in Europe, Asia and the eastern United States. The dried, ripe fruit has been used in curative preparations since the ninth century. Its main purpose was to purge the digestive system of toxins that caused intestinal distress. Fresh berries were used for a syrup to soothe the throat. However, caution is advised as overuse of this plant can cause poisoning.

♀   WENDY: From the root name *Jennifer*.
♂   WES: From the root name *Wesley*.

♥ ♂ **WESLEY** **Wes, Westleigh, Westley:** *Wesley* is an Old English place name that means "west meadow." It started out as a surname given to families who came from one of several places in England called Westley, which is a variation of the name.

The most famous people to bear the surname *Wesley* were the founders of the Methodist Church: the evangelist and theologian John Wesley (1703–1791) and his brother Charles (1707–1788), a preacher and hymn writer, respectively. In honor of them, parents began using *Wesley* as a given name while the brothers were still alive. At first, only members of the Methodist Church adopted the name, but eventually Catholic converts started naming their sons *Wesley* instead of the saints' names they were used to.

In the late nineteenth and early twentieth centuries, American missionaries spread the name *Wesley* to other countries, including the Orient. In English-speaking countries, *Wesley* has been in regular use for many years. Along with the names of other Protestant heroes, such as *Luther* and *Calvin, Wesley* has been borrowed by non-British immigrants to substitute for their ethnic-sounding names.

The name cropped up in American Jewish families in the 1940s, and today, parents of many faiths name their boys *Wesley*—a sign that the name has completely shed its early religious associations.

Variations of the name include *Wesly, Wessley,* and *Westley,* popular in England since the late 1970s. The nickname is *Wes.*

Number

Eight. Eights are strong-willed, courageous, and fair-minded. John Wesley was born under this number.

Astrological sign

Capricorn. People of this sign achieve their goals through persistence. Capricorn is ruled by the number eight.

Color

Mahogany. Shades of brown are linked to Capricorn.

Stone

Andalusite. This stone varies in color from pale yellow-brown to bottle green, dark brown or greenish red. It has the unusual property of changing color when tilted in the light and the same stone might appear yellow, green or red. Most andalusite stones are opaque, rodlike crystals or waterworn pebbles. The pebbles are used most often for gemstones. Pebbles are found in Sri Lanka and Brazil and crystals come from Spain, Austria, Brazil, and the United States. An opaque yellowish gray type is called chiastolite and occurs in long prisms which make a cross when cut and polished.

 Element

Aluminum. Aluminum is present in andalusite. Modern mystics attribute powers to this silvery-white metallic element including the ability to boost mental concentration.

 Herb

Meadow-wort *(Filipendula ulmaria)*. Meadow-wort is common in European meadows and the eastern United States. The entire plant has medicinal value and was helpful for flu, respiratory problems, arthritis, and fever. Its creeping rootstock was used by some to make cleansers for wounds or eye rinses. Its yellow-white or reddish flowers bloom from June to August.

♂ WESTLEIGH: From the root name *Wesley.*

♂ WESTLEY: From the root name *Wesley.*

♂ WILEK: From the root name *William.*

♂ WILEY: From the root name *William.*

♂ WILHELM: From the root name *William.*

♂ WILHELMUS: From the root name *William.*

♂ WILKES: From the root name *William.*

♂ WILKIE: From the root name *William.*

♂ WILKINSON: From the root name *William.*

♂ WILL: From the root name *William.*

♀ WILLA: From the root name *William.*

♀ WILLABELLA: From the root name *William.*

♀ WILLAMINA: From the root name *William.*

♂ WILLEM: From the root name *William.*

♥ ♂ **WILLIAM** **Bill, Billy, Ellma, Guglielma, Guglielmo, Guillaume, Guillelmina, Guillermo, Helma, Helmina, Helminette, Liam, Min, Mina, Minnie, Velma, Vilhelm, Vilma, Wilek, Wiley, Wilhelm, Wilhelmus, Wilkes, Wilkie, Wilkinson, Will, Willa, Willabella, Willamina, Willem, Williamson, Wills, Willson, Willy, Wilma, Wilmar, Wilmette, Wilmot, Wilna, Wilson, Wim, Wylma:** The name *William* consists of the Germanic elements meaning "will" and "helmet." It literally means "resolute protector." *William* was brought to England by the Normans in 1066. Oddly, it became the most popular male name among the conquered English, even though the Conqueror himself was named *William.* Not surprisingly, it was also the number one name among the Normans.

William the Conqueror (1027–1087) was the first of four English kings named *William.* As Duke of Normandy first, he defeated and killed England's King Harold at the Battle of Hastings. Because he was illegitimate, he was also called "William the Bastard." A strict but capable ruler, he revamped England's military and landholding systems, erecting many castles and forming a strong feudal government.

In the following centuries, *William* continued to be immensely popular in England. A testament to its renown is the fact that, on a festival day in Henry II's court (twelfth century), 120 knights named *William* showed up for dinner.

The success of *William* can both be measured by and explained by the number of kings and saints who have borne the name. One of the four English kings with the name, William of Orange, moved from Holland to become King of England in 1689. In Germany, William I became king of Prussia in 1861, and his grandson William II succeeded him in 1888. Numerous saints also bear the name. Among them are the Italian Saint William of Vercelli (1085–1142), an orphan who became a hermit and founded an order of monks called the Hermits of Monte Vergine or Williamites. The Scottish Saint William of Rochester (canonized in 1256) was murdered by his adopted son David. A mentally ill woman found his body and cared for it, then was miraculously cured.

By the thirteenth century, *William* had spun off into several surnames, including *Wilkins* and *Wilkinson*. At this time, though, it was surpassed by *John* as the most popular English name. Then, between the sixteenth and the nineteenth centuries, the name ran neck and neck with *John* for first place, with the two names comprising one-fifth of all the male names in use.

English parents began to tire of the name *William* by the early twentieth century, but this didn't happen in the United States until twenty years later. The name reached a low point in England in the 1970s, but when Charles and Diana named their firstborn *William*, a revival began, though the name has not yet been restored to its former glory. *William* fares better in the United States, where it ranks consistently among the top one hundred names for boys. Both African American and white parents use it equally in the United States.

Literary references to *William* and its nicknames include Will Scarlet, Robin Hood's companion, and Bill Sikes, the burglar in *Oliver Twist*. The name *William* also inspired the expressions "silly billy," referring to William IV, a king not known for his intelligence, and "hillbilly," describing a person from a backwoods area. *Will, Willy, Bill,* and *Billy* are common nicknames.

Liam, the Irish Gaelic short form of *William,* has become quite popular as an independent name on both sides of the Atlantic, given a boost recently by the actor Liam Neeson. In France, the name is *Guillaume;* in Italy, *Guglielmo;* in Spain, *Guilermo; a*nd in Germany, *Wilhelm.* The English feminine forms are *Willa* and *Wilma.*

 ## Number

Eight. Many eights have iron wills and the ability to drive themselves. They are born leaders and can conquer the impossible.

 ## Astrological sign

Taurus. Most Taureans have a practical streak a mile wide. However, Taurus's tie to Venus adds romance to their souls. William Shakespeare, William Randolph Hearst and William Seward were all Taureans.

 ## Color

Williamsburg blue. Shades of blue are tied to Taurus and nobility.

 ## Stone

Williamsite. This gem is usually translucent green with veins or spots of white, blue, or black. As a member of the serpentine group, Williamsite has a rich gemological history dating back centuries. Native Americans wore serpentine with coral to ensure survival in harsh environments when they were away from home. Ancient artisans carved it into statues, jewelry, or used it as polished beads for trading. Serpentine amulets found in ancient tombs were transition stones possibly used to help the entombed's soul make a safe journey to the hereafter. Williamsite is the rarest of the serpentines and is found in Italy, England, and China.

♛ Element

Gold. Gold is an ore fit for kings, saints, presidents, and poets. It makes a beautiful setting for Williamsite.

Herb

Helmet flower *(Scutellaria lateriflora)*. The helmet flower plant grows wild in North America. It has a fibrous, yellow rootstock and pale purple or blue flowers. Native Americans used it for convulsions from fevers or nervous conditions. Some early herbalists thought it was effective against rabies and other forms of uncontrollable dementia.

♂   WILLIAMSON: From the root name *William*.

♂   WILLS: From the root name *William*.

♂   WILLSON: From the root name *William*.

♂   WILLY: From the root name *William*.

♀   WILMA: From the root name *William*.

♂   WILMAR: From the root name *William*.

♀   WILMETTE: From the root name *William*.

♂   WILMOT: From the root name *William*.

♀   WILNA: From the root name *William*.

♂   WILSON: From the root name *William*.

♂   WIM: From the root name *William*.

♀   WINIFRED: From the root name *Jennifer*.

♥ ♂ **WINSTON** **Winton, Wintsen, Wynston, Wynstonn:** *Winston* is an Old English name whose origin and meaning are still being debated. The name of a hamlet in Gloucestershire, England, *Winston* probably started as a surname that meant "Wine's settlement," after the man called *Wine* who lived there. However, *wine* meant "friend" in Old English, and *stan* or *stane* meant "stone." So it may be that *Winston* means "friend stone," or "firm friend."

There was also an Old English first name, *Wynnstan,* made up of the elements *wynn,* "joy" and *stan,* "stone." But this name didn't survive to modern times.

As a first name, *Winston* originated in the famous Churchill family and traveled up through generations. The first Sir Winston Churchill (born in 1620) was named after his mother, Sarah Winston, who came from the hamlet of Winston mentioned previously. Sir Winston's son John, the first Duke of Marlborough, had Winston as his middle name. But Sir Winston Spencer Churchill (1874–1965), prime minister of England in the 1940s and 1950s, is the man who made the name a household word.

Churchill's dynamic leadership during World War II popularized the name throughout the English-speaking world. During the German occupation of Holland, Dutch parents defiantly named their boys *Winston,* and the name has remained more prominent there than in England.

Today, *Winston* has faded in popularity in England, except among West Indian families. It's uncommon in the United States, although it does crop up occasionally in African American families.

The English variations are *Winton* and, occasionally, *Winstone*. The nicknames are *Winnie* and *Win*.

 Number

Six. Sixes are sincere and always determined to carry out their plans. While they can be obstinate, they attract many admirers.

Astrological sign

Sagittarius. Jupiter's influence leads many Sagittarians to greatness. They make excellent strategists in war or peace. Sir Winston Churchill was a Sagittarian.

Color

Grape. Purple is linked to Jupiter in metaphysical lore. Stones of this color were used by early healers to relieve headaches.

Stone

Plum axinite. This gem's name comes from its axhead-shaped crystals. While brown is the most common color of axinite, it also occurs in a deep plum shade. Axinite is hard, but often too brittle for gem cutting. However, it's popular with collectors. Axinite can be found in Cornwall, England.

Element

Brass. The element of fire rules brass on a metaphysical level and is an excellent ore for a fiery Sagittarian. Brass was used as a substitute for gold in magic or healing rituals.

Herb

Whinberry (*Vaccinium myrtillus*). Also called bilberry, this shrublike plant grows in sandy northern areas of the United States and forest meadows of Europe. The leaves and berries were helpful in several remedies. Fresh or dried berries mixed with grated or powdered apples aided digestion. A berry tonic was believed to be good for typhoid fever. Leaf teas were used for coughs, nausea, and stomach cramps. Cold teas were suggested as gargles and for cleansing skin infections and burns.

♂ WINTON: From the root name *Winston*.

♂ WINTSEN: From the root name *Winston*.

♂ WITT: From the root name *Dwight*.

♀ WYLMA: From the root name *William*.

♂ WYNSTON: From the root name *Winston*.

♂ WYNSTONN: From the root name *Winston*.

♀♂ XAN: From the root name *Alexander*.

♂ XANDER: From the root name *Alexander*.

♀ XANDRA: From the root name *Alexander*.

♂ XIMENES: From the root name *Simon*.

♂ YAKOV: From the root name *Jacob/James*.

♂ YANNI: From the root name *John*.

♀ YARINA: From the root name *Irene*.

♀ YEKATERIN: From the root name *Katherine*.

♀ YELENA: From the root name *Helen*.

♀ YETTA: From the root name *Henry*.

♀ YETTIE: From the root name *Henry*.

♂ YGOR: From the root name *George*.

♂ YITZHAK: From the root name *Isaac*.

♀ YLISABETTE: From the root name *Elizabeth*.

♂ YOCHANAN: From the root name *John*.

♂ YOSEF: From the root name *Joseph*.

♀ YOSEPHA: From the root name *Joseph*.

♀ YSABEL: From the root name *Elizabeth*.

♀ YUDI: From the root name *Judith*.

♀ YULIA: From the root name *Julian*.

♂ YURI: From the root name *George*.

♂ YURIK: From the root name *George*.

♂ YUSUF: From the root name *Joseph*.

♂ YUSZEL: From the root name *Joseph*.

♀ YVONNE: From the root name *Eve*.

♂   ZACARIA: From the root name *Zachary*.

♂   ZACCHEUS: From the root name *Zachary*.

♂   ZACH: From the root name *Zachary*.

♂   ZACHAIOS: From the root name *Zachary*.

♂   ZACHARIAH: From the root name *Zachary*.

♂   ZACHARIAS: From the root name *Zachary*.

♥ ♂ **ZACHARY** Zacaria, Zaccheus, Zach, Zachaios, Zachariah, Zacharias, Zack, Zekariah, Zaz, Zeke: *Zachary* is the English form of the New Testament Greek name *Zacharias,* which came from the Hebrew name *Zachariah* or *Zechariah*. The name means "God has remembered." The Greek and Hebrew forms of the name figure prominently in many biblical stories. The Book of Zechariah is part of the Old Testament. In the New Testament, Zacharias, son of Barachias, was a martyr murdered by the Jews between the temple and the altar.

But the most famous New Testament story is about Zacharias, father of John the Baptist. The angel Gabriel told Zacharias that his wife would bear a son and that they should name him John. But Zacharias's wife was barren and they were both old, so he didn't believe the angel. As punishment, God struck Zacharias dumb. His voice returned eight days after his son was born, when he christened him

John. Afterward he wrote the hymn of praise known as the "Benedictus."

Over the centuries, the name evolved into the English form *Zachary*. The Reformation period in the sixteenth century evoked a revival of Greek and Roman names, including *Zachary*, and in 1679, the name was listed in the appendix of Littleton's *Latin Dictionary* as one of the most common Christian names for men. In England, *Zachary* was popular enough at this time to also become a surname.

By the seventeenth century, *Zachary* was a well-used Protestant name, especially among country people who continued to revere Old Testament names. Its use continued into the eighteenth and nineteenth centuries, when the English brought it to the United States and it became a favorite among pioneer families.

The most famous American to be named *Zachary* was President Zachary Taylor (1784–1850). Called "Old Rough and Ready" by his men, Taylor was a soldier for forty years, fighting in the Mexican War and the War of 1812. As a soldier, he helped open the West to settlement; as a president, he took a stand against slavery. He died after only sixteen months in office, but the name *Zachary* lives on.

Although the name fell from grace in the United States in the early twentieth century, it was revived in the 1940s, possibly because of the famous actor Zachary Scott. In the 1980s, the name began a steady rise in popularity and now it is one of the one hundred most popular names for boys in this country.

Boys and men named *Zachary* are typically called *Zach* (or *Zack*) for short. Another, less common nickname is *Zaz*.

☺ Number

One. People of this number command respect from those around them, and usually get it. Ones are highly focused, determined, and can be stubborn.

☾ Astrological sign

Sagittarius. People born under this sign can be unconventional and sometimes tactless; however, they are sincere. Zachary Taylor was a Sagittarian.

✳ Color

Saffron. Shades of yellow are helpful in stimulating memory. Some ancients wore yellow turbans to sharpen their mental powers.

◆ Stone

Lilac jadeite. Jadeite or jade was believed to aid the mind in making quick and accurate decisions. Ancient traders often carried pieces of this gem and would conceal it in their right hands while transacting business. Early healers mixed jadeite powder with water as a calming tonic for upset stomachs. Egyptians of yore believed that jadeite would instill peace and guide departing souls to their place in the hereafter.

♔ Element

Tin. Tin is the metal metaphysically linked to Jupiter, ruling planet of Sagittarius. It was once thought to have powers that aided seers in predicting the future.

❧ Herb

St. Benedict's thistle *(Cnicus benedictus)*. This annual plant grows throughout southern Europe and parts of Asia. Its yellow flowers bloom from spring to late summer. Tea made from the herb of St. Benedict's thistle was helpful for digestive troubles, chronic liver or gall bladder ailments and fever. The plant was also used to make poultices and teas to cleanse wounds and sores.

♂ ZACK: From the root names *Isaac* and *Zachary*.

♀ ZAHRA: From the root name *Sarah*.

♂ ZAK: From the root name *Isaac*.

♀♂ ZAN: From the root name *Alexander*.

♂ ZANDER: From the root name *Alexander*.

♀ ZANDRA: From the root names *Alexander* and *Cassandra*.

♂ ZANE: From the root name *John*.

♀ ZANNA: From the root name *Susannah*.

♀ ZARA: From the root name *Sarah*.

♀ ZARITA: From the root name *Sarah*.

♂ ZAZ: From the root name *Zachary*.

♂ ZEKARIAH: From the root name *Zachary*.

♂ ZEKE: From the root name *Zachary*.

♂ ZINDEL: From the root name *Alexander*.

♀ ZITA: From the root names *Rose* and *Theresa*.

♥ ♀ ZOE **Zoelie, Zoeline, Zoelle, Zoey, Zoya:** The name *Zoe* comes from the Greek word meaning "life." It was originally used by Jews from Alexandria, Egypt, as a translation of the name *Eve,* which has an almost identical meaning. According to the Book of Genesis, Adam named his wife Eve, which meant "the mother of all living." None of Eve's daughters copied this prophetic name for a long time, and when the Alexandrian Jews finally discovered it, they translated it from the Arabic word *howwa,* meaning "life," into *Zoe.*

Early Christians named their daughters *Zoe,* alluding to their hopes of eternal life and in honor of two saints. One Saint Zoe was a Roman woman thrown into the Tiber River and drowned in A.D. 280. The other was a Christian slave in

Asia Minor during Emperor Hadrian's reign (A.D. 117–138). Zoe and her husband Hesperus refused to eat the food their master offered to the gods when their son was born. So he ordered them and their two sons, Syriacus and Theodulus, tortured and then roasted in a furnace.

The name *Zoe* was being used in Rome at the close of the classical period (seventeenth century), although at first it was just a pet name. It wasn't popular in English-speaking countries until the mid-nineteenth century, when English parents adopted it. *Zoe* finally became fashionable in the late 1960s, and by 1980 its popularity was rapidly increasing in England and the United States.

Although *Zoe* seldom appears in literature, the English poet Lord Byron's poem, "Maid of Athens," includes the dedication, "Zoe, I love you." The name *Zooey* was made famous as a man's name in J. D. Salinger's novel *Frannie and Zooey*.

Zoe is sometimes written with an umlaut mark above the final *e*, indicating that this letter should be pronounced. Since umlauts are not a feature of American written English, parents have chosen instead to spell the name phonetically when naming their girls, resulting in the variant spellings *Zoey, Zoie, Zowie,* and *Zoee*.

The English forms of the name are *Zoe, Zoa, Zoela, Zoeta, Zolita, Zolida,* and *Zoi*. The Greek form is *Zoe*, pronounced "Zo-ee."

◎ Number

One. In modern numerology circles, the image of the great White Flame is associated with one and represents creativity.

☾ Astrological sign

Pisces. One of Pisces's ruling planets is blue-green Neptune. This planet can influence religious inspiration in those of this water-based sign.

Color

Tiber blue. Like the waters of the mighty Tiber River, shades of deep blue encourage healing and peacefulness of spirit.

Stone

Green opal. In some modern lore, the opal is considered a gem of bad luck. This idea may have come from a passage in Sir Walter Scott's novel *Anne of Gierstein*. However, in ancient gemological history the opal is a stone that brought psychic visions, enhanced beauty and attracted money, luck, and power. An old legend calls the opal, "Eve of the Gods," and connects it with the conception of all life. Because the iridescent opal flashes all hues, it carries the qualities of every color, making it a supremely magically charged gem.

Element

Platinum. Platinum is the metal associated with Pisces and the perfect complement for the all-powerful opal.

Herb

Motherwort *(Leonurus cardiaca)*. This perennial grows in the northern United States and throughout Europe. The leaves and flowering tops have curative properties. Preparations of either part of the plant were used to aid stomach cramps and some heart problems. It was also recommended for easing menopausal discomfort, shortness of breath, and respiratory congestion. Some may have allergic reactions to this plant.

♀ ZOELIE: From the root name *Zoe*.

♀ ZOELINE: From the root name *Zoe*.

♀ ZOELLE: From the root name *Zoe*.

♀ ZOEY: From the root name *Zoe*.

♀ ZOFI: From the root name *Sophia*.

♀ ZOFIA: From the root name *Sophia*.

♀ ZONDRA: From the root name *Alexander*.

♀ ZOYA: From the root name *Zoe*.

♀ ZSA ZSA: From the root name *Susannah*.

♀ ZSOFE: From the root name *Sophia*.

♀ ZSOFIA: From the root name *Sophia*.

♀ ZUSA: From the root name *Susannah*.

♀ ZUZA: From the root name *Susannah*.